P9-CKX-184

Dante
Philomythes and Philosopher
MAN IN THE COSMOS

Dante
Philomythes and Philosopher
MAN IN THE COSMOS

PATRICK BOYDE

*Professor elect of Italian in the University of Cambridge
and Fellow of St John's College*

CAMBRIDGE UNIVERSITY PRESS

Cambridge
London   New York   New Rochelle
Melbourne   Sydney

Published by the Press Syndicate of the University of Cambridge
The Pitt Building, Trumpington Street, Cambridge CB2 1RP
32 East 57th Street, New York, NY 10022, U.S.A.
296 Beaconsfield Parade, Middle Park, Melbourne 3206, Australia

First published 1981

Printed in Great Britain
at the Alden Press, Oxford

British Library Cataloguing in Publication Data
Boyde, Patrick
Dante philomythes and philosopher.
1. Dante Alighieri. Divina commedia
I. Title
851'.1   PQ4390   80-40551
ISBN 0 521 23598 7

Contents

Preface

I HAVE COME TO THINK OF THIS BOOK SIMPLY AS *Dante Philomythes* (which I pronounce so that it scans like *Samson Agonistes* and rhymes with *Shanty Bill o' High Seas*). Some of my friends found the projected title 'intriguing'; others thought it might be 'daunting'; and all of them were a little perplexed. So I decided to begin this preface with a brief explanation of my choice.

'Philomythes' has yet to appear in any dictionary of the English language. It is in fact the medieval Latin transliteration of a late Greek form that had grown up alongside the classical *philomythos*; and I prefer its full and virile sound to that of any of its potential rivals such as 'philomyth', 'philomyther' or 'mythophile'.

The meaning of the word will be readily divined from its roots. Just as the *philo-soph-os* was a lover of true knowledge, so the humbler *philo-myth-os* was a lover of myth, or a lover of the old stories and legends, or, as we might say today, a lover of fiction. It is not difficult, either, to see how these two terms might have been paired and contrasted in earlier debates about the Two Cultures. But my title is to be understood as a specific allusion to the opening chapters of the *Metaphysics* where Aristotle attempted some kind of reconciliation between them. 'The lover of myth', he wrote, 'is in some sense a lover of true knowledge, because a myth is composed of wonders.'

As it happens, I first came across this sentence in the Latin paraphrase and commentary by St Thomas Aquinas in which the subject and predicate are reversed, thus: 'the lover of true knowledge is in some sense a lover of myth' – *philosophus aliqualiter est philomythes*. This is certainly not a correct translation of Aristotle. But my argument will be that, in the case of Dante at least, the proposition is valid in both forms. And the book has been written to throw some light on that *aliqualiter*, and to indicate in *what* sense Dante was inseparably philosopher and philomythes, or philomythes and philosopher.

We shall return to the sentence and its context in due course, and we shall discover exactly what Aristotle meant by wonder and knowledge, how they relate to sensation, memory, experience and art, and what influence these concepts may have exercised on Dante before and during the composition of his *Comedy*. For the moment, however, it is enough to establish the point that Dante's poetry and his thought will be treated throughout as equal partners demanding an equally thorough analysis.

The book has grown out of lectures given to undergraduates in the Department of Italian at Cambridge and to the wider audiences who have come so faithfully to hear our public *Lecturae Dantis* over the past fifteen years. It is a longer and heavier work than the one I set out to write, but it is still intended to meet the needs of a similar cross-section of readers elsewhere in the English-speaking world. Those who are already familiar with the *Comedy* in whole or in part will have some initial advantage, as will those who have made some study of Italian or of medieval philosophy – virtue must have its reward. But I have done all I can to emulate my author and to write for anyone with an 'innate desire to find things out', whatever the present state of his or her knowledge may be; and I have tried to take nothing for granted apart from a serious interest in Dante and a certain relish for detail.

My thanks are due to the friends who read some or all of the chapters in draft and helped me to make many improvements: Stephen Bemrose, Piero Boitani, Peter Brand, Judith Davies, Roger Griffin, Joan Hall, Jon Hunt, Robin Kirkpatrick, Guy Lee, Malcolm Schofield, David Sedley. And I owe a special debt of gratitude to Kenelm Foster and Uberto Limentani, who not only made constructive criticisms of the whole draft, but have given me their friendship, advice and encouragement throughout the years in which the book has been evolving into its present form.

P.B.

> . . . it's as well at times
> To be reminded that nothing is lovely,
> Not even in poetry, which is not the case.
>
> (W. H. Auden)

Introduction
Dante and Lucretius

Diagnosis and prescription

THERE IS NOTHING NEW IN THE CONTENTION THAT IT IS IMPOSSIBLE to separate the study of Dante's poetry from the study of his thought. Benedetto Croce did manage to persuade a whole generation of critics in Italy that the ideological framework and content of the *Comedy* had proved an obstacle to the free expression of Dante's poetic genius; but, in the longer term, Croce's attempt to banish content, structure and context from any discussion of the poem as poetry has only served to convince subsequent generations of their importance and indispensability. In 1980, we are no longer scornful of those early readers of the *Comedy* who sought to express their admiration by describing its author as 'a supreme philosopher, although a layman', 'a man of piercing intellect and tenacious memory, and most assiduous in his studies', 'a theologian to whom no doctrine was unknown', 'a poetic philosopher by profession'.[1]

The moment is, then, a propitious one, but it is still scarcely fashionable to insist, as I shall do, that Dante is first and foremost a poet of the intellectual life, or that most of the distinguishing features of his mature poetry derive from his study of philosophy. And although the sky is generally clear, so to speak, there remain some patches of cloud and mist to be dispersed. The specialists on whom we depend for the correct interpretation of Dante's philosophical terminology, arguments and conclusions are sometimes naive and inflexible in their response to nuances of tone, to possible ambiguities and inconsistencies, or simply to the richness and multiplicity of meaning that characterizes great poetry. Literary critics, on the other hand, who show themselves to be subtle and sensitive in their close reading of the text may seem curiously little interested in *what* Dante is saying or *why*. In Italy, Dante's Catholicism can become a serious stumbling-block to readers outside the schools and universities, and many young Italians seem to repudiate the *Comedy* as part of the process by which they lose their religious faith. English students tend to misread Dante in different and contrasting ways: either they become alienated by the rigour, abstraction, schematization and reverence for authority that are among the hallmarks of thirteenth-century thought; or they are dazzled and blinded by their first discovery of the clarity, certainty and universal order embodied in the medieval world view. In general, also, many people misunderstand Dante's position because they are unable to draw back far enough from his work to see the resemblances between his culture and our own, or because they never study his thought in sufficient detail to be able to distinguish his attitudes and ideas from those of his teachers and opponents.

These in my view are the symptoms of a mild but persistent malaise that afflicts the study of Dante today at all levels of competence. And my diagnosis of the symptoms naturally points to the remedy here proposed. In this introduction I shall give a preliminary sketch of my personal understanding of the interrelationship between 'true knowledge' and 'poetry' in the *Comedy*; and I shall do this in the form of an extended comparison between Dante and Lucretius. In the eleven chapters that follow I shall offer a detailed and systematic exposition of the ideas and beliefs that lie at the heart of all Dante's thought – his ideas and beliefs, that is, concerning the place of man in the cosmos. That will make up one-half of the book. The other will consist of a no less detailed but deliberately *un*systematic analysis of the many different ways in which Dante used and transformed this conceptual raw material to form the body of his poem. The two halves are not separated. In some chapters it is the exposition of ideas that comes first; in others it is the literary analysis; in others again they are presented simultaneously. But each presupposes and complements the other at all times, and every chapter is a compound of both elements.

The contents of this book are no more original than the proposition from which it takes its departure and which it is intended to illuminate. Although many of the details, connections and emphases occurred to me for the first time in the heat of composition, there can be no doubt that the seeds had been sown by my predecessors in the field, whose work I had read and only imperfectly remembered or understood. A book of this kind is built from materials that have been quarried by countless scholars, critics, commentators and popularizers from the fourteenth century down to the present day. But the enterprise will have been justified if the expository sections are clear and correct and if the more literary analysis is found to be stimulating and persuasive. If a cure proves effective, it does not greatly matter whether its success was due to a new drug, a traditional herbal remedy, or to the bedside manner of the physician.

Dante and Lucretius: the nature of the comparison

The names of Dante and the Roman poet, Lucretius, are often associated. They are the 'thinking' poets, the 'philosophical' poets *par excellence*. They are perhaps the only two writers who are allowed the titles of greatness in poetry and professional competence in philosophy. But the first vital point to grasp is that there was no direct link between them. Whereas Dante knew the works of Virgil intimately, it is quite possible that he never consciously registered the name of Lucretius; and it is quite certain that he could not have known more than a few lines from the *De rerum natura*, as quoted by one of the Latin grammarians or a Father of the Church: in Dante's lifetime the poem seems to have survived in just three manuscripts, all buried in monastic libraries north of the Alps. If there are any essential similarities between Lucretius's poem and the *Comedy*, they cannot be ascribed to the influence of the one work on the other. They would have arisen because two men of genius and of kindred temperament made a similar response to a similar experience of life, poetry, politics and philosophy in cultural situations that in certain key respects are uncannily alike.

In what follows I shall try to describe the similarities that I find important, and to suggest why they should be central to our appreciation of both poems. But to avoid any misunderstanding, I must make it clear from the outset that the differences between the two cases are far more striking, and, in the long run, more important. The two ideologies, for example, are almost diametrically opposed on every major issue from the structure of matter to the creation of the universe, from divine providence to the meaning of history, and from the nature of human happiness to the immortality of the soul. Dante's poem is a work of fiction, telling a story that is anything but a framework on which to hang philosophical discourses. The *De rerum natura* is didactic and expository throughout; its structure is that of a treatise; and the philosophy which it expounds is far narrower in range, less demanding intellectually, and a great deal less satisfying. However, it is precisely because of these radical differences, because Lucretius had no influence on Dante, and because his philosophy is so much simpler and his poem more straightforwardly didactic, that he can help us to see Dante in a different and helpful perspective.

The resemblances to be described will be presented under four main heads. I shall point first to certain parallels in the political and social circumstances of Dante's Florence and Lucretius's Rome. I shall then summarize what we know, or what we can reconstruct, about the early development of the two men, and I shall argue that they both underwent a kind of 'conversion' to a philosophical system at a time when they had already reached maturity as poets. Next, I shall call attention to important common elements in the two distinct bodies of knowledge which Lucretius and Dante sought to master and expound, and I shall dwell in particular on the close relationship between the ethical thought and the physical science. Finally, I shall discuss the state of language and literature in the two cities, and consider the nature of the challenge to which both poets had to respond as they strove to express or recreate in

3

vernacular verse the concepts and insights that they had discovered in the sophisticated prose of a foreign culture-language.

I must also give notice that the various points of comparison and contrast will not be spelt out in detail until after I have given a connected account of Lucretius's circumstances, thought and poetry under the four heads that have just been indicated. The reader may rest assured, however, that nothing will be said about the Roman poet that is not relevant to a fuller understanding of Dante.

Lucretius: the political and cultural background

We know next to nothing about Lucretius from reliable, independent sources. But he seems to have been a Roman citizen, who lived in the first half of the first century B.C., and, in spite of some dissentient voices, a majority of scholars believe that he came from the kind of background that assimilated him to the Roman governing class. And as in the case of Dante, these simple assumptions concerning period, place and social class are vitally important.[2]

Rome was still a republic and had extended its power by force of arms to cover not only Italy but the whole of the Mediterranean basin. The energy of its citizens was nothing less than extraordinary, revealing itself not only in Rome's continuing strength and expansion abroad, but in the bitter dissensions at home, where we find electoral corruption, constitutional gerrymandering, and abuse of high office for personal advantage, against a background of an unceasing struggle for power between individuals acting in the name of a class or party.

Lucretius's early years were marked by a war (91–87 B.C.), in which Rome's immediate neighbours in Italy fought to obtain the privileges of Roman citizenship, and by the bitter and violent internal strife – at times erupting into civil war – which is associated above all with the names of Marius and Sulla. After Sulla's *coup d'état* and brief dictatorship, the rule of the senate was re-established in 79 B.C., but the party struggles continued, and in the year 63 a conspiracy headed by Catiline nearly led to an insurrection in the city itself. Not long after Lucretius's death, Julius Caesar, the political heir to Marius, was to defy the Senate and cross the Rubicon (49). Again there was open civil war, first between Caesar and Sulla's lieutenant, Pompey; then, after Caesar's short-lived triumph, between Octavian and Mark Antony. Peace would come only with Octavian's victory at Actium in 31 B.C. and at the price of a permanent dictatorship.

And yet within those same years of domestic struggles leading to the downfall of republican institutions, Pompey had conducted a victorious campaign in the Near East (67–62); while Caesar finally subdued Gaul and made successful punitive expeditions into Germany and Britain

4

(59–50). It was also a time of renewed activity in all branches of literature, which had languished after the death of Plautus, Ennius and Terence, the great authors of the second century (Terence was the last of the three to die, in 159 B.C.). Greek had remained the language of higher education, and the relationship of Greek to Latin was almost exactly like that of medieval Latin to the Romance vernaculars in Dante's time.[3] But now, in the last years of the republic, there was a deliberate and concerted effort to make the Latin language and Latin literature in all respects equal to Greek. Lucretius's contemporaries were Varro, Cicero, Caesar, Catullus and Sallust, all of whom were born between 116 and 86 B.C. His was the generation that finally forged a language equal to all the demands of poetry and philosophy, the language that would be used by the great writers of the Augustan age, from Virgil (born in 70 B.C.), to Horace, Livy, Propertius and Ovid (born in 43).

Lucretius: a late convert to philosophy?

In the *De rerum natura* Lucretius reveals himself as a man in the maturity of his powers who can address a prominent noble as friend and equal, or at least as a 'client' would address his 'patron'. He has clearly lived in the world and will appeal naturally and confidently to his own personal observations and to the experiences he has shared with his readers: *vidi* and *ut videmus* come to his lips with equal readiness. He is a master and lover of language, proud of his skill as a poet, and no less eager for recognition and the laurel crown than Dante and Petrarch were to be.[4] And his poem champions an ethic which ran clean counter to official Roman morality, with its insistence on civic duty, fortitude, military prowess and the due observance of religious rites, as it also ran counter to the actual way of life of the Roman upper class which was characterized by greed, ostentation and 'freebooting political ambition'.[5] Lucretius tells us nothing directly about himself or his life, but these facts together with other aspects of his poem make one suspect that his early life had been not unlike Dante's. Wary though we must be of conjecture, it is not groundless to speculate that as a boy and youth his education had been practical and literary in bias rather than philosophical; that as a young man he had written poetry imitating the admired models of the day, with a particular regard for the satires of Lucilius and above all for the epic verse of Ennius (for whom Lucretius expresses a reverence very like that of Dante for Virgil);[6] and that in his adult life he underwent something approaching a religious conversion to the moral system of the Greek philosopher Epicurus (341–270).[7] And it is a matter of fact and not conjecture that he made it his mission to spread the 'good news' among his fellow Romans, using his mastery of poetic language and form to win their attention, to mingle instruction with delight, and to move them to reform and renew themselves within through the power of his advocacy. *Mutatis mutandis*, all these points can be paralleled in the case of Dante and his poem, and in both cases they have far reaching consequences.

Epicurus's ethic: (a) Happiness

We must now look a little more closely at Epicurus's teaching and the nature of Lucretius's response, concentrating obviously on those features which will most illuminate Dante's more complex response to the Christian Aristotelianism of his day.

Epicurus was first and foremost a moral philosopher who taught the science of living. And like the founders of almost every other philosophical or religious sect in antiquity, he regarded his teaching as a demonstration of the way to achieve happiness.

It must be noted that he himself did not use this word. He preferred to speak of 'pleasure' (*hēdonē, voluptas*); and his conception of pleasure was passive and negative. Both the key terms in his philosophy begin with the negative or privative particle *a*-, since pleasure is said to consist in *aponía*, meaning freedom from physical pain or want, and in *ataraxía*, meaning freedom from mental anxiety and stress.

But although his concept of *voluptas* may seem to be far removed from Aristotle's *felicitas* or from the *gaudium* and *beatitudo aeterna* later to be promised by Christian writers, we must not be misled by Epicurus's taste for understatement and his laudable concern to find a minimum definition in which all men can concur. Nor must we be misled by the perversions and distortions which his teaching suffered at the hands of his enemies – perversions which gave 'Epicurean' its current meaning of one 'who lives for the pleasure of the senses alone'.[8] His emphasis clearly falls on *ataraxía*, not on *aponía*, on mind and not on body. It is abundantly clear from Epicurus's writings that for him happiness or pleasure demands a secluded and frugal life lived in the company of like-minded people who have abandoned the pursuit of possessions and political power for the sake of friendship and meditative contemplation. Epicurus did not deny the existence of the gods, and his account of their mode of being is clearly a sublimated view of the happiness possible to man on earth (as Lucretius will put it: 'nothing should prevent us from leading a life worthy of the gods – *dignam dis degere vitam*', III, 322). It is less sublimated and less sublime than Dante's vision of the joys of the blessed in heaven, but it is no different in principle. And it is certainly not ignoble or unworthy when described by Lucretius – or by Tennyson, in this free imitation:

> The Gods, who haunt
> The lucid interspace of world and world,

Where never creeps a cloud, or moves a wind,
Nor ever falls the least white star of snow,
Nor ever lowest roll of thunder moans,
Nor sound of human sorrow mounts to mar
Their sacred everlasting calm.[9]

Epicurus's ethic: (b) 'The truth shall make you free'

The other essential feature of Epicurus's ethic is its claim to be founded on the truth. And this in two senses. It rests on the facts about human nature as determined by dispassionate rational inquiry, setting aside all wishful thinking and all forms of fear. And recognition of those incontrovertible but unwelcome facts is the first indispensable step on the road to happiness. Ignorance does not know the limits set by nature to our power and possessions; ignorance attributes disaster to the gods and seeks to propitiate them by undignified and barbarous sacrifices; ignorance lives in fear of punishment in an afterlife and cannot be happy.[10] What Epicurus says in effect is: human nature is like this; this is the happiness possible to man; this is what you must do if you want to achieve that happiness.[11] At its noblest (which is to say, as expressed by a Lucretius) the essence of his teaching can be conveyed in the sublime promise made by Jesus and reported in the gospel of St John (8.32): 'And ye shall know the truth, and the truth shall make you free.'

'If only men could know', writes Lucretius; 'if only men could know the causes of the heaviness they feel in their minds, if only they knew where that dead weight of misery in their hearts comes from, they would not lead the kind of lives we now see them lead, not knowing what they want and always moving from place to place as if they could set the burden down':

> *Si possent homines*, proinde ac sentire videntur
> pondus inesse animo quod se gravitate fatiget,
> *e quibus id fiat causis quoque noscere* et unde
> tanta mali tamquam moles in pectore constet,
> *haud ita vitam agerent*, ut nunc plerumque videmus
> quid sibi quisque velit nescire et quaerere semper
> commutare locum quasi onus deponere possit.   (III, 1053–9)

Moreover, it was not just the ethical teaching that Lucretius took from his master. Epicurus also taught him the pure love of wisdom, the delight of knowing a truth as true, of seeing with the eyes of the intellect, of hunting down a truth by following its tracks, penetrating the dark recesses of its hiding place and dragging it into the light of day; of seeing how one fact illuminates others so that the dark night of unreason no longer conceals the path, and the journey ends in a vision of the inner-most secrets of nature:

> ... the lessons, one by one,
> Brighten each other, no dark night will keep you,
> Pathless, astray, from ultimate vision and light,
> All things illumined in each other's radiance.[12] (I, 1115–17)

Epicurus's physical philosophy

As these lines show, the truth which allows one to dwell in the calm temples of the wise is not narrowly conceived. It takes in the whole universe and the whole of experience. The proper study of mankind is man, but the facts of human nature which lead to the Epicurean defini-tion of happiness cannot be understood until one has grasped the facts about birth, growth and death in the rest of the cosmos. These cannot be understood unless it is known that the universe consists of matter and empty space and nothing else, and that matter itself is composed of an infinite number of almost infinitesimally small, indivisible particles (atoms), which are in eternal motion.[13]

The first two books of De rerum natura are given over to the study of atoms and their properties. And when Lucretius deals directly with man in the third book, his first concern is to show that man is no exception to the universal laws. He marshals more than twenty arguments to prove that the human frame, including what we call the 'soul' and the 'mind' (anima and animus), consists of atomic particles and vacancy and nothing else; that the 'soul-particles', dispersed as they are throughout the body, cannot survive as a separate entity after the dissolution of all the other atoms that form the body; and that death is final: only the atoms are indivisible and eternal. These are the physical facts on which the ethic rests. But the ethic itself is extremely simple and does not require or receive a detailed exposition. Topics drawn from the natural sciences still predominate in the three remaining books; and although the poem was probably left unfinished, there can be no doubt that these proportions are deliberate and justified. Epicurus set forth the *whole* nature of things: 'suerit/... omnem rerum naturam pandere dictis'. And Lucretius who follows in his master's footsteps will not let his reader escape until he has heard the 'full flood of his arguments'. 'Right reason and the nature of things compel', 'vera tamen ratio *naturaque rerum*/cogit ...'.[14] 'I will try to hold you with my verses,' he writes, 'while you take in the whole nature of things and see the practical benefit':

> ... dum percipis *omnem*
> *naturam rerum* ac persentis utilitatem. (IV, 24–5)

So it was to the moralist Epicurus that Lucretius owed his full discovery of nature and the scientific study of the working of the universe. His delight in the subject is everywhere apparent, and nowhere more so than in his response to the whole. The mingled emotions of horror and *divina voluptas* which Lucretius feels as he follows Epicurus, 'travelling in mind and thought throughout the whole immensity and far beyond the flaming ramparts of the universe', are superbly conveyed in his poetry. As a poet he is nowhere more exciting than when he writes of the eternity that has gone before us and will come after, or when he writes of infinite space and the eternal movement of the atoms:

There is therefore a limitless abyss of space, such that even the dazzling flashes of the lightning cannot traverse it in their course, racing through an interminable tract of time, nor can they even shorten the distance still to be covered:[15]

> est igitur natura loci spatiumque profundi,
> quod neque clara suo percurrere fulmina cursu
> perpetuo possint aevi labentia tractu
> nec prorsum facere ut restet minus ire meando.   (I, 1002–5)

Lucretius and sensation

Like Dante, Lucretius is always admired for his frequent and vivid rendering of concrete detail. Unexpected similes and descriptions show us the shifting iridescent colours round a pigeon's neck, the twitching and growling of dogs as they dream, children running out to meet their father and filling his heart with a silent sweetness, children afraid of the dark, or wetting the bed in their sleep, the passing cart which shakes the whole building, hot iron screaming when plunged into cold water, or forcibly submerged logs leaping out of the water on release. All these and many others like them came to Lucretius from his study of philosophy.[16]

Happiness, we remember, depends on knowledge; and all knowledge depends on the senses.[17] Our senses cannot detect the processes by which puddles dry in the wind or clothes become damp in the sea air. They cannot see the ring, ploughshare or paving-stones being worn away over the years; they cannot see food being carried to every part of the body. But they do detect the products or the results of these processes. And from these results we may infer by use of our reason that the ultimate constituents of matter are those atomic particles moving in the void, even though they 'lie far below the threshold of the senses'.[18]

Of course we have to be on our guard. We have to understand the process of sensation itself (and Lucretius will devote two-thirds of the fourth book to the subject). Otherwise the senses may lead us astray. Even if we set aside the special case of the sufferer from jaundice, a rectangular tower appears rounded if seen from a distance; at a greater

9

distance, a flock of sheep and frisking lambs can seem no more than 'whiteness motionless against a green hill', and at a greater distance still even the tumult of an army exercise can appear as 'brightness still on the plain'. Stars seem to move against the clouds, and an oar thrust under water seems to bend. Boys who have made themselves giddy think that the walls are spinning and that the roof is about to collapse. But all these are recognized as 'illusions'; and it is the senses themselves that uncover the deception. Paradoxically, the greatest threat to the truth may come from the mind, from the erroneous interpretation which the mind 'adds to' the evidence, seeing and hearing only what it expects to see or hear.[19]

It is for these reasons, then, that Lucretius will never weary of repeating that we must put our trust in the senses. Unless the senses tell the truth, all reasoning must be false.[20] If we doubt, deny or set aside their evidence, we shall remain in a state of ignorance and superstition. Superstition breeds fear; ignorance makes us pursue impossible goals by impossible means: both lead to misery. That is why Lucretius will boldly affirm at one point that the senses are the foundations of life and happiness: '*fundamenta* quibus nixatur *vita salusque*'.[21]

This attitude to the senses, in turn, explains why his poem is so rich in close and accurate representation of what we see, hear, touch, taste and smell. The detailed descriptions are not there simply to give delight (although they do give delight; and what could be more appropriate in an Epicurean poem than *blanda voluptas*?). Nor are they there simply because Lucretius is a superb teacher who can always find fresh examples and analogies from familiar experience which will help an inexpert audience to grasp and retain abstruse philosophical concepts. Many of his so-called similes are not similes at all in the conventional sense. He does not pick out likenesses between unlike and distinct actions or things. He is citing instances from everyday life of the cosmic laws and processes which we must try to understand, but which escape our attention because of their very familiarity, or because of their magnitude, or because they lie below the threshold of perception. He is not giving us descriptions in addition to the physical and ethical doctrine. He is giving the foundations on which those simple doctrines rest. The reader must learn to put his trust in what he can see and above all in what he can touch. Then his *vita* and *salus* will be assured.[22] He will not attribute natural phenomena to the activity of the gods, nor attempt to influence their decisions and thereby seek out tyrannical masters of his own invention.[23]

Epicurus's rejection of physical determinism

Vita salusque. As we have seen, the physical doctrine may bulk large, but it remains subservient to the ethical teaching. There was, however, one point at which Epicurean physics and ethics threatened to drift apart or even come into outright opposition. This was over the crucial problem of human freedom, which every ethic must in some sense affirm, as against determinism, which is what many a theory of physics seems to entail. It may be possible to reach agreement that pleasure is the only certain good, and that pleasure consists in freedom from pain and anxiety. But such agreement is of very slight value if it appears that there is nothing men can do to achieve that freedom. Lucretius wrote with a mixture of confidence and underlying desperation that 'if men could only know whence and from what causes comes that dead weight of misery in their hearts, they would not live as we now see them do'. But are men in fact able to change their lives and modify their habits and temperaments?

The originators of the atomic theory would have replied in the negative. Leucippus and Democritus were apparently thoroughgoing determinists. Everything in the universe had to be explained in terms of atomic particles moving in the void. And atomic movement was of two kinds only: either it was due to the weight of the atoms which, if they were unimpeded, would carry them 'downwards' at a uniform speed; or it was the result of random collision and repulsion. Everything therefore came about by necessity or chance, *fatum* or *casus*, weight or collision.[24] Man was no exception.

Epicurus accepted the atomic theory and agreed that man was no exception. But the facts of empirical observation demanded that he should recognize the existence of something called 'will', *voluntas*, which is found not only in man but in all animals, that is, in all living organisms which contain atoms of the kind that can form an *anima*. To account for the existence of will as a third source of movement in the universe, Epicurus proposed a simple but profound modification to the original atomic theory. The atoms must be able to swerve or deviate from that straight 'downward' fall in the void (Lucretius will use the verbs *declinare* and *inclinare*). The amount of the deviation is almost infinitesimally small, but it is sufficient.[25] At one stroke Epicurus thought he could explain how the first collisions ever occurred between the falling atoms, and also suggest a basis in physical theory for the possibility of human freedom – a way in which the chain of physical causes might be broken that would otherwise extend *ex infinito* and *ad infinitum*.[26]

Lucretius's affirmation of human freedom

Epicurus's theory is sketchy and inadequate to say the least, and it was often ridiculed by his opponents. But we are not concerned here with its adequacy as a scientific or ethical hypothesis. Our concern is with what Lucretius made of it in his poem, and with what we can learn from *De rerum natura* about Dante and his *Comedy*. And in this regard we can limit ourselves to three observations. First, Lucretius affirms human freedom with confidence and conviction. Something must exist which breaks the decrees of fate (*fati foedera*).[27] Otherwise,

What is the source of the free will possessed by living things throughout the earth? What, I repeat, is the source of that will-power snatched from the fates, whereby we follow the path along which we are severally led by pleasure, swerving from our course at no set time or place but at the bidding of our own hearts?[28]

> *libera* per terras unde haec animantibus exstat,
> unde est haec, inquam, *fatis avulsa voluntas*
> per quam progredimur quo ducit quemque voluptas,
> declinamus item motus nec tempore certo
> nec regione loci certa, sed ubi ipsa tulit mens? (II, 256–60)

He refuses to accept that the mind is subject to an internal necessity in all things; and he will speak without any inhibition of the *studium mentis* and of our *innata potestas, arbitrium* or *consilium*.[29]

Second, Lucretius tackles the problem of human freedom not in the abstract and in isolation, but in the context of a particular theory of physics which at this one crucial point seemed to threaten the moral theory rather than support it. It is also important to notice that the concept which he has to defend is the will as such – the will as a distinct source of motion. He is not arguing, as Dante will have to argue within *his* system, that man has *free* will, while animals act only from instinct. For Lucretius, that was not the issue. The essence of his physical and ethical doctrine was, as we have seen, that man is no exception.

Third, his grasp of Epicurus's teaching is complete, and his exposition is nowhere more lucid or forceful than in his descriptions of the will in action. The two examples which he gives to demonstrate from familiar experience that the mind does indeed have the power to act independently are brilliantly chosen and presented. He cites the case of men coerced or forced to move when we can see from their outward bearing that it is against their will, and that there is something in our breast which can struggle and resist and rein in our limbs.[30] Or, conversely, he describes racehorses at the beginning of a race straining forward with their minds more eagerly than their bodies can at once follow. In the first example the mind acts as a restraining bridle, in the second it functions as a spur; and Aristotle and Dante no less than Epicurus and Lucretius will accept that all human actions stem from these two mental impulses, to pursue or to avoid, *seguire* or *fuggire*. Both examples can be readily analysed in terms of the movement of atomic particles, with the atoms of 'mind' or 'soul' moving one way while the heavier atoms of the body are inert or are dragged in the opposite direction. The brief simile of the racehorses in their special Roman starting-boxes (*carceres*) is clearly drawn from first-hand experience, not the texts of the philosophers; and it would surely have been vivid and compelling for the audience which he had in mind. It is a fine example of how a philosophy can help a poet to see for himself and also determine the mode of his vision:

Observe, when the starting barriers are flung back, how the race-horses in the eagerness of their strength cannot break away as suddenly as their hearts desire.[31]

> nonne vides etiam patefactis tempore puncto
> carceribus non posse tamen prorumpere equorum
> vim cupidam tam de subito quam mens avet ipsa?   (II, 263–5)

Lucretius recognizes that our physical constitution varies from one individual to another, so that a man with a higher than average proportion of heat-atoms will, for example, be more disposed to the emotion of anger. Even where education and upbringing have given an equal polish, he says, different individuals will be prone to different faults. These imprints or traces left by nature cannot be banished by reason nor entirely rooted out. Nevertheless, they are so slight or so faint that there is nothing to prevent us from living a life worthy of the gods.[32]

Man has a measure of freedom from fate or chance. He is therefore *worth* helping. It is also *possible* to help him by instruction and persuasion, since he is able to direct his steps towards the good and the true once he has been shown the path. And help is what he most desperately needs.

'Mortalibus aegris'

The mainspring of Lucretius's poem is his sense of compassion for the wretchedness of man: the phrase *mortalibus aegris* was his before Virgil made it his own.[33] In general and metaphorical terms he sees all men carrying a weight of suffering in their hearts. Our *anxia corda* are lacerated by stabs of desire and superstitious fears. We are tossed on the dark waves of disquietude, tormented by guilt and by fear of the wrath of the gods, and we cannot drink at length from the pure fountain of pleasure because a bitter taint rises from the depths. Even in the midst of material comforts, we are unable to enjoy life calmly, equably and with peace of mind, because we are like a contaminated and leaky vessel that can never be filled and that spoils everything that is poured into it. And the chief cause of this general distress is the fear of death and the fear of retributive punishment in an afterlife. Lucretius's task is therefore to lead men to a life that is 'sweet and sure' and to purify the tainted vessel of the heart; and this he seeks to do not by force of arms but by words:[34]

> I must now
> Make use of poetry to clarify
> The nature of intelligence and spirit,

Of mind and soul. The fear of Acheron
Must, first and foremost, be dismissed; this fear
Troubles the life of man from its lowest depths,
Stains everything with death's black darkness, leaves
No pleasure pure and clear.[35]   (III, 35–40)

More specifically, Lucretius feels the special ills of his own turbulent, aggressive and acquisitive society. In his portrait of the avaricious man, he shows him as seeking always what is absent, as viewing poverty as a tarrying before death's door, and as being tormented by an insatiable thirst for good things in ignorance of the limits set by nature, 'raking together possessions and redoubling wealth at the price of civil war, heaping slaughter on slaughter'. He tells of the quest for status and honours or for supreme political power, leading men 'to struggle on the narrow path of ambition'. Should they gain the summit he knows that they may well be hurled down again by the force of envy, to be savagely trampled on by the mob they had terrorized. Perhaps, he says, they will cling to life even when exiled in disgrace, ready to betray friends and relatives in a last desperate attempt to stave off death. Or perhaps, absurdity of absurdities, they will seek to be free of the fear of death by committing suicide.[36] And all in vain – *frustra, incassum, nequiquam* – as the poet will constantly exclaim.[37] There is no need to wait for an afterlife to experience the torments of Hell, for 'Hell is here on earth in the life lived by the ignorant':

hic Acherusia fit stultorum denique vita.   (III, 1023)

The analysis has an all too familiar ring. It is almost identical with that which Dante gives of his Florence; and it lives on in the clichés of pulpit and leading article throughout the 'advanced' societies of the industrial West. But there is nothing of the cliché in Lucretius. The passages summarized above are his deeply felt and personal condemnation of the 'glory that was Rome' in the middle of the first century B.C. And so it is small wonder that this most un-Roman Roman, this Roman *natione non moribus*,[38] should have begun his poem with a sustained hymn of praise to Venus, with a vision of Mars for ever overcome by the wound of love, and with a prayer to the goddess that she should speak fair words to the god of war in this evil hour for the city, 'imploring an untroubled peace for the people of Rome':[39]

petens placidam Romanis . . . pacem.   (I, 40)

'Egestas linguae'

If we are to do justice to Lucretius's originality we must return to another aspect of Roman culture in his lifetime. As we noted earlier, when Lucretius was a young man (let us say in 75–70 B.C.), the language of higher education and, in particular, the language of philosophy was still Greek. This meant that a Roman who did not have a good command of Greek was cut off from all but the most elementary study of philosophy, and that the Latin language had been allowed to remain a vernacular, lacking a full range of syntactic forms, and lacking above all the necessary abstract vocabulary: for example, Lucretius had no ready-made and philosophically neutral words at his disposal for such fundamental notions as 'universe' and 'atom'. He had to write in Latin if he was to fulfil his self-imposed task and bring peace of mind to his fellow citizens. But the task was a daunting one precisely because of the poverty of the language and the newness of his matter – *propter egestatem linguae et rerum novitatem*. These difficulties were also a stimulus and a challenge, of course. He felt that he was exploring territory where 'no one had set foot before'. Just as Epicurus was the first to discover these truths, so, in his own mind, Lucretius was the first man to turn them into his native Latin.[40]

He made good the deficiencies of Latin vocabulary by the occasional transliteration or calque translation from the Greek, and by frequent recourse to periphrasis, catachresis and metaphor. He adapted the traditional and by now rather old-fashioned language of poetry with its almost Germanic compound adjectives and heavily alliterative epic formulae to expound philosophical and scientific concepts. He juxtaposed words from this elevated and archaic register of the language with words, idioms and constructions drawn from everyday colloquial speech, and with technical terms proper to the mechanical arts. As a result his language is uneven, at times even clumsy and rough. But it is almost always fresh, tingling with a kind of nervous tension born of a struggle with the ineffable. It is arresting, rebarbative and shocking by turns, but never easy or complacent. It is the language of a writer who rejoiced that he was drinking from virgin springs and plucking new flowers:

> . . . iuvat integros accedere fontis
> atque haurire, iuvatque novos decerpere flores. (IV, 2–3)

Barely a generation after his death, the linguistic situation was to change beyond recognition. The Latin language came of age both in prose and in verse. It became capable of 'expressing the highest and most abstruse concepts fittingly, fully, and elegantly, almost as well as Greek'.[41] Poets now concerned themselves with decorum, balance, restraint and harmony. The privileged or under-privileged moment of the *De rerum natura* had passed forever.

Honey or thunderbolts?

In theory there was nothing to prevent Lucretius from writing in prose.

It would in fact have been the natural medium. Epicurus himself had written in bare, inexpressive prose; and it was in prose that other Latin Epicureans sought to disseminate his lifesaving truths. In practice, it is most unlikely that the idea ever crossed his mind. Poetry was his mistress, imperious and irresistible, not something he could take or leave. We must remember also that, just as Virgil would compose the *Aeneid* in emulation of the Homeric epics, and Dante would write in emulation of Virgil, so Lucretius must have set out quite consciously to write a poem in Latin hexameters that would be worthy of the great didactic poets of ancient Greece: Hesiod, Parmenides and Empedocles. Indeed, this may have been the main reason for his decision to use verse.

But with hindsight it is possible to see that the choice of verse was absolutely essential to his missionary purpose. The audience whom he sought to reach and 'convert' were members of the Roman upper class, men with a practical, non-vocational, literary education. He had to offer them literary pleasure if they were to read him at all. He knew that his matter was forbidding and rather bitter, that readers would drag their feet and shy away, or turn aside doubting his words. 'Give me your ears and attention', he writes, 'lest you deny that these things can occur, and walk away with a heart that rejects the truth, although the fault lies in you.' Readers of this kind will readily fall back into their old superstitious beliefs.[42] And for reasons such as these, Lucretius himself speaks of his poetry as a sweet coating to the pill; or rather, true to the medical practices of his own day:

Physicians, when they wish to treat children with a nasty dose of wormwood, first smear the rim of the cup with a sweet coat of yellow honey. The children, too young as yet for foresight, are lured by the sweetness at their lips into swallowing the bitter draught. So they are tricked but not trapped, for the treatment restores them to health. In the same way our doctrine often seems unpalatable to those who have not sampled it, and the multitude shrink from it. That is why I have tried to administer it to you in the dulcet strains of poetry, coated with the sweet honey of the Muses.[43]

The simile is certainly persuasive, and it has been taken up by many later writers whose conscious aim it has been to blend instruction with delight. But as an account of Lucretius's poetry it is scarcely more than a quarter-truth. His poetry is more like dynamite than honey: from his own vocabulary I would choose the words 'thunderbolt' and 'energy' – *fulgur* and *vis*. Lucretius uses all the varied resources of poetic language to convey not just the content of Epicurus's physical and ethical teaching but his own passionate response to that teaching, this being the response that he hoped to arouse in his readers: delight in the exercise of the intellect in pursuit of the truth, delight in the study of the natural world and its causes, and above all deliverance from fear, guilt, anxiety and stress. Like other great poets, Lucretius found that the use of verse gave him a wider not a narrower range of expression. He does not seek to be elevated or poetic all the time. Where circumstances require, his language is bare and uncoloured, although the conventions of verse allow him a freer and more emphatic word-order, and the discipline of verse gives his writing a greater tautness and concision than it might otherwise have had. We can feel these qualities even in the following one-line statements of axioms that are fundamental to his theme, 'Nothing except matter can touch and be touched', or 'Change implies disintegration and therefore death':

> tangere enim et tangi, nisi corpus, nulla potest res. (I, 304)

> quod mutatur enim dissolvitur, interit ergo. (III, 756)

But verse allows him to pass smoothly and rapidly into many different and more affective modes: arguments cast in question and answer form, impassioned declamation and exhortation, solemn liturgical celebration, sarcasm and paradox, or an intimate and deeply felt meditation. He uses all the resources of metre, rhythm, assonance, alliteration, repetition, antithesis, metaphor and simile, colloquialism and archaism to sweep his reader along where he will. In all these modes his natural unit is the long paragraph, and nothing shorter than the following already truncated passage can give an idea of his power:

So the war of the elements that has raged throughout eternity continues on equal terms. Now here, now there, the forces of life are victorious and in turn vanquished. With the voice of mourning mingles the cry that infants raise when their eyes open on the sunlit world. Never has day given place to night or night to dawn that has not heard, blended with these infant wailings, the lamentation that attends on death and sombre obsequies.

> sic aequo geritur certamine principiorum
> ex infinito contractum tempore bellum.
> nunc hic nunc illic superant vitalia rerum
> et superantur item. miscetur funere vagor
> quem pueri tollunt visentes luminis oras;
> nec nox ulla diem neque noctem aurora secutast
> quae non audierit mixtos vagitibus aegris
> ploratus mortis comites et funeris atri. (II, 573–80)

Lucretius and Dante: recapitulation and preview

Throughout this account of Lucretius and the *De rerum natura* I have concentrated on those features for which I can see a close and significant parallel in Dante and the *Comedy*. Some of these resemblances have already been pointed out parenthetically; the remainder will emerge only in the main part of the book. Later references to Lucretius will tend to lay the stress once again on the many and profound differences between the two poets; but these contrasts will only prove illuminating if the original comparison is accepted as valid and important. And so it will perhaps be helpful if I now recapitulate the main points about Lucretius by restating them in a form of words which could also be applied to Dante.

My case then is this. Like Lucretius, Dante was a member of the ruling class in a dynamic, aggressive and bitterly divided city-republic to which he was tied by an emotional bond compounded of love and loathing. As a young man he made his mark as a poet, writing in his mother tongue in the fashionable genres of the day. Subsequently he underwent what may fairly be described as a 'conversion' to philosophy. Through his study of a philosophical system which was already fully elaborated but was available only to those who knew the international language of high culture, the poet was awakened to a delight in the use of his intellect and in the attainment of certain knowledge by deduction and dialectic. His powers of sensation were sharpened as he learnt to think of the senses as instruments for obtaining the raw material from which that certain knowledge is derived. And his attention was turned to all the phenomena that fall within the province of the natural sciences. Philosophy and science were loved for their own sake, for the sake of the truth that all men naturally desire to know. But the chief cause of the poet's fervent commitment to the system was its ethical teaching to which all else was subordinate. This ethic taught the nature of human happiness and the way to achieve it; and it made that achievement dependent on knowledge. It said: this is the nature of the universe, this is the nature of man, and *therefore* this is the way you must live if you want to be happy. The truth will make you free. Ignorance will leave you in misery and slavery. Learn to live in peace.

The poet responded from the innermost core of his being to this eudaimonist, naturalistic ethic which was so profoundly at odds with the way of life in his own society. He made it his lifework to bring that knowledge and happiness to his fellow citizens, to those who lived by appearances and by the promptings of instinct. His teaching would always find its point of departure in the concrete, particular world familiar to his readers. His language, necessarily, was the vernacular, although this posed almost insurmountable problems of expression because of its lexical and structural deficiencies. And his medium was verse, through which (to reduce a very complex matter to the very simple terms which he himself would use) he could give not only instruction but delight, and through which he could convey his own emotional response to the doctrine, and bring about not only a change of mind but a change of heart.

Like Lucretius, Dante was in error concerning many points of fact. But neither poet was wrong in his desire for the kind of knowledge that would enable him to embrace the whole universe and all its parts simultaneously, *pariter summam et singula, universaliter et membratim*;[44] nor again were they wrong in their quest for ethical principles grounded on that total knowledge. This is the truth that all men still desire to know. And one reason why the two poems continue to grip the imagination is that they offer a symbolic prefiguration of what the universal vision might be like, and what we should feel if we possessed unshakeable principles that could lead all mankind to live in peace, fulfilment and purposeful activity in harmony with the rest of the universe.

Dante: the political background

Dante was born in Florence in 1265. At that time Florence was a republican city state of immense vitality, and a great deal of the citizens' superabundant energy was expended in the struggle for internal political power. This struggle is bewildering to follow in detail because it took place at many levels: between individuals, between families, and between the three main classes in Florentine society (the older nobility; the merchants and bankers; the artisans, tradesmen and labourers). It was further complicated by *ad hoc* alliances between the various leaders or factions and neighbouring powers; and antagonisms were polarized and perpetuated by the traditional allegiances of certain families or classes to the cause of either the Emperor (Ghibellines) or the Papacy (Guelphs).

At the same time, all these individuals, families, factions and classes sought power on a legal and constitutional basis, even if this did entail changing the laws and the constitution at frequent intervals. Crisis succeeded crisis, but a political solution was always found. No one was willing to trust a fellow Florentine to administer justice impartially, but everyone could agree to call in a professional *podestà* and *capitano del popolo* to preside over the magistrature and enforcement of the law for a year at a time. There was a very strong sense of civic pride, and the greater part of the citizens' energy was channelled into more fruitful activities or at least directed outwards.[45]

Throughout the thirteenth century Florence was seeking to extend its influence and direct rule to the south and west, and it was therefore engaged in unending disputes and sporadic warfare with the neighbouring communes of Arezzo, Siena, Pisa, Lucca and Pistoia. This territorial expansion and sustained outward thrust was made possible by the great and increasing wealth of the Florentine merchants who were becoming the main international financiers of Western Europe. And yet the foundation of the city's prosperity was the skill and industry of its working class, since the activity of the bankers and financiers was still rooted in the production and marketing of high-quality woollen cloth; the raw wool or woven cloth being imported from abroad to be processed, dyed and finished by the artisans of Florence, and then re-exported as a luxury article.[46]

Florence was also a political force in Europe where the instrument of her power was money. Unlike the Roman republic of Lucretius's day, she did not seek to make new conquests, but simply to obtain economic advantages in the form of concessions and privileges granted to her merchants. She relied not on fighting men (indeed she was employing mercenaries even in Dante's lifetime for the minor local wars), but on diplomacy and the giving or withholding of credit. Hence the best indices of her great power and prosperity are those recorded by the social and economic historians. In the year 1260 Florence began to mint her own gold coin, the famous *fiorino d'oro* which was to remain one of the principal international currencies for centuries afterwards. The population increased rapidly throughout the thirteenth century and had reached an estimated 100,000 inhabitants by the year 1300. New city walls were begun in 1284 to enclose the many suburbs which had sprung up round the twelfth-century walls; and the enclosed area was to be eight times greater than before.

Many of the best known buildings in modern Florence go back to the second half of the thirteenth century. The *Palazzo del capitano del popolo*, now known as the *Bargello*, was completed in 1255. The great cathedral was begun in 1296, the *Palazzo vecchio* in 1298; the Dominican church of *Santa Maria Novella* was begun in 1279, the Franciscan *Santa Croce* in 1296. The citizens' pride in their commune is well expressed in the crude hexameters which we can still read on a stone set in the walls of the *Bargello*, claiming that Florence possesses the sea, the land, indeed the whole globe; that all Tuscany rejoices in her rule; that she sits as securely as Rome, and will celebrate triumphs for ever, compelling all things to accept her judgement under the certain rule of law:

> ... Florentia ...
> quae mare quae terram quae totum possidet orbem,
> per quam regnantem fit felix Tuscia tota;
> tamquam Roma sedet semper ductura triumphos,
> omnia discernit certo sub iure conhercens.[47]

My comparison of Dante's Florence and Lucretius's Rome may have caused a few raised eyebrows: it would not have surprised a contemporary Florentine.

Later we shall lay stress on the many darker aspects of life in Florence in the closing years of the thirteenth century. Dante was to be a victim of the political strife and was rejected by the city he loved. He took his revenge in bitter and satirical description of all her faults: the family feuds and party warfare, the corruption of her officials, the violence in the streets, the aggressive foreign policy, the confusion resulting from massive immigration from the countryside, the ostentation of the newly rich, and above all the universal devotion to the cause of self-enrichment, the worship of money symbolized by the fact that the commune's *fleur de lys* was impressed on the golden florin and gave the coin its name. But there was also a positive side, and Dante was a child of his city: a city rich in individuals, brimming with self-confidence, bold in innovation, a world in itself. It is no coincidence that we can apply the same range of epithets to Dante's *Comedy* and Dante's Florence; and we may be sure that neither the man nor the poem would have been what they were if Dante had been born in any other city or at any other time.

Dante's first age and first love

Dante was born into an undistinguished family on the fringe of the noble or aristocratic class (and this borderline status helps to explain much that would otherwise be puzzling about his education and career and his lifelong obsession with the concept of nobility, to which his attitude was always a little ambiguous). We know very little about his early education, but we can make some informed guesses and some reasonably certain deductions from our knowledge of his social rank and of his mature writings.

In his formative years he must have received a grounding in Latin grammar and rhetoric, although a telltale remark in a work written when he was about forty would seem to indicate that he had not been a very proficient Latinist in his youth. He would certainly have picked up some knowledge of the related vernaculars of Provence and Northern France. He would have acquired the sort of general knowledge about astronomy, geography, history and ethics that we find in *Le Tresor*, an encyclopaedic compilation written in French by Brunetto Latini, who held various official positions in Florence during the 1270s and 1280s. A famous canto in the *Comedy* indicates that Dante learnt much from Latini personally, even though the contact is likely to have been an informal one rather than that of master and pupil. We must also assume that Dante learnt a good deal from oral traditions, from sermons preached in church, and from his association with older men of comparable rank who would have had much experience of commerce and public affairs and who may have travelled extensively in Italy and Western Europe. But although his studies must have taken him to the university city of Bologna in the 1280s, the all-important facts about his early education and culture were that it was largely informal, unsystematic, lay, literary, and conducted in the vernacular. He did not receive a professional, vocational training at a university in medicine, law or theology.

His vocation was poetry; and he entered early into his chosen domain. Before he was twenty he began to make his name in literary circles, writing in the vernacular and composing poems in the fashionable genre, the lyric of courtly love. A few of his very earliest poems survive, and they are conventional and derivative in almost every respect. But within a few years Dante, together with his older friend, Guido Cavalcanti, had worked an almost complete transformation in the themes, language and style of the traditional lyric. By the time he was twenty-five he had written some of the most beautiful poems in Italian literature; for works like the *canzone, Donna pietosa e di novella etate* or the sonnets, *Tanto gentile e tanto onesta pare* and *Deh peregrini che pensosi andate* would have kept his name alive even if he had written nothing else.[48]

With hindsight Dante came to see that all his early poetic activity had been directed towards one end: the mastery of a medium through which he could convey the nature of his love for a young woman, a few months younger than himself, whose beauty and transparent goodness seemed nothing less than miraculous. Her name was Bice (in all probability, Bice Portinari). Little by little Dante was to understand and express the full import of that name; for behind the Florentine diminutive 'Bice' he discovered 'Beatrice', a name active in meaning and rich in suggestion, which we might paraphrase as 'she who brings joy and salvation'.

The paraphrase has religious overtones – and quite deliberately so. Dante's feelings for Beatrice grew from love-longing and love-service to love-worship. And, with a boldness that is quite disarming, he drew on Christian concepts, symbols and expressions to consecrate his love. Beatrice was something 'new', a *cosa nova* (where the adjective means 'wonderful, without precedent and without peer'). She seemed to have come down from heaven to make the miraculous known, *a miracol mostrare*. She offered him 'new' matter, *materia nova*, for 'new' poems, *nove rime*, in a 'new' sweet style, a *dolce stil novo*. Through his love for her he felt he had entered into a 'new' life, a *vita nuova*, a phrase which can mean simply 'youth', but which can also carry all the overtones of St Paul's 'newness of life'.[49]

The death of Beatrice and the 'Vita Nuova'

Such then was the young Dante and such were his achievements at the moment when he passed from his first age, *adolescenzia* (which on his reckoning lasted from birth until his twenty-fifth year) into his second age, *gioventute*, or the 'prime of manhood' (which, again on his reckoning, would last until he was forty-five).[50] This transition was to be marked by a catastrophe in both senses of the word; that is, by a disaster which changed the whole course of his life. Within a few days of Dante's twenty-fifth birthday, on 8 June 1290, Beatrice died. Her death was to be the first of two fortunate misfortunes to which we owe the *Comedy*. It brought his first age to a close in a way that no birthday could ever have done. It virtually compelled him to make a fresh start. It led to developments so unexpected that within a very few years he found that the interests, culture and poetry of his manhood were sharply opposed to those of his youth.

This radical change in direction and the virtual break with his past did not take place overnight. In the short term, Beatrice's death led him through grief, mourning, self-pity and the temptation of love for another woman – all duly explored and recorded in poetry – to a new serenity founded on a deeper understanding and a deeper love. Within a year he could speak of her death as an assumption into heaven; and with new insight he would see it as the necessary climax of her life. In heaven her beauty was greater and her beatifying influence increased.[51] She was still his inspiration, still the matter of his verse. Only now did he discover the hidden pattern and meaning of his development as a poet. So, taking a series of thirty-one poems which documented all the main stages and events from 1283 to some time in 1292, he introduced and linked them with passages of poetic prose to tell the story of his growth in understanding and his consequent or, rather, contemporaneous growth as a poet. The result was his first masterpiece, the *Vita Nuova*; and, as we have seen, the ambiguous title proclaims that his 'youth' had been given over to the love of Beatrice, and that through her he had found 'newness of life'.[52]

The little book is the highly stylized and highly selective record of what Dante regarded as the essential meaning, the *sentenzia*, of his 'first age'. As such it gives little or no hint of the change that was to come and that in all probability had already begun. In the last chapter, it is true, Dante does anticipate a development. In fact he promises one. But this is simply a projection into the future of the line along which he had been travelling. Through study, he tells us, he will make himself worthy of the role he has now assumed – the poet of Beatrice in glory. God willing, he hopes to write in her praise what has never been said of woman before: 'io spero di dicer di lei quello che mai non fue detto d'alcuna'.[53] One day, as we know from the *Comedy*, he was to make that promise good. But he was not to reach his goal along the trajectory he had foreseen, and the gravitational centre of his intellectual and poetic activity over the next fifteen or twenty years was to be not Beatrice, but her declared rival.

Dante's second age and second love

In an effort to overcome his enduring grief at the death of Beatrice, Dante turned to two well-known books of consolation: the dialogue *On Friendship* by Cicero; and, more important in its effects, the *Consolation of Philosophy* by Boethius. Looking for silver, as he himself put it, he found

gold. Looking for comfort and a 'remedy for his tears', he found philosophy and his intellect.[54]

Boethius's work was the ideal introduction. It is cast in the form of an
extended conversation between the author, who is languishing in prison
on a charge of high treason (for which he was subsequently executed),
and an allegorical lady soon to reveal herself as Philosophy. Dante could
identify with the author and protagonist in his wretchedness at the blow
dealt him by fortune, and he could then follow Boethius step by step on
the spiritual and intellectual journey which enabled him to rise above
misfortune and accept it. The dialogue form is an ideal medium for the
beginner in philosophy, and the book also appealed strongly to Dante
because passages of dense argument alternate throughout with meditative and exhortatory passages in verse, thirty-nine in all. Gently, and with
the 'honey of the Muses', it led him to the very heart of the subject. The
Consolation deals with most of the issues that were to remain central for
Dante: the problems of fortune and human happiness, of evil and divine
providence, of human freedom and divine foreknowledge. The goal of
human activity is said to be happiness, *beatitudo*;[55] and all ethical
problems are discussed in the perspective of the order which obtains in
the universe as a whole: 'mankind would be happy if only men's minds
were governed by the love that governs the heavens':

> O felix hominum genus,
> si vestros animos amor,
> quo caelum regitur, regat![56]

But the book's chief attraction was neither its paraphrasable conclusions, nor its literary charm, but its intellectual rigour. For the first time
(or so we are led to believe) Dante tasted the joys of rational inquiry into
the nature and causes of things, into the truth that lies behind appearances and is often contrary to the opinions of common men. He learnt the
beauty of the exact definition and of strictly logical procedures. Reading
the earlier books he would have had the satisfaction of following every
stage in an argument through to its inescapable conclusion; in the fifth
book he would have glimpsed 'higher' truths which were still too difficult
for him to grasp fully, but which were for that very reason all the more
attractive. In a revealing simile Dante later compared these two pleasures
to the two beauties in a woman's smile;[57] and we may perhaps sample
both of them in the following brief but very characteristic paragraph from
the third book:

Just as in geometry some additional inference may be drawn from a theorem that
has been proved, called in technical language . . . a corollary, I too will give you a
kind of corollary. Since it is through the possession of happiness that people
become happy, and since happiness is in fact divinity, it is clear that it is through
the possession of divinity that they become happy. But by the same logic as men

become just through the possession of justice, or wise through the possession of wisdom, so those who possess divinity necessarily become divine. Each happy individual is therefore divine. (*Omnis igitur beatus deus.*) While only God is divine by nature, as many as you like can become so by participation.[58]

It was in these circumstances, then, that Dante learnt for himself the truth of Aristotle's dictum that 'all men naturally desire to know'. Having felt the pure and lasting excitement of knowing a truth as true, he came to accept wholeheartedly, and as a personal discovery, that speculation and contemplation – the use of the intellect to seek out, know and enjoy the truth – was man's highest activity, the only activity that could give enduring satisfaction and happiness. In a word he became a 'philosopher', 'a lover of wisdom', *amatore di sapienza*, as he would later say, dwelling on the etymology of the word. He was a convert to philosophy, 'whose goal is that perfect loving which admits no interruption or shortcoming, in a word, *true happiness won through contemplation of the truth*': '. . . fine de la Filosofia è quella eccellentissima dilezione che non pate alcuna intermissione o vero difetto, cioè *vera felicitade che per contemplazione de la veritate s'acquista*'.[59]

He began to frequent the Franciscan and Dominican schools, *le scuole de li religiosi*, and to attend what he called the disputations of the philosophizers, *le disputazioni de li filosofanti*. In two or three years of intensive study, which adversely affected his eyesight for a time, he read the basic texts and mastered the repertoire of concepts, technical terms, modes of argument and forms of debate which constitute the common denominator of that astonishingly rich, elaborate and diversified body of knowledge which historians of philosophy call 'scholastic thought'.[60] By 1296 at the latest (the probable date of his own first philosophical work) the foundations were laid, and thoroughly laid, on which he would continue to build for the remaining twenty-five years of his life.

In due course we shall grapple in considerable detail with many of the more important axioms, propositions and conclusions. We shall have to lay stress on the diversity and even the incompatibility of the heterogeneous elements which make up the scholastic system, and to dwell on the intellectual weakness of that synthesis as well as its strengths. We shall see that there were many different but overlapping syntheses – different scholasticisms – and that Dante himself was eclectic in his choice of materials and often original in the use he made of them. We shall also have to insist on his continuing growth and development in those last twenty-five years, taking note of shifts of emphasis, of new interests, of the retraction of beliefs once vigorously affirmed. For the moment, however, it will be better to remain at the distant vantage-point imposed by the terms of our comparison between the *Comedy* and the *De rerum natura*, and to use the simpler paradigm of Lucretius and Epicureanism to pick out what seems essential and enduring in Dante's prolonged love affair with Lady Philosophy (remembering that the image of a 'love affair' is Dante's own).

Dante as 'lover of wisdom'

Dante fell in love with a fully elaborated system of thought which was at once philosophical and theological, and which claimed to be universal and certain.[61] It offered not only truths, but the whole truth; and each and every part of the system was fully intelligible only in the context of the whole. Dante learned about the Creator and all of his creation in space and time. He applied himself to the study of logic, mathematics, being, matter, causality, change, astronomy and astrology, optics and sensation generally, physiology, embryology, psychology, history and politics.

But for him, grown man and citizen of Florence that he was, there was always a centre to which everything referred and from which everything radiated. And that centre was man. Of all the works he read in his late twenties it was the *Nicomachean Ethics* of Aristotle, as expounded by Aquinas, that engaged him most deeply and left the most lasting impression. The most difficult and the most pressing of all the questions to which he addressed himself were 'What shall I do for the best?' and 'What shall I do to find happiness?' To those questions Dante found answers that were as certain as the nature of the subject permits.[62] Right choices were not simply a matter of opinion, and happiness not simply a matter of good luck. When Dante in due course assumed the mantle of teacher, his goals were almost always ethical. At the end of his life he could assert that the *Comedy* was ordered to secure a practical not a purely speculative end, and that it therefore lay within the province of ethics: '*genus* vero *phylosophiae*, sub quo hic in toto et parte proceditur, est *morale negotium*, sive *ethica*; quia *non ad speculandum*, sed *ad opus* inventum est totum et pars'. In his forties he said, in a striking phrase, that 'morality was the beauty of philosophy'; and when he drew up a graduated classification of the various sciences, he placed ethics above metaphysics and second only to the study of God and the revealed word of God.[63]

Nevertheless, while all his studies related in some way to man and the problems of living, the facts of ethics rested on the facts of the other sciences, and could not be fully understood except in the widest context. In any case Dante loved all knowledge for its own sake, simply because it was true. He was deeply stirred by the glimpses he caught of what was promised him as the final vision: the eternal, uninterrupted contemplation of the whole truth concerning the cosmos; the perception of the universal order, through which multiplicity and diversity become a unity, and of the great design through which the whole of creation could be said to resemble its creator.

The fervour of his response is all the more remarkable in that most of the works he studied were written by professionals for professionals. The language was Latin (which fulfilled the same role that Greek played in Lucretius's Rome). The style was technical, unemotional and drab (again the parallel with Epicurus's writings holds good). The mode of presentation was strict and often almost hypnotically monotonous. It was satisfying to the professional, but forbidding to the uninitiated. All the excitement lay in the ideas and their interrelations, not in the way they were presented.

Dante was soon to discover that he had chosen an exacting mistress. Philosophy demanded love for her own sake with no thought of reward: Dante came to feel scorn for those who studied jurisprudence, medicine or theology to gain a livelihood or advance themselves in society, 'per acquistare moneta o dignitade'. She also demanded that her lover should devote himself to her every part, because ' 'l vero filosofo ciascuna parte de la sua sapienza ama'; and again Dante was to speak scathingly of those dilettantes who pursue just one branch of knowledge, or of those who, like his former self, 'take delight in music and rhetoric for the making of songs'. Philosophy could brook no rivals: 'Wherever this love shines out all other loves grow dim or are extinguished, because its eternal object surpasses all others and is incommensurable with them' – '. . . lo suo obietto etterno improporzionalmente li altri obietti vince e soperchia'.[64]

Dante could not serve two mistresses. Just as Aristotle had been forced to choose between his reverence for Plato and his greater reverence for the truth – *amicus quidem Plato, sed magis amica veritas* – so Dante had to choose between his love for Beatrice in glory and his new love for philosophy. He had to say in effect that he loved Beatrice – *amica quidem Beatrix* – but he loved wisdom more – *sed magis amica sapientia*.[65] In short, philosophy demanded that he should entirely forsake his early love, his early culture and his early poetry. In the middle 1290s, as the poems he wrote at the time make abundantly clear, Dante was unable to regard his new passion for philosophy as a natural development from his early interests. For him it was a new start. The second age brought a second love.[66] It was only in his *third* age (strictly, from 1310 until his death in 1321), and only in the *Comedy* itself, that he felt able to heal the breach and to reconcile the second Dante with the first.

'Courtship', 'praise' and 'love-service' of philosophy

From our vantage-point, however, it is possible to see that the breach had been far from complete. Dante had been a poet in his first age, a love-poet writing in the vernacular. And it was as vernacular love-poet that he reacted to his discovery of philosophy. Once he had conceived philosophy as a woman (and the identification was there in Boethius, not to speak of the sapiential books of the Bible and a long allegorical and iconographical tradition), he could interpret his feelings as a kind of love. He already had at his command the literary techniques and resources to give those feelings expression. The first poems that he wrote for his new mistress are modelled on the three main types of love-poem in the tradition of courtly love: poems of supplication and courtship; poems of praise; and poems of service.

It is perhaps a little fanciful to describe the earliest of these poems as 'poems of courtship'. There is no question obviously of Dante pleading his suit and seeking to win philosophy over with fair speeches. Nevertheless, there was a distinct opening phase in his second love, and it is extremely interesting. Dante felt guilty of infidelity towards the dead Beatrice; and he was almost deterred by the sheer difficulty of some of the concepts with which he had to wrestle. His complex feelings of guilt, attraction and repulsion are worked out in the *canzone*, *Voi che 'ntendendo il terzo ciel movete* and in the *ballata*, *Voi che savete ragionar d'amore*. But the analysis and representation of these feelings is carried through without any departure from the modes of his youthful love-poetry. There is little or nothing on the surface to indicate that the new lady who has 'transformed his life' is different in *kind* from Beatrice.[67] Dante has innovated and created a new species of allegorical poetry simply by doing nothing. Or, to be a little less cryptic and a little more precise, he has begun to write what we can only call allegories by changing the matter of his poetry (love for wisdom replaces love for a mortal woman), while preserving the familiar situations, and the characteristic language, texture and form of his earlier work.

We find the same relationship between new matter and old form in the poems which mark the second phase, written when Dante had put aside self-doubt and surrendered himself unconditionally to philosophy. Being a love-poet, what he wrote was a poem of praise. And the splendid *canzone*, *Amor che ne la mente mi ragiona*, 'Love which speaks in my *mind*', glorifies philosophy in the same words, rhythms and hyperbole which had earlier been used to celebrate Beatrice living and Beatrice dead. The 'sweet new style' created for Beatrice has perhaps its finest monument in this paean to her victorious rival.

Emancipation from the earlier poetic modes came only in the third phase, with the works we may think of as arising from his 'service'. What form could love-service take when his mistress was *Sapienza*? For Dante there was only one answer, and here once again the analogies with Lucretius are suggestive. He had to communicate his new knowledge to those who had no access to it: those who were prevented by the demands of family and society, which left them no leisure for study, 'sì che in ozio di speculazione esser non possono'; and those who lived far from centres of learning, in a place 'da gente studiosa lontano'. It was a vast audience.

28

In the first chapter of the *Convivio*, from which these quotations are taken, Dante says that such men are 'innumerabili', and that they constitute the greater part of mankind, 'de li uomini lo maggior numero'. They were all being starved of food for their specifically human appetite, the appetite for knowledge. And if this hunger was to be satisfied – the sustained metaphor is Dante's own – they would have to be given food in a form they could digest: otherwise '[la] vivanda . . . da loro non potrebbe esser mangiata'.[68] They would have to be given instruction in their native tongue since they had no Latin. Nor would it be enough simply to translate the works which Dante had read: they would still be too long, too difficult, too technical, too remote. Dante would have to select what was essential and to find new examples accessible to a contemporary audience. He would have to use the literary forms with which it was familiar and in which it took delight; to find words to convey his excitement in hunting down a truth and his joy in possessing it.[69] He would have to convey his sense of the unity of all knowledge, because it was the interrelationship of the disciplines and facts which was new and marvellous to him, not simply the facts themselves. He would have to demonstrate the relevance of all branches of knowledge to ethics, and the relevance of ethics to everyday life. He would have to convince people of the urgent need to reform themselves and their institutions if they were to lead a happy life as human beings in accordance with the facts about human nature and about man's place in the universal design. His aim, in his own words, was to lead men 'a scienza e a vertù', and to save them from the death of ignorance and from vices ('salvo da la *morte de la ignoranza* e da li vizii').[70] He would satisfy the hunger of thousands, who included 'princes, barons, knights and many other noble people, and not only men but women'. He would bring a 'new light, a new sun, rising where the old sun sets, giving light to those who live in shadows and darkness because the accustomed sun does not shine for them'.[71]

It was an immense undertaking. And clearly Dante himself could never have foreseen just where his evangelical zeal would lead him, nor just what solutions he would find. But there is also a sense in which there was no problem at all, and still no break in the continuity of his development. He knew this audience intimately. It was the audience of his love-poems. It shared the assumptions, tastes and general knowledge that had been his own until he had passed his twenty-fifth year. He had left his fellows behind, but he knew their wretched life at first hand: 'conosco la misera vita di quelli che dietro m'ho lasciati'.[72] If he was to teach them through delight, and ultimately persuade them to *act* in accordance with what they had learnt, all he had to do was to go on writing poetry. Accordingly, his very first offerings in the 'service' of Lady Philosophy were two poems, each of about 150 lines: *Le dolci rime d'amor* and *Poscia ch'Amor del tutto m'ha lasciato*. Significantly, both poems open with a statement of intent addressed to the readers of his love-poems. And the two concepts which he chooses to define and defend are values which are central to the ethos of the courtly love tradition: respectively true nobility, *gentilezza*, and true charm, *leggiadria*.

Dante and Lucretius contrasted

All but a handful of the works which Dante wrote from this time to his death were composed, in some sense, in the service of Wisdom. But between those two ethical *canzoni* and the *Comedy* there lies an abyss; and it is of course the *Comedy* which we have been comparing to the *De rerum natura*. If we are to cross that abyss, we must use the Lucretian model in its negative aspect, adopting it, that is, as a term of contrast to throw the many crucial differences into relief.

To account for the *De rerum natura* we need posit only one 'conversion-in-maturity' (although of course the period of study and assimilation may have lasted several years). The philosophical system which Lucretius drew on was simple and self-contained, as we have seen; and it was presented in its definitive form in the writings of one man, Epicurus. It was still relatively unfamiliar to the Roman public, and indeed it sought to subvert civic values and the polytheistic religion of the state. There were models for the philosophical poem in Greek literature. And for all these reasons, it was not only possible, but necessary and desirable, that Lucretius should expound the physical premises and the ethical conclusions in a systematic way.

Dante's situation was quite different. He read many works by many different thinkers from many different centuries. He never committed himself to the school of any one contemporary teacher. The works he studied were known in schools and universities all over Western Europe, and (with certain exceptions that we shall study in due course) there was no necessary gulf or opposition between the religious beliefs and the commonly accepted notions of the layman on the one hand, and the teaching of the philosophers and theologians on the other. As a result, Dante never set out to give a systematic, comprehensive exposition of all he had learned about God, the universe, human nature and human history. He concentrated instead on certain topics which were of pressing importance for his lay audience, or, in the case of his three Latin treatises, on areas which had never been treated by anyone else to his own satisfaction. And the relationship of the particular topic or area to the rest of knowledge was taken for granted and emerged only indirectly.

Moreover, Dante's interests changed and developed profoundly with the passing of time. His thinking became more personal, more original, and broader in scope. He never wavered in his Christian beliefs, never changed his mind on a major issue, and never ceased to be a typically thirteenth-century intellectual. But the early years of his studies were marked by a wholehearted devotion to Aristotle, a great confidence in human reason, and a desire to find the way to human happiness in this life; whereas the last years, and in particular the *Comedy*, show a greater reliance on the revealed word of God and on Christian writers, a certain mistrust of the unaided human intellect, an awareness of sin and the need for grace, and a correspondingly greater emphasis on the attainment of an enduring happiness in the life hereafter.

Unlike Lucretius again, Dante did not immediately find the ideal medium for his activity as 'evangelist' and philosopher. After the two *canzoni* on nobility and charm he did not write any more purely expository verse. They were followed after some years by two important poems devoted to moral virtues and their correlative vices, *Doglia mi reca ne lo core ardire* and *Tre donne intorno al cor mi son venute*. But the first is a moral sermon, a diatribe against avarice; whilst the second is an intensely personal allegory on the theme of justice, human and divine. From these he turned to vernacular prose (a new and splendid medium in his hands) in the form of commentaries to his philosophical poems; thence to prose in Latin. And so his eventual return to the vernacular and to verse, and the happy choice of a narrative fiction that was also allegory and autobiography, constitute the fourth or fifth attempt to find the ideal vehicle through which to bring the 'liberating truth' in the most effective way to the widest possible audience.

These successive formal experiments were of course intimately related to the developments in his thinking and to consequent shifts of emphasis. And these in their turn were determined in very large measure by the personal disasters that befell him and by the complex vicissitudes of his life. Lucretius followed Epicurus who preached disengagement from the political life of the republic. Dante followed Aristotle for whom man is by nature a 'political animal', a 'compagnevole animale', as Dante once translated the phrase.[73] As a true Florentine, he accepted to the end of his days that the city was the smallest social unit that could make possible a 'vita di felicitade'. And member of the minor nobility though he was, he enrolled in the guild of physicians and apothecaries at some time in the year 1295, and thereby qualified to participate in the government of his city. There seems little doubt that his study of Aristotle would have encouraged him to take this step; and there is no doubt at all that his subsequent involvement in politics was to have a decisive influence on his development as a thinker and writer.

Florentine politics and Dante's exile

Dante rose fairly rapidly to positions of responsibility. From 1296 to 1301 he served on several important councils. In May 1300 he represented the commune on an embassy to San Gimignano; and in the summer of that year he was one of the six priors who for two months at a time governed the republic. It was a difficult moment. The ruling Guelph party had split into two main factions headed by the Donati and the Cerchi, and known respectively (for reasons that need not detain us) as the Blacks and the Whites. The Blacks had the support of the pope, Boniface VIII, one of the most unscrupulous and dynamic politicians ever to sit on the papal throne, and author of a famous bull (*Unam sanctam ecclesiam*, 1302) which restated with greater force and intransigence than ever before the claim that the pope is the supreme ruler or supreme arbiter in temporal affairs, no less than in spiritual. Dante was a White.

Rivalry between the two factions led to ever more frequent public disorders (graphically described for us by Dante's fellow White, the chronicler Dino Compagni). And one of the decisions that Dante had to take during his term of office as prior was to banish the ringleaders of both sides. The White leaders were soon readmitted. The Blacks remained in exile for nearly eighteen months. When they returned it was thanks to the complicity of a French prince, Charles of Valois, who had been allowed to enter the city with a force of armed men on 1 November 1301 as the pope's representative and peacemaker. The Donati entered the city by night. There was an uprising and a brief reign of terror, followed by a series of political trials.

Dante seems to have been absent from Florence at the time of the *coup* (in all probability he had gone to Rome on a last desperate mission to Boniface). He was charged in his absence with various offences including embezzlement of public funds. He was sentenced at first to a heavy fine and two years banishment. Six weeks later, on 10 March 1302, he was condemned to death at the stake should he ever fall into the commune's power. So ended his five years of direct participation in the conduct of affairs in Florence. Disgraced, poor, dependent on a series of aristocratic patrons for his salty bread, he lived the rest of his life as a political exile and never set foot again in his native city.

Renewed studies: the 'Convivio' and 'De vulgari eloquentia'

For the first two years he remained with the other White exiles seeking ways to return to Florence by negotiations or by force. But after a series of rebuffs and military defeats he abandoned them to become 'a party on his own'.[74] He resumed his studies, and it is possible that he was again in Bologna for a time; he may even have crossed the Alps to study in Paris. And in the years between 1304 and 1308 he embarked on two very ambitious projects, both of which he failed to complete.

The first was the *Convivio*. It takes the form of a prose commentary to the philosophical poems of which we have already spoken, and it is the main source of our information about Dante's love affair with philosophy. It is the finest and most characteristic product of his second age. Of the fifteen books which he had planned, Dante completed only four, and this is scarcely surprising when we consider the scale of the enterprise. For example, in his commentary on the literal meaning of the first line of the first poem – 'You who by intellection move the third heaven' – he gives an extensive account of the heavens and of the nature and functions of the angelic intelligences who control their movement; and later, in the allegorical exposition of the same line, he devotes two long chapters to the Seven Liberal Arts together with physics, metaphysics, ethics and theology.[75] As the title proclaims, it is indeed a 'banquet' or 'feast' of learning; and we shall draw on it extensively in the main part of this book. It is also a superb piece of Italian prose. In making knowledge available to those who had no Latin, Dante raised the still relatively unformed and despised vernacular of Italy to hitherto undreamt-of heights, bringing it to a level of perfection and maturity where it could truly express even the most lofty and unfamiliar concepts 'almost as well as Latin itself', 'quasi come per esso latino'.[76]

In his defence of his use of Italian, in the first book of the *Convivio*, Dante still admits the superiority of Latin; but in the other unfinished work of these first years of his exile, Dante wrote in Latin to establish the pre-eminence of the vernacular. This is the much shorter *De vulgari eloquentia*, literally 'Concerning eloquence in the mother tongue', which he abandoned towards the end of the second book of the four which he had originally conceived. It is fascinating in its wide range, originality, boldness and concision. We find Dante theorizing about his chosen medium from five distinct points of view. First he writes as a philosopher concerned with natural language in the abstract as it affects every man, since language is recognized as the distinctively human mode of communication needed by neither animals nor angels. Then he is the historian tracing with biblical help the diversification and diffusion of the main linguistic families in Western Europe. Next he is the vernacular author trying to find a norm amid the thousand and more dialects of his peninsula, examining the chief claimants and rejecting them all in favour of a supra-regional *koiné* which he calls the 'illustrious vernacular'. Then he is the rhetorician analysing and justifying the different levels of style, and describing the words and structures appropriate to each. And finally he writes as poet or *versificator*, assessing the merits of different lines of verse and explaining the principles which govern the rhyme-scheme and rhythmical structure of the *canzone*-stanza.

International politics: the Emperor Henry VII

We do not know the reasons which led Dante to abandon the *De vulgari*

33

eloquentia and the *Convivio*. But his decision may have been influenced by his renewed involvement in politics, at the European level this time, and as propagandist rather than as active participant.

In November 1308 the Count of Luxembourg was duly elected as the new Holy Roman Emperor. He is known to history as Henry VII. It was the first time since the death of Frederick II in 1250 that the supreme office had been entrusted to an able and ambitious ruler. With the blessing of the French pope, Clement V, Henry announced his intention (May 1310) of crossing into Italy there to receive homage, administer justice, and be crowned in Rome itself. Dante, not unnaturally, formed the passionate hope that Henry's coming might bring about his own return to Florence on honourable terms. And in October 1310, shortly before the Emperor came to Milan, he wrote a highflown epistle in Latin, addressed to the rulers and people of Italy, urging them to welcome the Lord's Anointed with joy and thanksgiving. This was followed in March and April of 1311 by two more such letters addressed to the Florentines and to Henry himself.[77]

Henry enjoyed a triumphant success in the first few months of that year, as city after city in the North acknowledged his authority and allowed their political exiles to return. But the traditionally Guelph cities, led by Florence, and soon abetted by the pope, refused to submit. Support for the Emperor began to fall away after his first military reversals; and in the autumn of 1312 Florence successfully withstood a siege. Dante's high hopes were finally extinguished with the news of Henry's death from a fever in August 1313. There was never to be another opportunity for him to return to Florence with honour. His sentence of banishment was confirmed in November 1315 (this time death for defying the ban would be by decapitation), and it was explicitly extended to his children. Dante spent his remaining years north of the Apennines at the court of Can Grande della Scala at Verona, and later at Ravenna with Guido Novello da Polenta. It was there that he died at the age of 56 in the summer of 1321.

'Monarchia'

He had lived long enough to bring to completion two other major works – the *Monarchia* and the *Comedy*. Both reflect the hopes and disillusionment occasioned by the rise and fall of Henry VII, but they do so in totally different ways.

The *Monarchia* is a Latin treatise and it deals with the government of the world. The first book argues that if mankind is ever to live in unity and peace, and to fulfil the divine purpose for which man was created, there will have to be a supreme ruler whose jurisdiction and power will extend throughout the inhabited world. The second shows that this supreme ruler, this 'monarch', should be the Roman Emperor; and that the Roman conquest and subjugation of the world had been willed and ordained by God. The third book demonstrates that the Emperor's authority is not delegated to him by the pope but derives directly from God. It argues that the universal 'state' no less than the universal church is willed by God, but that they are both autonomous, and that the Pope should not therefore meddle in politics.

The work is certainly written from the heart. Dante could attribute his exile from Florence to the interference of Pope Boniface, and the failure of Henry's expedition to the duplicity of Pope Clement. But, in marked contrast to the political letters, the tone of the greater part of the book is objective and dispassionate, and the problems are examined *sub specie aeternitatis*. No direct reference is made to any of the events in Dante's lifetime, and as a result we do not know when the work was conceived, or written, or finally released. Some scholars hold that it must have been composed before Henry's campaign or during the first relatively success-ful years, certainly not later than 1312. Others believe that it belongs to his last years; and in this regard it must be said that the only piece of firm evidence in the manuscripts (a parenthesis now restored to the text in the critical edition) indicates that the twelfth chapter of the first book did not finally leave Dante's hands until he had written the fifth canto of the *Paradiso*; and few scholars would want to date that canto much before 1317.[78]

As we shall see, the dating of the *Monarchia* is of considerable importance for the proper interpretation of Dante's intellectual develop-ment in the last ten years of his life. But it is beyond any dispute that many of the ideas expressed in the first and second books had already been formulated in outline in the fourth book of the *Convivio* and in the political letters of 1310 and 1311. And even if the whole work was not in fact committed to parchment before 1316 or later, it is still not unreason-able to see it as another act of 'love-service' for Lady Philosophy, in unbroken line of succession to the philosophical poems, the *De vulgari eloquentia* and the *Convivio*. Like these works it is a fruit of the complex interactions between Dante's life and thought in the twenty years that make up his *gioventute*, his 'second age', which strictly speaking lasted from 1290 to 1310, but is perhaps marked off more significantly by the moment of his renunciation of Beatrice in about 1293 and by the death of the Emperor Henry VII in 1313.[79]

Dante's third age: the 'Comedy'

Now, it is anything but obvious that the *Comedy* follows in the same unbroken line of development. Indeed, the opening words of the poem tell us that in his thirty-fifth year, that is, in the very middle of his second

35

age, Dante had lost the straight way in a dark wood of sin, and that he was unable to climb the sunlit hill of virtue and happiness without the aid of divine grace. Little by little we learn, in effect, that the 'undergrowth' of that wood was a not very dense tangle of lust and dissolute living, whereas the 'trees' that truly concealed the way were his pride and presumption – in particular his intellectual presumption.

In the great confession-scene, played out at the end of the *Purgatorio*, Dante makes himself confess through his tears of remorse, that 'as soon as Beatrice had been hidden from him' by her death, 'his steps had been turned aside by the false allure of "present things" ':

> Piangendo dissi: 'Le presenti cose
> col falso lor piacer volser miei passi,
> tosto che 'l vostro viso si nascose.'   (*Purg.* XXXI, 34–6)

And in the context of the whole poem it becomes clear that these '*present* things' include even the noblest of Dante's this-worldly aspirations in his second age – those of a blameless moral life, political service of the community, the perfection of his art, the disinterested quest for the truth. Such 'present things' are not rejected as valueless, but they are shown as having a 'false allure' whenever they are pursued as ends in themselves, and whenever they are conceived as objectives that can be attained by man's unaided efforts, or as goals that will bring an enduring happiness by satisfying man's every longing and need.

The subject of the *Comedy* is precisely the now crucial '*absent* things', the state of human souls in the afterlife, where a truly everlasting happiness of a very different kind is the reward of those who sought God and acknowledged their frailty and dependence on Him, and where those who ignored Him or turned their backs on Him are condemned to everlasting misery, deprived of all hope, and probably visited with active torments.[80]

Dante's master and guide on the fictitious journey through Hell and Purgatory is not Aristotle, the man whom he had earlier called 'the glorious philosopher, to whom Nature opened her secrets more than to any other', and the 'master and guide of human reason'. Instead it is Virgil, the unconscious prophet of the birth of Christ, and, above all, the greatest poet of antiquity: for Dante's choice symbolizes, among many other things, his return to poetry and to the vocation of his youth. Similarly, but even more significantly, his guide through the Heavens is not Lady Philosophy, but her once defeated and now triumphant rival, Beatrice, the girl who had come down from heaven to earth to show forth miracles, and who had died early to make good a defect in heaven. And these are just some of the most striking signs of a change in outlook and intention which informs the whole work.[81]

There are, in short, good grounds for arguing that the *Comedy* is the result of a new departure, and that it is radically '*dis*continuous' with the *Convivio*, the *De vulgari eloquentia* and the *Monarchia*.[82] In recent years, therefore, a number of distinguished scholars and critics have inclined to the view that Dante must have undergone a spiritual crisis of self-doubt, remorse and despair, which was perhaps precipitated or aggravated by the failure and then the death of Henry VII, and by the consequent collapse of Dante's hopes of a political solution to his own misfortunes. In this reconstruction of events, Dante emerged from the crisis – thanks perhaps to some such revelation or vision as the poem records – with a new vigour and confidence in his powers, born of a renewed faith in God and in divine providence. Inspired with the conviction that God had singled him out, like St Paul, as his 'chosen vessel', he turned once again to poetry in order to teach mankind the way to an eternal freedom and happiness, by presenting the judgement of God in fictional and dramatic form, and by telling the story, again in fictional disguise, of his own error, sin and deliverance.[83]

It must be stressed that there is absolutely no external confirmation that Dante underwent a second, *religious* conversion at some time in his mid-forties (i.e. between about 1308 and 1312). Such a conversion is simply a hypothesis (like that posited for Lucretius) which seeks to account for the spirit and content of the poem. Like the Lucretian hypothesis, it is open to the objection that it is based on a very narrow and literal-minded view of the nature of poetic inspiration. And it raises far graver chronological problems than those presupposed by the more commonsensical, traditional view of Dante's development and of the relationship between the poem and his works in prose.[84]

Nevertheless, the hypothesis does have a great deal to recommend it, provided that we handle it with caution, treating it as a 'model', or as what Plato called a 'likely story', rather than as a single, datable event. And, for my own part, I find it helpful, and entirely consistent with Dante's own ideal reinterpretation of his life, to think of the *Comedy* as belonging in spirit to Dante's '*third*' age, his *senettute*, the age which for most men begins in the forty-fifth year. This implies that I do accept that Dante's aims and view of human nature in the poem are significantly different from those evident in the 'minor' works we have discussed so far, and that I do not dissent from the view that the beginning of this ideal third age was marked by a 're-conversion', which was almost as far-reaching in its consequences as the well-documented 'conversion' to philosophy with which his *gioventute* began.

On the other hand, I am reluctant to lay too much stress on the 'discontinuity' of Dante's development. His return to Beatrice, and his adoption of a more specifically Christian or other-worldly point of view, seem to me less important than his return to poetry and his re-emergence as a 'philomythes'. And I find nothing to withdraw from the comparisons

I have made between Dante's poem and that of Lucretius. The *De rerum natura* is certainly didactic, purely philosophical, anti-religious, anti-historical and impersonal, but it remains close in spirit to the *Comedy* – much closer than it is to the didactic and philosophical works of Dante's middle period. It was only in the *Comedy* that Dante drew level with and surpassed Lucretius in depth of feeling and in power and originality of expression. Only now did Dante build his poetic method on the Aristotelian dictum that 'nothing is in the intellect that was not in the senses beforehand', seeking to hold and instruct his readers by the sharply focused, detailed presentation of sensory experience, often in the form of concrete similes and examples drawn from everyday life.

If Dante did pass through a crisis resolved only by a religious experience, and by hope in the world to come, he did not reject or ignore this world as a result. From the sixth canto to the ninety-eighth the vicissitudes of the commune of Florence are recalled time and time again. The major cities of Italy, the rulers of European kingdoms from Norway to Cyprus, and a succession of popes and Emperors are all attacked or praised for what they did to destroy or foster conditions of justice and peace here on earth.

Again, it was only in the *Comedy* that Dante matched the intensity of Lucretius's feeling for human suffering and misery, outdoing him in the terrifying presentation of its nature and consequences in his vision of Hell. And it is only in the poem that Dante writes with comparable fervour, urgency and beauty of the happiness that men could find if only they would use their intellects, recognize the facts, and live their lives in conformity with the truth – the truth that the poem itself will lay bare.

'*By profession, a poetic philosopher*'

If we do choose to think of the *Comedy* as the product of Dante's 'third age', we must still make allowance for the likelihood that Dante composed or edited the *Monarchia* in the same years that he was at work on the *Purgatorio* and the early cantos of the *Paradiso*. And we must also take notice of the existence of two further works, which, if they are not wholly or partly forgeries, must have been written in the last years of Dante's life. Both are in Latin, and both are quite short – not more than a dozen pages in a modern edition. The first is a letter to Dante's patron, Can Grande della Scala, allegedly accompanying a gift of the first canto of the *Paradiso*. It was composed between 1315 and 1317, and it gives an introduction to the whole poem, followed by a detailed and learned commentary on the first twelve lines of *Paradiso* I. The second work is the *Quaestio de situ et forma aquae et terrae*, the text of a lecture (as we should now say) which was apparently delivered in Verona on 20 January 1320. Here the author sets out and defends his views on a question of natural science: granted that Aristotelian physics would lead us to expect that the sphere of water would completely enclose and cover the sphere of earth, by what means was the land-mass of Europe, Asia and Africa raised above the sea? Both works are highly technical and intellectual in character, and they are both very reminiscent of the books that Dante wrote in the service of Lady Philosophy.

In the present state of our knowledge, it is not possible to prove the authenticity of these *opuscula* beyond reasonable doubt.[85] But the traditional attributions are well supported and not to be lightly set aside; and, in any case, their testimony is not decisive in establishing the temper of Dante's mind in his full maturity. Even if we ignore their evidence, it is still clear from the poem itself that, for Dante, man is by nature an intellectual being, whose goal it is to know and contemplate the truth. Twice in the last cantos of *Paradiso* he insists that knowledge is prior to love.[86] Speeches of a doctrinal nature become more and more frequent as the action of the poem unfolds. And while it is true and significant that Beatrice has displaced Lady Philosophy, she has done so only by a process of assimilation: the Beatrice who is Dante's guide from heaven to heaven in the *Paradiso* is a blue-stocking who delivers no less than five major philosophical discourses in the first seven cantos.

We must also beware of making a false opposition between Dante the 'philosopher', in his second age, and Dante the Christian 'apologist' or 'theologian', in his third. In both capacities, his point of departure was always a written authority, whether this was the word of God, or the word of Aristotle.[87] In both cases, the vocabulary is technical and the mode of argumentation is rigorous and exacting. His profession of Christian faith and charity towards the end of the poem couples philosophical and scriptural authorities in a most revealing way: 'By philosophical arguments and by authority descending from on high', he will say; or 'in this belief, I have proofs from physics and metaphysics, and from the truth that rains down from above'.[88] Dante never accepted the heterodox views of certain teachers in the Parisian Faculty of Arts in his lifetime, who taught that reason and revelation might reach conflicting but equally valid conclusions. For him truth was one. The difference between the *Convivio* and the *Comedy* in this respect is not between philosophy and theology, but between good prose and great poetry.

In short, there is no escaping the fact that the author of the *Comedy* is a repentant sinner but an unrepentant intellectual. As Marsilio Ficino said of him (in a phrase already quoted in the first paragraph of this introduction) he was 'by profession, a poetic philosopher'. This view is confirmed in Dante's affectionate but detached and critical portrait of himself as the protagonist of the poem, since the dominant trait in the protagonist is his thirst for knowledge. Dante-character is portrayed as a 'lover of wisdom' in the broad sense that all men can lay claim to that title, inasmuch, that is, as all men have 'a natural love engendered by the desire to know'.[89] What we are shown in the poem is the process by which that love was requited and he became an *amatore de la sapienza* in the narrow sense. The *Comedy* is the story of a journey on which he travelled from ignorance and bondage to a state of freedom in the final apprehension of the whole truth, the full and simultaneous perception of all things seen in their unchanging essence in the mind of God.[90] The protagonist is a philosopher *in fieri*. The author who narrated that personal journey to the Truth was a philosopher *in actu*. To revert to the language of the *Convivio*, he was one who 'by diligence and study had won the love of wisdom and received the gift of understanding'.[91]

There is nothing incompatible with the Christian religion in this conception of man's nature, happiness and destiny, as will be confirmed by the following eloquent paragraph from a work that Dante used and admired – the prologue to the *Summa contra gentiles* by St Thomas Aquinas:

The pursuit of wisdom is the most perfect of all human pursuits, just as it is the most sublime, the most profitable, and the most delightful (*Inter omnia hominum studia sapientiae studium est perfectius, sublimius, utilius et iucundius*). It is the most perfect, since a man already shares in true happiness in proportion to the extent that he devotes himself to the pursuit of wisdom; hence we read in Ecclesiasticus (14.22) 'Blessed is the man that shall continue in wisdom'. It is the most sublime, because it is in this pursuit above all others that a man approaches a likeness to God, who 'made all things in wisdom'; and since likeness is the cause of love, the pursuit of wisdom above all others unites man to God by friendship. Hence it is said in the Book of Wisdom (7.14) that 'Wisdom is an infinite treasure to men: they that use it become the friends of God'. It is the most profitable, because by wisdom itself man is brought to the kingdom of immortality, since it is written in the same book (6.21) that 'the desire of wisdom leads to the everlasting kingdom'. And it is the most delightful, because (8.16) 'the conversation of Wisdom has no bitterness, and her company no tediousness, but joy and gladness'.[92]

The biblical texts quoted by St Thomas also point to the conclusion that there is nothing in this profoundly intellectual conception of human nature that is incompatible with poetry.

PART 1
The cosmos

I

Wonder and knowledge

The living dead

WE DO NOT USUALLY THINK OF THE *Comedy* AS A GHOST-STORY, BUT that is what it is. Out of a cast of hundreds, the protagonist Dante is the only creature of flesh and blood. All other human beings are referred to as 'souls', 'shades' or 'spirits' (*anime, ombre, spiriti*). They are the living dead – ghosts.

The clear distinction between fact and fiction in our modern consciousness has led to a curious paradox. Relatively few educated people firmly believe in the existence of disembodied beings, and even fewer would publicly claim to have seen one: the philosophy of science has made sceptics of us all. But our scepticism does not prevent us from watching horror-films or from reading tales of mystery and imagination; and as a result, there must be very few people who could not say in advance what they would feel if they ever were confronted by a ghost. We have been conditioned to expect shock and fear in the first instance, manifested in such physical symptoms as a cold sweat, a pounding of the heart or a temporary seizure of the limbs. Subsequently, we should expect an onrush of other emotions that might range from amazement and astonishment through bewilderment, dread and suspense to wonder, marvel and awe, depending on the circumstances and on whether or not the ghost seemed well-intentioned. Modern English has no single word that is sufficiently rich to denote such a complex of physical and mental reactions; but Dante's Italian offers us a choice of two – *maraviglia* and *stupore*.

The living dead of the *Comedy* can arouse many different emotions in the reader, and *stupore* may certainly be one of them. But our *stupore* will not have been caused by the fact of their being ghosts. This would be quite contrary to Dante's intentions. In the world beyond the grave, it is a condition of existence to be a 'shade'; and it is a matter of definition that the familiar and the normal no longer excite marvel. The odd man out there is Dante the traveller. And so, by that reversal of expectation which is one of the main resources of authors who set their fictions in an imaginary world in order to gain a fresh perspective on our own, Dante the traveller is not awed or astonished at the ghosts *qua* ghosts. Instead, it

43

is they who react with *stupore* when they become aware that Dante is there in the flesh, solid, heavy and drawing breath.

A day of marvel

This inversion of the *stupore*-motif is little used in the *Inferno*, partly because visibility is poor in the underworld, but mostly for other more important reasons.[1] It becomes prominent only when Dante and Virgil have climbed up from the centre of the earth to the sunlit mountain island of Purgatory in the unexplored waters of the southern hemisphere. Indeed, during the first of the three days that they pass on the island – the day spent on the foreshore and on the lower slopes of the mountain – the motif is so insistent that it may be fairly described as a dominant theme.[2]

Dante and Virgil emerge from their long climb shortly before dawn on Easter Sunday at an hour when it is still dark enough for the planet Venus and a constellation of four bright stars to be clearly visible. Almost immediately the two travellers are challenged by Cato, the Stoic guardian of the lower slopes. He cannot distinguish the living Dante from the dead Virgil, and he assumes that they are both damned souls escaping from Hell. There is no perception on his part, and hence no *stupore*.[3]

As the sun reaches the horizon, there appears a miraculous vessel. It is piloted at immense speed by an angel, and it is ferrying a precious cargo of newly dead souls. The souls disembark, and, being uncertain how to proceed, they seek information from Dante and Virgil. The sun, we are told, is now well above the horizon; and while Virgil is explaining that he and his charge are 'strangers here themselves', the souls are able to see that Dante is breathing and therefore still alive.[4] They grow pale in wonder:

> L'anime che si fuor di me accorte,
> per lo spirare, ch'i' era ancor vivo,
> *maravigliando* diventaro *smorte*.　　　(*Purg.* II, 67–9)

This is the simplest statement of the theme in its inversion; and it is followed immediately by a more complex version in what would normally be its regular form. In other words, Dante himself experiences *maraviglia*, and shows it in his face, when three times he seeks to embrace the insubstantial shadow of his musician friend, Casella, and three times closes his hands on his own breast in vain:[5]

> Ohi ombre vane, fuor che ne l'aspetto!
> tre volte dietro a lei le mani avvinsi,
> e tante mi tornai con esse al petto.
> Di *maraviglia*, credo, mi dipinsi.　　　(II, 79–82)

In the next canto we learn more about the insubstantial shadow-bodies and witness Dante in the grip of a momentary terror because he has failed to grasp that an *ombra* will allow light to pass through it and hence will not cast a shadow. As the two poets hurry on their way towards the mountain, with the sun now high and at their backs, Dante suddenly notices that there is only one shadow on the ground before him. He swings round, fearing that he has been abandoned by his guide, and his panic-stricken loss of trust draws from Virgil a heartfelt speech of comfort, reproach, despair and resignation that ranks among the most important documents for the study of Dante's conception of human nature. For the moment, however, we need only note that Virgil's brief account of the properties of shadow-bodies prepares us for the return of the *stupore*-motif in its inverted form – the *maraviglia* that the souls feel on seeing a living person.[6]

Virgil and Dante are drawing close to the mountain, with the sun now shining over their left shoulders. High on the rocks above them Dante catches sight of a group of souls who are moving forward very slowly and who pause as the newcomers approach. Virgil calls up to them seeking directions for the ascent, and the leaders of the group inch their way forward again. They are followed timidly by the other souls who are compared to a flock of sheep coming out of the fold and imitating the movements of those in front, stopping and starting as they do without knowing why. When the leaders become aware of Dante's shadow, they come to a halt and draw back in amazement, until Virgil reassures them with the words, *non vi maravigliate*. In this case, then, *stupore* is expressed not in words, nor in pallor, but in arrested movement; and Dante twice underlines the fact that the souls do not understand the 'wherefore' of their actions. We shall see later that *maraviglia* is always a product of ignorance.[7]

After a strenuous climb, the travellers pause on a ledge running round the mountain, and Virgil seizes the opportunity to explain why the sun, which has now climbed through fifty degrees of its daily course, is passing to the north of them. He is interrupted by a voice coming from a group of souls who had passed unobserved because they were sitting in the shade of a huge boulder. Dante and Virgil go over to them, and the speaker proves to be an old Florentine friend of Dante called Belacqua. Because they are all in the shadow cast by the boulder, Belacqua does not realize that Dante is still alive, and the reunion takes place in an atmosphere of affectionate mockery rather than *maraviglia*. But when Dante moves off again into the noon-day sunshine, one of the group notices his shadow and calls out from behind.[8] Dante turns round to see them all 'looking in amazement at him, only at him, and at the light which was "broken"':

> Li occhi rivolsi al suon di questo motto,
> e vidile guardar *per maraviglia*
> pur me, pur me, e 'l lume ch'era rotto.　　　　　(v, 7–9)

This time the sense of wonder is captured by the narrator's use of metaphor, emphasized by the rhyme, and by the unexpectedly simple repetition of the monosyllables *pur me, pur me*.

Scarcely has Dante recovered from a sharp rebuke from Virgil, when another group approaches singing, or rather chanting, a plainsong *Miserere*. They too notice that Dante's body does not allow the sun's rays to pass through, and their chant breaks off in a long, hoarse *Oh* of astonishment. Immediately two of them rush forward as messengers asking, 'tell us about your condition':

> Quando s'accorser ch'i' non dava loco
> per lo mio corpo al trapassar d'i raggi,
> mutar lor canto in un 'oh!' lungo e roco;
> e due di loro, in forma di messaggi,
> corsero incontr' a noi e dimandarne:
> 'Di vostra condizion fatene saggi.'   (V, 25–30)

Here for the first time, Dante does not name the emotion in the course of describing its manifestations; and with that interjection, *Oh*, used, as the grammarian Donatus had described long before, to express the passions of the mind, we are close to the verbal expression of wonder.[9]

But the broken utterances of a man speaking while still in the grip of marvel are reserved for the poet, Sordello, in a scene of a different kind in the seventh canto. Sordello has greeted Virgil with impetuous warmth, interrupting him simply on hearing that he was a fellow Mantuan. When Virgil is finally allowed to reveal his identity, Sordello becomes 'like a man who sees something so totally unexpected that he is seized with wonder, believing and yet refusing to believe, saying "It is", "No it can't be"' (and the elements of paraphrase in my translation still fail to convey what Dante expresses simply through dislocations of syntax, rhythm and word-order):

> Qual è colui che cosa innanzi sé
> subita vede ond' e' si maraviglia,
> che crede e non, dicendo 'Ella è ... non è ...',
> tal parve quelli ...   (VII, 10–13)

Thereafter, Sordello is so completely overwhelmed at finding himself in the presence of the greatest poet of Rome that he simply ignores Dante (pointedly addressing Virgil with the singular pronoun), and does not realize until later that Dante is alive and in the flesh.[10]

The sun has been throwing long shadows and is now sinking low in the sky. Sordello explains that no further ascent will be possible once the sun is below the horizon, and he leads his two companions towards a valley hollowed out in the mountain side. There, in the little sunlight that remains, he points out the souls of some notable European rulers. The sun sets and the three poets move in among these souls in the now murky

air.[11] One of them peers hard at Dante. They turn towards each other.
And a flood of relief and astonishment sweeps over Dante the poet as he
remembers the scene and breaks in on the narrative to exclaim: 'Ah Nino,
judge and gentleman, how I rejoiced when I saw you were not among the
damned':

> Ver' me si fece, e io ver' lui mi fei:
> giudice Nin gentil, quanto mi piacque
> quando ti vidi non esser tra' rei! (VIII, 52–4)

To adapt the famous definition of poetry by William Wordsworth, here
we have 'marvel recollected in tranquillity'.

In the darkness, Nino cannot see that Dante is alive, and he assumes
that his friend has come on the long voyage by the angelic vessel, as
described in the second canto. Dante reveals that he is still *in prima vita*,
and once again sudden astonishment is registered through movement as
both Nino and Sordello draw back on hearing his reply. Then the day
draws to its close with one last variation on the *stupore*-theme, as Dante
shows us the emotion of marvel as felt by a Christian soul whose salvation
is assured. There is no hint of alarm or fear in Nino's words as he calls out
to a friend sitting nearby: 'Get up, Conrad; come and see what God in his
grace has willed':

> E come fu la mia risposta udita,
> Sordello ed elli in dietro si raccolse
> come gente di subito smarrita.
>   L'uno a Virgilio e l'altro a un si volse
> che sedea lì, gridando: 'Su, Currado!
> vieni a veder che Dio per grazia volse.' (VIII, 61–6)

Dante philomythes

It is almost impossible even for a chess grandmaster to reveal his
distinctive powers and style in the first half-dozen moves of a game.
Similarly, there is bound to be a certain predictability in the exchanges
that serve to get personal encounters under way in the *Comedy*, even
when Dante is not deliberately restricting himself, as in these examples,
to variations on a single theme. If we needed immediate evidence of
Dante's mastery as a poet and story-teller, we should have to follow each
of these encounters into the phase of the 'middle game' and analyse what
passes between Virgil and Cato or Sordello, or between Dante and the
friends with whom he is so unexpectedly reunited.

Nevertheless, there are many minor felicities in the truncated passages
we have just considered, and many features that are characteristic of
Dante's art at all times. His style is habitually spare and direct, and yet his
concern for narrative detail and verisimilitude is usually compatible with
a rich vein of symbolism (in these cantos, the sun which plays such an

important part in the mechanism of the plot is also a symbol of divine grace). A love of variety goes hand in hand with a well-developed sense of design, and episodes are often grouped into a formal pattern of the kind we have seen. Dante's psychological insight rarely falls below the high level evident in these brief studies of individual human behaviour in situations that are strange beyond expectation or beyond belief. And it is, of course, for his power to draw from the life and to tell a story swiftly and convincingly that we value Dante today. These are the talents for which we should look in vain among other enthusiastic and intelligent students of philosophy in the early years of the fourteenth century – the talents that earn for Dante the epithet 'philomythes'.

It must be emphasized, however, that we should also look in vain for these qualities in other poets or story-tellers of the period, and that the passages we have read show the decisive and beneficial influence of Dante's study of philosophy in several distinct but overlapping ways. In the first place – and this point is valid for the poem as a whole – Dante may have found encouragement in Aristotle's authoritative view that it was simply part of human nature to take delight in the imitation or representation of reality (*repraesentatio enim naturaliter homini delectabilis est*). The *Poetics* were not influential at this time, but Dante would have known from other sources that, for Aristotle, the poet's specific task was to excite the sense of wonderment, and that mimesis or *repraesentatio* by use of language was the distinctive property of poetry as such.[12]

In the second place, it becomes abundantly clear from a study of Dante's earlier writings that his insight into human psychology cannot be attributed to his keen but untutored observation alone. The later chapters of the fourth book of the *Convivio* provide a full but compendious survey of the virtues, good qualities and laudable emotions that characterize the man who possesses true nobility of mind. Both the list and the treatment derive ultimately from Aristotle's *Rhetoric* and *Ethics*, but Dante already shows considerable originality in the way that he apportions these qualities among the four ages in human life. Some are revealed in the first age, *adolescenzia*, some in *gioventute*, others in *senettute*, and others not until a man has reached threescore years and ten. *Stupore* is included in this survey, and it is categorized as one of the three elements in the composite emotion of *vergogna*, 'shamefastness', which in turn is one of the four desirable states of feeling that should mark out the noble man in his first age. The context could scarcely be more rigorously systematic or more redolent of the medieval classroom.[13]

Let us now read what Dante had said concerning *stupore* in that earlier text-book analysis:

Wonderment is a state in which the mind is stunned because it has seen, heard or otherwise perceived great wonders (*lo stupore è uno stordimento d'animo, per grandi e maravigliose cose vedere o udire o per alcuno modo sentire*). To the extent that they seem 'great', they induce a feeling of reverence; to the extent that they seem 'wonders', they excite a desire to know about them. Hence the kings in ancient times used to adorn their palaces with works that were resplendent with gold, precious stones and artifice, so that visitors would be filled with awe, and therefore with reverence, and so that they would inquire about the king's honourable state. (*Con.* IV, xxv, 5)

A moment's reflection will show that all the main points in this brief paragraph were faithfully translated into representational terms in the encounters between the living Dante and the ghosts of Antepurgatory. Dante's journey through the afterworld is certainly *grande e meraviglioso*, since the only analogues which he himself suggests are the journey to Hell of Aeneas, St Paul's being 'caught up into Paradise', and the summation of both in Christ's Harrowing of Hell, Resurrection and Ascension. His choice of a strikingly 'physical' word like *stordimento* (which could be used of the consequences of a blow on the head) points forward to his clinically precise rendering of the physical manifestations of *stupore* in pallor, recoil, inarticulate gasps and broken speech. The apparently pedantic distinction between *vedere*, *udire* or *in alcuno modo sentire* is later exploited to vary the presentation of the souls' discovery that Dante is alive. The close connection between *stupore* and the state of *riverenza* is reasserted in the later stages of the encounters with Cato and Sordello.

The same chapters of the *Convivio* also provide a clue as to why Dante should have given such prominence to the emotion at this stage in the poem. There is, after all, something rather odd in the consistent reaction of the souls. *Stupore*, it is made clear, is not a virtue. As a state of feeling, it is praiseworthy only in the very young. It should in any case fade rapidly in a noble heart.[14] But the apparent oddity disappears when we remember that all the souls whom Dante meets on the first day in Purgatory are confined to the lower slopes of the mountain and are held back from the processes of purgation. Metaphorically speaking, they remain on the threshold of their 'new life'; or, better, they are in the 'first age' of that 'new life'. In the same way, Dante the character is here portrayed during the first phase of his ascent to Paradise. And so he and the souls are endowed with the same good qualities that are given to noble souls in the first age of their earthly life in order to help them 'through the gateway and along the path by which we enter the city of virtue'.[15] According to the fourth book of the *Convivio*, these qualities are *obedienza*, *soavità* and *vergogna*.[16] *Stupore* is one of three elements in *vergogna*. And that is one reason why it receives such a strong stress.

'Propter admirari incoeperunt philosophari'

There is, however, a second and more important reason. This is suggested by the only words in the *Convivio* paragraph to which we have yet to call attention: '. . . to the extent that these things seem wonderful they excite a desire to know about them (*fanno voglioso di sapere di quelle*), and to ask questions about them'.[17]

Marvel is always the effect of ignorance, since it is aroused only when we have noticed something we had not noticed before. If it were only an effect, however, it would be a dead end, and there would be nothing more to say. But it is also a cause. Marvel awakens the desire to find out. It kindles the intellectual appetite, the distinctively human appetite, which seeks to understand and to know the truth for its own sake. As such, marvel is perhaps the most positive and valuable emotion we can ever feel. Without love of truth, there would be no knowledge; and the love of truth would lie dormant without marvel. This may seem an excessive gloss to thrust upon the simple words *fanno voglioso di sapere*; but behind the phrase there lies the following text from the second chapter of Aristotle's *Metaphysics*:

Philosophy (the love of wisdom) arose then, as it arises still, from wonder. At first men wondered about the more obvious problems that demanded explanation; gradually their inquiries spread farther afield, and they asked questions upon such larger topics as changes in the sun and moon and stars, and the origin of the world. Now a man labouring under astonishment and perplexity is conscious of his own ignorance (it is for this reason that the lover of myth is in some sense a philosopher, for myth is composed of marvels); and if men philosophized in order to escape from ignorance, they were evidently in search of knowledge for its own sake and not for any practical results they might derive from it.[18]

It will be seen that the pregnant words alluded to in the preface – *philomythes aliqualiter philosophus est* – are embedded in the parenthesis at the heart of this passage, but for the moment we must confine our attention to the opening sentence. In the literal translation by William of Moerbeke it runs 'Nam *propter admirari* homines nunc et primum incoeperunt philosophari'; and in the paraphrase by Aquinas: '. . . ipsi etiam philosophi *ex admiratione* moti sunt ad philosophandum'.[19]

Dante certainly knew this text and he alluded to it several times in his other works.[20] When he wants to lay stress on marvel as a cause rather than as an effect, he will sometimes use *ammirazione* and the verb *ammirare* to render *admiratio* and *admirari* in precisely the sense they have in the passage we have just quoted.[21] And that little phrase *propter admirari cepere phylosophari* (to give it in the form in which Dante quoted it) generates a great deal of poetry in the *Purgatorio* and the *Paradiso*.

The representation of *maraviglia*, *stupore* and *ammirazione* does not cease after that first day.[22] The only difference is that the emotion is reserved increasingly and then exclusively for the character Dante.[23] Gradually, too, it receives less emphasis than the cognate but more 'advanced' emotion of perplexity or doubt (*dubbio*, *dubitazione*), which is aroused when the explanation of the marvel seems inconsistent with our previous knowledge and calls our previous assumptions into question. Time and time again Dante shows us his *stupore* and *dubbio* acting as the stimulus to excite his thirst for knowledge. This demands satisfaction on matters which become increasingly arduous and fundamental, rising from the order of the universe through free will, providence, divine justice and predestination to the nature of the angels and the first creation. The last appearance of a verb of marvelling comes two-thirds of the way through the final canto (*Par.* XXXIII, 96), for marvel becomes unnecessary and impossible only when Dante has been granted the lightning flash of total understanding that enables him to grasp the mystery of the Trinity and Christ's two natures. The story of the *Comedy* is the story of a journey to knowledge. Knowledge begins in the sense of wonder. And this is the main reason why wonder is expressed in so many forms during the first day of Dante's ascent, and why it remains so important for the characterization of Dante the traveller throughout the poem.[24]

Knowledge and causation

Now that we have dealt in detail with 'wonder', we must pass on to 'knowledge'. Dante proclaimed his allegiance to Aristotle in the first book of the *Convivio* by taking the first sentence of the *Metaphysics* as his opening words: 'All men by nature desire to know' – 'Sì come dice lo Filosofo nel principio de la *Prima Filosofia*, "tutti li uomini naturalmente desiderano di sapere".' But what did Dante and Aristotle mean by the verb 'to know' (the relevant verbs in Latin and Italian being *scire* and *sapere*)?

When it is used in a philosophical context and without qualification, *scire* means to possess perfect and absolute knowledge. The corresponding noun, *scientia*, therefore denotes a demonstrable certainty, and it marks a contrast with words like *opinio* or *qualiscumque cognitio* which denote lesser, imperfect degrees of understanding.[25] Aristotle himself attempts a definition of the verb in the opening paragraph of his *Physics* and in the second chapter of the *Posterior Analytics*: 'We think we know something', he writes, 'when we know its primary causes and first principles right back to its elements.'[26] And again: 'We think we know a fact without qualification . . . when we think that we know its cause to be its cause, and that the fact could not be otherwise.'[27]

It will be seen that his definition rests upon the term here translated as 'cause' or 'causes', and it will come as no surprise to learn that our modern everyday use of the word coincides only very imperfectly with the senses that Aristotle had given to the term and which were common currency in Dante's lifetime. Aristotle, in fact, distinguished four main types of cause, all of which have to be known before we possess that perfection of knowledge which is *scientia*.[28] Or, to put it another way, before we can say we 'know' something, we must be able to give an answer to four questions: What is it made of? Who or what made it? What was it made for? and What is its structure or form? A simple example will serve to make this clear and to introduce the Aristotelian terminology.[29]

A casserole or earthenware cooking pot is made from a special substance familiarly known as potter's clay; no other mud-like compound has the same properties, not even ordinary clay. It is made by a potter; no inanimate force could make it, nor could an animal, nor could an unskilled human being. It is made in order to stew meat and vegetables. And its purpose largely determines its form or structure: it must be glazed (unlike a flower pot); it must be reasonably capacious (unlike a cup); it must have high sides and a lid (unlike a frying pan); it must have a reasonably thick bottom to prevent the food from burning; and it must be sufficiently robust to withstand frequent heating, cooking and scouring. The china clay is its matter or *material cause*. The potter is its maker, or mover, or *efficient cause* (if we need to distinguish the contribution made by wheel, fire and kiln as regulated by the potter, we refer to them as *instrumental* causes). The stewing of food is the goal or end (Latin *finis*) or *final cause*. And the functionally determined structure or shape which makes it what it is, is called the form or *formal cause*. From Aristotle's point of view, then, the potter is not the sole cause, as we all too readily assume. Matter, form and purpose all determine the pot in different and compatible ways; and it is only when we understand them all that we know that the casserole 'could not be other than it is', *nec aliter posse se habere*.[30]

It is not always so easy to distinguish the four causes. Any artefact with many distinct parts requires a much more complex analysis of its form. Living organisms are more difficult still (not least because three of the causes seem to be identical: the formal, final and efficient causes of an animal are all the mature animal viewed in different ways).[31] In any case, our explanation of the pot would be of no help to anyone who did not already know the meaning of 'stewing', 'potter' and 'potter's clay'. Again, the full understanding of the formal cause of the casserole depends on our prior knowledge of many things which are not pots, and of many pots which are not casseroles, since it is this knowledge that enables us to identify the genus and the species by a process of comparison and contrast. More often than not, an explanation of one thing reveals our ignorance of the causes of the alleged causes; and investigation of these leads us on to explore the causes of those. Indeed, the process of inquiry into efficient causes would be literally infinite, if Aristotelian and Christian alike had not agreed that there must be a First Cause which is itself uncaused, or which is the cause of its own being, and which precludes the possibility of an infinite recession of caused causes.[32]

It will be obvious that Aristotle's theories concerning perception, cognition and certain knowledge take in far more than his theory of causality, of which we have in any case barely scratched the surface. But enough has been said to make it clear that any philosophy erected on a theory of knowledge of this kind must of its very nature be systematic. Everything is interrelated and interdependent. Strictly speaking, certain knowledge of any fact depends on certain knowledge of every fact. This is why the fully fledged philosopher must be able to see the whole and the parts simultaneously – *pariter summam et singula*. And this is also why the journey towards the acquisition of that total knowledge can begin with the inquiry into any fact whatsoever, since the pursuit of the causes of the causes will proceed and ramify until all the causes are known – all, that is, except the self-caused First Cause, whose existence can be inferred, but who remains on this view of knowledge literally unknowable.

The hunt for man

The certain knowledge that transformed Dante's life and poetry and that he sought to represent and explain in the *Comedy* was knowledge about man and about human happiness, and these are the concepts we must learn to understand if we are to enjoy his poem to the full. At the very least we should be able to do for man what we have just done for the casserole, even though the description of man's four causes will inevitably be more detailed and complex. But it will have become clear from what has been said, that if we are to focus on man, we must not begin with him. Otherwise, our inquiry will spread wider and wider, and farther and farther away, like the ripples when a pebble is thrown into a pond.[33] We must not flush man from his lair immediately (and the hunting imagery is borrowed from both Dante and Lucretius).[34] We must encircle the wood with nets and close gradually in on our prey.

To understand man's *material* cause, we shall have to learn about the properties of the four elements and their compounds (Chapters 2–4); and to understand these, we must consider the fifth element that supplies the matter of the heavenly bodies (Chapter 6).

To understand man's *formal* cause, we must know something about the rest of the cosmos, since we shall only grasp what is distinctive and specific to mankind when we are aware of other genera and species ranging from worms to angels. The relevant data will be presented in the remaining chapters of the first part of the book (5 and 7).

In the second part, we shall concentrate our attention on man's *efficient* causes. Having reviewed the underlying 'picture-language' (Chapter 8), we shall make a thorough study of the two distinct modes of coming into being – 'creation' and 'generation' – that separately account for the production of all creatures except man (Chapters 9 and 10). In the final chapter, we shall see that man is unique because he owes his being to both generation and creation; and we shall explore the consequences of this dichotomy for the understanding of his *final* cause, which is synonymous with human happiness.

The wood is a large one, then, and the nets have to be cast correspondingly wide. For much of the volume, man will appear only fleetingly; and the reader is asked to take it on trust that all the axioms, notions and facts to be presented are the bare minimum necessary for a proper understanding of Dante's anthropology. But there are compensations. The material is fascinating in its own right as part of the history of ideas. Much of it has to be known in order to understand the literal meaning and topography of the *Comedy*. Some of it is the raw material, the 'dust of the earth', into which Dante has breathed the spirit of great poetry. And in reading certain chapters, it should not be forgotten that Dante followed Aristotle and Aquinas in his affirmation that human reason feels more delight in what little it can see of things immortal and divine, than it does in all the many certainties concerning things which are judged by the senses:

E avvegna che quelle cose, per rispetto de la veritate, assai poco sapere si possano, quel cotanto che l'umana ragione ne vede ha più dilettazione che 'l molto e 'l certo de le cose de le quali si giudica secondo lo senso, secondo la sentenza del Filosofo in quello de li Animali.[35]

'Felix qui potuit rerum cognoscere causas'[36]

There can be no doubt that Dante was the conscious beneficiary – as well as the unconscious victim – of the Aristotelian theory of causes. He himself calls attention to the fact that his early definition of nobility (*c.* 1296) had taken in all four causes: 'questa diffinizione *tutte e quattro* le cagioni, cioè *materiale*, *formale*, *efficiente* e *finale*, comprende'; and the definition of philosophy in Book III of the *Convivio* does the same in a much more original way.[37] In Book IV of that work he brushes aside an objection to the legality of the world dominion of the Roman people by insisting that their use of force had been an *instrumental*, not an *efficient* cause.[38] A notoriously difficult speech in the second canto of the *Paradiso*, concerning the dark patches on the surface of the moon, also turns on the question of which cause was responsible. Dante had earlier believed that these patches should be attributed to the *material* cause, that is, to varying degrees of rarity and density in the moon's matter; but, in the *Comedy*, he insists that they are the product of the *formal* cause, the *formal principio*; or, in other words, that they are an aspect of the moon's structure.[39] Dante also gives a fairly circumstantial account of the Aristotelian causes in his two late works in Latin, the letter to Can Grande and the *Quaestio*.[40]

In the *Comedy*, the thirst for knowledge which is aroused in Dante the protagonist is quite often expressed as a desire to know or see the *cause*. There is no pedantic ostentation, of course, and the more obvious technicalities are suppressed: words like *cagione* and *effetto* appear, but not *cagione efficiente*. However, the tone of some of these references can be quite cool and prosaic. The Roman poet, Statius, is made to keep close to the language of the philosophers when he remarks that 'indeed things often appear which give false occasion of doubt because the true causes are hidden':

> Veramente più volte appaion cose
> che danno a dubitar falsa matera
> per le vere *cagion* che son nascose.[41]   (*Purg.* XXII, 28–30)

Similarly, Dante's question concerning Man's 'first disobedience and the fruit' is formulated for him by Adam in these terms: 'You want to know the proper cause of God's great disdain' ('. . . la *propria cagion* del gran disdegno'). And Adam's answer begins with the words: 'The tasting of the tree was not *per se* the cause of so great a banishment' ('non . . . fu *per sé la cagion* di tanto essilio').[42] In each case, the scholastically exact *causa propria* or *causa per se* stands in remarkable contrast to the short poetic periphrasis with which it is juxtaposed.

Precision of language is never a bar to expressiveness in Dante. When he begins his ascent through the heavens, he hears the harmony of the spheres, and is enveloped in a lake of light. 'The "newness" of the sound and the great light', he tells us, 'kindled in me a desire to learn their *cause*, sharper than anything I had ever felt before':

> La novità del suono e 'l grande lume
> di lor *cagion* m'accesero un disio
> mai non sentito di cotanto acume.   (*Par.* I, 82–4)

The technical word *cagione* takes its place alongside apparently neutral words like *novità*, *suono* and *lume*, but they are all quickened into life by the ellipse of the verb of 'knowing' or 'learning' (Dante writes *un disio . . . di lor cagion*), by the metaphor of *accesero*, and above all by the rhythm and word order of the last line. This throws *mai*, 'never', into strong relief, and places the rare word *acume* in the final rhyming position; and all these features combine to make the urgency of the desire a poetic fact.[43]

More than once Dante prefers to speak in even more basic language of 'the why', the *propter quid*, rather than 'the cause'. This simpler variant was twice used in the description of that group of souls whose movements were compared to a flock of sheep.[44] It is also used with great daring in one of many circumlocutions for God, the unknowable First Cause, who is referred to as 'He whose "primal why" is hidden and unfathomable':

> . . . colui che sì nasconde
> lo suo primo perché, che non li è guado.[45]

In other contexts, Dante will pass into metaphor, using the word 'root'; so, for example, the French prince Charles Martel will speak of 'di vostri effetti le *radici*'.[46] The most memorable of these 'root'-metaphors comes at the beginning of the second speech by Francesca in the fifth canto of the *Inferno*. Paraphrasing the question put by the character Dante, she seeks his sympathy with the words: 'If you have so great a desire to know the first *root* of our love, I shall answer as well as my tears allow':

> Ma s'a conoscer *la prima radice*
> del nostro amor tu hai cotanto affetto,
> dirò come colui che piange e dice.   (*Inf.* v, 124–6)

The syntax, vocabulary and rhythm of her lines echo some of the words that Aeneas addressed to Dido in the second book of the *Aeneid*: 'sed si tantus amor casus cognoscere nostros'.[47] The new element is precisely the insistence on 'first roots' or 'causes'. It is a not insignificant reminder that the poet who created Francesca was the poet who asked that he should be shown the *causes* of human perversity, in order that he in his turn might show those causes to others:

> ma priego che m'addite la *cagione*,
> sì ch'i' la veggia e ch'i' la mostri altrui.   (*Purg.* xvi, 61–2)

2

The elements

Usque ad elementa

LET US RETURN TO THE OPENING OF ARISTOTLE'S *Physics* AND THE sentence to which Dante refers in the *De vulgari eloquentia*: 'We think we know something when we know its primary causes and first principles right back to its elements'; (. . . *cum causas primas et prima principia cognoscimus, et usque ad elementa*). In the previous chapter we treated the three nouns here as roughly synonymous and concentrated on the meaning of the word *cause*. We must now try to distinguish them one from another and focus on the word *element*.[1]

In his own little dictionary of the most important philosophical terms, Aristotle points out that in ordinary usage the word 'element' belongs with the concept of 'material cause'. It refers to the 'cause out of which', and as such it must always be immanent in the thing of which it is predicated: no one would call a potter the 'element' of his pot. On the other hand, 'element' is not a synonym for 'material cause'. We do not speak of bronze as the 'element' of a bronze statue, because we know that it is an alloy of copper and tin; and, by the same token, we do not speak of potter's clay as the element of a pot. An element must be the first and simplest constituent. It must be capable of independent existence (unlike the abstraction 'primary matter'); but it cannot be resolved or divided into other simpler species.[2]

Aristotle takes an example from speech, and it will be helpful to follow his lead and analyse one complete, meaningful proposition into its written elements, e.g., 'Theundertakerwalksbeforethehearse'. Traditional grammatical analysis resolves it first into words or parts of speech, thus: 'The undertaker walks before the hearse.' The word 'undertaker' can be divided into two separate English words, *under* and *taker*; and *taker* can be analysed into the independently meaningful verb *take* and the nominal suffix *er*, which may have a constant meaning in combination with certain verbs. *Under* can be split into two syllables, *un* and *der*, each of which is here meaningless; and these syllables in their turn into the letters *u n d e* and *r*. There, for Aristotle, the analysis stops. The letters are the elements out of which the whole statement is compounded, and they satisfy all the conditions on which we have agreed: they are capable of

57

independent existence; they cannot be further sub-divided; they remain 'within' the statement; and quite clearly they do not of themselves give the statement the meaning which is its form.[3]

The nature and origins of Aristotle's theory

So far we have met with nothing to which we need object, and nothing indeed that conflicts with our present-day use of the word 'element'. And all might have been well, if Aristotle had pursued his investigation quite independently. But true to his normal practice, he tried to extract the truth from the muddled thought of his predecessors. Having carefully rejected the atomic theories of Democritus and Leucippus, he took over three ideas of genius, which he purified and combined with great skill to produce a theory of matter which is unacceptable to the lover of truth, but which is still deeply satisfying to the lover of myth.[4]

The three essential components of his theory derived from intuitions for which Aristotle gives credit to Thales, the Pythagoreans and Empedocles (and it is characteristic of Dante's love for ancient philosophy that he in his turn should do honour to them all, even though he knew very little more about them than he could read in Aristotle and his commentators). Thales, the first natural philosopher, introduced the idea that there must be one single stuff, indestructible and eternal, underlying all the forms which matter assumes in the world, and underlying all the transformations which matter undergoes in the never-ending cycle of birth, growth and death: he was wrong only in his candidate, 'water'.[5] Pythagoras and his school elaborated the Presocratic intuition that all existing things are the product of *incorporeal* qualities, and, more precisely, that they are the product of incorporeal qualities acting in opposing pairs. The dualism of many philosophies and heresies in the following centuries, together with the negative and positive charges of electro-magnetic theory and nuclear physics, have their origins in the Pythagorean polarities, such as 'finite and infinite', 'odd and even', 'unity and plurality', 'light and darkness', and 'good and evil'.[6] Finally, the poet-philosopher, Empedocles, is credited with having been the first man to extend the number of basic elements to four, the still familiar Fire, Air, Water and Earth.[7]

Let us now see how Aristotle refines and harmonizes these ideas, beginning with the polarities or contrary qualities (which, in Latin, are usually referred to as *contraria, contrarietates* or *qualitates contrariae*). Since he was pursuing material elements, conceived as the simplest bodies that actually occur in nature, and since bodies are tangible by definition, Aristotle limited his survey of contrary qualities to those which can be perceived by touch. He argued that all such tangible qualities, including 'hard and soft', 'rough and smooth', 'coarse and fine', could be reduced to just two fundamental polarities: Hot and Cold, Dry and Wet. Then he reasoned that, if contraries are the principles of things (*existentium principia*), each of the simple bodies he sought must possess two of these four contrary qualities. And since polar opposites cannot coexist – a body cannot be simultaneously hot and cold – there can be only four possible combinations of these four qualities, and there must be neither more nor less than four simple bodies. One of them would be hot and dry – a description which seems to fit Fire. Another would be hot and wet, which, with a little good will, might seem to accord with Air. The third would be cold and wet – Water, obviously; and the last would be cold and dry: clearly, Earth. Empedocles had landed a lucky blow. The four elements are indeed Fire, Air, Water and Earth; and Aristotle had provided the explanation why it 'could not have been otherwise'.[8] The following traditional diagram will perhaps prove easier to follow than any verbal description of the relationship between the contraries and the elements:

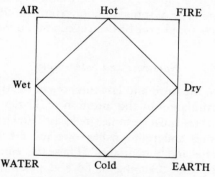

Figure 1. The four elements and the four contraries.

This is also a convenient place to make two further clarifications. First, although Aristotle and the medieval philosophers frequently speak of the four elements by that name (*quatuor elementa*), the technical and completely unambiguous term is 'simple bodies', *corpora simplicia*. This term contrasts implicitly with all other bodies, which are *corpora mixta*, that is, compounds built up from the 'simple bodies' as words and sentences are built up from letters. Second, the element Earth is not to be identified with the soil of the ground, which is a *corpus mixtum*. It is 'similar in nature', but no more. By the same token, Water is not water and Air is not air (it has been pointed out that Aristotle comes close to speaking of these 'simple bodies' as we would speak of the three 'states' of matter – solid, liquid and gaseous). Fire, too, is 'such as fire, but not fire'.[9]

Among Empedocles's misapprehensions about the four elements was his belief that they were stable and permanent. By contrast, Aristotle taught that the simple bodies were capable of transformation one into another (this doctrine of the transmutations of the elements was to be the ultimate theoretical basis of the science of Alchemy).[10] If Earth were to lose its quality of coldness (a glance at the diagram may be helpful here), it would no longer be cold and dry, but *hot* and dry. In other words, it would become Fire. Anyone who has watched a log or a piece of coal burning will have a reasonably accurate notion of the process involved.[11] Similarly, if Water were to lose its wetness it would become dry and cold, which is to say Earth. In this case, the process of freezing by which water turns to ice is the obvious example from everyday experience; just as the formation of steam illustrates the way in which Water can become Air on exchanging cold for heat. The metamorphoses to which water is subject by alternate freezing and thawing, evaporation and condensation, make it easy to accept that such elemental changes are reversible and can continue indefinitely. And from this perception it requires only a small leap of the imagination to grasp and assent to Aristotle's deduction that there can be a continuing *cycle* of transmutation from one element to another, in which no matter would ever be destroyed and no matter created.[12]

Substrate and potentiality

Before we come to the third and last component of Aristotle's theory of matter – his reformulation of the intuition of Thales and other earlier philosophers that there must be some single stuff underlying all the forms that matter assumes and relinquishes – we must briefly examine the notions of 'substrate' and 'potentiality'. These two concepts are essential to Aristotle's theory of 'Coming to be and passing away'; and it is precisely in the work bearing this title (in Latin, *De generatione et corruptione*), that he gives his fullest account of the elements and the contraries. Neither concept is difficult to understand in a general or provisional way, particularly if we approach them through the kind of examples that Aristotle himself used.

When a tree is made into planks, and the planks are made into a bed, there is clearly something which persists through these changes; and that something is wood, which is the material cause of the tree, the plank and the bed in turn, *underlying* each successive form. In the context of change, we call wood the 'substratum' (in Latin, *subiectum*, meaning quite simply 'that which is placed beneath').[13] And in every comparable case of simple alteration, there will be a clearly identifiable substratum of matter, which will be the necessary condition for any change to take place, just as it is the necessary condition for the existence of the original form and of the new form (for Aristotle, the forms of trees, planks and beds can exist only in matter).

The same principle seems to hold in the more complex kind of change which Aristotle calls 'generation' and 'corruption' (that is, 'coming into being' and 'passing away'). When blood is changed into sperm, the matter itself assumes a new structure in a way that the wood did not when it was made into a bed. But nothing is destroyed when blood ceases to be blood, and nothing is created at the moment when sperm becomes sperm. And pursuing this line of reasoning, Aristotle declared that in *every* case of change studied by the physicist, there must always be a material substrate underlying both the form that ceases to be and the form that comes into being. So much then for the concept of a substrate.[14]

Now it is clear that not all matter is equally suited to receive every form.[15] Sperm can only be formed from blood. If we want to make a knife or a saw (favourite examples these), we must make it out of iron. Even the hardest wood would be useless; bone is difficult to shape; softer metals would not maintain their cutting edge.[16] Of all natural materials, only iron has the 'right potential'; that is, only iron has those particular qualities, properties or 'powers' (*potentiae*) which enable it or predispose it to take on the form of a knife or saw, and to carry out their respective functions. When we have grasped this point it is not difficult to understand the slightly paradoxical way of talking which allows Aristotle and his disciples to say that 'iron is potentially a knife'. Once the iron has assumed the form of a knife, it is said to be a knife 'in act' (*in actu*); but before then it can be informatively described as a knife 'in potency' (*in potentia*).[17]

In the same way, we can see that iron ore was potentially iron before it was smelted, and that certain unnamed mineral compounds were iron ore in potency before they became iron ore in act. And pushing the analysis right back to the elements, *usque ad elementa*, it must be true that these unnamed compounds existed potentially in Earth, Water, Air and Fire before coming into being. Indeed, it becomes apparent that since all things which exist in our world have different compounds of the four elements as their material cause, the four elements must be all things in potency: that is, they have the capacity or the potentiality to assume all existing material forms.

We can summarize these points by returning to the familiar substance, wood, and clarifying the circumstances in which an Aristotelian would want to call it 'matter', or 'substrate', or 'potency'. In the analysis of a particular object, he would speak of it as *matter* or the 'material cause', thereby contrasting it with 'carpenter' and 'comfortable sleep' (which are the efficient and final causes) and above all with the formal cause, the structure by virtue of which it is a bed. Matter is the correlative of form. In the analysis of the successive changes by which a tree became a bed, he thinks of wood as the *substrate*, and he is making a contrast, not with 'form', but with 'change' and 'alteration'. When it is considered in the present tense, so to speak, wood is called 'matter'; but it is called 'substrate' in the passage from past to present. And in the perspective of the future, it becomes *potentiality*. In other words, when the Aristotelian thinks of the many items of furniture which might be made from wood, he is thinking of it as 'potentiality', and contrasting it with the 'actuality' or the real and present existence of those items.

Primary matter

Holding fast to these concepts and distinctions, we may now revert to the four elements and the cycle of their transformations. We have established that whenever one body is changed into another, there must be a substratum.[18] But in the case of the transmutations of the elements, that substratum cannot itself be a body (it cannot, that is, be analysed as matter possessing a certain form, because the elements are by definition the *simplest* bodies). Nor can the substratum possess any tangible qualities, since whatever possesses tangible qualities must be a body, and vice versa. Having no qualities, it is not predisposed or fitted to receive any one form rather than another. Its potentiality is therefore absolute and unconditional; and it can be spoken of as 'pure potentiality' (*potentia pura*). Pure potentiality is, of course, an abstraction; but it is a necessary abstraction, and has as much right to a name as any other. So while we must be on our guard, and beware of thinking of this quality-less, incorporeal, pure potentiality as something capable of independent existence apart from the finite simple bodies and their compounds – Dante twice feels it necessary to insist that this pure potentiality is at all times fully actualized – we may take Aristotle's lead and call the substratum of the elements 'primary matter', in Latin, *materia prima*.[19]

On first acquaintance, it is admittedly a rather difficult concept. Dante confessed that he found one of the problems related to 'la materia prima de li elementi', to be so daunting that he nearly abandoned his philosophical studies in despair. Like eternity and God, he tells us, prime matter is a concept which we are compelled to affirm, but which we cannot contemplate steadily. Our human intellect is dazzled by the notion of 'pure potentiality', just as our human eyes are dazzled by the sun.[20] But it is by no means impossible to grasp it by analogy, *in universali et in typo*, which is all that is required of readers of the *Comedy*.[21] Within Aristotle's own system of ideas, 'primary matter' is no more difficult than such modern abstractions as 'minus quantity' or a 'gross national product'. The really arduous problems lay in wait for the Christian Aristotelians of the thirteenth century, who were committed by their faith to the proposition that God had created the world from nothing (a belief which Aristotle had rejected as impossible).[22] Christian philosophers had to grapple with such questions as whether primary matter had in some sense enjoyed an independent existence before it contracted the contrary qualities which made possible and necessary the formation of the four elements, or how 'pure potentiality' could proceed from a supreme being and First Cause who was defined as 'pure actuality'.[23] But for the time being we can ignore the *efficient cause* of matter, whether primary or secondary, since we must discover a little more about the properties of the four elements and about the universe which they underlie.

Heat and cold, lightness and gravity

Each of the four elements is perfectly homogeneous and possesses its two constituent contrary qualities in a perfectly uniform and regular way, such that every part has exactly the same properties as every other part, and the whole is no more than the sum of the parts.[24] But the four contraries are not all on the same footing as each other. Dry and Wet are passive qualities, while Hot and Cold are active. Strictly speaking, then, the efficient causes of all transformation and change are the contrary qualities of Heat and Cold. They dominate and 'master' the passive qualities. And it is to their activity (varying from hour to hour and season to season, as we shall see, according to the movements of the sun and moon) that we must ascribe the necessary transience of 'li elementi' and 'quelle cose che di lor si fanno', on which Dante insists with superb lucidity in the seventh canto of the *Paradiso*:[25]

> Io veggio l'acqua, io veggio il foco,
> l'aere e la terra e tutte lor misture
> venire a corruzione, e durar poco. (VII, 124–6, cf. 133–4)

In the *corpora mixta*, and especially in plants and animals, it is natural to associate Heat with life, generation and coming to be; while Cold is linked with death, corruption and passing away. This is certainly an oversimplification, but it will be helpful rather than misleading, provided we remember that the activity of Heat and Cold is complementary: a new body comes into being when its form supplants the form under which its matter had existed until that moment; and therefore no new body can be generated except by the corruption of other bodies.[26]

At the level of the *corpora simplicia* and their mutual transformations we cannot speak of Heat as the positive pole, and Cold as the negative. All we can safely say is that the action of Heat is to rarefy, expand and dilate, while the action of Cold is to condense, shrink and contract. And both Hot and Cold seem to be more 'masterful', more fully themselves, so to speak, when they are combined with Dry: Fire is hotter than Air, and Earth is colder than Water.[27]

The two cold elements possess 'weight' or 'gravity'. We are sometimes warned not to posit any necessary link between heaviness and the tendency of the cold radical to contract, but it is difficult to resist the temptation. The element, Earth, in which Cold is more conspicuously cold, is said to possess weight naturally and absolutely. It is not heavy relative to the other elements; it is simply heavy. Being homogeneous, every part of Earth is heavy to the same degree, and any two equal portions of Earth must be equal in weight. Water is also heavy, but less so than Earth. Conversely, Fire, in which Heat is more conspicuously hot, possesses the quality of lightness naturally and absolutely; while the hot and wet element, Air, is light, but less light.[28]

Changing his terminology, Aristotle will say that the four elements all possess a natural tendency to move in a straight line until each comes to rest in its 'natural place', where it will be united with all other free particles of the same element. Cold and Hot are opposites, so they move in opposite directions. The colder of the two cold elements (Earth) moves inwards or 'downwards' (*deorsum*), until it comes to rest at or around the centre (and the centre is defined tautologically as that point to which all cold and heavy bodies move in a straight line, or as the 'natural place' where the natural movement of Earth comes to a halt). But if Cold is centripetal, heat must be centrifugal. So the hotter of the two hot elements, Fire, moves outwards or 'upwards' (*sursum*), until it reaches the extremity or circumference, which is defined no less tautologically than the centre.[29] Water and Air move down and up respectively but with less vehemence, because they are less cold and less hot than the dry elements. Whichever terminology we use, however (heavy and light, or movement up and down), it is important to remember that the force which carries Fire to the extremity is no less positive and active than the force which takes Earth to the centre: Aristotle's lightness is not the same as weightlessness.

This natural movement of the elements can also be described metaphorically. Each element is then said to have a natural 'inclination' or an instinctive 'love' for its proper place, or for other parts of the same element with which it seeks to be united (love being the force which impels like to unite with like).[30] But expansion and contraction, lightness and heaviness, upward and downward natural movement, and elemental love may all be understood as different ways of talking about the same inherent properties of the four elements, and it is helpful to relate them all to the primary active polarity of Heat and Cold.

The concentric spheres

If we continue to ignore the transmutations and combinations of the elements (as we have done in discussing heaviness and lightness), and if we accept Aristotle's proof that matter is finite, and that there can be no void, we shall expect to find that the natural, centripetal movement of the homogeneous element Earth will have created a single, perfect, solid and motionless sphere at the 'centre', and that the centre of Earth – the point to which all weights are drawn – will be the centre of the universe: granted its homogeneity and absolute heaviness, it could not naturally assume any other form.[31] Water, being heavy but less heavy, should also have formed a perfect and motionless sphere surrounding and pressing on the solid core of Earth. Similarly, Fire should have created a perfect motionless sphere at the extremity, since its every part will have sought with equal 'desire' to be at an equal distance from the centre. Air should have formed a perfect sphere inside that of Fire, pressing equally upwards on it; and, granted that 'Nature abhors a vacuum', the outer circumference of the sphere of Water and the inner circumference of the sphere of Air should be in perfect contact at every point. In short, the natural properties of the elements should have caused them to arrange themselves in four, perfect, motionless, concentric spheres which constitute their respective 'places'.[32] A diagram will make this clear.

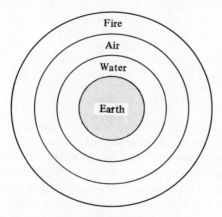

Figure 2. The four elements in their spheres.

Notwithstanding the action of external forces which have somewhat disturbed the natural arrangement, this is what observation confirms. Dry land has emerged to touch the Air, but the vast surface of the sea is none other than the convex surface of the sphere of Water. And we, the human observers, live out our lives at or near the point where Heat and Cold can interact through the medium of the passive quality, Wetness, which is present in both Water and Air.

Elemental love in prose and poetry

Dante alludes to the natural properties of the four elements in many passages, and two of these are of particular interest because they illustrate the difference between *giving* information, which is the role of prose, and *transfiguring* information in an act of celebration and worship, which is one of the functions of poetry.

In the *Convivio*, Dante touches on the natural movements of the elements in these words:

Everything has its specific love . . . The simple bodies have an inalienable natural love for their proper places, and hence Earth always descends to the centre, while Fire has a natural love for the upper circumference, bounded by the heaven of the moon, and therefore always climbs towards that heaven.

Onde è da sapere che ciascuna cosa . . . ha 'l suo speziale amore. Come le corpora simplici hanno amore naturato in sé a lo luogo proprio, e però la terra sempre discende al centro; lo fuoco ha amore a la circunferenza di sopra, lungo lo cielo de la luna, e però sempre sale a quello. (*Con.* III, iii, 2)

In the *Paradiso*, Beatrice is made to speak of the instinct that carries every part of creation to its appropriate haven, and she continues: 'Instinct it is which carries Fire towards the moon; this is the motive force in mortal hearts; this is what binds the earth and makes it one.'

> (. . . e ciascuna
> con *istinto* a lei dato che la porti).
> Questi ne porta il foco inver' la luna;
> questi ne' cor mortali è permotore;
> questi la terra in sé stringe e aduna.   (*Par.* I, 113–17)

It is more than usually difficult to talk about the terzina in isolation from the rest of Beatrice's discourse, but let us concentrate our attention on the two passages as quoted and try to analyse the differences between them. Those in vocabulary are not decisive. The prose passage combines neutral words like *terra*, *fuoco* and *luogo* with verbs that we use of human agents (*discendere* and *salire*) and with specialist terms like *circunferenza*, *corpora simplici*, *naturato* and *speziale*. But the absence of these last terms in the verse is not significant. The range of lexical items is essentially the same; and while the verbs, *stringere* and *adunare*, may be thought more expressive than anything in the prose, most people would regard *istinto* as less 'poetic' than *amore*, and *permotore* is certainly more exclusively 'scientific' than any word in the extract from the *Convivio*. Nor is the difference simply that between explaining a fact for the first time, and merely alluding to it in passing. Dante is not directly concerned with the elements in either case. He is reminding the reader of well-known facts about Earth and Fire as part of a wider argument about the role of love as a motive force in every part of the universe.

The important differences are those in organization – differences in sound, metre, rhythm and syntax. The *Convivio* prose is loosely made and rather sprawling, with an awkward link, for example, between *centro* and *lo fuoco*. The clauses and phrases are irregular in length and asymmetrical in construction; and, as a result, the repetition of *amore (naturato)* and of the linking phrase, *e però sempre*, strikes one as clumsy rather than elegant. There is no heightening of the rhythm (of the kind Dante certainly achieves in emotive passages in prose, whether in Latin or in the vernacular), and there is no attempt to make the reader aware of the sounds – certainly nothing of the pleasure given by the complex assonances of '*ne' cor mortali è permotore*'.

The *Paradiso* passage is an incantation, and its organization would be immediately evident even if it were not printed as verse. Formal balance is obtained by the perfect coincidence of clause and line, by the triple anaphora of *questi*, and by the fact that in each line the variable rhythmic pulses are deliberately made to fall in the same positions (there are stresses on the first, fourth and sixth syllables in each case). On the other hand, the syntax of each clause is pleasingly varied, and an obvious climax is reached in the third line, where a more pronounced caesura after the monosyllable *sé* is followed by not one verb, but a pair, in an order that satisfies the ear as well as the mind (*aduna e stringe* would not do). Semantically, too, it is probably important that the movement of Fire is described before that of Earth, since this creates a feeling of expansion followed by contraction, of motion followed by rest.

What distinguishes the poetry from the prose is not the concepts, nor the words, but concision, relevance, formal patterning and what we can only call verbal music. Needless to say the terzina also gains immeasurably in its immediate context, for it is only the third terzina of four which carry one idea triumphantly forward; and it is preceded by one of Dante's finest and most Lucretian evocations of cosmic immensity and order in the splendid sustained metaphor and the magnificently irregular rhythms of:

> onde si muovono a diversi porti
> per lo gran mar de l'essere, e ciascuna
> con istinto a lei dato che la porti.　　　(*Par.* I, 112–14)

'Hence they move to different havens over the great sea of being, and each with instinct to carry them on their journey.'

Fiction and fact in Dante's underworld

Dante imagined his Hell as a subterranean void of colossal dimensions. It is shaped like a funnel or an inverted cone, and its bottom coincides with the centre of the earth. We are not told the diameter of the base of this cone (and the problem has exercised the ingenuity of commentators ever since the fifteenth century), but we do learn that if a straight line drawn from the centre of that base to the apex of the cone were to be produced, it would connect Jerusalem in the northern hemisphere and the mountain island of Purgatory in the southern hemisphere. Figure 3 will make this clear.

Hell is divided into nine distinct zones in the form of broad, horizontal terraces which run the full circle round the cone (as shown in figure 4). Each zone is the place where a particular category of sin is visited with an appropriate punishment; and Dante's debt to Aristotle's *Ethics* and scholastic habits of thought is nowhere more evident than in his comprehensive classification of human sins, all of which are carefully assessed and graded in such a way that the lower the circle is, the more offensive is the sin, and the more severe the divine punishment. Dante had many models for his underworld in classical literature, in the Bible, and in Christian theology and art; but none of them show anything like this precision and rigour in respect of size, shape and exact location, or in respect of the superbly articulated moral structure, made concrete in the diminishing, deepening circles.

When we examine the layout and physical structure of Hell in detail it

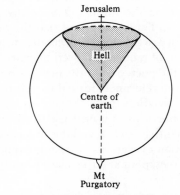

Figure 3. Jerusalem, Hell and Purgatory.

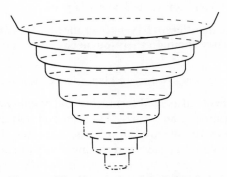

Figure 4. The nine circles of the infernal cone.

is therefore somewhat surprising to find that Dante has made very little attempt to reconcile his poetic fiction with his scientific knowledge. He tells us that Hell was made by God, and that it assumed its definitive shape at the time when Lucifer and the rebel angels fell from Heaven.[33] But he never explains how the existence of this huge 'pit' (to use the biblical term) could be harmonized with the Aristotelian teaching that our globe is a solid core of the element Earth. And he makes little or no use of his knowledge of the distances involved. Twice in a short space he states the exact dimensions of a cross-section of the infernal cone. But although the circumference dwindles from twenty-two miles to eleven within a single circle of Hell, we are not told how far we are from the centre at this point, and therefore no further inferences can be drawn. Dante does indeed suggest the existence of immense spaces in the underworld, both horizontally, as in the journey across the marshy river of Styx to the walls of the city of Dis, and vertically, as in the exciting downward flight on the back of Geryon; but we are certainly not made to *feel* that we have descended more than 3,000 miles in the journey to the centre of the earth.[34] The journey up from the centre is described in a mere half dozen lines, and it took the travellers a little less than twenty-four hours.

The infernal rivers provide another nice example of Dante's ability to turn a blind eye to the Aristotelian doctrine concerning the four elements. Dante has reinterpreted and rearranged the four rivers of the Graeco-Roman underworld in a most original and satisfying way. Acheron, Styx, Phlegethon and Cocytus have become just one river, manifesting itself under different names at different levels. But the account of its source and direction of flow is not Aristotelian, nor even remotely scientific in character: it is quite deliberately allegorical and biblical. On the island of Crete, we are told, stands the image or statue of an Old Man (deriving from Nebuchadnezzar's dream as related in the Book of Daniel), who symbolizes the history and progressive decline of the human race. His head is made of gold, his shoulders and arms of silver, his chest of copper, his legs of iron, and his right foot of clay. Each part of his body is cleft by a single deep fissure dripping with tears. It is these tears, representing the sufferings of mankind through the ages, which provide the source of the single river in Dante's underworld.[35] The river flows down to the bottom of the pit – just as 'la gente grossa' would expect. Yet, it could be argued that on Aristotelian principles, all water remaining under the surface of the earth would flow *upwards*, since its natural love for its proper place would carry it to the surface of our globe.[36]

The final manifestation of this one infernal river – Cocytus – forms the last of the ten zones in Dante's Hell. It is a vast lake, frozen over like a Russian river in winter-time.[37] Dante dwells insistently on the cold, describing its cruel effects on the two travellers and on the sinners who are embedded in the ice; and it might seem that he is at last exploiting the doctrine of the four elements and the four contraries. Since Cold is associated with heaviness, what could be more 'natural' than that the centre should be the coldest part? But Dante shuns any such naturalistic explanation. We learn that the instrumental cause of the cold is the icy wind (a fact which occasions a certain *stupore* in Dante the traveller, who is suddenly credited with enough scientific knowledge to realize that all wind, all *vapore*, should be still at this depth).[38] And in fact the cause of the wind has nothing whatever to do with Aristotelian meteorology.

Fixed in the centre of the earth, like a worm in the core of an apple, is the Prince of the fallen angels, Lucifer. From the waist up, he towers above the ice, as ugly now as he had once been beautiful; he is a terrible parody of the Trinity with his three monstrous heads; and his body is covered in thick shaggy hair like a wild animal. He has three pairs of gigantic wings, not feathered like an angel's, but leathery like those of a bat; and it is the flapping of these wings that gives rise to the cold wind, which is in turn a cruel parody of that other *vapore*, the Holy Spirit, that emanates from God and sustains the universe in order and love.[39] Everything seems to be expressed in the language of myth;[40] everything is charged with negative symbolism: ugliness, cold, darkness together remind us that here at the centre of the universe we are at the greatest possible distance from the goodness of God.

It is at this moment in the narrative, half-way through the last canto of the *Inferno*, that Dante suddenly chooses to exploit the most important 'scientific' fact about the centre of the earth, namely, that it is the centre of gravity. Symbolism gives place to suspense for more than forty lines while Dante describes how he and Virgil made their way out of Hell. The virtues of the writing are very different in kind from those we have examined up to this point, and they are perhaps best suggested by a version in idiomatic, modern prose. We may plunge into the story half-way through a speech by Virgil:

'But night is coming on again, and it's time that we were on our way, for we've seen everything.' I did as he wished and clasped my arms round his neck while he watched for the right moment and place. When Lucifer's wings were fully spread, Virgil caught hold of his shaggy flanks and climbed down from one tuft of hair to another between the matted fur and the frozen surface of the lake. When he reached the point where the thighs swell out, on the thickest part of the hips, Virgil made a great effort and worked his head round to where his feet had been. Then he caught hold of the fur as though he were climbing, so that I thought I was going back to Hell. 'Hold on tight', he said, panting with exhaustion, 'these are the stairs we've got to climb to get away from evil.' Soon he crawled out through a cleft in the rock, set me down on a ledge, and then made his way to my side. I looked up, thinking I would see Lucifer just as before – and saw his *legs* sticking upwards! Those of you who still haven't grasped the nature of the point we had passed will realize how stupefied I was. 'On your feet', said Virgil, 'there's a long way to go, and the path will be difficult; and the sun has been up for an hour and a half already.' It was no palatial hall we were in, but a natural cave with an uneven floor and hardly any light. 'Before I tear myself away from the abyss', I said when I had got to my feet, 'tell me enough to put my mind at rest. Where is the ice? And how can Lucifer be stuck upside down like this? And how can the sun have risen so soon after setting?' And he answered: 'You think you're still on the other side of the centre, where I first caught hold of the "worm in the core". You were still on that side while I was coming down, but when I turned round, you passed the point to which all weights move from every side.' (*Inf.* XXXIV, 68–111)

Action of a realistic kind, conveyed in a succession of short clauses with the simplest possible links, is punctuated by a naturalistic dialogue that is heightened only by the occasional touch of humorous exaggeration, which writers of adventure stories believe to be characteristic of men of action in a dangerous situation. There is no ostentation of learning, no didacticism. The only hint of scientific language comes in the very last line with Virgil's brief explanation about the centre of gravity. But the science is there; and in this passage we discover that Dante can use scientific knowledge in more or less exactly the same way that it is used by a competent writer of science-fiction today. Just as an author in the 1950s would try to imagine the sensation of weightlessness in space travel, and to invent some situation in which this could be dramatized and made vivid to his readers, so Dante imagined what it would be like to feel absolute heaviness in the course of his *Journey to the Centre of the Earth*. It is a measure of his relaxed confidence in his powers that he can combine this task with a reminder that, since Purgatory is removed in latitude by 180° from Jerusalem, it will be day there when it is night here.[41]

Words and blood

Many cantos earlier in the *Inferno* there is another moment of suspense and drama. Having crossed the infernal river at a point where it is filled with boiling blood, Dante and Virgil pass into an almost impenetrable wood. Harpies, half women and half birds of prey, perch on the gnarled and thorny branches, tearing off the leaves and feeding on them. No human shape is anywhere to be seen, but the air is filled on all sides with the sound of human voices screaming in anguish. Where do the voices come from? Are there people hiding behind the trees? In answer to Dante's unspoken fears and conjectures, Virgil makes him break a small branch from a large tree nearby. The protagonist is then terrified and appalled as the tree itself screams out in pain and reproach. Its words issue from the gash inflicted by Dante; and from the same wound there flows, not sap, but human blood.

71

At this horrific moment in his narrative, Dante introduces a simile which has won universal admiration. It is so sharply observed, so familiar, so apt to make one accept the whole 'truth' of the ghastly scene.

When a green log is burning at one end, it will weep at the other and whistle with the escaping wind; just so words and blood came out together from the broken branch.

> Come d'un stizzo verde ch'arso sia
> da l'un de' capi, che da l'altro geme
> e cigola per vento che va via,
>   sì de la scheggia rotta usciva insieme
>   parole e sangue . . .   (*Inf.* XIII, 40–4)

A prose translation can convey the central core of meaning and perhaps something of the relaxed precision and poise of the original. But the less flexible rules which govern word and phrase order in modern English prose make it difficult to catch the light stress on *verde*, or the opposition between *da l'un* and *da l'altro*, or the crucial delay of the subject in the second main clause – 'words and *blood*'. Similarly it would be stilted in English to use the formula 'just as . . . so' to render the *come . . . (co)sì* of the original. And while we can get close to the metaphor in *geme* (even a plumber will speak of a joint 'sweating' or 'weeping'), we have nothing sufficiently concrete and harsh for *scheggia* (literally a 'splinter'), and no precise word in modern usage for a burning log (who today says 'brand'?). Again, it is difficult to convey the quickening pulse of the third line where the patter of unstressed syllables is heightened by the alliteration of *v*; and it is impossible to match the imitative sound of *cigola*, let alone the latent onomatopoeia in *stizzo*, which is certainly actualized in this context.

The spareness, vigour and variety of the writing here clearly belong to a major poet at the height of his powers, and the close observation of everyday experience in the simile might seem to be at the opposite extreme to the abstractions and generalizations of a philosopher. If it is really necessary to take account of possible borrowings from another author, it would be natural to look where Dante the author openly invites us to look – in the third book of Virgil's *Aeneid*.[42] In short, Dante's simile is precisely the kind of text that one might choose in order to demonstrate that his greatness owed nothing to his philosophical studies, and everything to his consummate technique and to a fertile imagination well nourished by the classics of literature.

It is, however, probable that Dante took the simile over from the drab prose of Aristotle and his commentators. The burning log, as such, was a convenient example of the transmutation of Earth into Fire by the action of heat.[43] The spitting and hissing of the *green* log on the fire demonstrated that there are traces of all the elements in every compound body. One can always see the solidity of the predominant element of Earth in a piece of wood. But it is only when the flickering tongues of flame drive out the moisture and wind from a *stizzo verde ch'arso sia* that we are made aware of the presence of Fire, Water and Air.[44] In his work on meteorology, Aristotle also cites the burning of a green log as a precise analogue for the way in which wind is formed when the heat of the sun draws out exhalations from the ground; and Dante's choice of the word *vento* may owe something to that work, as will become more readily apparent in the following chapter.[45]

It may, of course, be objected that this identification of the source does not enhance our understanding of the episode in the *Inferno*, simply because the context in which Dante first encountered the simile of the burning log is totally unrelated to the horrific scene in which the protagonist is unwillingly involved. The trunk from which he broke the branch is not burning. It is extruding not air and moisture but words and blood. And as the drama unfolds, we discover that the 'tree' is not a tree at all: it is the monstrous fusion of a human spirit and a tree-like frame that serves as the eternal prison for the imperial chancellor, Pier della Vigna, who had sought in despair to put an end to his life, and who had succeeded only in separating his soul from his human body.

But if the simile leads us by association of ideas to think first of the *material* cause that is common to man and tree, then to recognize the greater importance of the *formal* cause that distinguishes man from tree, and finally to meditate on the intimate relationship between the formal cause and the *final* cause (between the bark, branches and sap that are sufficient for the purposes of tree life, and the limbs, blood and organs of speech that are required for human life), we may yet discover that there is a connection between the Wood of the Suicides and Aristotle's natural science, and that Pier della Vigna might not have destroyed himself if he had possessed a 'perfect knowledge of his causes, right back to the elements'.

3

Meteorology

The scope and influence of Aristotle's meteorology

LIKE 'PHYSICS', 'METEOROLOGY' IS ONE OF MANY ANCIENT AND medieval terms to survive in modern usage with a different and much restricted range of meaning. Aristotle has very little to say about 'meteors' in the four books of his *Meteorologica*, and his subject is a good deal wider than the 'weather'. For him, as for his predecessors, meteorology takes in all the transient phenomena which are caused by the action of Heat and Cold and which involve no more than the transformation of the 'simple bodies' one into another. Within his system of thought, it occupies an essential place between the study of the four elements as such, and the study of the compounds of the elements as they are found in minerals, plants and animals.

Apart from its intrinsic importance, there are two main reasons why the subject demands a separate chapter at this point. First, it was from meteorology that Dante drew much of the matter and imagery for two of the *canzoni* that he wrote to express his love for a hard-hearted 'lady of stone'. These poems are not only superb achievements in their own right, they are the earliest true forerunners of the *Comedy*. Here, for the first time, as he wrestled with the data of meteorology, Dante's poetry became simultaneously learned, concrete, passionate and technically daring. Second, and more important, almost all the phenomena described in the *Meteorologica* are recalled somewhere in the *Comedy*, and there are grounds for suggesting that this was part of a conscious design. Many of the more extended passages inspired by Aristotle's meteorology are of great power and originality, as we shall see; and whether or not the borrowings were made in a systematic way, the accumulated debt was a substantial one.

Condensation and evaporation

Aristotle's account of the causes of clouds, rain, mist, dew, frost, snow and hail is substantially correct and need not detain us long. When the heat of the sun falls on a large surface of water (or simply on the surface of the earth when the soil is wet), the action of Heat transforms the upper layer of water into vapour (*vapor*). *Vapor* is moist and hot; being hot it is light; and being light it will rise. When the *vapor* has reached a certain height, and the heat reflected from the earth grows less, the *vapor* will become colder, and, as the quality of Cold gains the upper hand, it will contract and condense and turn once again into water. At first, the process of condensation will lead to the formation of minute particles of water, and the air is then said to be 'impregnated', or 'pregnant' with water.[1] Where these minute particles gather together they become visible as cloud (*nubes*, *nuvola*); and if coldness, condensation and heaviness increase, the particles of water will combine into larger drops, and the drops of water will seek to find their own proper place in the sphere of Water: their own natural weight will cause them to fall as rain.[2]

If the *vapor* does not rise far above the surface, condensation may lead to the formation of mist, that is, of low-lying cloud. If it scarcely rises at all, and if condensation is due to the coolness of oncoming night, it will take the form of dew. But if the temperature falls very rapidly, that is, if the Cold is particularly vigorous, then the low-lying *vapor* will congeal into a solid, and become visible as frost.[3] When cloud-borne *vapori* are converted immediately into a solid by the action of intense cold in winter-time, the *gelati vapori* form large flakes and fall as snow. Hail must have a similar origin; but since it usually falls in summer-time, Aristotle inclines to the view that in this case the solidification of the *vapori* is due to a complex interaction of both heat and cold.[4]

In all meteorological phenomena which involve the process of evaporation and condensation, the explanations given by Aristotle are reasonably close to the conclusions of modern science and do not present us with any serious difficulties. The continued existence in modern European languages of the medieval Latin terminology (*evaporatio*, *condensatio* etc.) makes it particularly easy to assimilate his teaching. We must be a little cautious, however, in using the original terms, because they had different connotations within the context of the theory of the four elements. *Vapor* is not 'vapour'. For most English speakers, 'condensation' has lost the general meaning of 'growing dense'; and no one thinks of 'congealing' as being due to the action of cold (*congelatio*). The point to remember at all times is forcefully made by Dante in his *Quaestio*:

Uneducated people and those ignorant of physics believe that water ascends to the mountain peaks and to the source of springs under the form of water. But this is a childish belief, for water is actually *generated* in those places (*aquae generantur ibi*), as the philosopher proves in his *Meteorologica*, and its matter ascends under the form of *vapor*. (83)

When water has frozen, it is not correct to think of it simply as water; it has taken on the form of ice. The technical word for the process is *convertere*, and this is the verb Dante uses in the first of his *canzoni* for the 'lady of stone': 'The dead water is *converted* into glass, because of the cold that has locked it from without':[5]

> e l'acqua morta *si converte* in vetro
> per la freddura che di fuor la serra.　　　(*Rime*, C, 60–1)

In another poem from the same group, Dante specifies that 'in the frozen wastes near the north pole, water is *changed* into crystalline rock because of the intense cold, and air is *converted* into the cold element, so that water is predominant in those parts because of the cold':[6]

> 　　　　　. . . per algente freddo
> *l'acqua diventa cristallina petra*
> là sotto tramontana ov'è il gran freddo,
> e l'*aere* sempre in *elemento freddo*
> vi *si converte*, sì che l'acqua è donna
> in quella parte per cagion del freddo.　　(*Rime*, CII, 25–30)

Again, when Dante describes the melting of snow, as it is struck by the hot rays of the sun, he is careful to specify that the neutral substrate of snow is deprived of the colour and the coldness that were the essential properties of the *form* that made it snow. The substrate is first stripped 'bare'; then it is ready to be 'in-formed', that is, to receive the new form which will make it water:

> Or, come ai colpi de li caldi rai
> de la *neve* riman nudo il *suggetto*
> e dal *colore* e dal *freddo* primai . . .　　(*Par.* II, 106–8)

Before we leave the subject of the phenomena caused by evaporation and condensation, and more or less correctly explained by Aristotle, we can take note of the various optical displays created when sunlight or moonlight is reflected from minute particles of moisture suspended in the atmosphere. Many effects of this kind are discussed at length in the third book of the *Meteorologica*; and Dante was clearly influenced, both in choosing to describe them and in the manner of his description, by Aristotle's account of haloes round the moon, of rainbows, and in particular, of *double* rainbows, when a second, fainter rainbow appears outside the first, with the colours in reverse order indicating that it is formed by reflection from the first.[7]

Dry exhalations

We cannot understand Aristotle's account of lightning, thunder, winds and earthquakes (all of which figure prominently in the *Comedy*) until we have grasped his theory of 'dry exhalations'. On first acquaintance, the theory seems quite straightforward. Just as Water can be changed into a *wet* gas by the action of Heat, so Earth can be changed into a *dry* gas (the anachronistic term is convenient).[8] Whenever the sun is the source of the necessary heat, we speak of the two gases as 'moist exhalations' and 'dry exhalations' respectively. The dry exhalation is of course invisible; and it stands in the same relationship to smoke and fumes as the invisible moist exhalation does to steam.[9]

The least satisfactory part of the theory concerns the relationship of the two exhalations to the four elements and to the atmosphere. Strictly speaking, the moist exhalation or *vapor* is neither Water nor Air, but a kind of mean between them (*quoddam medium*). In the same way, the dry exhalation – sometimes called *fumus*, sometimes *vapore secco* – exists in a mean state with respect to the dry elements of Earth and Fire. The air we breathe usually contains an impure mixture of both exhalations. It is difficult if not impossible to interpret and reconcile in a perfectly consistent way all the pronouncements made by Aristotle and his followers on this subject.[10] The main point to grasp, however, is that Aristotle was prepared to trust his reasoning. For him the dry exhalations are no less real and incontrovertible than the moist exhalations, which, under the name of 'evaporation', we still accept today. He believed that the sun is constantly generating exhalations of both kinds. The amount produced will of course depend on the intensity of its heat, and this will vary according to the latitude, the season, and the time of day. The most abundant source of moist exhalations will be the Ocean near the Equator at the time of the equinoxes, while the desert sands of North Africa (Dante will specify Ethiopia) will be the richest source of the dry.

With these points in mind, we may turn to Aristotle's explanation of wind. He rejected the simple definition of wind as 'air in motion' for three reasons. First, what he would call 'wind' is confined to the lower atmosphere (defined as that which lies below the level of the highest mountain peaks), and he would not use the word to describe the motion of air in the upper atmosphere, which he believed to be swept round at a constant speed from east to west by contact with the sphere of Fire, which is itself swept round by contact with the innermost of the heavenly spheres in its diurnal revolution. Second, he limited the word to air which is flowing in a definite direction like a river. And third, he thought that the efficient and material causes of wind were not air in general, but the dry exhalations.[11]

Currents formed by these exhalations do of course displace and push before them large quantities of 'ordinary air', or even of air which is saturated by vapour, and this is why wind can feel cold on the face.[12] Nevertheless, from the scientific point of view, 'wind' must refer to a current of dry exhalations whose movement is the product of two forces. These are its own upward thrust towards the sphere of Fire, and a horizontal impulse which is either received from the constant motion of the upper atmosphere, or is caused by resistance from colder air above, which compels the rising exhalations to move sideways.[13] Aristotle deals in considerable detail with the wind's flow, with veering and backing, and with prevailing winds; and his treatment of hurricanes, whirlwinds and contrary winds has clearly left its mark on some famous passages in the *Inferno*; but these must not detain us here.[14]

Thunder and lightning are caused by the violent collision of wind with cloud. It sometimes happens that the upward movement of dry exhalation is arrested by a larger quantity of moist exhalation which cools, condenses and contracts, and becomes increasingly visible as black cloud. A cloud is coldest and densest in its uppermost layers, and it can thus form a barrier to the rising 'wind', which becomes trapped within the cloud, and subject to intense pressure as the *vapor* continues to contract. This pressure will then squeeze out the trapped dry exhalation with great force, either sideways or downwards, through the less resistant parts of the cloud (just as, says Aristotle, when we squeeze a fruit stone between our fingers, the pressure will carry it sideways or upwards against its natural tendency to move downwards). When the 'wind' rips open the wall of cloud, or when it strikes against a neighbouring cloud, we hear the noise of impact as thunder.[15] If the heat generated by its motion is sufficient to set the exhalation on fire, we see the 'vapori *accesi*' as lightning; and, of course, we see the lightning before we hear the thunder, even though the thunder was produced first. If, finally, the extruded wind should strike downwards, we call it a thunderbolt.[16]

Just as the human body can be convulsed by internal wind, so can the body of the earth. Dry exhalations may be generated under the earth, or surface exhalations may be driven downwards and flow inwards rather than out.[17] The subterranean winds force their way through the 'veins' of the earth, and in so doing they are the cause of earthquakes of all kinds. The shocks will be of greater or lesser severity depending on the amount of exhalation, on whether the underground passages are wide or constricted, and on whether the movement is horizontal, or, more rarely, vertical – in which case it may be accompanied by an upsurge of stones and water.[18] Dante makes dramatic use of Aristotle's theory in the *Comedy*, as we shall see, and many details are already present in these three lines from the first *canzone* which he wrote for the 'lady of stone': 'The *veins* spew forth the *fume-laden waters* because of the *exhalations* which the *earth* has in its *stomach*, hurling them upwards from the *abyss*.'

> Versan le vene le fummifere acque
> per li vapor che la terra ha nel ventre,
> che d'abisso li tira suso in alto.   (*Rime*, C, 53–5)

Dry exhalations are also the material cause of comets and shooting stars. Aristotle suggested that falling stars and shooting stars occur when a long envelope of combustible dry exhalation is ignited in the upper atmosphere. The flame spreads with immense rapidity along the envelope, exhausting its fuel as it goes, just as fire will spread across a field of stubble. In this way it produces the illusion that a single fiery object has moved through the sky. The efficient cause of the random and apparently spontaneous combustion must be the motion of the innermost of the heavenly spheres, which causes friction as it rubs against the upper atmosphere.[19]

Sometimes, however, this 'spontaneous' combustion will take place in a larger, denser pocket of suitable dry exhalations; and if the 'fiery principle' is neither too strong nor too weak, the pocket will burn like chaff in a large heap, producing the effect of a star with a 'beard' or with 'long hair' (which is what the adjective *comētēs* means in Greek). This kind of fire does not spread. Its apparent motion is simply that which it shares with the rest of the invisible upper atmosphere; and this is also the reason why a comet falls behind the movement of the stars.[20]

From comets Aristotle passes to a detailed examination of the nature of the Milky Way, concluding that it was properly part of meteorology and not astronomy, since it was due to an accumulation of dry exhalations in the upper atmosphere (in Dante's paraphrase, 'uno ragunamento di vapori *sotto* le stelle di quella parte'). But Dante does not follow Aristotle's teaching on this point. Instead, he accepts the correct explanation, as reported by Albert the Great; and he notes, with a certain relief at the extenuating circumstances, that one cannot know exactly what Aristotle had meant, since the two translations give different versions, and the error is probably due to the translators.[21]

We are now in possession of all the facts which we need to appreciate Dante's choice and presentation of meteorological phenomena in the *Comedy*.

Meteorology in narrative and simile

As the sun rises on the travellers' first day in Purgatory, Cato tells Virgil to take Dante down to the sea, there to gird him with a rush, the symbol of humility, and to cleanse his face of the filth that had clung there during his journey through Hell:

> Va dunque, e fa che tu costui ricinghe
> d'un giunco schietto e che li lavi 'l viso,
> sì ch'ogne sucidume quindi stinghe.   (*Purg.* I, 94–6)

When they arrive near the shore, Virgil gently places both hands on the dew-covered grass; and Dante, realizing his intention, stretches out his tear-stained cheeks to his master, enabling him to wipe them clean and lay bare once again the natural colour that Hell had hidden:

> ambo le mani in su l'erbetta sparte
> soavemente 'l mio maestro pose:
> ond' io, che fui accorto di sua arte,
>   porsi ver' lui le guance lagrimose;
> ivi mi fece tutto discoverto
> quel color che l'inferno mi nascose.   (124–9)

It is a moment of perfect solitude and intimacy, and of a childlike trust on Dante's part. It is the first, the most natural, and the most moving of all the ceremonies which mark the stages in Dante's own purification as he passes through Purgatory. Few readers, therefore, will dwell on the preceding terzina, which describes the poets' arrival in the 'shady place where the dew resists the sun and is slow to disperse':

> Quando noi fummo là 've la rugiada
> pugna col sole, per essere in parte
> dove, ad orezza, poco si dirada.   (121–3)

But we ought to take note of these little details, not only because they show a characteristic blend of personal observation with hints derived from Aristotle, but because this is the only place in the whole *Comedy* where Dante describes a meteorological event as part of the scene through which he as protagonist is travelling.[22] The reason for this proves to be almost disconcertingly simple: his journey occupies at least five days, but he is in the atmosphere only during the first day of Purgatory; and as we saw in the first chapter, that first day is dominated by the sun shining from a cloudless and undisturbed sky.

There are some apparent exceptions. The superb opening lines of the seventeenth canto of the *Purgatorio* describe a moment in the journey through an appeal to the experience of anyone who has walked in the hills:

Remember, reader, if you have ever been caught by a mist in the mountains, through which you could see as much as a mole does through its membrane, how, when the dense moist vapours begin to thin out, the sun's disc enters feebly among them . . . :[23]

> Ricorditi, lettor, se mai ne l'alpe
> ti colse nebbia per la qual vedessi
> non altrimenti che per pelle talpe,
>   come, quando i vapori umidi e spessi
> a diradar cominciansi, la spera
> del sol debilemente entra per essi . . .   (*Purg.* XVII, 1–6)

But the protagonist was not in a true mist, formed naturally by the condensation of *vapori umidi e spessi*. He is emerging here from a thick, choking cloud of black smoke, which acts as an instrument of purgation, and as such has a supernatural cause.

There is a similar case earlier in the cantica. Dante caught sight of a red light glimmering on the horizon, and he now compares it to the planet Mars, 'caught by the morning low above the sea in the west, and appearing more red than usual because of the density of the moist exhalations':

> Ed ecco, qual, sorpreso dal mattino,
> per li grossi vapor Marte rosseggia
> giù nel ponente sovra 'l suol marino.   (*Purg.* 11, 13–15)

The light is not Mars, however: it proves to be the angelic boat ferrying the souls of the newly dead to Purgatory. The same moist vapours are described as reddening the eastern sky at sunrise and tempering the brightness of the sun so that Dante could look directly at it for a long time; but the moment is being recalled in a simile portraying the first appearance in the poem of Beatrice, with her beauty still hidden by her veil.

Again, when Dante describes the kind of frost that settles in early February at a time when the sun's rays are tempered by the moist sign of Aquarius and the equinox draws nearer – the kind of frost which is so heavy that it resembles snow, except that it is quick to melt – the six lines of erudite and metaphorical description are merely the prelude to a sketch of the emotions of a shepherd, who is downcast on seeing what he thinks is snow, but who soon takes heart when the frost disappears; and this in turn is a simile to illuminate Dante's short-lived despondency on seeing Virgil first discomforted and then making a quick recovery. And when we read of an overcast sky swept clean by a gentle breeze from the north-west leaving the hemisphere of the air brilliant and clear ('come rimane splendido e sereno / l'emisperio de l'aere'), the simile is there to convey the feelings which accompany the lifting of a dark cloud of perplexity from Dante's mind.[24]

Meteorology and divine punishment

Weather cannot be dissociated from feeling. We are glad when the sky clears, and we feel oppressed and terrified by exposure to severe cold, by typhoons and floods, or even by thunder and lightning. From the earliest times, natural catastrophes have been interpreted as instruments of divine punishment for human transgression. In Dante's Hell, for example, the pagan Capaneus still defies Jupiter to take his vengeance by hurling thunderbolts until the arms of his giant smiths will be weary from forging them.[25] And so it is not surprising that 'adverse weather conditions' (as the modern meteorologists so lamely say) are the inspiration of many of the punishments in the *Inferno*.

The lowest circle of Hell was filled with *nebbia* (the *nebbia* that Virgil so gently wiped from Dante's cheeks) and the sinners are tormented by the intense cold. The cold numbs their senses, makes their teeth clatter, and freezes the tears over their eyeballs; it turns them livid in colour and bites off their ears – with the result, says Dante-author, that he now has a permanent dread of frozen swamps.[26]

In the last subdivision of the circle above, the torment is drought. The rising stench there is compared to that from rotting limbs in the 'hospitals' of Valdichiana, Maremma and Sardinia between July and September; and the forger, Master Adamo, is tortured by the constant vision of 'the fresh streams running down into the Arno from the green hills of Casentino, making their channels *cool* and *moist*':

> Li ruscelletti che d'i verdi colli
> del Casentin discendon giuso in Arno
> faccendo i lor canali freddi e molli,
> sempre mi stanno innanzi . . .   (*Inf.* xxx, 64–7)

High above them, in the third circle, the gluttonous are overwhelmed by a cold, heavy, accursed and eternal rain, never changing in quality or measure. Huge hailstones, filthy water and snow pour down through the murky air on to the sodden and stinking ground:

> Io sono al terzo cerchio, de la *piova*
> etterna, maladetta, fredda e greve;
> regola e qualità mai non l'è nova.
> *Grandine* grossa, *acqua tinta* e *neve*
> per l'aere tenebroso si riversa;
> pute la terra che questo riceve.   (*Inf.* VI, 7–12)

Above them, the souls of the unchaste are tossed by a hellish whirlwind of hurricane force that batters and smashes them, hurling them in all directions:

> La bufera infernal, che mai non resta,
> mena li spirti con la sua rapina;
> voltando e percotendo li molesta.
>
> . . .
>
> di qua, di là, di giù, di sù li mena.   (*Inf.* v, 31–3, 43)

Wind in Dante's poetry

Wind as a hostile force is presented in many different and revealing ways in Dante's poetry. Let us return for a moment to the first of the *canzoni* written for the 'lady of stone', and to the description there of the south wind as a bringer of rain and snow. Thanks to the heat of the sun, which is still intense in Equatorial Africa even in our northern winter, a body of dry exhalations arises from the sandy desert of Ethiopia to form what Dante calls a 'pilgrim' wind, a wind from overseas, which comes to darken our air. How does it do this? It passes over the Mediterranean bringing with it such an abundance of moist vapour (here called *nebbia*) that if there were no other wind to disperse it, it would completely enclose our hemisphere. This *copia di nebbia* then condenses and dissolves, falling in white flakes of cold snow and dreary rain, making it seem as if the air were sadly weeping:

> Levasi de la rena d'Etiopia
> lo vento peregrin che l'aere turba,
> per la spera del sol ch'ora la scalda;
>   e passa il mare, onde conduce copia
> di nebbia tal, che, s'altro non la sturba,
> questo emisperio chiude tutto e salda;
>   e poi si solve, e cade in bianca falda
> di fredda neve ed in noiosa pioggia,
> onde l'aere s'attrista tutto e piagne.   (*Rime*, C, 14–22)

The sun, the sand of Ethiopia, the wind that 'lifts itself', the atmosphere, the sea, the *copia di nebbia*, the opposing winds, the northern hemisphere, the process of dissolution into snow and rain are all meteorological facts presented in the correct order. But Dante has eliminated any superfluous glosses and organized the sequence of events into one syntactic period, with the action carried by the three main verbs (*Levasi . . . passa . . . e poi si solve*) which stand at the head of the principal metrical divisions of the stanza. He has secured a splendid contrast of sound in the seventh line to match the slow fall of the snow by introducing a most unusual succession of three pairs formed of adjective and noun; and he moves to a satisfying climax with the humanizing metaphors of the tenth line (*s'attrista . . . e piagne*), where for the first time we are made aware of the implied personification of the 'pilgrim' wind.

In the ninth canto of the *Inferno*, Virgil and Dante are denied entry to the city of Dis by a throng of fallen angels and by the three Furies, who threaten to display the head of the Gorgon, Medusa, and to turn Dante to stone. Virgil quickly covers Dante's eyes, and at this moment the terrified Dante hears a crashing tumult approaching over the dark waters of the Styx. It proves to be an angel sent by God to crush the rebellion.

The description of his approach was hailed by Erich Auerbach as the first authentically sublime moment in European literature since Virgil.[27] The vehicle of that description is a simile describing the onslaught of a sudden wind:

a crashing sound . . . like a wind, made impetuous by the opposition of hot exhalations, which strikes the forest and irresistibly tears, flattens and carries

THE COSMOS

away the branches. Driving dust before it, on it goes in pride; and it puts the
beasts and shepherds to flight:

> un fracasso d'un suon . . .

> . . .

> non altrimenti fatto che d'un vento
> impetüoso per li avversi ardori,
> che fier la selva e sanz' alcun rattento
> li rami schianta, abbatte e porta fori;
> dinanzi polveroso va superbo,
> e fa fuggir le fiere e li pastori.   (*Inf.* IX, 65, 67–72)

As the deliberately exaggerated translation suggests, the passage opens
with a flourish of quasi-technical vocabulary (*impetuoso per li avversi
ardori*); but the rhythm and syntax of this line are at least as important as
the meaning, since they delay the verb and thus 'imitate' the opposition of
the *ardori* by damming up the energy of the wind, which then strikes,
fiere, with redoubled violence in the next line.[28] The impact of an
irresistible force is conveyed by the anticipation of the object, *li rami*, and
by the sequence of three verbs, *schianta*, *abbatte e porta*, which sweep that
object away. And the moment of sublimity is reached in the following
line, 'dinanzi polveroso va superbo', which is absolutely extraordinary in
its syntactic isolation from what goes before, in the unexpected colloca-
tion of adjectives used as adverbs ('dusty' and 'proud'), and in the
unbroken march to the climax at *superbo*, which is once again a 'humanizing' metaphor.

The highest mountain

Purgatory 'proper' is entered through a gateway to which one ascends by
the three steps that Dante describes with elaborate symbolism in the
ninth canto. Above this gate, the mountain is encircled by seven narrow
terraces where the penitent souls expiate the seven capital vices and are
purified of their inclination to sin. We later learn (and the explanation is
put into the mouth of the Roman poet, Statius) that these terraces are
'free from all change'. More specifically:

No rain, hail, snow, dew or frost can fall above the level of the three steps that
form the brief stairway. Clouds do not appear, whether dense or rarefied; neither
does lightning, nor the rainbow, which so often shifts its domain on earth below.
Dry exhalations do not rise above the highest of the three stairs.

> Libero è qui da ogne alterazione:

> . . .

> Per che non pioggia, non grando, non neve,
> non rugiada, non brina più sù cade
> che la scaletta di tre gradi breve;

84

> nuvole spesse non paion né rade,
> né coruscar, né figlia di Taumante,
> che di là cangia sovente contrade;
>   secco vapor non surge più avante
> ch'al sommo d'i tre gradi ch'io parlai . . .

(Purg. XXI, 43, 46–53)

The eight phenomena that are *not* found on the mountain read like a list of chapter headings from Aristotle's *Meteorologica*; and although the rhetorical amplification is not inappropriate to the context, the repeated reference to the *tre gradi* is a little awkward, as is the rather gratuitous mythological periphrasis for the rainbow.[29] From a stylistic point of view, then, the lines could be regarded as little more than 'versified doctrine'. But the 'doctrine' is Dante's own invention. And seven cantos later we discover why the point was made with such insistence.

After another day's exertion, Dante has climbed beyond the seventh terrace, and has spent the night on the mountain-side not far short of the summit. At dawn he climbs again and soon emerges into a 'divine forest'. A steady breeze is blowing, which has made all the trees lean towards the west, and which draws a sweet music from their leaves to form an accompaniment to the song of the birds. Dante advances, and, after a few hundred yards, his path is blocked by a stream of running water. At this point the alert reader should feel a certain perplexity; for running water points to the existence of moist exhalations (which will fall as rain to replenish the source of the stream), just as inevitably as wind argues the presence of dry exhalations: whereas we have been told that Purgatory 'proper' is free from both. There is, however, no time for Dante to register this perplexity. As he lifts his eyes and looks beyond the stream, he catches sight of a girl who is singing while she gathers flowers. Her appearance is so unexpected, and she is so beautiful, that Dante is filled with *maraviglia* and his thoughts are only for her.

The girl, whose name is later quite casually given as Matelda, explains in her opening words that this divine forest is none other than the Garden of Eden, or Earthly Paradise, the place chosen as the proper place for mankind.[30] If Dante-character was filled with *maraviglia* simply on seeing Matelda, he ought to be thunderstruck by her revelation. To have located the Garden of Eden on the summit of Purgatory is one of Dante-poet's most daring and satisfying inventions. But the character-Dante does not react. Instead, he immediately puts an indirect question relating to the 'water and sounds in the forest, which are contrary to something I was told, and are undermining my new-won belief':

> 'L'acqua', diss'io, 'e 'l suon de la foresta
> impugnan dentro a me novella fede
> di cosa ch'io udi' contraria a questa.'   (*Purg.* XXVIII, 85–7)

The first part of Matelda's explanation is essentially a repetition of what Statius had said, with the significant addition of the purpose or final cause of this dispensation:

In order that man should live unmolested by the disturbances which are created beneath them by exhalations from water and from land, as they follow the heat upwards to the extent that their natures allow, this mountain rose so high towards the heavens, that it is free of exhalations from the point where the way is barred:

> Perché 'l turbar che sotto da sé fanno
> l'essalazion de l'acqua e de la terra,
> che quanto posson dietro al calor vanno,
> a l'uomo non facesse alcuna guerra,
> questo monte salio verso 'l ciel tanto,
> e libero n'è d'indi ove si serra. (*Purg.* XXVIII, 97–102)

Next, Matelda addresses herself to the causes of the breeze and *il suon de la foresta*:

Since the whole atmosphere revolves en masse together with the first of the heavenly spheres, except where the circle of Air is broken at any point [by mountains], the movement of the atmosphere strikes upon this lofty mountain, which is freely set in the 'living' air; and this makes the forest resound, because its leaves are dense.

> Or perché in circuito tutto quanto
> l'aere si volge con la prima volta,
> se non li è rotto il cerchio d'alcun canto,
> in questa altezza ch'è tutta disciolta
> ne l'aere vivo, tal moto percuote
> e fa sonar la selva perch'è folta. (103–8)

This is a wholly naturalistic explanation which is still firmly based on Aristotle's meteorology.[31] The cause of the running water, however, proves to be miraculous:

The water you can see does not rise from a spring nourished by vapour that has been converted by the cold, as is the case with a river that gains and loses in vigour. It flows from a fountain that is unfailing and sure. Every drop that it pours forth on either side is replenished from the will of God.

> L'acqua che vedi non surge di vena
> che ristori vapor che gel converta,
> come fiume ch'acquista e perde lena;
> ma esce di fontana salda e certa,
> che tanto dal voler di Dio riprende,
> quant' ella versa da due parti aperta. (121–6)

There are some lovely touches in Matelda's speech, and the whole episode tells us a great deal about the psychology of Dante the character, whose every advance in understanding comes from the attempt to reconcile some new and marvellous experience with the concepts and principles that make up his existing knowledge. But one would not single out these passages for their stylistic or psychological interest, nor would one describe them at such length merely to show the extent of Dante's interest in meteorology. The intention of Dante the poet, here as so often later in the *Paradiso*, is to make his readers aware of the abyss which separates the natural order from the order of God, and to warn them of the absurdities and dangers that follow if we attempt to measure the divine imponderables using human weights and scales. Dante the character makes this kind of mistake time and time again, in order that we may learn together with him. Both parts of Matelda's reply demonstrate that Purgatory is not just a mountain rising out of the southern Ocean, a mountain whose latitude and longitude can be determined exactly, since it lies at the antipodes to Jerusalem. The explanation of the 'wind' shows that Purgatory 'proper' only begins where other mountains cease. It must be unimaginably high; it is as much outside the confines of this world as it is within them. The explanation of the 'water' reminds us that everything on the mountain is provided and controlled by divine ordinance to secure a supernatural end – the restoration of man to the condition of 'righteousness' enjoyed by Adam before the Fall. Paradoxically, however, the effect of both explanations, the natural and the miraculous, is to make that fictive realm of the afterworld as concrete and particular as the only reality which we can know in this life, and to validate Aristotelian physics as the true explanation of natural phenomena. Here as elsewhere, the scientist is never more scientific than when he is concerned to stress the limitations of his science.

Meteorology and the language of prophecy

In a horrifying passage in the twenty-fourth canto of the *Inferno*, Dante describes how one of the thieves punished in the seventh subdivision of the ninth circle is first destroyed completely by fire and then immediately restored to his previous form. It proves to be Vanni Fucci, a 'man of blood and rages', who preferred the life of a wild beast to that of a man, and who is now made to confess that he is punished in this zone of Hell because he had been guilty of a sacrilegious theft from a church in the city of Pistoia, which lies about twenty miles north-west of Florence. Furious at having been recognized and having been forced to reveal his crime, Vanni Fucci takes his revenge by 'prophesying' some of the disasters that will soon fall on Dante. First, he declares, the Black Guelph faction will be driven out from Pistoia; then the White Guelphs will be expelled from Florence. For a time Pistoia will be the only major stronghold to remain in the hands of the Whites, but after a lengthy siege, the city will fall to a

Black army, including detachments from Florence and Lucca, and the fortifications will be destroyed. The leader of the Black forces on this occasion will be Moroello Malaspina, whose family seat is in the valley of the river Magra in the extreme north-west of Tuscany on the borders with Genoese territory.[32]

In the manner of prophecies and oracular utterances, Vanni's style is made deliberately elliptical, allusive and metaphorical. Pistoia is designated once by name and once by reference to the nearby field of Piceno. The exile of the Blacks is called a 'slimming' or 'losing of fat' (*si dimagra*), while the triumph of the Blacks in Florence is understated as 'a change of people and customs'. And the central idea of a battle in which Moroello Malaspina would be the victor, to the utter confusion of the White cause, is expressed through a sustained metaphor of a thunderstorm with lightning. In the valley of the Magra, the fiery planet Mars (rather than the sun) will draw up a mass of dry exhalations (here called simply *vapore*).[33] The resultant wind will move to the Campo Piceno surrounded by turbulent thunderclouds, and a bitter and harsh storm will rage, until the dry exhalations, compressed and squeezed within the moist cloud, will suddenly rip their way out, in the form of a thunderbolt now, which will strike down the White forces to a man:[34]

> apri li orecchi al mio annunzio, e odi.
> Pistoia in pria d'i Neri si dimagra;
> poi Fiorenza rinova gente e modi.
>   Tragge Marte vapor di Val di Magra
> ch'è di torbidi nuvoli involuto;
> e con tempesta impetüosa e agra
>   sovra Campo Picen fia combattuto;
> ond' ei repente spezzerà la nebbia,
> sì ch'ogne Bianco ne sarà feruto.
>   E detto l'ho perché doler ti debbia!   (*Inf.* XXIV, 142–51)

At first reading we are probably dazed by the oracular obscurity, and if anything makes an immediate impression, it will be the sounds. The language here crackles and roars with the deliberately harsh rhyme sounds of *-agra* and *-ebbia*, which are reinforced by multiple alliteration and assonance in line 145 (*Tragge Marte vapor* di *val* di *Magra*) and by the sudden change to a plunging dactylic rhythm in the following line, again with a phonetic echo between *nuvoli* and *involuto*. This is clearly not just a prophecy, but an act of spite, as is made clear by the last line with its stabbing initial *d*'s: 'and I have told you this to hurt you'. Nevertheless, the stylistic dominant of these lines is the sustained metaphor which, for all its extreme compression, remains true to the meteorological facts and demonstrates once again Dante's overriding concern with 'that which is the case'.

Lightning and velocity

In the last passage, the emphasis falls on the violence of the erupting exhalations, but elsewhere lightning is used in similes to describe the greatest imaginable speed, or a speed that is unimaginable, since it is said to be faster than lightning.[35] The 'messengers' who came to speak with Dante and Virgil in the fifth canto of the *Purgatorio* returned to their group 'faster than the "kindled exhalations" which cut across a clear sky after nightfall or across the clouds of an August thunderstorm as the sun sets'.[36] And in the heaven of the planet Venus, the souls of the blessed who are waiting for Dante and Beatrice suddenly abandon their circular dance and flash towards the travellers:

Winds, whether visible or not, never descended from a cold cloud with such speed, that they would not have seemed impeded and slow to anyone who had seen those divine lights come towards us, leaving their circling which they had begun with the Seraphim on high:

> Di fredda nube non disceser venti,
> o visibili o no, tanto festini,
> che non paressero impediti e lenti
> a chi avesse quei lumi divini
> veduti a noi venir, lasciando il giro
> pria cominciato in li alti Serafini.   (*Par.* VIII, 22–7)

Once again the allusions to the science of meteorology are precise, but they are kept to a minimum, and the long sentence is chiefly memorable for the way in which syntax, sound and rhythm reinforce the contrasts between speed and slowness.[37]

In her translation into *terza rima*, Dorothy Sayers makes a very creditable attempt to catch this succession of different tempi – allegro, adagio, allegro, adagio – which follow one another within the same sentence:[38]

> No visible or viewless blast from floes
>   Of icy cloud e'er darted but would seem
>   Heavily handicapped, lumbering and gross
> To one who'd seen those heavenly meteors skim
>   Our way, quitting their reel that was on high
>   Begun amid the exalted seraphim.

But the reason for quoting her version is that it shows all too clearly that rhythm and syntax alone are not enough, even in a passage like this; and Miss Sayers' success on the one front is offset by corresponding losses in point of diction. First, she is driven to padding: a glance at her version will show that she has introduced 'floes', 'heavily', 'gross' and 'on high'; and the swift *o no* has become 'viewless'. Second, words that would be at home in a text-book are replaced with stale poeticisms, or with rarer, allegedly more expressive words that would be inappropriate there: *non disceser venti* becomes 'no blast e'er darted'; *fredda*, *impediti* and *venire* become 'icy', 'handicapped' and 'skim'. And, lastly, where she prefers a word that is more technical than the original – as when 'meteors' is chosen for *lumi* – her choice greatly reduces the range of meanings and associations; and the adjective 'heavenly' for *divini* narrows that range still further. Quite simply, 'heavenly meteors' are not the same as *lumi divini*. Dante is altogether leaner and more scientific than his translator (and what is true of Dorothy Sayers here is also true of most other verse translations); he is less 'poetic' in the derogatory sense, and more poetic in the sense that his words reverberate with further symbolic overtones.

Earthquakes

Three earthquakes are described or alluded to in the *Comedy*. The first occurs when Dante and Virgil are standing on the banks of the river Acheron, and, to judge from the mode of description, it could be due to natural causes:[39]

When he had finished speaking, the gloomy plain shook so violently that memory still bathes me with sweat in fear. The tearful earth broke wind, which flashed out in a vermilion light that overpowered my senses; and I fell like a man seized by sleep:

> Finito questo, la buia campagna
> *tremò sì forte* che de lo spavento
> la mente di sudore ancor mi bagna.
>   La terra lagrimosa *diede vento*,
> *che balenò* una *luce vermiglia*
> la qual mi vinse ciascun sentimento;
>   e caddi come l'uom cui sonno piglia.

(Inf. III, 130–6)

The second certainly had a supernatural cause, for it was the earthquake that followed the 'darkness over all the land' at the moment of Christ's death on the cross; and Dante presupposes a knowledge of the following words from St Matthew's Gospel (27.45–51):[40]

Now from the sixth hour there was darkness over all the land unto the ninth hour. And about the ninth hour Jesus cried with a loud voice ... [and] yielded up the ghost. And, behold, the veil of the temple was rent in twain from the top to the bottom; and the earth did quake and the rocks rent (*et terra mota est, et petrae scissae sunt*).

Dante's imaginative reconstruction of the consequences of that earthquake in Hell, and the subtle and indirect ways in which he reveals what he has imagined, are highly characteristic of his mind and art. The first reference comes in the twelfth canto of the *Inferno*; but in order to understand that passage we have to recall two other pieces of information given earlier in apparently unrelated contexts.

In the fourth canto, Virgil has told us that while he was still 'new' in Hell (his death having fallen in 19 B.C.), the first circle was visited by a 'mighty figure crowned with the insignia of victory', who had taken with him the souls of Adam, Abel, Noah, Moses, Abraham and David, together with many others, and had made them blessed. The pagan Virgil cannot understand the full significance of this event, but to the Christian reader it is an unmistakable reference to the Harrowing of Hell. The *possente con segno di vittoria coronato* is Christ, who descended into Hell after he had yielded up His spirit, and delivered the souls of all those who had believed in the coming of the Messiah. Virgil has also revealed (in the ninth canto) that he had made this journey once before when the sorceress, Erichtho, who had the power to conjure up the souls of the dead, had compelled him to go to the very bottom of Hell. This earlier journey, he specified, had taken place shortly after his own arrival in Hell, and therefore before the Harrowing.[41]

Dante and Virgil make their way from the sixth to the seventh circles of Hell by scrambling down a gigantic scree. Virgil explains that at the time of his previous descent, the rock had not yet fallen. But if his understanding does not play him false, he continues, there had been an earthquake which had shaken the whole valley of iniquity on all sides shortly before the coming of Him who carried off from Dis the great spoil of the highest circle; and it was then that the ancient rock collapsed, here as elsewhere:

> Or vo' che sappi che l'altra fiata
> ch'i' discesi qua giù nel basso inferno,
> questa roccia non era ancor cascata.
>
> Ma certo poco pria, se ben discerno,
> che venisse colui che la gran preda
> levò a Dite del cerchio superno,
> da tutte parti l'alta valle feda
> tremò . . .
>
> . . .
>
> e in quel punto questa vecchia roccia,
> qui e altrove, tal fece riverso.   (*Inf.* XII, 34–41, 44–5)

All the threads have now been drawn together, and the final phrase, 'here and *elsewhere*', prepares us for the sensational adventures to be described ten cantos later, when we also have the final, independent confirmation that the earthquake which left such damage in Hell took place at the moment of Christ's death.

Virgil and Dante cross over the ten concentric, moat-like ditches or *bolgie* that make up the ninth circle of Hell by one of the several natural 'bridges' that arch their way from the outer circumference to the inner. On the bank of the fifth *bolgia*, which is filled with boiling pitch, they see for the first time the kind of devils that one finds in medieval paintings – angular, winged demons, armed with sharp hooks and even sharper tongues, whose task it is to ensure that none of the embezzlers punished here should emerge from the pitch to enjoy a temporary respite from their torment. Virgil goes ahead to parley with the devils on the inner bank of the *bolgia*; and having quelled a show of violence, he seeks directions from their leader, who is casually named as Malacoda. Malacoda explains that they will not be able to cross the next *bolgia* by the same spur of rock that had served them as a bridge up to this point: the sixth 'arch' has collapsed. As a matter of fact, he goes on, the twelve hundred and sixty-sixth anniversary of that collapse took place yesterday. But there is another spur round to the left that will afford them a crossing, and he will send ten of his devils to accompany them safely to the place. Dante the character is terrified by this offer of an escort, and events prove that his fears were well-grounded. Malacoda was lying (and the crestfallen Virgil will be reminded two cantos later that the devil is the 'father of lies'). The date was perfectly correct, even down to the indication of the hour. But every single one of the arches over the sixth *bolgia* had been destroyed by that earthquake 1,266 years before. Thus, when Malacoda instructed the leader of the patrol that the travellers should be safe until 'they reach the spur that crosses the *bolgia* unbroken', he was giving him unequivocal instructions to use whatever violence he wanted towards his charges. And in due course, after the poets have witnessed some scenes from a brilliant but gruesome knockabout farce – 'black comedy' in the modern sense of those words – they themselves become the victims of the devils' violence and have to make a precipitous escape by sliding down the side of the sixth *bolgia* to reach safety at the bottom. This undignified descent may seem almost infinitely far removed from the shudder that marked the death of the Son of God; but in the way that Dante has told his story it is nevertheless a remote consequence of that earthquake.[42]

These linked episodes can tell us a great deal about Dante's art as a story-teller – from the capacity to 'think big' and to speculate about the effects that this of all earthquakes would have produced in the underworld, to the capacity to 'think little' and to disclose the minutely contrived circumstances of the topography and plot in the least obtrusive way. Perhaps the most delicate touch, however, lies in the fact that all the explanations about the earthquake are given by characters who do not fully understand its significance, and that they present the information in a way which is both 'in character' and very revealing of their character. Malacoda backs his malicious lie, as good liars will, with corroborative detail that is convincing because it is perfectly true.[43] And Virgil's account of the earthquake, and of the coming of Christ, clearly demonstrates his own limitations. For him, the Son of God is no more than *un possente*. This 'naturally Christian soul', whose fourth Eclogue was believed to be a prophecy of the birth of Christ, could sense the *mystery* of the earthquake. 'On all sides', he told Dante, 'the deep valley of iniquity shook so violently that I thought the universe had felt love':

> da tutte parti l'alta valle feda
> tremò sì, ch' i' pensai che l'universo
> sentisse amor . . .   (*Inf.* XII, 40–2)

That is exactly right. But Virgil, who here represents a whole culture that had flourished without knowledge of the true God, continues with a reference to the doctrine of Empedocles, who believed that the world had several times been created from chaos and returned to chaos thanks to the contrary principles of Love and Discord; and this qualification shows that he had no inkling of the Divine Love that, in the Christian account, led to the unique creation of the world from nothing, and to the redemptive self-immolation of God.

The third and last earthquake is once again represented as part of the action of the poem. As Dante and Virgil pick their way past the prostrate bodies of the penitent who are purging the sins of avarice and prodigality on the fourth terrace of Mount Purgatory, the mountain is suddenly shaken by a prolonged tremor, as though it were falling. Dante feels the kind of cold fear that seizes a condemned man as he is taken to his death; and his fear is increased when a great cry goes up from all sides.

Confidence begins to return, however, when the cry continues as a song, and when he can make out the words; for the words are none other than those pronounced by the heavenly host to the shepherds who were abiding in the fields near Bethlehem: 'Glory to God in the highest'. Dante and Virgil pause, motionless and intent as the shepherds had been, until the song is complete and the tremor comes to an end:

> '*Gloria in excelsis*' tutti '*Deo*'
> dicean . . .
> No' istavamo immobili e sospesi
> come i pastor che prima udir quel canto,
> fin che 'l tremar cessò ed el compiési.
>
>   (*Purg.* XX, 136–7, 139–41)

By now, fear has given place to *maraviglia*; and *maraviglia*, as always, generates the desire to know the cause. Satisfaction for this natural thirst is swift to come. A soul overtakes them, walking upright and free; and even before he has introduced himself properly he explains the origin of the earthquake and the singing of the *Gloria*. In due course, he will name himself as Statius; and we have already studied the first part of his speech earlier in this chapter, where we learned that Purgatory 'proper', above the three steps that lead to the gate, rises so high that it is free from the transmutations of the elements that cause all meteorological phenomena. Statius now goes on to state explicitly that this immunity extends to natural earthquakes. 'I do not know why', he says, 'but although there may be greater and lesser shocks on the lower part of the mountain, up here there has never been a tremor due to wind hidden in the earth':

> Trema forse più giù poco o assai;
> ma per vento che 'n terra si nasconda,
> non so come, qua su non tremò mai.

> (*Purg.* XXI, 55–7)

On the other hand, earthquakes of the kind they have just experienced are not infrequent. Every time that one of the penitent souls feels that he has completed the expiation and purification of his sins, and is ready to ascend into heaven, the mountain shudders, and all the souls in Purgatory sing the *Gloria*. This is precisely what had just happened to Statius himself after he had spent some 1,200 years on the mountain.[44]

The cause is supernatural; and Dante derives his inspiration and authority not from the flat prose of Aristotle, but from the prophetic and poetic books of the Old Testament, and in particular from the Psalms. The prophets and Psalmist often speak of God's 'holy mountain' – *mons Dei, mons tuus sanctus* – and the locution clearly had its influence on Dante's decision to make Purgatory a mountain and no mere annexe to the underworld. In describing the rejoicing of all creation at the goodness of the Creator, the Hebrew poets frequently use metaphor and personification, and speak of the 'earth trembling' and the 'hills exalting';[45] and the two ideas of a 'mountain of God' and a 'mountain that exalts' are already associated in the sixty-eighth psalm. Indeed, the following verses can provide an almost complete commentary on our episode:

Let God arise, and let his enemies be scattered. . . . But *let the righteous be glad and rejoice before God.* . . . Oh sing unto God, and *sing praises* unto his Name. . . . He is the God that maketh men to be *of one mind* in an house, and bringeth the *prisoners out of captivity.* . . . *The earth shook*, and the heavens dropped at the presence of God. . . . The Lord gave the word. . . . *Why hop ye so, ye high hills?* This is *God's hill.* . . . Thou art gone up on high, *thou hast led captivity captive.* . . . Oh sing praises unto the Lord.[46]

And an even more striking parallel will be found in Psalm 114:

When Israel came out of Egypt . . . Judah was his sanctuary. . . . The sea saw that, and fled: Jordan was driven back. The *mountains skipped* like rams: and the little hills like young sheep. What aileth [you] . . . *ye mountains, that ye skipped like rams.* . . . *Tremble, thou earth*, at the presence of the Lord. . . . Not unto us, O Lord, not unto us, but *unto thy Name give the praise.*[47]

This is the psalm that was sung by the souls as they arrived near the shore of Purgatory in the angel's boat. And this is the psalm that Dante twice used to illustrate the allegorical meanings to be found in the Bible. In the *Convivio*, he said that the spiritual meaning of the opening verse was that 'when the soul departs from sin, it becomes holy and free'.[48] In the letter to Can Grande, he would suggest three extra levels of meaning, all of which are relevant to the interpretation of this episode:

Allegorically, it signifies our redemption through Christ. Morally, it signifies the conversion of the soul from the sorrow and wretchedness of sin to a state of grace. Anagogically, it signifies the passing of the sanctified soul from the servitude of this corruptible world to the freedom of eternal glory. (*Epist.* XIII, 21).

This is what has happened to Statius; and the mountain skipped and the earth trembled not because of 'wind in the belly', but, as Virgil had divined with regard to the earthquake of the Crucifixion, because it had 'felt love'.

4

Land and sea

'Questa parte del mare e della terra'

IT WAS UNEXPECTEDLY DIFFICULT TO DECIDE ON THE TITLE OF THIS
chapter. 'Geography' would have been too comprehensive. 'The earth'
might have been misunderstood as referring exclusively to dry land or to
the heaviest of the four elements, while 'The world' would have been too
abstract and too vague. 'The terraqueous globe' was precise but forbidding. 'An inquiry into the location and configuration of water and earth'
was also precise, and it had the great advantage of being the title of
Dante's last philosophical work; nevertheless, it had to be rejected as too
cumbersome. The successful candidate – 'Land and sea' – may sound
excessively informal, but it was suggested by a phrase in Dante's *Convivio*, and it has the merit of simplicity and precision.[1] The subject of this
chapter, then, is the slightly imperfect sphere, popularly called the 'earth'
or the 'world', which lies at the centre of the medieval cosmos. And our
main objective will be to visualize and understand Dante's mental picture
of the distribution of land and sea over the surface of that sphere, and to
investigate what use he made of that 'picture' in his poem.

The notion of a slight 'imperfection' in our globe is implicit in the very
adjective 'terraqueous'. Aristotle's theory of the natural movements of
the two heavy elements would lead us to predict that there was a *perfect*
sphere of Earth at the centre of the universe, surrounded by a perfect and
concentric sphere of Water. In fact, dry land has appeared above the
surface of the water, and some of the mountain ranges, like the Alps or the
Atlas mountains, rise to a considerable height into the sphere of Air. For
the time being, however, we can ignore these irregularities and their
supernatural cause. There is no need to retain the technical terminology
of geometry, and we may follow Dante's own example in thinking of the
earth as a 'ball', *palla*, whose surface happens to be formed of both land
and sea. We can remind ourselves also that even the highest of the natural
mountains is really no more than an inconspicuous bump with respect to
the size of the ball as a whole.[2]

Medieval estimates of the size of the earth are not in fact greatly
dissimilar to our own. Few of us can readily visualize the difference
between a ball with a circumference of 24,800 miles, corresponding to a

radius of nearly 4,000, which are the dimensions we learnt from our text-books at school, and a ball with a circumference of 20,400 miles, corresponding to a radius of 3,250, which are the figures that Dante gives in the *Convivio*. It is certainly a little small, but it 'sounds' about right.[3]

The major differences between our maps – whether the maps are real or mental – are to be found in the area and distribution of the land-masses. We have grown up to be familiar with five continents, three of which lie or extend well below the equator. But Dante knew nothing of the Americas, nothing of Australia, and nothing of central or southern Africa. For him the 'dry land' or 'uncovered earth' was essentially a single vast island, divided by the Mediterranean Sea into the three continents of Europe, Asia and Africa. This *terra discoperta* or *gran secca* was roughly semicircular in outline, and since medieval maps were drawn with east at the top, Dante could compare its shape to that of a waning half-moon (see figure 5). It extended through $67°$ of latitude from the equator to the Arctic circle, and through $180°$ of longitude from the city of Cadiz in the west to the delta of the river Ganges in the east. There was no dry land anywhere else. Dante believed that the other half of the northern hemisphere and the whole of the southern hemisphere were totally covered by the encircling Ocean.[4] The sketch map on p. 98 – 'oriented' in the medieval way – will help to make this clear.

Even if this sketch is accepted as a greatly simplified representation of Europe, Asia and North Africa, it reveals many surprising errors. For example, the true separation in longitude between Cadiz and the delta of the Ganges is only a little more than a hundred degrees. And this mistake is as nothing when compared to the evident misapprehension concerning the length of the Mediterranean Sea. For centuries, Italian seamen had been navigating the inland sea from one end to the other, but Dante could still take it on trust from his text-books that the Mediterranean extended through nearly 90 degrees of longitude. The true figure is about 42 degrees; but Dante believed that there were 45 degrees of longitude between Cadiz and Rome and another 45 between Rome and Jerusalem.[5]

It is not without relevance, of course, that Dante was born in Florence rather than in Venice or Genoa. But the accident of birthplace is not decisive, and it is probable that a Venetian intellectual would have passively accepted the same figures. The explanation for this gross and persistent error lies in the nature and spirit of schoolroom geography. Facts were copied from ancient sources and they were subordinated to the pursuit of meaning and order. The alleged shape and dimensions of the land-mass satisfied a thirst for symmetry and symbolism. At the time of the equinoxes, as Dante explains in the *Quaestio de situ et forma aquae et terrae*, the sun will be setting for the inhabitants of Cadiz at the same time that it is rising for the people who dwell near the mouth of the Ganges, and it will be exactly midnight in Jerusalem. For it is written in

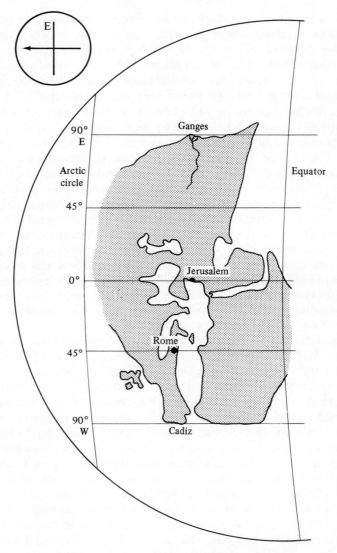

Figure 5. The 'half-moon' of the *terra discoperta*.

the Book of Ezekiel (5.5): 'This is Jerusalem: I have set it *in the midst of the nations and countries* that are round about her'; and the words of Jehovah had apparently been confirmed by non-Christian *cosmographi* and *astrologi*. So perfect was the matching of geographical space and historical time that the central event in the history of mankind – the Crucifixion of the Son of God – took place in the very centre of the *terra discoperta*.

98

Before we leave the geographers and their received ideas about the distribution of land and sea, it is worth noting that they did not attempt to study the whole of the *terra discoperta*. The confident assumption underlying the study of geography, whether ancient or medieval, sacred or secular, was that the earth existed for the benefit of man. And it was recognized that man was not prepared by nature to inhabit the extreme latitudes – neither the frozen wastes near the Arctic circle, nor the torrid deserts near the equator. And so geographers occupied themselves principally with what was called the *terra habitabilis*. This they divided into seven parallel 'belts', 'zones' or 'climes', each of which had its own characteristic 'climate', rendering it more or less suitable for human habitation.

It was known that man could survive, after a fashion, outside the latitudes of the *terra habitabilis*. Dante himself cites the case of the Scythians who live beyond the seventh zone – *extra septimum clima* – and the Garamantes who live close to the equator. But the Scythians, he notes, suffer an almost unbearable extreme of cold and have to endure days and nights of very unequal duration, while the Garamantes never cover themselves with clothes because of the excessive heat of the air. Conversely, the Roman people were fitted for their divinely-ordained role as rulers of the world by the temperate climate of central Italy. The exceptions, as always, prove the rule.[6]

Geography, language and politics

In the opening chapters of the *Convivio* Dante refers in moving words to his exile from the most beautiful and famous of the daughters of Rome, Florence, the city where he had grown to manhood and where he hoped to end his days in peace. Banishment had driven him as a stranger, and almost as a beggar, to nearly every part of Italy – or, to use his own phrase, to 'nearly every part to which this language extends' ('per le parti quasi tutte a le *quali questa lingua si stende*').[7]

The precise formulation is peculiarly important because it was in his writing about language that Dante first made use of his geographical knowledge and displayed his formidable ability to combine close observation and attention to detail with the boldest and most far-reaching generalizations.

The first book of the *De vulgari eloquentia*, written within a few years of the *Convivio* passage, does indeed confirm that he had put his enforced travels to good effect. He had become a connoisseur of the spoken language in all its manifestations. He is able to quote concrete examples, in the form of characteristic phrases or sentences, to illustrate the distinctive features of Italian speech in the fourteen principal regions; and his ear is sufficiently discriminating to catch the differences between speakers from different ends of the same city. When he reports that there are more than a thousand different varieties of spoken Italian, we accept the rhetorically rounded figure without hesitation. He writes with the authority of the expert who has been on the spot and listened for himself. It comes as no surprise to learn that Dante will later refer by name to more than two hundred Italian cities and rivers in the *Comedy* alone.[8]

Topography is not the same as geography, of course; and every true *scientia* requires a body of universal propositions as well as a collection of facts and specimens. But Dante is no less impressive as a theorist than as a field-worker. He recognizes that the city dialects of a given region have common features that constitute a species, and that all the regional dialects on what he calls the 'left' of Italy constitute a genus distinct from that formed by those on the right. He is also prepared to assert that there is an essence or form common to all the Italian *idiomata*, and that this common denominator has already been isolated and brought from potency to act in the writings of the best poets of the peninsula. The language of their poems is in fact treated as the norm against which the spoken dialects are measured and evaluated. Six centuries later Metternich could still dismiss the concept of 'Italy' as a 'geographical expression'. But Dante had seen that the unity of Italy was already a linguistic fact; just as he also realized that the diversity of dialects under which that unity lay concealed was a consequence of geographical features. The broad division of the dialects into 'left' and 'right', he tells us, is caused by the natural barrier and watershed of the Apennines.[9]

Earlier in the same work he had demonstrated the affinity between the dialects of Italy and those of southern and northern France by an analysis of common elements in the vocabulary; and he had drawn up what amounts to a general linguistic atlas of Europe showing the distribution of the three main linguistic families – Germanic, Slavonic and Romance. There is a splendid awareness of space in his brief account of the Germanic language area, bounded to the north and south, he tells us, by the Ocean and the frontiers of Italy and France, and stretching from the mouths of the Danube to the western shores of England. And his survey becomes truly universal when he considers the dispersion of mankind after the tragic rebellion of the Tower of Babel. It was then that human languages were first diversified and became mutually incomprehensible as a divine punishment for pride and presumption, and it was then that men were first scattered 'through all the zones of the world, the regions fit for habitation and the extremes': *per universa mundi climata, climatumque plagas incolendas et angulos.*[10]

Earlier still in the same work, Dante had told us that although he remained deeply attached to his native Florence, he was now convinced, through his reading of 'the poets and other writers who had described the world in broad outline and in detail', and through his own meditations on 'the various locations of places in the world and their relationship to the poles and to the equator', that 'there must be other more noble and delightful cities and regions than Florence or Tuscany'. And it is in this very sentence that he first makes his claim to be 'a citizen of the world' (*nos . . . cui mundus est patria*).[11]

This claim is made good in his later political treatise, the *Monarchia*. Its most striking feature is Dante's overriding concern to find a political solution for the ills of the *whole* of mankind. Having stated the case for a single world-ruler in abstract terms in the course of the first book, he goes on to argue that a single nation, the Romans, had been divinely ordained to establish justice and the rule of law throughout the *terra habitabilis*, and that their Emperor should be the 'Monarch' of all mankind.

In this way Dante's geography becomes the 'handmaid' of his politics. He argues, for example, that the world dominion of the Roman people had been foreshadowed in the progenitors and wives of Aeneas, the father of the Roman line. Asia had given him his immediate forbears, such as Assaracus, and it had given him his first wife, Creusa. Africa provided his second consort, Dido, and his most ancient relative in the female line, Electra, daughter of Atlas; while his remote ancestor, Dardanus, and his third wife, Lavinia, were both from Europe. 'Is there anyone', asks Dante, 'who can fail to detect divine predestination in that double concourse of blood from every part of the world?'

As so often, the rhetorical question does not disguise the weakness of the argument, which is more than a little bizarre even in a work of medieval political propaganda. But for the moment we are interested in Dante's knowledge and use of geography rather than his political views, and in this regard there are two points to be noted about the chapter under discussion. First, it shows once again Dante's power to handle large units and to 'think in continents'. Second, it marks the place where geography joins hands with poetry, since all Dante's assertions are backed by quotations from 'our divine poet and bard, Virgil'.[12]

Geography, place-names and poetry

Nothing could be less Virgilian, however, than Dante's celebration of the Roman conquests in the sixth canto of the *Paradiso*. Here, as elsewhere in the poem, Roman authority is imaged as the imperial Eagle; and, after a dense rehearsal of Rome's earlier triumphs over such antagonists as Brennus, Pyrrhus and Hannibal, Dante presents the decisive campaigns of Julius and Augustus Caesar as the rapid and victorious 'flight' of the Eagle from the rivers of Gaul to the Rubicon in north Italy, thence to Spain, Illyria, Thessaly and Asia Minor, and finally to Egypt and the shores of the Red Sea. It was a flight, says Dante, that neither pen nor tongue could follow.

Readers of Virgil will certainly approach the sustained metaphor and the long catalogue of geographical names with the liveliest and most pleasurable expectations. English readers may well have in mind such splendidly resonant and evocative passages in John Milton as these lines from his *Paradise Regained*, where Satan has taken the Son of Man up to a high mountain top to show him 'the monarchies of the Earth, their pomp and state':

> Here thou behold'st
> Assyria, and her empire's ancient bounds,
> Araxes and the Caspian lake; thence on
> As far as Indus east, Euphrates west,
> And oft beyond; to south the Persian bay,
> And, inaccessible, the Arabian drouth:
>
> . . .
>
> Persepolis,
> His city, there thou seest, and Bactra there;
> Ecbatana her structure vast there shows,
> And Hecatompylos her hundred gates;
> There Susa by Choaspes, amber stream,
> The drink of none but kings; of later fame
> Built by Emathian or by Parthian hands,
> The great Seleucia, Nisibis, and there
> Artaxata, Teredon, Ctesiphon,
> Turning with easy eye, thou may'st behold.
>
> (III, 269–74, 284–93)

But Dante has nothing to match this in *Paradiso* VI. His writing seems almost lifeless and inert by comparison, too full of facts. The flight simply does not take place for us as a poetic event:

> E quel che fé da Varo infino a Reno,
> Isara vide ed Era e vide Senna
> e ogne valle onde Rodano è pieno.
>   Quel che fé poi ch'elli uscì di Ravenna
> e saltò Rubicon, fu di tal volo,
> che nol seguiteria lingua né penna.
>   Inver' la Spagna rivolse lo stuolo,
> poi ver' Durazzo, e Farsalia percosse
> sì ch'al Nil caldo si sentì del duolo.   (*Par*. VI, 58–66)

It is then difficult not to feel a certain disappointment on first reading these and the following lines. But it would be wrong to dismiss the passage too quickly. The speaker in Milton's poem was Satan, and he was presenting with deliberate amplitude an enticing and idealized picture of 'Huge cities and high-towered, that well might seem / the seats of mightiest monarchs'. He goes on for nearly a hundred lines with even more dazzling rhetoric to describe the 'martial equipage', the 'warlike muster' and the 'forms of battle ranged' which Jesus will require to win such glorious prizes. But Jesus is not deceived. What he has been shown is no more than a mirage of power. And he dismisses both the temptation and the rhetoric as being 'plausible to the world, to me worth naught'. The 'cumbersome luggage of war' is 'argument of human weakness rather than of strength'.[13]

By contrast, Dante's speaker is Justinian (A.D. 527–65), the last great Emperor of the ancient world. His most admired and influential monument had been the codification of Roman law in the *Institutions* and the *Digest*. And in this canto it is part of his task to restate the argument of the second book of Dante's *Monarchia* and to show that Rome had conquered the world justly and by right (*iure*), not by force (*vi*). Justinian is preparing us for the paradoxes of the doctrine of the Atonement which will be expounded in the following canto; and he must establish, among other things, that Pontius Pilate did indeed possess the just and divinely given authority to punish Adam's Original Sin in the human nature of Christ.

If we now look again at Dante's account of the military campaigns, we shall see that he is deliberately seeking to achieve an effect of the utmost brevity and of scrupulous adherence to the historical facts.[14] The two Caesars had engaged in 'just' wars at a crucial moment in human history. They were the instruments of divine providence. The goal of their war-making was peace – *universal* peace. For Dante fervently believed, as we learn from the first book of the *Monarchia*, that the Roman Empire had for the first time brought peace throughout the world in preparation for the birth of the Saviour.[15] And so the 'poetry' of this passage lies not in the grandiloquent parade of geographical names, but in the lines that open and close the description of the Eagle's flight:

As the time drew near when it was the will of heaven that the whole world should share in its serenity, Caesar, by the will of Rome, took up the Eagle. . . . With [Augustus] Caesar the Eagle flew to the shore of the Red Sea; with him it brought such perfect peace to the world that the gates of the temple of Janus were locked.

> Poi, presso al tempo che tutto 'l ciel volle
> redur lo mondo a suo modo sereno,
> Cesare per voler di Roma il tolle.
>
> . . .
>
> Con costui corse infino al lito rubro;
> con costui puose il mondo in tanta pace,
> che fu serrato a Giano il suo delubro.

(*Par.* VI, 55–7, 79–81)

Geographical periphrasis in the Heaven of Venus

Dante gives great prominence to geographical periphrasis in the three encounters that take place in the heaven of Venus, to which he ascends after his encounter with Justinian. The passionate Cunizza describes the region of her birth with reference to the six rivers that flow through north-east Italy to the shore of the Adriatic Sea.[16] Poetically speaking, however, there is nothing to hold our attention. The Brenta, Piave, Adige, Tagliamento, Sile and Cagnano together achieve nothing of the power and pathos of that single reference to the river Po, 'seeking peace with its tributaries', in the opening words of Cunizza's counterpart in Hell, the impenitent Francesca:

> Siede la terra dove nata fui
> su la marina dove 'l Po discende
> per aver pace co' seguaci sui.   (*Inf.* V, 97–9)

Charles Martel, a young prince of the House of Anjou, had befriended Dante during a brief visit to Florence in the year 1294. He describes not his birthplace but the kingdoms over which he might have ruled: Provence, bounded by the Rhône and the Sorgue; southern Italy, between the outlying triangle of Gaeta, Bari and Catona, below the line of the rivers Tronto and Verde; Hungary, through which the Danube flows; and even perhaps Sicily the Fair, *la bella Trinacria*, had this not been lost through his grandfather's misrule some years before the two young men had met. All these vast lands 'had awaited him as their lord' – but in vain.[17] Charles died in 1295. The geographical periphrases are part of a great elegy for what might have been, and, in particular, for what might have been in Dante's own life had he enjoyed the fruits of a friendship with a ruler of such power. And Charles's speech is dominated by repetition of the conjunction 'if', beginning in the strangely broken phrases of his opening words: 'The world held me but a little space; and *if* it had been longer, much evil would not come to pass that will' (or rather, to be more literal, 'much evil will come about that would not have done'):

> Il mondo m'ebbe
> giù poco tempo; e *se* più fosse stato,
> molto sarà di mal, che non sarebbe.   (*Par.* VIII, 49–51)

The most interesting of the three periphrases is put into the mouth of the Provençal troubadour, Folco, or Folquet. It describes the city of his birth, and thereby serves to identify the speaker. First, he directs our gaze to the Mediterranean Sea. Then he establishes the latitude by indicating that his city lies on the *northern* coast. Simultaneously he gives us a first hint as to its longitude: it must be on what we would now call the French Riviera, since it lies between the river Ebro in north-east Spain and the river Macra in north-west Italy. Finally, he fixes the position by inviting us, in effect, to proceed more or less due north from the Algerian city of Bougie, which has almost the same sunset and sunrise as his native city. These co-ordinates of latitude and longitude are valid only for Marseilles. It was there that Folco was born, and there that he ended his days, no longer as a love-poet, but as bishop of the city and a stern persecutor of heretics.[18]

The details of this reference are erudite and extremely difficult. Unlike the resonant, classicizing toponyms that occur in Charles Martel's speech (e.g. *Trinacria*, *Ausonia*), the names of Ebro, Macra and Buggea are almost purely denotative. The poetic energy is stored in the opening vision of the Mediterranean, stretching between 'discordant' shores from west to east through fully ninety degrees. Folco combines metaphor and a rich verbal harmony to achieve an effect of precision and sublime simplicity, as he describes the inland sea as 'the greatest valley into which water may spread from the Ocean that puts its garland round the earth':

> 'La maggior valle in che l'acqua si spanda',
> incominciaro allor le sue parole,
> 'fuor di quel mar che la terra inghirlanda,
>   tra' discordanti liti contra 'l sole
> tanto sen va, che fa meridïano
> là dove l'orizzonte pria far suole.'   (*Par.* IX, 82–7)

The cosmic perspective

Folco's field of vision in these lines implies a viewpoint high in the heavens, and several cantos later the deliberate and explicit use of a heavenly vantage-point will form the occasion and the matter of two linked episodes, in which we are asked once again to imagine the distribution of land and sea over the 'ball' of our earth.

In the twenty-second canto, Dante the traveller has ascended through the last of the planetary heavens and arrived in the constellation of the Heavenly Twins, Gemini, which is being carried round the earth at immense speed by the diurnal revolution common to all the heavens. Beatrice invites him to look down and to see how much of the universe they have left beneath them. Dante obeys, and his gaze runs down past all the seven planets in their spheres to the terraqueous globe at the centre, which is so small that he smiles at its insignificance:

> Col viso ritornai per tutte quante
>   le sette spere, e vidi questo globo
>   tal, ch'io sorrisi del suo vil sembiante.   (*Par.* XXII, 133–5)

It is disclosed that Beatrice has chosen her moment well. The constellation is passing across the meridian of Jerusalem, and hence Dante is able to contemplate the whole of the *terra discoperta* laid out beneath his eyes, from the Atlas mountains in the west to the mouths of the Ganges in the east. None of these details are allowed to obtrude, however; everything remains implicit in the line, '*tutta* m'apparve da' colli a le foci'.[19] And the effect of the closing lines in this canto is curiously mixed. Dante does not want to leave us simply with a sense of the great expanse of the land-mass. After all, he has just smiled at the insignificance of the whole globe when seen in cosmic perspective. The word qualified by *tutta* in the line just quoted is not the neutral *terra* but *aiuola*, a 'threshing–floor'. The territorial struggles which occasion such ferocious wars between peoples and nations are all for the sake of a small patch of hard ground. Somehow, therefore, we must try to reconcile the emotions engendered by that dismissive *aiuola* with the feeling of cosmic space suggested by Dante's 'circling together with the Eternal Twins':

> L'aiuola che ci fa tanto feroci,
> volgendom' io con li etterni Gemelli,
> tutta m'apparve da' colli a le foci.   (*Par.* XXII, 151–3)

All the main features in this episode have their source in the extremely influential opusculum by Cicero known as the *Dream of Scipio*.[20] But there is no such model for the brief sequel some five cantos later.

Just before Dante leaves the Starry Heaven, Beatrice again invites him to look down. This time, however, she wants him to notice how far he has been carried round the earth by the revolution of the heavens: 'Adima / il viso e guarda *come tu se' volto*.' Six hours have gone by since he last looked down; and in that time Dante has been carried through ninety degrees of arc from the centre of the first inhabitable zone to its western extremity:

> Da l'ora ch'ïo avea guardato prima
> i' vidi mosso me per tutto l'arco
> che fa dal mezzo al fine il primo clima. (*Par.* XXVII, 79–81)

He is therefore over Cadiz. To the east he can see almost to the furthest shore of the Mediterranean. And to the west he can see the vast expanse of Ocean, the unknown Ocean, of which we have no first-hand knowledge, because, even though attempts have been made to sail those waters, no man has ever returned to tell his story.

Again one is driven to paraphrase and quotation from other parts of the poem in order to do justice to the daring of Dante's imagination and the bare simplicity of his writing. For the astonishing fact is that Dante's final glance at the terraqueous globe (the term is peculiarly exact here) leads him to recall what is perhaps the most celebrated episode in the *Inferno* – his encounter with Ulysses, and Ulysses's own narration of his last voyage over the Ocean to its tragic end. All Dante has to say here is that 'Beyond Cadiz I saw the mad course of Ulysses' ('io vedea di là da Gade il varco / folle d'Ulisse . . .'); and this is enough to demand the kind of response which has just been suggested.[21]

The voyage of Ulysses

As the present passage confirms, the figure of Ulysses had a deep and multiple fascination for Dante. His Ulysses is simultaneously a man of courage and resource, a representative of a great civilization that had nevertheless been cut off from divine grace, an orator whose power of persuasive speech gave him a dangerous hold over the minds and actions of his fellows, and a human being whose innate thirst for knowledge had declined into mere curiosity or a desire for sense-experience which led him to set aside the claims of family and society, to reject the occupations proper to an old man, and to defy the prohibition of the gods in pursuit of a 'world without people behind the sun'. To misquote Eliot, Ulysses attempted the 'wrong things for the right reasons'. And his ill-fated *viaggio* moves in subtle counterpoint to the divinely ordained *viaggio* of Dante himself, whose journey will take him through the realms of the afterlife towards the only true knowledge, a total intellectual grasp of principles and forms of a kind that can subsequently be communicated to other men in society in order to help them to find happiness and salvation. This is why Dante recalls his *controfigura* at this late moment in the *Paradiso*.

In due course we shall have to return to Dante's Ulysses in order to develop these points and substantiate them. But since modern criticism has tended to concentrate exclusively on the moral, theological and symbolic aspects of the figure of Ulysses, it will not be inappropriate to round off our geographical survey with a brief account of his heroic voyage, as it is told by Ulysses himself to the eager Dante in the twenty-sixth canto of the *Inferno*.

Dante's Ulysses begins the narrative of his last voyage at the point where he left the island of Circe, which lay in the gulf of Gaeta to the north-west of modern Naples (it must be remembered that Dante did not know the *Odyssey* at first-hand, and this was the point at which Ovid had abandoned his account of Ulysses's wanderings in the *Metamorphoses*).[22] With just one ship and a small but faithful crew, he set out again over the deep and open sea. But he did not set his course to the south and east in order to return to Ithaca and his patient wife, Penelope. Instead he sailed to the west. He saw both shores of the Mediterranean, as far as Morocco to the south and Spain to the north. He saw Sardinia and all the other islands which are bathed by that inland sea:

> ma misi me per l'alto mare aperto
> sol con un legno e con quella compagna
> picciola da la qual non fui diserto.
> L'un lito e l'altro vidi infin la Spagna,
> fin nel Morrocco, e l'isola d'i Sardi,
> e l'altre che quel mare intorno bagna.   (*Inf.* XXVI, 100–5)

And so he came, an old man now, with an old and weary crew, to the narrow straits (the Straits of Gibraltar, as we call them) where 'Hercules set up his marks as a warning to man not to proceed beyond'. Ulysses deliberately flouted this prohibition: 'I left Seville to starboard, having left Ceuta to port.' And with that last place-name (Ceuta or Setta is a small peninsula on the Moroccan coast facing the rock of Gibraltar), the familiar world, the world named and tamed by man, is left behind:

> Io e ' compagni eravam vecchi e tardi
> quando venimmo a quella foce stretta
> dov' Ercule segnò li suoi riguardi
>   acciò che l'uom più oltre non si metta;
> da la man destra mi lasciai Sibilia,
> da l'altra già m'avea lasciata Setta. (106–11)

The syntax and rhythm of the last two lines emphasize his conscious and deliberate defiance of the gods' decree. And this is made still more evident in the short and deservedly famous speech that Ulysses delivered to his crew, in order to persuade them to undertake a voyage which will give them first-hand 'experience behind the sun, of the world without people' ('esperienza / di retro al sol, del mondo sanza gente').[23]

His words achieved their effect. He addressed his men as 'brothers', and when the narrative resumes, the verbs change from first person singular to first person plural. It had become a common venture. All were now filled with Ulysses's own 'ardore . . . a divenir del mondo esperto'; and their decision is expressed in two magnificent lines, one stressing the deliberate and defiant resolution, the other catching the feeling of urgency and hinting at the fatal outcome: 'We turned our stern to the morning, and made our oars into wings for the mad flight':

> e volta nostra poppa nel mattino,
> de' remi facemmo ali al folle volo. (124–5)

Out over the nameless Ocean they plied their oars on a course between west and south.[24] By day, so we are given to understand, the sea and the sun were always the same. By night, however, the stars and the moon slowly changed to indicate their latitude and the passing of time. As they proceeded ever further to the south, the familiar stars around the north pole sank below the surface of the sea, while the stars around the southern celestial pole came into view. The moon, illuminated 'from below' by the light of the sun, waxed and waned in its monthly cycle.

After the moon's borrowed light had been kindled and extinguished five times, 'a mountain appeared to us, still dark because of the distance, higher than any I had ever seen'. A voyage of five months proved that there *is* land in the southern hemisphere after all:

> Tutte le stelle già de l'altro polo

> vedea la notte, e 'l nostro tanto basso,
> che non surgëa fuor del marin suolo.
>   Cinque volte racceso e tante casso
> lo lume era di sotto da la luna,
> poi che 'ntrati eravam ne l'alto passo,
>   quando n'apparve una montagna, bruna
> per la distanza, e parvemi alta tanto
> quanto veduta non avëa alcuna.   (127–35)

The crew rejoiced at the prospect of landfall, but their joy soon turned to lamentation. 'From the new-found land a whirlwind arose and struck the prow of our ship. Three times it spun her round in the swirling waters; at the fourth, it raised the stern aloft and plunged the bows down, as was Another's will, until the sea closed again above us.' The hero, or rather, the heroes, have met their heroic end, 'valiantly vanquished':

> Noi ci allegrammo, e tosto tornò in pianto;
> ché de la nova terra un turbo nacque
> e percosse del legno il primo canto.
>   Tre volte il fé girar con tutte l'acque;
> a la quarta levar la poppa in suso
> e la prora ire in giù, com' altrui piacque,
>   infin che 'l mar fu sovra noi richiuso.   (136–42)

Such is the poetry of land and sea.

Geography and theology

So far we have been looking at the uses to which Dante put the orthodox and uncontroversial geography of his day. Both in his reference to particular localities (as in the Mediterranean part of Ulysses's voyage) and in the projections based on his knowledge of the dimensions of the globe and the distribution of land and sea (as in the *folle volo* or *varco folle*), Dante remains faithful to that orthodoxy. But with the *montagna bruna e alta* we have come to what may fairly be called his major and original contribution to the subject; for, later in the poem, it will become clear that this mountain is none other than the mountain island of Purgatory, which we have already had occasion to describe in earlier chapters.

From the geographical point of view (which is all that concerns us here) we must realize that Dante has put forward a plausible answer to the two geographical questions which most exercised the theologians of his time: Where was Eden? And where was Purgatory? In other words, where precisely on the surface of the globe was the Earthly Paradise in which Adam and Eve were created and from which they were driven after the Fall, never to return? And where was the place appointed for the souls of penitent sinners to make satisfaction and expiation for their sins, before being 'justified' and 'sanctified' and ascending into Paradise to enjoy the everlasting bliss of the vision of God?

Dante's answer to these two questions is not one he would have affirmed as a demonstrable truth outside the fiction of his poem, nor did he believe it as an article of faith. But the solution he puts forward is a plausible one, geographically, in the sense that it is in harmony with all the accepted facts; and it is highly attractive because it satisfies that craving for symmetry and symbolic meaning which underlies so much of popular geography in the Middle Ages. Purgation – so Dante would have us not disbelieve – takes place on the terraces that encircle a mountain which rises to a prodigious height in the middle of the Ocean in the southern hemisphere. This mountain is situated exactly at the antipodes to Jerusalem.[25] Hence, when we know that Jerusalem lies, to use the modern co-ordinates, at 35° 13′ E and 31° 47′ N, we could place Purgatory on our maps at 144° 47′ W and 31° 47′ S.

This is Dante's first invention. And while its chief attraction and power lies in its symbolism, it has the useful practical consequence that it gave Dante a fourth point of reference on the globe, ninety degrees distant in longitude from both Cadiz and the Ganges. As we shall see, many of the periphrases indicating the time of day in the *Comedy* are based on the fact that when it is noon in Jerusalem, the sun will be rising in Cadiz and setting at the mouths of the Ganges, and it will be midnight in Purgatory.

His second contribution is scarcely less bold, and is astonishing in its simplicity. Eden has exactly the same longitude and latitude as Mount Purgatory, because the Earthly Paradise is situated on the summit of the mountain.

In a magisterial essay written in 1922, under the title 'Intorno al sito del Purgatorio e al mito dantesco dell' Eden', Bruno Nardi investigated the earlier history of Christian beliefs about the location of Eden and Purgatory.[26] He showed – what nearly always proves to be the case – that Dante was not completely original in his solution to the problems involved, and that he combined and developed traditions and beliefs that had been formulated in patristic times and in the earlier Middle Ages. Some Christian writers had already connected the two issues by arguing that Purgatory must be closely associated with Eden (the link lay in the 'flaming sword which turned every way, to keep the way of the tree of life', which was interpreted as a prefiguration of the refining, purgatorial fire spoken of by St Paul).[27] There was also general agreement that Eden lay in the east. More specifically, it was said to be inaccessible because it was cut off by seas, or mountains, or some impassable torrid region.[28] Finally, it was held, on the authority of the Venerable Bede, that Eden lay on a mountain that was unimaginably high, touching the sphere of the moon (that is, reaching as far as the outermost limit of the sphere of Fire).[29]

All these traditions clearly had a part to play in the conception of Dante's Purgatory; and all of them were scrutinized, criticized, reinterpreted and refined in the course of the thirteenth century, as the theologians endeavoured to reconcile these very vague and unscientific propositions with the 'facts' contained in Aristotle's *Meteorology* and in the geographical writings of the Arabs. But while we must recognize Dante's debt to these ancient traditions, and while it is necessary to understand the position which he took up in the context of the contemporary debate, it is perfectly clear from Nardi's study that there was no received, universally acceptable answer to any of these problems. We must not assume that Dante did no more than draw the inevitable conclusion from the given premises. No one had united the two locations in precisely this way. No one had set either of them at the antipodes to Jerusalem. No one else could have had the audacity to introduce this mountain, once conceived, as the mysterious, unexpected and unintended goal of the last voyage of Ulysses. And, as we shall see in due course, no one else had devised an account of the circumstances in which the mountain first rose from the water that could equal Dante's. Like the earthquake that shook the mountain, the mountain itself had a miraculous cause.

5

The natural world and the Scale of Being

The 'Comedy' as microcosm

IN HIS FAMOUS PREFACE TO WHAT WAS TO BE THE FIRST PRINTED commentary on the *Comedy*, the fifteenth-century humanist Cristoforo Landino wrote:

Dante's similes are so original that I can find no simile to convey their originality. His comparisons are beyond compare. They are more exact and more frequent than in any other poet and simply more true to life. They are wonderfully effective in expressing the poet's state of mind and are superbly adapted to their location. The similes in the *Inferno* are not drawn from the same sources as those in the *Paradiso*; rather, each seems fitted by nature to its context. Furthermore, Dante's comparisons often lay bare the workings of some natural agency, or instruct the reader about some thing in nature.[1]

Landino makes several distinct points in this paragraph, and it will be generally agreed that they are quite well taken. Dante's similes are both numerous and new. Many of them do reveal his powers of close observation. They are often informative; and, taken as a whole, they do enable him to enrich his poem about man and God with a profusion of references to 'the grass, the herb yielding seed, and the fruit tree yielding fruit, the fish of the sea, the fowl of the air, the cattle, the beasts and every creeping thing that creepeth upon the earth'.[2] It is undeniable, too, that readers new to the *Comedy* take immediate pleasure in Dante's evocation of the world of natural things – *le spezie de le cose* – that will form the subject of this chapter.

Landino also suggested that Dante had deliberately chosen to make his poem into a microcosm of the universe as an expression of thanksgiving and homage to the Creator: 'for God is the supreme poet, and the macrocosm is his poem'; 'Ed è Idio sommo poeta, ed è el mondo suo poema'.[3] For Landino, moreover, the wealth of natural kinds evoked in the *Comedy* is, of itself, a cause or sign of Dante's greatness as a writer: 'What natural scientist', he exclaims,

has written more lucidly about the generation and local movement of perfect and imperfect creatures or animate and inanimate bodies? What conjunction of the planets and stars or what revolution of the heavens has he failed to mention? Is there one transformation of the elements, is there a single atmospheric change producing hail, rain, wind or thunderbolts, or is there one mineral compound under the earth to which the experts have not found at least a passing reference in our poet? The soul has four powers and various properties and functions: all of them are accurately described in Dante.[4]

Once again Landino is making some sound observations; and once again he is spoiling his case by rhetorical exaggeration and, more importantly, by an unwillingness to discriminate. In the present chapter we must therefore ascertain *which* species of mineral, vegetable and animal existence are given pride of place, which of their many properties are described, and why; for it would be wrong to leave the impression that the *Comedy* is a miniature encyclopaedia, or that Dante shows much interest in the medicinal virtues, the talismanic powers, the religious symbolism, or the many unlikely anecdotes that loom so large in medieval lapidaries, herbals and bestiaries. We must also discover the abstract categories and 'scientific' axioms that underlie Dante's perception and representation of the natural world, for it is misleading to suggest that he was able to look and see with what the Bible calls a 'simple eye'.[5] And finally we must look at the language in which the similes and metaphors are expressed – at least, those involving metals, stones, plants and animals – in order to distinguish the inert and conventional from the new, and to do justice to the full range of Dante's writing.

Exposition of ideas and literary comment will be bound up more closely than in the preceding chapters, but insofar as the two components can be separated it will be convenient to reverse the order followed in the last three chapters and to begin with the poetry. Most of us are more familiar with starlings and doves than we are with 'homoeomerous bodies'; and the concepts will be easier to grasp if the relevant examples are fresh in our minds.

Metals and minerals in the 'Comedy'

Dante's Hell is, in effect, a vast mine reaching into the very bowels of the earth, but there are relatively few references to metals or minerals in the *Inferno*, and those that are mentioned are almost without exception coarse, heavy, base, defiling and *di colore oscuro*. The natural wall of the ninth circle is said to be an iron-bearing rock, and the city of Lower Hell is encircled by an artificial wall made of iron. The financial peculators are immersed in boiling pitch such as the Venetians used to caulk their galleys. Precious metals are recalled only where they give occasion for abuse. The Simoniacs are solemnly cursed because they sold the gifts of the Holy Spirit for *oro e argento*. The hypocrites are aptly punished by being compelled to wear for all eternity the crushing burden of mantles which are gilded to simulate gold, but which are in fact made of lead. And

Dante prepared a special *bolgia* for those who used alchemy to falsify metals, or who forged the florin and debased the gold alloy by the substitution of three 'carats of dross'.[6]

None of this is casual. Dante knew the classical myths in which a Golden Age of primitive innocence had given way to the Ages of Silver and Iron. And he reminds us of the traditional scale of values in the description he gives of the strange symbolic figure called the Old Man of Crete whom we mentioned earlier: it will be remembered that 'his head is formed of fine gold; the chest and arms are of pure silver, the midriff of copper; from there down, he is made of good quality iron, except that the right foot, the weight-bearing foot, is made of baked clay'. In short, those substances that are either found in Hell, or linked through imagery with Hell, are taken from the bottom of the scale where nothing redeems the *grossezza di materia*.[7]

The realms of hope and joy, by contrast, are associated with *precious* metals and stones; and the change is heralded at the very beginning of the *Purgatorio* where the dawn sky is compared to the 'sweet colour of the Oriental sapphire':

> Dolce color d'oriental zaffiro
>
> . . .
>
> a li occhi miei ricominciò diletto.   (*Purg.* I, 13, 16)

Colours give pleasure. Like light they can be perceived only by the noblest of the senses, the sense of sight.[8] To some extent precious stones are valued precisely because of the purity and intensity of their colour; and Dante seems to have been familiar with the professional secrets of contemporary painters, and to have known the materials they ground to produce the strong bright colours that survive undimmed on many altar-pieces after more than six hundred years. The flowers that adorn the ground of the little valley reserved for the Princes in Antepurgatory are said to be more brilliant than 'gold, fine silver, cochineal, white lead, indigo, the unclouded limpidity of lychnites, or of an emerald newly split'; and the hardness and sharpness of the implied colours are synaesthetically reinforced by the crisp rhyme-sounds of *biacca* and *fiacca* which are anticipated in the word *cocco*:

> Oro e argento fine, cocco e biacca,
> indaco, legno lucido e sereno,
> fresco smeraldo in l'ora che si fiacca.   (*Purg.* VII, 73–5)

For Dante, the purest green is always emerald; porphyry and rubies are the paradigm of redness; while sapphire contains the essence of blue. Blue is of course Mary's colour, while green and red are the colours of Hope and Love.[9]

More even than in the *Purgatorio*, precious stones find their *luogo connaturale* in the imagery of the *Paradiso*. They are doubly appropriate as symbols for the souls of the blessed because of their supreme worth, and because they participate most fully in the nature of light. The soft translucence of alabaster fitted it for use as a diffusing screen in front of a flame or fire. Transparent substances like glass, amber and crystal are recalled because they are like the element Air, and offer no resistance at all to the passage of light. The element of Fire predominates in sparkling stones, *lucidi lapilli*, which reflect the sun's rays so brilliantly that they seem to be independent sources of light.[10] This is the same property that Dante admired in the ruby, the *balasso* (a species of ruby), in the diamond, and also in gold. The similes involving the last four substances are strikingly alike in syntax and rhythm, and they illustrate how closely Dante collaborates with his chosen metrical form, either condensing his thought into a single line or verse, or expanding it to include technical terms (e.g. *raggio*, *rifrangere*) so that it fills a whole terzina:

quasi *adamante* che lo *sol* ferisse	(*Par.* II, 33)
qual fin *balasso* in che lo *sol* percuota	(IX, 69)
quale a raggio di *sole* specchio d'*oro*.	(XVII, 123)

parea ciascuna *rubinetto* in cui
raggio di *sole* ardesse sì acceso,
che ne' miei occhi rifrangesse lui.   (XIX, 4–6)

Plants and flowers in the 'Comedy'

All plants differ from all minerals in that they are alive (we shall discuss the meaning of 'life' in due course). But the specific virtues of plants differ more widely one from another than those of metals and stones, and it is not uncommon for two species to have properties that we regard as diametrically opposed, as, for example, when their stems are either downy or spiky, and when their fruit is either sweet or sour, nutritious or poisonous. Dante formalizes and intensifies such oppositions in his famous description of the Wood of the Suicides in Hell: 'The branches were not green but dark; the boughs not smooth but gnarled and twisted; there were no fruits, but poisonous thorns.'

Non fronda verde, ma di color fosco;
non rami schietti, ma nodosi e 'nvolti;
non pomi v'eran, ma stecchi con tòsco.   (*Inf.* XIII, 4–6)

He also uses a number of traditional metaphors which are based on this kind of contrast. The thorn-bush can stand for the heretic, while the orthodox are imaged as shrubs in the Catholic garden. Millet is a coarse grain fit only for animals, but wheat is the staple of human life; and in Christ's parable it represents the righteous who are garnered into the *arche ricchissime* of Paradise; whereas the tares that grow in the wheat-fields and are burned in a bonfire at harvest-time are a figure of the damned in Hell. More originally, Dante is the sweet fig who cannot produce fruit among the bitter sorbs of his fellow Florentines.[11] Other brief allusions remind us of the range of differing properties possessed by plants. Nettles sting (like the pricks of remorse). Oaks are robust, and ivy clings. The grape gives wine. The olive produces an oil which is all the hermit needs to survive. Its branch is the symbol of peace, and in classical times it had been the tree of Minerva and was therefore associated with wisdom. Classical associations also ennoble the evergreen myrtle and bay whose leaves are used to make crowns for victors in war or in poetic contest; while the palm remains the Christian symbol for the martyr's truly everlasting triumph.[12]

With the possible exception of the simile describing the tenacious grip of ivy, none of the allusions is in any way remarkable for its expression. Taken together, however, they do serve to clarify the fundamental assumptions which make such imagery possible. All individual plants of the same species are assumed to have identical properties; and the properties of distinct species are by definition distinct. 'By their fruits ye shall know them', said Jesus; and Dante will add: 'Wheat is judged by the grain.' Blossom can sometimes deceive; and after prolonged rain, trees may produce inedible fruit (*bozzacchioni*). But the plant world is ordered and secure; only among men can there regularly be degeneracy such that 'the plant is less than the seed'.[13]

Some of these powers of plant life are of course common to more than one species. The branch that straightens itself, after bending its tip to allow the wind to pass over, does so by a *virtù* that is *propria* to many if not all trees:

> Come la fronda che flette la cima
> nel transito del vento, e poi si leva
> per la propria virtù che la soblima.   (*Par.* XXVI, 85–7)

But here too there are distinctions to be made and limits to be observed. No tree can equal the humble rush in its capacity to sway and 'ride the blow'. It is this characteristic which allows the rush to survive even down in the soft mud on the very edge of the low-lying shore of Dante's Purgatory, where a plant with branches or a woody stem could never endure the buffeting of the waves:[14]

> Questa isoletta intorno ad imo ad imo,
> là giù colà dove la batte l'onda,
> porta di giunchi sovra 'l molle limo:
>   null' altra pianta che facesse fronda
> o indurasse, vi puote aver vita,
> però ch'a le percosse non seconda.   (*Purg.* I, 100–5)

This is probably the fullest and most satisfying portrayal of a plant and its adaptation to a particular habitat to be found anywhere in the *Comedy*, and it may be tempting to ascribe its greater detail and naturalism to the fact that it occurs not in a simile but in a description. In fact, however, the description also establishes the rush as a perfect symbol of humility; and it is for this symbolic property that the protagonist must gird himself with *un giunco schietto* before he can make his ascent of the mountain of God. And far from being a rush as we know it, this specimen is more like the Golden Bough that Aeneas plucked in preparation for his journey into the world beyond death. 'What a miracle', the poet exclaims in recollection of the scene; 'no sooner did Virgil pluck the humble rush than another was "reborn" on the same spot, identical to the one he had chosen':

> oh maraviglia! ché qual elli scelse
> l'umile pianta, cotal si rinacque
> subitamente là onde l'avelse.   (*Purg.* I, 134–6)

There are not many references to flowers in the *Comedy* but they make a vivid and lasting impression on the reader's mind. Dante treats them as a special case analogous to the precious stones among the minerals. They too are natural examples of pure colour. They too have associations of beauty and supreme value. In the Garden of Eden, Matelda gathers flowers to make herself a garland in an ideal picture of human innocence before the Fall. And when Beatrice appears on the triumphal chariot at the centre of the Mystic Procession, angels will virtually cover her in a cloud of flowers. The distinctive feature of flowers is, of course, the sweetness of their scent: in Italian, *fiori* rhymes with *odori*. Dante celebrates their fragrance in a simile of the May breeze 'tutta impregnata da l'erba e da' fiori' and again in his description of the Valley of the Princes, where 'Nature had not simply painted the ground with their bright colours, but had blended the sweetness of a thousand flowers into a single perfume unknown here on earth':[15]

> Non avea pur natura ivi dipinto,
> ma di soavità di mille odori
> vi facea uno incognito e indistinto.   (*Purg.* VII, 79–81)

Just as it was the distinctive yielding of the rush that Dante captured in his syntax, so the most revealing of his similes involving flowers are both evocations of their movement. When his despair gives place to a new surge of confidence at the outset of his journey, he compares himself to the 'flowers which have been weighed down and closed by the cold night, but which straighten and open on their stems when they are touched by sunlight':

> Quali fioretti dal notturno gelo
> chinati e chiusi, poi che 'l sol li 'mbianca,

> si drizzan tutti aperti in loro stelo,
> tal mi fec' io di mia virtude stanca.   (*Inf.* II, 127–30)

Much later, the courtesy and affection shown by St Peter Damian make the pilgrim's trust expand like a rose under the sun, when it finally becomes all that it had been in potency:

> E io a lui: 'L'affetto che dimostri
> meco parlando, e la buona sembianza
> ch'io veggio e noto in tutti li ardor vostri,
>   così m'ha dilatata mia fidanza,
> come 'l sol fa la rosa quando aperta
> tanto divien quant' ell' ha di possanza.'   (*Par.* XXII, 52–7)

How different Dante's rose is from that of the Renaissance poets, which was beautiful only while it remained a promise unfulfilled. And how different too from the more conventional image of a maidenhead, guarded by thorns and waiting to be plucked, that we find in the final scene of the *Romance of the Rose*. For Dante, the beauty and fragrance of the mature rose make it a fitting emblem for the Virgin Mary.[16] And his poem will draw to its close with an image that transforms the whole vast amphitheatre of the blessed in Paradise into a white rose. Beatrice leads the poet to the yellow heart of this sempiternal rose, and there, from the centre, he sees it 'spreading, rising petal above petal, and giving off the sweet fragrance of praise to the Sun who makes it always Springtime':[17]

> Nel giallo de la rosa sempiterna,
> che si digrada e dilata e redole
> odor di lode al sol che sempre verna.   (*Par.* XXX, 124–6)

Animals in the 'Comedy'

The essential feature of a plant is the root that holds it fast. Its movements are restricted to the upward or outward thrust towards the sunlight, and to the reassertion of its natural habit after external forces like the wind and waves have ceased to molest it. Animals, on the other hand, are by definition capable of movement from place to place. Their organs are accordingly more numerous and more complex than those of plants. This complexity permits a greater diversification of species. And the differences between the species are nowhere more apparent, at least to Dante's delighted eye, than in the many distinct forms of *locomotion*. Leaving on one side for the moment the flight of birds, Dante shows us the snake gliding and preening itself seductively, and the lion advancing with head held high. His greyhounds are eager and swift, while the lizard crosses the summer road like a flash of lightning. Pigs burst out of the sty, running and snapping at each other, but sheep come hesitatingly and timidly out of the fold, their heads lowered, first one, then two, then three . . .:[18]

> Come le pecorelle escon del chiuso
> a una, a due, a tre, e l'altre stanno
> timidette atterrando l'occhio e 'l muso.　(*Purg.* III, 79–81)

More often than not, Dante knows, the cause of an animal's movement is simply the desire for food or the fear of becoming food for another species, and many of the animals mentioned in the *Comedy* are paired in the relationship of predator and prey. They are images either of the devils and their victims in Hell, or of man's inhumanity to man. Dogs pursue the deer and the hare or the beggar-man and thief. The mouse tries to escape from the cat, the lamb from the wolf, and the wolf from the greyhound.[19] Frogs will lie watchfully near the edge of a ditch with nothing showing out of the water except their snouts, but when they catch sight of their natural enemy, the water-snake, they will scatter through the water and huddle on the bottom:[20]

> E come a l'orlo de l'acqua d'un fosso
> stanno i ranocchi pur col muso fuori,
> sì che celano i piedi e l'altro grosso . . .　(*Inf.* XXII, 25–7)

> Come le rane innanzi a la nimica
> biscia per l'acqua si dileguan tutte,
> fin ch'a la terra ciascuna s'abbica.　(*Inf.* IX, 76–8)

Dead metaphors involving wolves, sheep and shepherds were no doubt ten-a-penny in the pulpits of medieval Europe; and it must be freely conceded that many of Dante's animal images are hackneyed and trite. The fox is crafty, the lion valiant, the pig is a filthy swine. The ape imitates, the bee brings forth sweetness, and the insatiable hunger of the wolf makes it a symbol of human greed.[21]

When he is fully himself, however, Dante declares his originality by deliberately avoiding the proverbial associations of a given species, and giving us instead his own independent observations. He describes the snail not for its slowness but for the eerie power of withdrawing its horns into its head. Similarly, his ant is not a symbol of industry and dedication ('Go to the ant, thou sluggard'). Dante has noticed how ants will move in columns to and from the nest, and how an individual ant will sometimes pause to 'muzzle' a fellow ant proceeding in the opposite direction as if it were seeking news and information:

> così per entro loro schiera bruna
> s'ammusa l'una con l'altra formica,
> forse a spïar lor via e lor fortuna.　(*Purg.* XXVI, 34–6)

Passages like these show the sharp eye of the naturalist who will record such humble impressions as the wet fur of an otter, fish rising to the surface of a fish-pond, the wriggling twist of an eel, a dog scratching, an ox licking its nose, or two billy-goats butting each other.[22]

In physical size, the animals in Dante's menagerie range from the diminutive ant to the elephants and whales that he understood to be the largest creatures in the natural kingdom now that giants are extinct.[23] But the scale of *size* is far less important than the scale of *nobility*. An aristocrat would normally choose a lion or a mastiff for his coat of arms rather than a goose or a sow. To be compared to a steed might be flattering, but Vanni Fucci was nicknamed the Mule because of his *vita bestiale*. We do not resent comparisons with an ant or a bee. But we intensely dislike any form of association – whether literal or metaphorical – with other 'hostile' insects such as the flea, flies, horse-flies, gadflies, mosquitoes and wasps which are made to play a part in the torments of Hell, or which appear in derogatory similes.[24]

Many people will confess to a dislike for vermin but a positive hatred for snakes and creeping things. The Book of Genesis attributes this enmity to the part played by the Serpent in the Fall of Adam and Eve; and the souls in Antepurgatory are reminded of the Tempter's wiles in a nightly ritual in which two guardian angels put to flight a snake that tries to enter the Valley of Princes.[25] Dante found suitably sinister and repellent names in the poems of Ovid and Lucan for the snakes who appear on the heads of the three Furies, or who torment the souls of the thieves. Alongside such vernacular terms as *vipera*, *biscia* and *serpentello*, we have *idre*, *ceraste*, *chelidri*, *iaculi e faree*, and *cencri con anfisibena*.[26] He exploits our instinctive revulsion at the thought of merely touching a snake by describing in horrifying detail the process by which the body of one of the thieves is merged with that of a six-footed serpent to form a slow-moving monster that was 'like two and nothing', the very image of perversity:

> due e nessun l'imagine perversa
> parea; e tal sen gio con lento passo.   (*Inf.* xxv, 77–8)

Dante caps this metamorphosis with an even more blood-chilling spectacle. A second thief is stung in the navel by a thin, black snake. Smoke issues from the wound and from the snake's mouth while the two stare at each other in silence. Then, stage by stage, terzina by terzina, the snake takes on the form of a human body, while the matter of the man is transformed into a snake.[27] This amazing *tour de force* of description – and the poet himself boasts that he has surpassed the metamorphoses described by Ovid and Lucan – comes as the climax of nine cantos in which Dante has been deliberately prodigal in his use of animal images that are unflattering or degrading; and it finally reveals the purpose of that imagery. Those who deceive and hurt their fellow human beings are no more than wild animals. The life of sin is a *vita bestiale*.

Birds in the 'Comedy'

Few readers of the *Inferno* will have forgotten the first group of similes involving birds. In the second circle of Hell the souls of guilty lovers are tossed in the black air by a violent, gusting wind symbolizing the sexual passion that mastered them on earth. Dante-character's first sighting of the souls reminds him of a winter flock of starlings who remain in a dense, broad cluster while the individual birds swirl hither and thither in every direction. Then 'more than a thousand shades whom Love drove from this world' are carried past lamenting, and the poet compares them to a long line of migrating cranes who make a melancholy honking as they fly. Finally, two of the damned lovers, Paolo and Francesca, break away from the line in answer to Dante's appeal and come to speak with him. They approach 'like doves called by longing for their sweet nest and borne along by desire'; and they are caught by Dante's camera, so to speak, in the very instant of arrival, when their wings have ceased beating and are 'spread wide and still' to brake their flight:[28]

> E come li *stornei* ne portan l'ali
> nel freddo tempo, a schiera larga e piena,
> così quel fiato li spiriti mali
> di qua, di là, di giù, di sù li mena;
>
> E come i *gru* van cantando lor lai,
> faccendo in aere di sé lunga riga . . .
>
> Quali *colombe* dal disio chiamate
> con l'ali alzate e ferme al dolce nido
> vegnon per l'aere, dal voler portate.
>
> (*Inf.* v, 40–3; 46–7; 82–4)

As with the mammals and reptiles, so with the birds: Dante is clearly interested more in their movement than in their shape or colour; and in each of these three similes he calls attention to the diversity of the patterns of flight that characterize the different species. Nor are these the only examples. He portrays jackdaws as birds who roost in a flock and rise all together at dawn 'as their nature and customs dictate' (*per lo natural costume*); after this, he notes, some will fly away, some will return to their perches, and others circle in the sky above them. By contrast, the falcon is a proud and solitary bird. When his hood is removed, he arches his head, stretches his wings and preens himself. He soars aloft followed intently by the falconer's eye. He swoops down on his prey, climbing again in disgust if he misses his mark. He may return empty-taloned to the falconer's lure, or he may descend prematurely in wide circles, settling on the ground sullenly and disdainfully far away from his disgruntled master.[29]

Notwithstanding such variants between the species, the power of flight is taken to be common to all birds, and birds are taken to be the only two-legged creatures that can fly.[30] Now, the distinctive feature of flight as a form of locomotion is that it entails a movement *upwards*, a triumph over the downward tendency of the heavy elements, Water and Earth. Heaviness is usually a symbol of oppression, imprisonment and defeat. Hence flight has come to symbolize exultation, liberation and victory; and birds participate in that symbolic value. The Psalmist longed for the 'wings of a dove'. And in the action of the *Comedy*, Dante-character is portrayed metaphorically as a nestling who must first acquire feathers and wings and then use them to soar up to his Maker. He is taught to recognize and avoid the 'nets' and 'bird lime' that would trap him and hold him down.[31] As Hugh Shankland has pointed out, Dante's very surname, Alighieri, may offer a clue to his spiritual development, since it may be plausibly linked with the Latin word *aliger*, which means 'bearing wings', or 'wing-borne', the 'Messenger of the Gods'.[32] It is therefore appropriate that we should complete our brief survey of the natural world on a rising scale.

Birds excel in voice as well as in movement. The devils and damned in Dante's Hell croak like frogs, or bark, bay, snarl and howl like dogs; but his birds are credited with sweetness of song and harmony. Every sound is transformed by the magic of the human metaphors. The monotonous cooing of pigeons becomes a 'murmuring of affection', the honking of cranes becomes a poetic 'lay', while the noisy twittering of the swallows is changed into 'sad lays' – *tristi lai*. The Earthly Paradise would be incomplete without birdsong. The nightingale is recalled as the bird that most delights to sing; but the prize goes to the lark, who 'sings as she soars freely in the air and then falls silent in the final sweetness that fills her being with contentment':[33]

> Quale allodetta che 'n aere si spazia
> prima cantando, e poi tace contenta
> de l'ultima dolcezza che la sazia. (*Par*. xx, 73–5)

Above the lark we may rank two birds that Dante could only have known from the bestiaries and encyclopaedias, where they were given attributes that permitted a symbolic link with Christ. The pelican suggested a parallel with His self-sacrifice on the cross by its willingness to shed its own blood to feed its young. And pious readers were reminded of the Resurrection by the phoenix which, after more than five hundred years of life, would prepare a funeral pyre of aromatic boughs, immolate itself in the flames, and rise again from the ashes.[34]

The place of absolute supremacy, however, belongs to the eagle. It was known to be larger and more powerful than any other bird. It could fly higher and see further, and was reputed to be able to look directly into the sun. In classical mythology it was the bird of Jupiter. It was early chosen as the standard of the Roman legions, and it became the symbol of the Roman Empire. In the *Comedy*, it appears in similes which recall its main attributes and also in the extended metaphor for the conquests of the Caesars that we discussed in the previous chapter. In a miraculous sculpture representing the Emperor Trajan doing justice to the widow, it waves as a banner in the wind. It comes in a dream to lift Dante up into the sky. In the allegorical masque at the end of the *Purgatorio* it represents the Empire under Constantine. And in the Heaven of Jupiter the souls of the just rulers arrange themselves to present, not the circles or the cross of the two lower heavens, but a heraldic eagle, the *sacrosanto segno* of divine justice. For Dante, the eagle is quite simply the bird of God, *l'uccel di Dio*.[35]

Corporeity, form, quality and composition

All these diverse beings and things, from ironstone to the eagle, have one thing in common: they exist as compound bodies – *corpora composita*. The use of the noun, *corpus*, marks them off from God and the angels. The use of the adjective, *compositum*, distinguishes them from the four elements and the heavens (respectively *corpora simplicia* and *corpora caelestia*); it also excludes the pure abstraction of a '*mathematical* body'.

Let us begin with the noun and clarify the concept of 'corporeity', that is, of the main conditions of existence common to *all* natural bodies, whether they are simple, composite or celestial. For the medieval Aristotelian, any natural body is a whole (*totum*) analysable as a conjunct (*coniunctum*) of matter and form. By virtue of its matter, we may say, it possesses 'extension' or 'quantity', which simply means that it exists in three dimensions. By virtue of its form, it is finite and bounded by a surface. It is a 'complete magnitude' and a *continuum*. It occupies space; it is located in space; and no two bodies can be in the same place at the same time.[36]

Every body in nature has certain determinate properties or qualities. As we saw in the second chapter, some of them may be classified as active and others as passive, but they are all inherent in the *form* (matter as such, it will be remembered, is a mere potentiality to receive form). The concepts of form and quality or property are in fact inseparable. Some properties are common to more than one form, but no form can exist without a specific property, and no two distinct forms can share exactly the same combination of properties. Hence any two bodies that exhibit the self-same properties must have the self-same form.[37]

A few examples taken from our knowledge of the *simple* bodies will help to make these essential correlations clear. Any body that is simply hot and dry without any other property whatsoever must be Fire. For while the active radical (hot) is common to Air, and the passive radical (dry) is common to Earth, no other body is distinguished by *this combination* of the contrary qualities. Conversely, Fire can never be either cold or wet. Wet and cold in combination are the qualities proper to Water. And the fact that Fire and Water have mutually exclusive properties is the clearest proof that the universal substrate of primary matter is devoid of any qualities.

With the exception of the *corpora caelestia* all natural bodies are doomed to pass away. Their matter is indestructible and everlasting, but this matter will inevitably pass under a new form, taking on a different structure with its own inherent qualities. At the moment of that passage a new body comes into being and the former body ceases to exist.[38]

As far as possible, all questions relating to the processes of generation and corruption – to use the technical names – will be held over until the penultimate chapter. But the distinction between simple and composite bodies, and the subdivision of composite bodies, will be easier to understand if we return for a moment to Aristotle's theories concerning the process of *transmutation*.

In the first place, it will be recalled that not all qualities are surrendered at the moment when one element is transformed into another; for example, when Earth becomes Water, the new body remains qualitatively cold. It is in fact impossible for transformation to take place if there is no common radical. Fire cannot become Water immediately; it must first be transformed into either Earth or Air. With slight modifications, this principle is valid for all composite bodies as well. No body can be generated from another body unless that body is cognate or compatible with the new, in the sense that the supplanted form has properties in common with the new form.[39]

It will also be remembered that Aristotle's meteorology allowed for qualities that are *intermediate* between the extremes of the four contrary qualities. Water is said to be cold, but it is obvious that it remains unambiguously water at temperatures ranging from very cool to very warm. And the doctrine of 'exhalations' shows that there is a twilight zone in which it is impossible to say whether a body is more hot than cold or vice versa. A moist exhalation (*vapor humidus*) is a *medium*, something almost unclassifiable lying in a no-man's-land between Water and Air. It is a body but it cannot be called 'simple'. Equally, it cannot be called 'compound'. It takes in at most two of the elements. It is highly unstable. And it does not possess any properties that cannot be accounted for by postulating a mean position or state of equilibrium between one pair of the contrary qualities.[40]

By elimination, therefore, we find that a *corpus* may be classified as *compositum* when it satisfies the following conditions. It must contain a blend of all four elements.[41] It must be relatively more stable than the exhalations or the elements. And it must have at least one quality distinct from those of the elements in combination or in equilibrium. In the generation of one element from another, something is lost and something else takes its place. In the generation of a compound from the elements, or from an existing compound, something is added, and nothing is lost.

Complexion, powers and virtues, 'differentiae'

The primary qualities of the elements do of course *persist* in their compounds. Different *corpora composita* contain differing proportions of the four elements; and it is this proportion that determines the relative importance of a given primary quality in a given case. All composite bodies contain a certain quantity of Earth, and hence they all possess the quality of weight or gravity, but some substances are heavier than others because they contain proportionately more Earth. Again, all minerals contain both Earth and Water, but the brittleness of stones and rocks points to a preponderance of Earth, while the malleability of metals suggests a predominance of Water.[42]

Nor was it only among minerals or plants that qualitative differences between the species, or between individuals of the same species, were ascribed to differences in the proportions of the elements. The courage of a lion, for example, could be attributed to a predominance of the hot radical, while the cowardice or folly of an ass was attributed to a predominance of cold. One man could have more Fire in his make-up, another more Earth or 'common clay'.

At this point we must introduce a new term – *complexio*. It is derived from a verb meaning to 'embrace' or 'enfold', which in turn derives from a root meaning to 'plait' or 'knit together'. It was often used as a mere variant for *compositio*, and the adjective *complexionatum* could be interchangeable with *compositum*. Hence, the expression *corpora complexionata* could be synonymous with *corpora composita*. But there were also differences in usage that are worth registering and preserving. *Compositio* marks an opposition to *simplicitas*. *Complexio* was preferred when the writer wanted to stress that the form of a certain body requires a blend of the four elements in a more or less constant ratio, or when he wanted to lay the emphasis on the qualitative differences that result from quantitative factors. Thus a lion is said to be of a 'hot complexion', not of a 'hot composition'. And the medieval doctors would consistently use the word *complexio* (or *dispositio*) to describe those differences in physique, temperament or state of health that they attributed to variations in the balance of the elements in the individual's constitution.[43]

It is therefore vital to grasp that the primary qualities of the elements are not extinguished in their compounds (and this is one reason why we have to understand the material cause of a body before it can be the object of 'certain knowledge').[44] But it is even more important to insist that a *corpus compositum* must have other distinctive qualities which reside in its structure or 'formal cause', and which enable it to carry out a specific function in the universe and to reach its goal or 'final cause'.

The secondary qualities divide into two main classes. Some of them are called 'passive' (they may also be referred to as *potentiae*). It is these that predispose a body to 'obey', making it fit and ready to be acted upon by some higher body.[45] They are best understood as a refinement of the fundamental 'desire' for form which Aristotle posited in all matter, including *materia prima*, and which found its first expression in the passive polarity among the elements. The others are called *virtutes*, or 'active' qualities. They are analogous to the hot–cold polarity, and they enable a given body to exert an influence on others – to modify them, and in some cases either to convert them into its own substance or to use their matter to generate new bodies in its own likeness.[46]

The concepts are not in the least abstruse and may be illustrated by combining Dante's example of predators and their prey with what modern ecologists call the 'food chain'. Lions cannot live on grass, deer cannot live on minerals, and grass cannot live on elements in their elemental form (each pair of bodies is too unlike to be compatible). But the *potentiae* and *virtutes* of these bodies enable minerals to take up the elements, grass to absorb the minerals, deer to convert grass into their own substance, and lions to digest the flesh of deer. Every composite body is at once an 'agent', using other bodies to secure its own proper goal, and a 'patient' serving as a means to the end of some higher body. It is the combination of active and passive qualities that makes it possible for compounds to be subordinate one to another and for all of them to be subservient to man.[47]

The food chain can also serve to exemplify the essential point that the higher body is able to act upon the lower because it contains – *in potentia* at least – the main properties of the lower body.[48] Or, to put it another way, the qualities that characterize the lower body are taken up or 'subsumed' and presupposed in the higher. In fact, the higher body is 'higher' (*magis perfectum*), because its distinctive powers are added to existing powers and not substituted for them.

In many cases the classification of the properties of a compound body into 'active' and 'passive' will produce much the same results as a classification into 'higher' and 'lower'; and a similar list would be obtained by dividing them into 'specific' and 'generic'. But the coincidences would not be complete; and so, at the risk of labouring the obvious, we must note that in this context the adjective 'generic' denotes those qualities, be they active or passive, that are shared by several cognate forms, which are thereby defined as belonging to the same kind or 'genus'; while the adjective 'specific' denotes those qualities which distinguish a given body from its near relatives, especially from those immediately below it on the scale of complexity. The distinguishing quality is called the *differentia*, and it is essential to the definition of the species. In fact, the concepts of *differentia* and *species* are as inseparable as those of quality and form.[49]

Compound bodies: inanimate, vegetative and sensitive

The lowest or simplest kinds of composite existence are lifeless and inert. The only power of movement they possess is the heaviness they derive from the elements of Earth and Water in their 'complexion'. Like the four elements, they are perfectly uniform or homogeneous, in the sense that every particle of pure gold, for example, has exactly the same properties as every other particle, or as a mass of gold however large.[50] Among philosophers such bodies are called *corpora inanimata* or *corpora homogenea* (*homoeomera*); in less exalted company they are called *mineralia*.

Minerals were divided into metals and stones, and these were subdivided, as we have seen, into many species each with its own distinctive quality (and it is well known that even educated laymen were inclined to credit stones with some very strange properties indeed). In general, both the learned and the unlearned seem to assume that metals were 'higher' than stones; and they would probably have agreed that no two species were, strictly speaking, equal in rank. But there was of course no single comprehensive scale of value accepted by everyone; and the impossibility of setting up such a scale becomes obvious as soon as one goes into detail.

Above the minerals come the *corpora animata*. As their name suggests they have an *anima*, conventionally translated as 'soul' but perhaps better rendered by such locutions as 'vital principle', 'principle of life', or 'living form'. All these bodies have not just 'being' but 'life'.[51] They can all absorb nourishment, grow and multiply. To perform these different tasks they need different parts with specialized functions, and a *corpus animatum* will always have dissimilar parts. Some of these parts may themselves be homogeneous (like sap or pith) but the whole body is said to be *heterogeneum* or *anhomoeomerum*.[52]

The term chosen to designate the different functional parts was 'tool' or 'instrument' (by analogy obviously with man's use of hammer, chisel and saw), and this was the original meaning of the Latin word *organum*, taken over from the Greek *organon*. Hence a *corpus heterogeneum* is also properly called a *corpus organicum*, or *corpus organizatum*, a 'body with instruments'.[53]

The lowest kind of 'organized', heterogeneous, animate body is a plant. It cannot do more than take in food, increase in size, and reproduce itself.[54] Its distinctive organs are limited to roots, stem, branches, leaves, flower, fruit and seed. Its *anima* is said to be *vegetativa* or *vegetabilis*. But as we saw in the first part of the chapter, plants are far more diversified than minerals. The distinctive 'virtues' are far easier to recognize – significantly, the medieval herbals are much less fanciful than the lapidaries – and the differences in size or in longevity as between a rush and an oak are matched by a no less apparent inequality in point of complexity and 'nobility' of form.

Above the plants come those bodies which possess all the faculties of the *anima vegetativa* and, in addition, the power of self-movement. This power was regarded as the very essence of life, and thus such bodies are called not just *corpora animata* but *animalia*.[55]

Their *corpus* is still a *totum* with its own unity and integrity of form, but it is made up of substances as different from each other as blood, tissue, bone, nerves and hair. These homogeneous substances are structured into new and distinct sets of 'instruments', each containing numerous unlike parts – the organs of locomotion and the organs of sensation. In higher animals the two sets are always found in conjunction. Some lower animals, however, such as the oyster, are restricted to the senses of touch and taste; and since the organs of motion are never found in isolation from the organs of sensation, the 'vital principle' of animal life is known as the *anima sensitiva*.[56]

Sensitive life permits a diversity far greater than does vegetative life, and the inequality between the species is even more pronounced. The reproductive systems of the so-called 'perfect animals' are so complex that the various components are distributed between two bodies of different sex – the passive and inferior female, and the active, dominant male. Animals that have specialized organs of motion (legs) are superior to those that creep on their belly; and, in general, the more *operationes* an animal can perform, the more perfect it is held to be.[57] Thus, animals that possess only two senses are inferior to those with a full complement. And the five senses themselves form a pyramid resting on the base of touch, and climbing through taste, smell and hearing to reach the apex of sight.[58]

The higher the sense, and the more efficient its activity, the nobler or more honourable is the animal that possesses it. The sense of sight is the supreme power of the *anima sensitiva*. The eagle possesses the sense of sight in supreme degree. And this is why the eagle stands at the summit of sensitive life and is rightly described by Dante as the bird of God.

The Ladder of Being or the Scale of Nature

These ideas form part of the common stock of scholastic philosophy. Nearly all of them are expounded in Aristotle's *De anima*, which was one of his best known works in the thirteenth century; and there can be no doubt that they were familiar and congenial to Dante. Indeed, he demonstrates his theoretical grasp of the whole subject in several places in his prose works, both early and late, and in the *Comedy* itself. One of the main arguments in the *Quaestio* depends on the distinction between active and passive qualities, and on the principle that all homogeneous bodies have uniform properties in every part. In the first book of the *Monarchia* he dwells on the absurdity of defining a species by referring to the generic powers that it shares with other, less complex beings, without indicating its unique *differentia*. The same point is made in the fourth book of the *Convivio* in a chapter where Dante also alludes to Aristotle's geometrical simile of the pentagon which 'contains' the square, as the square 'contains' the triangle. In *Purgatorio* IV he repeats Aristotle's condemnation of those who misunderstood the concept of 'subsumption', and believed that an animal must have two distinct *animae*, one *vegetativa* and one *sensitiva*.[59]

But the work in which his preoccupation with these ideas amounts almost to an obsession is the third book of the *Convivio*. In the second chapter he offers the following almost hypnotically repetitive summary of what we have been calling the 'subsumption' of the powers (we will cut him short at the point where he passes on to the *human* soul):

In the second book of the *De anima*, where Aristotle analyses the capacities of the psyche, he asserts that its principal powers are three – life, sensation and thought. (He also adds motion, but this can be taken together with sensation, since every psyche that receives information through the senses, whether one or more than one, is also capable of movement; hence, motion is a power inseparable from sensation.) And, as Aristotle says, it is perfectly obvious that the powers are arranged in such a way that one acts as foundation for the next. The first can exist independently, but the second must rest on the first. Thus the vegetative power, which is the principle of life, is the foundation for sight, hearing, taste, smell and touch; but it can also exist as a psyche in its own right, as we see in all the plants. The sensitive power cannot exist without the vegetative, and it is not found in any inanimate body; and this sensitive power is the foundation for the intellectual power, that is, reason. In mortal, animate beings, the ratiocinative power is never found disjoined from the sensitive power; but the power of sensation does exist without reason, as we see in beasts, birds, fish, and indeed in all brute animals. And the psyche that takes in all these powers, being the most perfect of them all, is the human soul . . . (*Con.* III, ii, 11–14)

After a very circumstantial account of the appetites or 'loves' that characterize each level of existence (and we shall return to these in the penultimate chapter), Dante eventually goes on to give his own version of a very important axiom in the Aristotelian theory, which was usually stated in the form: *Natura non facit saltum*. Aristotle insisted, that is, that just as there was no void in nature, so there was no gap or 'jump' between the different levels of being. The exhalations formed an unclassifiable *medium* between the elements; the lodestone seemed to have the power of originating movement (which belongs by definition to animate bodies);

and the sponge lay on the boundary between plant and animal life. So, if one were familiar with the whole range of species found at each of the main levels of existence, one would see that each *differentia* in turn brought only a very small addition to the powers already found in some lower species.[60]

The simile that was used to make the arrangement comprehensible became a dead metaphor long ago, since few people now recognize that the 'degrees' on a 'graduated scale' were originally 'rungs' (*gradus*) on a 'ladder' (*scala*), or 'steps' on a flight of 'stairs'. But the image can be revived – and helpfully modernized – if we compare the levels of existence to the extending ladder used by firemen or in the building trade.

Each of the sections of such a ladder would correspond to one of the main levels of existence, while the rungs would correspond to the species. And just as the fireman moves from the ground to the top of the highest building by small and equal steps, so Nature ascends from the elements up to the most complex living organisms by small and even degrees. Such is the Ladder of Being, or the *Scala Naturae*. And Dante makes it clear that the differences between individuals in any given species are also differences of 'higher' and 'lower', or 'more' and 'less perfect', and that these individual differences are so contrived that the 'noblest' example of one species will possess powers that can scarcely be distinguished from those of the most defective specimen of the species on the next highest rung of the ladder. There is no break in continuity: *quodam continuo ordine progreditur*.

It will not be appropriate to quote from Dante's own description of these *gradi generali* and *gradi singulari* at this point, because the thrust of his argument is away from animals and plants towards angels and men, who form the subject of later chapters in this book.[61] For the time being, therefore, it will be enough to remark that Platonist thinkers had deduced that there must be still further upward 'extensions' of the ladder. In other words, they assumed that the *Scala Naturae* continued above the level of the most perfect men, reaching up beyond the physical heavens and beyond all material bodies into an order of purely intellectual beings, climbing always by the same even steps until it reached the First Intelligence, the summit of the created universe.

A typical Platonist or Platonizing Christian would probably have expounded these ideas in reverse order, proceeding from the top of the scale to the bottom. Rather than talk of the 'rungs' of a 'ladder' he would prefer the metaphor of 'links' in a 'chain' – a Golden Chain of Being – hanging down from the First Cause. But although descent is prior to ascent in the mind of the Platonist, he would still give more or less equal emphasis to both processes. Whichever image one prefers, the principle of a 'graduated' advance remains unaffected: the ladder or chain of nature is not two, but one.[62]

Dante was deeply in love with this Platonic 'extension' of the ladder into the intellectual order; and the third book of the *Convivio* is full of imagery and turns of phrase that derive from very un-Aristotelian sources. He does not describe the different species as simply being either more or less complex than each other because of the addition or subtraction of observable *differentiae*. The species are said to be 'closer to God', or 'further away'. They are more or less 'in His likeness'; they are more or less able to receive and reflect His outflowing goodness; they participate to a greater or lesser extent in the nature of light; they are more or less submerged in the 'grossness of matter'.[63] Expressions such as these (which do not contradict the Aristotelian categories) will, of course, be found on almost any page of the *Paradiso*. And we must remember that the whole action of the *Comedy* is conceived as an imitation of the Scale of Being, as it shows the protagonist climbing step by step, canto by canto, encounter by encounter, truth by truth, until he comes into the presence of God.

For the moment, however, we must hold fast to Aristotle and bring this chapter to a close with a brief and down-to-earth summary of our main findings. We saw, first, that Dante's poetic representation of the species of the natural world is marked by a meticulously close attention to the qualities that characterize and differentiate each species, and by a constant awareness of their place on a scale of nobility or excellence. Then we noted that these are precisely the features that distinguish Aristotle's classification of *le spezie de le cose*. Lastly, we have seen that, in Aristotle's theory, a distinctive *mode* of being and a distinctive *level* of being are simply two sides of the same coin. To be diverse necessarily means to be unequal, because the *differentiae* are either added or subtracted: *formae rerum sunt sicut numeri*.[64]

6

Concerning the heavens

The material cause of the heavenly body

WE HAVE NOW CONSIDERED ALL THE CENTRAL TENETS AND SOME OF
the more important ramifications of Aristotle's teaching concerning the
four elements. We have seen what their properties are, and how their
natural movements separate them into four concentric spheres, with the
solid core of Earth at the centre and the invisible envelope of Fire at the
extremity. We have noted the major exception to that natural ordering – the emergence of Earth above the sphere of Water in our northern
hemisphere. We have seen how, in the vicinity of this *terra discoperta*
(where the hot and wet element, Air, comes into contact with the cold and
dry element, Earth), the four elements are being continually transmuted
one into another to produce the many different phenomena described by
the science of meteorology. We have also seen how the elements enter
into relatively stable compounds under increasingly complex forms to
make possible the generation of minerals, plants and animals. In fact, we
have now studied the '*material* causes' and, to some extent, the '*formal*
causes', of nearly all the things that are accessible to our senses and that
awaken our natural desire to understand them. We are almost ready to
perfect our knowledge of these objects and beings by passing on to
consider their '*efficient*, *instrumental* and *final* causes' – to discover, that
is, Who made them, and How and Why.

There remains, however, one very important class of objects in the
universe that we have yet to study in a systematic way, even though we
have been forced to refer to them on many occasions when discussing the
imaginative use that Dante makes of his scientific knowledge. These are
the sun, moon, planets and stars.

They are clearly 'bodies', and since they emit heat and light, some
early Greek thinkers had supposed that they were made of the element of
Fire, or of some compound in which Fire predominated. But there were
grave objections to this view. Why did these bodies move at all if they
were in their proper place? Why did they move in circles at a constant
speed, rather than in a straight line up or down with ever increasing
velocity? The records of many centuries showed that they were unchanged in form and number, but how could they continue to 'burn'

without ever being exhausted? In short, how could they be free from the cycle of generation and corruption to which all *corpora composita* are subject, and from the cycle of transmutation which governs the *corpora simplicia* themselves?[1]

Aristotle warned his readers that they must not look for *certain* answers to such questions about the heavenly bodies. The most they should expect was a hypothesis that respected all the observable facts and was consonant with the fundamental laws of physics. But his arguments were once again so compelling that his conclusions came to be accepted as dogma by all those who, like Dante, believed that 'Nature had opened her secrets to him more than to any other philosopher'.[2]

These conclusions and the all-important reasoning are set out in a work which was known in the Latin West as *De caelo et mundo* or simply as *De caelo* (Dante uses both forms). The title is a significant one because it shows that Aristotle was more interested in astrophysics, as we should now say, than in astronomy. His subject was 'the bodily heaven' rather than 'the heavenly bodies'; and his main concern was to complete the account of matter, motion and the general properties of natural bodies that he had begun in the *Physics*. The movements of the sun, moon, planets and stars are relatively minor matters compared with the general theory of which they form a part. And the work opens – rather disconcertingly for the unwary reader – with a lengthy demonstration that there must of necessity be a *fifth* element in the universe, a fifth 'simple body', in addition to the now familiar Fire, Air, Water and Earth.

The first and most important proof of the existence of a *quintum corpus simplex* makes use of certain axioms that Aristotle had established in his analyses of motion. By definition, all physical bodies exist in three dimensions, and all physical bodies can move. All movements, even one as complex as that required to describe a helix, can be analysed as a combination of three 'simple' movements. These are (*a*) rectilinear motion *away* from a centre point; (*b*) rectilinear motion *towards* that centre; and (*c*) circular motion *around* the centre. Each simple body possesses, again by definition, the power of only one simple motion (and conversely, the natural motion of a simple body is by definition 'simple').

Now, we have seen that the natural movement of the four elements is limited to *rectilinear* motion, either away from or towards the centre. Given the correspondences we have noted, it would seem impossible that there should exist in nature a simple *circular* motion, unless there also exists in nature a simple *body* which exhibits that motion. There must therefore be a *fifth* simple body in the universe, which possesses the power of circular motion.[3]

A three-dimensional physical body with the natural and inalienable property of circular motion, so Aristotle argues, must assume the *form* of a perfect sphere. The perfect sphere formed by this fifth body must lie outside and beyond the spheres formed by the other four; and, granted the impossibility of a void, its inner or concave surface must be in contact at every point with the outer or convex surface of the sphere of Fire. It follows that the fifth sphere must be concentric with the inner four (otherwise it could not rotate); and the still centre of its rotation must coincide with the centre of the sphere of Earth. It is to the outermost sphere that we give the name *caelum* in its widest sense, and this is the subject of Aristotle's treatise.[4]

Still with scarcely more than a glance at the heavenly luminaries and their movement, Aristotle goes on to deduce the other properties of this *quintum corpus*. Circular motion has no contrary or opposite (in the sense that rectilinear motion *away* from a point is unequivocally the opposite of rectilinear motion *towards* that point). And whereas rectilinear motion through a finite space must be finite in duration, the circular motion of a finite body can continue for ever. Again, the natural movement of the four elements ceases when they have come to their natural place in the universe, and the goal of rectilinear motion is stillness. But the rotation of a spherical body will neither move it away from its natural place nor cause it to return there. Hence a *natural* circular motion has no *terminus* or goal, and it must therefore continue for ever.[5]

From these and other considerations, Aristotle reasons that circular motion is prior to and more perfect than rectilinear motion, and that the 'fifth body' is prior to and more noble than the four elements. In truth, it alone fully deserves the name of a 'simple' body, because it does not embody a contrariety or polarity of any kind. It is neither heavy nor light, hot nor dry, wet nor cold. Having no contraries, either within or without, it cannot be described as an 'element' in something else. It is perfectly immutable, and cannot be increased or diminished. It must always have existed in its present form, and it will exist in that form for ever. It is uncreated and indestructible, Aristotle concludes, *ingenitum et incorruptibile*. Its only property or 'virtue' is the power of perpetual motion in a circle. And it is for this essential property that Aristotle justifies and perpetuates the traditional name for this 'divine' substance – 'aether'.[6]

The Empyrean

In the course of the first book of the *De caelo et mundo*, Aristotle makes an apparent digression which in fact serves to demonstrate that his description of the general form of the universe and his account of its 'material causes' are complete and definitive. There is nothing more to be said on either topic. It is physically impossible that matter should exist under any other form than those of aether, the four elements, and their compounds. No physical, material body can be infinite in extent. The natural movements of the *corpora simplicia* must have brought *all* Earth to the centre of our universe, and *all* Water, Air and Fire to their respective spheres (the only exception being the *terra discoperta*). Aether, too, is a physical body, and is finite in extent. And if we ask whether any body lies beyond the outer circumference of the sphere of aether, beyond the *caelum*, the answer is very simply, 'No'. There are no other universes.[7] We cannot even speak of a 'place' or 'void' or 'time' existing beyond the heaven. 'Whatever is there', Aristotle maintained, 'is of such a nature as not to occupy any place, nor does time age it; nor is there any change in any of the things which lie beyond the outermost motion; they continue through their entire duration unalterable and unmodified, living the best and most self-sufficient of lives.'[8]

As Dante noted in the *Convivio*, these words could easily be interpreted as a premonition of revealed truth. Educated Christians of Dante's time, who accepted as a matter of fact that the universe was material, spherical and unique, also held as an article of faith that beyond the physical heaven lay Paradise, or Heaven, or, more technically, the *caelum Empyreum*, or Empyrean. They also held that this was the abode of God, the angels, and the souls of the blessed.[9]

It is of course a little taxing to conceive a 'non-existent somewhere outside space', and it is virtually impossible to give such a concept expression in language. The majority of medieval theologians, and with them the younger Dante, will speak of the *caelum Empyreum* as a *locus* or even a motionless *corpus* with its own *materia*. It is only in the closing cantos of the *Paradiso* that Dante seems to liberate himself from these inconsistencies and find a greater purity of expression. Together with Beatrice he will issue from what he calls the 'greatest body' (the outer rim of the physical heaven) into a heaven that is 'pure light':

> . . . Noi siamo usciti fore
> del maggior corpo al ciel ch'è pura luce:
> luce intellettüal, piena d'amore . . .   (*Par.* xxx, 38–40)

But we are not yet ready to tackle such concepts as 'intellectual light', 'divine love' or the 'infinity of God'; and we must content ourselves for the time being with a brief extract from the *Convivio* which illustrates the conceptual and linguistic difficulties of the subject, and gives us a revealing glimpse of the different strands in Dante's philosophical culture during his middle years:

It must also be said that, beyond all these heavens, Catholics posit the existence of the *caelum Empyreum*, that is, 'the heaven of flame' or 'heaven of light'. They also affirm that it must be motionless, because it contains within itself, uniformly and in every part, all that its matter desires. . . . The place of that supreme Godhead, who alone has perfect knowledge of himself, is still and at peace. According to the infallible teaching of Holy Church, this is the place of the blessed spirits; and Aristotle too seems to sense this, as his attentive readers will agree, in the first book of the *De caelo et mundo*. This is the supreme edifice of the universe, in which the whole universe is contained, and beyond which there is nothing; it is not in space, but was formed in the First Mind alone, which the Greeks call Protonoè. (*Con.* II, iii, 8, 10–11)

The planetary and stellar spheres

Now that we have grasped the main features of Aristotle's theory concerning the shape, matter and properties of the vast aetherial sphere, we may return to the problems posed by the sun, moon, planets and stars that constitute its only visible parts.

As regards their shape, Aristotle argued that the luminaries must themselves be spherical and not flat discs; and as regards their matter, he concluded that they must be made of aether just like the rest of the invisible bodily heaven. His commentators assume that aether will be more densely massed in the luminaries than elsewhere; and this seems a reasonable assumption provided that one is not rash enough to accept – as Dante did in his middle years – that variations in the density of celestial matter are sufficient to explain the differences between the luminaries and the rest of the heaven, or the differences in size and influence between one luminary and another, or, finally, such purely internal differences as may be seen in the irregular markings on the surface of the moon. All these must be ascribed to differences in the '*formal* cause'.[10] And this will lead the most influential of Aristotle's commentators to maintain that each luminary has its own specific form, and that each luminary is the unique representative of a distinct species. All of them do have the same material cause, however, and all of them belong to the same genus. It is by virtue of their *generic* form that they all emit light and heat.[11]

Aristotle himself did not inquire closely into the movement of the luminaries. In the *De caelo* he wrote as a theoretical physicist; and he left the many problems of detail to the professional astronomers. But he did enunciate certain general principles that provided the framework within which later astronomers sought to interpret their observational data. The laws of motion, which Aristotle had formulated in his *Physics*, led him to deny that the luminaries could move independently by pushing their way through aether like a ship through water. As we have seen, the luminaries themselves were made of aether, and *all* aether had the power of unending natural motion in a circle. Consequently, astronomers had to accept that the whole *caelum* was in eternal orbit.

It was well known, however, that some of the luminaries moved at different speeds and that they lay at different distances from the earth, as could be seen during occultations and eclipses. Aristotle was therefore compelled to lend his great authority to the view that luminaries with the power of independent motion were firmly set (*infixae*) in distinct spheres, and that they were carried round the earth by the revolution of those hollow spheres. These spheres were of course concentric with each other and with the spheres formed by the four elements around which they moved. They were all made of the same matter, aether, and they all belonged to the same genus. As a result, they all revolve eternally, at a constant speed. But since the spheres were *formally* distinct, and each constituted a distinct species, they could and did orbit at different velocities.[12]

The great majority of the heavenly luminaries – the stars – did not change position with respect to each other, and they never came between the earth and one of the other lights. It could therefore be deduced that they were all set in one sphere which lay outside the others; and this was known as the 'Heaven of the Fixed Stars' or the 'Starry Heaven' (*cielo stellato*). Aristotle believed that this was the outermost of the spheres, the *sphaera suprema*, and that its outer or convex surface was the boundary of the universe, the limit of matter, place and time.[13]

Each of the seven 'wandering stars' or planets (and these included the sun and moon) was thought to be set in a distinct sphere. Three of them lay outside the sphere carrying the sun, and three inside. Proceeding from the outer to the inner, the order of the planetary heavens was determined as follows: Saturn, Jupiter, Mars; Sun; Venus, Mercury, Moon.

To explain some of the more bewildering motions of the luminaries, Aristotle was prepared to posit a further forty-seven revolving spheres lying between the eight spheres that carry the planets and the stars, but

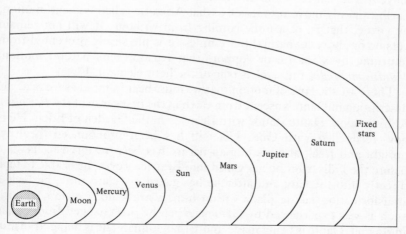

Figure 6. The planetary and stellar spheres.

these were lost to view in the popular conception, which can still be represented as in figure 6.[14] The only serious limitation of such a schematic diagram is that it makes the medieval universe seem too small and the distances between the heavens too uniform. It is therefore worth noting that Dante's main authority puts the mean distance of the moon from the earth at nearly 159,000 miles. The distance to the outer edge of the heaven of the sun was given as 3,965,000 miles; and to the inner edge of the stellar sphere, as no less than 65,357,500 miles.[15]

Body into body will go

The *Paradiso* tells the story of how Dante travelled through the bodily heaven – the 'pure country' or 'round aether', as he calls it – to pass beyond it into the Empyrean and the presence of God. The first two events on this journey are closely linked, and both involve a miraculous suspension of the physical and astrophysical laws which have just been described. Neither episode requires any knowledge of the science of astronomy as such; and it will therefore be convenient, before we abandon Aristotle for Ptolemy and Sacrobosco, to interrupt the exposition of facts and theories, and to consider once again the ways in which Dante exploits his scientific knowledge in the service of his poetry.[16]

Although many people have chosen to speak of the '*Vision* of Dante Alighieri', the narrative of the *Comedy* is quite unlike that of a medieval dream-poem. The fiction maintained throughout the work is that Dante was not 'dreaming' or 'seeing' but making the journey to God *in the flesh*. Now, the element which predominates in the human body is Earth; and, as we have seen, Earth is heavy by nature. It has a natural tendency to move to the centre of the universe, a natural love for its proper place. Earth can only move upwards by what Aristotle called 'violent' motion, by virtue, that is, of a force coming from without. It will not remain outside or above its natural place unless it is physically prevented from returning by some tie or support that frustrates its natural motion. *Mutatis mutandis*, the same is true of the light element, Fire.[17]

These are the laws of motion that we must bear in mind as we read the description of Dante's ascent from earth in the first canto of the *Paradiso*. At high noon, Dante stands with Beatrice in the Garden of Eden. He is now reconciled with God. His will has been pronounced 'healthy, upright and free', and his human nature has been restored to its state before the Fall. After he has gazed into Beatrice's eyes, he is able to look directly into the sun; and after he has gazed a second time, he feels a transformation taking place within him, a miraculous metamorphosis such as was experienced by Glaucus when he was changed from a man into a god. Dante is being made 'more than human'; he is being 'transhumanized'. Suddenly the sky becomes like an immense lake blazing with the sun's light, and his ears are filled with a supernatural harmony.[18] What is happening?

Beatrice is swift to relieve her ward's anxiety. The heavens are not falling. He is no longer on earth, as he mistakenly believes. He is now hurtling to his 'proper place' with the same velocity that a flash of lightning leaves *its* proper place when atmospheric pressures force it down to earth:

> Tu non se' in terra, sì come tu credi;
> ma folgore, fuggendo il proprio sito,
> non corse come tu ch'ad esso riedi. *(Par.* I, 91–3)

These brief and simple words, uttered with a smile, remove one cause of doubt in Dante's mind but immediately ensnare him in another. How can his heavy body rise above the 'light bodies' of Air and Fire?

> . . . ma ora ammiro
> com'io trascenda questi *corpi levi.* (98–9)

Beatrice's reply is itself one of the marvels of the *Paradiso* and one of the most remarkable passages ever written of poetry inspired by ideas. We have glanced at it already, in Chapter 1, and we shall return to it again. But for the moment it will be enough to paraphrase that part of her answer which is directly related to Dante's question.

All things move to their appointed goal, or port of destination, thanks to an innate love for their proper place, a love which is inseparable from their nature and inherent in their 'formal cause'. Man's natural place is with God, and it is towards God that his natural love will move him. If he behaves as though he were no more than his 'material cause', Earth, this is partly because he has been created free to ignore the promptings of that primal impulse, but mostly because he is weighed down by the burden of Original Sin inherited from Adam. Dante, however, has been freed from that burden. Nothing now obstructs him or holds him down; and so his natural love is carrying him up through the spheres of Air and Fire and through the aetherial heaven to his natural goal. Hence, Beatrice concludes, 'you should not feel any greater wonder at your ascent, than when you see a stream flowing downhill from a high mountain. If you had remained below, now that you are free from any impediment, that would have been a "wonder" as great as finding stillness in living fire on earth':

> Non dei più ammirar, se bene stimo,
> lo tuo salir, se non come d'un rivo
> se d'alto monte scende giuso ad imo.
> Maraviglia sarebbe in te se, privo
> d'impedimento, giù ti fossi assiso,
> com' a terra quïete in foco vivo. (136–41)

Rockets are not necessary. It is enough to untie the knots that hold the airship down. Or, in Dante's own metaphor, 'they are being carried by a concreated and perpetual thirst to the God-like realm on high, almost as swiftly as you see the heavens move':

> La concreata e perpetüa sete
> del deïforme regno cen portava
> veloci quasi come 'l ciel vedete. (II, 19–21)

In this first canto, then, Dante uses his narrative craft to make the moment of ascent as 'marvellous' and 'awe-inspiring' to the reader as it had been for him as protagonist, and he then concentrates the whole weight of his learning to show that the apparently 'marvellous' was perfectly in accordance with the laws of nature. In the next canto he introduces a miracle in an almost offhand way, as though it were a familiar event, and then limits himself to the observation that one day even the most inscrutable of the divine mysteries will be as easy to understand as the most self-evident axiom.

As he is carried upwards by that concreated thirst, with the speed of a crossbow-bolt that seems to quiver and rest in its target almost before it has been aimed and fired, Dante's attention is suddenly caught by a *mirabil cosa*.[19] There is no attempt to heighten the suspense. Beatrice immediately urges her charge to 'turn his mind in gratitude to God, for he has joined us with the first star':

> 'Drizza la mente in Dio grata', mi disse,
> 'che n'ha congiunti con la prima stella.' (II, 29–30)

As the rather odd locution suggests, they have penetrated the moon's body. The 'eternal pearl' has received them into itself. They are *in* the moon. And this, quite simply, is a miracle. Like Dante, the moon is a material body; and it was an axiom of Aristotelian physics that no two bodies could occupy the same place at the same time. As Aquinas explains, 'two bodies cannot be together in the same place by reason of their dimensions. If these dimensions are equal, they can differ only as to their place. We cannot imagine two lines of equal length as being different lines, unless we imagine them in different places. . . . When one body is thrust into another, the receiving body must yield: otherwise two bodies would be in the same place at the same time.'[20] And it is clear that Dante had some similar text in mind when he wrote 'I was there in the body, and the reader may not be able to conceive how one dimension suffered another, as must be the case when one body penetrates another':

> S'io era *corpo*, e qui non si concepe
> com' una *dimensione* altra patio,
> ch'esser convien se *corpo* in *corpo* repe. (37–9)

It is possible for a *glorified* body – such as the body of Christ after his

Resurrection, or of all human beings after the Day of Judgement – to be in the same place as another body; but even this requires a miracle. And here we are dealing with two *natural* bodies.[21]

Dante's presentation of this 'wonder' is remarkably detached. In his capacity as narrator, he confines himself to three similes, all of which tend to reduce the impact of the miraculous. It was, he says, as though a cloud had covered them, a cloud that was brightly burnished, like a diamond glinting in the sun, but which, still like a diamond, was solid and dense. His entry into the moon did not compromise its eternal integrity or unity any more than a shaft of sunlight can destroy the unity of water which it illuminates:[22]

> Parev' a me che nube ne coprisse
> lucida, spessa, solida e pulita,
> quasi adamante che lo sol ferisse.
> Per entro sé l'etterna margarita
> ne ricevette, com' acqua recepe
> raggio di luce permanendo unita. (31–6)

As commentator on the action, Dante simply remarks that the evident miracle should sharpen our desire to understand that greater miracle by which Christ became fully human and yet fully divine; and he assures his readers that in the presence of God we shall be able to have 'certain knowledge' of those mysteries which we must now take on trust as articles of faith. They will not need any 'demonstration'; they will be self-evident, just like the 'first truths' to which we immediately give our assent (such as the proposition that the whole must be greater than the part):[23]

> accender ne dovria più il disio
> di veder quella essenza in che si vede
> come nostra natura e Dio s'unio.
> Lì si vedrà ciò che tenem per fede,
> non dimostrato, ma fia per sé noto
> a guisa del ver primo che l'uom crede. (40–5)

In the last twenty lines of the whole poem Dante will give his poetic all in the attempt to suggest the experience of an illuminating flash in which he came to understand how our nature was united with God in the person of Christ. For the moment, however, the prefiguring miracle is handled with great restraint, because the lessons that he now wants to impart are different: it is 'natural' for an omnipotent God to work miracles; one day it will be 'natural' for men to understand their hidden causes.

The planetary heavens in Cicero and Dante

Before we resume our inquiry into the movements of the heavenly spheres, we may return to the episode, already discussed in Chapter 4, in which Dante looked down to the earth from the Heaven of the Fixed Stars and smiled at the 'mean appearance' of the 'threshing-floor which makes us so ferocious'. As was noted earlier, the whole passage is openly modelled on a paragraph in Cicero's *Dream of Scipio*, and it is extremely instructive to compare the original with Dante's 'imitation'.

In Cicero's work, the younger Scipio dreams that he has been caught up into the region of the stars, where he receives instruction from the mouth of his great ancestor, Scipio Africanus, who is the speaker in this excerpt:

Beneath the Starry Heaven are seven other spheres which revolve in the opposite direction. One of these globes is the light which on earth they call Saturn's. Next comes the star called Jupiter's, which brings fortune and health to mankind. Beneath it is the star, red and terrible to the dwellings of man, which you assign to Mars. Below it and occupying the middle region is the Sun, the Lord, Chief and Ruler of the other lights, the mind and guiding principle of the universe, of such magnitude that he reveals and fills all things with his light. He is accompanied by his companions, as it were – Venus and Mercury in their orbits; and in the lowest sphere revolves the moon, set on fire by the rays of the sun.[24]

It will be seen that Cicero is direct and simple. He refers to all seven planets in descending order, using the traditional names that had been taken over from the Graeco-Roman pantheon. He gives particular prominence to the sun, in its central position, and dwells on the astrological influences of the three outer planets. References to astronomy are kept to a minimum (*viz.* the retrograde motion of the planets; the closeness of Venus and Mercury to the sun; the borrowed light of the moon).

Dante's debt to Cicero – and something of his originality – will be evident even in a prose translation. He picks up the allusion to the moon's borrowed light; he calls attention to the orbits of Venus and Mercury; he treats the outer planets as a separate group. But with one exception, he refuses to insult his readers' intelligence by using the proper names of the planets. Instead he employs what we may call a patronymic periphrasis, that is, an allusion to the mythological personage who was the father or mother of the classical god who had become identified with the planet. He makes virtually no mention of astrology; and in his reference to the moon, he returns to the problem of the dark patches, and to his own earlier mistakes about their cause; he also adds the information that the other face of the moon is perfectly clear.

I saw the daughter of Latona, shining without that shadow which led me to believe that some parts were less dense than others. I endured the dazzling aspect of your son, Hyperion, and I saw, O Maia and Dione, how it is possible to move near and about him. Then there appeared Jupiter, tempering between his father and his son; and then the variations in their positions became clear.' (*Par.* XXII, 139–47)

The most important changes, however, can only be appreciated when one reads the original Italian in its context. Dante exploits the metrical form, using the terzina to group the sequence of facts into three paragraphs. He makes a judicious use of repetition to secure both symmetry and variety (*vidi . . . e vidi . . . quindi . . . e quindi*), and then to obtain a powerful climax (*quanto . . . quanto . . . e come*). Most important of all, he manages to suggest a sense of the eye scanning through space. The episode begins with the protagonist 'returning with his gaze past all the seven spheres to our globe, and smiling at its paltry appearance':

> Col viso ritornai per tutte quante
> le sette spere, e vidi questo globo
> tal, ch'io sorrisi del suo vil sembiante.   (*Par.* XXII, 133–5)

Then Dante manages to convey the steady tracking of his gaze as it returns from earth to his present position, naming the planets in ascending order. Finally, he adds a synoptic view of the whole planetary system: 'And all seven revealed their size, their speed, and their distance from each other.'

> Vidi la figlia di Latona incensa
> sanza quell' ombra che mi fu cagione
> per che già la credetti rara e densa.
>   L'aspetto del tuo nato, Iperïone,
> quivi sostenni, e vidi com' si move
> circa e vicino a lui Maia e Dïone.
>   Quindi m'apparve il temperar di Giove
> tra 'l padre e 'l figlio; e quindi mi fu chiaro
> il varïar che fanno di lor dove;
>   e tutti e sette mi si dimostraro
> quanto son grandi e quanto son veloci
> e come sono in distante riparo.
>   (139–50)

The conception and what we earlier called the 'power to think big' are something that Dante in this case shares with his source. But the factors which are decisive in determining the effect of his lines are his and his alone. He is simultaneously more attentive than Cicero to the purely formal values, and more concerned with the astronomical facts.

The difficulties of geocentric astronomy

It is almost impossible to acquire a sympathetic understanding of ancient and medieval astronomy without some knowledge of the true causes of the phenomena for which they were trying to account. And since even the simplest outline of modern theories may prove a little difficult to understand, it may be helpful to begin by trying to imagine the following rather homely 'experiment'. (It is modelled in content and style on a not dissimilar experiment involving three mirrors and a candle that Dante describes in a notorious passage in the second canto of the *Paradiso*.)

Go into a large, empty dance-hall with many light-fittings in the ceiling and round the walls. Switch on the lights, which will represent the stars visible from a point in the northern hemisphere. Take a standard lamp (the sun), place it in the middle of the floor, and switch it on. Ask an assistant to take a pocket torch (representing either Venus or Mercury) and to keep walking slowly anticlockwise in a fairly tight circle round the standard lamp. Ask another assistant to take a cycle rear-lamp or other red torch (representing Mars) and to carry that in a circle round the standard lamp, still anticlockwise, but more slowly and much further out.

Pick up a terrestrial globe, keeping the stand horizontal so that the axis of rotation remains inclined at the correct angle. Twist the stand together with the supporting 'arm' in a very slow circle, thus causing the whole globe to 'precess' in a clockwise direction. Simultaneously, rotate the globe anticlockwise on its axis. With the globe rotating and precessing, walk anticlockwise round the standard lamp between your two assistants, at a speed such that you will complete nearly two revolutions to every one revolution of the assistant with the red torch. Now persuade a third assistant – you will need an agile person – to take a lighted candle (representing the moon) and to walk anticlockwise rapidly round and round *you*, while you continue to walk round the standard lamp.

Next, try to imagine how the candle, the torches, the standard lamp and the hall lights would appear to move, if your eye were fixed at one point on the surface of the upper hemisphere of the rotating, precessing globe as you carry it round. Finally, try to devise a mathematical model which would enable you to predict the intervals at which the rear-lamp will come into line of sight with the pocket torch or the candle, on the assumption that your eye was motionless, and that all the apparent movements were caused by those various sources of light orbiting round you at constant speeds and in perfect circles. You will then have a hazy mental image of the solar system as we know it today, and some inkling of the difficulties faced by all those pre-Copernican astronomers who accepted a geocentric model of the universe.

The movements of the earth and the solar system

For reasons of space, it will not be possible to explain and illustrate the whole range of Dante's knowledge and use of astronomy in the *Comedy* (the latest writer on the subject required not half a chapter but two whole volumes).[25] We shall therefore ignore the revolutions of the lesser planets and the complex theory of 'eccentrics' and 'epicycles' that were necessary in geocentric astronomy to account for their varying speeds and distances from the earth, and for their 'stations' and 'retrogradations'; and we shall concentrate on the three heavens that were most important from the point of view of astrology and of Dante's poetry – the *primum mobile*, and the spheres of the sun and the fixed stars. To understand the Ptolemaic explanation of their observed movements, we need to be familiar with a small number of astronomical terms and a few facts about the solar system and the movements of our own planet. These facts and terms may be presented under the following heads.

(*a*) *The celestial sphere and the stars*. Even the nearest of the stars (apart from the sun) are so remote that for our purposes we may continue to treat them all as unmoving and equidistant from the earth. To this day, the astronomers' maps and charts perpetuate the Aristotelian and Ptolemaic fiction that the stars are set in a sphere onto which we can project a grid of co-ordinates that enable us to indicate the unchanging position of every star in the sky. Under the name of a 'celestial globe', one can still purchase a model of Dante's 'Starry Heaven' from any good map shop. The whole celestial sphere is still divided into zones of irregular size and shape that bear the names given by ancient astronomers to certain configurations of stars, visible to the naked eye, even though it is clear that the stars in these 'constellations' are unrelated to each other in any way. In short, the stars in their constellations can still be treated as the unmoving 'backdrop' against which, and in terms of which, we perceive and describe the movements of bodies within our solar system.

(*b*) *The annual revolution of the earth round the sun: 'ecliptic' and 'Zodiac'*. The earth is a planet of a star which we call the 'sun', around which it revolves once every $365\frac{1}{4}$ days. Although the terms are only relevant to an observer in the northern hemisphere, it will be convenient to describe the direction of this orbit as being anticlockwise. If the position of the sun as seen from the earth is plotted at regular intervals against the 'backdrop' of the stars, the sun will appear to move from *west to east*, *anti*clockwise, at a little less than one degree a day or thirty degrees a month. The apparent course of the sun may be traced onto a star map of the relevant constellations. It is known as the 'ecliptic'. The constellations through which the ecliptic passes, and through which the sun seems to move, have always been accorded pride of place. They are twelve in number, and since they lie at approximately equal intervals, it was possible to divide the ecliptic vertically into twelve equal segments, each extending through thirty degrees of longitude, and each named after the appropriate constellation. The position of the sun could then be roughly indicated, in words rather than in figures, by saying, for example, that it was '*in* Gemini' or '*in* Leo'. These twelve constellations are the famous or infamous constellations of the Zodiac.[26] Most of these points are illustrated in figure 7.

(*c*) *The earth's diurnal rotation: poles, equator, sidereal and solar days*. The earth *rotates* about its own axis, and it is this axis which determines the fixed points of reference for the familiar system of co-ordinates that we use to locate the position of any place on the surface of our globe. The extremities of that axis are the north and south 'geographical poles'. The great circle which lies equidistant at all points from these poles is called the 'equator'.[27] Lines of latitude run parallel to the equator. A terrestrial 'meridian' is a great circle (or segment of a great circle) which passes through both poles and therefore cuts the equator at right angles.

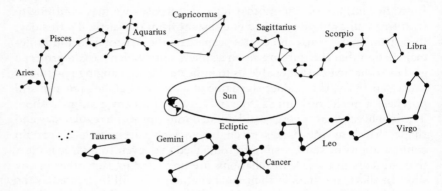

Figure 7. The earth, sun, ecliptic, and constellations of the Zodiac.

The 'celestial poles' are imaginary points on the imaginary celestial sphere obtained by projecting the line of the earth's axis; thus, the north celestial pole must be directly above the north geographical pole. The 'celestial equator' is an imaginary great circle described on the celestial sphere in the same plane as the terrestrial equator. Similarly, a 'celestial meridian' is a great circle on the celestial sphere passing through both celestial poles. More familiarly, it may also be described as the line running from north to south through the observer's zenith. The position of the geographical poles and therefore the position of the terrestrial equator do not change. But we shall see that when the orientation of the earth's axis in space is altered, the *celestial* poles and the *celestial* equator are displaced by the same angle. Figure 8 below will illustrate many of these points.

The earth rotates from west to east (anticlockwise from the viewpoint of an observer in the northern hemisphere), with the effect, of course, that the whole celestial sphere seems to revolve about the earth from *east to west*. It completes one rotation in 23 hours 56 minutes; and this is the interval, known as a 'sidereal' or 'periodic' day, at which any given star will be seen to cross the observer's meridian. As we know, however, the *solar* day, that is, the interval between successive crossings of a given meridian by the sun, lasts for 24 hours.[28] The difference between the two days arises because the earth continues its *revolution* around the sun, and by the end of a sidereal day the true bearing of the sun will have changed by nearly one degree: it will lie not due south, at 180°, but at 179°. The earth must therefore *rotate* for a further four minutes (this being the time it takes to rotate through one degree) before the sun will once again lie on the observer's meridian. It is very important to grasp that the duration of the solar day is the product of both movements, with extra rotation being required to cancel out the effect of revolution.

(*d*) *The axis of the earth's rotation: seasons, solstice, tropic, equinox.* It is worth speculating briefly as to what would have happened if the axis of the earth's rotation had been set at right angles to the plane of our orbit round the sun (which is how modern astronomers define the ecliptic). The solar day would still have been longer than the sidereal day, but the ecliptic would have coincided with the celestial equator, and the sun would always have been directly over the terrestrial equator. The whole earth would always have had days and nights of equal duration, and there would have been no seasons. In fact, as we know, the axis is offset at an angle of $23\frac{1}{2}°$; consequently, the two great circles of equator and ecliptic cut each other at this angle, as shown in figure 8. The apparent path of the sun, therefore, lies both 'above' and 'below' the celestial equator, and the sun can be overhead as far as $23\frac{1}{2}°$ to the north and south of the terrestrial equator. Beyond these limits of latitude the elevation of the sun at noon will vary by forty-seven degrees in the course of a year. In southern England, for example, it will be as high as 63° on midsummer day and as low as 16° on midwinter day. At these times the sun will be directly overhead at the Tropic of Cancer and the Tropic of Capricorn respectively (see figure 8). The technical names for these days in the year, or these points on the earth's orbit, are 'summer solstice' and 'winter solstice' respectively, the names being derived from the fact that the sun appears to 'stand still' (*sol + sistere*) before returning in the opposite direction; while the word 'tropic' was originally the adjective from the Greek noun *tropos* meaning a 'turn' or 'turning-point'. Far from the whole earth always enjoying days and nights of equal duration, the area near the north pole has a single summer day lasting six months while the south pole has a winter night of the same length, and vice versa. Daylight and darkness are equal only on the two days in the earth's annual orbit when the sun is directly overhead at the equator; and these are the points or days known as the spring and autumn equinoxes.

(*e*) *The precession of the equinoxes.* There is one further complication arising from the earth's rotation on its axis, and from the angle at which the axis lies to the plane of the earth's orbit round the sun. As was hinted earlier, in the description of the 'experiment', the earth is not only rotating and revolving but performing an extremely slow gyration like that of a spinning top or a toy gyroscope. Unlike the top or gyroscope,

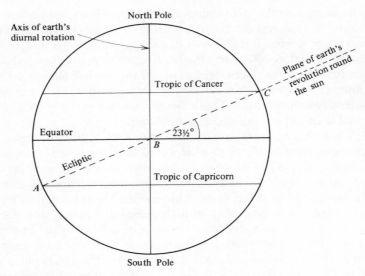

Figure 8. Equator, ecliptic, tropic.
N.B. The sun will be directly overhead at A on the day of the winter solstice, at B on the days of the equinoxes, at C on the day of the summer solstice.

however, the inclination remains constant at $66\frac{1}{2}°$ to the plane of the ecliptic.

The best way for a layman to visualize this movement and its consequences is to swivel the supporting arm of a terrestrial globe through 360°, taking care to keep the stand horizontal and concentrating on the north pole, the inclination of the equator, and the position of the point where the ecliptic crosses the equator. It will then be apparent that the celestial poles (which are simply projections of the terrestrial poles) trace out a circle on the celestial sphere, resembling the base of a cone which has its apex in the centre of the earth (see figure 9). It will also be found that stars which used to lie close above the celestial equator (which by definition lies in the same plane as the terrestrial equator) move to a position close below the equator and then return. The plane of the ecliptic remains constant, and the sun will always be in line of sight with one of the constellations of the Zodiac. But these constellations will seem to move round the belt of the Zodiac like beads on a rosary. On the day of each successive spring equinox the sun will be in line of sight with a different point, and it will apparently pass slowly backwards through the constellations. The equinoctial points move westwards round the celestial equator; the equinoxes will 'advance' in time; and the whole phenomenon is described as the 'precession' of the equinoxes.

The earth's gyration changes the points of origin for the *celestial*

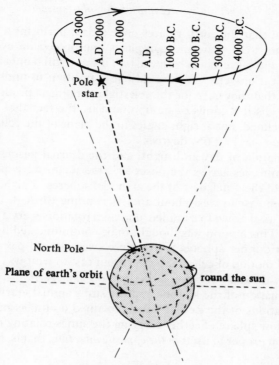

Figure 9. Precession.

co-ordinates (the celestial poles and the equinoctial points), and, as a result, the lines of longitude and latitude on the celestial sphere have to be continuously redrawn. Fortunately for the owners and compilers of star atlases, however, the gyration is very, very slow. It takes 25,800 years to complete one precession. The equinoxes advance in time by only twenty minutes a year, and will therefore move forward by one day in the life-span of the average individual. In those seventy years the equinoctial points will have been displaced by approximately one degree. But astronomy has a long history and the cumulative effect of precession is very striking. In the fifth century B.C., the position of the sun on the day of the spring equinox was used to mark the boundary between the constellations of Aries and Pisces, and this was called the 'first point of Aries'. In the second century B.C., Hipparchus discovered that the spring equinoctial point had moved westwards into Pisces, and by Dante's time it lay almost in the middle of that constellation (see figure 7). And as we shall see, the discovery of the precession of the equinoxes led to a very important revision of Aristotle's cosmography.

149

The geocentric account of the solar system

We have seen that the earth rotates once a day, performs a revolution round the sun every year, and completes one precession every 25,800 years. Dante and his teachers believed that it was a still point at the centre of the spherical universe. We are now in a position to understand the explanations that they gave for the celestial phenomena produced by the earth's three distinct kinds of motion, and by the fact that the axis of rotation is inclined, not at right angles to the plane of the ecliptic, but at an angle of $(90-23\frac{1}{2}=)$ $66\frac{1}{2}$ degrees.

The alternation of day and night, and the diurnal passage of all the heavenly luminaries across the observer's meridian, were attributed to the rotation of the outermost of the aetherial spheres. This was believed to rotate from east to west about an axis running through the celestial poles; and it was known to complete one such rotation every 23 hours and 56 minutes. This motion was thought to be communicated by contact to the concentric inner spheres which were swept round passively by its impetus. All motion of celestial bodies from east to west was assumed to be caused by the daily rotation of the *sphaera suprema*.[29]

The alternation of the seasons and the sun's annual journey through the constellations of the Zodiac were explained on the assumption that the vast hollow sphere of aether carrying the sun is rotating more slowly with a motion proper to itself *in the opposite direction*, that is, from west to

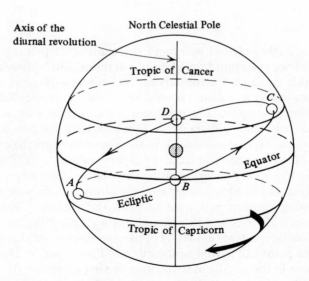

Figure 10. The 'proper' (SW–NE) and 'passive' (E–W) motions of the Heaven of the Sun. (Cf. figure 8.)

east. This rotation takes place about poles that are offset at an angle of $23\frac{1}{2}°$ to the celestial poles. The shining body of the sun itself is set on the equator corresponding to the poles of its 'proper motion'; and this equator is in effect identical with the ecliptic. Since the ecliptic or the equator of the solar sphere is inclined at an angle of $23\frac{1}{2}°$ to the celestial equator, the proper motion of the solar heaven carries the sun not only from west to east (at approximately $1°$ a day) but also from south to north and back again, as will be clear from figure 10.

The daily revolution of the sun, as we observe it from the earth, is the result of a smooth combination of the two simple, circular motions. The received or 'passive' motion carries it round the earth from east to west in an orbit parallel to the celestial equator. The 'proper' motion from west to east causes it to fall behind the stellar sphere by approximately one degree of longitude or four minutes a day; and the obliquity of that proper motion causes it to move either towards or away from the celestial equator, and therefore to vary in altitude from the point of view of an observer on the earth. As a result, the sun circles the earth with a screwing motion in a series of flattened spirals, ascending or descending according to the time of the year.[30]

Dante and the movements of the sun

Dante was always fascinated by this 'circulation of the sun'; and it will once again be convenient to interrupt the exposition of facts in order to consider his own description of the sun's apparent motions, and to examine some of the passages in the *Paradiso* where he turns his attention to the 'oblique circle of the ecliptic' and the consequences of that obliquity here on earth.

The long fifth chapter of the third book of the *Convivio* takes the form of an excursus to clarify a line from one of Dante's *canzoni* in praise of Lady Philosophy, in which he had spoken of 'the sun which circles the *whole* earth': '. . . 'l sol che *tutto* il mondo gira'.

Having explained such fundamental concepts as the celestial and geographical poles, the position of the equators, and the oblique path of the ecliptic which is cut by the celestial equator to form semicircles above and below, Dante invites us to imagine how the sun would appear to an observer at one of the terrestrial poles or at the equator. On the days of the equinoxes, the observer at the equator would see the sun rise and pass directly overhead: Dante compares its course to that of a wheel on a vehicle, where the axis is horizontal and the revolution is confined to the vertical plane. The observer at the north pole would not see the sun at all from the first day of the year until the spring equinox on 21 March. On that day he would see the top half of the sun go right round him through 360 degrees, its disc being cut in two by the horizon. In this case, Dante compares the sun's course to that of a millstone revolving in the horizontal plane about a vertical axis. For the next $91\frac{1}{4}$ days, says Dante, the sun will be visible without interruption, and it will spiral its way higher and higher into the sky. On the day of the summer solstice, having attained an altitude of $23\frac{1}{2}°$, it will appear to our observer much as it does in Italian latitudes at the *winter* solstice.[31] When this turning point has been reached, it will screw its way down again (still visible continuously) for the next $91\frac{1}{4}$ days, and then disappear completely for the six months following the autumn equinox. During those six months, an observer at the south pole would see exactly the same phenomena, save that the sun would circle from right to left instead of the other way.[32]

The north and south poles, Dante explains, have an equal day and night, each of six months' duration. The equator always enjoys equal days and nights of exactly twelve hours. All other places on the earth's surface have days and nights of varying proportions, depending on their latitude and the time of year. But in the course of a whole year, every point on the earth's surface will have had an equal number of hours of daylight and darkness.[33] The chapter ends with a passionate exclamation expressing Dante's wonder and gratitude for God's providential design:

By divine foresight the universe is so ordered that when the heaven of the sun has completed one revolution and returned to a given point, every part of the ball on which we live will have received an equal measure of light and darkness. Oh Ineffable Wisdom who established this order, how feeble is the human mind to comprehend You! And you, for whose benefit and delight I write, in what blindness you live, never lifting your eyes to these things, keeping them fixed in the morass of your ignorance! (*Con.* III, v, 21–2)

Dante returns to these themes and emotions in the arresting introduction to the tenth canto of the *Paradiso*, which marks the beginning of an important new stage in the structure of the cantica. The preceding cantos describe Dante's arrival in the planet Venus and his meetings – discussed in Chapter 4 – with Charles Martel, Cunizza and the troubadour bishop, Folquet of Marseilles; and the ninth canto ends abruptly with the last words of Folquet's violent imprecation against the topsy-turvy values which induce the Pope, the spiritual leader of mankind, to abandon the Holy Land to the infidel, while he conducts a minor 'crusade' against his fellow Christians and fellow countrymen.

Following the sequence of ideas in the *Convivio* chapter, but in reverse order, Dante opens the tenth canto with what is virtually a brief hymn to the Trinity and to the order revealed in the circling heavens:

Gazing on His Son with the Love that one and the other eternally breathe, the primal ineffable Good created all that revolves through mind and space with an order so perfect that no one can contemplate it without sensing Him:

Guardando nel suo Figlio con l'Amore
che l'uno e l'altro etternalmente spira,
lo primo e ineffabile Valore
    quanto per mente e per loco si gira
con tant' ordine fé, ch'esser non puote
sanza gustar di lui chi ciò rimira.   (*Par.* x, 1–6)

Then Dante invites the reader in a direct apostrophe to lift his eyes to
the wheeling heavens on high, and, more precisely, to the point where the
two contrary motions of the heavens intersect; to the point, that is, where
the ecliptic cuts the celestial equator.

Leva dunque, lettore, a l'alte rote
meco la vista, dritto a quella parte
dove l'un moto e l'altro si percuote.   (7–9)

'See', he continues, 'how the oblique circle carrying the planets branches
off from that node to satisfy the entreaties of the world':

Vedi come da indi si dirama
l'oblico cerchio che i pianeti porta,
per sodisfare al mondo che li chiama.   (13–15)

With the third line of this terzina ('per sodisfare . . .') Dante turns to
consider the *reasons* for the obliquity of the ecliptic. But he does not spell
them out. Instead he insists on a paradox. For a moral agent, the best path
is always the 'straight' path – the '*diritta* via' described in the opening
lines of the *Comedy*. The deviant or twisting path ('strada *torta*') leads to
the 'sea of deviant love' ('il mar de l'amor *torto*') and to damnation. But
the path of the sun and the other planets must be 'twisted', because
otherwise many places on earth would be deprived of their light, warmth
and influence (*virtù*), which would have existed in vain, because many
potential plants and animals – or many of their *potential* faculties – would
have remained unactualized and dead. If the obliquity had been greater
or lesser, the order of the universe would have been diminished, both in
the heavens and on earth:

Che se la strada lor non fosse torta,
molta virtù nel ciel sarebbe in vano,
e quasi ogne potenza qua giù morta;
    e se dal dritto più o men lontano
fosse 'l partire, assai sarebbe manco
e giù e sù de l'ordine mondano.   (16–21)

But the reader must 'sit on his school-bench' and ponder the matter for
himself. Dante passes swiftly on to concentrate on the sun. Five ideas are
presented in quick succession: the sun's pre-eminence among the
luminaries; its communication of *valore* to the world; its role in the
measurement of days and years; its position at the spring equinox; and

the spiralling motion that will lead it daily higher into the northern hemisphere. Paradox and admonishment are put aside. Information, celebration and description come together in verse of a sublime solemnity like that of the opening terzinas. And then these qualities yield abruptly to the facts of the narrative, which is unexpectedly resumed with the simplest words – 'and I was with the sun':

Nature's chief minister, who imprints the world with the heavens' power and by whose light we measure time, conjoined with the point recalled above, was circling up the spiral path which brings him ever sooner into sight; and I was with him:

> Lo ministro maggior de la natura,
> che del valor del ciel lo mondo imprenta
> e col suo lume il tempo ne misura,
>   con quella parte che su si rammenta
> congiunto, si girava per le spire
> in che più tosto ognora s'appresenta;
>   e io era con lui . . .
>
>   (28–34)

The phrase 'con quella parte che su si rammenta / congiunto' refers us to line 8 and thence to *Paradiso I* – to the moment when the narrative of the whole cantica was resumed, after the opening statement of its theme and the appeal to Apollo. The sun's primacy is there expressed with a single resonant metaphor: it is the 'lantern of the world'. Through further metaphors we learn that, at the time of Dante's journey, the sun had reached that point where it could best 'temper' the 'wax' of the universe and best 'stamp its seal' upon it, because it was in conjunction with a 'better star' and was 'running a better course'. All these details point to the time of the spring equinox, and this is confirmed by what we are told elsewhere in the poem. But Dante also chooses to fix that moment in purely astronomical terms: it is the time, he says, when the sun rises from a point 'which joins four circles with three crosses'.

At the two equinoxes, the sun crosses the great circle of the equator in its annual path along the ecliptic: that makes two circles and one cross. By definition, the 'equinoctial colure' is the great circle of longitude which passes through the poles and cuts the equator at the equinoctial points: three circles and two crosses. The fourth circle is the horizon, that is, the *astronomical* horizon, defined as a great circle whose circumference is equidistant at every point from the observer's zenith; and the third cross is where the horizon cuts the equator (see figure 11).[34] These four circles can intersect at the *same* point only at the spring and autumn equinoxes.

The details of this interpretation are not free from objection, but there can be no doubt that Dante did have some precise astronomical configuration in mind.[35] He was not a bungler, and this is no mumbo-jumbo. At the same time, of course, there is an incantatory element in the union of

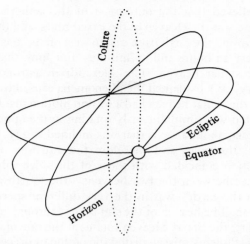

Figure 11. The circles of the equator, the ecliptic, and the equinoctial colure.

four circles and three crosses, which gives this passage a certain fascination long before one is able to understand it. There can be no doubt also that the 'circles' and 'crosses', like the numbers 'four' and 'three', have symbolic connotations which are highly relevant to the poem as a whole. And while we cannot pause to analyse the rhythm and syntax, or the metaphors and echoes from Virgil and the Bible, they too make an essential contribution to the splendour of these lines.[36] In short, the three-dimensional astronomical geometry of these vast invisible circles does not create great poetry of itself. But neither does it destroy the poetry. There is no contradiction. The narrative of the *Paradiso* opens with lines that are suggestive and precise, exact and beyond paraphrase, appealing as always to the ear, the imagination and the intellect:

> Surge ai mortali per diverse foci
> la lucerna del mondo; ma da quella
> che quattro cerchi giugne con tre croci,
>   con miglior corso e con migliore stella
> esce congiunta, e la mondana cera
> più a suo modo tempera e suggella.   (*Par.* I, 37–42)

Precession in geocentric astronomy: the 'cielo stellato' and 'primum mobile'

After this pause for refreshment, we must return to the postulates of a geocentric astronomy and consider the modifications made to Aristotle's model of the universe as a result of the discovery of the precession of the equinoxes.

Aristotle believed that the outermost of the aetherial spheres, the *sphaera suprema*, was the Heaven of the Fixed Stars, and that it swept the inner heavens round the earth from east to west on the axis of the celestial poles once every 23 hours and 56 minutes. For him, that was the only motion of the stellar heaven. The Alexandrian astronomer, Ptolemy (second century A.D.), explained the phenomena caused by precession by assuming that the stellar heaven had a second motion just like the heaven of the sun. It too was simultaneously rotating in the opposite direction, from west to east, about an axis that was inclined at $23\frac{1}{2}°$ to the celestial poles. In fact, the poles and therefore the equators of this second, retrograde motion coincided with those of the solar sphere. The only major difference between the two heavens – the fourth and the eighth counting from the earth – was in the very different speed of the retrograde revolution. The heaven of the sun rotates through a little less than one degree a day; the Starry Heaven rotates at the rate of one degree in a hundred years (Ptolemy miscalculated the period of precession as 36,000 years, instead of 25,800 years).

Dante deals at some length with the Heaven of the Fixed Stars in the second book of the *Convivio*, where he discusses the nature of the Milky Way and reports that the 'sages of Egypt' have catalogued 1,022 stars which are visible from the first zone of the *terra habitabilis*.[37] But his main interest lies in the slow retrograde motion, and in the poles and equator of that motion. In the first place, he knows that the ecliptic (or the equator of the sun's 'proper' motion) lies in the same plane as the equator of the retrograde motion of the stellar sphere, and that the constellations of the Zodiac must therefore lie along this equator (which, as we shall see, is the equator 'proper' to the heaven of the stars). And he develops an impressive argument to show that the particular importance of the constellations of the Zodiac is due to this 'equatorial position', and not to the coincidence that one or other of these constellations must be in conjunction with the sun:

Every heaven . . . has a circle which can be called the 'equator' of its heaven. This circle is equidistant at every point of its circumference from both poles, as you can see for yourself by twisting an apple or some other round object. It will be clear on reflection that in every heaven this equator moves more rapidly than any other part. The nearer a part is to the equator, the more rapidly it moves; whereas the further it is away, and the nearer to the pole, the slower it is, since the arc of its revolution is smaller, and yet it must of necessity revolve in the same time as the equator. It is also true that the nearer any part of the heaven is to the equator, the nobler it must be in comparison with the poles: it moves faster; it is more fully actualized; it has more life and form; it is in contact with a greater area of the heaven above it, and in consequence it exerts a greater influence (*più è virtuoso*). Hence the stars of the Starry Heaven have more influence (*son più piene di vertù*), the nearer they are to this equator. (*Con.* II, iii, 13–15)

Dante also turns his attention to chronology. Like other Christians of his day, he believed that the world had been created in 5198 B.C.; in A.D. 1300, therefore, it had been in existence for a mere 6,500 years. He also believed that the End of the World was nigh; and so he points out that the Starry Heaven has only revolved through one-sixth of its independent retrograde course, and would probably never complete one revolution, 'for we are in the last age of the world, and in truth we are awaiting the consummation of all celestial movement' (*Con.* II, xiv, 13).

This reflection inspired Dante to write an eloquent passage in praise of the *diurnal* motion of all the heavenly bodies. But before we can understand the details of that text, we must explore one further consequence of the discovery of precession and one very important addition to Aristotle's 'bodily heaven'.

Ptolemy gave his blessing to the view that the Starry Heaven had *two* distinct motions, but he, and more particularly his more philosophically-minded successors, could not accept that these were both 'proper' motions. Influenced by Neoplatonist modes of thought, they assumed that the outermost sphere – whichever it was – must be the source of all movement in the universe that it contains, and that it must owe its movement to a supreme being who was eternal, simple and one. They also argued that such a being could only communicate a motion that was one, simple and eternal. They were therefore led to the inescapable conclusion that there must be a *ninth* sphere lying outside the Starry Heaven. It had to be a 'body'; it had to be made of aether; it had to be concentric with the other eight heavens which it contained. It also had to be perfectly uniform and therefore without luminaries; and it was credited with the one, perfect, simple and eternal motion. This ninth heaven thus became the 'first moved thing', or *primum mobile*, and it was by this name that it was most often known in Dante's time.[38]

Dante himself gives a beautifully lucid account of this heaven in the same second book of the *Convivio*. Having noted Aristotle's mistakes, he goes on:

Later, Ptolemy realized that the eighth sphere had more than one motion, seeing that its revolution departed from the upright circle which sweeps everything from east to west. Constrained by the principles of philosophy, which insists that there must of necessity be an absolutely simple first-moved-thing (*uno primo mobile semplicissimo*), he postulated the existence of another heaven outside the Heaven of the Stars, which would make this revolution from east to west, completing it in the time of 23 hours and $\frac{14}{15}$ of an hour, to the nearest fraction. So that in his view, which has prevailed in astronomy and philosophy ever since the movements of the Starry Heaven were detected, there are nine moving heavens.
... The ninth heaven cannot be perceived save by the motion described above. Many people call it the 'crystalline' heaven, as being 'diaphanous' or 'completely transparent'. ... It has fixed poles that never move in any respect

.... Its movement is swift almost beyond comprehension. (*Con.* II, iii, 5–7, 9, 13)

It is therefore the *primum mobile* which provides the motive force for the diurnal revolution of all the heavenly bodies; and it plays a paramount part in securing the providential ordering of the universe, as Dante explains in the final paragraph of the section devoted to the Heaven of the Fixed Stars:

The *primum mobile* with its movement regulates (*ordina*) the daily revolution of all the heavens, as a result of which they are able to receive and transmit here below the influence of their every part. If this were not so regulated by the revolution of the ninth heaven, little of their influence would descend here, and they would be little seen. So that, if this heaven had remained motionless, a third part of the Starry Heaven would never have been seen on any part of the earth [i.e. the *terra discoperta*]. Saturn would be hidden from every place on earth for $14\frac{1}{2}$ years at a time, Jupiter for six years, Mars for nearly a year, and the sun for 182 days 14 hours. . . . Venus and Mercury would conceal and reveal themselves for almost the same period as the sun, and the moon would be hidden from all people for $14\frac{1}{2}$ days. In truth, there would be no generation and no life, whether of animals or plants. There would be neither night nor day. There would be no week, month or year. The whole universe would be out of joint (*disordinato*), and the proper movement of the other heavens would exist to no purpose. (*Con.* II, xiv, 15–17)

The ninth heaven in the 'Comedy'

In the *Comedy* Dante calls the ninth heaven by its proper philosophical or astronomical name only on the last of the many occasions on which he refers to it, when he tells us that the *primum mobile* derives its life and power from the Divine Light which shines upon its convex surface:

> . . . al sommo del *mobile primo*,
> che prende quindi vivere e potenza.　　(*Par.* XXX, 107–8)

Elsewhere he will describe it by periphrases which allow him to mention virtually all the properties with which it had been credited by its 'inventors'. The concept of an invisible heaven excited Dante as much as the hypothetical 'black holes' fascinate the amateur astronomer today; and his periphrases are fittingly alert and fervent in tone. The earliest comes in the last sonnet of the *Vita Nuova*, where it is called 'the sphere that circles widest', *la spera che più larga gira*. Later it is 'the swiftest heaven' or 'the heaven that hastens in the highest place' (*il ciel velocissimo, il ciel che più alto festina*). It is 'the greatest body', *il maggior corpo*, and 'the body in whose power lies the being of all that it contains' ('un corpo ne la cui virtute / l'esser di tutto suo contento giace'). And perhaps most beautifully of all, it is 'the royal surcoat of all the revolving spheres (*volumi*), that which glows and quickens most in the breath of God and in His modes':[39]

> Lo real manto di tutti i volumi
> del mondo, che più ferve e più s'avviva
> ne l'alito di Dio e nei costumi.   (*Par.* XXIII, 112–14)

When Dante-character ascends into the first eight heavens, he knows that he has been received into the very heart of a luminary, that is, into the denser aether of a planet or star. But the ninth sphere is absolutely simple in its form as well as its motion. All its parts are supremely 'alive' and exalted, and they are so perfectly uniform that Dante cannot tell which part of the heaven Beatrice has chosen:

> Le parti sue vivissime ed eccelse
> sì uniforme son, ch'i' non so dire
> qual Bëatrice per loco mi scelse.   (*Par.* XXVII, 100–2)

There is something a little awkward and contrived in this passage, because it seems all too obvious that the narrative has been contrived to highlight the philosophical fact, and to provide the occasion for a learned discourse. But any feeling of unease is immediately dispelled by the superb assurance of the explanation that follows. In five terzinas, Beatrice draws together all the main facts and ideas that have just been summarized. She begins with a paradoxical proposition that has all the pregnant concision of its Aristotelian source: 'The nature of the universe holds the centre still and moves all else around it; and this nature has its origin here in its outer limit [its beginning lies in its end]':

> La natura del mondo, che quïeta
> il mezzo e tutto l'altro intorno move,
> quinci comincia come da sua meta.   (*Par.* XXVII, 106–8)

Next, she passes into the densely metaphorical, lyrical language of Neoplatonist theology to recapitulate what Dante had said about the Empyrean in the *Convivio*: 'The heaven, in which we now are, is not located in some other space, but only in the mind of God. It is there that the love is kindled that drives it round, as also the energy that it communicates to the universe. It is encircled by a precinct of love and light, just as this heaven encircles the lower heavens; and that precinct is encompassed by God, who alone is its governing intelligence':

> e questo cielo non ha altro dove
> che la mente divina, in che s'accende
> l'amor che 'l volge e la virtù ch'ei piove.
> Luce e amor d'un cerchio lui comprende,
> sì come questo li altri; e quel precinto
> colui che 'l cinge solamente intende.   (109–14)

Then Beatrice reverts to ideas and terms that have their source in Aristotle's study of motion and time:[40] 'Its movement is not computed in terms of some other movement; rather, it provides the measure for all other movements, just as we analyse ten as the product of its factors, five and two [its half and its fifth]':

> Non è suo moto per altro distinto,
> ma li altri son mensurati da questo,
> sì come diece da mezzo e da quinto.　　(115–17)

And finally she introduces a brilliant metaphor of a Platonist stamp that we shall have to expand in the form of a simile. 'Time is like a tree growing upside down. Its visible "leaves" are in the luminaries of the lower heavens, and it is by their revolutions that we actually reckon the days, months and years. But the "roots" of time are hidden in the invisible "vase" of the *primum mobile* [its beginning lies in its end]':

> e come il tempo tegna in cotal testo
> le sue radici e ne li altri le fronde,
> omai a te può esser manifesto.　　(118–20)

This is perhaps the most difficult passage we have yet encountered, but it is in no way confused or obscure. Dante has here forged a unique synthesis of Aristotelian and Neoplatonist modes of expression to celebrate what must be one of the purest fantasies ever to issue from the human intellect and imagination. The whole aetherial mass of the spherical *caelum* was, in a sense, the product of Aristotle's poetic imagination; and the 'discovery' of the *primum mobile* could be compared to the completion of a great poem by another not inferior hand.

The cosmic clock: (a) 'moontime'

We must now turn from the *primus motus* of the *primum mobile* to 'li altri moti . . . mensurati da questo', and from the 'roots' of the tree to its 'leaves'–that is, from the problems of space and movement to the measurement of time.

One consequence of Dante's concern for realism in telling the story of his adventures is that there are many precise references to the lapse of time on his journey through Hell and Purgatory; and most of them are given by reference to the various 'faces' and 'hands' of the 'cosmic clock.' The easiest way to tell the time of day is to look at the position of the sun; and we have seen in the first chapter just how insistently Dante registered the direction and altitude of the sun's rays throughout his day in Antepurgatory, from the first gleams of light before dawn on the shore, to the falling of dusk on the mountain side. The 'time of night' can also be inferred from the position of the moon, and, with a little more expertise, from the position of the constellations of the Zodiac. But let us keep to the moon.

Like the heavens of the sun and fixed stars, the lunar heaven has two distinct motions: the 'passive' diurnal motion about the celestial poles, and its 'proper' periodic revolution from west to east in a plane close to the ecliptic. The moon receives most of its light from the sun; it is 'new' when it is almost directly in line of sight with the sun, and it is 'full' when it is diametrically opposite. It should therefore be clear that a full moon will always rise as the sun sets. Now, the period of the moon's *sidereal* revolution is 27 days 8 hours. As a result, we can calculate that it will 'fall behind' the stars every day by about ($\frac{360}{27\frac{1}{3}}=$) thirteen degrees; and it will therefore rise, on average, about fifty minutes later every day.[41] Hence, if we knew that three days had passed since the moon was full, we should expect it to grow very dark after sunset, since the moon would not rise for another two and a half hours.

This is the realistic explanation of the circumstances surrounding the last of Dante's encounters on his day in Antepurgatory. The air grew so dark, it will be remembered, that Nino Visconti did not perceive that Dante the traveller was there in the flesh. The opening of the next episode duly establishes that Dante subsequently fell asleep at moonrise, which occurred two and a half hours after the sun had set.[42] But that information merely confirms what had already been given, by implication, in earlier references to the 'time of night' and to the season of the year in the narrative of the *Inferno*.

To understand those references (which are very revealing of Dante's mind and of his craft as a story-teller) we must remind ourselves that the time told by the sun, moon or stars is always 'local' time; and, as we saw in Chapter 4, Dante is at pains to stress the *relativity* of local time. Thanks to their strategic placing at intervals of ninety degrees, the sun rises in Jerusalem when it is overhead at the Ganges; it will then be sunset over Mount Purgatory, and midnight in Cadiz. It follows that one must always specify for which place – that is, for which *longitude* – the sun is rising or setting. It also follows that if we were in Jerusalem on a cloudy night and were informed that the sun had just set in Cadiz, we could deduce that it was just past midnight local time. And this would be analogous to the situation in Dante's Hell. Local time there is Jerusalem time. Dante the traveller cannot see any of the luminaries while he is in the underworld. But Dante the *poet* is omniscient in this respect; and by endowing Virgil with the same omniscience, he secures some very striking effects.

In the first reference to the lunar clock, Virgil tells his charge that the moon was full on the *previous* night, and that it is now setting in the waves beyond the Spanish coast. That evening, therefore, it must have *risen* – for the longitude of Jerusalem, and at the latitude of the equator – at about fifty minutes after sunset. Since we are later told that the action of the poem unfolds shortly after the equinox, we can fix the time of sunset at shortly after 6.00 p.m. – let us say, at 6.05 p.m. Allowing for the fact that the moon's proper motion during the night will have retarded its setting by a further twenty-five minutes, we can deduce that the time in Hell, as in Jerusalem, is approximately 7.20 a.m.[43]

Nine cantos later, Dante is told, again by Virgil, that the moon is 'beneath their feet': 'E già la luna è sotto i nostri piedi' (*Inf.* XXIX, 10). This can only mean that the moon has been carried, by the impetus it receives from the *primum mobile*, through a further ninety degrees, from the meridian of Cadiz to the meridian of Purgatory. This in turn means that a further six hours have passed, to which we must add another twelve minutes for the retardation caused by the moon's proper motion: the local time, in Hell and Jerusalem, is therefore approximately 1.35 p.m.

Five cantos later still (*Inf.* XXXIV, 68), the travellers have reached the centre of the universe and stand in the presence of Lucifer. Just before they commence the laborious descent and ascent past the centre of gravity – as described in the passage translated and discussed in Chapter 2 – Virgil urges Dante on with the information that 'night is rising again'. Since we are told that 'night' in this sense is the point opposite to the sun, and since we may assume that the sun set for Jerusalem at 6.10, the time is about 6.20 in the evening.

After their strenuous but relatively short scramble down Lucifer's shaggy sides, Virgil suddenly declares that 'the sun is already returning to mid-tierce'. There is a double surprise here: first, Virgil refers to the position of the sun, rather than the moon or the night; second, mid-tierce means 7.30 in the *morning*. How is it possible, asks the pilgrim, for the sun to have gone from evening to morning in so brief a time? Virgil then explains to the incredulous Dante that 'you are now under the hemisphere *opposite* to the one covered by the land mass . . .; it is *morning* here, when it is *evening* there': 'Qui è da *man*, quando di là è *sera*'. In short, now that Dante is in the southern hemisphere he must adjust to local time, which is 'Purgatory time'. The scramble past Lucifer took just over an hour, but the clock has been 'put back' so to speak, by twelve hours.[44]

It now becomes clear that the whole sequence of lunar references was meticulously plotted in order to prepare for this moment of bewilderment and enlightenment, of doubt and resolution. But it is also clear that Dante had a symbolic purpose in giving all the indications of 'Hell time' by reference to the moon, the stars, or the night. And if we wonder why this should be, it is enough to refer back to the 'prophecy' made by Farinata degli Uberti. Dante, he declares, will discover for himself how difficult is the art of return from political exile before the passing of fifty lunar months, or, more literally, 'before the face of *the lady who rules here* has been kindled fifty times'.[45] In classical mythology, the moon-goddess, Diana, is identified with Hecate, the goddess of the underworld; and she is *la donna che qui regge*. The moon's faint and borrowed light is also symbolic of the deprivation of all the souls in Hell, just as the sun is the symbol of the grace that strengthens and illumines the penitent souls in Purgatory.

The cosmic clock: (b) the 'ideal' Easter

The astronomical references in those linked passages are wholly representative of Dante's art in that they show his concern for narrative detail and convey a range of wider, symbolic meanings. Usually there is no conflict between these two functions. For Dante, the particular event, the concrete object, or the scientific fact is simultaneously the natural symbol. But it is important to realize that where a potential conflict between fact and symbol does arise, Dante is prepared to depart from the truths of physical science in order to obtain the higher truths of ethics and theology. This will become clear if we glance at the scholarly controversies over the fictional date of the Comedy.

We have seen that the journey took place shortly after the spring equinox, and that the moon was full on the evening when Dante followed Virgil into the underworld. These two facts together are conclusive proof that the journey began in Holy Week, because Easter is a movable feast, and Easter Day must always fall on the first Sunday after the first full moon following the spring equinox. A reference made by the devil Malacoda to the anniversary of the earthquake at the time of the Crucifixion makes it absolutely certain that Dante's first full day in Hell was a Good Friday; and the same reference, together with other allusions to datable events, makes it virtually certain that the year in question is 1300.[46] In theory, therefore, there should be no room for dispute. In the ecclesiastical calendar used in Dante's lifetime, the day of the spring equinox was given as 21 March. According to the same calendar, the moon was full on Thursday 7 April 1300; Good Friday was actually celebrated on 8 April, and Easter Sunday on 10 April. Dante therefore descended into Hell on the evening of 7 April 1300.[47]

This solution is the one accepted by most Dantists today, but in 1897 it was strongly challenged by a distinguished astronomer, Filippo Angelitti; and three of his objections still demand attention. Even if one accepts 21 March as the date of the equinox, Easter Day in 1300 fell nearly three weeks later. In that period, the sun would have moved fully twenty degrees away from the equinoctial point defined by the intersection of the four circles that form three crosses. Moreover, Dante knew perfectly well from the astronomical tables in use in his day that the equinox did not really occur on 21 March. Over the centuries since the reform of the calendar by Julius Caesar, the introduction of an excessive number of leap years had pushed the day of the equinox backwards until it fell on 13 March.[48] In reality, therefore, the sun was nearly twenty-eight degrees distant from the equinoctial point on Sunday 10 April 1300.

Finally, the contemporary astronomical tables also show that Venus was close to superior conjunction with the sun in April 1300 and would have been visible only for a few minutes as an *evening* star: Dante insists that he saw Venus bright in the morning sky from the shore of Mount Purgatory.

Angelitti than went on to point out that in the following year Venus was indeed a morning star in the appropriate period, and that the moon was full on 24 March. This is appropriately close to the conventional equinox, and only eleven days after the true equinox; and Angelitti therefore proposed that the first full day of Dante's journey was 25 March 1301. Unfortunately, however, the *Church* calendar gave the date of the full moon in that year as Monday 27 March, and Good Friday was observed on 31 March.

There is, moreover, a crucial objection to both the dates proposed (and, indeed, to any other date). When referring to the stars of the Zodiac in the narrative of the *Comedy*, Dante always writes as though the sun were literally in line of sight with Aries at the time of his journey. In fact, he knew perfectly well that it must have been in line of sight with Pisces thanks to the steady precession of the equinoxes earlier described.[49] In other words, Dante deliberately chose to ignore the difference between the *constellation* of Aries, still visible in the sky, and the *sign* of Aries, which is what astrologers call the area stretching through thirty degrees of longitude to the east of the vernal equinoctial point (a point which professional astronomers still call the 'first point of Aries'). He ignored this fundamental distinction (as he ignored many other important details) because to have done otherwise would have been to confuse his readers, to sow doubts concerning the perfect order of the heavens, and to sacrifice a chain of symbolic correspondences. It is therefore misguided to press the astronomical data given in the *Comedy* in an attempt to make them accord with the facts given in the ecclesiastical calendar or in the astronomical tables which Dante consulted. What we are asked to imagine is an 'ideal' Easter week, in an ideal universe, with an ideal calendar, such that in the year 1300 Good Friday fell on 25 March.

Dante deliberately chose to represent such an ideal Easter, because he wanted to forge as many symbolic links as possible between 'the Christ', the 'Anointed One', who alone offered the possibility of salvation, and himself, as a representative Christian sinner. Thus, the year 1300 is appropriate because it was the beginning of a new century and possibly of a new era.[50] It had been designated a Jubilee Year by Pope Boniface VIII, who granted an indulgence to pilgrims who would perform certain rites in the city of Rome. In May or June of that year Dante was to become thirty-five and reach the culmination of his physical, intellectual and moral development. He would be exactly 'mid-way upon the journey of our life', at the point when the individual reveals most clearly the common essence of his species. In March or April 1300 he would still be thirty-four, and therefore the same age as the Saviour on the day of the Crucifixion.[51]

It is likely that Dante intended his readers to deduce that Good Friday fell on a 25 March, because it was on that very day, so the Church believed, that Christ was crucified and descended into Hell: Dante's day in the 'pit' and his re-emergence on the shore of Mount Purgatory would then coincide with the anniversaries of the Passion and the Resurrection. Moreover, 25 March is the day on which the Church commemorates the Annunciation, the Incarnation of the Word: Christ died on the thirty-fourth anniversary of his conception. It must be remembered, too, that the Florentines counted the years from the *Incarnation* of the Lord and not from his Nativity: in Florence, 25 March was the first day of the New Year.

If Good Friday falls on 25 March, Easter Day will fall just one week after the conventional date of the spring equinox. And Dante clearly wanted the day of Christ's Resurrection—and the day of every Christian's rebirth as a moral being in Christ—to coincide as closely as possible with the day on which the whole of the *terra habitabilis* enters into its *dolce tempo novello* and the annual cycle of generation begins anew. As we have seen, the sun, who is Nature's chief minister, is then in his most powerful position and conjunction. And it only remains to remark that this was the position and conjunction of the sun at the moment when the universe was created.[52] One complex strand of temporal symbolism binds Dante to Christ, and connects his journey towards the 'love that moves the sun and the stars' with the three great acts of divine love in time—the Creation of the World, the Incarnation and the Crucifixion.

The cosmic clock: (c) counting the years

To indicate long periods of indefinite duration Dante will occasionally speak of 'centuries': for example, twenty-five centuries separate his own extraordinary journey from its analogue in the classical past, the moment when the Argonauts became the first men to venture across the sea in ships. But his normal unit of measurement is the obvious one, the 'year'. St Francis renounced his father's fortune and married Poverty 'one thousand one hundred years and more' after her 'First Husband' had died on the Cross. Dante entered the Underworld exactly 'one thousand two hundred and sixty-six years' to the day after Christ's descent and the liberation of the patriarchs from Limbo. Adam had dwelt there in torment and in hope of that coming for 'five thousand years and more' from the moment when he tasted the forbidden fruit in Eden.

For greater solemnity and greater precision, however, Dante may prefer the definition to the word itself. When he comes face to face with Adam, he learns that after his death Adam had languished in Limbo for precisely 'four thousand three hundred and two revolutions of the sun', and that, 'while on earth, he had seen the sun return along all the stars of his path nine hundred and thirty times'.[53]

Dante had used the same way of speaking in a late sonnet addressed to his friend and fellow poet Cino da Pistoia, saying that he had been inseparable from Love 'since the ninth revolution of his sun':

> Io sono stato con Amore insieme
> *da la circulazion del sol mia nona.*   (*Rime*, CXI, 1–2)

This in turn is certainly an allusion to the opening of the *Vita Nuova*: 'Nine times since my birth had the heaven of light returned almost to the same point, with regard to its proper motion, when the glorious lady who rules my mind first appeared to my eyes.'

But the sun is not the only face on the cosmic clock. Indeed, the very next sentence from the *Vita Nuova* goes on to fix Beatrice's age at the time of their first meeting by reference to the proper revolution of the Heaven of the Fixed Stars, which moves through only one degree in a hundred years: 'She had been in this life long enough for the Starry Heaven to move eastwards for the twelfth part of one degree; and so she appeared to me almost at the beginning of her ninth year; and I saw her almost at the end of my ninth year.'[54]

Later, in the *Convivio*, when he wrote of the interval between the death of Beatrice and the beginning of his love for that other noble lady, symbolizing Philosophy, he felt it appropriate to make the computation by reference to the proper, epicyclical motion of the planet Venus, 'the star which *comforts love*': 'the star of Venus had twice revolved upon that circle which makes it appear now in the morning and now in the evening'.[55] By the same instinct, he makes his ancestor Cacciaguida measure the interval between the Incarnation of Christ and his own birth by referring to the revolutions of his tutelary planet. According to his great-great-grandson, this Cacciaguida was a knight who died on the second Crusade. Dante the traveller meets him in the Heaven of Mars, together with others who fought for the faith. And there Cacciaguida declares, in perhaps the most elaborate of these time references: 'From the day when the angel said "Hail Mary" till the birth by which my mother, now in Paradise, was delivered of her burden, this fire of Mars returned to rekindle his flame beneath the paws of the Lion five hundred and fifty and thirty times' (it seems pedantic to add that this yields a date of A.D. 1091):

> . . . Da quel dì che fu detto '*Ave*'
> al parto in che mia madre, ch'è or santa,
> s'allevïò di me ond' era grave,
>   al suo Leon cinquecento cinquanta

166

e trenta fiate venne questo foco
a rinfiammarsi sotto la sua pianta.   (*Par.* XVI, 34–9)

The heavenly luminaries as terms of comparison

'The souls of the righteous . . . are in peace . . . and run to and fro like *sparks* among the stubble.' 'Then shall the righteous *shine forth as the sun* in the kingdom of their Father.' On the day of the Last Judgement, the bodies of the blessed are to be 'raised in glory'. Supported by such biblical texts as these, Christian artists had sometimes painted Christ, or Mary, or even the blessed, surrounded by an aureole or 'glory', that is, a stylized zone of light resembling the familiar halo or nimbus, but represented as emanating from the whole body rather than the head.[56] As so often, Dante was influenced by such textual authorities and iconographical traditions; but he follows them only to improve upon them.

In the Heaven of the Moon, Dante-character is slow to recognize the spokeswoman of the first group of the blessed who come to greet him there, even though she is a childhood friend–Piccarda Donati. She is hidden by her own increased loveliness and by an indefinable air of divinity–a *non so che divino*–that 'shines' in her face. When she is able to help Dante by answering his questions, she smiles with such delight that she seems 'to *burn* in the first *fire* of love'. 'Shining', 'burning' and 'fire' might be no more than metaphors, but when she refers to her more illustrious companion, the Empress Constance, simply as 'this other *splendour*', the status of the term is becoming ambiguous.[57]

In the next planetary sphere, that of Mercury, the shades or shadow-bodies (*ombre*) of the blessed are first described as being visible within the bright radiance that issues from each in proportion to its joy:

> vedeasi l'ombra piena di letizia
> nel folgór chiaro che di lei uscia.   (*Par.* V, 107–8)

But when their spokesman, the Emperor Justinian, is filled with greater joy at the prospect of being able to assist Dante, he shines with an increased radiance so intense that his human form is concealed, and he becomes hidden within his own dazzling light:

> Sì come il sol che si cela elli stessi
> per troppa luce . . .
>
> . . .
>
> per più letizia sì mi si nascose
> dentro al suo raggio la figura santa.   (133–4, 136–7)

From this moment in the narrative, Dante the traveller will be unable to discern the human lineaments of the blessed, until his eyes have been tempered by the light of glory in the Empyrean itself. The souls who are 'closer' to God experience a greater joy; and that joy itself is the cause of the radiance that hides them.[58]

From this moment, too, Dante the poet never uses *ombra* as a synonym for *anima* or *spirito*; and for the most part he refers to the blessed, whether singly or collectively, as 'lights', 'lamps', 'splendours', 'lightnings', 'flowers' and 'fires', or by the names of various precious stones. In the middle heavens, the individual 'lights' of the blessed arrange themselves in wonderful and spectacular displays. In the Heaven of the Sun they form three concentric spinning circles. In Mars they assume the shape of a Greek cross. In Jupiter they really do 'run to and fro like sparks in the stubble': they arrange themselves so as to spell out in turn the letters of the phrase 'Love Justice, ye that judge the earth', *Diligite iustitiam qui iudicatis terram*. Then, having paused for a moment in the shape of the final M they go through further movements to transform the letter into the shape of an heraldic eagle, which is miraculously able to speak with one common voice. Needless to say, the patterns formed by the individual lights call forth many superb similes from Dante, and some of the finest are drawn from his knowledge of the heavens and of astronomy.

When the souls who make up the imperial Eagle cease for a moment to speak with their one voice and break into choral song, the change from a collective unity to individuals in concord is likened to the disappearance of the sun and the reappearance of the stars at sunset: 'When he who gives light to the whole world sinks from our hemisphere, so that the day is extinguished on all sides, the sky, which had been lit by him alone, swiftly reveals itself again through many lights in which the one light shines':[59]

> Quando colui che tutto 'l mondo alluma
> de l'emisperio nostro sì discende,
> che 'l giorno d'ogne parte si consuma,
>   lo ciel, che sol di lui prima s'accende,
> subitamente si rifà parvente
> per molte luci, in che una risplende.   (*Par.* xx, 1–6)

In Mars, each of the broad bands of light formed by the thousands of individual souls is compared with the greatest exactitude and sense of cosmic space to the Milky Way 'gleaming white between the poles'. And when the soul of Cacciaguida descends from a position at the right arm of this cross to where Dante stands at its foot, he is said to be like a shooting star. But Dante immediately corrects the image (a 'shooting star' was then thought to be an illusion caused by meteorological phenomena) and he makes it plain that Cacciaguida was 'a star in the constellation shining there', 'un *astro*/de la *costellazion* che lì resplende'.[60]

In the Heaven of the Sun, the almost imperceptible coming of a *third* circle of lights is compared first to the brightening of the horizon at dawn, and then to the re-emergence of the stars at nightfall. The souls who appeared to form the first and inner circle were described as 'burning suns', *ardenti soli*, brighter than the heart of the sun itself, against which they stand out, not because of any difference in colour, but through their greater radiance, 'non per *color*, ma per *lume* parvente'. Their circular dance of rejoicing around Dante and Beatrice at the centre was likened to the revolution of the circumpolar stars. And when that first circle, formed by the souls of twelve great teachers, is surrounded by another circle of twelve lights, Dante invites his readers to imagine a constellation like Corona Borealis, but 'reduplicated', and with much brighter stars. This provides an occasion for Dante to air his astronomical learning, as he refers to the twenty-four most prominent stars visible from the northern hemisphere.[61] Unfortunately, however, the parade of erudition is matched by a virtuoso display of his command of syntax: a single sentence unfolds over twenty-four lines, making it impracticable to quote. It will therefore be more appropriate to conclude this brief survey of similes drawn from astronomy by recalling the best known and most beautiful of them all. The first appearance of Christ surrounded by *all* the souls of the blessed is compared to the full moon amid the stars, which are referred to metonymically as the Goddess Diana (under another of her names, Trivia) smiling among her eternal nymphs:

> Quale ne' plenilunïi sereni
> Trivïa ride tra le ninfe etterne.   (*Par.* XXIII, 25–6)

The stars around the southern pole

Not content with describing imaginary constellations for the purposes of a simile, Dante is bold enough to devise new configurations of stars and set them in the unknown southern hemisphere of the Starry Heaven. In the 'sweet sapphire-blue' of the pre-dawn sky over Purgatory, Dante the traveller notices first the luminaries that are familiar: Venus, as a morning star, is so bright that she seems to 'veil' the constellation of Pisces. But when he swings to the right and gazes south in the direction of the 'other pole', Dante becomes aware of four stars never seen before save by Adam and Eve:

> I' mi volsi a man destra, e puosi mente
> a l'altro polo, e vidi quattro stelle
> non viste mai fuor ch'a la prima gente.   (*Purg.* I, 22–4)

If the east seemed to 'smile' in the clear light of Venus, the whole sky now seems to 'rejoice' in their flaming lights: '*goder* pareva 'l ciel di lor fiammelle'; and the inhabited land of the northern hemisphere is called a 'widowed place', since it is bereft of the opportunity of gazing on these stars.

Needless to say, there has been much speculation as to whether Dante had heard or read travellers' tales about the Southern Cross or whether he made an inspired guess about its existence. But such questions need not detain us. Dante does not specify that the stars form a cross, and he clearly invented them as vehicles for a very precise allegory, to which every detail of the description just recalled is also subservient.

This allegorical meaning is soon clarified. Dante turns to the north and sees the white-bearded, white-haired, patriarchal figure of Cato. He is the stern guardian of the lower slopes of the mountain, that is, of the terraces that lie outside Purgatory 'proper'. In the *Convivio*, Dante had admired his unbending virtue, *rigida onestade*, and had declared that no man was more worthy to serve as a 'type' of God. He was the man who loved freedom and chose to die by his own hand rather than submit to tyranny. He was the embodiment of the four 'pivotal' or 'cardinal' virtues – self-restraint, courage, prudence and justice – the virtues which Adam and Eve had briefly possessed before the Fall, and which are now unheeded and unknown.[62] When we read in the poem that Cato's face was lit as brightly as if the sun were shining on it, but that the light which so adorned him came from these four holy stars, there can be no doubt that they symbolize the cardinal virtues:

> Li raggi de le quattro luci sante
> fregiavan sì la sua faccia di lume,
> ch'i' 'l vedea come 'l sol fosse davante.   (*Purg.* I, 37–9)

This interpretation is reinforced by the parallel scene which occurs later on the same day, when Dante is still in the Valley of Princes but closer to the gate of Purgatory itself. Night has fallen and Dante's 'greedy' eyes turn once again to the polar region. This time he sees '*three* stars with which the southern pole is all ablaze': 'tre facelle / di che 'l polo di qua tutto quanto arde'. And he is told that 'the four brillant stars you saw this morning are now low over there, while these have risen where they were':

> . . . Le quattro chiare stelle
> che vedevi staman, son di là basse,
> e queste son salite ov' eran quelle.   (VIII, 91–3)

The four virtues, in short, have given way to three *superior* virtues.

Both episodes are finally explained in the course of the complex masque that occupies the last five cantos of the *Purgatorio*. Beatrice is there accompanied on her left by a group of four ladies dressed in purple, and, on her right, by three others dressed in white, green and red. As the group of four escort Dante from his immersion in the river Lethe, they sing: '*Here* we are *nymphs*, in the *sky* we are *stars*' ('Noi siamo qui ninfe e nel ciel siamo stelle'). And they continue: 'We were ordained *ab aeterno* as handmaids of Beatrice; we shall lead you to her eyes; but the three on the other side will sharpen your gaze to experience the light of joy her eyes contain; for they see more deeply.'[63] In other words self-restraint, courage, prudence and justice are indeed virtues, but they are subordinate and do not suffice of themselves. Man will not be saved and set free except through the greater, religious virtues of Faith, Hope and Love – 'and of these the greatest is Love'. By the same token, Cato was indeed the embodiment of pagan virtue, but his stern austerity is not the highest good. It must take on the love and joy that Dante will represent in Purgatory and Paradise.

In Dante's art, as we have repeatedly seen, symbolism does not exclude realism, and realism does not preclude symbolism. The 'constellated virtues' in the southern sky do not necessarily violate any principle of Ptolemaic astronomy. We must remember that Purgatory lies about thirty-two degrees south of the equator, and that the southern celestial pole will therefore be only thirty-two degrees above the horizon. If we assume that the two constellations lie at about twenty-five degrees from the poles – at much the same distance as the closest stars in the best-known circumpolar constellations in the northern hemisphere – then the first constellation could have been seen at an altitude of about sixty degrees in the morning, and would have revolved to a position just a few degrees above the horizon at sunset, while the second constellation, which might have been close to the horizon at dawn, could have risen by evening to the place where the first had been.

But there are certain difficulties in this purely naturalistic interpretation. On both occasions, morning and evening, Dante stresses that his eyes sought the *pole*; and the natural inference is that both constellations were sited *close* to the pole, and not removed by as much as twenty-five or thirty degrees. If this inference is correct, and if the *stellae* were *fixae* like all the familiar stars, then Dante could not have failed to see both constellations at the same time.[64] It is therefore possible that Dante wanted us to think of the constellations and their appearance as being in some sense miraculous. They may seem to be more permanent than the seven ladies who appear in the masque (*that* was clearly enacted for Dante alone); but perhaps their movements are governed directly by God, rather than controlled by the passive motion of the eighth heaven. Such an interpretation would certainly accord with the praeternatural intensity of their light-rays, and with Dante's treatment of the earthquake in Purgatory. Dante did not dedicate himself to the study of corporeity, matter, motion and time with a view to discrediting miracles by showing that everything in nature was subject to nature's law. He studied the physics of natural bodies – from the *corpora simplicia* to the *corpora caelestia* – in order that he might better understand and better represent the direct and miraculous interventions of God.

7

The angels

The Keeper at the Gate

MORE THAN TWO HOURS AFTER SUNSET AT THE END OF HIS FIRST LONG day in Purgatory, exhausted by the events and emotions described in Chapter 1, Dante the pilgrim falls asleep in the Valley of the Princes in the company of Virgil, Sordello, Nino Visconti and Currado Malaspina. Nearly twelve hours later he wakes in a state of alarm. He has been dreaming that he was seized by an eagle who carried him up – like Ganymede before him – into the fiery region of the sky, where he and the eagle seemed to burst into flames; and it is the 'imagined blaze' that wakens the dreamer.

His fear and bewilderment are increased as he finds himself in a strange place accompanied only by Virgil. But his mentor is quick to reassure and explain. The dream had reflected real events, for, while he was sleeping, Dante had in fact been carried high up the mountain by St Lucy. The *imaginato incendio* was his veiled perception of her radiance, or perhaps simply a consequence of the sun's rays falling on his eyelids, since it is now more than two hours after sunrise.[1] Dante has been brought from the lower slopes to Purgatory itself; and Virgil urges him to look at the rocky cliff that surrounds it, and to see the entrance at a point where there is a break in its wall:

> Tu se' omai al purgatorio giunto:
> vedi là il balzo che 'l chiude dintorno;
> vedi l'entrata là 've par digiunto.   (*Purg.* IX, 49–51)

The two poets set off up the slope and, as they draw nearer, they discover that what had seemed a mere opening is really an elaborate gate. Three steps of different colours lead up to the threshold which is guarded by a silent watchman. As Dante's eyes open still wider – 'e come l'occhio più e più v'apersi' – he registers that the watchman is seated above the topmost step, but he finds that he cannot look steadily either at his face or at the drawn sword which he holds in his hand.[2]

The keeper's voice rings out, challenging the travellers with an air of authority that reminds us of Cato on the shore of Mount Purgatory, and also, more distantly, of Minos on his judgement-seat in Hell. 'You there,

tell me what you want. Where is your escort? Are you sure that your
ascent will bring you no harm?':

> 'Dite costinci: che volete voi?',
> cominciò elli a dire, 'ov' è la scorta?
> Guardate che 'l venir sù non vi nòi'. (85–7)

There is no menace in his words, however, and no attempt to undermine
Dante's confidence in his guide. Indeed, as soon as Virgil has briefly
explained St Lucy's intervention, the keeper shows his courtesy by
expressing the hope that she may further guide them towards the Good,
and he bids them 'come forward to the steps':

> 'Ed ella i passi vostri in bene avanzi',
> ricominciò il cortese portinaio:
> 'Venite dunque a' nostri gradi innanzi'. (91–3)

The three steps are now described in greater detail; and our eyes follow
those of the protagonist, rising from the polished white marble of the first
to the dark, rough and deeply fissured rock of the second, and up to the
massive block of porphyry that forms the third, in colour flaming red,
like blood spurting from an artery. There on its diamond-like surface rest
the two feet of the *angel of God*. Only now is the 'cortese portinaio'
identified:

> Lo terzo, che di sopra s'ammassiccia,
> porfido mi parea, sì fiammeggiante
> come sangue che fuor di vena spiccia.
> Sovra questo tenëa ambo le piante
> *l'angel di Dio . . .* (100–4)

Didactic narrative: (a) the angel of humility

Once he has passed through the gate of Purgatory, Dante will climb in
turn to the seven ledges or terraces that run round the mountain and form
the places appointed for purification and expiation. As he completes part
of a circuit on these terraces, and as he comes to the flight of steps that
lead up to the next, he will meet seven more angels. All these encounters
will follow the pattern and mood established by the first, and they are
carefully composed to make up a well-rounded set of variations on a
theme. The writing throughout is marked by great delicacy and beauty,
and, in particular, by an element of suspense or surprise, which is
achieved, as in the episode we have just read, by deliberately withholding
information known to the narrator, and by adhering faithfully to the
sequence of impressions as they struck the protagonist at the time. In
fact, the narrator seems to go almost out of his way to show the senses in
action, to demonstrate how they support and supplement each other,
and, above all, to make us aware of their limitations.[3]

It is not particularly difficult to see why Dante should lay such emphasis on human sensation in his representation of angels. But for the moment it will be better to go on following his example, and to read the episodes naively and without prior expectations. It will be enough if we are aware in advance that the seven encounters provide an unusually coherent and systematic demonstration of the didactic method that underlies Dante's narrative technique throughout the *Comedy*. Learning should begin with concrete experience. The reader must be steered into working things out for himself. He will understand the abstract concepts only if he has been helped to draw them out (*abstrahere*) from the sense-impressions he has received from a series of particular individuals belonging to the same class. Dante will give us precise information about the nature, origin and functions of the angels, but only after he has built up a store of images and connotations in our minds.[4]

Before we climb to the Circle of the Proud for the first of these meetings, we must follow Dante as he passes into Purgatory. First, he prostrates himself and in mercy's name begs for the gate to be opened. Then the angel takes the point of his sword and traces the letter P seven times on Dante's forehead, uttering as he does so the enigmatic command: 'See to it that you wash these wounds away when you are within':

> Sette P ne la fronte mi descrisse
> col punton de la spada, e 'Fa che lavi,
> quando se' dentro, queste piaghe' disse. (112–14)

He produces the two keys entrusted to him by St Peter and opens the great door. The metal pivots of the hinges move in their sockets with a thunderous roar which dissolves into a singing of the hymn, *Te Deum laudamus*, accompanied as if by an organ, in such a way that the melody is heard but some of the words are lost. It will not be the last celestial music we hear as Dante takes leave of an angel and begins a new ascent:

> Io mi rivolsi attento al primo tuono,
> e '*Te Deum laudamus*' mi parea
> udire in voce mista al dolce suono.
> Tale imagine a punto mi rendea
> ciò ch'io udiva, qual prender si suole
> quando a cantar con organi si stea;
> ch'or sì or no s'intendon le parole. (139–45)

Some four hours later Dante has completed his conversations with the souls of the proud on the first circle. He follows Virgil swiftly, but with head bowed in contrite recognition of his own fierce pride in his family and his art; and as he walks he studies graven images on the ground, which represent thirteen notorious examples of human vainglory, presumption and hubris visited by divine retribution. Suddenly Virgil bids him lift his head: 'Look, an angel is making ready to meet us':

> Drizza la testa;
> non è più tempo di gir sì sospeso.
> Vedi colà un angel che s'appresta
> per venir verso noi . . .   *(Purg.* XII, 77–80)

On this occasion, therefore, we know in advance that we are dealing with an angel.

Immediately afterwards, we are told that the angel's task is to speed the poets on their way to the next circle. We also learn that he is beautiful, dressed in white, and, 'in aspect, radiant and trembling like a morning star'. His gesture and words of welcome are simple and simply expressed; and nothing could be more direct than the three self-sufficient lines that describe how he performed his duty:

He opened his arms, then opened his wings. He said 'Come. The steps are near. Climbing will be easy now.' . . . He led us to where the rock was cut away. He touched my forehead with his wings. He promised me that my journey would be safe:

> Le braccia aperse, e indi aperse l'ale;
> disse: 'Venite: qui son presso i gradi,
> e agevolemente omai si sale.'
>
> . . .
>
> Menocci ove la roccia era tagliata;
> quivi mi batté l'ali per la fronte;
> poi mi promise sicura l'andata.   (91–3, 97–9)

The language is free from artifice, and these lines come close to the sublime simplicity of the Gospels. Nevertheless, they both convey and conceal a piece of information that must now be discovered by the protagonist, in the most delightfully indirect way, in order to restore the element of surprise.

Scarcely have the two travellers turned their backs on the angel and begun to climb, when they hear the words of the first beatitude: 'Blessed are the poor in spirit, for theirs is the kingdom of heaven.' As with the *Te Deum* earlier, the words are sung, and sung with a beauty that language cannot express. And Dante-poet breaks in on his narrative to point out the contrast between the songs that now accompany his entry into the circles of Purgatory, and the fierce lamentations that he heard in the mouth of Hell:

> Noi volgendo ivi le nostre persone,
> '*Beati pauperes spiritu!*' voci
> cantaron sì, che nol diria sermone.
> Ahi quanto son diverse quelle foci
> da l'infernali! ché quivi per canti
> s'entra, e là giù per lamenti feroci.   (109–14)

The steepness of the climb is emphasized by means of a long simile which reminds Florentine readers of the flight of steps that lead up to the church of San Miniato from the south bank of the Arno. But as the pilgrim climbs he feels himself lighter than he did when he was walking round the first circle on level ground. He seeks enlightenment, asking: 'Master, what weight has been lifted from me so that I can now climb with hardly any weariness or strain?':

> Ond' io: 'Maestro, dì, qual cosa greve
> levata s'è da me, che nulla quasi
> per me fatica, andando, si riceve?'   (118–20)

Virgil's reply is informative but studiously oblique:

When the remaining Ps–which have now almost faded away–have been completely cancelled from your face, as the first has been, your feet will be so subject to your will, that they will feel not weariness but delight in taking the thrust.

Slowly understanding begins to dawn as we remember the angel's wings.

With a remarkable disregard for personal dignity, Dante compares his reactions to those of a man who begins to suspect from the gestures of people in the street that he must have something on his head of which he was unaware. Where the sense of sight is helpless, the sense of touch must come to the rescue. Tentatively he raises the fingers of his right hand to feel his temples and finds that, of the seven letters incised there by the angel with the keys, only six remain:

> e con le dita de la destra scempie
> trovai pur sei le lettere che 'ncise
> quel da le chiavi a me sovra le tempie:
> a che guardando, il mio duca sorrise.   (133–6)

Like Virgil, we can only smile at a discovery related with such a happy combination of artlessness and art.

Didactic narrative: (b) the angels of love and forgiveness

In the next two encounters Dante's sight will fail him in a more dramatic way. In the first case, he is walking westwards round the Circle of the Envious and his eyes have already been made uncomfortable by the low rays of the early-evening sun. Suddenly the level of illumination before him increases. He tries to shield his eyes with his hand, but to no avail, because light from the new source is also bouncing up at him from the reflecting surface of the stone terrace. Dante's sight is powerless to identify the cause of its own distress, and he must turn for reassurance and explanation to Virgil, who will reply with just a hint of ellipsis: 'Don't be amazed if you are still dazzled by one of the heavenly retinue; it is a messenger coming to invite us to ascend':

> 'Non ti maravigliar s'ancor t'abbaglia
> la famiglia del cielo', a me rispuose:
> 'messo è che viene ad invitar ch'om saglia.' (*Purg.* xv, 28–30)

In the second case, he is moving round the Circle of the Wrathful in a state of withdrawal from external reality, his attention being wholly given over to contemplation of three visions that have appeared by supernatural agency in his *interior* sense of 'imagination'.[5] Then, in just the same way that we can be roused from sleep if a bright light falls on our closed eyelids, Dante is awoken from his trance by a light more brilliant than anything experienced here on earth. As he looks about him to find his bearings, a voice says: 'This is the way up.' With his usual impetuosity, Dante swings round to look at the speaker face to face, but his power of vision is again extinguished, and he is temporarily blinded by what he sees, just as if he had looked directly into the sun. Virgil's voice immediately breaks in on his sense of hearing, however, with the words: 'This is a divine spirit. He is showing us the way to climb without waiting to be asked, and he is hiding himself in his own light':

> Questo è divino spirito, che ne la
> via da ir sù ne drizza sanza prego,
> e col suo lume sé medesmo cela.　　(*Purg.* XVII, 55–7)

Dante turns unseeingly to the first step, but with his other senses he feels as it were the moving of a wing and a breath of air over his face, and he hears the words of the appropriate beatitude, which, here as on every circle, brings the episode to a close: 'Blessed are the peacemakers who have no wrongful anger':

> e tosto ch'io al primo grado fui,
> 　senti'mi presso quasi un muover d'ala
> e ventarmi nel viso e dir: '*Beati
> pacifici*, che son sanz' ira mala!'　　(66–9)

Didactic narrative: (c) the angel of moderation

The following two encounters are briefly reported rather than represented at length, and the surprises they offer are of a different kind.[6] The narrator is clearly varying the pattern he has laid down and holding something in reserve for the most sensuous of all these encounters, which will take place on the terrace where the sinners suffer the greatest degree of sense-deprivation – on the Circle of the Gluttonous. At the point where we pick up the story, Dante and Virgil have been joined by a third poet, Statius, in the circumstances which were described in Chapter 3.

We were walking well spaced out, each of us lost in contemplation, and we had covered more than a mile, when a sudden voice said 'What are you thinking about, you three all alone?', making me jump in alarm like a timid wild animal. I lifted my head to see who it was; and you have never seen anything so brilliant or so red – not even glass or metal in a furnace – as the figure I saw, who continued: 'If you should wish to go higher, you must turn aside here. This is the way for those who seek peace.'

> Drizzai la testa per veder chi fossi;
> e già mai non si videro in fornace
> vetri o metalli sì lucenti e rossi,
>   com' io vidi un che dicea: 'S'a voi piace
> montare in sù, qui si convien dar volta;
> quinci si va chi vuole andar per pace!'   (*Purg.* XXIV, 136–41)

His aspect robbed me of my sense of sight, and I turned to my teachers like a man who walks as his ear directs him. Then, as if it were the first intimation of a May breeze, heavy with the fragrance of flowers and grass, and stirring to announce the coming of dawn, I felt a puff of wind in the middle of my forehead, and I distinctly felt the moving of feathers which filled the air with ambrosia. And I heard: 'Blessed are those who are so illumined by grace, that the prompting of taste does not cloud their heart with the smoke of excessive desire, and whose hunger is always for what is just':

> L'aspetto suo m'avea la vista tolta;
> per ch'io mi volsi dietro a' miei dottori,
> com' om che va secondo ch'elli ascolta.
>   E quale, annunziatrice de li albori,
> l'aura di maggio movesi e olezza,
> tutta impregnata da l'erba e da' fiori;
>   tal mi senti' un vento dar per mezza
> la fronte, e ben senti' mover la piuma,
> che fé sentir d'ambrosïa l'orezza.
>   E senti' dir: 'Beati cui alluma
> tanto di grazia, che l'amor del gusto
> nel petto lor troppo disir non fuma,
> esurïendo sempre quanto è giusto!'   (142–54)

More than ever before, the loss of sight seems to sharpen Dante's other senses; and it is no accident that *sentire*, the common verb of sensation, occurs in four successive lines towards the end of the passage. For the first time the sense of smell is called into play; and the beatitude has been paraphrased in such a way that it introduces the sense of taste and the verb proper to *its* specific love (*l'amor del gusto, esuriendo*).

It is tempting to go on to the last of these encounters, or to go back to the angels whom Dante saw from afar as they ministered to the souls in Antepurgatory.[7] But we have reached the point where the gathering of further information is less urgent and less rewarding than the analysis and the interpretation of what we have already collected. It is time to move from the particular towards the universal and to ask ourselves what we have learned about the nature of the angels from the five encounters we have witnessed.

Perhaps the most essential quality exemplified by all five angels is what the Authorized Version would call their 'loving-kindness'. Their only command is 'Come'; they are swift to move forward and extend their invitations unbidden; their words and song fall sweetly on the ear; and they are most gentle with the patient as they 'wash away' his seven 'wounds'.

At the same time they are figures of authority and majesty. We could not imagine Dante-character pausing to pass the time of day with them. Their manner is not forbidding, but it is certainly not familiar. And this impression is of course intimately bound up with the way in which they have been presented by Dante-poet.

We know from the *Vita Nuova* that Dante was an amateur artist capable of 'drawing figures of angels in his tablets', and there can be no doubt that he was familiar with the representation of angels in contemporary art.[8] Their feathered wings, their bright garments, their youth and beauty, their association with music-making and song could all come from that source. But his angels are not the demure adolescents of uncertain sex found in much thirteenth-century painting. We have not seen them steadily face to face, because they have been hidden by their own radiance. They inspire awe and wonder. Dante has done more than merely affirm that an angel is a *divino spirito* or one of the *famiglia del cielo*. He has made us experience the fact through our nerve-ends. And in the last analysis, as we shall see, the most important single fact about angels is that they transcend the human condition.

Angels in the Bible

Dante was well aware that whenever a cause is more than human, it cannot be apprehended or understood in itself, but must be approached through a study of its effects (in this case, the effects on the senses of the protagonist).[9] And so it should come as no surprise to discover that Dante has supplied very few details about the appearance of the five angels. Almost everything he has disclosed can be found in a single sentence from the Gospel of St Matthew which Dante had translated in the fourth book of his *Convivio*. The Evangelist relates how 'Mary Magdalene and the other Mary' had come to Christ's burial place on the morning of the first Easter Day; and he continues: 'And, behold, there was a great earthquake: for the angel of the Lord descended from heaven, and came and rolled back the stone from the door and sat upon it. His countenance was like lightning, and his raiment white as snow' (28. 2–3). In Dante's version, it runs: 'L'angelo di Dio discese di cielo, e vegnendo volse la pietra e sedea sopra essa. E 'l suo aspetto era come folgore, e le sue vestimenta erano come neve' (*Con.* IV, xxii, 15).[10]

It is of course on the authority of the Bible alone that Christians believe in the existence of angels; and we must now remind ourselves of the biblical data on which all subsequent speculation depends. In general terms, the Bible represents angels as doing God's word and will and acting as his servants or administrators. Their simplest task is delivering messages, and the Greek word *angelos* meant no more than 'messenger', as Dante was well aware. As messengers they appear sometimes in dreams or visions, sometimes in person; and the messages they bring may be injunctions, prophecies or simple announcements. The most important announcement in human history was of course the Annunciation, and the best known of these 'legates' was the Archangel Gabriel.[11]

They were also sent to guide, protect and succour those in need. Elijah and Jesus were fed in the wilderness; Jesus and Paul were strengthened in their hour of trial. Angels led the children of Israel out of Egypt, saved the three Jews in the Fiery Furnace and twice freed St Peter from prison. The best-known guardian angel was Raphael who assumed human form for some considerable time as he helped young Tobias to win a bride and heal his father's blindness.[12]

Their third main task was to destroy the enemies of the Lord and of his chosen people: on one occasion they massacred 185,000 Assyrians in their camp. The warrior-angel par excellence is Michael. He is said to have contended with Satan for the body of Moses, and to have driven Satan and his angels out of Heaven. At the End of Time, he will bind Satan in the bottomless pit and seal it over him.[13]

There is evidence of popular belief that angels accompanied the souls of the dead 'into the bosom of Abraham'; and some of those who saw an angel were afraid that their last hour had come.[14] In the New Testament we read that angels will play a prominent part in the struggles that will precede the Second Coming and on the Judgement Day itself, when they will carry the virtuous into Heaven and drive the damned into Hell. In this role they dominate the vision of St John in the Book of Revelation.[15]

The narrative books of the Bible do not record many angelic visitations, and angels usually appear singly, or at most in groups of two or three. But it is worth remembering that Jacob dreamt he saw angels of God ascending and descending on a ladder set up upon the earth with its top touching Heaven, since this gives us some idea of their true number and of the frequency of their missions to earth. And on the morning of Christ's Nativity the angel who gave 'good tidings of great joy' to the shepherds was accompanied by a 'multitude of the heavenly host praising God and saying, "Glory to God in the highest, and on earth peace to men of good will"'.[16]

The poetic and prophetic books confirm that the heights of heaven are indeed full of spiritual creatures. Sometimes they are referred to as 'angels' and sometimes as 'sons of God' or 'sons of the Most High'. There are, in addition, two special groups who remain close to the throne of the

Almighty, the Seraphs—mentioned only by Isaiah—and the Cherubs. The whole host is apparently dedicated to the perpetual contemplation of the Lord and to the worship and praise of His name and works, to which end they sing this other hallowed form of words: 'Holy, holy, holy is the Lord of hosts: the whole earth is full of his glory.' But the fact which most impressed all the prophets who were granted a vision of the host in heaven was that the angels were 'almost innumerable': 'Thousands of thousands' ministered to 'the Ancient of Days', and 'ten thousand times one hundred thousand stood before Him'.[17]

As regards their outward shape and appearance on earth, it is sometimes made quite clear that the angels assume human form, while sometimes it is left uncertain. In either case they may be wearing white clothing, and they can be recognized by the brightness of their faces, as we saw in the sentence from St Matthew. When they are engaged on a mission of retribution they may carry a drawn sword. But the biblical narrative does not usually *represent* the angel in any way. An *angelus Dei* may be the subject of some verb of saying or doing that could equally well be attributed directly to God or to the Holy Spirit; and there are a number of passages where the author oscillates between the two conventions open to him.[18] The only significant exception will be found in this rather longer description from the Book of Daniel:

I beheld a certain man clothed in linen, whose loins were girded with fine gold of Uphaz: his body also was like the beryl, and his face as the appearance of lightning, and his eyes as lamps of fire, and his arms and his feet like in colour to polished brass, and the voice of his words like the voice of a multitude (Daniel 10.5–6).

The prophets say nothing concerning the appearance of common angels in heaven. But Isaiah describes the Seraphs as each having *six* wings: 'with twain he covered his face, and with twain he covered his feet, and with twain he did fly'. And Ezekiel describes in bewildering detail the multiple wings, hands and faces of four composite 'living creatures' that he clearly understood to be Cherubs. These *animalia*, however, were later interpreted as symbols of the four Evangelists; and, since Dante appropriated them as such, we need not go into detail.[19] It is perhaps enough to remark that the prophets' visions of creatures in heaven are decidedly not realistic nor anthropomorphic, and that the reader retains an impression of geometrical shapes, hypnotically repeated numbers, and a profusion of emblematic metals and stones.

Biblical angels in the 'Comedy'

The *Comedy* is rich in allusions and references to the texts that have just been summarized, and Dante was clearly at pains to remind his readers of the main inferences concerning the nature of angels that can be drawn from the biblical evidence. In a carefully graduated series of epithets and brief descriptive phrases he describes them as 'envoys from Heaven', 'officials from paradise', 'members of the retinue of Heaven', 'divine spirits' and 'ministers and messengers of eternal life'.[20]

The ladder that Jacob saw in his dream is the model for the *scaleo d'oro* down which the souls of the contemplatives come to greet Dante in the heaven of Saturn, and up which Dante will himself ascend to the constellation of Gemini. The visions of Ezekiel and St John are the duly acknowledged sources for his account of the Mystic Procession and the Sacred Pageant in the Garden of Eden; while the chorus-like interventions of the angels which punctuate the dramatic confrontation between the irate Beatrice and her contrite lover owe something to the Song of Songs and to the celestial host that appeared to the shepherds. The gatekeeper's insistence that the pilgrim should not look behind him after he has entered Purgatory is clearly derived from the command which the angel gave to Lot when he delivered him from Sodom.[21] It is also possible that the idea of placing angels on the terraces came to Dante from a well-known passage in Ezekiel: 'Thou hast been in *Eden*, the Garden of God; every precious stone was thy covering. . . . Thou art the anointed *cherub* . . . thou wast upon the *holy mountain of God*.'[22]

The three archangels are jointly cited as 'Gabriel, Michael and the other who healed Tobias' in the passage where Beatrice is made to insist that it is right to portray spiritual beings in human form—*con aspetto umano*—because all our knowledge must begin in the experience of the senses. Michael is named in two other places, and it is by no means implausible to assume that he is the mysterious envoy who crossed the Styx dry-footed to put down the insurrection by the demons whom he had driven into Hell. The place of honour, however, is reserved for Gabriel. His part in the Annunciation is twice recalled in scattered references, and it is represented by the expedient of introducing a description of a miraculous low-relief sculpture of the scene.[23] Gabriel also makes two appearances in the action of the poem itself—once when he comes to escort Mary back into the Empyrean, and once when he renews his devotions there.

The first of these appearances is an extraordinary achievement, even for Dante.[24] The scene is set in the Heaven of the Fixed Stars, where Dante and Beatrice have been welcomed by the souls of *all* the human beings who have succeeded in returning to their Maker (their number includes Christ, in his human person, and the Virgin Mary). As in all the higher spheres, the souls are perceived as so many 'lamps', or 'fires' or 'splendours'. Their human form is hidden from the pilgrim by the light they themselves emit, and they are differentiated one from another only by the size and intensity of this radiance or glory. After the withdrawal of

Christ, who was imaged as a 'sun' so bright that he outshone and hid the other 'stars', Dante's eyes turned to the greatest of the remaining 'fires' – the 'living star' which concealed the Virgin. As he gazed:

a torch descended through the heaven, formed in a circle as though it were a crown. It cast a girdle about Mary and circled round her. The sweetest melody ever heard here below – the melody that most draws the mind to itself – would have seemed like a cloud ripped apart and thundering, compared to the playing of the lyre which crowned the fair sapphire that ensapphires the brightest heaven of all:

> per entro il cielo scese una facella,
> formata in cerchio a guisa di corona,
> e cinsela e girossi intorno ad ella.
> Qualunque melodia più dolce suona
> qua giù e più a sé l'anima tira,
> parrebbe nube che squarciata tona,
> comparata al sonar di quella lira
> onde si coronava il bel zaffiro
> del quale il ciel più chiaro s'inzaffira. (*Par.* XXIII, 94–102)

'I am angelic love. I circle the noble joy that issues from the womb that was the term and chamber of our Desire. And I shall continue so to circle, Mistress of Heaven, until you follow your Son and make the supreme sphere more divine by your entry there.' With these words the circling melody sealed itself, and all the other lights made Mary's name resound:

> 'Io sono amore angelico, che giro
> l'alta letizia che spira del ventre
> che fu albergo del nostro disiro;
> e girerommi, donna del ciel, mentre
> che seguirai tuo figlio, e farai dia
> più la spera supprema perché lì entre.'
> Così la circulata melodia
> si sigillava, e tutti li altri lumi
> facean sonare il nome di Maria. (103–11)

In this way, the *aspetto umano* of the protagonists of the Annunciation is dissolved into a living star, a burning torch, a sapphire, a joy, a crown, a girdle and a lyre. Perfect angelic love is expressed through the perfect circular motion found in the heavenly spheres.

There are sources in the prophetic books of the Bible for Dante's use of the pure forms of geometry and the cold beauty of precious stones. Mary was hymned as Queen of Heaven long before Dante's day; and it was Latin hymnody that gave him models for such phrases as 'il ventre / che fu albergo del nostro disiro'. Perhaps Dante was subconsciously influenced by paintings of the Assumption of the Virgin, or the Coronation of the Virgin, since both motifs seem to be present in this passage. But it is obvious that Dante alone is responsible for the poetic fusion of all these elements, for the sweetness of the words (thrown into relief by the harsh sound of *squarciata*), for the effortless spinning of the subordinate clauses, and for the metaphorical union of sound and sight which turns both the message and the messenger into a *circulata melodia*.

The 'Celestial Hierarchy': (a) St Paul and Dionysius

Before we finally leave the biblical sources of Dante's angelology we must take note of three brief but influential passages in the letters of St Paul. In these texts the apostle refers to spiritual creatures using five names that we have not yet encountered. Four of them are abstract nouns expressing the idea of 'strength' or 'authority': 'Principality', 'Virtue', 'Power' and 'Dominion'. Three of these are joined by a concrete noun 'Thrones' (also associated by metonymy with the idea of 'authority') in the following context:[25]

The Father . . . hath delivered us from the power of darkness, and hath translated us into the kingdom of his dear Son, in whom we have redemption . . .; for by him were all things created that are in heaven, and that are in earth, visible and invisible, whether they be *thrones*, or *dominions*, or *principalities*, or *powers* . . . (Colossians 1.12–16).

The earliest interpreters of these enigmatic texts seem to have been in agreement on the main points. They all accepted, that is, that the five words did denominate distinct categories among spiritual beings, and that each of the five groups must exist to fulfil some distinct role or function in the divine order. They further agreed that the five groups could not be equal in worth, but that, collectively, they ranked between the Seraphs and the Cherubs at the top and the Archangels and Angels at the bottom. And they were at one in the belief that the names must be descriptive of the functions of the five groups, whether these functions were exercised in the court of heaven or in the economy of the universe at large. There was, however, an area of relatively uncontentious disagreement concerning the precise definition of those functions or tasks (the difficulty being caused by the semantic overlap of all five terms), and concerning their rank with respect to each other (the difficulty being caused by the differing order in which the names appear in the Pauline texts).

We do not need to inquire very deeply into the various solutions that were proposed, but we shall not understand an important chapter in the *Convivio*, nor some forty lines in Beatrice's first discourse about the angelic choirs in the *Comedy*, until we have learned a little more about the rival interpretations of these disputed points.

In Dante's time the most highly regarded work on the subject of angels was the much quoted, but little read, *Celestial Hierarchy*. This work is now known to be the work of a Greek Christian, deeply imbued with the spirit and terminology of Neoplatonist philosophy, who wrote at some time in the late fifth or early sixth century A.D. The unknown author, however, passed his treatise off as the work of one Dionysius the Areopagite, an Athenian who had been converted to Christianity by St Paul.[26] It was this false assertion that gave the work its unique prestige, because Dionysius claimed to have received his information directly from the apostle, and St Paul was known to have been 'caught up into heaven' where he had seen for himself. The book became available in the West during the early ninth century thanks to a Latin translation by John Scotus Eriugena, and it had come to exercise great influence by the late twelfth century.

Now, the addition of the five Pauline names to the four mentioned earlier meant that there was biblical authority for the existence of *nine* groups of angels; and the chief importance of the *Celestial Hierarchy* was that the author (whom we may as well continue to call Dionysius) insisted that the nine groups were divided into three 'hierarchies', each of three 'orders', as shown in this table:[27]

Thrones	*Powers*	*Angels*
1 Seraphs	4 Dominions	7 Principalities
2 Cherubs	5 Virtues	8 Archangels
3 Thrones	6 Powers	9 Angels

In the course of his difficult work Dionysius gives several different accounts of the 'angelic nature and ministry', and these accounts are not fully compatible with each other. In one section he treats all the angels as 'contemplative', and he distinguishes them by their mode of cognition and by the different objects of their speculation, which become progressively more particularized in the lower orders. Elsewhere, he tends to treat them all as 'active', and he compares the three hierarchies to the three tiers in the established church, the deacons, the priests and the bishops: the lowest prepares or 'purifies'; the second 'illuminates'; the third 'perfects'.[28]

In his more detailed discussion of the meaning of the nine names, however, where he follows the principle that 'the proper names of the several orders designate their properties', Dionysius seems to oppose contemplation to action, as higher is opposed to lower.[29] Thus, the two highest orders are defined through their relationship to God: the Seraphs, interpreted as 'burning', 'ardent', are most closely united to God in love; while the Cherubs, whose name is interpreted as 'fullness of wisdom', excel all other creatures in their knowledge of the divine secrets. The two lowest orders are defined through their relationship to man: the Angels deliver messages to private individuals, the Archangels to men of consequence; but both are mere executives. To the five middle orders—those bearing the Pauline names linked with 'power'—Dionysius rather lamely assigns the task of mediation: *medio modo se habent*. They are compared to the officers in an army who translate the strategical thought of the general first into tactical objectives and then into the particular commands issued to the fighting soldiers.[30]

The 'Celestial Hierarchy': (b) Dante

In the second book of the *Convivio*, Dante devotes two chapters to the subject of angels, and he takes up a position which is notably independent of Dionysius. He accepts, as everyone did, that the nine orders are grouped into three hierarchies, and he differentiates them in terms of the objects of their contemplation. But he follows St Gregory in his ranking of the Pauline orders, relegating Thrones to the seventh position and promoting Powers in their place; and he develops a line of thought, found in Hugh of St Victor, St Bonaventure and others, to argue that the orders and hierarchies must be distinguished and grouped in accordance with the way in which they contemplate the Trinity.[31] 'The divine majesty', he writes,

exists in three Persons, of one substance, who may be considered in three ways. One may contemplate the supreme power of the Father, as does the first hierarchy (the first in point of nobility . . .). One may contemplate the supreme wisdom of the Son, as the second does; and one may contemplate the supreme and most fervent love of the Holy Spirit, as does the last. . . .

And since each person in the Holy Trinity can be considered in three ways, there are three orders within each hierarchy. . . . The Father may be considered having regard only to himself; and this is how he is contemplated by the Seraphs. . . . One may consider him in relation to the Son, as being distinct from him and yet one with him; and this is how the Cherubs contemplate him. Finally, one may consider him in relation to the procession of the Holy Spirit, who is also united with him and yet distinct; and such is the contemplation of the Powers. The Son and the Holy Spirit may be considered in the same threefold way.

This is why there have to be nine kinds of contemplative spirits, to gaze into the Light that is seen in its wholeness only by the Light itself. (*Con.* II, v, 8–10)

Dante did not lose his rather naive interest in the names and ranks of the angelic choirs, but by the time he came to write the *Paradiso* he had clearly changed his mind about the status of his authorities. Beatrice places *Serafi* and *Cherubi* at the head of the list, as always; but *Troni* replace *Podestadi* in the third position. In fact, Dionysius's sequence is asserted throughout:

The God-like creatures of the second hierarchy are, first, Dominions, and then Virtues, with Powers as the third order. Principalities and Archangels circle in the two penultimate rings of the sacred dance, while the last is wholly the disport of Angels:

> In essa gerarcia son l'altre dee:
> prima Dominazioni, e poi Virtudi;
> l'ordine terzo di Podestadi èe.
>   Poscia ne' due penultimi tripudi
> Principati e Arcangeli si girano;
> l'ultimo è tutto d'Angelici ludi.   (*Par.* XXVIII, 121–6)

As will be seen even in these relatively simple terzinas, the laboured and repetitive prose of the *Convivio* has given way to a poetic language that is as daring and outlandish as the Latin translations of the *Celestial Hierarchy*. And Dante's change of allegiance is finally spelt out in the closing lines of Beatrice's speech:

Dionysius gave himself over to the contemplation of these orders with such fervour that he was able to name and distinguish them as I have done. Gregory ventured to differ; but when he opened his eyes in this heaven, he was forced to smile at himself. You must not be astonished that a mere mortal, still on earth, could proclaim a secret of such magnitude; for it was revealed to him, together with many other things concerning these spheres, by one who had seen them here in heaven. (130–9)

Dionysius is therefore reinstated as the supreme authority on the celestial hierarchies, because he had been the disciple of St Paul. But it is worth noting that Dante will still maintain a certain independence of his source. While he makes Beatrice insist that the Seraphs are closer to God in the ardour of their love for Him, he also makes her insist that their love is greatest because they 'see most deeply into the Truth that satisfies every intellect'. In other words, their love for God is greater than that of the Cherubs because their knowledge of Him is greater; and in this way Dante has undermined the claims to supreme knowledge usually made on behalf of the second order.[32]

Again, while Dante does not restate in the *Comedy* the trinitarian arguments of the *Convivio*, he certainly had not abandoned them. Critics have noticed that the structure and layout of the *Paradiso* are deeply influenced by the same pattern of thought. The grouping of the souls of the blessed who come to greet Dante in each of the planetary heavens is not determined by astrological associations alone, and the topics discussed in the doctrinal passages are not treated in a random order. The three lowest heavens are primarily dedicated to Love and the Holy Spirit; the next three belong to Intellect and the Son; while the three highest are reserved for the Power of the Father.[33]

Demonology

There remains one last purely Christian or purely religious component in

Dante's beliefs concerning the angels. Within a matter of seconds of their creation, he tells us, a large body of the angels, perhaps a tenth of the total number, rose in proud rebellion and were driven out of heaven into the 'pit'. That 'pit' is of course the underworld of Hell; the fallen angels are the devils or demons; and the Devil par excellence is their leader, Lucifer, once the Prince of Light, now the 'Emperor of the Dolorous Realm', where he is known by the new and sinister names of Satan and Beelzebub.[34]

Angels fell from all nine orders. There are nine circles in Dante's Hell. His Satan has the six wings of a Seraph, and a demon from the eighth circle is described as 'one of the black Cherubim'. It is therefore plausible that Dante intended us to deduce that the devils stationed in any one circle are all drawn from one order, and that the sequence of the hierarchies is maintained in such a way that the highest circle is manned by 'legionaries' from the lowest order of angels.[35]

To these nine legions we must add the 'evil choir of angels who were neither rebels to God nor loyal to him, but who stood for themselves':

> . . . quel cattivo coro
> de li angeli che non furon ribelli
> né fur fedeli a Dio, ma per sé fuoro.   (*Inf.* III, 37–9)

Fittingly, 'they too are driven from Heaven in order not to mar its beauty; but they are not received into the depths of Hell, lest the damned should gain some glory from their presence there':

> Caccianli i ciel per non esser men belli,
> né lo profondo inferno li riceve,
> ch'alcuna gloria i rei avrebber d'elli.   (40–2)

Instead they inhabit a no-man's-land, the so-called Vestibule or *Antinferno*, which lies between the gate of Hell and the first coil of the infernal river where Charon ferries the souls over the Acheron.

There will be no need for us to go deeply into Dante's demonology. Devils make only one brief appearance in the action of the *Inferno* until the protagonist reaches the ten 'pockets of evil', or *Malebolge*, which form the penultimate circle; and Dante's inspiration is drawn not from his reading in theology, but from painting, folk-tales and the popular religious drama.[36]

The devils are horned, winged, fleet of foot, and sharp of shoulder. In certain cases they are allowed to go and collect the souls of the damned from the upper world; and they may even snatch the soul of a traitor in the very instant of his treachery, leaving a devil behind to inhabit the body until the day appointed for its natural death. They will struggle with angels – another folk-motif – for the possession of a soul whose fate is uncertain; and while they lose the contest for the young Buonconte da

Montefeltro, a Ghibelline general who died of wounds received in battle, but who had time to shed a tear of true repentance before he expired, they triumphantly carry off the soul of his father, the crafty and calculating Guido, notwithstanding his Franciscan habit and the absolution he had received from the Pope himself.[37]

In Hell, their task is to oversee the torments of the damned. They are shown as armed with whips in one instance and with iron hooks in another. Where the punishment consists of immersion, they are described as thrusting the souls back below the surface like cooks prodding meat down into a stew. Their activities are reported with great gusto in Dante's long account of his adventures in the fifth *bolgia* where a group of ten devils, with grotesque names, are allowed to run riot. They lie to Virgil about the path he should follow; they threaten the terrified pilgrim; they express themselves in the highly-spiced, scurrilous language of the Florentine 'underworld'; they catch a sinner, but allow him to slip away; they fight among themselves, until two of them fall into the boiling pitch. They give chase to the two poets, who are forced to make an undignified getaway by sliding down the slope into the next ditch. But the devils' impotence is stressed in our final glimpse of the band as they glare down at their intended victims. They are powerless to pursue their prey any further. Against their will they remain 'ministers of high providence'; and their sphere of action is strictly limited. They are like the gargoyles on a Gothic cathedral, harmless to those who have a clear conscience, and useful in spite of themselves.[38]

In fact, it may not be too far-fetched to claim that all the devils described in the first cantica are there to further the cause of the good. They are as black in appearance and in heart as their heavenly counterparts are white; and they exist in order to sharpen our awareness of the angelic *candore*. Their cruelty should excite a contempt that will enhance our admiration for the gentleness and consideration shown by the guardian angels in Purgatory. And such a deliberate contrast of negative and positive images is nowhere more apparent than in Dante's presentation of Lucifer.

Once the highest of the high, he is now the lowest of the low, a 'vile worm' stuck fast in the very centre of the earth and of the universe, at the furthest point from God. Once the most beautiful being in the whole of creation, he is now revoltingly ugly. He has three heads in a grim parody of the Three-Person God; but the possession of six eyes merely gives him extra vents for his tears, and the three mouths are no longer vehicles of praise, but instruments of torture for the souls of the arch-traitors who are crushed and mauled between his jaws. His three heads are of different colours; but the white, green and red of the theological virtues, or the white, gold and living flame of the angels in heaven, have given place to black, off-yellow and a sinister vermilion. He still retains his six Seraph's wings, but they are bat-like now; and their beating produces neither a gentle breeze with ambrosial fragrance, nor the vivifying breath associated with the Holy Spirit, but a cold wind that turns the last section of the infernal river into the frozen ice of Lake Cocytus.[39]

Angels, demons and the pagan gods

We turn away now from the Bible and works of theology to the more strictly philosophical aspects of the subject, and to texts where angels are known by such names as 'movers', 'mirrors', 'essences', 'intelligences', 'separate substances' or even 'subsistences'.[40] It will be possible to gather the main topics under just three heads, and it is helpful to recognize that all of them derive from the philosophers of Greece and Rome, and, in particular, from their independent critique of polytheistic religion.

Looking behind the absurdities, complexities and contradictions evident in the proliferation of local deities and cults, the philosophers had begun to search for some common denominator, some kernel of truth, in the traditional stories about gods or supernatural beings and the part they were alleged to play in the creation of the universe, in the advent of natural disasters, or in the reversals of fortune so common in human affairs. Among the followers of Epicurus, as we saw in the Introduction, rationalism and scepticism led to a total rejection of superstitious beliefs and practices. Plato and Aristotle already spoke of God in the singular, and the Stoics were to elaborate the concept of a universal Providence. Educated men were groping towards the kind of philosophical monotheism that would later find expression in a memorable line which the poet Lucan puts into the mouth of Cato, and which Dante would quote in the form: 'Everything you see and everywhere you go is Jupiter'–'Juppiter est quodcunque vides, quocunque moveris.'[41]

In many cases the cultural heritage could be safeguarded by treating the myths as moral fables, or as allegorical fictions embodying some truth about physical forces.[42] There seems to have been a reluctance, even among advanced thinkers, to dismiss all those tales about spirits and gods as being totally without foundation. And it is significant that Epicurus himself admitted the existence–though not the causal activity–of a race of gods.

Thirteenth-century Christians had no hesitations or doubts in interpreting the same evidence; and Dante's position is wholly typical of his culture. From his vantage-point it was clear that the gods of Virgil's Rome were 'lying and false', in the sense that Jupiter, Mercury, Mars and Venus did not exist and had never existed. The 'ancient peoples' really did live 'in ancient error'. But a dispassionate eye could see that they had not been completely deluded. Supernatural agents had been at work; it was simply that they had not been correctly identified. The fact that the

pagans sought to appease malevolent deities and the gods of the underworld showed that they had experience of demons; while their 'sacrifices
and votive cries' to the kindlier Olympians argued their awareness of
angels.[43]

'Substances separate from matter'

The first group of purely philosophical problems all relate to the question
'What is it like to be a spiritual being?' By the thirteenth century, the
rather vague and tentative answers put forward by the Fathers of the
Church could no longer satisfy those who sought to reconcile their belief
in angels with their adherence to the rediscovered logic, physics and
psychology of Aristotle.

A Christian Aristotelian had first to make up his mind whether angels
had an aetherial body (as some more traditional theologians still inclined
to believe) or whether they were not wholly incorporeal.[44] If they were
incorporeal, he had to justify the apparent impossibility that a form could
enjoy independent being as a distinct substance (and not simply as an idea
in the Divine Mind) without some material substrate in which the form
was realized. Once he had extricated himself from such logical and
metaphysical traps, and had committed himself to the view that angels
were 'substances separate from matter', he was faced with a series of
questions in physics. Was it possible to say that a pure form, without any
dimensions, existed in space? If so, how many such 'dimension-less'
forms could be in the same place at the same time? Can an immaterial
form move? And, if so, how long would it take to move from one location
to another?[45]

Dante displays very little interest in problems of this fundamental, but
more abstruse kind, but he does commit himself to two points of fact.
Angels, he makes it clear, are incorporeal and immortal (or rather
'incorruptible'). To these conclusions he adds two more undisputed
facts: angels have an intellect, and they have a will.[46] With respect to the
first pair of propositions, angels are of course *un*like man; but with respect
to the second, they are so *like* man that they share with us those very
features which distinguish us from the animals and make us human.[47]
Not unnaturally, therefore, Dante concentrates his attention on the
interaction of the four truths. He tries to establish what it must be like to
know and to will without the restrictions imposed by a mortal body. He
studies the angelic mode of knowing and loving in order to gain a better
understanding of our human condition. For, if the demons are in the
Comedy to illuminate the angels, the angels are there to illuminate man.

As incorporeal beings, then, angels do not possess the bodily organs of
sensation. They have nothing which corresponds to the eyes or ears, nor

to the 'common sense' or the 'imagination'. Their knowledge is in no way circumscribed by the inherent limitations of material 'receptors' (the limitations of which were so consistently exposed in Dante's encounters with the guardian angels on the terraces). As incorruptible beings, dwelling in the immediate presence of God, they do not slowly elaborate concepts from their sense-experience of particular things; and they do not refine those primary concepts by a process of composition and division. They do not reason and they never learn. They intuit all the universal forms of things as they exist in the mind of God, and they know particular truths as they are reflected there. They are never wearied by their contemplation, and the 'light' will never fail them. Their intellection is direct, simultaneous and eternal. In the *Monarchia*, Dante describes it as being 'without intermission', *sine interpolatione*.[48] In the *Purgatorio*, he makes Beatrice say to the angelic chorus in the Garden of Eden: 'You are ever alert in the eternal day; neither sleep nor night can steal from you a single step that the world takes on its paths':

> Voi vigilate ne l'etterno die,
> sì che notte né sonno a voi non fura
> passo che faccia il secol per sue vie. (*Purg.* XXX, 103–5)

In the *De vulgari eloquentia*, Dante makes it plain that angels do not need anything akin to human language, with its sensible signs, to express and communicate concepts:

The angels' intellect has the inexpressible power of making its glorious concepts known in the instant. By virtue of this power, one angel is fully revealed to another, either directly in himself, or indirectly in that most brilliant Mirror (*speculum*) in which all the angels are reflected without diminution of their beauty, and at which they all fervently gaze (*speculantur*), having no need of a linguistic sign. (I, ii, 3)

In the *Paradiso*, Dante marks out one last contrast between the angelic and the human ways of knowing. Angels do not have a memory:

Ever since they were first gladdened by the sight of the divine countenance, from which nothing is hidden, they have never turned away from it. Their vision is never intercepted by some new object, and so they have no need to recall concepts which have been displaced by other concepts:

> Queste sustanze, poi che fur gioconde
> de la faccia di Dio, non volser viso
> da essa, da cui nulla si nasconde:
>   però non hanno vedere interciso
> da novo obietto, e però non bisogna
> rememorar per concetto diviso. (*Par.* XXIX, 76–81)

There are some limitations imposed even on the angelic mind. An angel can never achieve the fullness of God's own self-knowledge. Some truths lie so deep in the abyss of His eternal decree that they are cut off from every created vision, and they are hidden even from the highest Seraph whose eye is fixed most closely on God:

> quel serafin che 'n Dio più l'occhio ha fisso,
> a la dimanda tua non satisfara,
>   però che sì s'innoltra ne lo abisso
> de l'etterno statuto quel che chiedi,
> che da ogne creata vista è scisso.

(Par. XXI, 92–6)

The Psalmist said that man was 'created a *little* lower than the angels', '*poco* minore che li angeli' in Dante's translation. But it will be evident that there is an element of hyperbole in this claim if it is referred to man's rational powers here on earth.[49]

The angels have a faculty for loving as good what the intellect knows as good and conformable to their nature.[50] It is known by the same name as the equivalent faculty in man – *voluntas*, or the 'will'; and, as we shall see more fully in the final chapter, it is the ground or condition of their freedom, responsibility and worth. But its operation is as different from that of the human will as the angels' 'intuition' is different from our 'inquisition', or as eternity is from time.[51]

If we make use of the (strictly speaking) inappropriate categories of 'past', 'present' and 'future', the exercise of will by the separate substances might be described as follows. Within instants of their creation, the rebel angels freely chose and willed *not* to give their Creator the love and reverence that was His due. They were immediately driven out of Heaven and will never return. At the same moment, the loyal angels acknowledged their dependence on God and their loving gratitude for the gift of being. They sought spiritual union with Him, showing a fervour proportionate to the depth of their understanding of His nature, which in turn depended on the species, order and hierarchy in which they had been created. As a reward for that freely offered love and service, God gave them 'illuminating grace' – again in the measure of their love and deserving – such that their wills were thereafter immutable. They can never turn aside from God; they have a 'firm and full will', *ferma e piena volontate*. They will never abandon the expression of their eternal love.[52]

Human beings may be tempted to turn away from God and yet live on to turn back again and be saved with the help of His grace. The demons will never know grace or salvation. The angels will never know temptation. But it must be re-emphasized that these temporal categories are not appropriate to the separate substances. They do not experience a 'then', a 'now', or a 'sometime'. There was or is no interval between their creation, their willed choice, and the receiving of grace or damnation in accordance with their deserts. Considered as speculative beings, they do not have a history.

The separate substances as intelligences and movers

There is, however, a sense in which angels are the source of time and change and of all the recurrent movements in the history of the universe. To put the matter very baldly, Dante believed that some of the separate substances lead an active rather than a contemplative life. They initiate and sustain the various 'proper' motions of the heavenly spheres, and by so doing they are the cause of the effects that these motions produce here on earth. And this in turn implies that they are the universal causes of the whole continuous cycle of coming into being and ceasing to be.

The theory that angels caused the revolutions of the celestial spheres had become fairly widely accepted in the universities of Western Europe by the later decades of the thirteenth century (although there was still strenuous resistance on the part of some theologians). It was the result, clearly, of a fusion of Christian belief with elements drawn from various non-Christian sources—notably, Greek and Arab astrology; the account of celestial motion propounded by Aristotle; and Neoplatonist theories involving an emanation of intelligences from the One. Dante himself was well aware of this mixed parentage, and it will be instructive to follow his own account of the theory and its evolution as he presents it in the second book of the *Convivio*.

This second book takes the form of a commentary to one of the *canzoni* Dante wrote to record his love for Lady Philosophy, and a good half of the commentary is devoted to an exposition of the poem's opening line, which runs, in translation, 'You who by thought move the third heaven'. After he has expatiated on the 'third heaven', Dante addresses himself to the subject and verb of the line, and asks himself: 'Who are these beings that move it?', 'chi sono questi che 'l muovono?' His answer begins:

The first point to grasp is that the Movers of these heavens are substances without matter, that is, intelligences, whom ordinary people call angels:

... li *movitori* di quelli sono *sustanze separate da materia*, cioè *intelligenze*, le quali la volgare gente chiamano *Angeli*. (*Con.* II, iv, 2)

Once he has established the identity of these four terms, Dante goes on to give a very brief sketch of their independent histories before they were merged to form the 'United States of Truth'. Typically, he is concerned to show that reason and experience had anticipated revelation and were not in conflict with it. [53] The ancient philosophers had disagreed amongst themselves, and no one of them had been able to grasp the whole truth about spiritual creatures, but they had reached a number of conclusions that were still valid:

Different people have held different views about these creatures, just as they did about the heavens, although the truth has now been discovered. There were certain philosophers, among them, it would seem, Aristotle in his *Metaphysics* (although a passing remark in his *De caelo* suggests that he may have held other opinions), who believed that the number of these creatures corresponded exactly to the number of distinct circulations in the heavens—just so many and no more. They held that any other creatures would have existed eternally in vain, that is, without performing any task or activity (*operazione*); and they thought this was impossible, since their being was their activity. (iv, 3)

In the first book of the *De caelo*, as we saw in Chapter 6, Aristotle had not dissented from the popular view that there might be some form of divine life existing outside the heavens, and therefore outside the boundaries of time and space. In the second book he asserted positively that the heavens were *animate* bodies. In other words, he said that the motion of a given sphere is caused by an intelligent being, that this being is the soul or form of the sphere, and that it is therefore part of the physical universe.[54] In the twelfth book of his *Metaphysics,* however, where we find his mature thought on the celestial motions and their relation to a Prime Mover, Aristotle has modified both his earlier positions; and he makes it clear that each of the spheres is moved by an intelligence who is separate from that sphere, and who is eternal and unmoving. The separate substances now have a role to play in the workings of the cosmos, but they are not the form of any physical part.[55] So much then for the contribution made by Aristotle. Now let us see what Dante has to say about the Platonists:

There were others, like Plato, a man of outstanding genius, who agreed that there must be one intelligence for every distinct movement of the heavens, but who went on to postulate the existence of as many intelligences as there are distinct species of things (by 'species' we mean classes: thus, all men form one species, all gold another, all magnitudes another, and so with everything). They believed that the intelligences controlling these spheres had brought those spheres into being, each its own. And they argued that all other things are brought into being by these other intelligences in the same way, each being the cause and exemplar of its own species. Plato called these intelligences 'ideas', which is to say 'universal forms' or 'universal natures'. (iv, 4–5)

As an exposition of Plato's theory of forms, this may leave a little to be desired. But the confusion is due as much to the extreme compression as to any misunderstanding on Dante's part of the information he had received at second hand. And if we recognize that he is trying to summarize a whole current of thought, rather than the distinctive contribution of one man, we shall find that he has in fact mentioned most of the relevant features in the cosmogonies of Plato's later disciples.

It is, then, true that Plato posited the existence of a world of absolute, eternal realities that he called Forms or Ideas, and that these include not just the archetypes of all the species of plants, minerals and animals, but abstract categories like magnitude, beauty, unity or goodness. It is also true that Plato did suggest, in the long myth of creation that makes up his *Timaeus*, that the Supreme Craftsman was assisted in the production of things by the celestial bodies (who are treated as divine beings) and by lesser gods; and Plato did teach that material things are produced as copies of the universal Forms or paradigms.[56]

This myth was profoundly modified in later Platonism, where the act of creation was imaged as an 'out-flowing' or 'out-shining' of being from the One. In the philosophy of Plotinus (d. A.D. 270), the One gives rise to Intellect, Intellect gives rise to Soul, and Soul is responsible for the formation of bodies in the visible world, and, by 'implication', of the matter of the whole universe.[57] Later thinkers, such as Iamblichus (d. 326), multiplied the number of separate emanations or processions lying between the One and the most perfect bodies in the material world–the heavens. In effect, as we noted in Chapter 5, they assumed that the Scale of Being must extend upwards into the intellectual order; and they postulated many different degrees of purely *intellectual* existence lying between the heavens and the One to match the many degrees of *sensible* existence between the heavens and the element of Earth.[58] In the thought of Proclus (d. 490), which exercised a considerable influence on the *Celestial Hierarchy* of Dionysius, and which was known to Dante and his age through a short anonymous compilation called the *Liber de causis*, these intelligences are represented as a hierarchy of secondary causes, who receive being and energy from above, and communicate being and energy to those who are below them on the ladder. Each intelligence is also said to be 'full of forms', *plena formis*; and in this way a connection is re-established with the Platonic Forms and with the gods or divine beings who collaborated with the Craftsman in the *Timaeus*.[59]

The whole composite theory was later enriched by Arab philosophers who were to make more explicit the obvious parallels between this hierarchy of intelligences and the 'separate substances' who, in Aristotle's theory, move the heavenly spheres. Once this identification had been made, it also became possible to incorporate the popular science of astrology and its humbler teachings about the 'influences' rained down from the planets and the stars. As a result, astrological teachings could be modified and rendered harmless in the eyes of Moslem (and, later, of Christian) theologians. It was no longer necessary to conceive the heavenly bodies as independent deities or blind physical forces, since they could now be presented as the instruments used by the intelligences in their causal activity. The astral 'influences' are simply one aspect of their never-ending work of inducing or impressing forms in matter. By the early eleventh century, Avicenna (d. 1037) could combine the doctrines of Plato and Aristotle, astronomy and astrology, 'intelligences' and 'movers', to arrive at the following synthesis. God is the immediate cause of the first intelligence. The first intelligence is the immediate cause of the soul and body of the *primum mobile* and of the second intelligence. The second intelligence is the immediate cause of the soul and body of the Starry Heaven and of the third intelligence. This process continues through the planetary spheres and their intelligences, until we reach the Heaven of the Moon. The ninth intelligence produces the body and soul of the lunar sphere and the 'agent intellect', who is then responsible for the induction or impression of the forms of sublunary existence.[60]

Dante was not entirely misinformed, therefore, when he attributed to Plato and his followers the discovery of Forms and Intelligences and the recognition of the part they play in the causal activity that produces *le spezie de le cose*. A short passage from the third book of the *Convivio* will serve to document his familiarity with the *Liber de causis* and his clear grasp of the specifically Platonist elements in the complete synthesis:

As we can read in the *Liber de causis*, each of the celestial Intellects knows what is above and below himself. He knows God as his cause and the lower beings as his effects. Now, God is the cause of all things in the most universal sense. Hence, by knowing God, an Intelligence knows all things in himself, insofar as the limitations of his individual nature permit. Hence, all the intelligences know the human form as it is framed as an idea in the Divine Mind. And the intelligences who move the spheres know it better than all the others do, because they are the immediate causes of this as of every other generated form. They know the human form in the fullness of its possible perfection, and it is this they take as their exemplar and paradigm.

All that is lacking here is the formal identification of these Platonist intelligences with the Christian angels; and this follows in the very next sentence where we read:

The pattern and exemplar of human nature exists in the mind of God, and thus in the minds of all the intelligences, especially those *angelic minds who use the heavens to manufacture things here on earth*, '. . . massimamente in quelle menti angeliche che fabbricano col cielo queste cose di qua giuso'. (*Con.* III, vi, 4–6)

To witness the final ceremony in this 'treaty of union' (if we may pursue the image of Dante's theory as being a federation of formerly independent states) we must return to the second book of the *Convivio*. Having dealt with the Platonists, Dante takes note of the evidence provided by the pagan religions, and then puts forward some arguments of his own to show that there are purely rational grounds for the belief that there must be an almost infinite number of *contemplative* intelligences in addition to those who 'fabbricano col cielo le cose di qua giuso'. The arguments are very revealing of their author, but not very convincing (as Dante is the first to admit), and they need not side-track us here, since the same conclusions are immediately restated on the authority of

Jesus himself, who disclosed that his Father had 'many legions of angels'.[61]

It is at this point that Dante expounds the teaching of the Church with regard to the angelic hierarchies, and contributes his own interpretation of the way in which they contemplate the Three Persons of the Trinity. Then a passage from the Psalms, in which the heavens themselves are said to 'declare the glory of God', allows him to relate the nine celestial spheres and their movers to the nine orders of angels. He continues:

> It is reasonable to believe that the Movers of the Heaven of the Moon are drawn from the order of Angels, that those of Mercury are drawn from the order of Archangels, and that the Movers of Venus are the Thrones.

Now, in Dante's scheme, this third order of angels (later to be named as Principalities rather than Thrones) contemplate the Holy Spirit. Hence:

> These Movers are one in nature with the love of the Holy Spirit, and they perform their connatural activity by causing the movement of the third heaven. This movement is filled with love, and hence the form of the heaven acquires the power to inflame, by which the souls of creatures here on earth are kindled to love in accordance with their dispositions. And because the ancients realized that this heaven was the cause of love here below, they said that Love was the son of Venus. (*Con.* II, v, 13–15)

Pagan worship of Venus and Cupid, astrological beliefs in the power of a planet to excite sexual desire, Aristotle's explanation of how the heavens move, Plato's implied simile of a team of builders and masons who realize the blueprints of a Master Architect, the Neoplatonists' vision of an emanation of intelligences from the One and of their causal activity as links in an unbroken chain of being, a mystic's dream of a celestial hierarchy of spiritual beings who contemplate and worship the Almighty on his throne—these are the most important components of Dante's angelology, and they are all implied in this brief passage, where they are seen to be held together and rendered innocuously orthodox by their subordination to the providential design of the Christian Trinity.

L'essemplo e l'essemplare

We must now leave Dante in his role as philosopher and historian of ideas and return to Dante philomythes. We began this chapter by considering his poetic representation of the angels in their biblical role as 'ministers and messengers of eternal life', and we shall bring it to a close by examining his representation of the angels as the Neoplatonist movers of the heavenly spheres.

Almost immediately after his arrival in the *primum mobile*, Dante becomes aware that Beatrice's eyes are shining with a reflected light whose source must lie behind him. Turning round, he finds the same kind of spectacle that had been enacted for him in the Heavens of the Sun, Mars and Jupiter. A point of dazzling light, infinitesimally small and infinitely bright, is surrounded by nine concentric circles, each of which is formed by thousands upon thousands of living lights, later to be called 'sparks'—*scintille*.[62] Since these nine circles are circling round the point of light, the reader is tempted to assume that the display is a working model of the universe, illustrating the nine spherical heavens as they revolve around the still earth at the centre. But Dante as narrator insists on three features that are inimical to this assumption. First, as we have noted, the still centre is luminous. Second, the period of revolution is not the same for all the circles; and the circle which is actually moving fastest is not, as one would expect, the outermost, corresponding to the *primum mobile*, but the innermost: in fact, each sphere in turn is said to revolve more slowly, the further it is removed from the centre.[63] Third, the radiance emitted by the *scintille* who make up each circle diminishes in intensity in proportion to their distance from the central point of light.

Dante-character is perplexed by these inconsistencies:

If the universe were structured in the order I see in these wheels, my appetite would be satisfied by what has been set before it. But in the world accessible to the senses, one sees that the spheres are more godlike [in their increasing brightness and speed] the further they are from the centre. So, if my desire is to be assuaged in this wondrous temple of the angels, bounded by Light and Love alone, you must explain how the original and the copy do not follow the same mode. Left to myself, I should speculate in vain.

> . . . Se 'l mondo fosse posto
> con l'ordine ch'io veggio in quelle rote,
> sazio m'avrebbe ciò che m'è proposto;
>   ma nel mondo sensibile si puote
> veder le volte tanto più divine,
> quant' elle son dal centro più remote.
>   Onde, se 'l mio disir dee aver fine
> in questo miro e angelico templo
> che solo amore e luce ha per confine,
>   udir convienmi ancor come l'essemplo
> e l'essemplare non vanno d'un modo,
> ché io per me indarno a ciò contemplo.
>
> (*Par.* XXVIII, 46–57).

The correspondences between the *exemplar*, the model or original idea, and the *exemplatum*, the copy or realization of that idea, are indeed rather bewildering here. The *scintille* that spin and glow with decreasing velocity and radiance in these nine circles are not the souls of the blessed, but the nine choirs of angels, with the Seraphs nearest the centre, and the Angels at the extremity. They are not representing the nine heavens, but 'miming' their own eternal functions in a special visible form; for, as we have seen, the angels are the 'movers' of the heavenly spheres, and each order controls the revolution of one heaven. The point of light is not the terrestrial globe, but a manifestation of God. As Beatrice explains, in words taken almost *verbatim* from Aristotle, He is 'the point from which the heavens and all nature depend'.[64] Once these identifications have been made, it is less difficult to see why 'l'essemplo e l'essemplare non vanno d'un modo'.

God is infinite and the first cause of all things. The 'body' which most resembles him and is most 'divine' must be the most active, the one that exercises the greatest influence on other bodies. In the material, sensible universe, so Beatrice reasons, this must be the largest and most swiftly-moving body. And since the universe is built up of concentric spheres, the largest, swiftest body can only be the *sphaera suprema*, the *primum mobile*, which communicates the divine energy to all the heavens that lie within it, and sweeps them all round in its diurnal motion.[65] It is natural to assume that this most God-like or divine of the physical bodies must lie 'nearest' to God. Hence, we usually conceive or imagine God as the uncircumscribed but all-circumscribing *circumference*, who embraces and enfolds the world of space, movement and time, in the stillness, infinity and eternity of the Empyrean.[66]

But this is only one convenient projection. It has no exclusive validity. God is also the point of origin and *centre* of all things; and this is precisely what Dante is trying to convey through this alternative projection. The angelic orders form a hierarchy, no less than the heavens that they move; and their motion cannot be other than circular. Their greater and lesser resemblance to God is still expressed by their relative distances from him, and by their relative velocities. In the non-material supra-sensible world, however, it is not the immensity of the angels' extension into three-dimensional space that constitutes the God-like feature, but the intensity of their radiance: God is here revealed as a point of *light*. The brightest and fastest-moving circle of the angels who know and love God the most is therefore the one *closest* to the centre, the one whose circumference is no greater than a halo round the moon. Nevertheless, these are the movers of the *primum mobile*. The innermost circle in this projection corresponds to the outermost heaven in the other. But let us read Dante's superbly lucid and balanced lines:

The corporeal spheres are broad and narrow in proportion to the energy and influence that extends to their every part. The greater is their goodness, the greater is the benefit they confer; and assuming that all its parts are equal in perfection, the greater body must contain the greater benefit.

> Li cerchi corporai sono ampi e arti
> secondo il più e 'l men de la virtute
> che si distende per tutte lor parti.

> Maggior bontà vuol far maggior salute;
> maggior salute maggior corpo cape,
> s'elli ha le parti igualmente compiute.   (*Par.* XXVIII, 64-9)

'Therefore, the heaven that sweeps the rest of the universe round with it in its course corresponds to the angelic circle that knows God most and loves him best. If you measure the influence rather than the apparent size of the *substantiae* who show themselves to you in circular form, you will see a marvellous correspondence of greater to more, and smaller to less, as between every heaven and its intelligence.'

> Dunque costui che tutto quanto rape
> l'altro universo seco, corrisponde
> al cerchio che più ama e che più sape:
>   per che, se tu a la virtù circonde
> la tua misura, non a la parvenza
> de le sustanze che t'appaion tonde,
>   tu vederai mirabil consequenza
> di maggio a più e di minore a meno,
> in ciascun cielo, a süa intelligenza.   (70-8)

The new projection does not replace the old. Dante has not recanted any of his beliefs 'concerning the heavens'. He will stress that in this vision God only *seemed* to be enclosed by the angels whom he encloses.[67] We are compelled to talk about God and to represent Him through finite images, that is, through comparison with His handiworks. But even when we use the pure, immaterial images of geometrical forms, we must be on our guard. We must be prepared to withdraw them or deny them as soon as they have been affirmed, lest they compromise the infinity of God. We must use the resources of paradox. This last spectacle in Dante's journey through the physical heavens is his own way of reminding us of the ancient paradoxical definition of God, best known in its formulation by Alan of Lille: 'God is an intelligible sphere, whose centre is everywhere and whose circumference nowhere'; 'Deus est sphaera intelligibilis, cuius centrum est ubique, et circumferentia nusquam.'[68]

PART 2

Coming into being

8

Images of God as maker

Metaphorismatics

THE GREEK POET AND PHILOSOPHER, EMPEDOCLES, ONCE ATTEMPTED to explain the saltness of seawater by saying that 'the sea is the sweat of the earth'. The striking phrase found no favour with Aristotle, however, who commented dryly that 'such a statement is perhaps satisfactory in poetry, for metaphor is a poetic device; but it does not advance our knowledge of nature'.[1]

The clear-headedness and native caution evident in this typical reprimand were not without influence on subsequent philosophers, but even Aristotle's greatest admirers seem to have been powerless to resist the blandishments of simile, metaphor and myth when they turned their minds to the subject of the First Creation and the origin of species. And from one point of view, it is scarcely too much to say that all philosophical and theological speculation about the Beginning of Things has been bedevilled by the persistence of mythical and metaphorical modes of thought inherited from earlier and more primitive phases in the history of Western culture and religion.

It is, of course, possible to vindicate the use of figurative language in this kind of context, and Dante justifies his own ever more daring use of fiction and metaphor in the *Paradiso* by sketching out two of the more familiar lines of defence. The first may be called the argument from linguistic need. 'We can see many things with our intellect', he writes in the epistle to Can Grande, 'for which language has no signs; and Plato makes this clear enough by his use of metaphorical locutions (*per assumptionem metaphorismorum*), because he saw many things by the light of his intellect that he was unable to express in plain language (*sermone proprio*).'[2] The second may be called the argument from human nature. It had long been used by theologians to defend the parables of Jesus or the tropes and figures found so abundantly in the poetic and prophetic books of the Bible, and it forms the nucleus of Dante's poetic in the *Comedy*.[3] He enunciates it in these terms:

This is the way you have to talk to the human mind, because the information from which true knowledge is subsequently abstracted all derives from concrete

205

objects perceived by the senses [literally: 'because only from sense perception does the mind grasp what it then makes fit for the intellect']. This is why the Scriptures make concession to your mode of knowing, and speak of God as having 'feet' and 'hands', while intending something quite distinct.

> Così parlar conviensi al vostro ingegno,
> però che solo da sensato apprende
> ciò che fa poscia d'intelletto degno.
> Per questo la Scrittura condescende
> a vostra facultate, e piedi e mano
> attribuisce a Dio, e altro intende.   (*Par.* IV, 40–5)

We cannot enter here into a full discussion of the status of figurative language in works of philosophy and theology. But these few seminal texts and references may already be enough to indicate the scope and relevance of the subject, and to make it plain why our study of Dante's ideas concerning creation and generation must begin with a survey of the 'picture-language' underlying the sometimes rather elusive abstract concepts.

The treatment of this vast topic will of necessity be simple in the extreme. We shall not normally distinguish simile from metaphor. The most fossilized of dead metaphors will be treated on the same plane as some of Dante's most sublime utterances. We shall proceed on the assumption that all the images were current among Christian writers long before the thirteenth century, and we shall not be concerned to assess the extent of Dante's originality in their use. Similarly, we shall not probe deeply into the very diverse provenance of the various images, although the sources may range from the Book of Genesis to Plato's *Timaeus*, from traditional myth to a philosopher's allegory, and from everyday experience to a far-fetched poet's conceit. With one exception, also, we shall avoid the many semantic problems surrounding the definition of 'image' and 'concept' and the relationship between them.

The solitary exception to these self-denying ordinances is that we shall constantly return to the fact that an image is never emotionally neutral. No matter how circumspectly and clinically a comparison may be presented, the 'vehicle' will always carry with it a penumbra of associations and overtones, which will inevitably be transferred onto the 'tenor', that is, onto the concept or process which requires explanation or illustration. Very often, the penumbra is just as important and just as persuasive as the hard core of intended meaning; and it will therefore be necessary to comment briefly on these connotations and to indicate in each case whether they are broadly flattering or unflattering – *ad laudem*, or *ad vituperium*.

The main objective of this chapter, however, is to make the reader familiar with the eight images, or 'clusters' of images, that appear again and again in the writings of Dante and his masters, where they illustrate various aspects of God's activity as Maker or First Cause, or serve to clarify the relationship between Him and the universe considered as His handiwork or effect.

Light: (a) its nature and properties

The most important family of images habitually used in the contexts just described are those which can be conveniently gathered under the general heading of 'light'. Some of them are easily understood by anyone who has not been blind since birth. But many others do not reveal their full significance until one has some knowledge of medieval writings about the nature and properties of light.

These writings may be divided into three groups. The philosophers disputed among themselves concerning the definition of light. Was Aristotle correct to call it 'transparency in act'? Was light itself a 'substantial form' in which luminous bodies 'participated'? Or was it an 'active quality' inherent in the form of bodies like the sun or the stars?[4] The theologians, for their part, puzzled over the relationship between this familiar, 'sensible' light and what they called the 'light of reason', the 'light of grace', and the 'light of glory'.[5] At a humbler level, however, there was a wide measure of agreement, because the Latin West had inherited from the Arabs a substantial body of experimental facts concerning the behaviour of light.

Dante was familiar with writings of all three kinds, and he had a special predilection for the simple, geometrical propositions that made up the science of 'perspective', as the subject was then called.[6] From this applied science he learnt to use some of the more common words for light in their technical acceptations in order to distinguish three aspects or three phases in the diffusion of light. These distinctions are usually ignored by the layman, but they are worth recording because they offer a simple and helpful framework within which to classify the light images that are our concern.

Dante tells us in the *Convivio* that, according to the usage of the philosophers, the comprehensive term for light in all its manifestations is *lume* or, in Latin, *lumen*. When we need to specify light in the body of the sun or in a candle-flame, that is, in its active source or *fontale principio*, it is called *luce* (*lux*). When we refer to the light emanating from that source, as for example in the case of the sunlit air or the area illuminated by a candle, then we should call it *raggio* (*radius*): in English, it is more natural to speak in the plural of 'light-rays', or perhaps of 'radiant light'. And when, finally, we want to indicate light reflected (*ripercosso*) from the surface of an opaque body, we call it *splendore* (*splendor*). The whole passage is worth quoting in the original:

Dico che l'usanza de' filosofi è di chiamare *luce* lo lume, in quanto esso è nel suo fontale principio; di chiamare *raggio*, in quanto esso è per lo mezzo, dal principio al primo corpo dove si termina; di chiamare *splendore*, in quanto esso è in altra parte alluminata ripercosso. (*Con.* III, xiv, 5)

The relationship between the second and third of these categories does not present any difficulties. Reflected light is produced automatically whenever a ray of radiant light falls upon a reflecting surface. But how are we to conceive the production of *il raggio* from *la luce*? One answer is to be found in works like those of Robert Grosseteste, who stated that 'the intrinsic activity of light is to multiply itself and to diffuse itself immediately in every direction' (*lux . . . cuius per se est haec operatio, scilicet se ipsam multiplicare et in omnem partem subito diffundere*). Wherever there is even a *point* of 'light', therefore, it will instantly emit 'rays' all around itself and thus generate a sphere of 'radiant light' (*a puncto lucis sphaera lucis . . . subito generatur*).[7] Of its nature, light possesses the power to multiply itself—a *vis multiplicativa*.

Light: (b) 'God is light'

'Of all the things accessible to our senses in the world', Dante writes in the *Convivio*, 'none is more fitting to be a symbol (*essemplo*) of God than the sun.'[8] And when he addresses God directly as 'Light Eternal' in the last canto of the *Paradiso*, the metaphor is so familiar that we hardly perceive it as a metaphor at all. On occasion, Dante will revitalize this hallowed use of light-imagery by introducing technical terms borrowed from the science of perspective. For example, the Apostles' Creed already speaks of the Second Person of the Trinity as 'light from light' (*lumen de lumine*); but Dante will visualize the Son as a 'circle conceived as if it were *reflected* light' (*come lume reflesso*); and it is difficult not to see the influence of texts like those of Grosseteste on his first indirect vision of God as 'a point irradiating light' (*un punto che . . . raggiava lume*). However, the main point to establish for the moment is that nothing was more traditional than to speak of God as 'light'.[9] And while a cautious Aristotelian like St Thomas Aquinas was at pains to stress that such speech was metaphorical, there were other influential works in the thirteenth century which did not hesitate to affirm that God is Light literally and not figuratively: *Deus . . . lux . . . dicitur proprie et non translative.*[10]

Now, if God is conceived as a point of light, and if light has the power of self-diffusion, then it becomes possible to think of the First Creation as an 'out-shining' or 'illumination'. Dante can speak of God as the 'First Light who irradiates the angelic choirs in their entirety'; and he can say that 'His will is the cause of every created thing by an act of irradiation' (*. . . essa, radiando, lui cagiona*).[11] Such claims are bolder in their expression than anything to be found in the Bible. But it may be remembered that in the account given in the Book of Genesis, God's first creative command was 'Let there be light'; and by suggesting that light existed before the sun and moon, this sublime verse had opened the path for a thorough-going Neoplatonist interpretation of the biblical story.

When it is used of the creative act, the most important connotations of the light-image are those of effortless ease and of instantaneity. However great the distance involved, so it was then believed, illumination takes place in the instant; and as soon as something receives light it is fully lit (*illuminatio . . . fit in instanti . . .; nam simul aliquid illuminatur et illuminatum est*).[12] Or as Dante puts it: 'There is no interval between the coming of a ray of light into glass, amber or crystal and its being there completely':

> E come in vetro, in ambra o in cristallo
> *raggio resplende* sì, che dal venire
> a l'esser tutto *non è intervallo*.
>
> (*Par.* XXIX, 25–7)

It is significant, also, that this simile occurs at the very heart of Dante's own account of the First Creation, at the point where he insists (picking up the noun *raggio*, used literally, with the verb *raggiare*, used metaphorically) that there was no separation in time between the raying forth of prime matter, the heavens, and the angels; all three issued into complete being instantaneously and simultaneously:

> Così 'l triforme effetto del suo sire
> ne l'esser suo *raggiò insieme* tutto,
> sanza distinzïone in essordire.
>
> (28–30)

The same image clarifies not only the nature of God's creative act in the beginning but also the relationship between Him and the universe in time. His power and will sustain the universe, which will exist only so long as God continues to irradiate His divine energy. The eighth-century Platonist, John Scotus, expresses the idea through metaphor: 'The subsistence of all things sensible and intelligible is simply the illumination and diffusion of God's goodness.' In Dante's own century, Aquinas would use simile to make the same point with greater caution and exactitude: 'Every created thing is in the same relationship to God as is the air to the sun which illumines it. The preservation of things by God is not due to any new action but to the continuation of the action by which He gave being.' If the source of light were ever to be switched off, the sphere of radiance that is the universe would immediately cease to exist.[13]

Light: (c) The scale of luminosity

Everyday experience of light considered as *radius* made it easy to understand and accept the inequality of the different parts of creation. All things might share in the nature of the Creator, but they did not all share to the same extent. Reading by candlelight taught everyone that the level of illumination declines in proportion to one's distance from the flame. It was obvious, too, that some substances—like the glass, amber and crystal of Dante's simile—allow light to pass apparently undimmed, while others admit light only partially, and others again deny it any passage. A polished surface, like a precious stone or a mirror, reflects sunlight with dazzling intensity; a matt surface does not. A light colour reflects more light than a dark colour. In short, wherever one observed the behaviour of incident and reflected light, it was possible to detect a scale of greater and lesser intensity that was apparently inherent in the nature of light outside its source. There was a scale of luminosity, a scale of transparency, of reflection, and of hue. In each case the *radius* or *splendor* could be either brighter or dimmer, more or less like the *lux* whence it originated.

It was also clear that a great deal depended on whether the source was distant or close. And since it was axiomatic that no two bodies could be in the same place at the same time, it followed that all things were either more or less close to their source (*più al principio loro e men vicine*), and that therefore all things were *necessarily* more or less radiant than each other. The light-image suggested that all differences in form and kind are at bottom differences in degree. The scale of luminosity was therefore the perfect symbol of the scale of being.[14]

Some idea of the lengths to which even orthodox theologians were prepared to go in pursuit of these analogies can be gathered from the following much-quoted texts from St Bonaventure, the great Franciscan teacher, who was a contemporary and rival of St Thomas Aquinas in the Parisian schools during the 1260s, and who would become his collaborator and peer in the action of Dante's *Paradiso*:

God is light in the most literal sense (*propriissime*), and those things which draw nearest to Him share most in the nature of light. All the bodies which make up the universe are more and less noble according to whether they participate more or less in the nature of light. Light is the substantial form of all bodies. In proportion to their greater or lesser participation in light, bodies enjoy a truer and more elevated 'being' among existing things. Hence, the noblest of bodies, the Empyrean, is luminous to the highest degree, while the least noble, Earth, is most opaque. Bodies that lie between these extremes participate in light either more or less in proportion to their greater or lesser nobility. Of all things possessing body, light is the noblest form.[15]

There are a number of matters here over which Dante would have disagreed. But his own thinking was permeated by this kind of speculation; and there are passages in the *Convivio*, as there are in Aquinas's sober paraphrase of Aristotle's work *On Sensation*, which show the same vocabulary, concepts and animating spirit. When Dante writes that 'the divine light penetrates the universe in proportion to its merit', we must recognize the source in texts like these, which constitute what is often called 'The Metaphysics of Light'.[16] And these same texts also lie behind the opening lines of the *Paradiso*, in which Dante achieves his own unique blend of precision and sublimity:

The radiance of the All-mover penetrates the universe and shines out more in one place and less in another. I was in the heaven that receives most of His light . . . .

> La *gloria* di colui che tutto move
> per l'universo penetra, e *risplende*
> in una parte *più* e *meno* altrove.
> Nel ciel che *più* de la sua *luce* prende
> fu' io . . .
>
> (*Par.* I, 1–5)

Before leaving the subject of inequality, which is one of the central themes of Dante's poem, we may take note of another light-simile which was used to illustrate the concept that not even the blessed in Heaven will be equally blissful when they enjoy the vision of God. It came with all the authority of St Paul, and it runs:

There are also celestial bodies, and bodies terrestrial: but the glory (*gloria*) of the celestial is one, and the glory of the terrestrial is another. There is one glory (*claritas*) of the *sun*, and another glory of the *moon*, and another glory of the *stars: for one star differeth from another star in glory.* (1 Corinthians 15.40–1)

Light: (d) relaying by reflection

The sun, moon and stars offered a starting point for yet another important extension of light-imagery. The moon, it was known, shines with a borrowed light. It was held that the stars too derived their light in some sense from the sun.[17] And since the sun is clearly not the First Cause, it must receive its light from a higher power. At a less exalted level, the light by which one reads a book may be reflected from the wall behind, which is lit from the window, which admits light from the air, which is illuminated by the cloud-cover, which filters light from the sun. In each case the immediate and visible source of light is not the ultimate source, and it may be reflected rather than radiant light. In terms of radiodiffusion, the proximate source is not the transmitter, but a relay station – no more than a link in a chain.

To put it another way: light is essentially active, and it has the power of transforming every body that it touches – provided its surface is not black or matt – into a *de facto* source of light for some other body not directly illuminated by the primary source. If we now take illumination as the type of *all* causal activity, and if we mentally transpose these elementary observations into the context of the medieval universe, it will be seen that the relaying of light by reflection from mirror to mirror could provide a model in terms of which one could understand the transmission of energy in all natural processes. God is imaged as the Divine Light, pure, simple and eternal. His sustaining energy is beamed from the Empyrean to the outermost of the heavenly spheres. Under the direction of the nine angelic orders, each one of whom presides over the movement and operation of one heaven, this energy is relayed by reflection from one luminary to another until it reaches the sphere of Earth at the centre. Each luminary is conceived as an 'instrument' (*organo*), energized from above and energizing below:

> Questi *organi* del mondo così vanno,
> come tu vedi omai, *di grado in grado*,
> che *di su* prendono e *di sotto* fanno.   (*Par.* II, 121–3)

They function like a series of mirrors, *ad modum speculorum*. God does indeed conserve the universe 'by the same action through which he gave it being'; but He now acts at many removes through the agency of His ministers.[18]

Dante drew extensively on these ideas when he came to expound the opening lines of the *Paradiso* in the letter to Can Grande. The section is too long and difficult to quote here in its entirety, but the following sentences will document his familiarity with the interrelated thought and imagery:

The power to cause effects is a kind of ray (*radius quidam*) emanating from the First Cause, which is God. . . . Directly or through intermediaries, everything that exists receives its being from Him; because every secondary cause exerts the influence it receives from the First like a body receiving and reflecting a ray of light (*ad modum recipientis et reddentis radium*) . . .

It is clear that every essence and every causative power proceeds from the First. It is also clear that the lower Intelligences receive their essence and power as if from a body radiating light (*quasi a radiante*), and that they relay the rays they receive from the higher Intelligence to the one below them in the manner of mirrors. All this is clearly indicated by Dionysius in his work, *On the Celestial Hierarchy*. . . . Such then is the rational demonstration that the divine light (*divinum lumen*)—that is, the divine goodness, wisdom and power—must shine out everywhere (*resplendere ubique*).[19]

In the *Paradiso* itself, the separate components may be condensed into passages like the following, where the compression and the novelty of the language are so daring and so arduous, that they can dazzle the eyes of the unprepared mind:

See the transcendent generosity of God's eternal power, since He has created so many mirrors in which He is refracted, while remaining One in Himself as before:

> Vedi l'eccelso omai e la larghezza
> de l'etterno valor, poscia che tanti

>   speculi fatti s'ha in che si spezza,
>   uno manendo in sé come davanti.   (*Par.* XXIX, 142–5)

The mortal and immortal parts of creation alike are no more than the radiance of
the Idea to which Our Lord gives birth in an act of love. For in its goodness, the
Living Light – flowing from its Source, yet never disjoined from that Source, nor
from the Love that completes the Trinity – focuses all its out-shining on nine
orders of being, as if reflected in mirrors, while remaining eternally one:

>   Ciò che non more e ciò che può morire
>   non è se non *splendor* di quella idea
>   che partorisce, amando, il nostro Sire:
>   ché quella viva *luce* che sì mea
>   dal suo *lucente*, che non si disuna
>   da lui né da l'amor ch'a lor s'intrea,
>   per sua bontate il suo *raggiare* aduna,
>   quasi *specchiato*, in nove sussistenze,
>   etternalmente rimanendosi una.   (*Par.* XIII, 52–60)

Light: (e) negative and positive connotations

The tone of these passages is lyrical and emphatically 'positive'. But the
same image of light reflected from one body to another could also lead to a
less favourable view of these secondary causes, a view that would ascribe
the many imperfections in the world to the deficiencies inherent in these
agents and in the relay system. Some part of the divine energy – so the
image could imply – must be absorbed and dispersed by each of the
relaying bodies in turn. The lower heavens will reflect the divine power so
feebly that their causative influence can be frustrated. They become
causae impedibiles, that is, they will produce their effect not infallibly and
every time, but more often than not.[20] Although the luminaries or the
angelic intelligences are themselves immortal, and enjoy a 'necessary'
being, their effects here on earth are destined to pass away and are merely
'contingent' – *brevi contingenze*, as Dante calls them in the lines immediately following the second of the passages quoted above.[21]

Even if one were not seduced by the characteristically Arab version of
Neoplatonist creation theory, in which it was held that each successive
Intelligence and heaven was actually the cause of the Intelligence and
heaven immediately below it, it was still tempting to ascribe the diversity
and shortcomings of the *brevi contingenze* to the relay system, shifting the
responsibility and the blame from the One to the 'order of secondary
agents' (*secundorum agentium ordo*). As it passes from mouth to mouth – if
we may switch the image to one that Dante uses in the *Convivio* – the
divine Word becomes distorted and garbled until it is scarcely intelligible.[22]

Light-imagery also encouraged another persistent heresy about the

First Creation, which was all the more insidious just because it was less extreme. If light has a *vis multiplicativa*, and if God is literally light, then it must be impossible for Him *not* to irradiate, diffuse, and multiply Himself. God could not have existed *ante omnia saecula*, as the Creed insists. He could not *not* have created. On this view, creation becomes a purely mechanical necessity, and ceases to be the free expression of the Creator's love and generosity.[23]

It will be apparent, then, that a professional philosopher or theologian might well have regarded the images of light with some misgivings. They could so easily trap the unwary into heterodox or heretical assumptions about the nature of God as Creator. But the possible snares and pitfalls could never have led to a total ban on their use: they were so easily understood, so persuasive, and, above all, so satisfying to the emotions. At all times and in all cultures, one is tempted to generalize, the connotations of light have been positive. Light suggests life, deliverance, truth and joy. 'Of all things', writes the anonymous but influential author of the *Liber de Intelligentiis* in the early thirteenth century, 'light is the most delightful to our senses.' While the Book of Genesis records with no less gravity than simplicity: 'And God saw the light, that it was good.'[24]

The very last words in Dante's *Comedy* are 'the sun and the other stars'; and his final perfect vision of God came in a flash of 'lightning'. We have no difficulty at all in assenting to the climactic chain of repetitions with which Beatrice announces to Dante that he has come from the greatest intensity of physical light, experienced in the *primum mobile*, into the Empyrean and the presence of God:

We have emerged from the greatest body into the heaven that is pure light: an intellectual light filled with love; a love of the true good, filled with joy; a joy that transcends every sweetness.

> Noi siamo usciti fore
> del maggior corpo al ciel ch'è pura luce:
> luce intellettüal, piena d'amore;
> amor di vero ben, pien di letizia;
> letizia che trascende ogne dolzore.   (*Par.* xxx, 38–42)

These are the permanent associations of light. A universe imaged as radiance, and a creation imaged as light, cannot be other than good. For the good, like light, is self-multiplying: *bonum est diffusivum sui*.[25]

Water

Many of the verbs used to indicate the irradiation of light were originally drawn from our second family of images, those which are in some way connected with the flow of water.

In this group, God is compared, implicitly or explicitly, to a bottomless well or a never-drying spring of water. He is what the Book of Revelation calls the 'fountain of the water of life', or, in Dante's words, the *fontana vivace* or the *etterna fontana*. His first creative act is compared to the overflowing or outflowing of the spring; and thus the universe may be imagined as a river 'proceeding out of the throne of God', like the 'pure river of the water of life' seen by St John the Evangelist.[26]

As will have been evident in the passage from *Paradiso* XIII just quoted, the verbs may be as recondite as *meare*, or as neutral and innocuous as *descendere* (which is often more specific in this context than might at first appear). More often they will be *fluere*, with its derivatives *effluere* and *influere* (whence our 'influence'), or *defundere* and *effundere*, or *decurrere*, or again *manare* and *emanare* (whence the modern 'emanate').[27] The transferred use of these verbs was so common that the metaphorical element might often be forgotten. But it was never dead, only in suspended animation; and it could swiftly be brought back to life by the presence of another word from the same semantic field.

No less than the image of God as light, the image of the Creator as a fountain-head makes it plain that the universe is preserved 'by the continuation of the same action which gave it being'. God is an *etterno fonte*, and the universe will never exhaust him. This idea is enunciated with particular clarity by John Scotus in a simile that illustrates many of the recurrent words:

The whole river flows from the source (*totum flumen ex fonte manat*). The water rises there (*aqua surgit in fonte*), and then flows along the river bed (*per eius alveum defunditur*) without interruption for ever, extending as far as may be desired. In the same way the divine goodness, essence and life, which are in the Fountain-head of all things (*in fonte omnium*) flow down and along (*defluunt et decurrunt*).[28]

The many channels in the deltas of rivers like the Po and the Nile provided a convenient analogue for the way in which the forms and energy that issued undifferentiated from their Divine Source would later diverge and ramify to make possible the multiplicity and diversity of existing species. And the universe as a whole found its splendidly evocative equivalent in the Ocean – the 'great sea of being', as Dante calls it – over which all creatures move seeking their different havens.[29]

The same chapters of the Book of Revelation that speak of the 'river of life flowing from the throne of the Lord' also declare that God is at once Alpha and Omega, that is, 'the First and the Last, the Beginning and the End'.[30] The apparent contradiction might seem to defy representation within the terms of our comparison. But metaphorical language readily adapts itself to paradox. It is easy to think of God as *fons et origo*: it is just as easy to think of Him as the Ocean or *pelagus* into which all rivers flow, limitless in extent, unfathomable in depth.[31]

Now, it was characteristic of all Neoplatonist cosmologists to assert that just as the universe had issued from the One in an outpouring of love, so the whole universe longed with a reciprocal love to return into its Source. The outward movement was answered by a movement back: the *effluxus* or *exitus* was matched by a *reditus* or a *reversio*—in aspiration, if not always in physical movement. On the Last Day, indeed, so some believed, the universe would actually flow back into the One and cease to have an independent existence. This pattern of ideas could be expressed by simply 'reversing the flow' of the river in the simile.[32] And this solution will be found in some of the loveliest lines in the *Paradiso*, where Piccarda Donati explains to the pilgrim that the 'peace' of the blessed lies in conforming their desires to the Will of God. His Will is the 'sea' to which everything moves, whether it be created directly by Him or 'made' indirectly by nature:

> E 'n la sua volontade è nostra pace:
> ell' è quel *mare* al qual tutto si *move*
> ciò ch'ella crïa o che natura face.   (*Par.* III, 85–7)

There is no need for the flow of 'water' from God to his Creation to be imaged as a stream or river. Dante speaks of truth, grace and love 'raining' from Heaven. In one crucial passage he pairs *piovere* with *distillare* to express the outpouring of the creative Word and Power; and he can use *piovere* as an active verb when referring to the celestial influences and 'virtues' descending to earth from the physical heavens. The noun *pioggia* is usually employed in its literal sense (although once Dante promises to 'rain' on to others the 'rain' of instruction that has fallen on him), but the synonymous Gallicism, *ploia*, is used metaphorically, and it will provide a convenient cue for us to consider the associations of water-imagery.[33]

These associations are not necessarily 'good' or 'positive'. Water will not retain the forms impressed in it. The sea may be an image of sin. The Flood destroyed virtually all human and animal life at the time of Noah. But when Dante speaks of 'lo *refrigerio* de l'etterna *ploia*', we are reminded that water-imagery tends to suggest relief, rebirth, purity, and the washing away of the stain of sin (hence 'ab-solution'); and in almost all cases the connotations are appropriate to a benevolent Deity.[34]

The bowshot

Our third group of images is of a very different kind and much more restricted in number and scope. God becomes the Archer, or the Bow, or even the Bowstring; and His creative act is compared to the loosing of an arrow. Hence Dante can speak of 'that *Bow* which *shoots* forth all creatures, not just those lacking intelligence':

216

> né pur le creature che son fore
> d'intelligenza quest' *arco saetta*.   (*Par.* I, 118–19)

There is good biblical authority for attributing arrows and a bow to God, although the divine shafts were usually instruments of retribution, not of creation. The comparison also had the advantage of being vivid and concrete to a contemporary audience, because the crossbow and its bolts were standard military equipment in Dante's time (English readers should remember that it is unlikely that Dante was thinking of the longbow and the cloth-yard shaft). It is from this more immediate source that the image acquired its first, highly desirable association, that of 'speed'. It is clear from many literal references to the crossbow in the *Comedy* that it was regarded as the fastest mode of propulsion by human agency, in that the bolt seemed to reach its destination almost before it had left the bow, or at least before the bowstring had stopped quivering.[35]

But its primary connotation is one that was totally absent in the case of light-imagery. An arrow is not fired at random, but at a definite target (*segno, bersaglio*); and a target is perhaps the most obvious and easily understood example of a goal or objective (*fine*). Whenever Dante speaks of a bow, whether in literal or figurative contexts, he tends to lay emphasis on the purpose successfully achieved.[36] Everything that the divine Bow shoots forth hits the bull's-eye. 'It reaches an end that was foreseen, like something aimed at a target.' 'The power of this Bowstring directs everything it looses to a joyful end':

> . . . quantunque quest' *arco saetta*
> disposto cade a *proveduto fine*,
> sì come cosa in suo *segno* diretta.   (*Par.* VIII, 103–5)

> . . . la virtù di quella *corda*
> che ciò che *scocca drizza* in *segno* lieto.   (I, 125–6)

This constant stress on intention and purpose suggests that the most important influence on Dante in his use of this simile was that of Aristotle and his commentators or disciples. The following excerpt from Aquinas's commentary to the *De caelo* provides perhaps the best gloss:

God does nothing in vain. He acts by means of his intellect, and thus with an end in view. Similarly, nature performs nothing in vain, because it acts as impelled by God in His capacity as Prime Mover; just as an arrow does not fly in vain, since it is loosed by an archer at some definite target.[37]

Numbers: (a) the one and the many

We turn now to numbers and to some of the many ways in which they were used to express the relationship between God and Creation. Ancient writers speak of the unit 'one' as the starting point or *principium* of number: *unitas* (or *ipsum unum*) *est principium numeri*.[38] The infinite sequence of whole numbers was said to 'proceed' from one; and, by borrowing his verb from the language of light, Dante can say that 'five and six are "irradiated" from one, when this is understood':

> . . . così come raia
> da l'un, se si conosce, il cinque e 'l sei.   (*Par.* xv, 56–7)

At the same time it was traditional to revere the Supreme Being as 'The One' or 'The Monad'. As we have seen repeatedly, He is regarded as the source of all things in the universe, yet He 'remains eternally one'. He is conceived as unique, simple, indivisible – so much so that it is not possible to distinguish even conceptually between cause and effect in God, or between His essence and His being. It was therefore easy to make the semantic jump from 'one', in the sense of 'unit', to 'one' in the sense of 'unity' or 'indivisibility', and to imagine the First Creation as the procession of number from the One.[39] John Scotus is once again brief and explicit: 'The universe is created by the One, just as all numbers spring from the Monad, and all lines from the centre' (*Ab uno enim universitas creata est, sicut a monade omnes numeri, et a centro omnes lineae erumpunt*).[40]

Aristotle wrote that 'the species of things are like numbers' (*species rerum sunt sicut numeri*).[41] And when this much-quoted dictum is detached from its original context, it helps to establish the point, made in Chapter 5, that if there is a diversity of species, they *cannot* be equal in worth. Whichever two species we choose to examine, one of them must be 'closer' to God and more 'like' Him than the other; similarly, whichever two numbers we take, one of them must be closer than the other to the *unitas quae est principium numeri* (it will be seen that by this way of reckoning, five is prior and superior to six). The analogy also suggests that different species are evaluated by comparing them with God, who is the Measure of all things, just as the unit 'one' was said to be the *prima mensura numeri*.[42] All these modes of thought and speech combine in a sentence like the following from Dante's *De vulgari eloquentia*:

In every genus there must be one thing (*unum*) in terms of which all the others are weighed and compared, and which we accept as the measure of all the others (*omnium aliorum mensura*); just as in the case of numbers all are measured by one, and they are said to be greater or lesser according to whether they are far from or close to one (*sicut in numero cuncta mensurantur uno, et plura vel pauciora dicuntur secundum quod distant ab uno vel ei propinquant*). (*Dve*, I, xvi, 2)

All the whole numbers from two to infinity were thought to have this in common, that they denote a 'plurality'. It is of their essence that they refer to *many* things, in the sense in which 'many' is opposed not to a 'few', but to 'one'; for it is equally of the essence of 'one' that it excludes plurality. Seen in this way, the gulf between 2 and 999,999,999 is less than the gulf between 1 and 2, because unity and plurality were conceived as opposing extremes.[43]

This perspective permitted the most welcome extensions to the analogy obtaining between God as One and the universe as number, because it tended to preserve and indeed widen the gulf that separates the uncaused First Cause from even that part of His creation which is 'nearest' to Him and most 'deiform'. God is Truth, and the angels contemplate the truth in Him. But, as we saw in Chapter 7, the answers to some questions cannot be seen 'even by the Seraph whose eyes are fixed most closely on God; the answers lie so deep in the abyss of God's eternal decree that they are cut off from the vision of *every* created being'.[44] Translated into number-imagery, the same opposition might be expressed like this: 'Multitude or plurality is caused by a unity; but unity is opposed to plurality. Unity provides the measure for all numbers, and it alone cannot be measured by number' (*Multitudo . . . ex uno causatur. Uni enim multitudo opponitur. Sola unitas est quae non mensuratur a numero, sed ipsa omnes numeros mensurat*).[45]

Dante shared the almost mystical reverence for the One which seems such a constant feature of Neoplatonist sensibility and thought. In particular, this feeling animates much of the first book of the *Monarchia*, where he argues that mankind is one genus and must seek political unity throughout the world under the rule of one man – the 'monarch'. It is therefore not altogether surprising to discover that he was affected by the concomitant unease and suspicion in the presence of multiplicity, which is equally characteristic of Neoplatonism through the ages. Consciously he remained deeply committed to the biblical view that Creation was 'very good'; but subconsciously he seems to have entertained misgivings about the goodness of a universe which could not be perfect because it was neither 'simple' nor 'one'. These misgivings rise to the surface when he surrenders to the hypnotic language of number metaphor, as in this remarkable passage from the *Monarchia*:

The perfect being is perfect unity (*maxime est unum*), and the perfect unity is perfect goodness, and the further anything is removed from perfect being, the further it is from being one (*ab esse unum*) and being good. Therefore, within each kind of being the best is that which is most one, as the philosopher maintains in the *Metaphysics*. Hence unity (*unum esse*) seems to be the ground of goodness, and multiplicity (*multa esse*) the ground of evil; for this reason Pythagoras in his Correlations places unity (*unum*) on the side of goodness and multiplicity on the side of evil (*ex parte . . . mali plurale*), as we are told in the first book of the *Metaphysics*. Hence we can see that to sin is to despise and abandon unity for the sake of multiplicity (*peccare nichil est aliud quam progredi ab uno spreto ad multa*). (*Mon.* I, xv, 1–3, translated by Donald Nicholl.)

This mistrust of multiplicity as such is perhaps the most important of the 'negative' connotations inherent in the analogies derived from number.

Number: (b) proportion and harmony

It is not always true that a higher number is less 'like' one than a lower number; and this fact too has its implications for our analogy. Dante expresses a common opinion when he records that all odd numbers are inherently superior to even numbers because the 'supremely simple quantity, which is one, is more evident in odd numbers than in even' (*simplicissima quantitas, quod est unum, in impari numero redolet magis quam in pari*).[46] Moreover, it could not be fortuitous that God had laboured six days to create the world, because six was one of just three 'perfect' numbers between 2 and 1,000.[47] All square numbers and all cube numbers were thought to have a special significance for the kind of reason Dante gives in the *Vita Nuova* when he is explaining the constant association of Beatrice with the number nine (the passage loses in translation because Dante is punning on the two senses of the word *fattore*, used first in the mathematical sense of 'factor', then in the sense of 'Maker', 'Creator' or 'Worker'):

Three is the root of nine because it makes nine when multiplied by itself without any other number. . . . So, if three is the sole factor of nine, and if the sole 'factor' of miracles is Three, that is Father, Son and Holy Ghost, who are Three and One, Beatrice was accompanied by the number nine to show that she too was a nine, that is, a miracle, whose sole 'root' is the miraculous Trinity. (*VN*, XXIX, 3)

For Christian writers, the validity of such speculations had been confirmed by one of the most quoted texts in the Bible: 'Thou hast ordered all things in measure and number and weight (*omnia in mensura, et numero, et pondere disposuisti*).[48] Thus encouraged, the interpreters of the Bible had discovered an allegorical significance in almost every number mentioned in the Sacred Book. It was also felt that almost any number discerned in the Book of Nature might conceal a deeper meaning. One further example, again from Dante, will suffice to illustrate the habit of mind.

As we noted earlier, the astronomer Ptolemy had described 1,022 stars that are visible to the naked eye from the latitude of northern Egypt. Dante took the catalogue from his source, Alfraganus, and he treated it as though it were a complete and exhaustive list of all the stars in the eighth heaven. He then suggested that the total is significant in that the three numbers of which it is composed – 2, 20 and 1,000 – symbolize the three kinds of 'movement' distinguished by Aristotle. The number 2 represents 'local' movement, 'which must be from one point to another'. For more complex reasons, 20 signifies the movement of 'alteration'; while

1,000 stands for the movement of 'growth', 'since 1,000 is the highest number, and no further growth is possible except by multiplying that number'.[49]

So far we have kept within the territory of ancient arithmetic, confining our attention to the study of number and of individual numbers. The other mathematical sciences in antiquity were geometry, and, perhaps more surprisingly, astronomy and music. In different ways they all entailed the study of the *relationship* between numbers, that is, of all types of ratio and proportion, and of the principles of harmony. As will be readily imagined, the possible extensions of the analogy in these fields become almost impossible to count. And perhaps it is a little misleading to go on speaking of an 'analogy' between numerical proportions and the structure of the universe. Many thinkers were convinced that numbers were in some sense the elements of all things. 'Take away number', says Isidore, 'and all things perish'; while Dante reports that Pythagoras believed that '"odd" and "even" were the principles of natural things, since he considered all things to be number' ('Pittagora . . . poneva li *principii* de le cose naturali lo *pari* e lo *dispari*, considerando tutte le cose esser *numero*').[50]

Pythagoras was indeed regarded as the first begetter of this strange amalgam of mathematical intuition and unbridled fancy, which stands in the same relationship to modern physics as alchemy does to chemistry; and it will be worth quoting Aristotle's brief account of his position:

Contemporary with the early philosophers and even prior to them were the so-called Pythagoreans, who led the field in mathematics and whose studies convinced them that the principles of that science were of universal application.

Numbers, of course, are of their very nature the first of those principles; and the Pythagoreans thought they saw in numbers, rather than in fire or earth or water, many resemblances to things which exist and which come into being. They also realized that the properties and ratios of musical scales depend on numbers. In a word, they saw that other things, in respect of the whole of their natures, resemble numbers, and that numbers are the primary elements of the whole of nature. Hence they considered the principles of numbers as the principles of all things, and the whole universe as a harmony or number (*et totum caelum harmoniam esse et numerum*). Moreover, they collected and systematized all the instances they could find of correspondence between numbers or harmonies and the properties and relations of the heavens and the whole universal order. (*Metaphysics*, I, 5, 985b 25, translated by John Warrington.)

Aristotle went on to expose the logical inconsistencies in these claims; but the ideas continue to exercise their fascination over the lay mind even today, and Dante refers to this passage on several occasions without ever recalling Aristotle's critique.

We need not advance any further into this field, because most of it lies beyond the scope of our present inquiry. But we have already seen enough to understand how the 'positive' connotations of imagery based on proportion and harmony might serve to counterbalance or neutralize the 'negative' connotations inherent in the images derived from number and multiplicity, all of which tended to cast doubt on the goodness of creation. Observation of the principles of proportion, and the subordination of parts to a whole, could give the universe an 'order' which allowed it to function as 'one': *totum universum est unum, unitate ordinis.*[51] The lost resemblance to the divine unity of being could be recovered if the diverse parts satisfied the laws of harmony. These ideas are expressed with Dante's habitual density in the opening terzina of the first doctrinal speech in the *Paradiso*: 'All things observe order among themselves, and this is the form that makes the universe resemble God':

> . . . le cose tutte quante
> hanno *ordine* tra loro, e questo è *forma*
> che *l'universo a Dio fa simigliante.*   (*Par.* I, 103–5)

The logical infrastructure of these ideas may be studied in the first book of the *Monarchia* where Dante distinguishes two kinds of order – an order of parts among themselves, and an order of parts to a whole – and then insists that the *ordo totalis* is superior in worth to the *ordo partium inter se*, since it constitutes its goal and perfection.

Hierarchy

Both kinds of order can also be illustrated through the brief simile that Dante introduces in this passage. It is of Aristotelian origin, but is still easily understood. Every serving soldier must possess a definite rank which determines his relationship to every other member of the army. This hierarchy of rank permits an unbroken chain of command from the highest to the lowest, such that the general's orders will be carried out even though they are relayed from brigadiers to lieutenant-colonels and from them to majors, captains, subalterns and NCOs, right down to the privates, gunners and sappers. It is obvious that it is only in this way that many individuals can act as a military 'unit' and carry out the will of one man. And it will be obvious also that the structure based on rank – the *ordo partium exercitus inter se* – exists only to enable the general to put his plan of campaign into effect: the *ordo totalis* is the *ordo ad ducem.*[52]

Medieval society was much simpler and much more stable than that of the industrialized democracies in the West today; and whereas we are compelled to study a corporate body *within* our society in order to grasp the organization and *raison d'être* of a strict hierarchy, medieval men could simply look to society at large. We may pursue the phantom of 'status'; they knew their 'station in life'. Details vary from place to place and from one century to another, and the struggle for power made practice more complex and varied than theory, but we may assume that most people were familiar from everyday experience with a hierarchical society which they would have recognized in the following paradigm. Supreme authority was vested in the king or emperor. He was surrounded by his vassals, the dukes, marquesses, earls, counts and barons of the realm. Below them on the social scale came the knights, followed by the professional classes and the richer merchants. Then came tradesmen, craftsmen and yeomen, and, finally, peasants, labourers and feudal serfs.

When God was imaged in human terms drawn from the living fabric of medieval life, nothing could be more natural than to speak of Him as the emperor or eternal king—*lo rege etterno*, or *lo 'mperador che sempre regna*. But the analogy also suggests that He sits in the innermost chamber of a 'court' (*l'aula più secreta . . . di questa corte*), surrounded by his *conti* and *baroni*. Everyone and everything in His kingdom is ordered by degree, *di grado in grado*, or *di soglia in soglia*; for this is the will of its King and the pleasure of its subjects:[53]

> . . . come noi sem di *soglia* in *soglia*
> per questo *regno*, a tutto il *regno* piace
> com' a lo *re* che 'n suo voler ne 'nvoglia.   (*Par.* III, 82–4)

The structure of medieval society furnished a model which tended to reinforce the likelihood that there was a hierarchy in heaven. But the particular associations attached to images derived from the *social* scale extended much further than those attached to the scale of luminosity or the scale of number. Emperors do not collect taxes in person nor enact municipal by-laws, just as generals do not engage in hand-to-hand fighting.[54] And so the analogy made it seem plausible that a Supreme Being would deal with his lower creation at several removes through a chain of subordinates.

Conversely, an individual who sought redress for some official injustice would find that his complaint led him higher and higher up the chain of command; and the experience might teach him that a cause is always superior to its effect. If he pursued the quest far enough, he might come to the general or emperor prepared to accept the ultimate responsibility for the action he complained of, someone prepared to say with President Truman that 'the buck stops here'. And this might give him the confidence that no sequence of causes and effects can be infinite, and that one will in the end arrive at an uncaused First Cause.

These hypothetical experiences, and the lessons they might teach, are put forward with deliberate informality for the moment, but they do in fact contain the substance of three of the most important axioms in medieval debates about causality. These may be translated as: (i) 'The cause is nobler than the effect'; (ii) 'A first principle does exist, and the causes of things are not an infinite series, nor infinitely various in kind';

(iii) 'Nature proceeds from one extreme to another through intermediate stages.'[55] Today, none of these propositions would be regarded as self-evidently true; and all of them require the kind of apologetic introduction and exemplification that has just been offered. The fact that they were accepted so readily in earlier centuries is due in no small measure to the 'hidden persuaders' of imagery and, in particular, to the representation of God as emperor, and of the universe as His hierarchical empire.

The analogy could also encourage error and heresy, since it could easily imply—as it did to the great Moslem philosopher, Avicenna—that 'the lowest effects *cannot* proceed directly from the First Cause, but only through secondary or intermediate causes'. This would entail the consequence that God does not and cannot act directly in earthly life or in human affairs.[56]

To some extent, however, the political analogy itself could suggest a solution to this difficulty. It would be exceptional for an emperor or king to involve himself directly in the personal or purely local affairs of his subjects; but it was not impossible, and it was not unknown. The Emperor Trajan was said to have delayed his departure for the wars at the very last moment on hearing the reproaches and pleas of a poor widow who seized his bridle and demanded retribution for the murderers of her son. Dante gives us a splendidly vivid re-enactment of the scene in the *Purgatorio*; and we know that he pinned his own hopes of return to Florence on the success of the Emperor Henry VII. A brief excerpt from a petition he wrote to the Emperor's wife on behalf of another supplicant will illustrate the association of ideas, and show how easy was the transference from the earthly emperor to the Ruler of all things.

Yet was it not unseemly that the pinnacle of the ranks of human society (*humanorum graduum . . . apicem*) should thus incline itself, since from hence, as from a living fountain, the exemplars of sacred civilization must be transmitted to those below (*inferioribus emanare*). To return adequate thanks is beyond the power of man, but I deem it to be not unnatural for man sometimes to make prayer to God for help in his insufficiency. Now therefore let the court of the starry realm (*regni siderii . . . aula*) be assailed with just and holy prayers, and may the zeal of the suppliant obtain that the Eternal Ruler of the world (*mundi gubernator aeternus*) may recompense so great a condescension with proportionate reward. (*Epist.* VIII, 3–4, translated by Paget Toynbee.)

In short, both the emperor and God were known to intervene directly in the affairs of the humblest part of their 'Empire': appeals were not in vain; nor was prayer.

The wax seal

Our sixth family of images is as simple, close-knit and concrete as those involving arrows and the bow, and it has the great merit of focusing attention on the activity of a single efficient cause in the production of a particular material effect.

The cause in this instance is represented by a metal stamp—an imperial seal, perhaps, or the personal signet ring of a Pope. The matter into which its 'influence will descend' exists under the suitably 'complexioned' form of good-quality wax, which has been properly 'disposed' by heating to a certain temperature. The signet is pressed into the shapeless, semi-molten blob and then withdrawn. As a result, the piece of sealing-wax is transformed into an official seal, the guarantee of authenticity on an imperial edict or a papal bull.[57]

The process could hardly be simpler. But there are several related points to notice which will become important when this mode of production is taken as the paradigm of all kinds of causation and used as a simile of God's *productio rerum*.

It will be clear, first, that production involves the imposition or communication of a new form to pre-existent matter, and that the form communicated in this case is simply the form of the cause itself (strictly speaking, in reverse). The wax becomes a seal by taking on the likeness of the signet. Causation involves the transmission of a likeness. This is the meaning of a cryptic but crucial 'law' of causation which recurs again and again in scholastic philosophy: *omne agens agit sibi simile*, literally, 'every agent acts like itself', or 'every cause causes in its own image'. In one of Dante's paraphrases, it runs: 'When we say that influence passes from one thing to another, we mean that it draws the things into its own likeness' ('. . . "discender la virtude" d'una cosa in altra non è altro che *ridurre quella in sua similitudine*').[58]

The simile also suggests that all effects of the same cause will be alike, since they must all share the form of their common exemplar (and, as we shall see, this has consequences for any discussion of the relationship between individuals and their common species).[59] But there is a further and more important inference to be drawn, which emerges in another of Dante's attempts to paraphrase the axiom. Reversing the direction of inquiry, so to speak, he writes: 'Every effect, considered precisely as an effect, receives the likeness of its cause' ('*ciascun effetto*, in quanto effetto è, *riceve la similitudine de la sua cagione*'). Now, if every *exemplatum* carries the *similitudinem exemplaris*, it must be possible and legitimate to make deductions about a hidden, unknown or unknowable cause from the study of its known effects. And another scholastic dictum states that 'anything whatsoever can be investigated through the traces it leaves' (*per sua vestigia unumquodque investigari potest*).[60]

Dante followed a long tradition stretching back to Plato in using the impression of a seal as a metaphor of God's creative act. The 'divine goodness that stamps the universe' has left all things 'imprinted' with His 'worth'. All things become what they are in accordance with God's eternal pleasure, and they carry the likeness of His imprint:[61]

> ... l'*imago* de la *'mprenta*
> de l'etterno piacere, al cui disio
> ciascuna cosa qual ell' è diventa.   (*Par.* xx, 76–8)

God is unknowable by man because He 'dazzles our intellect'. But if the universe carries His stamp, it must be possible to discover something of His nature by studying the world and the heavens. This is the principle underlying all 'natural' theology. It is clearly restated by Dante in the *Monarchia*, in a sentence where the obligatory reference to the authority of St Paul is clarified by the image of signet, wax and seal in the form of a brief, explicit simile:[62]

It is true that the will of God in itself is invisible, but 'the invisible things of God are perceived and understood through His works'; for although the seal is hidden, the wax on which it is impressed gives us a clear knowledge of what remains hidden (*nam, occulto existente sigillo, cera impressa de illo quamvis occulto tradit notitiam manifestam*). (*Mon.* ii, ii, 8, translated by Donald Nicholl.)

The same simile had been used by Aristotle to illustrate the way that mental images are retained in the memory. And it is perhaps from this source that the simile acquired the connotation of permanence, which is obviously highly desirable when it is applied to God. A footprint in the dust is as transient as foam on water, or smoke in the air; but when Dante has grasped a truth, his brain holds it as retentively as if it were 'wax stamped by the signet which does not change the figure impressed':[63]

> ... Sì come *cera* da *suggello,*
> che la figura impressa *non trasmuta,*
> segnato è or da voi lo mio cervello.   (*Purg.* xxxiii, 79–81)

Similarly, when the Divine Goodness sets its seal *directly*, the imprint does not move:

> ... *non si move*
> la sua *imprenta* quand' ella *sigilla*.   (*Par.* vii, 68–9)

Wax is not transformed into gold when it is stamped with the golden seal. It remains wax. And the image-cluster is also important for what it suggests about the role of the 'material cause' in relation to the supervening 'efficient cause'.

The signet will not always leave a perfect likeness of itself. If the wax is of poor quality, or if the temperature is wrong, the outlines will be blurred. In other substances, like mud or stone, it will leave no impression at all, or only the faintest traces. This varying response of different kinds of matter to the same cause provides an excellent illustration of a law of causation which was often quoted in conjunction with *omne agens agit sibi simile.* It states: 'An influence is received in accordance with the mode of being of the recipient' (*quicquid recipitur secundum modum recipientis recipitur*).

Dante paraphrases the law and applies it to the activity of God with these words: 'although the divine goodness proceeds from a principle which is perfectly simple, it is received in different and unequal measure by the recipients'.[64] And he illustrates the point with reference to a famous *canzone* by Guinizzelli, who had used the example of the sun:[65] 'All day long the sun strikes the mud; vile it remains.' By contrast, Dante will say, 'when the heat of the sun is joined with the juice of the grape, it becomes wine':

> Fere lo sol lo fango tutto 'l giorno:
> vile reman, né 'l sol perde calore.   (*Al cor gentil*, 31–2)
>
> guarda il calor del sol che si fa vino,
> giunto a l'omor che de la vite cola.   (*Purg.* XXV, 77–8)

If the replication of many seals by the impression of one signet is taken as the model for the multiplication of individuals in a common species, it becomes easier to grasp the import of another typically dense axiom of Aristotelian origin: 'Matter individuates', or, 'The principle of individuation is matter' (*materia est principium individuationis*).[66]

The analogy also helps us to understand why the differences between individuals were so often ascribed purely to material causes, that is, to the varying proportions of the four elements or the four 'humours' in each individual's 'complexion' or 'constitution'. As we have noted earlier, this almost unconscious materialism was endemic among medical doctors, and it was equally apparent in their diagnoses of the various kinds of change and ill-health that might befall one individual. These were ascribed to 'distempers', 'disorders', and 'indispositions'–all of which are terms referring to imbalances in the humours, and to the undue preponderance of one of the four contraries, Hot, Cold, Wet and Dry. Many of the common remedies were no less 'materialistic', consisting as they did of purging, blood-letting and a careful attention to diet.

The attitudes to matter, form and individuation fostered by the example of the signet, wax and seal were not without dangers when they were carried across to influence speculation about God and the universe. The analogy preserved the uniqueness of God, who is seen to remain unchanged and undiminished however many times His likeness is reproduced. But it does tend to convey the idea that the differences between individuals do not form part of God's plan, and that they come about by chance. The variations are seen not as being directly opposed to God's intention (*contra intentionem Dei*), but as being in some sense 'beyond' or 'apart from' His intention (*praeter intentionem Dei, fuori d'intenzione*).[67]

The analogy could also lend support to the view that matter was in some sense resistant to form, instead of 'desiring form as the female desires the male'.[68] Variant copies are not just different one from another, they are more or less faithful to the exemplar, more or less perfect. It is tempting to attribute any individual imperfections or failures to the 'fluidity' of matter; and then, passing by easy stages to more and more emotive terms, to blame them on the 'inequality of matter', or on its 'resistance', or even its 'disobedience'.[69]

Metaphorical language of this kind can easily become the vehicle for that persistent dualism in human thought that would oppose matter to form, or matter to spirit, as darkness is opposed to light, and evil to good. With his conscious mind Dante rejected such antitheses as false. As a Christian and an Aristotelian, he believed that matter was good. But there was a Platonist in his make-up as well, not to speak of a common humanity (and there are few people whose experience of hunger, lust, pain and fatigue has not led them to feel that their spirit was still willing, but the flesh was weak). Even in prose he can write: 'If the human form, individuated and modelled on its exemplar, is not perfect, the fault lies not in the exemplar, but in matter which individuates.' Or again: 'We must not blame an ugly man for his ugliness; we must lay the blame on the bad disposition of the matter of which he is made, which was the origin of nature's fault' ('. . . dovemo *vituperare* la *mala disposizione* de la *materia* onde esso è fatto, che fu principio del *peccato* de la natura').[70]

In verse, he conveys a weary resignation more typical of Petrarch, when he contrasts 'the pure light of the Heaven that is never obscured' with 'the darkness or the shadow of the flesh, or its poison':

> Lume non è, se non vien dal sereno
> che non si turba mai; anzi è tenebra
> od ombra de la carne o suo veleno.   (*Par.* XIX, 64–6)

And he will say that the 'imprint' of the divine Idea (*il segno ideale*) shines out with varying intensity in different seals, because the 'wax' of generated beings and the signet or sealer (*chi la duce*) are not always in the same relationship. If the wax were perfectly disposed, and if the signet were in the ideal condition, the brightness of the signet's form (*la luce del suggel*) would show undimmed; but this never happens in nature:[71]

> La *cera* di costoro e *chi la duce*
> non sta d'un modo; e però sotto 'l *segno*
> *idëale* poi più e men *traluce*.
>
> . . .
>
> Se fosse a punto la *cera* dedutta
> e fosse il cielo in sua virtù supprema,
> *la luce del suggel* parrebbe tutta;
>   ma la natura la dà sempre scema . . .

> (*Par.* XIII, 67–9, 73–6)

My paraphrase suggests that 'signet' and 'sealer' should be distinguished in this passage, and that neither is identical with the *segno ideale*, which does not exist outside the Mind of God. In fact, the two terms refer respectively to the physical heavens and to the angelic Intelligences who use those heavens as their instruments; and Dante will often use the sealing-image of natural generation. He speaks of the sun in particular as 'tempering and setting his seal on the wax of the universe' and as 'imprinting the world with the heavens' power'.[72] And in one dense passage the whole system of the revolving spheres is called 'circular nature', which is 'signet' to the 'wax of mortal things':

> la circular natura, ch'è *suggello*
> a la *cera* mortal . . .   (*Par.* VIII, 127–8)

The image can thus blur the fundamental distinction between generation and creation, and this constitutes another potential threat to clear and consistent thought.

Seed and plant

Of all the many modes of coming into being or causing an effect, perhaps the most familiar is the growth of a plant from a seed. It is not surprising, therefore, that the majority of Dante's references to seeds, roots, branches, leaves, flowers and fruit are to be understood quite literally. It is only when he uses such terminology of *God's direct* activity in the universe, in particular of His part in the formation of man, that we find ourselves in the presence of the images that make up our seventh group.

Now, some of the most important concepts and axioms relating to causation were first formulated by Aristotle as a result of his biological researches and his attempts to understand propagation by seed. The life-cycle of plants still provides the best examples—*examples* not analogies—to illustrate these concepts when they occur in some abstract and technical argument. And since the concepts and axioms are the starting point for the metaphorical extensions of plant-language, it will be helpful to recall some of them here by way of introduction.

An acorn is the immediate and indispensable cause of an oak tree. Somehow or other, it contains within itself the power to realize the whole form of the oak; and there is a sense in which the mature oak exists potentially within the acorn—its growth is no more than the actualization of that potentiality. It is certain that nothing but an oak can grow from an acorn, and that acorns grow only on oaks. Again, the acorn exists *in order to* become an oak, and the oak is thus the purpose or the 'end' or the 'final cause' of the acorn. When that 'end' has been reached, the oak will have achieved its 'perfection', and the potential of the acorn will have been fulfilled. The oak may increase in girth ('augmentation'), but it will not grow any higher. Lastly, we may note that the mature oak, like all other mature plants, has a final cause outside itself: it exists to provide a commodity for use by human beings.

From those few propositions one may exemplify the concepts of 'form' and 'matter', 'potency' and 'act', 'growth' and 'augmentation','purpose' and 'perfection' – in fact, many of the key-ideas in the scholastic analysis of causation and generation. But there are three aspects of plant growth which we must single out in particular for their metaphorical implications. First, the cause remains mysterious, even when we have named the stages and can predict the effects. And for this reason the 'seed' is a much more suggestive image of God's direct causal activity than is the 'seal'. It suggests a power immanent in the world of change, and not simply an impersonal force acting from without. Second, the phenomenon of plant growth offers the perfect example of a complex process unfolding in accordance with a predetermined plan in order to achieve a definite purpose. Dante will constantly associate 'seed' and 'goal'; and when the image is transferred to God, this natural association of ideas can suggest that there is a providential design unfolding through the centuries in the life of the whole universe, even though this is hidden from the eye of a mere human observer at any point in time.[73] It suggests that everything exists for a purpose, and that the means to achieve that purpose are to hand. We may not understand the process, but we may be confident of the outcome. Many bold deductions in the thought of Dante and his teachers rest upon the premiss that Nature does 'nothing in vain' – *nil frustra* or *nil otiose*.[74]

Plant life also threw up a number of individual exceptions to this and other general rules. Some seeds fall on stony ground; some are eaten by birds; some are choked by weeds. Some trees produce poor fruit. In any case, growth does not begin till the spring, and it ceases in autumn. Observations such as these prepare us for other concepts and axioms. They indicate, for example, that the *virtus informativa* or 'formative power' within the seed is not the sole cause of the mature plant: there are other 'contributory' or 'concomitant' causes (*concausae*). 'Accidents' may frustrate the course of nature. The individual specimens differ in that they realize the potential of the species unequally, *secondo più e meno*. Individuals can also deviate from the general plan. And the proud, sweeping generalization that 'Nature does nothing in vain' had to be modified with the rider *ut in pluribus*, i.e. 'in the majority of cases'. All these notions too could be exploited metaphorically, whether to hint at imperfections and to express doubts about the goodness of Divine Providence, or to accommodate the principle of human freedom.

Encouraged by the luxuriant plant-imagery found in both parts of the Bible, Dante made free use – in places, extravagant use – of metaphors and similes based on the life of plants in order to express God's role in the life of man. Our bodies develop from the seed of our natural fathers. But it is God, the 'altissimo e glorioso Seminadore', who sows the 'seed of nobility' in man, the seed that should grow into the fruit of human happiness.[75]

God is the giver of our specifically human nature, and He tends and sustains our humanity while it grows. He sends a saint like Dominic to be His labourer (*agricola*) in the vineyard, to cut off the dead leaves, root out the thorn-bushes of heresy, and to irrigate the earth with the pure water of truth. He will even endeavour to graft new life onto a stock that would otherwise be barren or worthless. He will burn the tares in an eternal fire, but gather the wheat and the fruits of the earth into His store-house. The angels sprout in His eternal spring.[76] God is therefore not only the Sower, but the 'Gardener in the eternal garden', the 'fronds' of which are all the manifestations of His goodness in the universe:

> Le *fronde* onde *s'infronda* tutto *l'orto*
> de *l'ortolano etterno*, am' io cotanto
> quanto da lui a lor di bene è porto.   (*Par.* XXVI, 64–6)

In the *Convivio* (and again in the *Paradiso*), Dante takes the blooming of the rose as his favourite metaphor of a life come to fulfilment in maturity. Having reached forty-five years of age, a man must 'open like a rose that can no longer remain closed, and spread the perfume generated within'.[77] Texts such as this are the key to the great pageant in the Empyrean when Dante finally sees the blessed 'in the form of a white rose, its petals rising and swelling in more than a thousand rows above the yellow heart, and giving off a fragrance of praise to the Sun', while the angels 'like a swarm of bees moving to and fro between the flower and the hive where their labour is turned to sweetness, swoop down into this vast flower adorned with so many petals, and then rise again to where their Love dwells in eternity':

> Nel *giallo* de la *rosa* sempiterna,
> che si digrada e dilata e *redole*
> *odor* di lode al sol che sempre verna . . .
>
> In forma dunque di *candida rosa*
> mi si mostrava la milizia santa
> . . .
>   sì come schiera d'*ape* che *s'infiora*
> una fïata e una si ritorna
> là dove suo laboro *s'insapora*,
>   nel gran *fior* discendeva che *s'addorna*
> di tante *foglie*, e quindi risaliva
> là dove 'l süo amor sempre soggiorna.
>   (*Par.* XXX, 124–6; XXXI, 1–2, 7–12)

This is Dante's final image of what the seed of nobility sown by God will achieve when it has come from potency to act.

Deep below the coruscating surface of these metaphors and similes there lurks one of the more fascinating and difficult elements in the thought of St Augustine, his doctrine of the 'germinal forms' or 'seminal reasons'–the *rationes seminales*.[78] Augustine's teaching on this point was variously interpreted in the Middle Ages; but the metaphor seems to convey that the forms of all the things that come into being with the passage of time were somehow present in the matrix of matter from the Beginning, and therefore that *all* things had in fact been created simultaneously, even though most of them were created only *in potentia*. Dante never alludes to the *rationes seminales*, and we do not know what interpretation he himself would have given. His silence on the subject may be significant, however, for the Augustinian doctrine, narrowly interpreted, would have been inimical to his own sharp distinction between the First Creation and the subsequent generation of things in time.

The craftsman

Images of light suggest that creation was inevitable rather than a free act of love. Arrows and numbers seem too cold and mechanical when applied to God. The 'social' image makes Him seem too remote and unapproachable; while both the seal and the seed make it difficult to understand–if we accept that *omne agens agit sibi simile*–how a unique, immortal Deity can be the cause of a multiplicity of transient beings.

All such disadvantages disappear, however, if we replace those images with that of God as a human craftsman, an *artefice* or *artista*, exercising his *arte* or craft–a potter, perhaps, as in many of the biblical metaphors, or a smith, as in the Aristotelian tradition.[79] At a stroke, His creative act becomes the conscious, voluntary action of an intelligent, loving being. St Thomas Aquinas brings these implications out into the open with his habitual economy when he notes that 'God is the cause of things by means of His intellect and will, just as the craftsman is of the things made by his craft' (*Deus est causa rerum per suum intellectum et voluntatem, sicut artifex rerum artificiatarum*). And Dante confirms the association when he writes that 'nature takes its course from the divine intellect and from its craft' ('. . . dal divino 'ntelletto e da sua *arte*').[80]

The connotation of love is no less strong in Dante. This Master-Craftsman loves the product of his art so much that he never lets it out of his sight; and we too are invited to share in his delight:[81]

> e lì comincia a vagheggiar ne l'*arte*
> di quel *maestro* che dentro a sé l'*ama*,
> tanto che mai da lei l'occhio non parte.   (*Par.* X, 10–12)

The analogy also enables us to consider from a new and rewarding standpoint the resemblance that must exist between a cause and its effect. A painter may use his skill to capture the likeness of a sitter, or to draw a purely imaginary form. Similarly, a potter may agree to copy the form and dimensions of a pot set before him as a model, or he may execute a unique and original design. To us the four situations may seem distinct, but the scholastic philosopher would say that in every case an *artista* was making a copy of an exemplar, whether that exemplar existed outside him, or only in his mind (*sive . . . extra, sive . . . interius mente conceptum*).[82] And the schoolman would also argue that in every case the significant exemplar was the mental form in the craftsman's head – his *intentio*, in scholastic terminology. In a much-quoted tag, Avicenna stated the principle in terms of house-building: 'The house that is made from walls and stone is generated from the house in the mind of the builder' (*in anima artificis*). Dante, himself an amateur painter, put it like this: 'No painter could set down a form, if he did not first take on "intentionally" the form as it should be.'[83]

It is obvious that no pot resembles the human form of the potter; and it is equally obvious that a single potter can produce many different types of pot without compromising his identity or integrity. In other words, the form and the likeness that the craftsman, *qua* cause, communicates to his handiwork, *qua* effect, is not like that of a metal die, stamp or signet; it is that of a mental idea. And there is no limit to the number of distinct ideas that he may hold in his mind. Once again Aquinas demonstrates the relevance of the comparison to our understanding of God's mode of creation: 'An exemplar is the same as an idea; and St Augustine defines "ideas" as the "principal forms contained in the Divine Intelligence".'[84]

If we lay emphasis on the craftsman's tools and on the materials in which he works, as when we think specifically of a smith forging knives from iron with the aid of furnace, bellows, hammer and anvil, then the image can be readily adapted to exemplify the processes of nature and their dependence on God.[85] Dante makes this quite explicit in the following passage:

It must be pointed out that nature, like art (*ars*), may be considered under three aspects. In the case of art these are the mind of the artist, the instrument he uses and the material on which he works (*in mente scilicet artificis, in organo et in materia . . .*). In nature the corresponding aspects are the mind of the first mover, who is God, and then the heavens, which are a sort of instrument for communicating the image of eternal goodness to the third aspect, that of fluctuating matter. (*Mon.* II, ii, 2, translated by Donald Nicholl.)

Hence, too, Dante can describe miracles as 'work, where Nature never heated the iron nor beat the anvil'.[86]

The continuation of the passage from the *Monarchia* reveals all too clearly that the craftsman-image, no less than that of the wax-seal, can become a vehicle for the expression of what we called a 'suspicion' or 'hostility' with regard to matter. Once again we meet the notion that matter is able to frustrate God's intention:

Now when there is a perfect artist employing a perfect instrument, any imperfection in the work of art must be attributed to the matter, and since God is supreme perfection and His instrument, the heavens, never lacks the requisite perfection . . . it follows that any imperfection in things here below must be the fault of their matter and is no part of the intention of the divine author or the heavens (*restat quod quicquid in rebus inferioribus est peccatum, ex parte materiae subiacentis peccatum sit et praeter intentionem Dei naturantis et caeli*). (*ibid.*, 3)[87]

In the *Comedy* Dante hints at the same attitude to matter with a new metaphor – its 'deafness'. 'The form of the finished work often differs from the artist's *intentio*', he writes, 'because matter is deaf to respond':

> Vero è che, come *forma* non s'accorda
> molte fiate a l'*intenzion* de l'*arte*
> perch' a *risponder* la *materia* è *sorda*.　　(*Par.* I, 127–9)

The image can be further adapted so that all deficiencies and imperfections in the universe are attributed to the Craftsman himself. And Dante came close to this when he made his St Thomas say that 'Nature never achieves the perfect copy, because She works like a craftsman who possesses the "know-how" but has an unsteady hand':

> Ma la *natura* la dà sempre *scema*,
> similemente operando a l'*artista*
> ch'a l'*abito* de l'*arte* ha *man che trema*.　　(*Par.* XIII, 76–8)

In this case the possessor of the unsteady hand is Nature rather than God – the secondary causes, not the First Cause. But there could hardly be a more revealing example of the risks incurred by Dante and the authors of the Bible when they 'attributed *hands* and *feet* to God'. Nevertheless, the risk had to be taken, for 'this is the way you have to speak to human minds': 'Così parlar conviensi al vostro ingegno.'[88]

9

Creation: 'Paradiso' XXIX, 1–57

The problems presented by Genesis 1.1

THE BOOK OF GENESIS KNOWS NOTHING OF THE FIVE ELEMENTS
arranged in thirteen concentric spheres, nothing of the Scale of Being,
and nothing of the relayed influences of the seven planets and the twelve
constellations of the Zodiac. It speaks of angels, but it does not tell us
how, why or where they were created. Its concept of creation–if it is
proper to talk of a 'concept'–veers between the simple giving of orders
and the activity of a craftsman moulding or shaping some pre-existent
material. It never hints at irradiation, emanation, semination, the procession of number or the projection of missiles. More than this, its opening
words read like an unequivocal challenge *ante litteram* to the fathers of
Western philosophy. Against Aristotle and the Peripatetics it asserts that
the world did have a beginning, and that the Prime Mover was also a
Creator; against Plato and the Neoplatonists it insists that the earth too
was made by God directly and not by his underlings. Nothing could be
more plain and uncompromising than the first verse: 'In the beginning
God created heaven and earth' (*In principio creavit Deus caelum et
terram*). No one could call himself a Christian and deny that stark
affirmation. It was, after all, echoed in the opening words of the Creed: 'I
believe in the one God, the Father almighty, Maker of heaven and earth,
and of all things visible and invisible.'

Like any other intellectual of his time, therefore, Dante faced enor-
mous difficulties in thinking or writing about the Creation. He had to
harmonize the first tenet of his faith with his up-to-date scientific
knowledge of the 'facts' about the universe and with his philosophical
concepts, axioms and rules of argument, almost all of which were
ultimately derived from the Greeks. Apart from the Trinity and the
Incarnation, few subjects placed a greater strain on the medieval genius
for reconciling authorities that today we would regard as irreconcilable.

It will help us to understand certain features of Dante's account of the
Creation if we first take note of some of the different interpretations that
had been put forward for the key-words in that first verse. The precise
meaning of *caelum* and *terra* was called into question by their recurrence a
few sentences later, where we read that it was on the second day that God

235

made the firmament and called it 'Heaven' (vv. 7–8), and that it was only on the third day that he ordered the dry land to appear and called it 'Earth' (vv. 9–10). What God did on the *first* day – 'in the *beginning*' – was to call light into existence and to separate light from darkness.

One resolution of the apparent contradiction was given by the Greek Father, John Chrysostom. He made the practical point that the first verse functions as a preview of the whole Creation, which is then described and particularized in the rest of the chapter. St Thomas Aquinas clarifies his point by introducing once again a craftsman-simile. If we say, 'The craftsman built this house: first he laid the foundations, then he raised the walls, and then he added the roof', no one will think that he built the house before he laid the foundations. The two cases are similar, and there is no inconsistency.[1] In any case, a large body of interpreters, headed by no less an authority than St Augustine, held that the different labours itemized in the first chapter of Genesis had in fact all taken place simultaneously, since it was written in the Book of Ecclesiasticus – or at least in the Vulgate translation – that 'He who lives for ever made all things at once' (*creavit omnia simul*). On this view the Six Days of the Genesis account indicate the order of nature, not a temporal succession.[2]

Nevertheless this common-sense solution of the difficulty did not win universal assent. St Augustine, indeed, favoured a much more daring interpretation. He inclined to the view that, whereas *caelum* and *terra* were used in their proper acceptation in verses 8 and 10, at their first appearance they signified 'the still undifferentiated angelic nature' and the 'prime matter of corporeal beings'. The great attraction of this bold proposal was that it made good the otherwise baffling omission of any reference to the creation of angels in the Genesis narrative.[3]

Why did the author of Genesis – universally held to be Moses – choose to express himself in this way? The answer runs like a leitmotif through medieval exegesis of this chapter. He was writing for an uneducated people. He had to condescend to their weakness. He had to use concrete, 'bodily' terms and convey abstract concepts under the similitude of things they knew. And in this particular case he avoided any mention of the angels in order not to give the Jews excuse for idolatry, a vice to which they were naturally prone. Thus the first sacred writer to avail himself of concrete imagery in order to be understood by untutored minds was none other than Moses himself; and he had done so on the first possible occasion, in the very first line of the Bible.[4]

Even from these brief examples it is not difficult to understand why St Thomas demanded that an interpreter of the Book of Genesis should remain flexible and undogmatic. Such a commentator must at all times uphold the truth of the Word of God; he must not cling to any interpretation which is demonstrably untenable, lest he bring the Bible into disrepute with the infidel; but he could and should be willing to entertain several distinct explanations of a controversial passage.[5] St Thomas himself provides an illuminating practical example of the required tolerance in his résumé of the different meanings which can be attributed to the word *principium* in that same first verse; and in so doing he introduces a further guiding principle which throws light on Dante's treatment of the subject – the 'exclusion of error'.

Principium is interpreted in three different ways, he reports, to rule out three distinct errors (*tripliciter exponitur ad excludendum tres errores*). Some philosophers affirmed that the universe has always existed, and that there was no beginning of time. Others have held that there were *two* creative 'principles', one of good things, the other of evil. A third group have said that material things were created by God through the agency of spiritual creatures. To guard against the first error, *in principio* is to be glossed as 'in the beginning of time'; to preclude the second, we should take *principium* as a synonym for the Word, that is the Son, or Second Person of the Trinity, in whose Intellect and Wisdom are contained the exemplars of *all* created things; while the third error is excluded by paraphrasing *in principio* as 'before all other things'. For it has been said, St Thomas concludes, that four things were created in the beginning – heaven, prime matter, angels, and, by implication, time.[6]

The monstrous jagged shape in the foreground of Holbein's famous portrait of *The Ambassadors* is revealed as a skull when the spectator moves to a point well to the right of the painting. In much the same way, the apparent oddities and distortions in Dante's main account of the First Creation will cease to appear as deformities if we grasp the nature of his perspective and take up the viewpoint suggested by the foregoing examples.

We must remember that Dante was a thirteenth-century intellectual, familiar with the complex theology of a long exegetical tradition, and steeped in the philosophical thought of his own time. In this regard, it is worth recalling that in his paraphrase of the Creed, recited in the twenty-fourth canto of the *Paradiso*, he omits any mention of the specifically Christian 'Father almighty, Maker of heaven and earth, and of all things visible and invisible'. Instead, he substitutes a purely Aristotelian 'unmoved Prime Mover' ('io credo in uno Dio / solo ed etterno, *che tutto 'l ciel move, / non moto* . . .'); and he goes on to refer to 'proofs physical and metaphysical' of the truth, before claiming the authority of the Word of God. He commits himself to one interpretation of the Genesis story; but he too is most anxious to ward off error, and his account is prefaced and punctuated with qualifications which serve to 'exclude' less orthodox views which were circulating in the Arts Faculty at Paris, in the Medical School at Padua, or in popular heretical movements. The central truth that he wishes to put across in a form free from error is in reality quite simple, and can be summarized in the words of St Albert alluded to by St Thomas: 'Four things are of like age–prime matter, time, the heavens, and the angels.'[7]

If he makes just one reference to the text of Genesis, this is largely because the topic arises in connection with the creation of the angels, and, as we have seen, there is no open reference to angels anywhere in that first chapter. Finally, it will become apparent that his intellectualism is tempered by a desire to reach a relatively uncultivated audience and to write with an elevation and beauty worthy of his theme; and thus the specialized vocabulary of scholastic philosophy alternates with a very bold use of picture-language.

Prelude: the point of space and time

Dante's main account of the Creation comes very late in the *Comedy* and cannot be fully understood or appreciated without reference to its context in the narrative of the poem. The scene is set in the *primum mobile*. Beatrice and Dante converse against the background of the last of the great geometrical spectacles that are enacted for the pilgrim's benefit as he ascends through the physical heavens. God, it will be remembered, has appeared as a point of light, infinitesimally small but infinitely bright, while the angelic orders are perceived as nine circles of fiery light spinning around that point.

With the last line of Canto XXVIII Beatrice has completed her first long discourse about the angels, in which she answered Dante's questions about the inverse relationship between the fiery circles and the heavenly spheres, and satisfied his unspoken doubts about the ranking of the nine choirs of angels by listing their names in the descending order established by Dionysius. Dante-character longs to discover more of 'the truth about these circles', but he is given no time to formulate his questions. In the *proemio* to Canto XXIX Beatrice fixes her gaze upon the dazzling point of light that overpowered Dante's sight, and there, in God, in the place 'where every *when* and every *where* are concentrated in a point', she sees what it is that he wants to hear.

Dante's questions are often anticipated by Beatrice or others of the blessed, but there is nothing stereotyped in this prelude. It links the exposition of doctrine to the narrative action, and it foreshadows the language, imagery and themes of Beatrice's reply in the most subtle and original way.

The twenty-ninth canto opens with a complex astronomical simile giving information which allows us to calculate the length of time that Beatrice's eyes remained fixed on God. We wrestle with a mythological periphrasis, proper names of constellations, new-coined verbs and a battery of technical terms ranging from 'hemisphere' to 'zenith', and discover that we are asked to imagine the conjunction of the heavens at the time of the spring equinox, with the full moon and the sun lying diametrically opposite each other on the horizon: they are like the two round pans of an apothecary's balance suspended in perfect equilibrium from the zenith, as shown in figure 12.

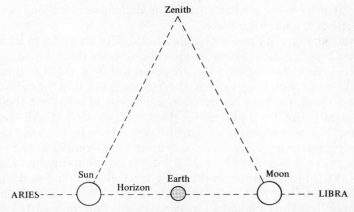

Figure 12. The sun and moon in perfect equilibrium at the spring equinox.

When Latona's two children [Apollo and Diana, the Sun and Moon], lying under Aries and Libra respectively, make themselves a common girdle of the horizon, the zenith holds them in balance for a moment until they each slip from the girdle and change hemispheres. For just so long did Beatrice remain silent, her face radiant with a smile, gazing intently on the point that had overcome me. Then she began: 'Without asking, I shall tell you what you want to hear, for I have seen it there where all space and all time meet in a point.'

> Quando ambedue li figli di Latona,
> coperti del Montone e de la Libra,
> fanno de l'orizzonte insieme zona,
> quant' è dal punto che 'l cenìt inlibra
> infin che l'uno e l'altro da quel cinto,
> cambiando l'emisperio, si dilibra,
> tanto, col volto di riso dipinto,
> si tacque Bëatrice, riguardando
> fiso nel punto che m'avëa vinto.
> Poi cominciò: 'Io dico, e non dimando,
> quel che tu vuoli udir, perch' io l'ho visto
> là 've s'appunta ogne *ubi* e ogne *quando*.   (*Par.* XXIX, 1–12)

How long, then, would the two 'planets' remain in perfect equilibrium before the sun set and the moon rose? How long, indeed, does any heavenly body, or any moving body whatsoever, remain in exactly the same position? Strictly speaking, the answer can only be 'for a mathematical instant'. And despite a forcefully argued objection by Manfredi Porena it seems that this, the traditional interpretation, does give the sense required here.[8] This last astronomical periphrasis does not measure the lapse of time on Dante's journey, nor the passing of the centuries; it does not fix a specific, unrepeatable *nunc* in the life of the universe; it indicates a moment without duration, a 'point of time', exactly analogous in the temporal order to the mathematical point, defined as something possessing location without magnitude.

At this juncture in the story Dante and Beatrice are about to leave the 'greatest body' in the universe and pass beyond the three dimensions of corporeal space into infinity. We are about to follow them as they rise from the swiftest-moving heaven, the 'root of time', into the stillness of eternity. Dante the poet has given us a foretaste of *infinity* in the most paradoxical form by representing the Uncircumscribed, All-circumscribing Deity as a point infinitesimally small.[9] Here he gives us a no less surprising foretaste of *eternity* by conjuring up a moment in and out of time, a moment of infinite brevity or infinite duration (neither description is exact, but the former is the more 'marvellous'). And so the pause that separates Beatrice's first and second speeches is not ridiculously short, not 'less than a comma', in Porena's mocking phrase. It lasts an eternity.

Porena also attacked Dante for the misplaced ostentation of erudition in this prelude to the canto. He reminds us that the sun and moon are in opposition at every full moon, not just at the equinox. And he points out that in the precise conjunction which Dante describes, the moon would be invisible as it would suffer a total eclipse. So much for those who admire Dante for his scientific rigour! But Porena seems to have been temperamentally hostile to any passage of poetry that makes demands on the reader's intellect; and his healthy refusal to indulge in indiscriminate admiration of every line that Dante ever wrote blinds him here to the wider implications of the simile and its relevance to the speech that is to come. Dante chooses both sun and moon because they are the 'two great lights' made by God 'to divide the day from the night', and to be 'for signs, and for seasons, and for days, and years' – in short, to measure time. He shows them in conjunction with Aries and Libra because this is where they were placed in the firmament at the moment of creation, when these *cose belle* were set in motion and time began.[10] This is the moment Beatrice is about to describe. And Dante's choice of simile is no more casual than his decision to indicate God with the periphrasis 'là 've s'appunta ogne *ubi* e ogne *quando*'.

The unfolding of God's eternal love

In the next five lines Beatrice combines affirmation and refutation to 'unveil the sweet face of fair truth'.[11] She defines God's purpose in creating the angels, and at the same time she 'excludes' no less than four interrelated sources of misunderstanding. Two of them relate to the *ubi* and *quando* of the creation. It is as nonsensical, she implies, to speculate about the 'when' of creation, as it is to inquire what God did 'before' He created, or to ask 'how long' he existed 'beforehand'. The universe has not always existed; it is not coeval with God; but He exists in eternity, outside time – 'in sua etternità di tempo fore'. Similarly, it is vain to ask 'where' the creation took place. God is infinite. He has no poles, no co-ordinates, no bounds. He is outside every possible limit or boundary, 'fuor d'ogne altro comprender'.

The third mistake – hinted at perhaps in the word *comprendere* – is to suppose that God acted out of necessity or under any sort of constraint. On the contrary, we learn, creation was an act of free will, done at His pleasure, 'come i piacque'. The fourth error concerns God's purpose, and its refutation leads into a statement of the truth. He did not create the angels in order to increase His goodness – '*non* per aver a sé di bene acquisto'. This cannot be ('esser non può'), because there cannot be any augmentation of an infinite amount. His true motive was to enable His 'ideas' to exist independently outside Himself and to body forth His likeness in three ways – in their being as such, in their self-awareness, and in their nature. God named himself to Moses simply as 'I AM', and the angels were created in order that they too might announce 'I exist', *subsisto*. By that declaration they show that they also resemble God in the *consciousness* of their existence. Since God is imaged as light, they can be called His radiance or effulgence, His *splendore*. They have the power to shine out, or to shine back, with a reflected light (*risplendere*); and it is in that outshining that their 'declaration' of conscious being is made.[12]

It would seem quite impossible to unite biblical allusion, scholastic Latin, light-imagery, personification and word-play more densely or more effortlessly than in the phrase 'ma perché suo splendore / potesse, risplendendo, dir "*Subsisto*"'. But Dante surpasses himself as he comes to the main clause of this long sentence; and the energy dammed up behind the preliminary qualifications and 'exclusions' discharges itself in the stupendous line describing the creative act. In creating the angels, God, who is eternal love, 'opened Himself in new loves':

> s'aperse in nuovi amor l'etterno amore.

The reflexive verb *aprirsi* could not be 'plainer', but it is totally unexpected and amazingly rich in meaning and connotation. It is appropriate to so many of the image-families that we discussed in the previous chapter. It can suggest the irradiation of light, the welling-over of a spring, the procession of number, or the unfolding of a flower. In the context it also carries overtones of intimate human relationships – the disclosure of a secret, a declaration of love, even the opening of arms that precedes an embrace. For Dante insists that Creation was an active outpouring of love.[13]

God is Love, as we read in the first Letter of St John (4.8). His effects resemble Him so closely that they can be called by the same name. And yet the abyss that separates the Creator from His creatures is not forgotten. He is eternal, they are 'new-made'; He is singular, they are plural. One could not find a more sublime application of the twin laws of causality which state that a cause causes in its own likeness, and that an effect receives the likeness in accordance with the limitations of its own nature. But to dwell on the exactness or the profundity of the thought here might be almost as sacrilegious as it would be to investigate the part played by rhythm, assonance and asymmetrical repetition in making this line the fitting climax to one of the most beautiful and most extraordinary sentences anywhere in the *Comedy*:

> Non per aver a sé di bene acquisto,
> ch'esser non può, ma perché suo splendore
> potesse, risplendendo, dir '*Subsisto*',
> in sua etternità di tempo fore,
> fuor d'ogne altro comprender, come i piacque,
> s'aperse in nuovi amor l'etterno amore.   (*Par*. XXIX, 13–18)

The 'triform effect'

Beatrice next returns briefly to the absurdity of confounding time and eternity. 'God did not lie torpidly inert before his act of self-revelation', she says, for no "before" nor "after" could precede His "moving upon these waters"':

> Né prima quasi torpente si giacque
> ché né prima né poscia procedette
> lo discorrer di Dio sovra quest' acque.   (19–21)

This more prosaic terzina, with its teasingly oblique allusion to the text of Genesis, provides a quiet transition to the next section of Beatrice's speech, where she will affirm that while it is literally nonsensical to speculate as to what God did 'before' creation, it is also mistaken to believe that the angels were created for 'many centuries *before* the rest of the world was made'.[14] The word 'before' is conceptually possible in the second case, but it is still unacceptable because other parts of the universe came into being simultaneously. And so, in order to exclude this further error concerning time, Beatrice is forced to widen her terms of reference, and to reveal which other parts of the universe issued directly from God in that same outpouring of His love. From the angels we pass at last to an account of the whole of the First Creation.

The next five terzinas are rather difficult. Indeed, it may seem as if Beatrice were going out of her way to avoid plain words and to conceal the identity of these other parts of the universe by using periphrases which involve a dense accumulation of metaphor and a double layer of scholastic terminology. But there is no obscurity in her thought, and the difficulties will evaporate if we take them one by one in the proper order.

The most important point is made without recourse to figurative or technical language. The number of components created in the same instant was neither more nor less than three.[15] God, as cause, produced a threefold effect, a 'triforme effetto'. And since we know that the angels constitute one of these three parts, our quest is limited to the identification of the other two.

The similes and metaphors used in these lines will be familiar from Chapter 8, and they should not present any serious obstacles. As we saw, the creative act may be compared to a bowshot. But a normal crossbow can fire three arrows only by loosing them one after the other. We are therefore asked to imagine a special weapon with three strings capable of shooting all three arrows at once. Our mental picture of creation as an emanation, that is, as an outpouring of water, must also be replaced by that of the irradiation of light. However rapidly water is poured into a vessel, some time must elapse before the vessel is filled. But there is no interval – so it was then believed – between the coming of the ray of light to a transparent object and its illuminating every part of that object however large it may be.[16] In just this way, the triform effect 'rayed forth' (*raggiò*) from the Lord without admitting any differentiation as to its beginning ('sanza distinzïone in essordire').

We come now to the periphrases involving scholastic terminology. In the first line of the passage, the three components are elliptically described as 'pure form', 'pure matter', and 'form and matter conjoined' ('forma e materia, congiunte e purette'). The adjective 'pure' can only be applied to a form possessing no matter. Elsewhere, it might refer to the pure abstraction of a geometrical form; but in this context it must denote a 'substantial form', that is, a form that subsists outside the mind, a form enjoying a distinct, independent existence. As we have seen, thirteenth-century theologians defined spiritual creatures as 'substances separated from matter', and they habitually referred to them as *substantiae separatae*. It is therefore certain that the locution 'pure form' must indicate the angels.

The phrase 'pure matter' might be used to describe a raw material that was free from admixture or impurity. But in the context of this passage it can refer only to matter possessing no form. In other words, it must denote the unknowable, unimaginable, indestructible substrate of the four elements known to Aristotle and the scholastics as *materia prima*. Hence we can identify the second component as 'primary matter'.

The characterization of the third component as 'form and matter conjoined' does not permit such certainty. As it stands, the expression could refer to any or all of the *corpora composita* that make up the world of everyday experience. It could also be applied to the *corpora simplicia*, or four elements, since they too are a compound of matter and form. The precise meaning is clarified in the sequel, however, where it becomes clear that the choice of *congiunto* is deliberate, and that the word implies a more intimate, durable union than does the apparent synonym *composto*.

In her second set of circumlocutions Beatrice passes from 'matter' and 'form' to the three possible permutations of 'potency' and 'act'; and here an example may help to bridge the conceptual gap. To the experienced eye, a lump of iron is *potentially* a knife. But the knife does not come into being until the iron takes on that particular form. It is therefore the form that *actualizes* the potentiality of the material; and the form may be called the *act* of its body. A material form such as that of a knife does not, however, exhaust the potential of its matter. The iron can always be melted down again; and, in any case, it is subject to change and decay through normal use and through the action of rust. The angels, by contrast, are 'pure' form, entirely divorced from matter. They cannot be considered as something else *in potentia*. In this sense it is meaningful for Beatrice to describe the angels as 'substances' in which 'pure actuality' was produced; and it is also meaningful for her to say that they were the 'summit of the universe' (a phrase we can also understand in purely spatial terms).[17]

Primary matter is once again presented as the polar opposite to the angels. It is not determined by *any* form, and it is in a state of potency with respect to *every* material form. It can therefore be called 'pure potentiality'; and it can be said to have occupied the lowest position ('pura potenza tenne la parte ima').

From this we may infer that the still unnamed third component will occupy the middle, and that it will consist of 'potency and act conjoined'. Our inference is duly confirmed – with an all-important addition. Beatrice asserts that the bond which tied this act to this potency, and this form to this matter, was such that it will never be untied:

> nel mezzo strinse potenza con atto
> tal vime, che *già mai non si divima*.   (35–6)

Notwithstanding the metaphorical form, the statement is perfectly precise. It excludes any possible reference to the *corpora composita* or to the *corpora simplicia*. The only matter that never slips from under its form is the fifth element, aether; the only form that never loosens its hold on matter is that of the heavenly spheres. The third component can only be the physical heavens considered as one entity – *il cielo*.[18]

Such then is the argument of these five dense terzinas. All that remains, now that the footholds have been cut, and the pitons hammered home, is to enjoy the view from the summit: the vast panorama opened up by the imagery; the unobtrusive use of repetition that binds the key-words together; and the varied 'order and construction' of the syntactic and metrical units.

Like three arrows from a three-stringed bow, form and matter, pure and conjoined, shot forth into perfect being. And just as a ray of light shines out in glass, amber or crystal in such a way that there is no interval between its coming and its being there completely, so the threefold effect rayed out from its Lord with no distinction as to beginning. The separate substances were created in their ordered hierarchy; they were the summit of the universe in whom pure actuality was produced. Pure potentiality held the lowest part. Between them a bond seized potency and act that will never be unbound.

> Forma e materia, congiunte e purette,
> usciro ad esser che non avia fallo,
> come d'arco tricordo tre saette.
> E come in vetro, in ambra o in cristallo
> raggio resplende sì, che dal venire
> a l'esser tutto non è intervallo,
> così 'l triforme effetto del suo sire
> ne l'esser suo raggiò insieme tutto
> sanza distinzïone in essordire.
> Concreato fu ordine e costrutto
> a le sustanze; e quelle furon cima
> nel mondo in che puro atto fu produtto;
> pura potenza tenne la parte ima;
> nel mezzo strinse potenza con atto
> tal vime, che già mai non si divima.　　(*Par.* XXIX, 22–36)

'Whatsoever God doeth, it shall be for ever'

In these first thirty-six lines of Canto XXIX the passing of time has been denied three times in three different ways. No time elapsed while Beatrice fixed her eyes on God; time did not exist before creation; there was no interval between the creation of the angels and that of the heavens. Only now, after reiterating this last point, does Beatrice make her first reference to an event that took place *in* time. In less time than it takes to count up to twenty, she says, one section of the angels rebelled and were driven from Heaven to cause an upheaval in the lowest of the elements ('de li angeli parte / turbò il suggetto d'i vostri alimenti'). The others, a majority, remained; and it was then that they began their 'circling' around God, which they are now displaying in visible form before the delighted eyes of Dante the pilgrim.[19]

The time reference could hardly be more precise – and it could hardly be more tantalizing. In the remainder of her discourse, Beatrice confines herself to the angels, and we learn no more about the universe at large. We can safely deduce from earlier references to the fall of Lucifer that 'il suggetto d'i vostri alimenti' refers to the lowest-lying element, Earth, and not to primary matter, the 'substrate of the elements'; and hence we can be sure that the four elements had assumed their forms and taken up their natural places before these twenty seconds had elapsed.[20] What we cannot tell from this canto is whether any time elapsed between the emanation of the triform effect and the performance of what the theologians called the *opus distinctionis*, that is, the formation of the elements and the distinction of the species of minerals, plants and animals. And therefore we cannot tell whether these tasks were carried out by God himself, directly, and in the same instant of creation, or whether the angels and the heavens played any part in activating the potentiality of prime matter.

The question is of the utmost importance, as we can see if we turn to a remarkable passage earlier in the *Paradiso* in which Beatrice had anticipated many of the points made in this canto. There she declared:

Casting forth all envy and burning with love, the goodness of God flashes out to reveal the beauties that are eternal. *Everything which flows directly from his goodness will have no end*; for where the divine goodness sets its seal, the imprint does not move.

> La divina bontà, che da sé sperne
> ogne livore, ardendo in sé, sfavilla
> sì che dispiega le bellezze etterne.
> *Ciò che da lei sanza mezzo distilla*
> *non ha poi fine*, perché non si move
> la sua imprenta quand' ella sigilla.　　　　(*Par.* VII, 64–9)

Images of burning, irradiation, unfolding, flowing and sealing follow each other in one of the most densely metaphorical passages in the *Comedy*, and few readers will be able to grasp all their implications. But even on a first reading there can be no misunderstanding the plain language of the sentence italicized. The crucial general principle is that all those things which God creates with His own hands shall never cease to be.[21] This explains why the still unspecified 'beauties' are 'eternal' ('bellezze *etterne*'). This is why the heavens are no less sempiternal than the pure actuality of the angels. The heavenly spheres are composite, material and corporeal; but the knot that binds their matter to their form was tied by the fingers of God, and it will never come undone.[22]

Now, this general principle would be virtually meaningless if the converse were not also true. It follows, therefore, that everything which does not proceed *sanza mezzo* from God is mortal and is doomed to pass away. Dante does not deny that God is the 'Maker of *all* things, visible and invisible'. But he does make it clear that not all things are made by

246

God directly, without intermediaries. And so it is of the utmost importance to discover the '*efficient* cause' of any being or thing in the universe, and to know whether it was produced by God directly or indirectly, *sanza mezzo* or *con mezzo* (in Latin, *immediate* or *mediate*).[23]

It will be evident, on reflection, that the general principle is simply one instance of the law which governs all causality – *agens agit sibi simile*. God is eternal. All those effects of which He is the sole cause will therefore participate in His eternity to the extent permitted by their nature as created beings. Unlike Him they have a beginning (they are '*nuovi* amor', 'cose *nove*'); but like Him they are without end.

There is no lack of biblical authority for this axiom, for it is written in the Book of Ecclesiastes (3.14) that *omnia quae fecit Deus perseverant in aeternum* ('all things made by God shall endure eternally'). But historians of medieval thought have shown that orthodox theologians of Dante's own day did not choose to apply the principle in the same way.[24] Dante is looking back to the Platonizing theologians of the school of Chartres in the *twelfth* century and to their commentaries on Plato's *Timaeus* or on the *Consolatio philosophiae* by Boethius.[25] And, more important, his thesis is virtually indistinguishable from an axiom that is central to the thought of the Moslem Neoplatonist, Avicenna. This states: 'Whatever comes directly from an immutable being must itself be immutable' (*a stabili inquantum stabile non est nisi stabile*).[26]

We shall find that it is possible to reconstruct the broad outlines of Dante's position with regard to the *opus distinctionis*, and that his rigorous application of the principle just described did in fact lead him into heterodoxy.[27] But before we can attempt this reconstruction we must make ourselves thoroughly familiar with the processes of generation and corruption which are operating at any given moment in the subsequent life of the universe, and we must discover exactly what part is played by the angels, the heavens and seed in the production of individual beings in time.

10

Generation and universal nature

Aristotle's account of generation

THE TERM 'GENERATION' COULD BE USED QUITE PROPERLY OF THE making of a rain-cloud, a sapphire, a dandelion, a greyhound or a poem. As a first approximation, it is scarcely too much to say that it could refer to the production of any being or thing which had not been created. Its precise area of meaning in any given context, in any given medieval thinker, could therefore expand or contract to match any corresponding contraction or expansion in the referential field of the term 'creation'. In a context where 'creation' was used in its widest sense to denote God's making in any form whatever, 'generation' would refer to the workings of nature. When 'creation' was used in its narrowest sense to indicate the production of something out of nothing—*ex nihilo* or *nullo praesupposito*—'generation' could refer to any process of formation in which some aspect or component of the new-made thing had pre-existed under some form or had been in any way presupposed—*aliquo praesupposito*. If 'creation' was reserved for the direct action of God as First Cause, 'generation' would be used of the activity of all secondary causes. And so, to revert to Dante's terminology, if 'creation' is reserved for the things that God makes *sanza mezzo*, 'generation' is the proper word for the production of all those things that he brings into being *con mezzo*.[1]

At the time of writing the *Convivio* Dante acknowledged that his views on generation were based on the 'opinion of Aristotle and the Peripatetics', and we must therefore begin our investigation by taking note of the main features in that account.[2]

Aristotle tried to limit the semantic range of the term by laying down certain conditions for its use that would be binding in every context. He insisted that 'generation' can only be used for the production of something that comes into existence as a body in the material universe, and that enjoys 'being' in the fullest and most concrete sense of the word. 'Greatness' cannot be generated, nor can 'felinity', but only a 'great cat' such as a lion. Moreover, 'generation' cannot be used of 'lion' in general, but only of '*this* lion', in this body, made of this matter, possessing these dimensions, occupying this space, existing at this moment, and not having existed before it was generated.[3] In other words, it can only be predicated of an individual being or thing—of the *substantia*, and not of the species. It can refer only to the production of a particular whole, a *totum* or *synolon*, analysed as a *compositum* of this matter and this form.[4] It must not be used of either matter or form independently. Matter is presupposed in the process of generation; it can only be 'transformed'. A form is transmitted from one existing *compositum* to generate another, but the form itself is not generated.[5]

In Aristotle's opinion, four conditions must be met before generation can take place. First, there must be a 'generant' (*generans*), that is, an existing *compositum* possessing the fully actualized form of the *substantia* to be generated.[6] Then, there must be some pre-existent matter which is suitable in complexion and which is ready to shed its existing structure in order to take on the new. No matter is either created or destroyed in the process, and the generation of one *compositum* entails the 'corruption' of an existing one.[7] Next, the *generans* and the *materia disposita* must be in contact at the crucial stage. Aristotle knew of course that most living organisms are generated from a seed, and that it is the seed alone which carries the mysterious 'informative power', as it was later called, which will be gradually unfolded in the course of growth. But this does not infringe the rule, because the seed is made within the mature plant or animal, and the seedling or embryo emerges directly from the seed. (In fact, the distinction between seedless generation and generation through seed is much less important in Aristotle's theory than might be expected.)[8] Lastly, there must be an *extrinsic* 'active principle' or 'cause moving towards' generation. In the case of living organisms that cause is heat; in the case of inanimate *composita*, both heat and cold are considered to be active principles.[9]

Heat produces the dry and moist exhalations from the surface of the earth and the sea; and variations in temperature govern all the transformations of the four elements. Where the exhalations are trapped below the earth, different applications of hot and cold produce metals from the moist exhalations and minerals from the dry.[10] Heat (with moisture) is required for the propagation of plants by cuttings, and to activate the *virtus informativa* of a plant seed, which can remain dormant for months or even years. Heat is also necessary throughout the gestation of the embryo before the egg is hatched or the young animal is born. In the case of birds and mammals, the heat is provided externally or internally by the vital warmth of the mother. But the ultimate cause of that warmth, and the immediate source of the heat required at all lower levels of generation, is to be found in the sun.[11] And Aristotle's position is fairly summarized in the famous dictum—in which we may substitute the name of any other composite being—'A man is generated by a man and the sun': *homo hominem generat . . . et sol.*[12]

It is not enough, however, to speak of the sun's *heat*. If the sun were stationary, the temperature would remain constant and there would be no generation and no corruption. And so we must understand Aristotle's 'active principle' as including the *movements* as well as the heat of the sun. Changes in temperature between night and day are caused by the sun's passive motion which it receives from the outermost heaven, and these changes determine the short-lived cycles of evaporation and condensation. The more significant variations in temperature, as between midwinter and midsummer, are the result of the sun's different elevation at noon as it passes on its annual path round the oblique circle of the ecliptic; and it is this that governs the seasonal growth of the crops and the breeding season of most animals.[13]

The heaven of the moon also has a part to play as a 'moving cause' in Aristotle's theory, since it communicates a semicircular motion to the sphere of Water and a circular motion to the sphere of Fire.[14] The first causes the twelve-hourly ebb and flow of the tides, while the second is transmitted to the sphere of Air and helps to determine the winds: in the upper atmosphere it is received—relatively weakly owing to the resistance of the medium—as a steady breeze blowing from east to west; in the lower atmosphere it interacts with the vertical movement of the exhalations to produce the frequent changes in the force and direction of the winds over the surface of the earth.[15]

The impact of astrology

As we have seen in other contexts, the Aristotelian model of the universe was never rejected in the Middle Ages but underwent important 'improvements' and extensions. And so it happened with his theory of natural generation. The theory was modified profoundly to accommodate ideas and attitudes deriving from the sacred writings of Judaism, Christianity and Islam, and from the developing sciences of medicine, alchemy and astrology. There can be no doubt that the most important modifications came from astrology, and it is this which we must now briefly take into consideration.

Superstitious beliefs about the influence of the planets and the stars had formed the core of the state religion of Babylon, and they were already known to Aristotle. They were refined and codified in Alexandria during the first centuries of our era, and they were widely disseminated in the Roman Empire. They enjoyed great prestige and they underwent further elaboration in the succession of Moslem cultures that extended from Persia in the seventh century to Spain in the eleventh and twelfth; and from Spain they spread throughout the whole of the Latin West. By Dante's lifetime almost every educated person in Europe seems to have accepted the fundamental premises of astrology, which were incorporated as self-evident principles into virtually all branches of natural science.[16] And as a result of this key-development, Aristotle's sane and coherent observations concerning the heat and movement of the sun were almost submerged by the much wider, vaguer, magical claims made on behalf of the other heavenly luminaries. All the planets and all the individual stars were now credited with a distinct role in the cycle of generation and corruption; and this role was by no means limited to that of an 'active principle' in the sense that Aristotle had given to the term.[17]

The attractions of the new model are not difficult to understand. It satisfied the human thirst for meaning and order in that it suggested a purpose for the existence of the stars and the other six planets.[18] And from the purely practical point of view, it seemed to provide a better explanation of the countless variations in nature. [19] The path of the sun is always the same, but one summer can be hotter or dryer than the next. From time to time there occur natural disasters such as typhoons and pestilences. Metals and minerals are found in differing quantities and in differing degrees of purity. Not all copulation results in pregnancy, and not every pregnancy in a live birth. The offspring of the same parents, even puppies from the same litter, can differ in size, appearance and vigour. All such variations could be accounted for on the hypothesis that the differences were the result of differing conjunctions of the heavens; and even today many people find this kind of explanation plausible and satisfying.

It is difficult, if not impossible, to find unambiguous and universally accepted accounts of the activity of these multiple celestial causes. A planet like Mars was said to be hot, while Saturn and the Moon were said to be actively cold; and such claims are not incompatible with Aristotle's view of the sun's role as a *principium activum*.[20] Similarly, it is not entirely inconsistent with Aristotle's approach to assume that the heavens possess a *virtus mineralis*, a power of generating minerals.[21] But alchemists and encyclopaedists go beyond this. They repeat the ancient Babylonian belief that each of the seven principal metals is caused by one of the seven planets; and while this is not to deny the necessity of an existing, material *compositum generans*, it certainly lays the emphasis on the contribution made by the heavens.[22] Less cautious writers express themselves as though each species of mineral were caused by a specific star, or by a distinct conjunction of the heavens.[23] And the implication of this view is that the form itself is communicated by the luminary and not by some existing sample of the metal or mineral in question. In other words, the luminary has become the *generans* and no longer the 'moving' cause.

The process by which the generative agent or *generans* was displaced from the earth to the heavens was completed by the Neoplatonist metaphysicians among the Arabs. For them, the true author of the form of a newly generated mineral *compositum* was one of the celestial Intelligences, the *dator formarum*, who used the luminary as an instrument with which to give body to his 'idea'. Fifteen centuries of philosophical, religious and scientific thought had led them back very close to the Platonist position that Aristotle had set out to refute.[24]

St Thomas interpreted Aristotle very faithfully in his commentaries, and even in his own independent writings he held fast to Aristotle's view.[25] But many of his Christian contemporaries disagreed with him or simply did not understand the distinctions he made. More often than not their language is figurative and resists precise paraphrase. Nevertheless, the clear implication of their metaphors of building, hammering, impressing and infusing is that the heavens are capable of 'inducing' forms from without, and not simply of 'moving towards' form.[26]

Dante's account of generation and the celestial influences

We have seen that Dante thought he was following the *verace oppinione* of Aristotle and the Peripatetics in his theories about generation; and it is certainly true that he quotes with approval and understanding a number of relevant texts from the *Metaphysics*, the *Physics* and the *De generatione*. In the *Convivio*, he insists that 'anything that makes something must itself be that thing perfectly'; that 'when one thing is generated from another, it is generated as having been in that first thing'; and that 'anything that is altered must be conjoined with the cause of its alteration'.[27] In the *Comedy*, he points out that Plato was mistaken in his belief that the human soul was given by Nature from the stars to be the form of a human body, and that it will return to its tutelary star at death. Nevertheless, it seems clear that, in Dante's view, Plato's mistake was limited to the generation of *human beings*. And a few cantos later, Dante will speak of *la virtù informante* of animals and plants as residing in the movement and light of the stars.[28] In short, we must recognize from the outset that Dante's views on generation are not always clear or consistent, and that his position was in some respects closer to that of the Arab Neoplatonists than to that of the Peripatetics.

Dante is still close to Aristotle in his insistence that the sun is the 'father of mortal life' and 'the chief minister of Nature'; and we have seen how much prominence he gave to the obliquity of the ecliptic. In several places Dante asserts that the other luminaries derive their light from the sun. But it is quite clear that he did not believe that the sun performed its role in generation unaided. On the contrary, he affirms time and time again that it is the heavens as a whole that 'by their movement produce generated things, both with seed and without'. The heavens function as a unified system in which energy is relayed from the higher to the lower. It is 'circular nature' in its entirety that 'sets its seal on the wax of mortal things'. In the *Monarchia*, Dante writes that 'the disposition of this world follows the disposition inherent in the circulation of the heavens'; and in the *Quaestio* he quotes Ptolemy with approval to the effect that 'the aspects of things here below resemble the aspects of things on high'.[29]

Dante makes it quite plain that a heaven does not act through the whole great body of its sphere, but only through its luminary. In the case of the stellar sphere, each star, or each constellation, possesses a distinct 'formal principle' which causes effects that are distinct in form; but, as we saw in Chapter 6, it is the stars that lie closest to the equator of the heaven's 'proper' movement–the constellations of the Zodiac–that are the most important. Narrowly considered, effects are caused by the light-rays emitted by a given planet or star. However, Dante frequently reminds his readers that the true cause of the *moto* and *virtù* of each sphere is the angelic Intelligence, who uses the heaven as his instrument in order to realize forms that he has intuited in the mind of God.[30]

Like all agents, a heaven causes by reducing things to its own likeness. But the degree of likeness that it communicates will vary from time to time and from place to place in relation to three main variables–the altitude of the luminary; the readiness of matter to receive its impression; and the position of other planets, which may either enhance or retard its influence.[31]

We must now go into a little more detail and attempt to reconstruct what Dante believed about the generation of *corpora composita* at each of the three main levels on the Scale of Being.

Concerning the production of inanimate bodies Dante himself has tantalizingly little to say, since he refers to only three examples: a magnet, a crystal and a precious stone. From these references we learn that minerals are indeed generated (i.e. that they were not all created in the Beginning), and that they have a special love for the place of their generation. It is this love which makes the lodestone turn towards the north. Crystals, too, are made in the frozen north by the action of extreme and prolonged cold, but Dante does not indicate whether the heavens have any other part to play in their formation.[32] The case of the *precious stone* is however more instructive, since it enables us to distinguish two distinct and successive operations. The sun initiates the process by 'drawing out all that is base' in the raw material, which must be a suitably complexioned compound in which Earth predominates. (This would be called the 'digestion' or 'disposition' of the matter.) Then, and only then, a star communicates the specific form of the stone. It is this form which carries with it the 'active qualities' or 'virtues' that are described in the medieval lapidaries.[33]

Dante has more to say about the role of the heavens when he deals with the generation of living organisms. First, he reminds us that although the seed is indispensable, it is not the sole cause since 'the *life* of every *living* thing here below is caused by the heavens'. The heavens 'induce the "first perfection" in fitly disposed things', he writes in the *Convivio*; and we must remember that 'first perfection' is one way of defining the soul or psyche, that is, the form and vital principle of a living body.[34] In the *Comedy* the same concept is expressed less technically, and yet more guardedly: 'The souls of plants and animals are drawn from the potentiality of complexioned matter by the rays and movements of the heavenly lights.'[35]

The heavens are also a concomitant cause of the '*second* perfection' of plants and animals, that is, of the full exercise of their characteristic activity when they have reached maturity. We are told that the 'power of Aries draws forth the leaves' in spring, and that the ' "great wheels" guide every seed to a goal, a goal that varies in accordance with the particular stars that accompany it'.[36]

The crucial verbs in these sentences are all used metaphorically ('drawing out', 'guiding', 'accompanying') but their literal meaning does become a little clearer after one has studied a paragraph in the *Convivio* which we may treat as Dante's account of the embryonic life of a mammal.[37] The seed, we learn, passes into the mother's womb where it finds suitably complexioned matter in the menstrual blood. First, it matures and 'disposes' the blood, by causing it to curdle and making it ready to receive the 'formative power' which the seed carries from the father. Then this *vertù formativa* prepares the organs of sensation and movement which are necessary for animal existence. Finally, the power of the heavens brings the soul into life from the potency of the seed: 'la vertù celestiale . . . produce de la potenza del seme l'anima in vita'.[38]

Now, this *vertù celestiale* is far from being constant or uniform: indeed, Dante's main objective in the chapter from which we are quoting is to explain the diversity of individuals by reference to variations in the heavenly influences. His next point, therefore, is that 'the disposition of the heavens to this effect can be good, better or best, varying as it does with the continual changes in the conjunctions of the planets and stars'; and so it comes about that the soul will be 'less pure' or 'more pure'.[39]

It would seem that Dante is here referring to the effect produced by the heavens at the moment of birth, when the infant animal is at last separated from its mother and begins to take nourishment through its mouth rather than through the umbilical cord (in the case of a human being this was the conjunction that an astrologer would need to know before he could cast a horoscope). But Dante also indicates other variables that help to make the soul 'more pure' and 'less pure'. These come into play much earlier – from the moment of conception, or even from the time when the seed is formed in the father. And these other variables are also subject to celestial influences in some respects.

It is now made clear that the seed itself possesses three 'virtues'. These are the formative power received from the father; the properties of the elements in its material complexion; and its 'natural heat'. Quoting Aristotle, Dante refers to this *calore naturale* as a *vertude celestiale*; and, as such, it will presumably vary in strength or efficacy in accordance with the differing disposition of the heavens.[40] The material complexion of the seed can be 'better or less good', and so too can the disposition of the father, which will vary according to his age, health, diet, the season of the year and even the time of day. The disposition of the father and the complexion of his seed are in fact very closely related, since they both depend on the proportions of the four humours or the four elements. And it seems clear that the constant variations in these proportions are largely determined by the celestial influences.[41]

Drawing together all these scattered and very uneven texts, we might summarize Dante's beliefs concerning the role of the heavens somewhat as follows. The heavens collaborate in the generation of plants and animals from the moment when the seed is formed. They help to determine the complexion of the future *substantia*. Through their heat they dispose matter to receive form. They draw out the soul from the potency of the seed; and they guide it towards maturity. Since the luminaries are never in the same position or the same conjunction for long at a time, their influence is unequal. One individual receives more and another less. And thus, of necessity, the heavens make individuals of the same species different and unequal. They cannot make an acorn grow into a plum tree. But it is thanks to their influence that one tree bears an abundance of good plums, while another produces inedible *bozzac-chioni*.[42]

There are some passages in Dante's work in which he seems to regret this inequality and to question its justice. His tone suggests that such inequality has come about by accident rather than design, and that it is, so to speak, a mere by-product of the way in which the heavens revolve.[43] But in the eighth canto of the *Paradiso*, where he tackles the problem directly, he adopts a more positive and triumphant attitude. The laws of causation dictate that *omne agens agit sibi simile*. And so the nature of every generated being tends to reduplicate that of its generant, and 'to follow in the same path'. But God in His providence – the word is repeated five times in the canto – gives the heavens power to overcome this tendency and to endow individuals diversely with different aptitudes and talents. This dispensation is necessary for the well-being and order of the universe. Far from being a by-product, differentiation is now seen as the *raison d'être* of the heavens and as the 'final cause' of the whole intricate system of revolving spheres.[44]

Determinism in the natural order

Everything that is generated under the heavens is generated under their influence and remains subject to their power. All movement is initiated by the heavens, since every generated being follows the promptings of its own instinctive nature in response to stimuli from without, and both the external stimulus and the internal response are determined by the movement of the heavens. Every generated being is therefore fully determined, and no generated being has any freedom of action.[45]

These more or less synonymous propositions contain the essence of Dante's beliefs about natural determinism. They are not difficult to understand, and they do not challenge or contradict our everyday experience of the non-human world around us. But modern terms like 'stimulus' and 'response' can lull the reader into a sense of false security; and the less familiar terms used by Dante and his teachers do in fact embody some concepts and assumptions that are markedly different from those current today. It is these notions that we must now investigate in detail, bearing in mind that they constitute the most important part of Dante's theory of generation and one of the corner-stones of his cosmological and ethical thought.

We must begin with the scholastic concepts of 'movement' and 'love', for these were much more closely associated in the thirteenth century than they are today and had a much wider range of reference. Following Aristotle, Dante and his teachers could refer to any change or action whatsoever as a kind of 'movement'. So all-embracing was this concept that 'natural science', or 'physics', was defined as the study of movement, or as the study of bodies in movement; and the objective of the natural scientist was to identify all the species of movement, and to discover the 'motive force' or 'motive' in every case. Movements were divided into those that were 'violent', in which the subject was purely passive and the motive force came wholly from without, and 'natural', in which the motive force was intrinsic. And it could be said that *every natural* movement or action is initiated by some kind of love: *omne agens, quodcumque sit, agit quamcumque actionem ex aliquo amore.*[46]

At this level of abstraction love can be universally defined as a 'force that unites': *Amor est virtus unitiva.*[47] In the simplest case, it manifests itself in the form of a desire to be united with something good in which the subject is deficient. This desire then becomes the intrinsic motive force that impels the subject to 'take steps' in order to obtain that 'good' and be one with it. The simplest example of the process is that of an animal moved by hunger. On seeing an antelope, a lion may rise, give chase, seize it, kill it and devour its flesh. He will then be 'united' with the protein, carbohydrate and other nutrients in which he was deficient. Desire will be satisfied, and it will give place to fruition; and that particular sequence of movements will come to an end. If there had been no such deficiency, the lion would not have felt hunger, and he would have remained motionless.

The nature of the 'good' will vary from subject to subject and from one case to another; so too will the kind of movement required before union takes place and desire is assuaged. But it will be found that for every subject the primary good and the primary object of desire is 'being'. Everything that 'is' desires to go on 'being'. Everything that has not yet attained the fullness of its being desires that perfection: *omnis natura appetit suum esse et suam perfectionem.*[48] In every case 'love of being' takes the form of 'self-love', *amor proprius* or *amor sui*; and these terms had none of the pejorative overtones that they have since acquired. Self-love expresses itself as the desire for self-conservation and self-fulfilment. It is quite simply the foundation of all other loves; and so Dante can speak of 'lo proprio amore di me medesimo, lo quale è *principio di tutti li altri*, sì come vede ciascuno'.[49] In other words, a desire for the continued existence of the self underlies all the particular desires for all the 'goods' with which a given subject will seek to be united; and a particular 'good' is good to the extent that it is truly a means conducive to that end.

It may be objected that the likely reactions of the antelope in our example demonstrate that some movements proceed not from love but from fear, since the antelope would certainly 'take steps' to 'separate' itself from the lion, and it would not stop running until it had reached a place of safety. But there is no contradiction. All fear, and all movements inspired by fear, are simply the consequences of our self-love. If we enlarge the concept of the 'unifying' power of love, so that it includes the desire to *remain* united with the good that is already possessed, we can see that *flight* from the force that seeks to remove that good is dictated by the love of being, no less than the *pursuit* of another good whose acquisition is necessary for survival or perfection. In both pursuit and flight, the movement ceases when the good is safely united with the subject. There is a sense in which the goal of all movement is rest.[50]

The natural love of being declares itself in a natural movement towards the natural *place* where the subject's being will be conserved; and the love, the movement and the place are all determined by its level on the Scale of Being. As one ascends from one *grado generale* to the next, the place becomes ever more particularized, and the power of movement ever greater.

In the case of the four elements, the natural place is the appropriate sphere, and natural movement is limited to up and down. It is important to remember that in Dante's system the weight or 'gravity' of Earth is simply its natural love, and that any given clod seeks to rejoin or to remain united with the bulk of the element in order to conserve its being and to resist transformation into one of the other elements.[51]

Minerals love the precise geographical location where they came into being. They lose their active qualities or 'virtues'–which are their main 'movements'–when they are carried away; but in their natural place they 'grow and acquire vigour and strength' ('crescono e acquistano vigore e potenza'). Although they exhibit no power of movement distinct from that of Earth, the magnet shows that at least one mineral can *turn* towards the place of its generation.[52]

The plants' love of place subsumes that of the elements and inanimate matter, but it is still further refined and particularized by the power which distinguishes its level of being–the power to absorb nourishment and grow to maturity. A plant must live where the earth provides food and moisture suitable for its complexion, and at an altitude and a latitude that guarantee the right degree of heat. 'Some', says Dante, 'keep to the water's edge; some prefer the tops of mountains, others the fields, and still others the lower hills. If they are transplanted, they either die or grow "sad", just as though they had been separated from a friend.'[53] Plants also show their love of being in the sense that their whole life-cycle is dedicated to the production of seed which will serve to multiply individual plants and thereby conserve the life of the species. Their most characteristic 'movements' are seen in their growth and self-reproduction.

Animals share the loves proper to the three lower levels, but their forms and complexions are more specialized, and their needs are correspondingly more particular; hence, no one place can satisfy their natural love of being. A herbivore must move on when the grass is exhausted; a carnivore must pursue its prey, while the prey must be able to flee to a place of safety. Some birds migrate every year to avoid extremes of heat and cold. Male must seek out female, since the reproduction of the higher species requires the collaboration of both sexes. Members of a gregarious species must locate their fellows in order to survive. All the higher animals are therefore endowed with the organs of locomotion so that they can move to the successive places and unite with the different 'goods' that conserve their being; and they are also endowed with the organs of smell, hearing and sight, in order that they may recognize these goods and places from a distance.[54]

The organs of sensation that characterize all animal existence are capable not only of discriminating between one object and another, but of establishing whether they are 'good' or 'bad' for the subject. They perform this second task primarily through the experience of pleasure and pain. The appropriate food–to return to the obvious example–will look nice, smell pleasant, feel agreeable, and taste good. The inappropriate food will look and taste repellent. An immature animal may be misled by its sense of sight or hearing, but it will discover any mistake through the pain subsequently felt by the sense of touch. As the animal grows up, its memory of past pleasures and pains will develop and enhance its inborn power of 'estimation' – *aestimativa* – and such mistakes will no longer occur.[55]

We are now sufficiently familiar with the details to retrace our steps and to summarize the precise links in Dante's thought between the concepts of natural love or instinct, natural movement, determinism, and the role of the heavens in generation.

Every non-violent action or movement is initiated by a desire for union with a 'good'. Nothing, except 'being' as such, is a good absolutely, desired by all things at all times. For each individual *substantia*, in every species of every genus, at each of the main levels of existence, those things are 'good' that conserve its being, and those things are bad that will harm or destroy it. Goodness and badness therefore depend on the mode of being proper to the given *substantia*. This mode of being is determined by the form, which carries with it a love of being, and a natural 'inclination' or 'leaning' – the words are used technically – for those things or states that are good for it, and a natural aversion to those things that are bad. This inclination is further limited and defined by the precise proportion of the four elements in the subject's complexion, since this helps to determine its temperament and therefore its particular likes and dislikes. The form also carries with it the faculties, organs and appetites which enable the given subject to know, seek out and unite with the appropriate 'goods'.

The subject does not choose its form, complexion or inclinations, and it does not control the instinctive workings of its organs. Even the highest animal, nearest to man on the Scale of Being, is at the mercy of an automatic chain of responses. A 'good', outside the self and beyond its control, comes within the purview of its senses; the senses apprehend that good as pleasurable; apprehension leads to desire; desire initiates movement; movement leads to union; union produces joy as desire gives way to fruition. Movement ceases when there is no longer any desire, and the animal will return to a state of repose until a new stimulus awakens a new response dictated by a new deficiency. On each occasion 'nature reasserts its power through the principle of pleasure', says Dante, 'and the living form of an animal has no other feet with which to walk'. It is therefore fully determined.[56]

The heavens control the generation and the life-cycle of all things in the natural order. As 'fires', or sources of heat, they certainly determine the receptivity of matter; and they call living forms into being from the potency of a seed. As 'hammers', or formative influences, they probably 'induce' the forms of inanimate *composita*. Their influences play upon every *substantia* throughout its existence, modifying its complexion and its desires from hour to hour and season to season. They are the ultimate cause of all violent movements in nature. In these ways they determine both the stimuli and the responses for all generated things. And all things may be said to be 'subject to their power', and 'more acted upon than acting'.[57]

Corruption, privation and death

There is one further very important sense in which all things in the natural order are determined. A 'bound' is set that 'they may not pass over'. Everything that has life must die.[58] Everything that is generated must be 'corrupted'. 'Formation' is inevitably followed by 'privation' of form.[59] Natural movements follow their causes of necessity; but natural *things*—the *corpora mobilia* themselves—do not enjoy the 'necessary' being that was attributed to the heavens and the angels. Their being is only 'contingent'; and Dante can refer to generated things as 'brief contingencies'.[60]

Various perfectly compatible explanations were put forward to account for the inevitability of 'corruption' (we cannot avoid the technical scholastic term), and, as always, it is important that we should be familiar with them. More often than not, the cause was located in the very nature of matter. As we saw in Chapter 8, picture-language suggested that matter was too 'slippery' or 'fluid' to retain the impression of form, or else that it was 'deaf' and would not heed the craftsman's commands. An Aristotelian could argue, less emotively, that if primary matter was 'pure potentiality', then no form could ever exhaust the capacity of any part to assume some other form: otherwise, its potentiality would not be 'pure'. And Dante does indeed say that contingent being is coextensive with primary matter.[61]

The inevitability of corruption may also be attributed to the natural movement of the elements. All four elements were present in every *compositum*, and at least three of them could not be in their proper place. These would have a connatural and ultimately successful tendency to disband and pull the matter away from under its form.[62] But the 'materialistic explanation' most frequently put forward explained corruption as the unavoidable consequence of the internecine strife between the four contrary qualities. The complexion of every generated thing contained both Hot and Cold, and both Moist and Dry. Sooner or later the Cold would triumph, provoking what we call 'natural death', unless it were forestalled by Heat gaining the upper hand, as when premature death results from a fever.[63]

There was, however, a good case for assigning corruption to the activity of the heavens. Once again, the causal link could be conceived in various ways. It was a logical deduction that, if the heavens were the remote or proximate causes of all movement, whether violent or natural, then they must be responsible for *un*-making as well as for making. Observation suggested that the presence of heat and light caused generation, and that their withdrawal caused corruption. In Aristotle's considered view, as we have seen, the chief cause of both processes was the obliquity of the ecliptic, which makes the sun higher and hotter in spring and summer, and lower and cooler in autumn and winter.[64]

Dante combines notions such as these with hints from astrology to construct his own original explanation for the necessity of corruption. If generation is caused by the circulation of the heavenly bodies, he argues, and if the effect must retain something of the nature of the cause, then generated things must in some sense be 'circular'. But as seen from any place on earth, the daily path of a planet or one of the influential constellations of the Zodiac describes an *incomplete* circle as it rises in the east, culminates in the south, and sinks out of sight in the west. And so the nature of generated beings is 'arc-like' rather than 'circular'.[65] They come into existence, grow and develop until they reach their culmination; then they decline, decay and pass away. Their 'setting' is as much a part of their nature as their 'rising'. 'Rotting' begins in the same moment that 'riping' ends. The period of adolescence is equal to the period of senescence.[66]

Explanations of yet another kind retain the heavens as the active cause of corruption, but strive to present this activity in a more favourable light. Nothing can ever be generated except by supplanting the form under which its matter had existed until that moment. 'The generation of one thing is the corruption of another': *generatio unius est corruptio alterius*. If nothing were ever corrupted, there would be no generation, and the heavens would move and rain down their influences in vain. The heavens, as makers, resemble their Maker to the extent that their nature allows. They cannot produce effects that last *senza fine*, but, by continuing to generate individual *composita* in perpetuity, they ensure that all the species shall continue to exist in perpetuity. If such generation is for a good end, then so too is corruption which is its inevitable corollary.[67]

We must learn to distinguish, moreover, between the 'nature' of each individual *substantia* and 'Universal Nature'. It is true that each subject desires and wills its own being. Ceasing-to-be comes about *praeter intentionem*, not *secundum intentionem*; but Universal Nature, to which all individual natures are subject, can and does intend their corruption as an integral part of its plan to actualize all the forms that lie in the potency of matter, and to keep the whole potentiality of prime matter actualized at all times.[68] And therefore all generated beings do in fact have 'another nature' that enables them to obey the universal command and to acquiesce in their own dissolution.[69]

The explanation to which Dante gives prominence in the *Comedy* is simpler and starker. There are two kinds of making and two ways of coming into being. Created things issue *directly* from God, and, as we have seen, they are incorruptible and sempiternal. Generated things issue from God *indirectly*, and because of this they will necessarily come to corruption. There are therefore just two modes of existence in the universe, which are described with sublime simplicity in a single hendecasyllable as:

> ciò che non more e ciò che può morire.   (*Par.* XIII, 52)

The distinction between the two kinds of making and their consequences is made most clearly in the seventh canto of the *Paradiso*. In the middle of a very long speech Beatrice has proclaimed:

> Ciò che da lei sanza mezzo distilla
> non ha poi fine, perché non si move
> la sua imprenta quand' ella sigilla.   (*Par.* VII, 67–9)

And before concluding she returns to these lines in order to anticipate a possible objection from Dante-character:

You may say: 'I see Water, Fire, Air and Earth and all their compounds come to corruption and last only a short time. But these things too are part of God's creation (*creature*). Hence, if those words were true, they ought to be immune from corruption.'

> Tu dici: 'Io veggio l'acqua, io veggio il foco,
> l'aere e la terra e tutte lor misture
> venire a corruzione, e durar poco;
>   e queste cose pur furon creature;
> per che, se ciò ch'è detto è stato vero,
> esser dovrien da corruzion sicure.'   (124–9)

But there is no contradiction.

The angels and the pure country [of the heavens] may be said to be 'created' in their whole being. But the elements and their compounds were given their form by a power (*virtù*) that was itself created. Their matter had already been created [as primary matter]. The power that gave them their form (*la virtù informante*) had also been created beforehand, in these luminaries that revolve around them:

> Li angeli, frate, e 'l paese sincero
> nel qual tu se', dir si posson creati,
> sì come sono, in loro essere intero;
>   ma li alimenti che tu hai nomati
> e quelle cose che di lor si fanno
> da creata virtù sono informati.
>   Creata fu la materia ch'elli hanno;
> creata fu la virtù informante
> in queste stelle che 'ntorno a lor vanno.   (130–8)

The elements and their compounds are 'what Nature makes'. The angels, the heavens and primary matter are 'what God's will creates'. The whole of the universe had earlier been described in another single line of verse as:

> ciò ch'ella cria o che natura face.   (*Par.* III, 87)

And we may recombine the hemistichs in this and the other 'cosmic' hendecasyllable to produce the following equations:

$$Ciò\ che\ non\ more = ciò\ ch'ella\ cria;$$

$$ciò\ che\ può\ morire = [ciò]\ che\ natura\ face.$$

Dante's view of the 'opus distinctionis': a reconstruction

Before we examine some of the ways in which these ideas and patterns of thought are transmuted into poetry, we must return briefly to the unresolved problem of Dante's views about the *opus distinctionis* in the First Creation.[70] The questions we must try and answer are such as these: What did happen in the period of not more than twenty seconds between the simultaneous creation of the 'triform effect' and the rebellion of some of the angels? More precisely, who formed the elements in their spheres, and who brought them into contact and mixed them for the first time? Who 'induced' or 'drew out' the forms of the first minerals and metals? Who made the prototypes of all species of plants and animals, that is, who made the first parents of each species from whose seed all their descendants would be generated?[71] Was it God, *sanza mezzo*? Or did He even then avail Himself of the *mezzi* constituted by the angels and the heavens? Were the prototypes created *in loro essere intero*, or was their mode of coming into being more like that of generation?[72]

Dante addresses himself directly to only one of these interrelated questions, but his approach and his conclusions could hardly be more revealing of his attitude to the distinction of species as a whole.

Earth is raised above the sphere of Water to form the *terra discoperta*; and it will be remembered that this land-mass is confined to the northern hemisphere and extends in a roughly semicircular shape from the equator to the arctic circle and through 180 degrees of longitude to the east and west of Jerusalem. In his *Quaestio*, Dante makes it clear that the 'final cause' or purpose of this unnatural elevation was to permit the four elements to come into contact, this being the necessary precondition for their entering into compounds, and forming the 'complexionate' matter required by all higher forms of existence.[73] Having established this point, Dante tries to determine the '*efficient* cause'. He rejects the idea that Earth could have raised itself by its 'natural love': every part of Earth is homogeneous and every part alike seeks the centre. The natural loves of the other three elements are disqualified on the same grounds. The claims of the moon are excluded because its path lies close to the ecliptic and it is therefore carried both north and south of the equator. If it had been the efficient cause, it would have drawn up land in the *southern* hemisphere as well; but, in Dante's view, there is no *terra australis*. The same argument rules out the other planets, which also revolve in a plane close to that of the ecliptic. The *primum mobile* is perfectly uniform in its matter, virtues and movement: it could not therefore have drawn up the Earth in one area only.[74] We are therefore left, by elimination, with just one candidate—the Heaven of the Fixed Stars. We know that each star has a distinct *virtus*, and we may therefore conclude that the partial elevation of the sphere of Earth was caused by certain of the stars in the northern celestial hemisphere.[75]

Dante was clearly more than a little embarrassed by this reductive argument which, among other weaknesses, does not explain why there is no land west of Cadiz or east of the Ganges. He felt it necessary to stress that he was restricting himself to the viewpoint of a natural scientist, and that his readers must expect only that degree of certitude which is possible when we reason from effects to causes.[76] On the other hand, it must be said that he does not rigorously exclude evidence deriving from divine revelation. He insists that the shape and position of the *terra discoperta*, no less that the position and dimensions of the whole universe, were determined by God, *ille dispensator . . . gloriosus*, and he is convinced that it must be the best possible solution in this as in every other particular: *hoc fecit tanquam melius, sicut et illa*. In the same paragraph, he also quotes directly from the text of Genesis where 'the Lord said, "Let the waters . . . be gathered together unto one place, and let the dry land appear"'.[77] And so, even when all allowances have been made for context, it is rather remarkable that Dante does not mention the obvious possibility—and the most natural interpretation of the text of Genesis— that none of the heavens played any part at all, and that God raised the dry land by Himself, *sanza mezzo, immediate*.

If Dante was willing to admit that the heavens and the angels participated in the first *mixtio* of the elements, there was nothing to hold him back from the conclusion that they also participated in the subsequent induction or institution of the first forms of composite beings, from those of the minerals to those of the mammals. And the same conclusion seems to follow inexorably from the axiom that 'Those things which issue directly from the Divine Goodness are immortal'. If the prototypes had issued directly from God, they would still be in existence, since the knot which ties their matter to their form would never have come untied. But this is self-evidently not the case (indeed, some species of monsters have died out completely).[78] Ergo, they could not have been made by Him directly. Or again: if God Himself had induced all forms in the beginning, and thereby actuated all the potentiality of prime matter, then all the resultant *composita* would have been 'safe from corruption', and no generation would ever have been possible.

It does therefore seem almost certain that Dante subscribed to the view that the whole *opus distinctionis* was performed *con mezzo*, and that the *mezzi* employed were precisely the angels, the heavens and prime matter—the 'triform effect', which has been involved in the processes of generation ever since. And it is important to grasp that this was not the orthodox view.[79] Even a relatively 'advanced' theologian like St Thomas made it absolutely clear that the distinction of species in the beginning was performed directly by God—more specifically, by the Second Person of the Trinity, the Son or Word.[80]

Of course, we do not know whether Dante was fully aware of all the conclusions implicit in his premises; nor do we know how he would have defended himself if he had ever been charged with heterodoxy. It is no less important to stress that there is nothing irreligious, or anti-Christian, in this position. Dante would almost certainly have begun his defence by quoting well-known texts from Job, Isaiah, the Psalms and St Paul, to remind himself and his judges that no man should presume to understand the mysteries of creation.[81] Had he chosen to uphold the view we have attributed to him, he would probably have emphasized that the *exemplaria* of all the species to be distinguished derived from the Mind of God or the Word; and he would have insisted that, whether we are discussing distinction or generation, the angels and the heavens are always to be conceived as workmen, using tools to realize the designs of the Supreme Architect. Dante would never have questioned that God was the *universal* cause of *all* things ('Dio è universalissima cagione di tutte le cose').[82] He could have pointed to the elegance and economy of this theory, and its ability to accommodate the observable facts. And he might have concluded his defence by remarking that there was nothing sacrilegious in the assumption that God had availed himself of the angels, the heavens and prime matter in order to produce the first individual *composita*, since they were created for this precise purpose, and God does nothing superfluous and nothing in vain.

The poet of Christian Neoplatonism

Whatever the precise philosophical and theological nuances of his views on the *opus distinctionis*, there can be no doubt that Dante was deeply committed to the Neoplatonist elements in his cosmology. The proof is in the poetry. There are certain themes that almost never fail to stir him profoundly. The divine gift of being in the emanation of creative love from the One; the answering love of this gift by the Many; the diversification of the divine energy as it descends from heaven to heaven; the degrees on the Scale of Being that make possible the harmony of all the different 'voices' in the cosmos; the underlying purpose discovered in every aspect of Universal Nature—all these move him to celebration rather than simple reaffirmation. His rhythms settle into more stately measures. The syntax is made of correlated and balanced structures. Difficult concepts are conveyed through metaphor in such a way that they capture the imagination even when they are imperfectly understood. Technical philosophical words still predominate, but the more prosaic terms are avoided in favour of those that are luminous, rich in suggestion, and satisfying to the ear.

We may test these assertions and recapitulate the main points made in this chapter by reading or re-reading a dozen or so passages from the *Paradiso*. They will be presented with a bare minimum of paraphrase and translation in a sequence that will enable us first to follow the descent of God's sustaining power from the Empyrean through the *primum mobile* and the Starry Heaven down to the earth, and then to contemplate the controlled, purposeful movement and the perfect design of every component in the whole hierarchical universe. There will be no analysis or comment of the kind attempted in other chapters; for this is one of the moments when a critic may best serve his author by standing aside and simply pointing to the text.

The Empyrean is a heaven of pure light—an intellectual light filled with the love of the True Good, a love that is full of joy, a joy that transcends all sweetness:

> . . . al ciel ch'e pura luce:
> luce intellettüal, piena d'amore;
> amor di vero ben, pien di letizia;
> letizia che trascende ogne dolzore.   (*Par.* xxx, 39–42)

This is the light that will finally reveal the Creator to man, the being who will find peace only in seeing Him:

> Lume è là sù che visibile face
> lo creatore a quella creatura
> che solo in lui vedere ha la sua pace.   (xxx, 100–2)

The same light communicates both movement and the power to cause all natural effects to the *primum mobile*, the 'greatest body', which connects the infinity of the Empyrean to the finite spheres that lie within its embrace. 'Within the heaven of God's peace there spins a body in whose "virtue" lies the being of all it contains':[83]

> Dentro dal ciel de la divina pace
> si gira un corpo ne la cui virtute
> l'esser di tutto suo contento giace.   (II, 112–14)

'This heaven is located only in the Mind of God, where the love that moves it and the "virtue" that it rains are kindled. It is enfolded in a sphere of light and love, just as it enfolds the other spheres':

> e questo cielo non ha altro dove
> che la mente divina, in che s'accende
> l'amor che 'l volge e la virtù ch'ei piove.
> Luce e amor d'un cerchio lui comprende,
> sì come questo li altri; . . .   (XXVII, 109–13)

Every part of the *primum mobile* is uniformly perfect, and uniformly filled with 'virtue'. It is nearest to God and it receives most goodness. As it sweeps the whole of the rest of the universe around with it, it exerts the greatest influence to conserve the well-being (*salute*) of the world. This is why it is the greatest body; and this is why it is controlled by the Seraphim, the angelic order which is closest to God, and supreme in knowledge and love of Him. It will of course be clear that the *moto e virtù* of the spheres must derive from Movers who are in a condition of blessedness, just as the hammer's art derives from the smith:

> Li cerchi corporai sono ampi e arti
> secondo il più e 'l men de la virtute
> che si distende per tutte lor parti.
> Maggior bontà vuol far maggior salute;
> maggior salute maggior corpo cape,
> s'elli ha le parti igualmente compiute.
> Dunque costui che tutto quanto rape
> l'altro universo seco, corrisponde
> al cerchio che più ama e che più sape: (XXVIII, 64–72)

> Lo moto e la virtù d'i santi giri,
> come dal fabbro l'arte del martello,
> da' beati motor convien che spiri.   (II, 127–9)

Down from the *primum mobile* and the Seraphim flows the energy that sustains the being (*esse*) of the universe which is now diversified into distinct essences (*essentiae*) that are associated with the many stars contained in the next heaven, each of which has a distinct 'virtue'. The planetary heavens, each acting in accordance with its distinct nature, differentiate this energy still further as they bring to perfection what they have sown. For these 'instruments of the Universe' are arranged step by step so that they receive from above and perform below:

> Lo ciel seguente, c'ha tante vedute,
> quell' esser parte per diverse essenze,
> da lui distratte e da lui contenute.
> Li altri giron per varie differenze
> le distinzion che dentro da sé hanno
> dispongono a lor fini e lor semenze.
> Questi organi del mondo così vanno,
> come tu vedi omai, di grado in grado,
> che di sù prendono e di sotto fanno.   (II, 115–23)

The 'living light' of God grows fainter as it flows from one level of actualized being to the next, down towards the extreme limits of its power; and as a result it ends by making 'brief contingencies', that is, the things generated by the movements of the heavens, with and without the co-operation of a seed:

> ché quella viva luce che sì mea
> dal suo lucente
>
> . . .
>
> quindi discende a l'ultime potenze
> giù d'atto in atto, tanto divenendo,
> che più non fa che brevi contingenze;
>   e queste contingenze essere intendo
> le cose generate, che produce
> con seme e sanza seme il ciel movendo.   (XIII, 55–6, 61–6)

But we must not dwell on their contingency or brevity. For *all* things, whether created and immortal, or generated and mortal, are simply the radiance of the Word who gives them birth in His love:

> Ciò che non more e ciò che può morire
> non è se non splendor di quella idea
> che partorisce, amando, il nostro Sire.   (XIII, 52–4)

All natures are formally distinct and greater or lesser in worth. Their *diversity* enables them to co-ordinate their respective activities, as they follow instinctive love to different destinations on the great sea of being. Their *inequality* enables the lower to be subordinated to the higher, and all natures to be subordinated to the whole. In these ways the universe achieves a single form, and the multiplicity of species comes to resemble the unity of the Creator:

> Le cose tutte quante
> hanno ordine tra loro, e questo è forma
> che l'universo a Dio fa simigliante.
>
> . . .
>
> Ne l'ordine ch'io dico sono accline
> tutte nature, per diverse sorti,
> più al principio loro e men vicine;
>   onde si muovono a diversi porti
> per lo gran mar de l'essere, e ciascuna
> con istinto a lei dato che la porti.   (I, 103–5, 109–14)

The being, and the *well*-being (*salute*), of all natures are willed and foreseen in the perfect mind of the Creator; everything He shoots forth reaches a destination that He foresees and wills, just like an arrow aimed at a target:

> E non pur le nature provedute
> sono in la mente ch'è da sé perfetta,
> ma esse insieme con la lor salute:
> per che quantunque quest' arco saetta
> disposto cade a proveduto fine,
> sì come cosa in suo segno diretta.   (VIII, 100–5)

Inequality is not inequitable. Even the lowest beings can rejoice in the order that relegated them to their lowly degree, for this is the will of the King on high. Nothing desires to be higher than it is. All things – whether created or generated – are moving in conformity with God's will, seeking peace there, as though they were rivers flowing into the ocean:

> E 'n la sua volontade è nostra pace:
> ell' è quel mare al qual tutto si mòve
> ciò ch'ella crïa o che natura face.   (III, 85–7)

This is the meaning of the proposition with which the *Paradiso* begins: 'The radiance of the All-mover penetrates the whole universe, shining out more in one part and less in another':

> La gloria di colui che tutto move
> per l'universo penetra, e risplende
> in una parte più e meno altrove.   (I, 1–3)

11

The makings of a man

The vain embrace

IN THE FIRST CHAPTER WE LEARNT TO THINK OF THE OPENING CANTOS of *Purgatorio* as a ghost-story in reverse. Instead of the ghost returning to his earthly haunts to terrify the living, it is Dante, a creature of flesh and blood, who penetrates the realms of the afterlife and alarms the souls of the newly dead who populate the shores and lower slopes of Mount Purgatory. They marvel and ask themselves by what miracle he has come among them. But with one exception the character Dante does not express wonder at the miracle by which they may survive and subsist as individual beings. This one exception comes of course at the moment when Dante seeks to embrace his old friend, Casella, and is dismayed to find that his arms return three times empty to his breast. The shades are delusory except to the eye: 'ohi ombre vane, fuor che ne l'aspetto!'.

Like the passages in the *Aeneid* and the *Odyssey* on which it is modelled, the episode is a little unsettling to the reader. It raises doubts about the nature of shadow-bodies that had not presented themselves before; for when most people read the *Inferno* or the sixth book of the *Aeneid*, they simply accept the souls in the underworld on the same terms as other characters in any work of imaginative fiction. They suspend disbelief, and they do not ask how the shadow-bodies may be visible and yet transparent, or intangible and yet subject to torments by the tangible qualities of heat and cold.[1] Least of all do they ask what a good Aristotelian ought to ask: if the soul is simply the structure by virtue of which a living *compositum* exists, and is 'what it is', how can it take on an independent existence at the moment when that *compositum* ceases to be and its structure is destroyed?[2]

Most readers probably dismiss the vain embrace from their minds and forget its disturbing implications as soon as the next scene begins. So too do most authors, including Homer and Virgil. But Dante was a very different kind of poet. For him, verisimilitude was a kind of moral imperative. Every part of his fiction had to have a firm outline – nothing is left indeterminate – and every part had to conform to the known facts. He could not write about Hell and Purgatory until he had found them a location on the map of the universe and determined their shape and size.

270

And he clearly felt a particular duty to explain and justify his assumptions about the condition of souls after death—*status animarum post mortem*—since this was the whole subject of his poem in its literal meaning. The problems posed by the shadow-bodies are not forgotten. Instead, a delicate trail of reminders and anticipations leads from the encounter with Casella in the second canto to the twenty-fifth canto where Statius makes a detailed and authoritative statement on the subject.[3]

As always, the long doctrinal speech is firmly anchored in the events of the story. In this case, Dante-character has just witnessed the terrible emaciation suffered by the penitent souls of the gluttonous on the sixth cornice of Mount Purgatory, and he is puzzled as to how a 'body' can grow thin when it has no need of nourishment anyway: 'Come si può far magro/là dove l'uopo di nodrir non tocca?'[4] But, as always, the reply takes us far beyond the relatively narrow terms of the question. The shade-bodies and their capacity for pleasure and pain are shown to be just one aspect of man's immortality. Man's immortality is a consequence of our unique mode of coming into being; and so too is everything else that is distinctively human in our nature. Our loves and our 'natural place', our language and its defects, our capacity to know the truth and the limits set upon our knowledge, our freedom to choose and the near impossibility of choosing well—these are all rooted in the same ground. Statius will lay bare the *principia* of human nature. This is the true *raison d'être* of the whole speech, and this is why we must examine his answer in the detail that it deserves.

Generation: (a) From the formation of seed to conception

All the main features of Dante's account of human reproduction derive ultimately from Aristotle's *Generation of Animals* as interpreted by thirteenth-century Christian commentators in the light of the medical writings of Galen and Avicenna. Within Aristotle's system, the power of self-reproduction is simply an extension of the power of self-conservation and self-perfection. Each involves the transformation of matter by its *assimilation* to the form of a living *compositum*, in obedience to the universal law of causation that 'every agent acts in its own likeness': *agens agit sibi simile*.[5] Statius therefore begins his speech with a dense and allusive summary of the stages by which food is transformed into blood and then blood is transformed either into flesh, sinews and bone, or into sperm.

The process by which an appropriate foodstuff is changed into the substance of a living organism is called 'digestion'. Digestion consists of a series of operations which are all analogous to the cooking of food before it is eaten, and which are therefore known as 'coctions', or 'decoctions', or 'concoctions'.[6]

The first takes place in the stomach where the nutrients contained in the food are transformed by the natural heat of the body into a milky substance called chyle, while the useless or noxious elements are turned into excrement and expelled. The second coction takes place in the liver where the chyle is converted into 'raw' or 'imperfect' blood. Some of this 'raw' blood passes from the right ventricle of the heart through invisible pores into the left atrium, where it comes into contact with air from the lungs and is transformed by a third coction into 'perfect' blood. This blood is imbued, as Statius reminds us, with a 'formative power'; and by far the greater part of it is carried along the veins and arteries to make and nourish the body by changing into the tissue, flesh, bones, sinews, muscles and organs of which the body is composed. But this collateral coction need not detain us here. We are concerned with a small quantity of the perfect blood which, in the sexually mature human being, remains in the heart and undergoes a further digestion.[7]

In the case of the male, the result of this fourth successive coction is the human seed, in which the formative power residing in perfect blood is intensified, so to speak, to the point where it can *transmit* form and generate a new *substantia* with the same specific form as the parent. In the case of the female, the fourth coction remains incomplete owing to a lack of natural heat. The result is menstrual blood, which constitutes the only matter that can assume human form, but which itself contains no active principle or formative power. From the heart, the central organ and 'perfect place' where nature makes provision for all parts of the body, the semen descends to the testicles, and the *menstruum* to the uterus; but these organs are no more than a conduit and a vessel respectively.[8]

These are all the facts to which allusion is made in the opening of Statius's speech, but the simile he uses there does require some further elucidation. The seed is in the same relationship to perfect blood as this blood is to chyle, or chyle is to the whole mass of food taken into the stomach. Each successive coction, that is, transforms the material left over and unused from the previous stage; and hence Aristotle can rightly refer to the end product as a remnant of the raw material. Semen, he says, is a 'residue of food': a *superfluitas cibi*, or *superfluum alimenti*.[9] It was obviously this dry phrase that suggested the rather precious simile in the following lines:

Perfect blood receives in the heart the power to communicate form to all human members, and it goes along the veins to 'become' those members. But some of this perfect blood is not subsequently drunk by the thirsty veins. It remains like food carried away after a banquet. It is digested still further and then descends to a place that it is fitter not to name.

> Sangue perfetto, che poi non si beve
> da l'assetate vene, e si rimane

quasi alimento che di mensa leve,
   prende nel core a tutte membra umane
virtute informativa, come quello
ch'a farsi quelle per le vene vane.
   Ancor digesto, scende ov' è più bello
tacer che dire . . .   (*Purg.* XXV, 37–44)

Generation: (b) The transformations of the embryo

Statius now describes the moment of conception. Still following Aristotle, he insists that the mother's role is purely passive. She contributes nothing except the place and the 'material cause'. Her menstrual blood is to the seed as patient to agent, or as matter to form. Indeed, the matter she provides is not even fitly 'disposed' until the seed has caused it to curdle. Only then can the seed give life to the resultant clot.[10]

Thence it trickles on to another's blood in the vessel appointed by nature. There the two bloods mingle together, the one disposed to act (thanks to the perfect place from which it springs), the other to be acted upon. Having reached and united with the mother's blood, the perfected blood [i.e. semen] of the father begins to work. First it coagulates the *menstruum* making it 'set' and constitute its matter. Then it communicates life.

         e quindi poscia geme
sovr' altrui sangue in natural vasello.
    Ivi s'accoglie l'uno e l'altro insieme,
l'un disposto a patire, e l'altro a fare
per lo perfetto loco onde si preme;
   e, giunto lui, comincia ad operare
coagulando prima, e poi avviva
ciò che per sua matera fé constare.   (44–51)

There is nothing in the least controversial in Statius's account of the formation of semen and the moment of conception. But when he comes to describe the embryo's development during the first seven months in the womb, he is forced to commit himself to one of several rival expositions of Aristotle's teaching.

The difficulties and the controversies, both medieval and modern, all have their origin in a fundamental weakness in the Aristotelian analysis of change. Aristotle made a rigorous distinction between changes in the size and appearance of a given *substantia*, which can be continuous and reversible, and the unique and irreversible transformation by which the *substantia* first comes into being or ceases for ever to exist. In scholastic terminology, 'generation' and 'corruption' are totally other than 'alteration' and 'augmentation'. Qualitative or quantitative changes, such as acquiring a tan or putting on weight, can never change the essential nature and the specific properties of a *substantia*. No change in colour, shape or smell can turn a rose into a mouse; no increase in size will ever turn a mouse into an elephant; no amount of indoctrination will ever enable a parrot to understand the words whose sounds he can imitate. No one *substantia* can cross the boundary between species and species, between genus and genus, or between one level of existence and another.

These distinctions are, however, difficult to apply to the changes undergone by an embryo during gestation. One week after conception, the embryo of an ape will exist as a *substantia*, for it is no longer part of the father, it is not part of the mother, and it is not simply the sperm enlarged. It has the power to absorb nourishment and to grow. Aristotle must therefore concede that the embryo subsists by virtue of a 'vegetative' or 'nutritive' soul. By the time of its birth several months later, it will have acquired the organs and power of sensation and movement. It will therefore possess a 'sensitive' soul; and it will seem to have defied the rule that no one *substantia* can pass from one category of existence to another. It was, in some sense, a plant before it was an ape. And, in that same sense, Aristotle had to say that the human embryo was an animal before it was a man: *prius animal quam homo.*[11]

Aristotle could escape from this apparent contradiction by appealing to his concept of potency and act. A week after conception, the embryo of the ape has a nutritive soul *in actu*, but it also has a sensitive soul *in potentia*. It is still on its voyage, still *in via*. A week-old seedling, by contrast, has a nutritive soul *in actu*, but it has already arrived on the shore: it is '*a riva*'. All its subsequent development is towards the *second* actuality, represented by its 'perfection' as a mature plant which is able to form seed and reproduce itself.[12]

But this clarification does not remove the difficulty altogether. Although all the properties of plant life are subsumed and presupposed in animal life, no *substantia* can have two substantial forms. There must come a point at which the embryo ceases to have a 'nutritive' soul and takes on a 'sensitive' soul. But a transformation of this kind involves the corruption of the first *substantia* and the generation of a new one. Only the matter persists. Formal identity is lost. And this loss of formal identity will happen not just once but many times, since the honest Aristotelian is forced to admit that the embryo does exist successively under many different forms, and that for each of these intermediate forms there must be an intermediate generation.[13]

Common sense protests against a theory that necessitates such a clumsy section and division of what is clearly a continuous process. But the common-sense view of generation can itself lead to absurdity within the Aristotelian framework. If we refuse to admit that the matter of the embryo exists under several distinct forms, and if we insist that the father generates the child, we may be inclined to say that the 'formative power' in the seed *becomes* the first plant-like form of the embryo, or that this form pre-existed in the seed itself. In this last case, we should have to concede that generation takes place at the moment when the seed is separated from the father (just as a second worm is generated at the very moment when a worm is cut into two). And, in general, we might be compelled to conclude that there is no such thing as generation at all, and to view the whole process from the ingestion of food to the birth of the child as a kind of continuous 'alteration'. Broadly speaking, the thirteenth-century Aristotelians divided into two camps on this issue. Those who were more concerned with sound reasoning, like St Thomas, emphasized the discontinuity in the development of the embryo. Others, like St Albert, who were perhaps more interested in the observable facts, tended to emphasize the continuity. Dante was closer to St Albert (as Nardi showed in a fierce polemic with Busnelli).[14] But it is important to remember that the area of agreement was far, far greater than the area of disagreement, and that neither party ever ventured to question the validity of Aristotle's logical categories or the truth of his biological observations.

Returning now to Statius's discourse, it will be seen that he certainly dwells on the distinct stages in the embryo's development. First, he says, it has a soul like that of a plant. Next it is like a sea-sponge (which was the standard example of a species that exhibited some power of sensation and movement without possessing organs or limbs). Then, and only then, does the foetus elaborate 'all human members' up to and including the articulation of the brain. To this extent, therefore, Statius does show himself to be aware of a *dis*continuity. But even when due allowance has been made for the extreme compression of his utterances, and for the restrictions of metre and rhyme, it will be seen that his phraseology, syntax and deliberate repetition of key-words do present the embryo's development as one continuous process:[15]

The active power becomes a soul, like that of a plant, except that it has not yet reached its journey's end, while that of a plant has already come to the shore. It goes on working until it can feel and move like a sea-sponge. At this point it begins to provide organs for the capacities of which it is the seed. Now, my son, the power that comes from the father's heart (where nature makes provision for all members) spreads throughout its length and breadth.

> Anima fatta la virtute attiva
> qual d'una pianta, in tanto differente,
> che questa è in via e quella è già a riva,
> tanto ovra poi, che già si move e sente,
> come spungo marino; e indi imprende
> ad organar le posse ond' è semente.
> Or si spiega, figliuolo, or si distende
> la virtù ch'è dal cor del generante,
> dove natura a tutte membra intende. (52–60)

Creation: (a) The intellect and the error of Averroes

The philosophical and artistic reasons for the stress on continuity are now made clear. Statius deliberately interrupts the flow of his exposition. He formulates the problem to which he is now going to address himself, namely, 'how does the embryo become a human being?' He heightens our anticipation by 'excluding' an influential error, and in so doing he introduces certain crucial concepts and assumptions concerning human nature, mind and speech. By this interruption he prepares us for the truly radical *dis*continuity in the embryo's development. The transitions from seed to 'plant' and from 'plant' to 'animal' are all part of nature's craft (*arte di natura*); but the transition from 'animal' to 'man' can only come about through the direct intervention of God. From generation we are about to pass on to creation.

The new concepts and assumptions all relate to the rational powers peculiar to the human soul, and they derive not so much from Aristotle's *Generation of Animals*, as from passages in his other writings, and, in particular, from two notoriously difficult chapters of the *De anima* (III, 4–5).

Man is distinguished from all other animals by his capacity to know and to reason.[16] By virtue of their sensitive souls, animals have *cognition* of *particular* objects; by virtue of their higher, human souls, men also attain *knowledge* of *universals*. Animals can apprehend and form a *mental image* (*phantasma*) of a stone. Men can do this and also form the abstract idea (*species intelligibilis*) of a universal nature common to all stones, a concept of 'stoniness'. An animal's mental image of a stone may be large, heavy and brown. But man alone can form *concepts* of size, weight and colour.[17]

The faculty by which we are able to form, combine, divide and express abstract concepts is best called the 'intellect', and its activity, 'intellection'.[18] We may add that the intellect is capable of knowing itself, and that the outward and visible sign by which we recognize its existence in others is human speech: Statius suggests that when we have understood how we are able to invest noises with meaning, we shall indeed know what separates an animal from a man.[19]

Vision is the activity of the eye, and, in general, all sensation is the activity of some organ of sensation. But intellection is not the activity of any specific organ: *non habet aliquod organum corporale*. It is not located in the brain. It is a faculty inherent in the whole soul. The intellect is not in any way corporeal. It is wholly immaterial, like the concepts which it 'abstracts' from the already dematerialized mental images. It is something 'divine', said Aristotle; it alone is 'immortal and perpetual'.[20]

There is, however, a certain parallelism between the formation of a visual image and the formation of a universal concept. Vision is only possible where there is an object, a seeing eye, and light. It requires, that is, a passive capacity for sight and an active force that makes the object visible. In much the same way, so Aristotle suggests, intellection presupposes a potentiality for knowing and a force that actualizes that potentiality. In medieval Latin, in the particular tradition to which Dante will allude, these two aspects of the intellect are called the *intellectus possibilis* and the *intellectus agens*–the 'possible' and 'agent' intellects.[21]

It was axiomatic, as we have often seen, that the properties, qualities or activities exhibited by a living organism were a consequence of its 'soul' or *anima*, defined as the 'first principle of life in living things'. And it was common practice to describe the 'soul' in terms of its distinctive activity–its *operatio propria*–and to ignore the *operationes* which it shared with organisms lower on the Scale of Being.[22] A man certainly does more than think and know. He eats, grows, feels and moves. But his *operatio propria* is intellection; and we may therefore say that he exists as a man because he has an *anima intellectiva*.[23]

It is also natural to name the soul after its highest part, and so we can say that man is man by virtue of his *intellect*.[24] And since each individual human being is clearly born with a capacity for knowing but with no actualized knowledge, Dante and his teachers could say that each man exists as an individual human being by virtue of his '*possible* intellect'. Hence, the embryo whose development we have been following from a plant-like existence to an animal-like existence will become human at the point where it develops or receives a '*possible* intellect'.[25]

Finally, Aristotle and all his followers assumed that the immaterial, God-like and immortal intellect could not be transmitted by a material vehicle such as the sperm, not even by the almost aetherial 'natural spirit' in the sperm. We are left with the conclusion, says Aristotle, that 'the intellect alone enters from outside': *relinquitur intellectus solus de foris advenire.*[26]

The error now to be 'excluded' was the brainchild of the twelfth-century philosopher from Moslem Spain, Averroes, whose Great Commentary to all Aristotle's works enjoyed such prestige in the Latin West that he was usually referred to simply as the Commentator.[27] Statius will here reacknowledge Averroes's intellectual stature, but reject his interpretation of Aristotle's enigmatic teaching concerning the *intellectus possibilis*.

Misled by Aristotle's reference to the intellect as having no corporeal organ, and as being separate from the body, Averroes treated it as though it were *completely* 'separate', just like one of the Neoplatonist Intelligences or *substantiae separatae*; and he asserted that there was just *one* possible intellect for the whole human race. Knowledge could be rented but not owned. Each individual human being could participate in the pool of intellect, but intellect was not in any way an essential part or faculty of his 'soul', and it was therefore quite unrelated to his individuality. Each man *knew* by virtue of the possible intellect, but he *existed* by virtue of a special kind of sensitive soul.[28]

Now, any living organism which is animated by a *sensitive* soul must be 'generated' in its entirety. Everything that is generated, as we have seen, is inevitably subject to corruption. And so Averroes held that, while the possible intellect was eternal, every individual human being was doomed to pass away. In short, there was no personal immortality.

Averroes's exposition may well have a good deal to recommend it as a faithful interpretation of Aristotle's thought, but his denial of personal immortality was obviously incompatible with Christian belief. St Thomas, as the leading Christian Aristotelian of his day, is unusually vehement in his condemnation of Averroes's interpretation, which he attacks again and again.[29] Dante's reactions may be readily imagined when we reflect that, if Averroes were correct, there would be no basis in fact for *any* part of his story of a journey through the afterlife. And so Statius continues:

What you still do not see is how, from being an animal, the embryo becomes capable of rational discourse. This is a point which led a wiser man than you into error, so that in his teaching he made the possible intellect distinct from the soul, because he could not see any bodily organ assigned to the intellect.

> Ma come d'animal divegna fante,
> non vedi tu ancor: quest' è tal punto,
> che più savio di te fé già errante,
>   sì che per sua dottrina fé disgiunto
> da l'anima il possibile intelletto,
> perché da lui non vide organo assunto.   (61–6)

Creation: (b) The breath of human life

With a phrase of biblical solemnity Statius now bids Dante 'open his heart to receive the truth'. Carefully picking up the thread of his discourse at the point where he had interrupted himself, he continues:

You must know that when the articulation of the brain is complete, God himself, the First Cause of all movement, turns his attention to the foetus. He rejoices over such a masterpiece of Nature's handiwork, and he breathes into it a breath, a *spirito*, which is newly created and filled with power. The *spirito* draws up into its own substance all that it finds active in the foetus, and becomes a single soul that lives, feels, and considers itself within itself [that is, a single vivifying principle, which subsumes the active powers of nutrition and sensation already present in the generated embryo, and which is capable of knowing itself as something 'separate' from any part of the body].

> Apri a la verità che viene il petto;
> e sappi che, sì tosto come al feto

278

l'articular del cerebro è perfetto,
  lo motor primo a lui si volge lieto
sovra tant' arte di natura, e spira
spirito novo, di vertù repleto,
  che ciò che trova attivo quivi, tira
in sua sustanzia, e fassi un'alma sola,
che vive e sente e sé in sé rigira.   (67–75)

This nine-line sentence contains perhaps the single most important doctrinal statement in the *Comedy*, and the vehicle is worthy of the content. It holds fast to the principle that the exact word is always the best (and it finds room for *feto, articular del cerebro, motor primo, attivo, sustanzia*). But the language of Aristotle and his philosophy is enriched with Christian elements. The choice of the metaphor, *spirare spirito*, deliberately recalls the creation of the first man, Adam, as related in the second chapter of Genesis, where we read that the Lord God 'formed man of the dust of the ground, and *breathed* into his nostrils the *breath* of life; and man became a living soul'.[30] The phrase *tira in sua sustanzia* would be at home and may even have its source in a theologian's account of the greater miracle of the Incarnation by which Jesus took human nature up into His Godhead.[31] The last line is almost an epitome of Dante's art. Using the simplest prepositions, conjunctions and verbs, he reproduces Aristotle's characterization of the nutritive, sensitive and intellectual powers in the human psyche; and yet the phrasing and rhythm of the line, coupled with the insistence that our psyche is formally *one*, recalls the language of Christian marvel and paradox in the presence of the mystery of the Three Persons in One God.[32] Finally, nothing is more characteristic of Dante's religious feeling than his stress on the Creator's joy.[33] He is *lieto* both at what He has made *con mezzo*, and at what He is about to create *sanza mezzo*; and the adjective achieves an effect out of all proportion to its simplicity, through its position in the sentence and at the end of a line, and because it is the only emotive word in the whole discourse.

The shadow-bodies and the role of the heavens

Statius now returns to his point of departure and the particular question concerning the nature and consistency of shadow-bodies in the afterlife. This second part of his speech must be approached in a rather different way. It is unlikely that Dante would have upheld the views which he here puts into the mouth of Statius in a prose work like the *Quaestio*. As a thinker, he is speaking tentatively – *dubitando* or *inquirendo*, not *determinando* or *assertive*. The explanation is like those given for the geography of Hell, for the earthquake on Mount Purgatory, or for the rising spring in the Garden of Eden. It is based on agreed facts, but it finds no explicit support in the Bible, in Aristotle, or in Dante's teachers. It is persuasive rather than cogent; and it relies heavily on imagery. It is in fact closer to the fiction of Virgil's *Aeneid* than to the theology of St Thomas. Nevertheless, we must briefly consider the answer he gives, since it is derived from the premises we have examined, and it does further clarify Dante's thought about the relationship of the several powers of the soul to each other, and the relationship of the whole unified soul to the body.[34]

Clearly, a distinction still persists between the 'generated' and the 'created' parts of the soul. At the moment of death, says Statius, when the soul is separated from the body, the three components of the intellective faculty – memory, intelligence and will – are enhanced or 'sharpened' in their activity, while the faculties of sensation are temporarily 'muted' and exist only *in potentia* or *in virtute*. But the distinction is short-lived, and the *alma sola* carries with it both the human and the divine elements – 'ne porta seco e l'umano e 'l divino'.

As soon as the soul reaches its destination, and takes up a place on the shores of Acheron or the shores of Mount Purgatory, it resumes its primary function as the *form* of a body. Its 'power to form all human parts' is not extinguished completely. On the contrary the *virtù formativa* communicates the form and dimensions of the earthly body to the air which surrounds it.[35] Metaphors and similes suddenly crowd the page. The soul is said to 'ray forth' its likeness, and to 'stamp itself' in the atmosphere. The shade-body is compared to a rainbow, and it follows the moving soul 'as a flame follows a fire'.

It is not a real body, of course; and the rainbow-image suggests that the particles of air do not themselves move as the soul moves. But the *virtù formativa* provides all the organs of sensation from touch to sight, just as it had done in the womb (once again the verb used is *organare*). Hence the 'shade' has the capacity to feel pleasure and pain, and to express those feelings by smiling or weeping. And the 'passion' of hunger can still cause emaciation in the case of the souls of the gluttonous, whose appearance was the occasion or pretext of the whole speech.

As part of Dante's fiction this solution may be judged both ingenious and ingenuous. As a product of his thought about man, however, it does confirm that the generated parts of the soul are indeed 'drawn up' into the created part, and that the unified human soul is most emphatically the form of a body. The *anima separata* is not a true *substantia separata*, as in the case of an angel.

It may seem surprising that Dante makes no mention of the part played by the heavens in the generation of a human embryo. But the omission is not significant. In this speech, in this context, he makes Statius confine his remarks to what is true of every human being. His task is to show that everyone is the child both of an earthly father and of a Father in Heaven. In the *Convivio*, in the passage discussed in the previous chapter, Dante had not been concerned with this common denominator. He had to explain why some individuals were different from and superior to others. Hence the emphasis fell on the variable factors – the disposition of the father, the complexion of the seed, and, in particular, the conjunction of the heavens. As we saw, the primary function of the heavens is to diversify individuals of the same species: that is the 'final cause' of their 'proper' movements.

Dante has not changed his mind about the influence of the heavens on mankind. Many passages in the *Comedy* make it plain that he still believed that the heavens lay the foundation of our complexion, temperament, aptitudes and inclinations, and that they do affect our health, vigour and state of mind in different ways at different times. Like all passionate lovers, Cunizza da Romano was overcome by the rays of Venus; the crusaders and other defenders of the Faith who appear to Dante in the Heaven of Mars derived their martial zeal from that heaven; Dante himself ascribed his own *ingegno* to the constellation of Gemini, which was in conjunction with the sun at the time of his birth.[36] His journey takes place at the ideal conjunction of the heavens. We may therefore assume that the planets and stars 'rain down' their 'virtues' on the human embryo in just the same way that they do in the case of the *animalia perfecta*. They remain a major element in the *arte di natura*, and their active contribution is also drawn up into the *spirito novo, di vertù repleto*.

'Man in Society' and 'Man and God'

The remaining pages of this book offer little more than a foretaste of the two further volumes that will be necessary to do justice to Dante's vision of man as an ethical and religious being and to his complex representation of 'human vices and human worth'. Both these volumes will follow the guiding principles and plan of the present work. Every chapter, that is, will offer an analysis of Dante's poetic achievement in some episode of the *Comedy*, and this analysis will be preceded, accompanied or followed by an exposition of the matrix of ideas from which the episode sprang. But the contents of each volume will be clearly contrasted, and they will reflect the dichotomy evident in all Dante's thinking about man.

The first will be subtitled *Man in Society*, and it will contain studies of man's life in this world and of his relationship with his fellow human beings. The topics will include: the human body, with particular reference to the 'spirits' and the senses; the intellect and human knowing; language; human loving in relation to the universal concepts of appetition, desire and union; judgement and choice, and the extent of our freedom and responsibility; man as maker; moral virtues and vices in the life of the individual; the nature and goal of society; justice, government and the rule of law; and, finally, the city, the nation-state, and the Universal Empire. Man will be seen from a timeless, ahistorical point of view as a being who moves towards a natural goal within the natural order; and most of the concepts to be illustrated will derive from the philosophy of Aristotle, in particular, from the *Ethics*.

The final volume will be called *Man and God*. It will consider the world beyond the grave, or the values of this world as judged from the standpoint of the absolute and the eternal. It will cover such matters as the nature of good and evil, and the meaning of original sin; the life and death of Jesus, and the history of the Church from the time of the apostles to Dante's own day; the theological virtues; penitence, confession, absolution, purification and justification; prayer and predestination; prophecy and prefiguration; the providential design in the history of the Jews and the Romans; the Last Judgement, the resurrection of the body, and the Beatific Vision. The viewpoint will be Christian and historical; the object of study will be divine grace and the ways in which it completes and complements the processes of nature; and the ideas will derive from the Bible or theology, rather than from rational inquiry or the Philosopher.

There is nothing in the least original in this proposed bipartition of the topics and passages that remain to be discussed, just as there is nothing original, as such, in the doctrine of 'Creationism'—which is the rather chilling name that theologians give to the theory expounded by Statius. But it is not always fully appreciated that Creationism is at the very heart of all Dante's thinking about human nature, or that the dichotomy in his treatment of the human condition is the inevitable consequence of his commitment to that theory—which, as he presents it, would be more accurately described as 'Generationism *and* Creationism'.

From our vantage point, it is possible to see that 'Dante was attached, simultaneously, to Christianity and to paganism' (this is the opening sentence of the profound study which gives its title to a new collection of essays by Kenelm Foster, *The Two Dantes*). But within Dante's own consciousness the polarity presented itself in rather different terms. He could not explain man's self-awareness or capacity for abstract thought except on the assumption that God had created every individual human soul. Having made that assumption, he could never forget all the other consequences which must, on his premisses, flow from the direct intervention of God. At the same time, he continued to attach great importance to the fact that man is generated as well as created. The soul is indeed 'one', as we have seen; but each man must live, develop, mature and act in the natural order, subject to the same conditions as all other generated beings. Dante was reluctant to accept that this first existence was a mere trial or testing ground. He was convinced that it had some intrinsic value and purpose. Reduced to syllogistic form, the bones of his position might be laid bare somewhat as follows:

Major premiss: *Agens agit sibi simile*; that is, every agent causes an effect by reducing something to its likeness, and therefore every effect must resemble its cause.

Minor premiss: Man and man alone has two efficient causes, since he is both generated and created.

Conclusion: Man and man alone has a dual nature and a double goal.

Our last task will be to put some flesh on these bones by attempting a brief preview of Dante's anthropology; and it will be convenient to begin by noting the resemblances to God in our human nature which are the result of His being the *direct* cause of our being.

Our likeness to God: (a) Knowledge and freedom

The first likeness is to be found in our capacity for self-awareness, abstract thought, and knowledge of the truth. The theologians had long made it clear that the 'image of God' within man lies in the intellect. No action can be called human unless it involves the exercise of mind. And the activity proper to mankind may be defined as the actualization of the potentiality of the God-given intellect.

Every human being has an intellectual appetite which craves satisfaction and which thereby prompts him to perfect or actualize his own 'possible intellect'. This may be achieved at various levels, each giving an ever greater degree of actuality and satisfaction – in ordinary conversation, for example; in taking decisions; in the process of arriving at some universal concept; or in the contemplation of a truth already understood. The proper object of the intellectual appetite is simply truth; and the full perfection of the intellect consists in pure contemplation. Notwithstanding certain grave difficulties, the conclusion cannot be escaped that the 'end' or 'final cause' of human existence is contemplation. 'All men naturally desire to know', as Aristotle insisted; and they will not find contentment and happiness as human beings until they are able to know the truth, the whole truth, and nothing but the truth.[37]

Our second likeness to God consists in our freedom. A *human* action should be as unconstrained as the free act of the creator. 'Freedom' has many senses. It means one thing when it is opposed to 'imprisonment' and another when it is opposed to 'censorship'. In fact, its meaning in any given context can only be established by reference to the contrary state implied by that context. In the present case this implied contrary is 'natural determinism' of the kind described in the previous chapter. Man is God-like and free in the sense that he is not determined by instincts. Like the higher animals, with whom he shares many needs and appetites, man performs all his actions out of some kind of love. He too must apprehend, incline, desire, move and find satisfaction in union with some particular 'good'. But, unlike the higher animals, man is not *compelled* to obey the instinctive responses provoked by external stimuli.

This freedom presupposes the possession of intellect. Man's intellect enables him to gain certain knowledge (*scientia*) about his own nature and the 'end' of human life; it also enables him to have knowledge about the class or species to which a particular object of attraction may belong; and, finally, it allows him to reflect, deliberate and form a reasoned judgement about the goodness or relative value of the attractive object, considered as a means to secure his end in life. (Most often, of course, deliberation will result in a choice made between two or more attractions.) Without such knowledge, and without such deliberation and rational choice, no action could ever be free.

But knowing is not the same as doing. It is not difficult to imagine a creature possessing perfect knowledge of ends and means, who might be totally inactive, or whose actions might be entirely controlled by instinct without regard to its knowledge. We therefore posit the existence of a second purely human faculty called *voluntas,* or the 'will', which is the principle of our freedom.[38] It must be like an animal's inclination or desire in the sense that it is the immediate cause of movement and action. It must stand in the same relationship to deliberation as an animal's desire does to apprehension and estimation. But it must by definition be distinct from desire, since it must be able to restrain or redirect the impulses of instinct. In Dante's words, 'it must control the threshold of assent'.[39] It must also be distinct from the intellect; otherwise, we should be victims of an *intellectual* determinism and compelled to put all our decisions into execution. The faculty of willing is in a sense higher than the faculty of knowing, and it must therefore be part of the intellective soul created directly by God.

It will be apparent that a 'free' act in this context is virtually synonymous with a 'voluntary' act. It can be performed only by an agent who has knowledge of the relevant general principles and of the particular circumstances, and who is acting after deliberation with a conscious end in view. As such, the free act may be *assessed* by other intellectual beings who possess the same knowledge. It may be judged good or bad, better or worse, more or less conducive to the end; and it may attract praise or blame in a way that no automatic or involuntary action ever can. The agent is moreover held responsible for the consequences of his free act. He may be justly rewarded or punished for what he chose to do. This is obviously an indispensable condition for the administration of justice, whether human or divine, and Dante reaffirms the fundamental principle in his letter to Can Grande where he tells us that the subject matter of the *Comedy*, considered as an allegory, is 'man, in so far as he incurs the penalties and rewards of justice, in accordance with his deserts, through the exercise of his freedom to decide (*per arbitrii libertatem*)'.[40]

Few writers who have upheld the reality of human freedom have shown themselves to be more aware of its narrow confines than Dante. He recognized that the will, no less than the intellect, is a potentiality to be actualized, rather than a gift already perfect at the time of birth. He knew that we often judge badly because our decisions are warped by pressures from the passions; and he knew that the will is often impotent to put sound judgements into effect. But he continued to assert that we are human to the extent that we possess knowledge and freedom. The intellect and the will are gifts from God in the act of our creation, and we cannot disclaim them or give them away except by ceasing to be human.

Freedom, indeed, is the greatest of God's gifts to man, as Dante proclaims in both the *Monarchia* and the *Comedy*. It conforms most closely to God's goodness and is most highly prized by Him.[41] No intellectual being has ever been or will ever be without the freedom that resides in the will:

> Lo maggior don che Dio per sua larghezza
> fesse creando, e a la sua bontate
> più conformato, e quel ch'e' più apprezza,
> fu de la volontà la libertate;
> di che le creature intelligenti,
> e tutte e sole, fuoro e son dotate. (*Par.* V, 19–24)

Everything that issues without intermediary from the Divine Goodness is completely free because it is not subject to the power of the heavens and their Movers:

> Ciò che da essa *sanza mezzo* piove
> *libero è tutto*, perché non soggiace
> a la virtute de le cose nove. (*Par.* VII, 70–2)

Our likeness to God: (b) God-longing and immortality

The third distinctive aspect of our *created* nature is perhaps no more than a consequence of the double likeness to God we have just described. The long climb of the intellect from truth to higher truth, and the many stages on the journey of the will from 'good' to higher 'good', both terminate in God who is the Whole Truth and the Supreme Good. The intellect and the will come directly from God; they make us like God; and they both have God as their proper object. Apprehension and desire draw us to particular generated things; knowing and willing lead us to the Author of all things.

This conclusion can also be stated in more emotive terms which will be familiar from our analysis of love as desire, movement and union, and from the doctrine of 'natural place'. In the *Convivio* Dante takes a Neoplatonist axiom as his point of departure. 'The first-given and supreme desire of everything is to return to its beginning or source (*lo ritornare a lo suo principio*).' Dante continues: 'God is the *principio* of our souls, and He creates them in His likeness, as the Bible testifies. . . . Therefore the human soul desires above all other things to return to its beginning in Him.'[42]

This love of God is our first love, our *prima voglia*. It is prior even to the love of being or love of self which is usually regarded as the ground of all other loves. Like the love of being, it is morally neutral. We cannot help being oriented towards God (although we are free to turn away), and we do not get any credit for this orientation.[43] The attraction is operative from the very moment of birth when the 'inexperienced soul, newly issued from the hands of Him who loved it before it existed, and alternating in child-like innocence between laughter and tears, shows the loving nature that it inherits from its joyful Creator by turning eagerly to all that gives it delight':

> Esce di mano a lui che la vagheggia
> prima che sia, a guisa di fanciulla
> che piangendo e ridendo pargoleggia,
> l'anima semplicetta che sa nulla,
> salvo che, mossa da lieto fattore,
> volontier torna a ciò che la trastulla.   (*Purg.* XVI, 85–90)

Once again it is worth stressing that Dante is never facile. He had experienced in himself the obstacles that must be overcome before a man can implement his love for God, tending the mere spark of inclination until it blazes into the fire of charity. Just as the needle of a magnetic compass can be deflected by a nearby piece of iron, so man is pulled back or drawn aside by the attraction of 'present things' with their false promise of assured and immediate satisfaction.[44] In any case, we cannot be said to 'will' what we do not understand; and many years must pass before the 'anima semplicetta che sa nulla' is able to gain even a dim awareness of the nature of God. Throughout our lives we are required to act on faith.

But Dante will still insist that even in societies that lived in ignorance of the revealed truth about God–societies where man's innate love for God remained no more than a confused aspiration towards a 'good' in which nothing would be lacking and the mind would be stilled–this aspiration was present as a vital and distinctive element in human nature.[45] His poem seeks to demonstrate that nothing but union with God can satisfy man's needs and longings. All other goods are limited, transient, and no more than means to that end. Hence, all other loves have to be judged good or bad depending on whether they are compatible or incompatible with our *prima voglia* and *desiderio supremo*. Charity is the root of virtue in the moral life.

Dante will also insist that the 'natural place' to which our first love should carry us does not lie anywhere on this earth, not even in the Garden of Eden. Our *sito decreto* is with God. In the fiction of his poem, therefore, Dante represents the 'concreated and everlasting thirst for the kingdom that is like God' as the sole and sufficient cause of his ascent through and beyond the physical heavens to the Empyrean. When man is made whole, and the whole man chooses and loves God, there is no longer any impediment to restrain his natural movement.[46]

In reality, as opposed to in his fiction, Dante accepted that no one had ever come to his 'proper place' while still in his body. In other words, no man had ever been able to satisfy his triple longing for the Truth, the Good, and the Cause of his Being while on this side of the grave; and this means that no man can have known complete fulfilment or happiness on earth. A happy ending to the 'comedy of human life' depends therefore on the last main resemblance between the Creator and the human soul.[47] God is eternal. We are in his image. Therefore we are immortal. Like the angels, the heavens and prime matter, we shall 'have no end'. Natural death does not suffocate the divine breath of life. It causes a temporary separation between the soul and the body. Our 'death-day' is a 'birthday' into a second life where we may see God face to face. Many Florentines in Dante's lifetime were followers of Epicurus and Averroes in the sense that they rejected the doctrine of personal immortality. But Dante regarded this disbelief as the 'most foolish, despicable and harmful of all bestialities': 'Dico che intra tutte le bestialitadi quella è stoltissima, vilissima e dannosissima, chi crede dopo questa vita non essere altra vita.' The tone of the long digression in the *Convivio* from which this sentence comes is so vehement that one wonders whether Dante was shouting to silence his own residual doubts. Certainly, one has to remember that he was writing as a man who had been banished from the place proper to his *earthly* existence, the city of his birth, for which he felt an emotion that could be dignified by the name of *carità*. His only hopes lay in that other *patria*, the 'true city of which everyone is a citizen'. Only if there was an afterlife could he hope to be compensated for his sufferings.[48]

It would be wrong, however, to lay too much stress on his private misfortune and bitterness. Dante felt a purely intellectual anguish at the thought that human life might really be extinguished altogether. Far from being the summit of creation, 'a little lower than the angels', man would be the most imperfect animal, since he would be tormented by appetites that could never be satisfied. For Dante, this is an 'impossibility that is horrible even to relate'; and this is why he declares: 'I believe, I affirm, and I am certain, that I shall pass to another and a better life after this one.'[49]

The intrigue of a classical play often became so complex, and the situation of the characters so desperate, that a happy ending could only be achieved by the intervention of some supernatural being who descended in a piece of stage machinery – a *deus ex machina*. The happy end of the drama of a Christian life is made possible, as we have seen, only by the 'deus *in* machina', the likeness to God within our bodily frame. But this same divine principle could also transform a comedy into a tragedy of revenge.

Immortality means that no one can be cheated of his true reward by the violence or oppression of another. But it is a blessing only for those who sought union with God, however faint-heartedly and ineffectually, for they alone will enjoy the Beatific Vision. Those who did not seek will not find. Those who resolutely turned their back on the Lord and His commandments will be punished after death for the wrongs they freely chose. They will not be able to escape the judgement-seat by taking their life, because suicide is impossible. They will never find release from the imprisonment and torments incurred through their second death. Hell, too, was made by the Divine Power of the Father, the Supreme Wisdom of the Son, and the Primal Love of the Holy Spirit. It was created *sanza mezzo* immediately after the 'triform effect' in the beginning, and it will endure forever. This is the 'hard meaning' of the words that Dante as pilgrim will read in dark characters over the entrance to the Underworld:

> Giustizia mosse il mio alto fattore;
> fecemi la divina podestate,
> la somma sapïenza e 'l primo amore.
> Dinanzi a me non fuor cose create
> se non etterne, e io etterno duro.
> Lasciate ogne speranza, voi ch'intrate.   (*Inf.* III, 4–9)

The last line is the key: 'Abandon all hope, you who enter.' Dante, as poet, will certainly expend great energy and take a grim pleasure in depicting the savage punishments meted out to the damned. But the floggings, immersions, mutilations and transformations that he describes belong to an age-old tradition in literature and in painting, and they are intended to terrify the imagination of an uneducated audience. The essence of Dante's vision of Hell is best seen in the condition of those souls who do not suffer any physical pain or indignity. They are condemned to 'eternal exile' from the 'Rome of which Christ is a Roman'. They have lost forever the 'good of the intellect'. They must live in desire without hope, and their fruitless desire is the cause of their eternal mourning. The worst torment is exclusion from the light, joy and love that Dante portrays throughout the *Paradiso*. These souls are forever denied the experience that Dante struggles to express in the last canto of his poem.[50]

The human person

All these likenesses to God are to be found in every human being. But the doctrine of Creationism is most satisfying and most original in the importance that it ascribes to the uniqueness of every individual. We are intellectual, free, God-loving and immortal by virtue of the substantial form that makes us exist as distinct beings. The differences between one man and another are so great and so varied that they cannot be explained—as they can with plants and animals—by reference to material complexions and astral influences. They derive from God himself. Each one of us originates in a distinct 'idea' in the Divine Mind. And this is tantamount to saying that each one of us constitutes a distinct *species*, distinguished by our form, rather than by the composition and dimensions of the matter in which the common form of the species is individuated. This is a very bold deduction, but it is one Dante himself puts forward—with suitable qualifications—in his *De vulgari eloquentia*: 'Man's actions proceed not from natural instinct but from reason. And reason is so diversified in individuals in respect of differentiation, judgement and choice that it almost seems as if each man rejoices in his own distinct species (*adeo ut fere quilibet sua propria specie videtur gaudere*).'[51]

Human individuality is certainly a case apart; and it had long been customary to call attention to its special status by designating human beings with a term that could not be used of animals or plants. Every human being is a 'person', a *persona*.

As early as the sixth century Boethius had defined *persona* as 'an individual *substantia* with a rational nature'; and his definition was often repeated by later theologians who endorsed his equation of 'personality' and 'rationality'. St Thomas reports, again following Boethius, that *persona* had originally signified the mask worn by actors on the Greek and Roman stage, and that it acquired the connotations of dignity and nobility from the fact that ancient tragedies represented famous and worthy men. More commonly—and more satisfyingly, though less correctly—*persona* was derived from the words *per se una*, that which is 'one of itself'. The word was also hallowed by its use to denote the Father, Son and Holy Spirit in the Three-Person God. When we speak of a 'human person', therefore, we are laying stress on his rationality, dignity, unity and likeness to God. And St Thomas summarizes all the claims made on behalf of the individual human soul when he writes that '"person" signifies that which is most perfect in the whole of nature (*persona significat id quod est perfectissimum in tota natura*)'.[52]

Every 'person' is the result of a miracle and has a unique value in the sight of God. This, ultimately, is why Dante chose to fill his poem with individual people rather than personifications of vices and virtues; this is why he could make himself the protagonist and represent himself in conversation with a humble Florentine girl and a Roman Emperor, with a personal friend like Casella, who died a few months before the fictional date of his journey, and with Adam, 'the first soul ever created by the First Power'.[53]

The goodness of man's 'natural' functions

To dwell at such length on these likenesses to God in every human person is to run the risk of exaggerating what is one of the weak points in Dante's anthropology, in that everything which we have found to be *distinctively* human in our nature is identical with what is 'angelic' in the nature of the angels. They too are directly created, as we have seen. They too are intellectual, free to will, God-loving and immortal. They too find fulfilment in a contemplative union with God. It may therefore appear that the souls of the blessed reduplicate the functions of the angels unnecessarily, and that the path they had to follow to attain beatitude was unnecessarily and unjustly arduous. And any redundance or injustice in the universe can only be ascribed to a fault or weakness in the Creator.[54]

It must therefore be re-emphasized that Dante gives great prominence to the fact that man is generated before he is created, and to the fact that the qualities and powers in his generated nature are drawn up into the *spirito novo* to make the single human soul. He reminds us that we have no less than *four* natures lying below the 'fifth and last, the truly human or angelic, that is, the rational nature', and that the complexion of the elements, the 'formative power' of the father's seed and the influences from the heavens all help to determine our temperament and aptitudes.[55]

Man must participate in the world of matter, change and time into which he is born. He cannot do other than follow a semicircular trajectory, rising from infirmity to strength and sinking again to infirmity; and throughout his life-span, his energy will ebb and flow with the rhythms of light and darkness, summer and winter, activity and repose. 'Man liveth not by bread alone'; but he cannot live without it, and he will perish unless he satisfies his corporeal needs, as indicated by the unconscious promptings of his appetites. He must use his organs and limbs to locate food, a shelter, his fellow men and a mate, and then to unite with each of them in the appropriate way. If he does not evade sudden attacks by involuntary reflex-action, he will die as an individual; if he does not copulate, mankind will die out as a species, since there will be no embryos in which God can perform His miracles. And if his parental instincts had not been as highly developed as those of the proverbial tiger, no infant would ever have survived long enough to actualize one iota of his possible intellect.

All these 'facts of life' were accepted and even welcomed by Dante. There is little trace of shame, distaste or disgust in his representation of our essentially animal feelings and activities. He took an evident delight in the activity of the senses and, as we have so often seen, his writing is

characterized by its concrete, sensual particularity. The passages anthologized at the end of the previous chapter also prove that he could and did
respond to the goodness of all the processes in the natural order, both as a
thinker and as a poet.

The 'winged caterpillar'

All that is vital in Dante's ethics, politics and Christianity springs from
his desire to recognize and to welcome the consequences of both generation and creation. Both modes of coming into being are held to be good
in themselves, and both remain good when they combine in the production of a human being. Man cannot renounce either 'patrimony'; and he
must endeavour to make the best possible use of the talents given in trust
by his earthly father and of those bequeathed by his Father in heaven.

Such at least is the ideal. But if we develop the parable of the talents, it
will become clear that the prudent administration of both incomes is
rendered difficult by problems of time and place. Man can enjoy his
earthly inheritance only for a fixed period of years, and even if he escapes
the blows of ill fortune and the ravages of inflation, it would seem that
exchange-regulations make it impossible for him to carry the balance
with him over the frontier into the next world. Conversely, the currency
of heaven will hold its value for all eternity, but it is difficult to spend in
the here and now. Should we therefore not bow to the exigencies of
reality and seek to preserve and enjoy two distinct accounts, one in the
present, and one in the afterlife?

Dante himself did not pursue the parable as we have just done, but if
we examine his use of another image we shall see that he was not unaware
of the difficulties inherent in his position. We shall also discover something of the ambiguity to be found in his solutions to particular aspects of
the general dilemma.

In the course of an impassioned aside to his readers, Dante exclaims:
'Don't you realize that you are caterpillars born to form the angelic
butterfly that soars defenceless to the seat of judgement?'[56]

> non v'accorgete voi che noi siam vermi
> nati a formar l'angelica farfalla,
> che vola a la giustizia sanza schermi? (*Purg.* X, 124–6)

If we examine the metaphor from the viewpoint of an Aristotelian
scientist, its tenor seems in perfect harmony with orthodox Christianity.
With his conscious mind, Dante is saying that the caterpillar exists in
order to become a butterfly, and that it already is a butterfly *in potentia*,
not a distinct being. Its first life is no more than a preparation for the
second (and the 'judgment' which it receives will relate to its doings as a
caterpillar).

If, however, we re-examine the image from a less specialized stand-point, it may seem to convey a different and indeed contradictory message. For the common reader there is probably no transformation more total, astounding or miraculous than the passage from caterpillar to butterfly. And we may suspect that, with his unconscious mind, Dante was drawn to the image just because it seems to maximize the contrast and the discontinuity between the conditions of our first existence and those to which we look forward in the life to come. We may also reflect that man's lot would be much easier if he were able to effect such a clear *temporal* separation of his two natures. How much simpler it would be if we could enjoy a first 'caterpillar-existence' on exactly the same terms as other generated beings, and then pass beyond the chrysalis of the grave to enter into a new 'butterfly-existence', in a different element and in another sphere, spreading our new-made wings of intellect and will as we rose effortlessly to the light of God.

But we have only to formulate the distinction in these terms to recognize how remote such an ideal would be from Dante's thought. It is no more likely that he would have advocated an unreflecting, uninhibited, 'red-blooded' life of the instincts than that D. H. Lawrence would have sought to persuade his readers to prepare themselves for the true life of perfect contemplation in the hereafter. Man does not have two successive souls and two successive natures adapted to his two successive existences. He has 'un' alma *sola*, / che vive e sente e sé in sé rigira'. The intellect and the will that characterize our soul must open their wings and attempt to make us airborne here on earth in our first life.

There is no single pattern to which man should seek to conform.[57] Dante accepts that man cannot live a fully human life unless he is a member of a moderately large, virtually self-governing community. This community—called the 'city', whether or not it is walled—exists both *because* its members are able and willing to perform different, specialized tasks, and *in order to* enable men to develop their distinct talents. Individuals are endowed at birth with an incredible diversity of temperaments and aptitudes, both to fit them for life in a city and to make the existence of a city possible. Some few individuals will be able to develop their purely intellectual powers to the utmost in a life of learning and of contemplation. The majority will actualize the 'practical' potential of the intellect and give expression to their will in such activities as agriculture, manufacture, commerce, defence, the professions, and administration.[58]

Despite these great and desirable differences, however, Dante assumes that *all* men, or all men worthy of the name, will become able to know, deliberate, choose and implement their choices. Every sane adult is assumed to have that minimum of freedom from natural determinism, and every sane adult is held responsible to the community for the acts that he freely performs, even where he has done no more than consent to the satisfaction of a sense-appetite.

In other words, there is a common denominator of intellect and will present in *all human* actions; and the exercise of this common denominator constitutes the specific function or *operatio* of the human species, which is quite distinct from that of the animals or that of the angels.[59] Our role is to join the two halves of the Scale of Being in our persons. We participate in the generated, sensible order by virtue of our body and its needs, and yet we simultaneously participate in the created, intelligible order by virtue of our minds. Our task here on earth is to live out a life-span which will resemble that of all generated beings, except in the crucial respect that it will be guided by the dictates of reason. We are to live *secundum rationem*.[60] We are to exist as conscious 'agents', and not as unconscious 'patients' of external forces or instincts. We are to live neither as caterpillars, nor as butterflies, but as 'winged caterpillars'.

'In my beginnings are my ends'

We are now ready to abandon picture-language for closely reasoned argument, and to proceed from these very tame and generic conclusions to Dante's most original and most important statement on the subject of man's divided nature.

Aristotle's philosophy is dominated, as we have repeatedly seen, by the idea that all things exist for a purpose. All things desire and move towards their 'end' or 'final cause'; and when they have reached it they no longer feel desire (which implies a lack) but completeness, joy, and happiness in fruition. It is therefore possible to say that all things desire happiness as their final cause. But Aristotle also held that the final cause of most *substantiae* – certainly of all sentient *substantiae* – consisted not in a state but in an activity. When a generated being comes from potency to act and is identifiable as a separate, autonomous organism, it is said to have achieved its first fulfilment or 'first perfection'; but it does not attain its second and ultimate perfection until it has reached maturity and begins to carry out that distinctive activity or *operatio propria*. Its fully actualized form is designed to enable it to perform that function without waste and without fail; and the correlation between 'formal cause' and 'final cause' is so close that an Aristotelian philosopher can assume that everything possesses, as part of its nature, the means to reach its end.[61] It will be seen, therefore, that the notions of 'actualized being', 'final cause' and *operatio propria* overlap almost completely, and that they are inseparably linked with the concepts of 'formal cause' and 'happiness'.[62]

If, therefore, we allow ourselves to say that man does have an *operatio propria* here on earth, we are also conceding that man has an 'end' in this life that will give him happiness, and that he possesses the means to reach that end. Man should be able to perfect his loving nature in the reciprocated affection of a disinterested friendship; he should be able to perfect his 'practical' intellect and his will by living a life of moral virtue; and he should be able to perfect his 'theoretical' intellect in the contemplation of truth for its own sake.

All these ideas derive from the *Ethics* of Aristotle, a work written more than three hundred years before the birth of Christ. And such was their impact on Dante that he regarded Aristotle not just as the 'master of those who know' but as the 'master of human life', precisely because he had shown us the *goal* of our existence.[63] But it will be obvious that claims such as these are a little difficult to reconcile with the more traditional teaching of the Church, which often represented this life as no more than a journey to a destination in another world, a journey on which the most we could hope was to save our souls from damnation by imploring the intercession of the Redeemer. Dante certainly felt the force of this starker vision of human life, and the whole action of the *Comedy* is subordinated to that interpretation. But even in his last years he was unwilling to turn his back on Aristotle. Caught between the rival claims of his religion and his philosophy—and this is how modern scholars explain the dichotomy or bipartition in his thought—Dante sought to extricate himself by arguing that *both* claims were valid because man, and man alone, had *two* ends (*duo fines*), each independent of the other. It followed therefore that man must have *two* natures, or at least a *duplex natura* which fits him to attain those ends. Not surprisingly, the two natures are those consequent upon his two *principia* or efficient causes—*generation*, which makes him a corruptible being; and *creation*, which ensures that he is incorruptible. All these ideas come together in the argument of the last chapter of the *Monarchia* from which we must now read the following paragraphs, since they are the only possible conclusion to this volume and the indispensable preface to the next.

Man is unique amongst all beings in linking corruptible things with those that are incorruptible (*homo solus in entibus tenet medium corruptibilium et incorruptibilium*); hence the philosophers rightly liken him to the line of the horizon which is the meeting-place of two hemispheres. For if man is considered according to his essential constituents, that is, his soul and his body, he is corruptible in respect of one, the body, but incorruptible in respect of the other, the soul. Thus in the second book of the *De anima* the Philosopher rightly says of the incorruptible constituent of man: 'and this alone, being eternal, is capable of separating itself from the corruptible world'.

Therefore man is, so to say, a middle-term between corruptible and incorruptible things (*medium quoddam . . . corruptibilium et incorruptibilium*), and since every middle-term participates in the nature of the extremes which it unites, man must participate in these two natures. And since every nature is ordered toward some ultimate goal, it follows that man's ultimate goal is twofold (*hominis duplex finis existat*); because since man is the only being sharing in both corruptibility and incorruptibility he is the only being who is ordered towards two ultimate goals (*solus inter omnia entia in duo ultima ordinetur*). One of these constitutes his goal in so far as he is corruptible and the other in so far as he is incorruptible.

Ineffable Providence has therefore set man to attain two goals (*duos igitur fines Providentia illa inenarrabilis homini proposuit intendendos*): the first is happiness in this life, which consists in the exercise of his own powers (*beatitudinem scilicet huius vitae, quae in operatione propriae virtutis consistit*) and is typified by the earthly paradise; the second is the happiness of eternal life, which consists in the enjoyment of the divine countenance (*beatitudinem vitae aeternae, quae consistit in fruitione divini aspectus*), which man cannot attain to of his own power but only by the aid of divine illumination, and which is typified by the heavenly paradise.

These two sorts of happiness are attained by diverse means, just as one reaches different conclusions by different means. We attain to the first by means of philosophical teaching, being faithful to it by exercising our moral and intellectual virtues (*ad primam per phylosophica documenta venimus, dummodo illa sequamur secundum virtutes morales et intellectuales operando*). We arrive at the second by means of spiritual teaching, which transcends human reason, in so far as we exercise the theological virtues of faith, hope and charity (*ad secundam vero per documenta spiritualia quae humanam rationem transcendunt, dummodo illa sequamur secundum virtutes theologicas operando, fidem spem scilicet et karitatem*).[64]

PART 3

Texts, references and notes

Introductory notes to Part 3

Attention is called to the following points

(*a*) Wherever practicable, straightforward references are grouped in such a way that there is only one note for each paragraph. These references are listed in the order in which the relevant passages are quoted, paraphrased or alluded to in the text (hence a reference to the *Purgatorio* may well come before one to the *Inferno*). Where such a list might prove disconcertingly long, each item is accompanied by an introductory word or phrase (as, for example, in notes 10 and 16 to the Introduction).

(*b*) The notes contain very few references to 'secondary' literature. Most of the topics covered in this book are treated authoritatively in one or more of the works listed under the heading *Suggestions for further reading*. The more advanced student who requires information about scholarly articles bearing on a particular subject is referred with confidence to the relevant entry in the splendid new *Enciclopedia dantesca* (6 vols, Rome, 1970–9).

(*c*) The space saved by these economies has been given over to the most important ingredient in this third part, namely, extensive quotation in the original from Dante's authorities and from his 'philosophical' works. It will become apparent that almost every paragraph in the expository sections of the text is underpinned by a number of brief excerpts from these sources, which serve to define the terms, state the facts, or illustrate the use of words and modes of argument. These texts are offered in the conviction that translation is always a betrayal, and that the analysis of ideas, no less than the analysis of poetry, demands close attention to the *ipsissima verba* of the original.

(*d*) In selecting and presenting these quotations, I have tried to keep in mind the needs of students who have a grounding in Latin grammar and syntax but who are as yet little acquainted with scholastic prose. I have avoided texts that are linguistically difficult; I have made extensive cuts (all duly indicated); and I have made free use of italics to call attention to the most important words and phrases. I have also quoted many passages documenting or illustrating elementary points that a historian of medieval thought would probably regard as beneath his notice.

(*e*) With two main exceptions, I have preserved the orthography and punctuation of the editions used. These exceptions are: (i) No indication is given when a quotation begins or ends in mid-sentence. (ii) Where the editor has preserved a medieval Latin *e* which corresponds to a classical Latin *ae*, I have in all cases substituted the more familiar classical spelling, in order to help the less proficient Latinists.

(*f*) The great majority of the passages here anthologized come from two main sources: the works of Dante himself (although these are assumed to be readily available, and are normally cited by a simple reference); and the physical and biological writings of Aristotle. I have not usually given the literal Latin translations of Aristotle's Greek, because they are often so cryptic as to be unintelligible as they stand. Instead, I quote from a Latin paraphrase of the text concerned, taken from an authoritative thirteenth-century commentary, and I give a multiple reference to the *lectio* and paragraph of the commentary, preceded by a reference to the book, chapter, page and line in the Bekker edition of Aristotle's works (these page and line references are reproduced in the margin of most modern editions and translations). The whole reference might therefore take the following form: *In De caelo*, I, 9, 279a 19–22, *lect.* 21, §207. In most cases, the chapter of the Aristotelian work, and the relevant *lectio*, would be the first texts that a reader would wish to consult for a fuller discussion of the topic in question.

(*g*) It is known that Dante used the commentaries of Averroes, St Albert and St Thomas Aquinas; and for some works, it is known precisely which commentary he adopted. It was my original intention to make use of this knowledge and to quote systematically from all three commentators, drawing on one commentator only in each chapter, as seemed most appropriate. But this proved a quite impossible undertaking: even when there was a reliable modern edition, the Latin translations of Averroes were too clumsy, and the works of St Albert were too digressive and prolix. It will therefore be found that I have almost always turned back to Aquinas; and all otherwise unattributed quotations from an Aristotelian commentary are by his hand. Two points should be made clear in this regard. First, there is nothing specifically Thomist about these paraphrases: they have been chosen as clear, economical and remarkably faithful expositions of Aristotle's thought. (Similarly, the excerpts quoted from Aquinas's two *Summae* are not to be understood as expressing a distinctively Thomist point of view, unless this is indicated quite explicitly.) Second, it is not my intention to suggest that Dante had actually read any of the passages quoted. In a book of this kind, one cannot investigate the precise wording of a presumed source, nor introduce any of the finer discriminations that become necessary at a more advanced level of study. Except where there is a specific disclaimer, therefore, or where the context suggests otherwise (as, for example, in many of the passages quoted in the notes to Chapter 8), all the excerpts quoted from authors other than Dante are presented in the belief that they are representative and uncontroversial formulations of concepts that were current among orthodox, Latin-speaking, Christian Aristotelians in the second half of the thirteenth century.

(*h*) For Dante's Latin works, I have quoted from the texts as they appear in the second volume of the *Opere minori*, recently published by Ricciardi (Milan–Naples, 1979: unfortunately, this edition arrived too late for me to draw on the abundant new material in the notes). For Dante's works in the vernacular, I have quoted from the editions of Petrocchi for the *Comedy*, Barbi for the *Vita Nuova* and *Rime*, and Busnelli and Vandelli for the *Convivio*. For Aquinas's *Summa Theologiae*, I have used the edition prepared by the Pontifical Institute of Medieval Studies in Ottawa (Ottawa, 1943). All other quotations from Aquinas are taken from the complete edition of his works published by Marietti.

Abbreviations used in Part 3

The following abbreviations are used in the notes:

A. Works by Dante

Con.	*Convivio*
Dve	*De vulgari eloquentia*
Epist.	*Epistolae*
Inf.	*Inferno*
Mon.	*Monarchia*
Par.	*Paradiso*
Purg.	*Purgatorio*
VN	*Vita Nuova*

B. Works by Aquinas

S.T.	*Summa Theologiae*
C.G.	*Summa contra Gentiles*

Philosophical commentaries:
(*a*) On the *Liber de causis*   *In De causis*
(*b*) On works by Aristotle (listed here in the order of Bekker's edition):

In Periherm.	*On interpretation*
In Poster.	*Posterior Analytics*
In Physic.	*Physics*
In De caelo	*On the heavens*
In De gen.	*On generation and corruption*
In Meteor.	*Meteorologica*
In De anima	*On the soul*
In De sensu	*On sense and sensation*
In De memor.	*On memory and reminiscence*
In Meta.	*Metaphysics*
In Ethic.	*Nicomachean Ethics*
In Pol.	*Politics*

The titles of works by other authors are given in full on the first occasion on which they are cited in each chapter. References to the same work in subsequent notes to the same chapter will give the author's name only, or, where this would be ambiguous, the author's name and a short form of the title.

Notes

Introduction

1. 'Questi fu grande letterato quasi in ogni scienza, tutto fosse laico; fu sommo poeta e filosafo' (G. Villani, *Cronaca*, IX, 136). 'Ne' suoi studi fu assiduissimo . . . Fu ancora questo poeta di maravigliosa capacità e di memoria fermissima e di perspicace intelletto . . . D'altissimo ingegno e di sottile invenzione fu similmente' (Boccaccio, *Vita di Dante*, XX). 'Theologus Dantes nullius dogmatis expers' (Giovanni del Virgilio, first line of Dante's epitaph). 'Dante Alighieri, per patria celeste, per abitatione florentino, di stirpe angelico, in professione philosopho poeticho . . .' (Marsilio Ficino, *Prohemio sopra la Monarchia . . .*, ed. P. A. Shaw, *Studi danteschi*, 51 (1978), p. 327).

2. The evidence is fully discussed by Cyril Bailey who concludes: 'All that can be said is that Lucretius was born in the 90's, and died somewhere between 55 and 50 B.C.' 'The weight of probability still lies on the side of the "orthodox" view that he was a Roman citizen, probably of aristocratic birth, who took his place naturally in the educated and literary circles of the city' (T. Lucreti Cari, *De rerum natura, Libri sex*, ed. C. Bailey (3 vols, Oxford, 1947, I, pp. 4, 8). The same verdict is given by W. E. Leonard (*De rerum natura*, ed. W. E. Leonard and S. B. Smith (University of Wisconsin, 1942), especially pp. 6–21); and by D. E. W. Wormell, 'The personal world of Lucretius', in *Lucretius*, ed. D. R. Dudley (London, 1965), pp. 35–67. In the introduction to his valuable commentary on Book III of the *De rerum natura* (Cambridge, 1971), Professor E. J. Kenney warns us that the 'poem . . . can and should be understood without reference to the personal circumstances of the poet' (p. 6); but he finds nothing to modify or withdraw. And he ends his section on 'The Poet' by restating the view that Lucretius writes as one who belonged to the aristocratic class, as 'a man who had witnessed and indeed been a party to the demoralization of a class in whose fate he was deeply interested. The agonies he describes sound like those of his own friends and kindred' (p. 9). T. P. Wiseman, however, argues that Lucretius was probably 'a good way from the top' of the social ladder ('The two worlds of Titus Lucretius', in *Cinna the Poet and other Roman Essays* (Leicester, 1974), pp. 11—45).

3. Dante was aware of the parallel: 'Contra questi cotali grida Tullio nel principio d'un suo libro che si chiama Libro di Fine de' Beni, però che *al suo tempo biasimavano lo latino romano e commendavano la gramatica greca* per simiglianti cagioni che questi fanno vile lo parlare italico e prezioso quello di Provenza' (*Con.* I, xi, 14).

4. He is justly proud of his *lingua suavis* (I, 413), *politi versus* (VI, 82–3), *lucida carmina* and his *suaviloquens carmen Pierium* with its *mel musaeum* (I, 934–5, 945–7). His *laudis spes magna* has made him seek an *insignis corona* for his head (I, 922–6, 929–30, repeated IV, 1–25; VI, 95). He begs Venus to give his poem *aeternus lepor* (I, 28).

5. The phrase is E. J. Kenney's in his commentary to III, 48–86, p. 81.

6. I, 117–26.

7. Perhaps one is saying no more than this: Lucretius is a great poet, not a versifier; and he writes with the total commitment and evangelical fervour that we associate with the proselyte or the man who has been reconverted to the faith of his childhood. Therefore one assumes that poetry came relatively early in his life, and philosophy relatively late. Obviously my view of Lucretius has been influenced by my knowledge of Dante's development, which we shall examine in due course. But I note that classicists with no axe to grind, and whose work I read long after forming the views set out in this section, come to similar conclusions. See for example, C. Bailey, vol. I, pp. 13-16, 171; Michael Grant, *Roman Literature* (London, 1958), pp. 145-7; D. West, *The Imagery and Poetry of Lucretius* (Edinburgh, 1969), pp. 32, 123-8. D. E. W. Wormell: 'Lucretius himself is fully committed, deeply involved in the sufferings of his fellow men, preaching a philosophy which is also a religion . . .' ('The personal world', p. 35); 'Lucretius is the spokesman of a movement which would like to evangelize the whole world; . . . initiation into Epicurean-ism is admission into a religious confraternity' (p. 42); 'Whether or not he was a convert to Epicureanism, he has the passionate conviction and enthusiasm of one who has under-gone a mystical religious experience, a revelation' (p.50). W. E. Leonard: 'He [Lucretius] believed himself saved, and Epicurus his savior. Epicurus must have come into his life at a critical moment . . .' (p. 29). 'It would seem that he stood about *nel mezzo del cammin*—midway upon the road of this our life . . . when Epicurus appeared to him, as Master Vergil to Dante, and spoke the golden words, the *aurea dicta*; . . . the initial clarification of thought, the purgation of spiritual distress, the awe at the revelation itself of the universe in boundless activity . . . must have been sudden and overwhelming, like a conversion, in which the experience of relief and exaltation for Lucretius, the man and thinker, revealed as suddenly the life task for Lucretius, the poet' (p. 30). '. . . Epicurus was a sudden impact on a life in need rather than a slow organic maturing in his nature. . . . I would not imply that Lucretius was already thirty-five when he first heard of Greek philosophy or of his philosopher. For a man in his set that would have been impossible. I mean simply that it had meant nothing integrated with his being' (p. 32).

8. Dante is remarkably dispassionate and just in his presentation of Epicurus. He defines the essence of his teaching on pleasure fairly (*Con.* IV, vi, 11-12). He speaks quite neutrally of Epicureanism as one of the three sects of the active life (together with the Stoics and disciples of Aristotle), who seek 'beatitudine' in the 'mondo presente' (*ibid.*, xxii, 15). And in a very startling passage in the third book of the *Convivio* he speaks of the three theological virtues thanks to which 'si sale a filosofare a quelle Atene celestiali, dove li Stoici e Peripatetici e Epicurii, per la luce de la veritade etterna, in uno volere concordevolemente concorrono' (III, xiv, 15). Again, Dante saw that the foundation of Epicurus's ethic was the denial of personal immortality, and defined his followers accordingly as those 'che l'anima col corpo morta fanno' (*Inf.* X, 14-15).

9. Tennyson, *Lucretius*, Oxford Standard Authors, p. 151. The passage imitated is *De rerum natura* III, 16-24, which in turn derives from the *Odyssey* VI, 42-6.

10. For ignorance of the 'limit', see V, 1430-3: 'ergo hominum genus incassum frustraque laborat/semper et in curis consumit inanibus aevum,/nimirum quia *non cognovit quae sit habendi*/*finis* et omnino quoad crescat vera voluptas'. For fear of the gods due to *ignorantia causarum*, see VI, 50-67, which pick up material from V, 82-90 and 1204-17. For the indignity and barbarity of sacrifices, see III, 51-4; IV, 1236-9; V, 1198-1203; and above all the deeply moving description of the sacrifice of Iphigenia, ending in the famous outcry: 'tantum religio potuit suadere malorum' (I, 80-101). For the fear of punishment in the afterlife, see I, 107-17; III, 830-1023.

11. Lucretius described Epicurus's achievement as follows: '*veridicis* igitur purgavit pectora dictis/et *finem* statuit cuppedinis atque *timoris*/*exposuitque bonum summum* quo

tendimus omnes/quid foret, atque *viam monstravit*, tramite parvo/qua possemus ad id recto contendere cursu . . .' (VI, 24–8).

12. Translated by R. Humphries (Lucretius), *The Way Things Are* (Bloomington, 1968). The hunting simile is developed in I, 404–9.

13. I, 418–21.

14. References in order: V, 52–4; I, 411–17; I, 498–9.

15. Translated by R. E. Latham (Lucretius), *The Nature of the Universe* (London, Penguin Books, 1951).

16. References in order (first lines only): II, 801 (pigeons); IV, 991 (dogs); III, 895, III, 87, IV , 1026 (children); VI, 548 (cart); VI, 148 (hot iron); II, 196 (logs).

17. Cf. I, 693–4, '*sensus* . . . unde *omnia credita pendent*'; I, 699–700, 'quo referemus enim? *quid* nobis *certius ipsis/sensibus* esse potest, qui vera ac falsa notemus?'; IV, 478–9, 'invenies primis *ab sensibus* esse *creatam/notitiem veri* neque sensus posse refelli.'

18. References in order (first lines only): VI, 623 (puddles); I, 305 and VI, 470 (clothes); I, 311 (slow wearing away); III, 702 (food); IV, 384, II, 312).

19. References in order (first lines only): IV, 332 (jaundice); IV, 353, 501 (tower); II, 322, 332 (sheep and army); IV, 443 (stars and clouds); IV, 438 (oar); IV, 400 (giddy boys); IV, 465 ('*opinatus* animi quos addimus ipsi').

20. '*Ratio* . . ./quae tota ab sensibus orta est./qui nisi sunt veri, ratio quoque falsa fit omnis' (IV, 483–5).

21. Cf. '. . . et violare *fidem primam* et convellere tota/fundamenta quibus nixatur *vita salusque*./non modo enim *ratio ruat* omnis, *vita* quoque ipsa/concidat extemplo, nisi *credere sensibus* ausis/praecipitesque locos vitare . . .' (IV, 505–9).

22. Christian readers may be astonished to find a phrase like *vita salusque* in Lucretius. But this bitter enemy of *religio* in the narrowest sense (='superstition') had a deeply religious sensibility in the widest sense; and this kind of language is not the property of any one creed. So Lucretius will speak with a liturgical majesty of Epicurus as god, father, conqueror, bringer of light and peace, deliverer from fear, comforter, purifier, teacher of the supreme good, and guide to the path: not quite *via*, *veritas* and *via* (cf. John 14.6), but not far removed either. The references in order are: V, 8 (deus); III, 9 (pater); I, 75 (victor); V, 10–12 ('quique per artem/fluctibus e tantis vitam *tantisque tenebris*/in *tam tranquillo* et tam *clara luce* locavit'); VI, 24–8. Perhaps the closest parallel to Lucretius's *vita salusque* to be found in the Bible is in *Proverbs* 8.34–5: 'Beatus homo qui audit me [=Sapientiam]; . . . qui me invenerit inveniet *vitam*, et hauriet *salutem* a Domino.' In general, the sapiential books of the Old Testament, and in particular the *Wisdom of Solomon* so beloved by Dante, are very close in inspiration and language to Lucretius.

23. Cf. V, 1186–1232; VI, 62: 'rursus in antiquas referuntur religiones/et dominos acris adsciscunt, omnia posse/quos miseri credunt . . .'.

24. II, 285

25. II, 244, 292.

26. II, 216–24; 240–5; 254–5.

27. II, 254. For the meaning of *foedera naturae*, see I, 586–7.

28. Translated by R. E. Latham.

29. References in order: II, 289–90; II, 268; III, 144; II, 286; 281; III, 94, 139, 450, 615.

30. II, 257–307, especially 284–8.

31. Translated by R. E. Latham.

32. All the material translated or paraphrased in this paragraph is taken from III, 307–22.

33. VI, 1. See also the outburst beginning 'o genus infelix humanum' in V, 1194.

34. References in order: III, 1056 (*mali* . . . *moles*); VI, 14, V, 45–6 ('quantae tum

scindunt hominem *cuppedinis acres* / sollicitum *curae* quantique perinde *timores*'); V, II and VI, 34 ('in pectore *fluctus*'); III, 55–93 and IV, 1135 ('*conscius* ipse animus *se . . .remordet*'); V, 1218–25, IV, 1133–40 ('medio de *fonte leporum*'); V, 1119, 1203, VI, 78 (phrases for 'equanimity'); II, 23ff. (material comforts); VI, 17–23 ('*vas . . . pertusum . . . taetro . . . sapore . . .*'); III, 66 ('dulci vita stabilique'); V, 18, 43, VI, 24 (purification); V, 50 ('dictis, non armis').

35. Translated by R. Humphries.

36. References in order: III, 59 ('avarities'); III, 957, 1082 ('aves quod abest'); III, 67 ('leti portas cunctarier ante'); II, 23, V, 48, III, 1003–4 ('explere bonis rebus satiareque numquam'); V, 1432–3 ('quia non cognovit quae sit *habendi*/*finis. . .*'); III, 59, 78, 1120 (honours); II, 10–14, III, 61–2, 998–9, 1120 (supreme power); V, 1132 (ambition); III, 75, V, 1126, 1140 (envy); III, 49–50 (exile); III, 83–6 (betrayal); III, 79–81 (suicide).

37. One of the most revealing recurrent constructions in the *De rerum natura* is the passionate paragraph which culminates in an epiphoneme or climactic exclamation of the type 'tantum religio potuit suadere malorum' (I, 101). These epiphonemes are often introduced by *nequiquam*–'in vain', because against the laws of nature: see II, 1148; IV, 464, 1110, 1133, 1188, 1239; V, 388, 846, 1123, 1231, 1271, 1313, 1332.

38. Dante, *Epist.* XIII, 1. There is of course a sense in which Dante was a Florentine by character as well as by birth; and similarly I do not disagree with W. E. Leonard when he writes (p. 27): 'Lucretius [is] the most Roman in character (so honest, fearless, austere, orderly) of the Roman poets.'

39. I, 34, 40.

40. References in order: I, 139, 926–7 (repeated IV, 1–2); I, 66–7; V, 336–7.

41. I translate literally from Dante's *Convivio* substituting 'Greek' for 'Latin': 'la gran bontade del volgare di sì si vedrà; però che si vedrà la sua vertù, sì com'è per esso altissimi e novissimi concetti convenevolemente, sufficientemente e acconciamente, quasi come per esso latino, manifestare' (I, x, 12).

42. I, 53–4, 331–3, 370, 398, 410, 944–5; IV, 912–15 ('tu mihi da tenuis auris . . .'); VI, 58–76 ('rursus in antiquas . . . religiones').

43. I, 936–47 (=IV, 11–22) translated by R. E. Latham.

44. Boethius, *Consolatio philosophiae*, V, m.3, 21; Dante, *Dve*, I, vi, 3.

45. This sketch is not intended to do more than point out similarities and dissimilarities between Dante's Florence and Lucretius's Rome. For an excellent account of the thirteenth-century communes in northern Italy, see D. Waley, *The Italian City Republics* (London, 1969). The relevant chapters of F. Schevill's *History of Florence* (New York, 1961) are still perhaps the clearest narrative (in English) of the political struggles in Florence itself. For the wider Italian context of the events in Dante's lifetime, one can recommend S. Runciman's *The Sicilian Vespers* (Cambridge, 1958), subtitled *A History of the Mediterranean World in the Later Thirteenth Century*. For a brief introduction to the history of Western Europe in the Middle Ages and the story of the contest between papacy and Empire, one might suggest Maurice Keen, *The Pelican History of Medieval Europe* (London, 1968). Many of the standard introductions to Dante have a good section on the relevant Florentine history, e.g. F. Maggini, *Introduzione allo studio di Dante* (Bari, 1948); T. G. Bergin, *An Approach to Dante* (London, 1965). For a full bibliography and critical evaluation of the field, see N. Rubinstein, 'Studies on the political history of the Age of Dante' in *Atti del congresso internazionale di studi danteschi* (2 vols, Florence, 1965), I, pp. 225–47.

46. See G. Luzzatto, *Storia economica d'Italia, vol.* I, *Il Medioevo* (Rome, 1948; 2nd edn Florence, 1963) chapters 7–10. F. Melis, 'La vita economica di Firenze al tempo di Dante', *Atti del congresso internazionale di studi danteschi* (2 vols, Florence, 1965), II, pp. 99–128.

47. The complete text of the inscription and many more 'economic indicators' will be found in the articles on *Fiorenza* in the *Enciclopedia dantesca*, and in *A Dictionary of Proper Names and Notable Matters in the Works of Dante* by Paget Toynbee, revised by C. S. Singleton (Oxford, 1968). The claims made on the Bargello tablet are sarcastically 'bettered' in *Inf.* XXVI, 1–3: 'Godi, Fiorenza, poi che se' sì grande / che *per mare* e *per terra* batti l'ali, / e *per lo 'nferno* tuo nome si spande!'

48. This characterization of Dante's early verse and indeed all the subsequent remarks about his lyric poetry are substantiated in the following publications: *Dante's Lyric Poetry* edited by K. Foster and P. Boyde (2 vols, Oxford, 1967). P. Boyde, *Dante's Style in his Lyric Poetry* (Cambridge, 1971). Both works have full indices.

49. All the expressions are Dante's. References in order: *Rime* XIV, 46; XXII, 8; *VN* XVII, 1; *Purg.* XXIV, 50 and 57; *Purg.* XXX, 115 (where *vita nova* = 'youth' = *adolescenzia* = *novella etade*, and contrasts with *seconda etade* in line 125 of the same canto).

50. *Con.* IV, xxiv, 1–6.

51. *VN* XXXIV, 11; *Purg.* XXX, 127–8.

52. My understanding of the stages in Dante's development as described in the *Vita Nuova* will be found in the closing pages of my essay: 'Dante's lyric poetry', in *The Mind of Dante*, ed. U. Limentani (Cambridge, 1965), pp. 79–112.

53. *VN* I; XLII, 2.

54. *Con.* II, xii, 5. Our only sources of information about Dante's 'conversion' to philosophy shortly after the beginning of his 'second age' are the poems he wrote at the time and his later exposition of them in the *Convivio*. It is obvious that the autobiographical matter in the *Convivio* is as selective and stylized as that in the *Vita Nuova*, but there is no reason to doubt the kernel of truth. This section is based largely on *Con.* II, xii.

55. 'Omnis mortalium cura, quam multiplicium studiorum labor exercet, diverso quidem calle procedit, sed *ad unum* tamen *beatitudinis finem* nititur pervenire' (*Consolatio* III, pr. 2).

56. These are the closing lines of the final poem in Book II. Dante quotes them in *Monarchia* I, ix, 3; and they are not without influence on the last line of the *Comedy*. The theme is in any case one of the leitmotifs of the poem. See also *Consolatio* I, pr. 4, first paragraph.

57. 'E qui si conviene sapere che li occhi de la Sapienza sono le sue *demonstrazioni*, con le quali *si vede la veritade certissimamente*; e lo suo riso sono le sue *persuasioni*, ne le quali si dimostra *la luce interiore* de la Sapienza *sotto alcuno velamento*; *e in queste due cose si sente quel piacere altissimo di beatitudine* ... Questo piacere in altra cosa di qua giù essere non può, se non nel guardare in questi occhi e in questo riso' (*Con.* III, xv, 2–3). The whole section is of the utmost importance for a proper understanding of Dante's 'love' of philosophy.

58. *Consolatio* III, pr. 10, translated by V. E. Watts (Penguin Classics, London, 1969), p. 102: cf. *Purg.* xv, 67–75; XXVIII, 136.

59. References in order: *Metaphysics* I, 1, 980a 22, quoted by Dante in *Con.* I, i, 1; *Con.* III, xi, 6, 14.

60. *Con.* II, xii, 7; III, ix, 15. The most important works Dante read can be ranged under four main heads: texts, commentaries, *quaestiones* and *summae*.

The texts were works by recognized authorities, usually classical. In philosophy the chief authority for Dante, as for most advanced intellectuals in the later thirteenth century, was Aristotle (cf. *Con.* IV, vi, 6–16), who was often referred to as 'the philosopher'. In these early years Dante made a thorough study of Aristotle's *Ethics* and *De anima*, and tackled his *Physics*, *Metaphysics* and the works on 'generation' and 'corruption'. He read them with the indispensable aid of the great commentaries by the Moslems,

Avicenna (980–1037) and Averroes (1126–98), and by the Christians who did most to assimilate the newly recovered corpus of Aristotelian writings to traditional Christian theology, namely, St Albert of Cologne (?1206–1280) and St Thomas Aquinas (1225–74). There were of course other texts and other authorities for other disciplines (e.g. Ptolemy for astronomy, and Galen for medicine).

The most characteristic and truly original vehicle of scholastic thought was the *quaestio*, and it is to these that one looks for independent thinking. A *quaestio* is best understood as a 'trial' or 'judicial inquiry' to establish the truth on some issue where the authorities seemed to be in disagreement and which was therefore the subject of contention. 'Expert witnesses' are summoned both for the 'prosecution' and the 'defence' in the shape of quotations taken from the relevant authorities – the Bible, the fathers of the church, the philosopher and his commentators. Arguments in more or less strict syllogistic form are developed on the basis of their testimony. Then the truth is ascertained and judgement is given. One 'witness' is shown to be in the right (provided his evidence is understood in a certain way), while the apparently contradictory evidence of the other authorities is shown, with the greatest respect, to be irrelevant, or based on a misunderstanding, or in the last resort, to be plain wrong.

Quaestiones can be grouped and arranged in self-supporting sequences in order to create a complete systematic presentation of some branch of knowledge: this is a *summa*. Today the best known of these syntheses is the *Summa Theologiae* by St Thomas Aquinas. It comprises 611 *quaestiones*, each of which may have up to ten constituent *articuli*. Dante, however, never refers to this *summa* by name. The *summa* which he knew was the one in which St Thomas attacks various non-Christian or heretical philosophers, and, in particular, the opinions of the non-Christian commentators of Aristotle and their latter-day followers – the *Summa contra gentiles* (see the *Enciclopedia dantesca, s.v.*).

61. Perfect knowledge, as we shall see in due course, requires absolute certainty, leaving no room for the *dubitazioni*, which rise in the first years of study, and then fall away leaving the now habituated intellect 'libero e *pieno di certezza*' (*Con.* II, xv, 5). Geometry and astronomy are both ranked high because of the high degree of certainty which they allow ('la Geometria è . . . sanza macula d'errore e *certissima* . . .'; 'l'Astrologia . . . [è] alta e nobile per la sua *certezza*, la quale è sanza ogni difetto . . .' *Con.* II, xiii, 27 and 30). The only truly perfect science is 'la Divina Scienza, che piena è di tutta pace; la quale non soffera lite alcuna d'oppinioni o di sofistici argomenti per la *eccellentissima certezza* del suo subietto, lo quale è Dio'. It is 'perfetta', 'perché *perfettamente* ne fa il *vero vedere* nel quale si cheta l'anima nostra' (*Con.* II, xiv, 19–20). At the time of writing the *Convivio*, Dante speaks of Christ's *teaching* (and not Christ himself) as 'the way, the light and the truth'; and this because his teaching brings certainty where otherwise none was to be had. 'Ancora, n'*accerta* la dottrina veracissima di Cristo, la quale è via, verità e luce: . . . verità, perché *non soffera alcuno errore . . . Questa dottrina dico che ne fa certi sopra tutte altre ragioni . . .*' (*Con.* II, viii, 14–15; and cf. II, v, 3).

62. Dante three times repeats the stern warning of Aristotle (*Ethics* I, 3, 1094b 23–7) that 'circa unumquodque genus *in tantum certitudo quaerenda est, in quantum natura rei recipit*' (*Quaestio*, 60; see also *Con.* IV, xiii, 8 and *Mon.* II, ii, 7).

63. References in order: *Epist.* XIII, 40; *Con.* III, xv, 11; II, xiv, 14–18.

64. References in order: *Con.* III, xi, 9–12; xiv, 7. Dante's rather exaggerated contempt for those who studied to gain a living is further evident in *Con.* IV, xxvii, 8–9; *Mon.* I, i, 5; III, iii, 8–9; *Par.* XII, 82–3.

65. Cf. *Ethics* I, 4, 1096a 16–18. The familiar quotation fairly summarizes Aristotle's position; but it is worth noting that Aquinas in his commentary (*lect.* 6, §75–8) insists that Plato had treated Socrates no less reverently, and no less firmly; and it is here that the

formula appears: 'amicus quidem *Socrates*, sed magis amica veritas' (§78). Dante refers to the text no less than four times: *Con.* III, xiv, 8; IV, viii, 15; *Mon.* III, I, 3; *Epist.* XI, 11. See also his commentary on the *canzone* which records the triumph of Lady Philosophy: 'che non dee l'uomo, per maggiore amico, dimenticare li servigi ricevuti dal minore [=Beatrice]; ma se *pur seguire si conviene l'uno e lasciar l'altro, lo migliore è da seguire*, con alcuna onesta lamentanza *l'altro abbandonando* . . .' (*Con.* II, xv, 6).

66. 'Dico e affermo che la *donna* di cu' io innamorai *appresso lo primo amore* fu la bellissima e onestissima figlia de lo Imperadore de lo universo, a la quale Pittagora pose nome Filosofia' (*Con.* II, xv, 12).

67. *Rime* LXXIX, 44. Reading the *canzone* and the *ballata* for the first time, one naturally assumes that the new 'gentile donna' is identical with the young lady whose compassion for his sufferings after the death of Beatrice kindled love in Dante (*VN*, XXXV–XXXIX). There is nothing in the prose of the *Vita Nuova* to suggest that this young lady was an abstraction.

68. *Con.* I, i, 11.

69. 'Oh quante notti furono, che li occhi de l'altre persone chiusi dormendo si posavano, che li miei ne lo abitaculo del mio amore fisamente miravano!' (*Con.* III, i, 3).

70. *Con.* I, ix, 7; II, xv, 4. The language of the second passage is extraordinary for its fervour: 'O dolcissimi e ineffabili sembianti, e rubatori subitani de la mente umana, che ne le mostrazioni de li occhi de la Filosofia apparite, quando essa con li suoi drudi ragiona! Veramente in voi è la *salute*, per la quale si fa *beato* chi vi guarda, e *salvo da la morte de la ignoranza e da li vizii*' (*Con.* II, xv, 4).

71. *Con.* I, ix, 5; xiii, 12.

72. *Con.* I, i, 10. Cf. further *Mon.* II, i, 3: 'cum videam populos vana meditantes, *ut ipse solebam*'.

73. *Con.* IV, iv, i, rendering *Politics* I, 2, 1253a 1–3. In his commentary Busnelli notes that Dante follows the vernacular translation of Egidio Romano's *De regimine principum* here in his preference for 'compagnevole'. The Latin translation of Moerbeke has '*civile* animal'. Aquinas will sometimes use '*sociale animal*'. For Dante's later unquestioning affirmation of the same views, see *Par.* VIII, 115–17.

74. *Par.* XVII, 69.

75. *Con.* II, ii–v, xiii–xiv.

76. *Con.* I, x, 12.

77. *Epist.* V–VII.

78. The parenthesis runs, quite simply: 'sicut in Paradiso *Comediae* iam dixi'. Even if this were an interpolation by another hand, the language of *Mon.* I, xii, 6 is extraordinarily close to that of *Par.* V, 19–24. For a review of scholarly opinion on the dating of the *Monarchia*, see the entry in the *Enciclopedia dantesca*, and also A. M. Chiavacci Leonardi, 'La "Monarchia" di Dante alla luce della "Commedia"', in *Studi medievali*, 3ª serie, 18 (1977), pp. 147–83, especially the appendix 'Nota sulla cronologia del trattato', pp. 181–3.

79. Like the 'temporal' or 'Church' hours of the day, the 'ages' may vary in duration from one individual to another: cf. *Con.* III, vi, 2; IV, xxiii, 15, xxiv, 7.

80. *Epist.* XIII, 24.

81. For the references to Aristotle, see *Con.* III, v, 7; IV, vi, 7–8; for Beatrice, seen *VN* XXVI, 6; XIX, 7.

82. I take the terminology from K. Foster, 'Dante Studies in England: 1921–1964', in *Italian Studies*, 20 (1965), pp. 1–16: see especially pp. 7–10.

83. For the link with St Paul, cf. *Inf.* II, 28, 32; *Par.* I, 73–5 (echoing 2 Corinthians 12.3), XXVI, 12; XXVIII,138–9.

84. For a lucid account of the rival theories, see A. E. Quaglio, 'Sulla cronologia e il testo della *Divina Commedia*', in *Cultura e Scuola*, 13-14 (1965), pp. 241-5.

85. For the relevant bibliography and discussion, see the introductions to these works in the new volume of Dante's *Opere minori*, vol. 2 (Milan-Naples, 1979), pp. 514-21, 693-6.

86. *Par.* XXVIII, 109-11; XXIX, 139-41.

87. 'In ciascuna scienza la scrittura è stella piena di luce, la quale quella scienza dimostra' (*Con.* II, XV, 1).

88. '*Per filosofici argomenti / e per autorità che quinci scende . . .*' (*Par.* XXVI, 25-6). 'E a tal creder non ho io pur *prove / fisice e metafisice*, ma dalmi / anche la verità che quinci piove' (*Par.* XXIV, 133-5).

89. *Con.* III, xi, 6.

90. 'Communiter omnes accipimus *sapientem* maxime *scire omnia, sicut eum decet, non quod habeat notitiam de omnibus singularibus*' (*In Meta.* I, 2, 982a 8-9, *lect.* 2, §36).

91. *Con.* III, xi, 8, 12-14.

92. *C.G.* I, 2, §8.

1 Wonder and knowledge

1. Only one character in Hell cries out spontaneously 'Qual maraviglia!' after fixing his eyes on Dante in the uncertain light; and that is Brunetto Latini. But his marvel is immediately eclipsed by the greater *stupore* of Dante the character on seeing his revered master of all people here in Hell and in this circle: 'Siete *voi qui*, ser Brunetto?' (*Inf.* XV, 24, 30). Dante dwells on the feeling of *maraviglia* felt by the schismatics and falsifiers (cf. XXVIII, 54, 67, 94–102); but they have to be *told* that he is alive. Guardians like Charon and the Centaurs remark on it without emotion (III, 88, XII, 80–5); while the fallen angels who defend the walls of Dis feel *stizza* not *stupore* (VIII, 82–5). With Francesca and Ciacco we cannot be sure whether they have noticed that Dante is a *living* visitor (V, 89, VI, 35–40). Farinata certainly knows that Dante is alive (X, 23), but it is an essential part of his character not to reveal *any* emotion (X, 36, 45, 74–5; only at line 88 does Dante draw a perceptible reaction). Pier della Vigna cannot see; and he is in any case too involved with himself, his own sufferings and his own reputation to be astonished that Dante can return to our world (XIII, 54, 76–8). In these ways Dante weaves ever new variations. Pope Nicholas III, upside down in his hole, mistakes the living Dante for the soul of Pope Boniface (XIX, 52–4). The hypocrites are uncertain whether Dante is dead or not (XXIII, 87–9); but in this encounter the emotion of 'maraviglia' is reserved for Virgil on seeing the crucified form of Caiaphas (124–6). In the cold ice of Cocytus the sinners cannot see clearly because their eye-balls are covered in frozen tears (XXXII, 46–51). Even when Dante has kicked Bocca degli Abati, the victim is not immediately sure whether his aggressor is alive (XXXII, 90). And in any case the traitors are dominated by a thirst for vengeance and the betrayal of others (109–23); there is no place in their hearts for *maraviglia*. Ugolino is glad to hear that Dante will return to the world because this will enable him to take revenge on the Archbishop Ruggieri (XXXIII, 7–9); Guido da Montefeltro, the fox outwitted, will speak only because he is 'sure' that no one will ever return from Hell (XXVII, 61–6).

2. One art will borrow its critical terminology from another, and it is difficult to avoid the language of music criticism, particularly of Wagnerian criticism, whenever one tries to describe the emergence, development and recapitulation of the many recurrent themes in the *Comedy*.

3. *Purg.* I, 13–27, 40–8. In this and the following notes, references are limited to the passages paraphrased in the text, and, in particular, to those that describe the emotion of wonder or that indicate lighting conditions and the passage of time.

4. II, 1–9, 55–7.

5. Here Dante is paying a debt to tradition, for, ever since Homer (*Odyssey* XI, 206) and Virgil (*Aeneid* II, 792–4; VI, 700–2), the thrice-attempted embrace of a shadow-body had become almost an obligatory element in such encounters beyond the grave. The vanity of such an embrace, which is established in this scene, is the precondition for the much more original and moving moment at the end of *Purg.* XXI.

6. III, 13–45.

7. III, 16–18, 55–99.

8. IV, 15, 101–5, 136–9, V, 1–6.

9. 'Interiectio est pars orationis interiecta aliis partibus orationis *ad exprimendos animi adfectus*, aut metuentis, ut *ei*; aut optantis, ut *o . . .*' Donatus, *Ars maior*, ed. H. Keil, in *Grammatici Latini* (8 vols, Leipzig, 1855–80), IV, p. 391.

10. It is not surprising that he should ignore Dante in lines 16–21. But his insistence on the singular pronoun becomes pointed at lines 42–8 and 53–7, after Virgil has said 'alcuno indizio / dà *noi . . .*' Sordello's astonishment on learning that Dante-character is still alive is registered at VIII, 63, quoted below. Sordello reacts in character even then, as he swings round to Virgil: Dante-poet does not overlook these fine details.

11. *Purg.* VI, 51, VII, 43, 52, 60, 85, VIII, 1–9, 49.

12. *Poetics* chs 1–4, 24, especially 1448b 5–10, 1460a 12–19. The sentence quoted in the text is a representative one from Aquinas, *S.T.* 1a. 1, 9, ad 1. Cf. *In Meta.* I, 2, 982b 19, *lect.* 3, §55 (the text quoted in the preface and below).

13. *Con.* IV, xxiv–xxviii; Aristotle, *Ethics* III, 6–v, 11; *Rhetoric* II, 2–11. Chapters 12–14 of *Rhetoric* II contain an analysis of character in relation to 'youth', 'prime of life' and 'old age', but Aristotle's account is not close to Dante in spirit or detail.

14. 'La vergogna è apertissimo segno *in adolescenza* di nobilitade. . . . Per vergogna io intendo tre *passioni* necessarie al fondamento de la nostra vita buona' (*Con.* IV, xxv, 3–4). 'Ma poi che furon di *stupore* scarche, / lo qual *ne li alti cuor tosto s'attuta*, (*Purg.* XXVI, 71–2).

15. 'Questa prima etade è *porta e via per la quale s'entra* ne la nostra buona vita . . . Dà adunque la buona natura a questa etade quattro cose, necessarie a lo *entrare ne la cittade del bene vivere*' (*Con.* IV, xxiv, 9 and 11). The passage continues with an anticipation of the opening lines of the *Comedy*: 'È dunque da sapere, che sì come quello che mai non fosse stato in una cittade, non saprebbe tenere le vie sanza insegnamento di colui che l'hae usata; così l'adolescente, che entra ne la *selva erronea di questa vita*, non saprebbe *tenere lo buono cammino*, se da li suoi maggiori non li fosse mostrato' (*ibid.*, 12).

16. For *obedienza*, see Dante's submission to the paternal admonitions of Cato in canto I (*Con.* IV, xxiv, 14–18 providing a very illuminating commentary); and again to Cato's 'correzioni e riprensioni' in canto II. For *soavità*, one thinks especially of the adverb 'soavemente' at I, 125 and II, 85, and of Manfred's '*sorridendo* disse' (III, 112). But the quality is omnipresent. 'Shame' in the normal sense of the word is felt by Virgil at the beginning of canto III, and by Dante in canto V.

17. The *Convivio* phrase 'domandatori de le condizioni' is echoed in *Purg.* V, 29–30 (*dimandarne, condizion*), cf. *Par.* V, 109–14; *Purg.* XIII, 130–1.

18. *Metaphysics* I, 2, 982b 12–22, translated by J. Warrington (London, Everyman Library, 1956), p. 55.

19. *In Meta.* I, 2, 982b 12, *lect.* 3, §55.

20. The only direct and explicit quotation comes in *Quaestio*, 61: 'quia per ipsos

inducimur in cognitionem causarum, ut patet, quia eclipsis solis duxit in cognitionem interpositionis lunae, *under propter admirari cepere phylosophari*'. But there are unmistakeable allusions in *Con.* II, xv, 11; III, vi, 12; xiv, 14.

21. A copy-book example will be found in *Par.* I where Dante introduces a question with the phrase, 'Già contento requievi / di grande *ammirazion*; ma ora *ammiro* . . .'(97–8), and Beatrice concludes her answer 'Non dèi più *ammirar* . . . Maraviglia sarebbe . . .' (136 and 139). But for a terzina where *ammirazione* is enacted as well as recorded, one must look to *Purg.* xxix, 55–7, where Dante turns to give a backward glance to Virgil after he has seen the Mystical Procession in the Garden of Eden. It is almost our last glimpse of Virgil in the poem: 'Io mi rivolsi *d'ammirazion* pieno / al buon Virgilio, ed esso mi rispuose / con vista *carca* di *stupor* non meno.'

22. As the terzina quoted in the previous note shows, Dante does not maintain distinctions between these three words which could and perhaps should have been observed. In his note to *Con.* IV, xxv, 4, Busnelli quotes a passage from Aquinas where *stupor* and *admiratio* are directly opposed: '*Admiratio* et *stupor* refugiunt difficultatem considerationis rei magnae et insolitae . . . *Admirans* refugit in praesenti dare iudicium de eo quod miratur, timens defectum, sed in futurum inquirit. *Stupens* autem timet et in praesenti iudicare, et in futuro inquirere. Unde *admiratio* est *principium philosophandi*, sed *stupor* est *philosophicae considerationis* impedimentum' (*S.T.* 1a 2ae, 41, 4, ad 4 and 5).

23. The penances undergone by the shades on the first four cornices of Purgatory make it impossible for the shades to set eyes on Dante. In heaven, the blessed see everything in the mind of God, and they can therefore no longer feel marvel.

24. In the Epistle to Can Grande, Dante insists that the subject matter of the *Paradiso* is *admirabilis* ('Cum ergo *materia* circa quam versatur praesens tractatus sit *admirabilis* . . .', 50); and he locates its *admirabilitas* in the fact that it describes such exalted and sublime matters as the conditions of the kingdom of Heaven ('*admirabilitatem* tangit, cum promittit se tam *ardua* tam *sublimia* dicere, scilicet conditiones regni caelestis', 51).

25. '*Scire* aliquid est *perfecte* cognoscere ipsum, hoc autem est *perfecte* apprehendere veritatem ipsius . . . *Scientia* est etiam *certa* cognitio rei' (Aquinas, *In Poster.* I, 2, 71b 9, *lect.* 4, §32). '*Philosophus* . . . est cognoscitivus . . . *per certitudinem*. Nam certa cognitio sive scientia est *effectus demonstrationis. Dialecticus* . . . procedit ex probabilibus; unde non facit scientiam sed quamdam *opinionem*' (*In Meta.* IV, 4, 1004b 20, *lect.* 4, §574).

26. 'Tunc enim cognoscere arbitramur unumquodque, cum *causas primas* et *prima principia* cognoscimus, et usque ad *elementa*' (*Physics* I 1, 184a 12–14, translated by Moerbeke). Dante alludes to this text in the following passage: 'quia *cognitionis perfectio* uniuscuiusque terminatur *ad ultima elementa*, sicut Magister Sapientum in principio *Physicorum* testatur' (*Dve* II, x, 1).

27. '*Scire* autem opinamur unumquodque simpliciter . . . cum *causam* arbitramur cognoscere propter quam res est: et quoniam illius causa est, et *non* est contingere hoc *aliter se habere*' (*Posterior Analytics* I, 2, 71b 9–12).

28. 'Quoniam autem causae quatuor sunt, de omnibus erit physici cognoscere; et in omnes reducens ipsum propter quid demonstrabit physice *materiam, formam, moventem* et *quod est cuius causa.*' 'Plainly, then, these are the causes, and this is how many they are. They are four, and the student of nature should know about them all, and it will be his method, when stating on account of what, to get back to them all: the matter, the form, the *thing which effects the change*, and *what the thing is for*' (*Physics* II, 7, 198a 21–4). This deliberately literal translation is by W,. Charlton (Oxford, 1970).

29. The example is not Aristotle's, who somewhat surprisingly does not analyse any one artefact into all its four causes, even though he gives a profusion of examples to

illustrate each cause in turn. But it is eminently biblical. Two references may suffice: Genesis 2.7; Isaiah 45.9.

30. 'Tunc quilibet opinatur se cognoscere aliquid, cum scit *omnes* causas eius *a primis usque ad ultimas*' (Aquinas, *In Physic.* I, I, *lect.* I, §6). Cf. *Con.* III, xi, I.

31. 'Sed tres in unam veniunt multoties. Quod quidem enim quid est, et quod cuius causa, una est: quod vero unde motus principium, specie eadem est his: homo enim hominem generat.' 'The last three [causes] often coincide. What a thing is, and what it is for, are one and the same, and that from which the change originates is the same in form as these. Thus a man gives birth to man . . .' (*Physics* II, 7, 198a 25, translated by W. Charlton).

32. *Metaphysics* II, 2, 994a I. 'Palam potest esse . . . quod sit *aliquod principium* esse et veritatis rerum; et quod *causae existentium non sunt infinitae*' (Aquinas, *In Meta.* II, 2, *lect.* 2, §299). Cf. Dante: 'Si ergo accipiatur ultimum in universo, non quodcunque, manifestum est quod id habet esse ab aliquo; et illud a quo habet; a se vel ab aliquo habet. Si a se, sic est primum; *si ab aliquo, et illud similiter vel a se vel ab aliquo. Et cum esset sic procedere in infinitum in causis agentibus, ut probatur in secundo Metaphysicorum*, erit devenire ad *primum, qui Deus est*' (*Epist.* XIII, 55).

33. Cf. *Par.* XIV, 1–3.

34. *De rerum natura* I, 402–9; *Dve* I, vi, xi, xiv, xvi; II, ii.

35. *Con.* II, iii, 2. Dante may well have had the reference at second hand, e.g. from the *Contra gentiles*: 'Apparet etiam alia utilitas ex dictis Philosophi in X *Ethicorum* [X, 7, 1177b 31–4]. Cum enim Simonides quidam *homini praetermittendam divinam cognitionem persuaderet et humanis rebus ingenium applicandum*, "oportere", inquiens, "*humana sapere hominem*, et mortalia mortalem"; contra eum Philosophus dicit quod "*homo debet se ad immortalia et divina trahere quantum potest*". Unde in XI *de Animalibus* [644b 32–4], dicit, quod, quamvis *parum* sit quod de substantiis superioribus percipimus, tamen *illud modicum est magis amatum et desideratum* omni cognitione quam de substantiis inferioribus habemus' *C.G.* I, 5 §32).

36. *Georgics* II, 490. It is often supposed that Virgil had Lucretius in mind when he wrote this passage.

37. *Con.* IV, xx, 10 glossing *Le dolci rime d'amor*, lines 119–20; III, xi, 13–14.

38. 'La forza dunque non fu *cagione movente*, sì come credeva chi gavillava, ma fu *cagione instrumentale*, sì come sono li colpi del martello *cagione* del coltello, e l'anima del fabbro è *cagione efficiente e movente*' (*Con.* IV, iv, 12). For his further use of the concept of an instrumental cause (*organum*), see *Mon.* II, ii, 2–3; *Par.* II, 121, 128.

39. 'Essa è *formal principio* che produce,/conforme a sua bontà, lo turbo e 'l chiaro' (*Par.* II, 147–8); cf. *Con.* II, xiii, 9.

40. *Epist.* XIII, 53–61, 69–70. *Quaestio*, 17, 59–68.

41. Petrocchi has preferred the reading *ragion*, justifying it not only on manuscript evidence (two of his mss have *cagion*, seven have *ragion*) but also because there is a 'più stretta e logica significazione che è nel vocabolo rispetto al più generico *cagion*'. My own view is that the texts quoted point towards *cagion*, which is anything but generic. Cf. further *Purg.* XXVIII, 89.

42. *Par.* XXVI, 109, 113, 115–16.

43. How important these details are may be seen by their absence in Cary's translation, which does justice to the bareness of the first line and a half, but then falls into banality: 'The newness of the sound,/And that great light, inflamed me with desire,/Keener than e'er was felt, to know their cause.'

44. 'e *lo* 'mperché non sanno'; 'non sappiendo 'l perché' (*Purg.* III, 84, 93).

45. Purg. VIII, 68–9.

46. *Par.* VIII, 123.
47. *Aeneid* II, 10.

2 The elements

1. *Physics* I, 1, 184a 13–15. In his commentary, Aquinas distinguishes the three terms from the outset, using his knowledge of the second book to suggest that *elementum* refers to the material cause, *principium* to the efficient cause, and *causa* to the formal and final causes: 'Sic igitur per *principia* videtur intelligere causas moventes et agentes . . . per *causas* autem videture intelligere causas formales et finales . . . per *elementa* vero proprie primas causas materiales' (*lect.* 1, §5).

2. 'Quatuor sunt *de ratione elementi*. Quorum primum est, ut sit causa sicut *ex quo*: per quod patet, quod *elementum* ponitur *in genere causae materialis*. Secundum est, quod sit principium ex quo aliquid fiat *primo*. *Cuprum* enim est *ex quo* fit *statua*; *non tamen est elementum*, quia habet aliquam aliam materiam ex qua fit. Tertium est, quod sit . . . intrinsecum . . . Elementa enim oportet *manere* in his quorum sunt elementa. Quartum est, quod habeat *aliquam speciem, quae non dividatur in diversas species*: per quod *differt* elementum a *materia prima*, quae nullam speciem habet, et etiam ab omnibus materiis quae in diversas species resolvi possunt, sicut *sanguis* et huiusmodi.' 'Sciendum est, quod cum in definitione elementi ponatur, quod non dividitur in diversa secundum speciem, *non est intelligendum* de partibus in quas aliquid dividitur *divisione quantitatis*: sic enim lignum esset elementum, quia *quaelibet pars ligni est lignum*: sed de divisione, quae fit *secundum alterationem*, sicut corpora mixta resolvuntur in simplicia' (Aquinas, *In Meta.* v, 3, 1014a 26–35, *lect.* 4, §§795–8, 800).

3. 'Dicimus enim *ipsas literas* esse *elementa vocis*, quia ex eis omnis vox componitur, et primo. Quod ex hoc patet, quia omnes voces in *literas* resolvuntur, sicut in ultima . . . *Literae autem non resolvuntur ulterius in alias voces specie diversas*' (*ibid.*, §799). See also *Metaphysics* I, 4, 985b 15; *De caelo* III, 3, 302a 10. In *De rerum natura*, Lucretius several times uses the example of letters, words and verses to illustrate how a finite number of indivisible atoms can combine in different *positurae* to form an almost infinite number of different bodies: see I, 197, 823–9, 912–14; II, 688–99, 1013–22.

4. The atomic theories are reviewed and rejected in *Metaphysics* I, 4, 985b 4–20 and again, in more detail, in *De caelo* III, 4, 303a 3–303b 8; *De gen.* I, 8, 325a 20–326b 28.

5. *Metaphysics* I, 3, 983b 7–984a 4. Dante puts Thales among the philosophers who surround Aristotle in Limbo (*Inf.* IV, 137).

6. 'Principia autem entium . . . confitentur philosophi esse *contraria. Omnes* enim dicunt entia et substantias entium ex *contrariis* componi . . . *Differunt* tamen quantum ad contraria quae ponunt. Quidam enim ponunt *par et impar*, sicut Pythagorici. Et alii *calorem et frigus*, sicut Parmenides . . . Alii *concordiam et discordiam*, sicut Empedocles' (*In Meta.* IV, 4, 1004b 30, *lect.* 4, §581).

In Aristotle's account, the first contraries to be recognized philosophically were 'rarity' and 'density', in which terms the early thinkers tried to explain the many forms assumed by the one element ('ponentes unam materiam . . . *ex illa materia una generabant aliam secundum diversas materiae passiones, quae sunt rarum et densum, quae accipiebant ut principia omnium aliarum passionum*' (*In Meta.* I, 4, 985b 12, *lect.* 7, §115). The atomists had kept to corporeal principles, but had chosen instead 'the full' and 'the void' (*ibid.*).

The Pythagoreans were the first to propose *incorporeal* principles, namely numbers ('Pythagorici . . . posuerunt principia rerum *incorporea* . . . [scilicet] *numeros* esse substantias rerum' (*In Meta.* I, 5, 985b 25, *lect.* 7, §§112, 119). Numbers, however, derive from a pair of contraries, 'odd' and 'even' ('principia vero numerorum dicebant esse *par et impar*, quae sunt primae numerorum differentiae', *ibid.*, §125). And from that fundamental opposition, members of the school derived ten pairs, including, apart from the five quoted in the text, 'right and left', 'male and female', 'rest and motion', 'straight and crooked', 'square and oblong'. In his prose works, Dante often refers to Pythagoras and his teaching, e.g.: *Con.* II, xiii, 18 ('*Pittagora* . . . poneva *li principii* de le cose naturali *lo pari* e *lo dispari*, considerando *tutte le cose esser* numero'); and *Mon.* I, xv, 3 ('qua re *Pictagoras* in *correlationibus suis* ex parte *boni* ponebat *unum*, ex parte vero *mali plurale*').

7. '[Aristoteles] ponit . . . opinionem Empedoclis quantum ad hoc quod *tria praedicta elementa*, scilicet *aquam*, *aerem* et *ignem*, *dicit esse rerum principia*, addens eis *quartum*, scilicet *terram*' (*In Meta.* I, 3, 984a 10, *lect.* 4, §88). Empedocles is named (along with Thales and others) in *Inf.* IV, 138; and he is referred to again for his very striking theory that the universe is produced and periodically destroyed by the contraries, Love and Strife, or Concord and Discord (XII, 42). Aristotle refers to this theory in *Metaphysics* I, 3, 985a 5–10; III, 4, 1000a 25–1000b 20; XII, 1, 1069b 21; XII, 10, 1075b 2.

8. *De gen.* II, 2–3. For a longer list of tangible qualities, see *Meteor.* IV, 8. For the metaphor of the lucky blow, see *Metaphysics* I, 3, 985a 10–16. The following typical sentences are taken from the Latin translation of the paraphrase by Averroes (cf. *Inf.* IV, 144): '*Nos quaerimus elementa corporum tangibilium in eo quod sunt tangibilia. Hic enim modus sensibilium communis est omnibus corporibus.* Nos autem quaerimus principia et elementa communia omnibus corporibus compositis naturalibus sensibilibus . . . Contrarietates ex quibus componuntur prima elementa sunt . . . haec: *calor* et *frigus* et *siccum* et *humidum* . . . Et etiam videmus quod *omnes contrarietates* quae sunt sub sensu tactus . . . *generantur* ab hiis et *revertuntur* in eas . . . *Compositiones* autem sive *coniugationes* quae fiunt ab istis sunt *sex, scilicet duae impossibiles* (calidum et frigidum, humidum et siccum), et *quatuor possibiles* . . .; quapropter manifestum est quod *numerus elementorum est quatuor*. . . Manifestum est quod istae quatuor qualitates sunt differentiae primorum corporum', Averrois Cordubensis, *Commentarium Medium in Aristotelis 'De generatione et corruptione' libros*, (ed. F. H. Fobes (Cambridge, Massachusetts, 1956), II, 2–3, pp. 100–7).

9. This point is made several times, e.g. in *De generatione et corruptione* II, 3, 330b 22–5. In H. H. Joachim's translation: 'In fact, however, fire and air, and each of the bodies we have mentioned, are not simple, but blended. The "simple" bodies are indeed similar in nature to them, but not identical with them. Thus the simple body corresponding to fire is "such-as-fire", not fire . . .' And again: '*Quartum elementum* supra aerem ordinatum *non proprie vocatur ignis*. Ignis enim significat excessum calidi, et est quasi *quidam fervor* et *accensio quaedam*; sicut glacies non est elementum, sed est quidam excessus frigoris ad aquam congelatam. Id autem ad quod sic se habet ignis sicut glacies ad aquam, non est nominatum, et ideo nominamus ipsum nomine ignis' (*In Meteor.* I, 3, 340b 20–5, *lect.* 4, §28bis).

10. *De gen.* II, 4, 331a 8; *De caelo* III, 6, 304b 23.

11. Cf. *De gen.* I, 5, 322a 15; 10, 327b 12.

12. *De gen.* II, 4, 331b 1. For the common ancient doctrine that nothing comes of nothing (*nihil fit ex nihilo*) see for example *Physics* I, 4, 187a 29 (Aquinas, *lect.* 9, §59).

13. This is a case of 'alteration' which Aristotle discusses and distinguishes from 'Coming into being' in *De gen.* II, 4–5. For 'wood' and 'bed' see note 21 below.

14. 'Causa continuitatis generationis, per modum *materiae*, est *subiectum*, quod transmutatur in contraria. Ex hoc enim contingit quod semper in substantiis *alterius generatio est alterius corruptio*, et e converso: nunquam enim materia est sub privatione unius formae, sine alia forma' (*In De gen.* I, 3, 319a 18, *lect.* 9, §69). In Dante's words: '*Cum omnes formae materiales* generabilium et corruptibilium, praeter formas elementorum, requirant materiam et subiectum mixtum et complexionatum . . .' (*Quaestio*, 47).

15. The principle is clearly stated by Dante: 'in ciascuna cosa, naturale ed artificiale, è impossibile procedere a la *forma*, sanza prima essere *disposto* lo *subietto sopra che la forma dee stare*: sì come impossibile la *forma* de l'oro è venire, se la materia, cioè lo suo *subietto*, non è *digesta e apparecchiata*; e la forma de l'arca venire, se la materia, cioè *lo legno*, non è prima *disposta e apparecchiata*' (*Con.* II, i, 10).

16. '*Vere* dicimus esse oculum cum videt, eum autem qui non videt, sicut oculus lapideus aut mortuus, non vocamus oculum nisi *aequivoce* et *metaphorice*, ut *serra lapidea vel lignea quae non potest secare*, est serra *aequivoce*' (*In Meteor.* IV, 12, 390a 14, *lect.* 16, §354). In *Contra gentiles* II, 30, Aquinas cites the even more patent absurdity of trying to make a saw out of wool: 'Necessitas . . . dependet . . . etiam *a conditione . . . recipientis* actionem agentis, cui vel *nullo modo inest potentia ad recipiendum* talis actionis effectum, sicut *lanae* ut ex ea fiat *serra* . . .' (§1077).

17. 'Omnia enim quorum materia est una communis, sic se habent quod unum eorum est *potentia* in alio; sicut *cultellus* est potentia in clavi, et *clavis* in cultello, quia utriusque *materia communis est ferrum*' (*In Meteor.* I, 3, 339b 1, *lect.* 3, §16).

18. 'Omne generabile fit ex contrario et *subiecto* quodam, sive *materia* . . . et similiter etiam omne corruptibile corrumpitur *existente aliquo subiecto*' (*In De caelo* I, 3, 270a 15, *lect.* 6, §59).

19. 'Sicut necesse est multitudinem rerum generabilium ut *potentia tota* materiae primae *semper sub actu sit*: aliter esset dare *potentiam separatam* quod est *impossibile*' (*Mon.* I, iii, 8). 'Sed intentio Naturae universalis est ut *omnes formae*, quae sunt *in potentia materiae primae, reducantur in actum*, et secundum rationem speciei sint in actu; ut *materia prima secundum suam totalitatem sit sub omni forma materiali*' (*Quaestio*, 45).

20. *Con.* IV, i, 8; III, xv, 6: 'Dov'è da sapere che in alcuno modo *queste cose nostro intelletto abbagliano*, in quanto certe cose si affermano essere che *lo nostro intelletto guardare* non può, cioè Dio e *la etternitate* e *la prima materia*.'

21. 'Sed sufficit quod dicatur in universali et in typo, idest *figuraliter*, idest *superficialiter* vel *similitudinarie* . . . Ad hominem pertinet *paulatim in cognitione veritatis proficere*' (*In Ethic.* I, 11, 1101a 28, *lect.* 17, §205; I, 7, 1098a 22, *lect.* 11, §132); Dante uses *typo* in this sense in *Mon.* I, ii, 1. Cf. also: 'Natura quae primo subiicitur mutationi, idest *materia prima, non potest sciri per seipsam, cum omne quod cognoscitur, cognoscatur per suam formam*; materia autem prima consideratur subiecta omni formae. Sed scitur *secundum analogiam*, idest *secundum proportionem*. Sic enim cognoscimus quod lignum est aliquid praeter formam *scamni* et *lecti*, quia quandoque est sub una forma, quandoque sub alia . . . Quod igitur sic se habet ad ipsas substantias naturales, sicut se habet *aes* ad *statuam* et *lignum* ad *lectum*, et *quodlibet materiale et informe ad formam*, hoc dicimus esse *materiam primam*' (*In Physic.* I, 7, 191a 8, *lect.* 13, §118).

22. *De caelo* I, 10, 279b 18.

23. See Chapter 9 below.

24. 'Ipsa autem corpora, quae *elementa* dicuntur, non *dividuntur* in alia corpora specie differentia, sed *in partes consimiles, sicut quaelibet pars aquae est aqua*' (*In Meta.* V, 3, 1014a 30, *lect.* 4, §800). Cf. further *De caelo*, 307b 20, 308b 10, 310b 8. '*Corpora* enim homogenea et *simplicia* . . . *regulariter in suis partibus qualificantur* omni naturali passione. Unde, cum *terra sit corpus simplex, regulariter in suis partibus qualificatur*, naturaliter et per se loquendo; quare cum gravitas insit naturaliter terrae, et terra sit corpus simplex, necesse est ipsam *in omnibus partibus suis regularem habere gravitatem* . . .' (*Quaestio*, 41–2).

25. 'Istarum *qualitatum duae* sunt *activae*, scilicet *calidum* et *frigidum*, et *duae passivae*, scilicet *siccum* et *humidum*.' 'Est ergo simplex et *naturalis generatio*, permutatio facta ab istis *virtutibus activis* . . . Cum igitur *activae obtinent supra passivas, tunc sequitur generatio*: quando autem passivae *vincunt* activas . . . tunc sequitur indigestio, quae est via ad

corruptionem' (*In Meteor.* IV, 1, 378b–379a, *lect.* 1–2, §§313–14). For Aristotle's classic statement of the importance of the spiralling movement of the sun, see *De gen.* II, 10, 336a 33.

26. 'Unius generatio est alterius corruptio'; see note 14.

27. 'Calidum et frigidum facit augmentum et decrementum; ita quod *calidum* proprie *facit augmentum*: eius est enim *dilatare et diffundere quasi movendo ad circumferentiam*; *frigidum* autem *causat decrementum*, quia eius est *constringere, quasi movendo ad centrum* . . . Calor naturalis active *causat augmentum per extensionem quamdam.*'

'Quamvis quatuor qualitatum elementalium duae conveniant singulis . . . in singulis tamen elementis *singulae harum qualitatum principaliter inveniuntur quasi propriae ipsis.* Nam *ignis* proprie *calidus* est, quia ignis est nobilissimum inter elementa et propinquissimum caelesti corpori [i.e. aether], ideo contingit ei proprie et secundum se *calidum* esse, quod est *maxime activum* . . . Aëri . . . secundum se . . . competit *humidum*, quod est nobilius inter qualitates passivas . . . *Aquae* . . . proprie et secundum se competit *frigidum*, . . . *terrae* vero . . . *siccum* . . .' (*In De sensu*, ch. 4, 442a 5 and 441b 10, *lect.* 10, §§144, 146 and 133–4).

28. *De caelo* IV, 1, 4 and 5. Dante refers to Fire and Air as 'questi corpi *levi*' (*Par.* I, 99) and dwells at length on the points made in this paragraph, e.g.: '*Gravissimum corpus* aequaliter undique ac potissime petit centrum: *terra est gravissimum corpus*; ergo aequaliter undique ac potissime petit centrum.' '*Potissima virtus gravitatis* est in corpore potissime petente centrum, quod quidem est terra . . .' 'Quare cum *gravitas insit naturaliter terrae*, et terra sit corpus simplex, necesse est ipsam *in omnibus partibus suis regularem habere gravitatem*' (*Quaestio*, 34, 37, 42).

29. *De caelo* IV, 1; cf. Dante: '*Grave* et *leve* sunt passiones corporum simplicium, quae *moventur motu recto*, et levia moventur *sursum*, gravia vero *deorsum*. Hoc enim intendo per *grave* et *leve*, quod sit *mobile*; sicut vult Phylosophus in *Caelo et Mundo*' (*Quaestio*, 25). 'Nam, sicut plures *glebas* diceremus "concordes" propter *condescendere omnes ad medium*, et plures *flammas propter coadscendere omnes ad circunferentiam*, si voluntarie hoc facerent . . .', there being just one 'qualitas . . . formaliter in *glebis*, scilicet *gravitas*, et una in *flammis*, scilicet *levitas*' (*Mon.* I, xv, 6).

30. Cf. *Con.* III, iii, 2 analysed below.

31. It will be simple or unique, because matter is finite; solid, because Earth is cold and dry; perfect, because Earth is homogeneous and 'aequaliter undique ac potissime petit centrum' (hence 'terra aequaliter in omni parte suae circumferentiae dist[a]t a centro'); motionless, because it has come to rest in its own natural place (*Quaestio*, 34–42). For 'the point to which all weights are drawn', see *Inf.* XXXII, 74–5; XXXIV, 110–11. For the centre of the earth as the centre of the universe, see *Quaestio*, 7. For Aristotle's proof that there can be no void, see *Physics* III, 4–8, IV, 6–9.

32. '*Aqua* enim est *circa terram* . . . *aër* autem *circumdat aquam, ignis* autem *circumdat aërem*; et secundum eandem rationem superiora corpora circumdant inferiora usque ad supremum caelum . . . *Haec corpora tangunt se invicem absque aliqua interpolatione alterius corporis, vel etiam vacui* . . . *Superficies* autem unius horum inferiorum corporum *est sphaerica*' (*In De caelo* II, 4, 287b, *lect.* 6, §357).

33. *Inf.* III, 4–8; XXXIV, 121–6; *Par.* XXIX, 49–57.

34. In *Con.* II, vi, 10 Dante states that the semidiameter of the earth is 3,250 miles.

35. *Inf.* XIV, 94–120.

36. Aristotle rejects the account given by Plato, who said (*Phaedo*, 111 D) that 'omnia flumina et mare *concurrunt sub terra ad aliquod principium*, quasi terra sit perforata a mari et fluviis. Hoc autem principium, quod . . . est principium aquarum omnium, *vocatur Tartarus*, qui est *quaedam magna multitudo aquae existens circa medium mundi*: ex quo

quidem principio dicit prodire omnes aquas quae non fluunt, sicut sunt mare et stagna, et quae fluunt, sicut fontes et flumina' (*In Meteor.* II, 2, 355b 32, *lect.* 3, §156). But the reason given for rejecting Plato's account is precisely the 'popular' one that water cannot run uphill: 'et sic accidet illud quod . . . *flumina sint superiora fontibus*, vel quod *sursum fluant*: et hoc est *impossibile*' (*ibid.*, §157). Aristotle is nevertheless clear that '*mare* videtur esse *locus naturalis* aquarum' (*ibid.*, and *lect.* 2, §148).

37. *Inf.* XXXII, 22–8.

38. *Inf.* XXXIII, 100–8.

39. *Inf.* XXXIV, 46–52. *Vapore* is used for the Holy Spirit in the paraphrase of the Lord's Prayer, *Purg.* XI, 6.

40. 'Philosophus est aliqualiter *philomythes*, idest amator *fabulae*, quod *proprium est poetarum*. Unde primi, qui *per modum* quemdam *fabularem* de *principiis rerum* tractaverunt, dicti sunt *poetae theologizantes*' (*In Meta.* I, 2, 982b 19, *lect.* 3, §55).

41. *Inf.* XXXIV, 96, 105, 112–18; see Chapter 6 below.

42. *Aeneid* III, 22–48; *Inf.* XIII, 46–8.

43. E.g. *In De gen.* I, 5, 322a 15, *lect.* 16, §112; I, 10, 327b 12, *lect.* 24, §169; *In Physic.* IV, 7, 214b, *lect.* 10, §518. *In Meteor.* II, 9, 369a 23, *lect.* 16, §245.

44. In his commentary Boccaccio uses the simile almost as a pretext for a little lesson on the 'qualities' and the 'elements'. 'Egli è vero che ogni animale vegetativo in nudrimento di sì attrae con le sue radici quella parte d'ogni *elemento* che gli bisogna; e perciò quella parte, che trae dal *fuoco* e dalla *terra*, consiste nella *solidità del legno*; e, senza alcun sentore, ardendo il legno, *si riprende il fuoco quello che di lui è nel legno*, e similmente *quello, che v'è terreo, converte in terra*. Ma dell'*umido* e dell'*aere* non avvien così, percioché, essendo l'*umido*, sì come da suo *contrario*, cacciato dal *fuoco*, ricorre a quella parte donde noi il veggiamo uscire, e per li pori del legno ne geme fuori. Ma questa *umidità* non fa nel suo uscire fuori alcun romore: l'*aere*, ancora per non esser dal *fuoco risoluto*, gli fugge innanzi . . .' (*Comento*, vol. 3, p. 135).

45. 'Quia igitur in istis locis qui sunt ad meridiem et septentrionem, plurima aqua descendit, oportet quod ibi etiam *plurima fiat exhalatio*; sicut *ex lignis viridibus et humidis maior exhalat fumus quam ex siccis*. Unde, cum *exhalatio talis* sit *principium ventorum*, rationabile est quod *plures et maximi ventorum* sint, qui flant a meridie . . . et a septentrione . . .' (*In Meteor.* II, 4, 361a 18–20, *lect.* 7, §187).

3 Meteorology

1. The role of the sun may be summarized as follows: 'Illud quod est *causa* sicut movens et principale et primum principium omnium harum passionum est *circulus zodiacus*, in quo manifeste movetur sol, qui et *disgregat resolvendo vapores* a terra, et *congregat eos per suam absentiam*' (*In Meteor.* I, 9, 346b 22, *lect.* 14, §96; cf. *ibid.*, 347a 1–10). *Vapor* is described in these terms: 'In prima enim *transmutatione*, secundum quam *aqua subtiliatur et elevatur*, medium est *vapor*: nam *ipsa exhalatio resoluta ab aqua vocatur vapor*, qui est medius inter aërem et aquam' (*ibid.*, I, 9, 346b 30, *lect.* 14, §99). For moisture drawn up from the sea, cf. *Purg.* XIV, 34–6; from the land, cf.: 'Et *sol* . . . etiam *ipsam terram desiccat*, attrahens humorem imbibitum in terra' (*In Meteor.* II, 4, 359b 35, *lect.* 7, §180). Dante uses the phrase *aere pregno* in *Purg.* V, 118; *Par.* X, 68. For reflected heat growing less in the upper regions of the atmosphere cf.: 'Alia causa calefactionis est *reverberatio radiorum solis a terra*; . . . (*radios refractos*, idest *reverberatos*, a terra) qui prohibent congregari nubes prope terram . . . Congregationes nubium fiunt ibi, ubi *radii repercussi a terra* iam desinunt habere virtutem calefaciendi' (*In Meteor.* I, 3, 340a 30, *lect.* 4, §26; cf. I, 12, 348a 15–20, *lect.* 15, §115).

2. 'Cum terra quiescat in medio, illud *humidum aqueum* quod est circa ipsam, tum a *radiis solis,* tum ab alia caliditate quae est a superioribus corporibus, *resolvitur in vaporem,* et sic *subtiliatum per virtutem calidi sursum fertur* . . . Vapor qui sursum fertur per virtutem caloris, deseritur a caliditate quae sursum eum ferebat . . . Sic igitur *deficiente calore calefaciente et elevante* vaporem aqueum, *vapor aqueus* redit ad suam naturam, coadunante etiam frigiditate loci; et *sic infrigidatur, et infrigidatus inspissatur,* et *inspissatus cadit ad terram.' '.* . . Quando *per modicas partes* vapores inspissati in aquam cadunt, tunc dicuntur . . . *guttae;* quando vero *secundum maiores partes* decidunt guttae ex vaporibus generatae, *vocatur pluvia'* (*In Meteor.* I, 9, 346b 24–35, *lect.* 14, §§97–8, 102; cf. *ibid.* I, 11, 347b 18; 12, 348a 5; II, 4, 360a 10). There is thus a *'circularis transmutatio* [quae] imitatur circularem motum solis' (§100).

3. 'Sed cum *nubes* condensatur in aquam, *id quod est residuum de nube,* quod scilicet in aquam condensari non potuit, est *caligo nebulae'* (*In Meteor.* I, 9, 346b 35, *lect.* 14, §99). '*Ros* et *pruina* contingunt ex hoc quod de die, sole existente super terram, *aliquid evaporat ex humido aqueo* propter solis calorem; quod quidem evaporatum *non multum suspenditur vel elevatur super terram* . . . Et ita, cum de nocte infrigidatus fuerit aër, *inspissatur ille vapor* elevatus de die, *et cadit in terram,* et vocatur *ros vel pruina* . . . Sed ros fit, quando vapor inspissatur in aquam, *et neque est tantus aestus quod vapor elevatus desiccetur, neque est tantum frigus quod vapor congeletur.* Et ideo oportet quod sit aut *in tempore* aut *in loco* calido . . . *Pruina* fit, quando vapor prius congelatur quam condensetur in aquam; et propter hoc fit in hieme et . . . in frigidis locis . . . Tam ros quam pruina fiunt cum *aër* fuerit *serenus* absque nubibus et pluvia, et *tranquillus* absque vento' (*ibid.,* I, 10, 347a 13, §§103–5).

4. 'Ex illo loco [sc. hoc inferiori aere vicino terrae] veniunt *tria corpora inspissata propter infrigidationem,* scilicet *aqua pluviae* et *nix* et *grando* . . . *Nix* enim et *pruina* proportionaliter sunt idem . . . Quando enim *tota nubes congelatur,* fit *nix;* quando vero aliquis parvus vapor circa terram congelatur, tunc fit *pruina* . . . *Grando* est sicut *crystallus* quidam, idest *aqua vehementer congelata* . . . Hoc accidit, cum vapor descendit in aërem calidum; . . . sic igitur *ex calido circumstante frigidum* et congregante ipsum, fiunt *magnae guttae* pluviarum et *violentae.* Sed cum *frigidum* magis *congregatur conclusum ab exteriori calido,* non solum subito condensantur nubes in aquam, *sed ulterius aqua congelatur* ex vehementi virtute frigidi inclusi, *et sic fit grando'* (*In Meteor.* I, 11, 347b 12–348b 30, *lect.* 15, §§110, 111, 119).

5. Cf. further: 'si *converti* quel vento in cotal voce' (*Inf.* XIII, 92); '. . . 'l pregno aere in acqua *si converse'* (*Purg.* V, 118); 'vena / che ristori vapor che gel *converta'* (*Purg.* XXVIII, 122–3).

6. These lines are from the canzone-sestina, *Amor tu vedi ben,* the third of the group written for the 'stony-hearted' lady. In place of rhyme, every line ends with one of just five words: *donna, tempo, luce, petra* and *freddo.* Each word is thus repeated twelve times in the final position according to a strict pattern which ensures that each of the five stanzas in turn is dominated by one of the key-words. The third stanza, as will be seen, is a kind of celebration of the power of the 'active quality' of Cold.

7. 'Intendit determinare de his quae fiunt *per refractionem luminis ex exhalatione humida* constante superius . . . *Halo* fit . . . ab aëre vaporoso, ingrossato a frigido in *nubem tenuem parvarum et regularium partium* . . . *Halo* saepius apparet secundum *circulum perfectum* . . . Fit autem halo *circa solem* et *lunam* et circa *astra* multum luminis habentia . . . In halo *non est illa varietas colorum* quae est in *iride'* (*In Meteor.* III, 2–4, 371b 18–375b, *lect.* 3–5, §§264–5, 274, 282). '*Iris* est . . . *apparitio ex refractione a nube opposita* . . . *causata,* ideo semper fit ex opposito ad astrum . . . Si fuerit nubes rorida, idest habens parvas guttulas semilucidas . . . et talis nubes posita fuerit ex opposito solis vel alterius astri

fulgidi, *ita ut fiat speculum* . . . tunc fiunt *colores iridis* in tali speculo. Sed quia illae parvae guttulae nubis sunt specula parva, et indivisibilia secundum sensum, ideo in illis *apparet color tantum, non autem figura* obiecti . . . *Iris nunquam apparet secundum circulum perfectum*, neque apparet in maiori portione circuli decisi per diametrum, sed sole oriente aut occidente apparet *sub figura semicirculi completa*, quae est maior portio circuli sub qua possit apparere . . . Aliquando videntur *duae irides* (sed plures duabus non apparent nisi raro) quarum *altera continet alteram*. Et utraque earum habet tres colores principales, eosdem quidem secundum speciem, et aequales secundum numerum, sed eius *quae est extra* et continet aliam, *colores sunt obscuriores* et minus apparentes quam illius quae est intra et continetur. Et *isti colores secundum situm sunt positi modo contrario* . . .' (*ibid.*, §§281, 266, 268). Dante uses his knowledge of how rainbows are formed in a brilliant simile in *Purg.* XXV, 91–3: 'e come l'aere, quand' è ben pïorno, / per l'altrui raggio che 'n sé si reflette, / di diversi color diventa addorno' (we cannot examine its highly daring application here). The moon-halo is described with equal precision in *Par.* X, 67–9: 'così cinger la figlia di Latona / vedem talvolta, quando *l'aere è pregno*, / sì che ritenga il fil che fa la zona'. And both moon-haloes and rainbows assist in the description of the supernatural *apparitio* where Dante has his first 'umbriferous' vision of the angelic orders circling around their Creator (*Par.* XXVIII, 22–4, 31–3). The *double* rainbow provides a familiar illustration for the two circles of singing lights which surround Dante in the heaven of the Sun: 'come si volgon *per tenera nube* [the Latin commentary speaks of a *nubes tenuis*] / *due archi paralelli* e *concolori*, / quando Iunone a sua ancella iube, / *nascendo di quel d'entro quel di fori* . . .' (*Par.* XII, 10–13). All the italicized details there derive from Aristotle; and the reminder that the outer circle is produced by reflection from the first forms the basis of the final appearance of rainbow-imagery, at the very end of the poem, to suggest the relationship between the Father and the Son: 'e l'un [giro] da l'altro come *iri da iri* / parea reflesso' (*Par.* XXXIII, 118–19; and cf. 127–8).

8. The word 'gas' was invented (with suggestions from the Greek *chaos*) by J. B. van Helmont, 1577–1644.

9. 'Sunt *duae species exhalationis: una* quidem *humida*, quae vocatur *vapor; alia* autem *sicca*, quae, quia non habet nomen commune, *a quadam sui parte vocetur fumus; nam fumus* proprie dicitur exhalatio sicca lignorum ignitorum. *Duae* autem hae *exhalationes non sic discretae sunt* ad invicem, quod humidum sit sine sicco, et siccum sine humido: *sed ab eo quod excedit, utraque denominatur* . . . Cum *exhalatio duplex* sit . . . una *vaporosa* et alia *fumosa* . . .' *'Aër* habet *aliquid vaporis* et *aliquid fumi. Vapor* eius est *frigidus et humidus* . . . et hoc convenit aëri inquantum est humidus . . . Sed *fumus* est *calidus et siccus*: siccus quidem propter terram, calidus autem propter ignem. Unde manifeste patet quod *superior aër*, qui est *calidus et humidus*, habet *similitudinem cum utroque*' (*In Meteor.* II, 4, 359b 27, *lect.* 7, §§179, 181, 183).

10. The difficulties are in part due to the basic error of fact, but also to ambiguities and uncertainties in their use of terms. *Fumus* can be used of visible smoke or invisible fumes, just as *vapor* can mean either 'steam' or 'water-vapour'. Dante will also use *vapore* to mean a '*dry*' exhalation. In most cases the context makes it clear which kind of exhalation is intended; otherwise Dante will specify 'vapori *umidi*' or 'vapori *secchi*' (cf. *Purg.* V, 110; XVII, 4; XXI, 52). On the only occasion when he uses *essalazioni* in the *Comedy*, it is referred to both dry and moist (Purg. XXVIII, 98). Both Aristotle and his followers will often forget that meteorological phenomena are caused by formal transmutations of the elements, whereby Air is *generated* from Water and rises because of its natural lightness; and they speak instead of the heat of the sun 'drawing' or 'attracting' the two different kinds of exhalation from the earth into the atmosphere. For the impurities in the atmosphere, cf. *Par.* XIV, 112–17.

11. '[Aristoteles] *excludit falsam opinionem* quantum ad hoc . . . quod *ventus nihil aliud est quam aër motus*. Et dicit quod *inconveniens* est, si quis existimet quod *iste aer qui circumstat unumquemque nostrum*, quando movetur est ventus; vel quod *unusquisque motus qui accidit in aëre*, sit ventus . . .' (*In Meteor.* II, 4, 360a 28, *lect.* 7, §184). 'Necessarium est quod *totus* aer qui est in circuitu terrae, *fluat circulariter motus*. Sed *ab ipso fluxu* excipit illum aërem qui capitur inter peripheriam . . . et sic *ille aër qui excedit omnem altitudinem montium, in circuitu fluit*: aër autem qui continetur *infra montium altitudinem, impeditur ab hoc fluxu ex partibus terrae immobilibus* . . . Aër qui excedit montes . . . ideo fluit in circuitu, quia *simul trahitur cum circulatione caeli*: ignis autem est *continuus*, idest contiguus, *cum corpore caelesti, aër autem cum igne*' (*ibid.*, I, 3, 341a 1, *lect.* 5, §30; cf. *Purg.* XXVIII, 7–8, 103–4). See also *Meteorologica* 344a 10. 'Sicut etiam *non existimamus fluvium* esse *aquam qualitercumque fluentem*, etiam si multa sit, sed solum *quando fluit ex aliquo principio determinato*, quod est fons ex terra scaturiens. *Sic* etiam est *de ventis: non enim est ventus*, si aër moveatur aliquo modo casu, etiam in magna multitudine, *nisi habeat principium, quasi fontem, exhalationem siccam elevatam*' (*ibid.*, II, 4, 360a 30, *lect.* 7, §184).

12. '*Venti secundum propriam naturam sunt calidi*: quia ventus est multitudo exhalationis siccae et calidae circa terram motae; *sed videntur* [ad sensum esse] frigidi, quia *movent secum aërem existentem plenum multo frigido vapore*' (*In Meteor.* II, 8, 367a 35, *lect.* 14, §235).

13. 'Quamvis exhalatio, quae est principium ventorum, *sursum elevetur in rectum*, tamen motus eorum non est in rectum . . . Exhalationes commoventes aërem *non movent ipsum in sursum aut in deorsum* . . . sed . . . *in obliquum* . . . Et *causa talis motus* est quod . . . *superior pars aëris fertur circulariter secundum motum caeli*; et . . . *iste* etiam *aër aliquid participat de motu superioris*, licet ista circulatio non compleatur' (*ibid.*, II, 4, 361a 23, *lect.* 8, §188).

14. *Meteorologica* II, 4–6; III, 1. A hurricane (*ecnephias, ventus violentus*) is generated as follows: 'si eadem exhalatio [sicca] spissior fuerit et minus subtilis, et segregetur ex nube multa simul absque interpolatione, et feratur deorsum velociter, *tunc fit ecnephias*, qui est spiritus fluens ex nube *secundum rectum deorsum* velociter' (*In Meteor.* III, 1, 370b 8, *lect.* 1, §251). As for the whirlwind (*typho, turbo*), 'quando *spiritus inclusus* in nube segregatur et *expellitur* a frigiditate loci et superioris partis nubis *ex amplo ventre nubis per angustum exitum et parvam scissuram*, et repercutitur ad aliquod corpus solidum, tunc fit quidam ventus in portis et viis *flans per modum turbinis*, qui dicitur *typho* . . . Cum pars prior non possit procedere ante, quia impeditur, neque possit retroverti, quia impellitur a sequenti, involvitur in sequenti, *et reflectit se ad latus ubi non invenit prohibens*: et sic causat *motum quasi circularem*.' The 'effectus mirabilis huius venti' is described vividly in these terms: 'sicut descendendo semper ducit secum aliquam partem nubis, ita quando reflectitur a terra *involvit secum omnia super quae cadit*, eradicando scilicet *arbores*, quandoque *evertendo* domos, *elevando saxa*. Et cum inciderit *ad mare*, *elevat* secum et involvit *magnitudinem aquae maris*: *quandoque autem elevat naves, propter quod multum timetur a nautis*; quia super quaecumque incidit, illa *motu circulari circumeundo et vim faciendo evertit*, et revertendo elevat ea sursum' (*ibid.*, §§253, 257). A passage like this is echoed in Dante's descriptions of the *bufera infernal* (*Inf.* V, 31–45), *vento impetuoso* (*Inf.* IX, 67–72) and the *turbo* that destroyed Ulysses and his ship (*Inf.* XXVI, 137–42).

Aristotle returns again and again to the subject of 'contrary winds': 364a 27, 364b 18, 365a 3, 366a 12, 368b 4, 370b 18. And while in general he insists that 'venti contrarii *non possunt simul flare*' because one wind will overcome the other, he does also speak of them in terms that recall *Inf.* V, 29–30: 'che mugghia come fa mar per tempesta, / se da *contrari venti* è combattuto'. For example: 'aliquando flant *supra terram et supra mare venti contrarii*, quorum unus *pugnando adinvicem* succumbit alteri'. As the commentator observes, 'videtur autem Aristoteles contradicere sibi: supra enim probatum est, quod *venti contrarii* non possunt simul flare, hic autem dicit quod inundatio aquarum accidit, quia *venti contrarii simul flant et adinvicem pugnant*'. The answer is that 'non possunt simul flare *diu et per longum tempus*, sed non inconveniens est quod *simul flent per parvum tempus*' (*In Meteor*. II, 8, 368b 5, *lect*. 15, §240).

15. 'Ambae . . . exhalationes simul elevantur, quia nec humida sine sicca, nec sicca sola sine alia ascendit . . . *Aggregatum* ex istis duabus exhalationibus *si sit humidum a praedominio*, tunc propter frigiditatem *convertitur in nubem* . . . *Nubes est densior in parte superiori* quam in inferiori . . . quia necesse est *nubem esse frigidiorem, et ex consequenti densiorem* in ea parte ubi deficit caliditas disgregans nubem . . . Sed *in parte inferiori nubes est rarior*, quia est minus frigida, et propterea, quia est minus densa, fulmina, ecnephiae et omnia huiusmodi quae fiunt ex sicca exhalatione, *propulsa a frigido moventur inferius*, quamvis exhalatio sicca sit nata moveri sursum propter naturam caliditatis. Sicut in simili accidit, quia *nuclei* et *parvi lapilli, dum comprimuntur inter digitos* ex una parte, exeunt ex alia quae est minus compressa et densa.

Alia pars [exhalationis siccae] quae est *grossior* . . . includitur in partibus aëris frigidi coagulantis nubem . . . Illa exhalatio sic *in nube inclusa*, propter frigiditatem nubis *exitum* petit, et *movetur huc et illuc*, et *facit magnam percussionem frangendo latera nubis*. Et *ex tali percussione et fractione* causatur *sonus, qui vocatur tonitruum* . . . *Tonitruum* igitur est *sonus* factus *propter . . . collisionem violentam exhalationis siccae ad latera nubis a frigido propellente*' (*In Meteor*. II, 9, 369a 12, *lect*. 16, §§244–5). It is texts like these that Dante had in mind when he spoke of 'le *guerre de' vapori*' 'colà dove *si tona*' (*Rime* CXI, 7–8).

16. 'Eadem *exhalatio sicca* quae *ex collisione* sua causat tonitruum, *extrusa et propulsata inferius . . . ignitur* debiliter in partibus subtilioribus et coloratur: sicut etiam apparet *in corpore ignibili violenter ac fortiter moto, quod propter motum ignitur*. Et hoc dicimus *coruscationem extrusam a nube* . . . *Coruscatio* secundum naturam *posterius generatur* quam tonitruum; quia tonitruum causatur ex violenta percussione ad latera nubis, *coruscatio autem est ignitio exhalationis extrusae a nube: extrusio autem et ignitio sunt posteriores percussura . . . Sed . . . visus in apprehendendo anticipat auditum*' (*In Meteor*. II, 9, 369b 5, *lect*. 16, §§246–7).

'Si *spiritus subtilis secundum substantiam*, et multus in quantitate, *extrudatur* a frigido quod est in ipsa nube, *generatur fulmen*, quod penetrat et frequenter adurit illud cui incidit . . . *Fulmen non est lapis vel aliquod corpus solidum*, sicut tamen multi crediderunt, sed est spiritus, idest *exhalatio sicca*, incensa et subtilis' (*ibid*., III, 1, 371a 18–30, *lect*. 2, §§259, 261).

17. 'Oportet enim intelligere quod *sicut in corpore nostro* et tremorum et pulsuum *causa est spiritus intercepti virtus, sic et in terra spiritum simile facere*, et hunc quidem terraemotum velut tremorem esse' (*Meteorologica* II, 8, 366b 15, translated by Moerbeke). The commentary by the pseudo-Aquinas interprets *spiritus* in the physiological sense, i.e. as 'spiritus vitalis'.

18. 'Sic *terra, calefacta* tum a caliditate solis, tum etiam ab igne, idest caliditate quasi in ea existente . . . *emittit multum spiritum*, idest multam exhalationem, non solum extra *sed etiam intra terram*. Aliquando ista exhalatio habet liberum egressum ex terra: et tunc totaliter exit, quia propter suam levitatem naturaliter movetur sursum . . . Aliquando autem *totaliter includitur intra, et non potest egredi*, quia *pori* et *exitus* terrae propter imbres *obturantur*: et *tunc fiunt magni terraemotus* . . . Exhalatio quae est in superficie terrae repellitur intus propter pluviam; ea quae prius erat intus, *in concavitatibus terrae angustatur compressa in parvo loco, et angustata quaerit locum maiorem, et pellit terram ut fluat exterius, et sic causat terraemotum*' (*In Meteor*. II, 8, 365b–366b, *lect*. 14, §§226, 231; cf. 367b 22, 368b 10).

'Quando *fortis* fuerit factus *terraemotus* . . . non statim cessat . . . Causa autem huius est, quia *intra cavernas terrae* inclusa est *magna multitudo exhalationis*, et *loca* etiam, in quibus recipitur illa exhalatio, sunt *parva*, et habent *exitus strictos et latera solida, quae cum difficultate franguntur*: et ex hoc *illa exhalatio non potest cito* et in parvo tempore *exire*, sed diu durat . . . *velut* cum in aliquo loco fuerit *magna multitudo aquae*, et *foramen* per quod exit fuerit *strictum*, non cito exit, sed *longo tempore durat exitus eius*' (*ibid.*, 367b 33, *lect.* 15, §238). '*Exhalatio dupliciter movet* terram, aliquando scilicet per modum *tremoris*, aliquando autem per modum *pulsus*; quia quando exhalatio movetur in terra *secundum latitudinem terrae*, et *percutitur ad alterum latus, tunc facit multas percussiones*, et facit *tremere* terram . . . Sed quando *exhalatio movet terram sursum*, tunc fit terraemotus per modum *pulsus*. Et *hoc fit raro*, quia difficile est *tantam exhalationem convenire in profundo ut possit terram proiicere sursum*. Sed quando hoc fit, *propellitur sursum multitudo lapidum*: sicut accidit in caldariis quae bulliunt, in quibus *gravia superius propelluntur* . . . In terraemotibus contingit aliquando *effluxio aquarum* . . . quia spiritus vel exhalatio erumpens, inveniens aquam in *superficie terrae, propellit* eam vel per se vel per eversionem terrae' (*ibid.*, 368b 23, §242; 368a 27, §240; cf. 366b 20, §232).

19. 'Oportet intelligere . . . *fumosam exhalationem* esse ut . . . *quandam materiam incendii*; et quod ordinatur in rotunditate quae est circa terram ultimo [i.e. in the sphere of Fire]; ita quod propter propinquitatem ad motum caelestem saepe exuratur . . . *Si praedicta materia* habeat magnam latitudinem et longitudinem, *videtur esse quaedam flamma accensa in caelo, sicut sum stipula ardet in area. Si vero non habeat multum in latitudine, sed solum in longitudine*, generantur et apparent illic *dali*, idest "titiones", et *aeges*, idest "caprae", et *sidera discurrentia* . . . Quando *exhalatio non fuerit continua* sed frequens et dispersa per modicas partes et multis modis, tam secundum longitudinem quam secundum latitudinem, quam etiam secundum profunditatem, *tunc fiunt sidera quae putantur volare*: eo quod *illa materia cito* consumitur, et *desinit esse ibi ubi prius accensa fuerat, sicut accidit de stuppa, si modicum de ea per longitudinem disponatur et accendatur: currit enim combustio, et videtur similis esse motui alicuius corporis ignei* . . . *Praedicta materia incendii, optime disposita* ad hoc quod igniatur, tali modo *exuritur*, quando fuerit *mota per calefactionem a circulari motu caeli*' (*In Meteor.* 1, 4, 341b 20, *lect.* 6, §40–2).

It is important to remember that Aristotle himself insists that he is only putting forward a hypothesis: 'De talibus, quae *sunt immanifesta sensui, non est exquirenda certa demonstratio et necessaria*, sicut in mathematicis et his quae subiacent sensui; sed sufficit per rationem demonstrare et ostendere causam, ita quod quaestionem solvamus *per aliquam solutionem possibilem, ex qua non sequatur aliquod inconveniens* per ea quae hic apparent secundum sensum' (*In Meteor.* 1, 7, 344a 5, *lect.* 11, §68).

20. '[Aristoteles] assignat *causam apparitionis cometae*. Et dicit quod quando *talis exhalatio fuerit condensata*, et propter motum superioris corporis *inciderit* in ipsam exhalationem *aliquod principium igneum*, ita scilicet quod ex aliqua parte incipiat exuri; sic quod *ignis non sit tam multus* ut cito exurat materiam, *neque* etiam *sit ita debilis* ut cito extinguatur priusquam accendatur, sed sit talis quod plus et diu possit *permanere cum quantitate ignis et dispositione materiae inspissatae*; cum hoc etiam quod *simul de inferioribus ascendat continue exhalatio bene disposita* ad hunc modum exustionis, ut scilicet diu duret, *tunc fit stella cometa* . . . Et est simile sicut si aliquis in *magnum cumulum palearum immiserit titionem*, aut aliud quodcumque ignitum principium; non enim statim discurret, quasi exurens paleam, sed *videtur ignitio diu in uno loco manere* . . . Si exhalatio sit *undique circumposita* "stellae", idest principio vel parti ignitae, videtur quasi "coma" unde et *cometes* dicitur; si autem disponatur *ad longitudinem* principii igniti, videtur exhalatio esse quasi "barba" stellae' (*In Meteor.* 1, 7, 344a 15, *lect.* 11, §71–2).

'Quando "stella cometa" est *per se ignis existens in aere*, sine aliqua superiorum stellarum, tunc videntur subtardantes . . . per hoc quod *latio inferioris mundi* qui est circa terram . . . est . . . *tardior motu caelesti*: quamvis enim circumvolvatur ignis et magna pars aëris per motum firmamenti, *non potest tamen attingere ad velocitatem motus caelestis* . . . ideo *cometa existens in aere remanet post corpora caelestia*, quae velocissime moventur; et sic *videtur habere motum contrarium firmamento*, sicut et planetae, *ex sola retardatione*' (*ibid*., 344b 10, §74).

Aristotle also recognized a second kind of comet which did move at the same speed as the heavens. This comet's 'hair' or 'beard' is still due to the burning of dry exhalation, but the efficient cause of the combustion is not friction but one of the stars (344a 35); and thus the fire spreads – exhausting its fuel – following the particular star (344b 9–10). This phenomenon might be described as a stellar 'halo' (344b 2–8), as long as one remembers that there are three differences between this kind of comet and the haloes that appear round the sun or moon. True haloes are caused by *reflection* in the *moist* exhalations in the *lower* atmosphere: 'stellar haloes' are produced by *combustion* of *dry* exhalations in the *upper* atmosphere.

Dante alludes to this kind of combustion in his account of the planet Mars: 'Marte . . . dissecca e arde le cose, perché lo suo calore è simile a quello del fuoco; e questo è quello per che esso pare affocato di colore, quando più e quando meno, secondo la spessezza e raritade *de li vapori che 'l seguono: li quali per lor medesimi molte volte s'accendono, sì come nel primo de la Metaura è diterminato*' (*Con.* II, xiii, 21).

21. 'Ista igitur *exhalatio adunata sub tali parte caeli*, facit ibi videri *lacteam claritatem*, sicut et exhalatio consequens aliquam stellam facit ibi videri comam' (*In Meteor.* I, 8, 346b 1, *lect.* 13, §89). Dante's account affords an interesting insight into the difficulties which beset the interpreter of Aristotle in the Latin West. 'Quello che Aristotile si dicesse non si può bene sapere di ciò, però che la sua sentenza non si truova cotale ne l'una translazione come ne l'altra. E credo che fosse lo errore de li translatori, ché ne la Nuova pare dicere che ciò sia uno ragunamento di vapori sotto le stelle di quella parte, che sempre traggono quelli: e questo non pare avere ragione vera. Ne la Vecchia dice che la Galassia non è altro che moltitudine di stelle fisse in quella parte, tanto picciole che distinguere di qua giù non le potemo, ma di loro apparisce quello albore, lo quale noi chiamiamo Galassia . . .' (*Con.* II, xiv, 6–7). The 'new' translation was, however, the accurate one. Dante again alludes to the perplexities caused to great minds by the Milky Way in *Par.* XIV, 97–9: 'Come distinta da minori e maggi / lumi biancheggia tra ' poli del mondo / Galassia sì, *che fa dubbiar ben saggi.*'

22. For the hints from Aristotle, see note 3 and phrases such as the following (it must be borne in mind that the scene takes place at dawn a few days after the Spring equinox, in latitude 30°S, at the *termini bassi* of the mountain, 'sovra 'l molle limo', and that the breeze is just strong enough to ruffle the sea): 'ut ita se habeat *accessus solis et recessus secundum motum diurnum ad generationem roris* et pruinae . . .'; '*ros* semper fit *in tempore temperato* et in locis temperatis'; '*ros* fit in omnibus locis *flantibus australibus ventis*, non tamen ita validis quod impediant congregationem vaporum . . .'; 'vapor ex quo generatur ros et pruina, elevatur *ex locis infimis et humefactis* . . .' (*In Meteor.* I, 9, *lect.* 14, §§103–7). *Diradarsi* is the technical verb for the 'thinning out' of moisture: cf. *Purg.* XVII, 5.

23. The example of the sightless mole was a favourite one in discussions on sensation, e.g. 'Unde et *talpa* . . . videtur habere oculos *sub pelle*; . . . sed . . . non fuit ei necessarius visus; et terra, si haberet oculos discoopertos, eius oculos offenderet' (*In De anima* III, 1, 425a 10, *lect.* 1, §573).

24. References in order: *temperanza di vapori, Purg.* XXX, 22–7; *brina, Inf.* XXIV, 1–6; *l'emisperio de l'aere, Par.* XXVIII, 79–84.

25. *Inf.* XIV, 52–60 (the technical word is *folgore=fulmen*).

26. References in order: XXXIII, 100–2; XXXII, 106, 47; XXXIII, 94–9, 114, 128; XXXII, 36, 70, 52, 71–2.

27. E. Auerbach, 'Camilla, or the Rebirth of the Sublime', *Literary Language and its Public in Late Latin Antiquity and in the Middle Ages*, trans. R. Manheim (London, 1965), pp. 183–223.

28. *Impetus* is a recurrent term for vigorous impulsion and motion. In moral contexts it has the connotation of that which is uncontrolled, e.g.: '[passio] in appetitu sensitivo, quae animum *suo impetu distendit quasi cum quadam violentia* ad aliquid movens' (*In Ethic.* IX, 5, 1166b 32, *lect.* 5, §1822); *Contra gentiles* III, 86, §2616; *Quaestio*, 48. *Ardori* must refer to dry exhalations, while the adjective, *avversi*, points to texts of the kind quoted at the end of note 14 and in note 15. But the phrase 'avversi ardori' is certainly more 'poetic' than technical, and would seem to have been influenced by a simile in the *Aeneid*, describing just such a conflict of winds in very unscientific terms, beginning, '*adversi . . . ceu . . . venti / confligunt*, Zephyrusque Notusque et laetus . . . / Eurus' (II, 416–18). Aristotle does recognize that a wind would grow stronger by being opposed, but Dante is probably thinking more of a river, or of human psychology in general, and of the particular situation where the angel's anger is provoked by resistance.

29. The figure is one of repetition by distribution. The procedure is nicely described by George Puttenham in *The Art of English Poesie* (1589) under the name *Merismus*, 'when we may conveniently utter a matter in one entier speach or proposition and will rather do it peecemeale and by distribution of every part for amplification sake'. Dante shows a master's hand here even in the varied placing of the seven *nons* and three *nés*.

30. References in order: *Purg.* XXVIII, 2, 7–42, 77–8; *Par.* I, 56–7.

31. See the second and third excerpts quoted in note 11; cf. also note 20.

32. *Inf.* XXIV, 91–120, 124, 129; *Par.* IX, 89–90. Dante was a guest of the Malaspina family in 1307–8; cf. *Rime* CXIII.

33. See *Con.* II, xiv, 6–7, quoted in note 21.

34. See notes 15 and 16.

35. 'Non scese mai con *sì veloce moto* / *foco* di *spessa nube*, quando *piove* / *da quel confine* che più va remoto / com' io vidi calar . . .' (*Purg.* XXXII, 109–12).

36. '*Vapori accesi* non vid' io *sì tosto* / di prima notte mai *fender sereno*, / *né*, *sol calando*, *nuvole d'agosto*' (*Purg.* V, 37–9).

37. Dry exhalations striking down from a cold cloud may be in the form of *lightning* or *thunderbolts* (see note 16), or also in the form of a *whirlwind* (which would certainly be 'invisible' and would match the *giro* of the souls in the Heaven of Venus: see note 14).

38. The vigorous attack of the first line is certainly helped by the inversion; and speed is suggested by the rhythm and light syllables of 'o visibili o no'. Then the course of the sentence itself is impeded by the complex form of the negative comparison, but seems to quicken again with the resolution at 'a chi avesse quei lumi divini / veduti a noi venir', with a strong enjambement. Finally, the movement stills in the last line and a half. Notice that none of the words has any connotation of speed or force – the effects are obtained by syntax and rhythm in collaboration with the meaning.

39. The fact that Dante is mysteriously transported into Limbo during his 'sleep' (he does not cross the Acheron by Charon's boat) makes it clear that the earthquake had a divine cause. But the phrase *diede vento* is an unmistakable allusion to the Aristotelian doctrine; and the flash of vermilion light could also be explained as the ignition of the escaping dry exhalation, just as lightning is kindled: see note 16.

40. With regard to the 'darkness over all the land', Dante bitterly attacked those modern theologians and preachers who explained it as due to an eclipse of the sun caused in the normal way by the interposition of the moon (*Par.* XXIX, 97–9). They lie, because

the light 'hid itself by itself' ('la luce si nascose / da sé), and the darkness lay over the *whole* earth *simultaneously* from the extreme west to the extreme east (100–2). A naturalistic explanation of the earthquake would have drawn similar indignation.

41. *Inf.* IV, 52–61; IX, 22–7. The conjuring of a spirit by Erichtho is described in Lucan's *Bellum civile*, VI, 507–830 (there is no mention of Virgil there). The story of the Harrowing of Hell is told in the apocryphal gospel of Nicodemus, and it was a favourite subject in medieval painting and drama. The germ of the legend will be found in Matthew 27.52–3.

42. *Inf.* XVIII, 1–18; XXI, 29–57, 64–90, 106–35; XXIII, 34–51, 144.

43. *Inf.* XXI, 112–14. The lie about the *scheggio intero* is told at line 125 and discovered at XXIII, 136.

44. *Purg.* XXI, 58–72.

45. Examples in order: Psalm 15.1; Isaiah 11.9. Psalm 65.13; 104.32.

46. Psalm 68, verses, 1, 3, 4, 6, 8, 11, 15, 16, 18, 32. The Vulgate (no. 67) has many slight variations, but not important enough to make one renounce Coverdale's English in the Book of Common Prayer. Note, however, that the phrase 'Why hop ye so, ye high hills' is rendered by *Quid suspicamini*.

47. Psalm 114, verses 1–4, 6–7; Psalm 115.1. In the Vulgate the verse beginning *Non nobis, Domine* is still part of the preceding psalm (numbered 113). The verb which Coverdale translates as 'skipped' is rendered by *exsultaverunt*; the imperative 'tremble, thou earth' is rendered by an indicative, *mota est terra*.

48. 'Spiritualmente s'intende . . . che ne l'uscita dell'anima dal peccato, essa sia fatta *santa e libera in sua potestate*' (*Con.* II, i, 7). Dante translated the phrase 'Judah was his sanctuary' in the second verse of the psalm as 'Giudea è fatta *santa e libera*'. These are the key-adjectives to describe the results of expiation and purification in Purgatory.

4 Land and sea

1. 'Prima dico che per lo *mondo* io non intendo qui *tutto 'l corpo de l'universo*, ma solamente *questa parte del mare e de la terra*, seguendo la volgare voce . . .' (*Con.* III, v, 3). Just as *mondo* could mean 'world' or 'universe' depending on the context, so *terra* could mean the element, 'Earth', a 'city', the 'world', or 'dry land' as opposed to the sea (cf. Genesis 1.9–10).

2. 'Sunt autem apud nos quaedam corpora sphaerica, quae tamen non perfecte habent sphaericam figuram: sicut *ipsum corpus terrae* dicitur esse *sphaericum, cum tamen habeat magnas elevationes montium et concavitates vallium. In corporibus etiam artificialibus* quae sunt apud nos sphaerica, inveniuntur aliquae *tumorositates vel depressiones*, quibus non obstantibus huiusmodi artificiata dicuntur esse sphaericae figurae, quia *huiusmodi additiones vel subtractiones secundum sensum quasi non apparent*' (*In De caelo* II, 4, 287b 15–20, *lect.* 6, §360). For Dante's informal use of *palla*, see *Con.* III, v, 11, 12, 19.

3. 'Con ciò sia cosa che la *terra* per lo *diametro* suo sia *semilia cinquecento* miglia . . .' (*Con.* IV, viii, 7). Dante's figures for the circumference are given in *Con.* III, v, 9–11, where he explains that the distance between two hypothetical cities at the poles is 'da qualunque lato si tira la corda, di *diecimila dugento miglia*': $10,200 \times 2 = 20,400$. It is as well to remember that we do not know which of the medieval miles Dante had in mind. Anyone who has learnt to distinguish between a Roman mile of 1,000 paces, an English statutory mile of 1,760 yards, and a nautical mile of 2,000 yards will know just how vague the unit of measurement can be. And experience shows that modern Italian readers have very little idea of the relationship between English miles and kilometres.

4. For *terra discoperta*, see *Con.* III, v, 8, 12, etc. For *gran secca*, see *Inf.* XXXIV, 112–14.

In Latin, Dante uses *terra emergens* or *terra detecta* (*Quaestio*, 13, 16, 17, 51, etc.). For the three continents, see *Mon.* II, iii (discussed in the text below) and phrases there like *quaelibet pars tripartiti orbis, Asia . . . Europa . . . Affrica; a qualibet mundi parte*. It was believed that 'Asia . . . was equal in size to Europe and Africa together' (E. Moore, 'The geography of Dante', in *Studies in Dante* (Oxford, 1903), vol. 3, 109–43, p. 124).

For the 'semilunar' shape of the land-mass, see *Quaestio*, 51 ('Figura terrae emergentis est *figura semilunii*'). Dante seems to have taken the rather puzzling description from Ristoro d'Arezzo (Moore, 'The geography of Dante', p. 122). For the extension in latitude and longitude, see *Quaestio*, 54–5: 'Ut comuniter ab omnibus habetur, haec habitabilis [terra] extenditur *per lineam longitudinis* a *Gadibus*, quae supra terminos occidentales ab Hercule positos ponitur, usque ad *hostia fluminis Ganges* . . . Igitur oportet *terminos praedictae longitudinis* distare per *clxxx gradus*, quae est *dimidia distantia totius circumferentiae*. Per lineam vero *latitudinis* . . . extenditur ab illis quorum cenith est circulus aequinoctialis [i.e. the equator], usque ad illos quorum cenith est circulus descriptus a polo zodiaci circa polum mundi, qui quidem distat a polo mundi circiter xxiii gradus; et sic *extensio latitudinis est quasi lxvii graduum et non ultra . . .*'. The *terra emergens* is said to cover approximately a quarter of the whole surface (*Quaestio*, 5). There are further references to the sea in the southern hemisphere in *Con.* III, v, 10; *Inf.* XXXIV, 123. The special case of Mount Purgatory in the fiction of the poem is discussed at the end of this chapter.

5. These figures emerge by implication from *Par.* IX, 86–7 (discussed below); *Purg.* III, 25; XV, 6.

6. For the sources of Dante's geographical notions, see E. Moore 'The geography of Dante'. For sunset in Cadiz and sunrise at the delta of the Ganges, cf. 'Quae quidem longitudo tanta est, ut *occidente sole* in aequinoctiali existente illis qui sunt in altero terminorum, *oritur* illis qui sunt in altero . . .' (*Quaestio*, 54). Of the many time-references in the *Comedy* using these facts, it will be enough for the present to cite *Purg.* II, 1–6. For the position of Jerusalem and the Crucifixion, see also *Inf.* XXXIV, 112–15; *Purg.* IV, 68–71, 79–84. In all these texts Dante makes free with words like *emisperio, orizzon(te), meridian cerchio, mezzo cerchio, Equatore*. For *cosmographi* and *astrologi*, see *Quaestio*, 53. Dante referred to a 'zone' as *clima* (in his Latin works and in *Par.* XXVII, 81) or *climate* (*Con.* III, v, 12). He took his notions concerning the seven zones of the *terra habitabilis* (*Quaestio* 5, 16, etc.) from the Arab astronomer whom he knew as Alfragano or Alfagrano (see *Enc. Dant.* and Toynbee-Singleton *s.v.*). Moore explains (p.131): 'Each "clima", going northwards, included such a space that the mean length of the longest day was half-an-hour longer than that of the longest day in the previous "clima" to the south.' The mean length of the longest day is 13 hours in the first 'clima', which begins at nearly 13° N, and 16 hours in the seventh which ends at 50° 30′ N – the latitude of Cornwall! Dante describes the lot of the Scythians and Garamantes as follows: '*Scithas*, qui extra septimum clima viventes et magnam dierum et noctium inaequalitatem patientes, *intolerabili quasi algore frigoris premuntur*, et . . . *Garamantes* qui, sub aequinoctiali habitantes, et coaequatam semper lucem diurnam noctis tenebris habentes, *ob aestus aeris nimietatem vestimentis operi non possunt*' (*Mon.* I, xiv, 6). On the Garamantes, see also *Con.* III, v, 12 and 18. For the 'virtues and properties' of Italy, see *Mon.* II, vi, 6–10 (which it is instructive to compare with Aristotle's *Politics* VII, 7).

7. *Con.* I, iii, 4.

8. References in order: (fourteen regions) *Dve* I, x, 7; (the two distinct dialects in Bologna) I, ix, 4; (far more than 1,000 primary, secondary and subsecondary variations) I, x, 7.

9. As we have noted, maps in Dante's time were still drawn with east at the top. In

central Italy the Apennines run on a line nearer to east–west than north–south. Hence on a medieval map this section of the range would be represented as an almost vertical line dividing Italy into left (north) and right (south): see *Dve* I, ix, 4; x, 5–7. For the elusive common denominator, see especially *Dve* I, xvi. Dante does not himself use the terms 'potency' and 'act' or 'species' and 'genus', but they are *redolentia ubique et necubi apparentia* (cf. I, xvi, i). For the Apennines as watershed and dividing line, cf: 'Dicimus ergo primo Latium *bipartitum* esse in *dextrum* et *sinistrum*. Si quis autem quaerat de *linea dividente*, breviter respondemus esse iugum *Apenini* quod ceu *fistulae culmen* hinc inde ad diversa stillicidia grundat aquas . . .' (*Dve* I, x, 4).

10. *Dve* I, vii, 1–8; viii, 1, 3, 5 (the points are made in reverse order in the text).

11. 'Nos autem, *cui mundus est patria* velut piscibus aequor, quanquam Sarnum ['the Arno'] biberimus ante dentes et Florentiam adeo diligamus ut, quia dileximus, exilium patiamur iniuste . . . quamvis ad voluptatem nostram sive nostrae sensualitatis quietem in terris amoenior locus quam Florentia non existat, *revolventes et poetarum et aliorum scriptorum volumina quibus mundus universaliter et membratim describitur, ratiocinantesque in nobis situationes varias mundi locorum et eorum habitudinem ad utrunque polum et circulum aequatorem*, multas esse perpendimus firmiterque censemus et magis nobiles et magis delitiosas et regiones et urbes quam Tusciam et Florentiam, unde sumus oriundus et civis . . .' (*Dve* I, vi, 3).

12. 'Invictissimus et piissimus pater [Aeneas] *quantae nobilitatis* vir fuerit, non solum sua considerata virtute sed *progenitorum* suorum atque *uxorum, quorum utrorunque nobilitas hereditario iure* in ipsum confluxit . . .' (*Mon.* II, iii, 7). '*Quaelibet pars tripartiti orbis tam avis quam coniugibus* illum nobilitasse invenitur. Nam *Asya* propinquioribus avis, ut Assaraco; . . . *Europa* vero avo antiquissimo, scilicet Dardano: *Affrica* quoque avia vetustissima, Electra . . .' (*ibid.*, 10). 'Prima . . . coniunx Creusa, Priami regis filia, de *Asya* fuit . . . Secunda Dido fuit, regina et mater Cartaginensium in *Affrica* . . . Tertia Lavinia . . . quae ultima uxor de *Ytalia* fuit, *Europae regione nobilissima*' (*ibid.*, 11–16). 'Quem in illo duplici concursu sanguinis a qualibet mundi parte in unum virum *praedestinatio divina* latebit?' (*ibid.*, 17). There are seven quotations from Virgil in this chapter, where he is referred to as *vates* and *divinus noster poeta*.

13. *Paradise Regained*, III, 261–2, 304, 308, 322, 393, 400–2.

14. Dante is in fact employing the rhetorical figure, *brevitas*, as may be seen in the following definition and example taken from the *Rhetorica ad Herennium*: '*Brevitas* est res ipsis tantummodo verbis necessariis expedita, hoc modo: Lemnum praeteriens cepit, inde Thasi praesidium reliquit, post urbem Bithynam Cium sustulit, inde reversus in Hellespontum statim potitur Abydi . . .' (IV, lxv, 68). See E. R. Curtius, 'Brevity as an ideal of style', in *European Literature and the Latin Middle Ages*, translated by W. R. Trask (New York, 1953), Excursus xiii, pp. 487–94. The Commentaries of Julius Caesar are proverbial for their air of terse objectivity.

15. *Mon.* I, xvi.

16. *Par.* IX, 25–30, 43–51.

17. *Par.* VIII, 58–75.

18. *Par.* IX, 82–93. These elaborate geographical periphrases return in the 'Lives' of St Dominic and St Francis. The periphrasis of Castile in canto XII, 46–54 opens with lines worthy of Folco. The rivers and cities of Umbria in canto XI, 43–8 give way to an elaborate word-play, in which Francis himself becomes the 'sun' and the place of his birth is not Assisi, but the 'Orient', *Ascesi*.

19. *Par.* XXII, 128–35, 154. The last line obviously permits a much more generic interpretation of the 'hills' and 'estuaries'. But the emphatic placing of *tutta* together with the sequel in canto XXVIII point conclusively to the interpretation given in the text. It has

been objected that it is impossible to see 180° round a sphere – from any distance! It is clear that Dante is imagining a flat map.

20. Dante's debt to the *Somnium Scipionis* will be analysed in Chapter 6 as part of the discussion of the astronomical data in this episode.

21. *Par.* XXVII, 77–84.

22. *Metamorphoses* XIV, esp. 312, 435–44.

23. *Inf.* XXVI, 116–17.

24. 'West', because their stern is turned to the rising sun; 'south', because they are 'always gaining on the left', 'sempre acquistando dal lato mancino' (*ibid.*, 126). This last phrase has a peculiar relevance: in Purgatory, Dante the traveller will always turn to the *right*; in Hell, always to the 'sinister' *left*.

25. 'Imagina Sïòn / con questo monte in su la terra stareˋ / sì, ch'amendue hanno *un solo orizzòn* / *e diversi emisperi . . .' Purg.* IV, 68–71.

26. It is now called simply 'Il mito dell'Eden' and will be found in Nardi's *Saggi di filosofia dantesca* (Florence, 1967), pp. 311–40.

27. Genesis 3.24; 2 Thessalonians 1.7–8; 1 Corinthians 3.12–15. See Nardi, pp. 313–17.

28. 'Est ergo Paradisus, ut Isidorus dicit in libro *Etymol.* [14, 3]: "locus *in Orientis partibus* constitutus, cuius vocabulum a graeco in latinum vertitur Hortus" . . . Dicendum [est] quod, sicut Augustinus dicit . . . "credendum est, quod *locus Paradisi* a cognitione hominum est *remotissimus*" . . . Locus ille *seclusus* est *a nostra habitatione* aliquibus impedimentis vel *montium*, vel *marium*, vel *alicuius aestuosae regionis, quae pertransiri non potest*' (Aquinas, *S.T.* 1a. 102, 1, resp.; ad 2–3; reference from Nardi, p. 321).

29. 'Ex quo possumus coniicere *paradisum* in oriente situm; . . . et . . . *in alto situm, pertingentem usque ad lunarem circulum*' (*Glossa ordinaria*, Migne P.L. 113, col. 86, quoting Bede and Rabanus Maurus, both of whom appear in Dante's *Paradiso* (X, 131; XII, 139): reference from Nardi, p. 321).

5   The natural world and the Scale of Being

1. 'Ha le sue similitudini sì nuove che a quelle non posso dare alcuna similitudine, né si possono sue comparazioni con alcuna comparazione esprimere: sono proprie e più che in nessun poeta frequenti, più ancora simili. Né solamente sono efficacissime in esprimere la mente dello scrittore, ma accomodatissime al luogo: il perché non delle medesime cose trae le comperazioni nello Inferno che quelle del Paradiso, ma in ciascuno le pone connaturali. *Praeterea* spesso dà comperazione nella quale o lui apre alcuna causa naturale o dà all'auditore cognizione e dottrina d'alcuna cosa naturale . . .', Cristoforo Landino, 'Proemio al commento dantesco', in *Scritti critici e teorici*, ed. R. Cardini (Rome, 1974), vol. 1, pp. 148–9.

2. Genesis 1.11–12, 20–8. All were created by God before man and set under man's dominion.

3. Landino, 'Proemio', *ed. cit.*, vol. 1, p. 142.

4. 'Qual fisico tutti e' moti naturali o secondo el luogo o secondo la forma o imperfetti o perfetti o animati o inanimati con più lucide ragioni mai scrisse, qual corso di stella, qual congiunzione, qual revoluzione di cielo è stata da lui pretermessa, qual transformazion d'uno in altro elemento, quale alterazione nell'aere, o di grandine, piove, venti, saette o d'altre simili, qual composizione di minère sotto la terra concreate hanno dimostro e' fisici che questo poeta non abbi almanco accennato? Ha l'anima quattro potenzie, ha vari offici e

varie proprietà, ma di tutte abbiamo vera cognizione apresso di Dante' (*ed. cit.*, vol. 1, p. 151).

5. Matthew 6.22 (*oculus simplex* in the Vulgate).

6. References in order; *Inf.* XVIII, 2, VIII, 78; XXI, 7-9, 16-18; XIX, 4, 95, 112; XXIII, 61-7; XXIX, 119, 137; XXX, 73-5, 88-90.

7. For the classical myth, cf. *Purg.* XXVIII, 139-44. For the Old Man of Crete, see *Inf.* XIV, 106-11, based on Daniel 2.31-5. For *grossezza di materia*, see *Con.* III, vii, 4-5.

8. *Rime* XC, 15. *Con.* III, ix, 6-10.

9. Emeralds: *Purg.* XXIX, 125; XXXI, 116. Porphyry: *Purg.* IX, 101. Ruby: *Par.* XIX, 4-6; XXX, 66. Sapphire (associated with Mary): *Par.* XXIII, 101-2. The colours of the theological virtues are referred to in *Purg.* XXIX, 121-9; XXX, 31-3. Marble can be 'whiter than white' (cf. *Purg.* IX, 95), while the oyster's pearl suggests the ideal complexion of a beautiful woman, and would be scarcely visible on her forehead (cf. *Rime* XIV, 47-8; *VN* XXXVI, 1; *Par.* III, 14-15).

10. The categories are suggested by *Con.* III, vii, 3-5. The references to the *Comedy* are, in order: *Par.* XV, 24; III, 10; XXIX, 25-7; XX, 16.

11. References in order: *Par.* XII, 100, 103-5 (thorns and shrubs); *Inf.* XIII, 99-100 (millet); *Par.* XXIII, 20, 131 (*arche*); *Inf.* XV, 65-6 (fig and sorbs).

12. References in order: *Purg.* XXXI, 70-1, 85 (nettle, oak); *Inf.* XXV, 58 (ivy); *Purg.* XXV, 77-8 (grape); *Par.* XXI, 115, *Purg.* II, 70, XXX, 31, 68 (olive); *Par.* I, 15, XXV, 9 (bay); *Purg.* XXI, 90 (myrtle); *Par.* XXXII, 112 (palm).

13. References in order: Matthew 7.20; *Purg.* XVI, 11, 4; *Par.* XXVII, 125-6, 148; *Purg.* VII, 121-2, 127.

14. '*Le piante . . . hanno amore a certo luogo* più manifestamente, secondo che la complessione richiede; e però vedemo *certe piante lungo l'acque* quasi cansarsi, e certe sopra li gioghi de le montagne, e certe ne le piagge e dappiè monti: le quali se si transmutano, o muoiono del tutto o vivono quasi triste, sì come cose disgiunte dal loro amico' (*Con.* III, iii, 4).

15. References in order: *Purg.* VII, 76-9, XXVIII, 55-6, 68, XXXII, 57-8 (colours); XXVII, 94-102, XXVIII, 40-60 (Lia and Matelda); XXX, 28-30 (Beatrice); *Par.* XIX, 22-4, XXX 65-7 (*fiori, odori*); Purg. XXIV, 147 (May breeze).

16. Tasso, *Gerusalemme liberata*, XVI, 14; *Romance of the Rose*, 21607-750; *Par.* XXIII, 73.

17. The image is prepared by the *fioretti* of *Par.* XXX, 111, and emerges for the first time in lines 115-17. It is restated in the opening of Canto XXXI and underlies the first twenty-one lines of the canto. It is recalled in XXXII, 15.

18. References in order: snake, *Purg.* VIII, 100-2; lion, *Inf.* I, 45; greyhounds, XIII, 125-6; lizard, XXV, 79-81; pigs, XXX, 26-7.

19. References in order: dogs, *Par.* IV, 6, *Inf.* XXIII, 18, XXI, 44-5, 67-9; cat and mouse, *Inf.* XXII, 58; wolf and lamb, *Par.* IV, 4-5, IX, 131, XXV, 5-6; greyhound and wolf, *Inf.* I, 49-51, 94-111, *Purg.* XX, 10-12, *Inf.* XXXIII, 29-36; cf. *Rime* CIV, 102. To these we may add: falcon and duck, *Inf.* XXII, 130-2; mouse, frog and kite, *Inf.* XXIII, 4-6.

20. The translation follows Boccaccio's commentary *ad loc.* for the translation of *biscia* and the interpretation of *terra* and *abbicarsi*. 'Dice qui l'autore la "*nemica biscia*" usando questo vocabol generale quasi di tutte le serpi, per quello della *idra*, la quale è *quella serpe che sta nell'acqua*, e che *inimica le rane* sì come *quella* che di loro *si pasce.*' '. . ."*s'abbica*", cioè *s'ammonzicchia* l'una sopra l'altra, ficcandosi *nel loto del fondo dell'acqua*, nella qual dimorano.' As Sapegno notes in his commentary, some of the details in these two similes are culled from Ovid's description of the newly created frogs in *Metamorphoses* VI, 370-81; but it is worth noting that there is no mention of the snake in Ovid, and that

Dante has clearly visualized for himself the action of the frogs, thereby transforming his literary source.

21. References in order: fox and lion, *Inf.* XXVII, 75–8, *Purg.* XIV, 46–7; pig, *Inf.* VIII, 50, *Purg.* XIV, 43, *Par.* XXIX, 125; ape, *Inf.* XXIX, 139; bee, *Purg.* XVIII, 58–9, *Par.* XXXI, 7–9; wolf, *Inf.* I, 49–51, 94–9; *Purg.* XIV, 50–1, XX, 10–12.

22. References in order: *Inf.* XXII, 35; *Par.* V, 100–2; *Inf.* XVII, 104, 49, 75; XXXII, 50.

23. *Inf.* XXXI, 49–57.

24. The first four animals named are mentioned in the *Comedy* as heraldic devices: *Inf.* XXVII, 46–50; XVII, 63–4. Significantly the *oca* and *scrofa* are the badges of once noble houses whose scions have turned to usury. For Vanni Fucci, see *Inf.* XXIV, 124–6. For stinging insects, see *Inf.* III, 65–9, XXVI, 28, *Purg.* XXXII, 133. To these we may add the *vermi* of *Inf.* III, 69, XXXIV, 108, and the *scorpione* of *Inf.* XVII, 26.

25. *Purg.* VIII, 94–108; Genesis 3, especially verses 13–15.

26. *Inf.* IX, 40–1; XXIV, 86–7; and cf. *colubro* in *Par.* VI, 77.

27. *Inf.* XXV, 94–135.

28. The similes demand a close reading in their context which it would be inappropriate to attempt here. For the migration of cranes, see also *Purg.* XXIV, 64, XXVI, 43–5; for the 'usato orgoglio' of doves (*colombi*), and yet for their affectionate nature, see *Purg.* II, 124–6, *Par.* XXV, 19–21.

29. Jackdaws, *Par.* XXI, 34–9; falcons, *Inf.* XVII, 127–32, XXII, 131–2, *Purg.* VIII, 104–8, XIX, 64–6, *Par.* XVIII, 45, XIX, 34–6. See also *Par.* I, 51, where some commentators have interpreted *pellegrin* as a peregrine falcon rather than a pilgrim.

30. Dante would have known one exception to each proposition, the ostrich and the bat (*Inf.* XXXIV, 49). See Isidore, *Etymologiae* XII, vii, 20, 36.

31. Psalm 55.6. Isidore derived *ales*, *alitis*, a 'wing', from *altus*, 'high', *Etymologiae* XII, vii, 3. The most important texts associating Dante-character and the flight of birds are: *Purg.* XII, 95; XXVII, 123; XXXI, 58, 61; *Par.* X, 74; XV, 54; XXXIII, 15, 139.

32. 'Dante *aliger*', *MLR*, 70 (1975), pp. 764–85; 'Dante *aliger* and Ulysses', *Italian Studies*, 32 (1977), pp. 21–40.

33. The unpleasant animal sounds are: *gracidare*, *Inf.* XXXII, 31; *latrare*, VI, 14, XXX, 20, XXXII, 105; *abbaiare*, VI, 28, VII, 43; *ringhiare*, V, 4 (cf. *Purg.* XIV, 47); *urlare*, VI, 19. In Isidore's view, only the swan has a 'song'. He says that many bird-names are derived by onomatopoeia from the sounds they emit, and he makes it plain that many of these sounds are not pleasant: *Etymologiae* XII, vii, 9, 16, 18, 42–8. The remaining references in this paragraph are, in order: *Par.* XXV, 19–21; *Inf.* V, 46; *Purg.* IX, 13–14; XXVIII, 13–18; XVII, 20.

34. Christ is called 'il nostro *pellicano*' in *Par.* XXV, 113. Many medieval paintings of the Crucifixion show the pelican piercing its breast – usually in a small insert at the head of the cross: cf. *Etymologiae* XII, vii, 26. For the phoenix, cf. *Etymologiae* XII, vii, 22. Dante alludes to himself as a phoenix in his letter to the Italian cardinals, meaning that he was unique of his kind. In *Inf.* XXIV, 106–11, the death and resurrection of the phoenix are the declared models for the punishment of Vanni Fucci.

35. References in order: the eagle's power of flight and vision, *Inf.* IV, 96, *Par.* I, 48, XX, 31–2, *Dve* II, iv, 11; its flight as conquest, *Par.* VI, 1–9, 31–111, *Epist.* VI, 12; with Trajan, *Purg.* X, 76–81; in Dante's dream, *Purg.* IX, 19–33; in the masque, *Purg.* XXXII, 112–17, 125–6, 136–41, XXXIII, 37–9; in the Heaven of Jupiter, *Par.* XVIII, 100–17; XIX, 1–39, 91–6, XX, 7–36, 139. It is called *l'uccel di Dio* in *Par.* VI, 4.

36. 'De *ratione corporis* est quod habeat dimensiones in omnem partem, non in longitudinem tantum ut *linea*, neque in longitudinem et latitudinem solum ut *superficies* . . .' 'Omne quod habet tres dimensiones est corpus . . .' (*In Physic.* III, 5, 205a 1, *lect.*

8, §355; IV, 1, 209a 5, *lect.* 2, §416). '*Corpus* quod est *magnitudo completa*, dupliciter sumitur, scilicet mathematice, secundum quod consideratur in eo sola quantitas; et *naturaliter, secundum quod consideratur in eo materia et forma* . . . Omne corpus naturale habet *determinatam quantitatem* et in maius et in minus. Unde impossible est aliquod *corpus naturale infinitum* esse' (*S.T.* 1a. 7, 3, resp.).

The use of *coniunctum* as a noun can be illustrated in the following typical sentence: 'Sicut . . . operationes corporales . . . *non sunt animae*, sed *corporis*, seu *coniuncti*, ita et . . . sentire et gaudere . . . non debent referri ad *animam*, sed ad *coniunctum*' (*In De anima* I, 4, 408b 10, *lect.* 10, §152). *Totum* renders Aristotle's *synolon*. 'Synolon, idest simul totum, idest . . . singulare compositum ex materia et forma . . . *Materia* enim per se *non potest esse separata a singularibus* . . . *Omnium eorum* quae sunt secundum suam naturam *sensibilia, formae non sunt separatae*' (*In Meta.* III, 4, 999b 18, *lect.* 9, §§453–5). '*Non* enim *est possibile* quod sit aliqua *domus* praeter *hanc domum sensibilem compositam ex materia et forma*' (*ibid.*). '*Secundum esse materiale* quod est per materiam contractum, *unaquaeque res est hoc solum quod est*, sicut *hic lapis* non est aliud quam hic lapis' (*In De anima* II, 3, 414a 30, *lect.* 5, §283). '*Continuum* a continendo dicitur: quando igitur multae partes *continentur in uno* et *quasi simul se tenent*, tunc est *continuum* . . . *Continua* sunt, quorum *terminus* est *idem*' (*In Physic.* V, 3, 227a, *lect.* 5, §691; IV, 13, 222a 10, *lect.* 21, §613). For the impossibility that two bodies should be in the same place, see *Physics* IV, 1–9; *Par.* II, 37–9.

37. These usages are well illustrated in these sentences from Aquinas (taken from L. Schütz, *Thomaslexikon, s.v. qualitas*): '*significare substantiam cum qualitate est significare suppositum cum natura vel forma determinata*' (*S.T.* 1a. 13, 1 ad 3); '*qualitas* dicitur "*differentia substantiae*", id est differentia, per quam *aliquid ab altero substantialiter differt*, quae intrat in definitionem substantiae' (*In Meta.* V, 14, 1020b 1, *lect.* 16, §987).

38. '*Generatio unius alterius est corruptio.*'

39. If the new body has *additional* powers, it is said to be the result of *generation*; if it has *fewer* powers, it is said to be the result of *corruption*. '*Alio modo dicitur generatio*, quando id quod ponitur in esse est *nobilius*, et e converso dicitur *corruptio*, quando quod ponitur in esse est *ignobilius*' (*In Meteor.* IV, 1, 379a 12, *lect.* 2, §314).

40. '*Differentiae elementorum sunt contrariae*, scilicet calidum et frigidum, et huius-modi, *et suscipiunt magis et minus* . . . Quando alterum elementum fuerit *simpliciter actu*, et alterum *simpliciter in potentia* fuerit, *tunc non potest esse mixtio*; quando vero unum *non est omnino actu*, nec per excessum praedominatur alteri elemento, *tunc generabitur quoddam* "*medium*", quod nec est simpliciter calidum, nec simpliciter frigidum, sed *quodammodo naturam participans utriusque*; . . . *illud* medium generatum non est sic in potentia sicut materia, nec simpliciter alterum elementorum, *sed medium inter ea* . . .' (*In De gen.* II, 7, 334b 8–20, *lect.* 8, §§238–9; cf. §§72, 180).

41. '*In quolibet mixto sunt omnia elementa* . . . *Omnia corpora mixta*, quaecumque sunt circa medium quod est terra, *necessario sunt composita ex omnibus simplicibus corporibus*, quae sunt *quatuor elementa*' (*In De gen.* II, 8, 334b 32–335a 32, *lect.* 8, §240). The whole chapter is important since it sets out the reasons for this belief. It is worth noting that there are a number of passages in the fourth book of the *Meteorologica* where the author speaks of compounds formed of *one* element (e.g. 388a 26; 389a 5–7; 389b 1, 7); but the context always allows the adverb 'predominantly' (*a praedominio*) to be supplied.

42. *Meteorologica* IV, 9–10.

43. '*Medium* autem illud *non est unius proportionis tantum*, scilicet quod *semper sit per aequalem* contrariorum *participationem*, neque est . . . uno modo tantum, sed diversis modis secundum *diversitatem proportionis contrariorum*: et sic est medium inter calidum et frigidum *secundum multiplicem proportionem* ipsorum. Ita enim intelligendum inter humidum

et siccum, quae *secundum mediorum diversitatem* quandam *in alia proportione* convenientia *faciunt carnem*, et *in alia proportione faciunt os*, et in alia faciunt alia, quorum *complexiones* variantur; sicut est *homo*, cuius complexio maxime vicina est temperamento, et *leo* qui est *calidae complexionis*, et *asinus* qui est *frigidae complexionis*' (*In De gen.* II, 7, 334b 25, *lect.* 8, §239). It is not yet time to inquire into the mysteries of the *human* complexion, but it may be worth clarifying four things. (*a*) Medical men spoke more of the four 'fluids' or 'humours' (Blood, Choler, Phlegm and Black Bile) than of the four elements. (*b*) They used *temperamentum* to mean the *perfect* equilibrium of the elements or humours. (*c*) They would use *complexio* (where today we say 'temperament') to describe *permanent* differences between individuals (who were 'sanguine', 'choleric', 'phlegmatic' or 'melancholy' depending on which humour predominated). And (*d*) they would use *dispositio* for *temporary* variations within the same individual, accounting among other things for what we still call an '*in*disposition'.

44. 'Non ergo manent elementa in mixto actu sine aliqua alteratione . . . Nec ambo nec alterum corrumpuntur omnino; . . . salvatur enim *virtus* eorum . . . Sicut igitur extrema inveniuntur in medio, quod participat naturam utriusque, *sic qualitates simplicium corporum inveniuntur in qualitate corporis mixti*' (*In De gen.* I, 10, 327b 25ff. *lect.* 24, §§171–2).

45. 'In ciascuna cosa, naturale ed artificiale, è impossibile procedere a la forma, sanza prima essere *disposto* lo subietto sopra che la forma dee stare: sì come impossibile la forma de l'*oro* è venire, se la materia, cioè lo suo subietto, non è *digesta* e *apparecchiata*; e la forma de l'arca venire, se la materia, cioè lo legno, non è prima *disposta* e *apparecchiata*' (*Con.* II, i, 10). 'Unde cum intentioni Naturae universalis *omnis natura obediat*, necesse fuit etiam praeter simplicem naturam terrae, quae est esse deorsum, *inesse aliam naturam* per quam obediret intentioni universalis Naturae; ut scilicet *pateretur* elevari in parte a virtute caeli, tanquam obediens a praecipiente' (*Quaestio*, 48).

46. The terms 'active and passive qualities' are usually restricted to the 'four contraries', while *virtutes* and *potentiae* occur with many shades of meaning in many other contexts – including some where they are almost synonymous. But the simplifications in this paragraph are supported by Dante's usage in the *Quaestio*, already quoted in note 45. Cf. further such phrases as: 'cum aqua sit corpus homogeneum . . . uniformiter oportet esse *virtuatam* . . .' (64; cf. 68); 'simul et *virtuatum* est caelum *ad agendum*, et terra *potentiata ad patiendum*' (76). Cf. further Aquinas: 'Subtrahere *ordinem* rebus creatis est eis subtrahere *id quod optimum habent* . . . Rerum enim quae sunt diversae secundum suas naturas, non est colligatio in ordinis unitatem nisi per hoc quod *quaedam agunt et quaedam patiuntur*' (*C.G.* III, 69, 2447; and cf. 2456).

47. 'Et ulterius non solum *anima est finis* viventium corporum, sed etiam *omnium naturalium corporum* in istis inferioribus . . . Videmus enim quod omnia *naturalia corpora* sunt quasi *instrumenta animae*, non solum in animalibus, sed etiam in plantis. Videmus enim quod *homines utuntur ad sui utilitatem* animalibus et rebus inanimatis; animalia vero plantis et rebus inanimatis; plantae autem rebus inanimatis, inquantum scilicet *alimentum et iuvamentum ab eis accipiunt*. Secundum autem quod agitur unumquodque in rerum natura, ita natum est agi. Unde videtur quod *omnia corpora inanimata* sint *instrumenta animatorum* et sint *propter ipsa*; et etiam *animata minus perfecta*, sint *propter animata magis perfecta*' (*In De anima* II, 4, 415b 16–22, *lect.* 7, §322).

48. Dante and Aristotle prefer the simile of the square that 'contains' a triangle, and the pentagon that 'contains' a square: 'Sì come dice lo Filosofo nel secondo de l'Anima, *le potenze de l'anima stanno sopra sé come la figura de lo quadrangulo sta sopra lo triangulo*, e lo pentangulo, cioè la figura che ha cinque canti, sta sopra lo quadrangulo; e così *la sensitiva sta sopra la vegetativa, e la intellettiva sta sopra la sensitiva*' (*Con.* IV, vii, 14). The passage in Aristotle occurs in *De anima* II, 3, 414b 30, and is paraphrased by Aquinas as follows:

'manifestum est enim in figuris, quod *trigonum*, quod est prius, *est potentia in tetragono*. *Potest enim tetragonum dividi in duos trigonos*. Et similiter in anima sensitiva, *vegetativa* est quasi *quaedam potentia* eius, et quasi anima per se. Et similiter est de aliis figuris, et aliis partibus animae' (*lect*. 5, §298).

49. The usages are illustrated in these sentences taken from L. Schütz, *Thomaslexikon* s.vv. *differentia, genus, species*. '*Differentia* est *quae constituit speciem*. Unumquodque autem constituitur in specie, secundum quod determinatur *ad aliquem specialem gradum in entibus*, quia *species rerum sunt* "*sicut numeri*, qui *differunt per additionem* et *subtractionem* unitatis" ' (*S.T.* 1a. 50, 2 ad 1). '*Differentia* sumitur a *forma* rei'; '*differentia* importat *distinctionem formae*' (*ibid*., 76, 1, *sed contra;*31, 2 ad 2). 'Semper autem id, a quo sumitur *differentia constituens speciem*, se habet ad illud, unde sumitur genus, sicut *actus ad potentiam*' (*ibid*., 3, 5, resp.). '*Genus* enim *dividitur in species* per *oppositas differentias*' (*In Poster*. I, 5, 74a 5–10, *lect*. 12, §100).

50. '*Corpora* enim *homogenea* et simplicia – sunt *homogenea* ut *aurum depuratum*, et simplicia ut ignis et terra – *regulariter in suis partibus qualificantur* omni naturali passione' (*Quaestio*, 41; cf. 64). 'Corpus . . . homoeomerum, idest *similium partium*, sicut aqua, cuius quaelibet pars est aqua' (*De caelo* I, 7, 274a 30, *lect*. 13, §129; cf. *Meteorologica* IV, 10, 388a 12).

51. 'Sì come dice Aristotile nel secondo de l'Anima [II, 4, 415b 13] "*vivere è l'essere* de li viventi" ' (*Con*. IV, vii, 11: Aquinas paraphrases: 'ipsum *vivere* est *esse* eorum', *lect*. 7, §319).

52. '*Anomoeomera*, idest membra *dissimilium partium*, puta *manus* aut *pes* aut similia . . . Unumquodque *membrum dissimilium partium componitur ex his quae sunt similium partium*, sicut *manus* ex *carne* et *osse* et *nervo*' (*In De gen*. I, 5, 321b 18–30, *lect*. 15, §105).

53. '*Omne corpus suscipiens vitam est organicum*'. 'Corpus *organicum* . . . habet *diversitatem organorum. Diversitas autem organorum necessaria est in corpore suscipiente vitam* propter diversas operationes animae . . . *Formae* vero *rerum inanimatarum*, propter sui *imperfectionem*, sunt principia paucarum operationum: unde *non exigunt diversitatem organorum* in suis perfectionibus' (*In De anima* II, 1, 412b 1, *lect*. 1, §§230, 231). Dante speaks also of a 'corpo . . . organizzato' (*Con*. III, viii, 1).

54. There is an order even within these three powers or activities: 'Inter *tres operationes* animae vegetabilis est quidam ordo. Nam prima eius operatio est *nutritio*, per quam salvatur aliquid ut est. Secunda autem perfectior est *augmentum*, quo aliquid proficit in maiorem perfectionem et secundum quantitatem et secundum virtutem. Tertia autem perfectissima et finalis est *generatio*, per quam aliquid quasi in seipso perfectum existens, alteri esse et perfectionem tradit' (*In De anima* II, 4, 416b 22, *lect*. 9, §347).

55. 'Propria autem *ratio vitae* est ex hoc, quod aliquid est natum *movere seipsum*' (*In De anima* II, 1, 412a 15, *lect*. 1, §219). There is, however, a class of animals (e.g. oysters) that cannot move from place to place, so that the whole scale should be described as follows: 'In quibusdam enim viventium inveniuntur tantum *alimentum, augmentum* et *decrementum*, scilicet in *plantis*. In quibusdam autem, cum his invenitur *sensus sine motu locali*, sicut in *animalibus imperfectis*, sicut sunt *ostreae*. In quibusdam autem, ulterius invenitur *motus secundum locum*, sicut in animalibus perfectis, quae moventur motu progressivo, ut bos et equus' (*ibid*., II, 2, 413b 2ff., *lect*. 3, §255).

56. 'Ad hoc igitur quod [animal] cognoscat ea, quae sibi sunt necessaria vel contraria secundum rationem corporis mixti, ordinatur sensus *tactus*, qui est cognoscitivus praedictarum differentiarum [sc. calidi et frigidi, humidi et sicci]. Ad hoc autem quod cognoscat conveniens nutrimentum, necessarius est ei *gustus*, per quem cognoscitur sapidum et insipidum quod est signum nutrimenti convenientis vel inconvenientis. Et ideo . . . *gustus et tactus ex necessitate consequuntur omnia animalis*' (*In De sensu* I, 436b 10, *lect*. 2, §21).

333

'*Omne* animal, inquantum est animal, *necesse est quod habeat sensum aliquem*. In hoc enim quod est sensitivum esse *consistit ratio animalis*, per quam animal a non animali distinguitur' (*ibid.*, 436b 8, §20). 'Nam *motivum non potest esse sine sensitivo; sensitivum autem potest esse sine motivo*: aliqua enim habentium sensum, habent etiam motum secundum locum, sed aliqua non habent . . . Hic enim motus [progressivus] non inest omnibus animalibus. Sed quae carent hoc motu, *habent aliquem motum localem*, scilicet *dilatationis* et *constrictionis*, sicut apparet in *ostreis*' (*In De anima* II, 3, 415a 2–8, *lect.* 6, §301).

57. 'Quanto anima est perfectior, tanto exercet plures perfectas operationes et diversas. Et ideo ad exercendum huiusmodi operationes, *necessaria* sunt ei *plura et diversa organa vel instrumenta corporalia* in corpore in quo est . . . *Anima* autem quae est in *animalibus anulosis* et in *plantis*, quia *parum habet de perfectione*, nec exercet diversas operationes, ideo *requirit corpus magis simile et uniforme . . .*' (*In De anima* I, 5, 411b 25, *lect.* 14, §208).

58. '*Animalia perfecta . . .* quae . . . habent motivum secundum motum progressivum *. . . excedunt animalia imperfecta, idest immobilia*, sicut illa animalia excedunt plantas et alia corpora mixta . . . Animalia immobilia habent quidem cognitionem eorum quae sunt necessaria solum secundum quod eis *praesentialiter* offeruntur; animalia autem progressiva accipiunt notitiam eorum etiam *quae a remotis* . . . Et sicut *omnibus* animalibus ad cognoscendum *necessaria*, quae pertinent ad *nutritionem*, secundum quod praesentialiter offeruntur, ordinatur *gustus*, ita ad cognoscendum ea quae offeruntur *a remotis*, ordinatur *odoratus* . . . Alii autem duo sensus, scilicet *visus* et *auditus*, ordinantur ad cognoscendum *a remotis omnia necessaria animali, vel corruptiva* . . . Manifestum enim est quod animalia per *visum* et *auditum fugiunt corruptiva quaelibet, et salubria prosequuntur.*' '*Visus* dupliciter *praeeminet auditui*. Uno quidem modo quantum ad necessaria, puta ad quaerendum cibum . . . alio modo . . . secundum se, quia *magis cognoscitivus est plurium* quam auditus . . . *Visus ideo secundum se est melior, quia potentia visiva sua apprehensione annunciat nobis multas differentias rerum, et diversorum modorum*' (*In De sensu* I, 436b 10–437a 10, *lect.* 2, §§23–4, 27–8). For the image of the pyramid, see *Con.* IV, xii, 17.

59. References in order: *Quaestio*, 41–8, 63–74 (cf. notes 45, 46 and 50 above); *Mon.* I, iii, 5–7; *Con.* IV, vii, 11, 14–15 (cf. note 48); *Purg.* IV, 1–18. In the passage from the *Monarchia*, Dante uses *vis ultima* or *ultimum* instead of *differentia*; but a *differentia specifica ultima* is synonymous with a *differentia constituens speciem* in Aquinas's usage. The attack in *Purg.* IV, 5–6, is on those, such as Plato, who believed that there are *three* distinct 'souls' in *man*. Following Aristotle, the error is refuted by Aquinas in *C.G.* II, 58 and *S.T.* 1a. 76, 3–4. The following sentence is characteristic: 'Nulla alia forma substantialis est in homine nisi sola anima intellectiva; et . . . *ipsa*, sicut *virtute continet animam sensitivam et nutritivam*, ita *virtute continet omnes inferiores formas*, et facit ipsa sola quidquid imperfectiores formae in aliis faciunt. *Et similiter est dicendum de anima sensitiva in brutis . . .*' (a. 4, resp.).

60. Cf. *Con.* III, iii, 3; *Quaestio*, 73; *Purg.* xxv, 56.

61. The passage occurs in *Con.* III, vii, 6. Instead we may quote from Aquinas's paraphrase of Aristotle: 'Ubi considerandum est quod ad hoc quod universum sit perfectum, *nullus gradus perfectionis in rebus intermittitur, sed paulatim natura de imperfectis ad perfecta procedit*. Propter quod etiam Aristoteles in octavo *Metaphysicae* [VII, 3, 1034b 33] *assimilat species rerum numeris*, qui *paulatim* in augmentum proficiunt' (*In De anima* II, 3 414b 32 *lect.* 5, §288). 'Sicut Philosophus dicit in septimo *de Historiis animalium, natura ex inanimatis ad animata procedit paulatim*, ita quod genus inanimatorum prius invenitur quam genus plantarum: quod quidem ad alia corpora comparatum videtur esse animatum, ad genus autem animalium, inanimatum. Et similiter a plantis ad animalia *quodam continuo ordine progreditur*: quia *quaedam animalia immobilia*, quae

scilicet terrae adhaerent, *parum videntur a plantis differre.* Ita etiam et *in progressu ab animalibus ad hominem,* quaedam inveniuntur, in quibus aliqua similitudo rationis appareat' (*In De memor.* I, 449b, *lect.* I, §298). Cf. further *C.G.* III, 97, §2725.

62. The classic study is A. O. Lovejoy, *The Great Chain of Being: a Study in the History of an Idea* (Cambridge, Mass., 1936).

63. See especially *Con.* III, vii, 2–5. We shall return to these images in Chapter 8. For the moment we may quote the following characteristic passages from St Bonaventure, St Albert and Aquinas (the quotations are taken from Bruno Nardi's *Saggi di filosofia dantesca,* pp. 108 and 203). 'Propriissime . . . *Deus lux* est, et quae ad ipsum *magis* accedunt, *plus* habent *de natura lucis.*' 'Corpora mundi, secundum quod *plus et minus participant de luce,* sunt *magis et minus nobilia* quantum ad esse substantiale, et *specie differentia,* sicut patet respiciendo *gradus* in corporibus mundi' (Bonaventure, *Sent.* II, d. 13 a. 1 qu. 1 ob. 3, and a. 2, *qu.* 2, *fund.* 6). 'Omnes . . . formae ab ipsa totius universitatis natura largiuntur; quo autem *magis* ab ea *elongantur,* eo *magis* nobilitatibus suis et bonitatibus privantur; et quo *minus recedunt,* eo *magis nobiles* sunt et *plures* habent bonitatum *potestates* et *virtutes . . .*' (St Albert, *De intell. et intellig.,* I, tr. 1, c. 5). 'Cum enim Deus sit actus purus, secundum hoc *aliqua magis vel minus ab eo distant,* quod sunt *plus vel minus in actu vel in potentia.* Illud igitur in entibus *est extreme distans a Deo* quod est in potentia tantum, scilicet *materia prima . . .* Corpora vero . . . *accedunt ad divinam similitudinem* inquantum habent formam, quam Aristoteles in I *Phys.* [192a 16–17] nominat "divinum quiddam"' (*C.G.* III, 69, §2457).

64. '*Distinctio* autem *formalis* semper requirit *inaequalitatem,* quia, ut dicitur in VIII *Metaph.* [1043b 34] "*formae rerum sunt sicut numeri,* in quibus species variantur per additionem vel subtractionem unitatis". Unde in rebus naturalibus *gradatim species ordinatae* esse videntur . . . Non enim esset *perfectum universum,* si tantum *unus gradus bonitatis* inveniretur in rebus'. '. . . *In constitutione* rerum. . . *est inaequalitas partium . . . propter perfectionem totius*' (*S.T.* 1a, 47, 2, resp., and ad 3).

6 Concerning the heavens

1. On the fiery nature of the heavens, cf.: 'Quod quidem sumitur a nomine [sc. "aether"] imposito ab antiquis, quod durat usque ad praesens tempus . . . *Sed Anaxagoras male interpretatus est* hoc nomen, attribuens ipsum *igni, quasi caeleste corpus sit igneum:* "aethein" enim in graeco idem est quod "ardere", quod est proprium ignis . . .' (*In De caelo* I, 3, 270b 25, *lect.* 7, §77). On their immutability, cf.: 'Secundum enim memoriam quam sibi invicem tradiderunt *astrologi,* dispositiones et motus caelestium corporum observantes, *in toto praeterito tempore non videtur aliquid transmutatum esse,* neque secundum totum caelum, neque secundum aliquam propriam partem eius . . .' (*ibid.,* 270b 15, §76).

2. 'Ista autem quae inquirenda sunt, *difficultatem habent*: quia *modicum de causis eorum percipere possumus,* et accidentia eorum magis sunt *remota a cognitione nostra,* quam etiam ipsa corpora *elongentur a nobis secundum corporalem situm.*' But 'reputemus dignum esse quod promptitudo hominis considerantis huiusmodi quaestiones magis debeat imputari verecundiae, idest honestati vel modestiae, quam audaciae, idest praesumptioni' (*In De caelo* II, 12, 291b 26, 292a 15, *lect.* 17, §§457, 450). See also Chapter 3, note 19. Aristotle was 'quello glorioso filosofo al quale la natura più aperse li suoi segreti . . .' (*Con.* III, v, 7).

3. *De caelo* I, 2. For Aristotle's preliminary studies, see *Physics* III–IV. For the helix (which is of relevance to the movements of the sun discussed below), cf.: 'Elix enim *videtur* esse una *linea simplex,* quia omnis pars eius est uniformis; et tamen linea elica nec est recta nec est circularis . . . sed *mixta ex recta et circulari.* Causatur enim elix *ex duobus*

335

motibus imaginatis, quorum unus est lineae circumeuntis columnam, alius autem est puncti moti per lineam; *si enim uterque motus simul et regulariter perficiatur, constituetur elica linea* per motum puncti in linea mota' (*In De caelo* I, 2, 268b 18, *lect.* 3, §25). For the three possible 'simple' movements, cf.: 'necesse est . . . simplicem motum localem quendam esse *a medio*, . . . quendam . . . *ad medium*, . . . alium . . . *circa medium* . . .' 'Necesse est motuum quosdam esse simplices, quosdam autem aliqualiter *mixtos*: sive ita quod motus mixtus non sit unus, sed habens diversas partes (sicut ille qui componitur ex *elevatione* et *depressione*, aut ex *pulsu* et *tractu*), sive ita quod motus mixtus sit unus, sicut patet de motu qui in obliquum tendit, et de motu qui est super lineam elicam' (*ibid.*, 268b 2, §§30, 32). For the connection between 'simple' bodies and 'simple' movements: 'Unde *simplicium corporum* necesse est esse *simplices motus*; *mixtorum* autem, *mixtos*' (*ibid.*, §32).

4. *De caelo* II, 4. 'Et primo [Philosophus] ostendit *caelum* esse *sphaericae figurae*; secundo ostendit quod haec figura *perfecte* in ipso existit . . . Dicit quod necesse est caelum habere sphaericam figuram, tum quia *ista figura* est maxime *propria* . . . *corpori caelesti*; tum etiam quia est *prima figurarum* . . .' (*In De caelo* II, 4, 286b 10, *lect.* 5, §344). '*Aqua* enim est *circa terram*, licet non ex omni parte cooperiat terram (quod est propter necessitatem generationis et conservationis vitae, maxime animalium et plantarum), *aër* autem *circumdat aquam*, ignis autem circumdat aërem; et secundum eandem rationem superiora corpora [i.e. the 'heavenly spheres'] circumdant inferiora usque ad supremum caelum . . . Haec corpora *tangunt se invicem absque aliqua interpolatione alterius corporis, vel etiam vacui* . . . Superficies autem unius horum inferiorum corporum est sphaerica; *illud autem quod continuatur*, idest sine interpolatione coniungitur, *corpore sphaerico continenti*, aut etiam quod movetur circa corpus sphaericum contentum, *necesse est esse sphaericum*' (*ibid.* II, 4, 287b 1–5, *lect.* 6, §357; see also 287a 5–10, §351). On the earth as the *medium quiescens* at the centre: 'Relinquitur ergo quod oporteat esse *aliquid quod naturaliter quiescat in medio*, si motus caeli est circularis et sempiternus. Hoc autem quod naturaliter quiescit in medio, est *terra* . . .' (*ibid.*, 286a 20, *lect.* 4, §335).

On the use of *caelum* in the singular to denote the whole body of the heavens: 'Secundo modo dicitur caelum non solum suprema sphaera, *sed totum corpus quod continuatur cum extrema circumferentia totius universi*, idest *omnes sphaerae caelestium corporum*, in quibus sunt luna et sol et quaedam stellarum, scilicet alii quinque planetae (nam stellae fixae sunt in suprema sphaera secundum opinionem Aristotelis) . . .' (*ibid.*, I, 9, 278b 12–22, *lect.* 20, §199). Dante will sometimes use 'il cielo' in the singular in just this sense: e.g. *Par.* I, 74; VIII, 106; XIII, 66; XXVI, 129; XXVIII, 42.

5. 'Impossibile est quod *motui circulari* sit *aliquis motus contrarius*' (*In De caelo* I, 4, 270b 32, *lect.* 8, §81). 'Nulla loci mutatio potest esse *continua* et *perpetua* nisi *circularis*' (*In Physic.* VIII, 8, 261b 27, *lect.* 16, §1104). The principle is often invoked in the *De caelo*, e.g.: 'Solus motus circularis potest esse perpetuus . . .' 'Super lineam . . . rectam finitam non potest esse motus infinitus *nisi per reflexionem, quae quidem non potest esse sine interpolatione quietis*' (II, 3, 286a 10, *lect.* 4, §334).

On stillness and rectilinear motion: 'Cum *quies* in loco sit *finis* motus localis . . .' (*ibid.*, I, 8, 276a 25, *lect.* 16 §156). 'Quaecumque enim mota quiescunt, *tunc quiescunt quando perveniunt ad proprium locum*, sicut patet in gravibus et levibus; sed *hoc non potest dici in primo mobili*, quod *circulariter movetur*, quia idem est unde incipit motus eius et in quod terminatur; ergo primum mobile movetur a primo motore *motu incessabili*' (*ibid.*, I, 9, 279b 1, *lect.* 21, §220).

6. '*Motus circularis* est *prior* naturaliter *motu recto*. Sed prior motus est naturaliter prioris corporis . . . Consequens est quod *motus circularis est proprius et naturalis alicuius corporis simplicis*, quod est *prius* corporibus elementaribus quae sunt hic apud nos' (*ibid.*, I, 2, 269a 20, *lect.* 4, §41). 'Corpori quinto non est aliquid contrarium.' 'Corpus primum,

quod scilicet *movetur motu primo* et perfecto, idest *circulari*, est *sempiternum*, quasi *non subiacens generationi et corruptioni*; neque etiam habet *augmentum*, neque *decrementum*; et non subiacet *senectuti*, neque *alterationi*, neque *passioni*.' 'Antiqui . . . nominaverunt supremum locum mundi "*aethera*", ponentes scilicet ei nomen ab eo "*quod semper currit sempiterno tempore*": "thein" enim in graeco idem est quod "currere" ' (*ibid.*, I, 3, 270a 20, 270b 1 and 22, *lect.* 6–7, §§59, 72 and 77). See also chapters 10–12 of the first book.

The Christian need make only one amendment, as Aquinas points out: 'Non tamen dicimus *secundum fidem catholicam*, quod *caelum semper fuerit*, nec dicamus quod semper sit duraturum . . . Non enim dicimus quod incoeperit esse per generationem, sed per effluxum *a primo principio*, a quo perficitur totum esse omnium rerum (*lect.* 6, §64; see Chapter 9 below).

7. 'Necesse est ulterius quod *elementa* sint *eadem* secundem speciem *ubique*, idest in *quolibet mundo*' (*ibid.*, I, 8, 276a 30, *lect.* 16, §161). 'Si enim primi motus, scilicet simplices, sunt finiti, necesse est quod *species corporum simplicium sint finitae*: et hoc ideo, quia motus ipsius corporis simplicis est simplex' (*ibid.*, I, 7, 274b 3, *lect.* 13, §130). 'Nullum corpus sensibile [est] infinitum' (*ibid.*, §136). 'Si enim corpora, quae sunt in quolibet mundo, sunt eiusdem speciei (videmus autem quod *omnes partes terrae*, quae sunt in hoc mundo, feruntur *ad hoc medium huius mundi*, et omnes partes ignis ad extremum huius), consequens erit quod etiam *omnes partes terrae* quae sunt in *quocumque alio mundo feruntur ad medium huius mundi* . . . Sed hoc est *impossibile*. Si enim hoc accideret, necesse esset quod *terra, quae est in alio mundo* ferretur sursum in proprio suo mundo . . . Necesse est ponere *unum solum medium*, ad quod feruntur omnia gravia ubicumque sint, et unum extremum ad quod feruntur omnia levia ubicumque sint. *Quo posito, impossibile est esse plures mundos* . . .' (*ibid.*, I, 8, 276b 10, *lect.* 16, §162). 'Sic igitur manifestum est quod *quaecumque corpora sunt in loco, sunt sensibilia*. Et ex hoc concludit [sc. Aristoteles], quod corpus infinitum non sit extra caelum; immo universalius, quod *nullum corpus sit extra caelum*. Cum enim corpus omne sit finitum vel infinitum, sequitur quod *nullum omnino corpus sit extra caelum*; . . . quia "extra" significat locum, *nihil autem est in loco nisi corpus sensibile*' (*ibid.*, I, 7, 275b 8, *lect.* 14, §144).

8. *De caelo* I, 9, 279a 19–22, translated by J. L. Stocks. '*Extra caelum neque* est *locus*, neque *vacuum*, neque *tempus*. . . Ea quae ibi sunt nata esse, *non sunt in loco* . . . Talia *non senescunt* in tempore, . . . neque est aliqua *transmutatio* eorum quae sunt super illam lationem . . . scilicet ultimae sphaerae . . . Illa entia quae sunt extra caelum sunt *inalterabilia* et penitus *impassibilia*, habentia optimam vitam . . . *per se sufficientissimam*, inquantum non indigent aliquo vel ad conservationem suae vitae vel executionem operum vitae' (Aquinas, *ad loc.*, *lect.* 21, §§207, 213, 214).

9. The classic study of the origin of this belief is that by Bruno Nardi, 'La dottrina dell'Empireo nella sua genesi storica e nel pensiero dantesco', now in *Saggi di filosofia dantesca* (2nd edn., Florence, 1967), pp. 167–214. There is much valuable material in A. Mellone, *La dottrina di Dante Alighieri sulla prima creazione* (Nocera Sup., 1950). See the same author's article on *Empireo* in the *Enciclopedia dantesca*.

10. 'Manifestum est quod *stellae* secundum molem suae magnitudinis sunt *sphaericae figurae*' (*In De caelo* II, 11, 291b 11–23, *lect.* 16, §442). 'Rationabile est quod *stellae* pertineant ad *naturam sphaerae* in qua situantur . . . consequens est quod habeant *eandem naturam cum sphaeris caelestibus*, et differant a natura quatuor elementorum' (*ibid.*, II, 7, 289a 15, *lect.* 10, §383). '*Corpora stellarum* videntur habere *differentiam* ad corpora sphaerarum caelestium, ex eo quod sunt lucida et videntur *spissiora* . . . In corporibus caelestibus, quanto est maior *congregatio* per modum inspissationis, tanto magis *multiplicatur luminositas* et virtus activa, sicut patet in *ipsis corporibus stellarum*.' '*Rarum* autem et *densum invenitur in corporibus caelestibus*, secundum quod *astra* sunt *spissiora et magis*

commassata quam sphaerae eorum: non tamen secundum differentiam contrarietatis, sed solum secundum additionem et deminutionem virtutis, secundum maiorem et minorem congregationem partium' (*ibid.*, §§384, 394).

A typical mistake is embodied in this objection refuted by St Albert: 'Corpus purum diaphanum non indiget ad hoc quod luceat, nisi quod sit spissum, sicut apparet in quibusdam lapidibus pretiosis. Cum igitur totus orbis sit purus et clarus et perspicuae naturae, *non indiget* stella eius, ut luceat, nisi quod sit spissa . . .' (*De caelo, lib.* 2, *tr.* 3, c. 6). In his *Convivio*, Dante agreed with Averroes as to the explanation of the 'dark patches' (*segni bui*): 'l'ombra che è in essa [sc. luna] . . . non è altro che *raritade del suo corpo*, a la quale non possono terminare li raggi del sole e ripercuotersi così come ne l'altre parti . . .' (*Con.* II, xiii, 9). This is the error which he reformulates and rejects in *Paradiso* II. His new explanation involves a very dense account of all the heavens and their *operationes*, and his argument depends heavily on Neoplatonist ideas that have no parallel in Aristotle. But the essence of his change of mind is simply that the cause is 'formal' not 'material'; 'essential', and not 'accidental' or 'contingent'.

11. 'Est tamen in eis [corporibus caelestibus] aliqua diversitas secundum naturam speciei, *licet conveniant in natura generis*; sicut conveniunt in communi ratione motus, quia omnia circulariter moventur.' 'Sic igitur dicendum est quod corpora caelestia sunt *unius naturae secundum genus, diversarum autem naturarum secundum speciem*' (*In De caelo* II, 7, 289a 18, *lect.* 10, §385; II, 11, 291b 11, *lect.* 16, §449). The context makes it clear that Aquinas (like Aristotle) is referring to the luminaries, not the heavens. '*Omnia* corpora caelestia, secundum *communem virtutem luminis*, habent *calefacere* . . .' (*ibid.*, §393).

12. 'Relinquitur quod . . . *sphaerae moveantur, sed astra secundum se quiescant*, quasi non per se motae, sed *moventur ad motum sphaerarum quibus sunt infixae*, non sicut alterius naturae existentes, sicut clavus ferreus infigitur rotae ligneae, sed *sicut eiusdem naturae existentes* . . .' 'Si igitur orbes quiescerent et stellae moverentur, si quidem stellae essent profundatae in corporibus sphaerarum, *sequeretur quod suo motu divellerent sive dirumperent ipsam sphaerarum substantiam*.' (*ibid.*, II, 8, 290a 1–7; 9, *lect.* 12, §§400, 401); cf. II, 9, 291a 10, *lect.* 14, §429. Aristotle also gives other reasons, chief among them that it would be impossible for the 'fixed' stars to maintain their relative positions if they were all moving independently (*De caelo* II, 289b 8).

13. The later 'discovery' that there must be a ninth sphere, without luminaries, is discussed below. See *Con.* II, iii, 3 for Dante's awareness of Aristotle's 'mistakes'.

14. There is a convenient summary of Aristotle's theory in D. Ross, *Aristotle* (London, 1923; 5th edn revised, 1949) pp. 96–7.

15. Alfragano, *Elementa astronomica* ('*Il libro dell'aggregazione delle stelle*') ch. 21, ed. R. Campani (Città di Castello, 1910), p. 146. The information is now clearly set out in C. Gizzi, *L'astronomia nel poema sacro* (Napoli, 1975), vol. 1, pp. 180–3. The numbers sound hypnotically long when written out in Latin. For example, the circumference of the inner surface of the stellar sphere is calculated as 410,810,570 miles; in Latin: 'Rotunditas magni orbis est quater centies et decies milies mille et octies centies et decies milies mille et quinquies centum et septuaginta miliaria.'

16. 'Il paese sincero' (*Par.* VII, 130) and 'questo etera tondo' (*Par.* XXII, 132) both refer to the *caelum* as a whole.

17. Dante quotes the Aristotelian definition of violence almost verbatim in *Par.* IV, 73–4. 'Se *violenza* è quando quel che pate / *niente conferisce* a quel che sforza', reflecting *Ethics* III, 1, 1110a 1–2, which Aquinas paraphrases: '*violentum est* cuius principium est *extra*; ita quod *ille qui patitur* inde, *nil conferat* ad actionem' (§405). For the nature of Fire in the *Comedy*, cf. *Purg.* XVIII, 28–30; *Par.* I, 115, 133–5, 141; IV, 77–8.

18. *Purg.* XXVII, 140; *Par.* I, 43–72.

19. *Par.* II, 23–4; V, 91–2.

20. 'Quod duo corpora non possint esse simul . . . est . . . solum *ex ratione dimensionum*, in quibus non potest esse diversitas si sint aequales, nisi secundum situm . . . Duae autem magnitudines *aequalis quantitatis* non possunt differre, nisi secundum situm. Non enim potest imaginari quod haec linea sit alia ab illa sibi aequali, nisi inquantum imaginamur utramque in alio et alio situ . . . Si duo corpora *aequalia dimensionata* sint simul . . . sequitur quod duo corpora sint unum . . . Universaliter tamen hoc verum est, quod oportet corpus *cedere* in quod alterum corpus immittitur, ne sint duo corpora simul' (*In Physic.* IV, 8, 212b 25, *lect.* 13, §541: the sentences have been re-ordered).

21. 'Corpus gloriosum ratione suae proprietatis non habet quod possit esse cum alio corpore glorioso in eodem loco . . . *Divina autem virtute fieri posset ut duo corpora gloriosa essent simul, vel duo non gloriosa* . . .' (*S.T. Suppl.* 83, 4, resp.: the whole *quaestio* is relevant to this episode). The following note on thunderbolts is also pertinent: 'Quod autem *fulmen* non sit corpus solidum vel lapis, patet: quia tale corpus non potest habere effectus, qui superius dicti sunt procedere a fulmine. *Non enim posset penetrare ad interiora nisi prius ruptis exterioribus: alioquin duo corpora essent simul in eodem loco, quod naturaliter non potest fieri*' (*In Meteor.* III, 1, 371a 30, *lect.* 2, §261).

22. This simile was widely applied to Mary's fecundation by the Holy Spirit when the Word was made Flesh. It thus prepares the way, by association, for Dante's allusion to the Incarnation in the following lines. By contrast, the adjectives *purus* (*diaphanus*), *spissus*, *politus* (*tersus*) and *lucidus* are all to be found in one section of St Albert's *De caelo* (II, *tr.* 3, c. 6).

23. A *vero primo* or *prima notizia* (*Purg.* XVIII, 56) corresponds to what Aquinas calls a *communis conceptio* in the following passage: 'Contra *communes animi conceptiones* non potest aliquid miraculose fieri, *ut scilicet pars non sit minor toto*, quia contraria communibus conceptionibus directe contradictionem includunt. Similiter nec *conclusiones geometricae*, *quae a communibus conceptionibus infallibiliter deducuntur*, sicut quod triangulus non habeat tres angulos aequales duobus rectis . . .' (*S.T. Suppl.* 83, 3, *ob.* 2).

24. 'Cui subiecti sunt septem, qui versantur retro contrario motu atque caelum; ex quibus unum globum possidet illa, quam in terris Saturniam nominant. deinde est hominum generi prosperus et salutaris ille fulgor, qui dicitur Iovis; tum rutilus horribilisque terris, quem Martium dicitis; deinde subter mediam fere regionem sol obtinet, dux et princeps et moderator luminum reliquorum, mens mundi et temperatio, tanta magnitudine, ut cuncta sua luce lustret et compleat. hunc ut comites consequuntur Veneris alter, alter Mercurii cursus, in infimoque orbe luna radiis solis accensa convertitur' (*Somnium Scipionis*, 17). The text and translation (save in a few minor details) are from the Loeb edition, ed. C. W. Keyes.

25. C. Gizzi, *L'astronomia nel poema sacro* (2 vols, Naples, 1975). I am almost wholly indebted to secondary works for the second part of this chapter, chief among them: E. Moore, 'The Astronomy of Dante' in *Studies in Dante* (Oxford, 1903) vol. 3, pp. 1–108; M. A. Orr, *Dante and the Early Astronomers* (2nd edn, London, 1956); F. Angelitti, 'Dante e l'astronomia', in the miscellany, *Dante e l'Italia* (Fondazione Marco Besso, Rome, 1921); I. Capasso, *L'astronomia nella Divina Commedia* (Pisa, 1967). The clearest, sanest, briefest and most practical introduction is currently that by G. Buti and R. Bertagni, *Commento astronomico della Divina Commedia* (Florence, 1966).

26. Modern astronomers define the ecliptic as the 'plane of the earth's orbit round the sun'; but on occasion they still find it convenient to speak of it in the traditional way as 'the apparent path of the sun among the stars'. Some of the constellations of the Zodiac, like Gemini and Leo, have bright stars and easily remembered patterns which are worthy of their fame. Others, like Cancer, which separates these two, are barely visible and quite unmemorable. The matter is of little importance, however, for the constellation is hidden when it is in conjunction with the sun. It will be noticed that the word 'Sign' is avoided (it used to mean no more than 'constellation') because in astrological parlance, as we shall see below, the Signs no longer coincide with the constellations, thanks to the precession of the equinoxes. See Sacrobosco, *Sphaera*, c. 2, ed. Thorndike, p. 89.

27. A 'great circle' is a technical term (already used in classical geometry and astronomy) denoting 'any circle, drawn on the surface of a sphere, whose plane passes through the *centre* of that sphere'. As will appear, all lines of longitude are great circles, but the equator is the only line of latitude to be a great circle.

28. 'A "periodic" or "sidereal" revolution is when a heavenly body has just gone once round its orbit. A "synodical" revolution is when it has come round again to the same position in reference to the earth and the sun . . . The familiar illustration which has been given from the hands of a watch will make this distinction clear at once. Suppose the hands together, say, at twelve o'clock. A "periodic" revolution of the minute hand occupies, of course, just one hour, and will be completed at one o'clock; but a "synodical" revolution will have been completed when the two hands are exactly together again, and that will evidently be a little after five minutes past one. So, in fact, 1 hour and $5\frac{5}{11}$ minutes is the "synodical" period of the minute hand in this particular case' (E. Moore, 'The Astronomy of Dante', p. 39).

29. The wording of this paragraph is carefully chosen so that it is valid for Aristotle, who believed that the eighth or Starry Heaven was the outermost sphere, and also for Ptolemy, Alfraganus and Sacrobosco who posited a ninth heaven, the *primum mobile*, as will be explained below.

30. The similes are both taken from Dante: 'a guisa d'una *vite* dintorno' (*Con.* III, v, 14); 'si *girava* per le *spire*' (*Par.* x, 32). For a more detailed account of the sun's movements, see Sacrobosco, *Sphaera*, c. 3, ed. Thorndike, pp. 95–112; *Con.* III, v.

31. 'Conviene anche che lo cerchio dove sono li Garamanti [= the equator] . . . veggia lo sole a punto sopra sé girare, non a modo di mola ma *di rota* . . .' (*Con.* III, v, 18). 'Pero convene che Maria [an imaginary city at the north pole] veggia nel principio de l'Ariete [i.e. at the spring equinox], quando lo sole va sotto lo mezzo cerchio de li primi poli [i.e. the celestial equator], esso sole girar lo mondo intorno giù a la terra, o vero al mare, *come una mola*, de la quale non paia più che mezzo lo corpo suo; e questa veggia venire montando a guisa d'una *vite* dintorno, tanto che compia novanta e una rota e poco più. E quando queste rote sono compiute, lo suo montare è a Maria quasi tanto quanto esso monta a noi ne la mezza terra, quando 'l giorno è de la mezza notte iguale' (*ibid.*, 14–15).

32. 'Poi per la medesima via par discendere altre novanta e una rota e poco più, tanto ch'elli gira intorno giù a la terra, o vero al mare, sé non tutto mostrando; e poi si cela e comincialo a vedere Lucia [an imaginary city at the south pole], lo quale montare e discendere intorno a sé allor vede con altrettante rote quante vede Maria. E se uno uomo fosse in Lucia dritto, sempre che volgesse la faccia inver lo sole, vedrebbe quello andarsi nel braccio sinistro. Per che si può vedere che questi luoghi hanno un dì l'anno di sei mesi; e una notte d'altrettanto tempo . . .' (*ibid.*, 16–17). Dante realized that this difference in the apparent direction of the sun's course holds good for an observer in the southern hemisphere *at any point* south of the Tropic of Capricorn; and he exploits this knowledge as the occasion for an important episode in *Purgatorio* IV, 55–84.

33. *Con.* III, v, 20–21.

34. By definition, the sun will 'rise to mortals' from the horizon. Horizon and equator must be inclined for observers everywhere except at the poles, where the two 'great circles' coincide exactly.

35. All the studies listed in note 25 have a discussion of the difficulties involved and of

rival proposals. Apart from the fact that two of the intersections are not 'crosses' in the strict sense (they are *incroci* not *croci*), the sun will rise to different mortals in different places, and only from one of these places will the horizon pass through equator, ecliptic and colure. The details may become clearer one day if a precise source is found, particularly one which uses *foce* (lines 37 and 44) in what looks like a technical acceptation.

36. 'Four' and 'three' suggest the cardinal and theological virtues (required for entry into Paradise), just like the four stars which illuminate Cato's head (*Purg.* I, 23, 37) and which give way to three stars over the Valley of the Princes (*Purg.* VIII, 89): see also *Purg.* XXIX, 121–32; XXXI, 103–11, XXXII, 25, 97–9. 'Surge ai mortali' echoes '*mortalibus* aegris/ *incipit* (*Aen.* II, 268–9), while 'la lucerna del mondo' echoes Christ's words: 'Vos estis *lux mundi*' (Matthew 5.14).

37. *Con.* II, xiv, 2, 5–8.

38. The main stages in the evolution of this doctrine are traced by Bruno Nardi in 'Dante e Alpetragio', *Saggi di filosofia dantesca* (2nd edn, Florence, 1967) pp. 139–66. The philosophical axiom underlying the argument is a particular case of the principle *Agens agit sibi simile* to be discussed in Chapter 8. In the form *Effectus immediatus a primo debet esse unus tantum et simillimus primo*, it was condemned by Bishop Tempier of Paris in 1277 (no. 64). Alpetragio applied the axiom to the movement of the heavens in the form: *ab uno motore primo simplici, in eo quod movetur ab ipso, non est nisi motus unus* (Nardi, p. 153n).

39. References in order: *VN* XLI, 10; *Par.* XXVII, 99; *Purg.* XXXIII, 90; *Par.* XXX, 39; II, 113–14. Later, in the passage analysed at the end of Chapter 7, the *primum mobile* will be described as 'costui che tutto quanto *rape* / l'altro universo seco' (*Par.* XXVIII, 70–1; and cf. *Con.* II, v, 17). The verb *rapire* reflects Dante's source: 'Sed primus motus [caeli ultimi . . . ab oriente per occidentem rediens in orientem] omnes alias [sphaeras] secum *impetu suo rapit* infra diem et noctem circa terram semel, illis tamen contra nitentibus . . .' (Sacrobosco, *Sphaera*, c. 1, ed. Thorndike, p. 79).

40. 'Est *unus primus motus*, qui est *causa omnis alterius motus* . . . Quicumque autem *percipit* quemcumque motum, . . . percipit esse transmutabile, et per consequens *percipit primum motum quem sequitur tempus* . . . Non autem tempus mensuratur secundum quantitatem cuiuscumque motus, . . . sed *solum quantitatem primi motus sequitur tempus* . . . Tempus est numerus loci mutationis . . . *Tempus enim est numerus primi motus*' (*In Physic.* IV, 2, 219a 5, 220a 1, *lect.* 17, 18, §§574, 576, 589).

41. The interval between two full moons is 29½ days (cf. *Con.* II, xiv, 17), but this is the moon's 'synodic' period (see note 28). Its 'sidereal' period is 27 days and 8 hours, as is correctly stated in Sacrobosco's *Sphaera*, c. 1, ed. Thorndike, p. 79. Note that the mean figure of 50 minutes (clearly used by Dante) is always valid only at the equator. In Dante's latitude, at the time of the spring equinox, it is closer to 90 minutes.

42. *Purg.* VIII, 49–51; IX, 7–11; cf. II, 4.

43. *Inf.* XX, 124–9. All the times and intervals suggested are rough approximations. The moon rose, for Jerusalem, at 0605+0050=0655 p.m. The interval from moonrise to moonset is 1200+0025 hours. The moon therefore set, for Jerusalem, at 0655+1225=0720 a.m.

44. *Inf.* XXXIV, 96, 104–5, 112–14, 118. Dante's subsequent climb to the island of Purgatory must last a little less than a day, from approximately 7.30 a.m., local time, to between 4 a.m. and 5 a.m., local time – well before sunrise.

45. *Inf.* X, 79–80.

46. 'Ier più oltre cinqu' ore che quest' otta, / *mille dugento con sessanta sei / anni compié* che qui la via fu rotta' (*Inf.* XXI, 112–14). That earthquake, as we saw in Chapter 3, took place at the moment of Christ's death. Dante believed (*Con.* IV, xxiii, 10–11, 15) that

Christ was crucified on his thirty-fourth birthday: 1266+34=A.D. 1300. Buti and Bertagno (p. 90n) give a convenient list of the other main allusions to the year.

47. Modern calculations show that the moon was really full on Tuesday 5 April 1300 and on Friday 24 March 1301. In the latter year, the ecclesiastical calendar gave Monday 27 March as the date of the full moon; and Good Friday was celebrated on 31 March. See E. Moore 'The Date assumed by Dante for the Vision of the *Divina Commedia*', in *Studies in Dante*, vol. 3, pp. 144–76; Table I, p. 177.

48. The sun crosses the spring equinoctial point once every 365.2422 mean solar days, and this is the true length of the solar year. If the civic year always had the same number of days, the day of the equinox would either occur later and move *forward* in the calendar by roughly one day every four years (assuming that the number was 'rounded *down*' to 365), or it would occur earlier and move *backwards* by roughly three days every four years (assuming that the number was 'rounded *up*' to 366). The Julian calendar assumed that the solar year lasted *exactly* 365.25 days; and it was hoped to keep the equinox on 21 March by the simple expedient of inserting one extra day in the calendar every fourth year. But the Julian year is in fact too long by .0078, that is, a little less than twelve minutes. The Julian calendar therefore has the effect of 'rounding *up*' the fraction of a day by allowing too many leap years; and 'rounding *up*' means that the day of the equinox was pushed slowly *backwards* until it had reached 13 March in Dante's time. Dante was well aware of the phenomenon and its cause: see *Par.* XXVII, 142–4.

49. E. Moore, 'The Assumed Date', pp. 169–170.

50. *Ibid.*, p. 175.

51. 'La nostra [sc. vita] . . . procede a imagine di questo *arco, montando e discendendo.* E però che lo maestro de la nostra vita Aristotile s'accorse di questo *arco* di che ora si dice, parve volere che la *nostra vita non fosse altro che uno salire e uno scendere* . . . Là dove sia lo punto sommo di questo arco . . . è forte da sapere; ma ne li più io credo tra il trentesimo e quarantesimo anno, e io credo che *ne li perfettamente naturati* esso ne sia *nel trentacinque-simo anno.* E muovemi questa ragione: che *ottimamente naturato* fue lo nostro salvatore Cristo, lo quale *volle morire nel trentaquattresimo anno* de la sua etade . . . E ciò manifesta l'ora del giorno de la sua morte, ché volle quella *consimigliare con la vita sua*; onde dice Luca e che era quasi ora sesta quando morio, che è a dire lo colmo del die. Onde si può comprendere per quello "quasi" che al *trentacinquesimo anno di Cristo era lo colmo* de la sua *etade*' (*Con.* IV, xxiii, 6, 8–11).

52. *Rime* C, 67. *Inf.* I, 37–40. Once again Dante ignores the distinction between the *constellation* and the *sign* of Aries.

53. References in order: Argonauts, *Par.* XXXIII, 95 (for 'secoli', cf. *Purg.* XXI, 80; *Par.* VII, 29); Francis, *Par.* XI, 64–6; Crucifixion, *Inf.* XXI, 112–14 (cf. IV, 52–63); Adam, *Purg.* XXXIII, 61–3, *Par.* XXVI, 118–23. The last passage shows that Dante believed that in 1300 the world was only 6,498 years old (930+4,302+1,266).

54. *VN* II, 1. Even at the time of writing the *Vita Nuova* Dante had learnt a good deal from Alfraganus about the Arabian and Syrian calendars, and thus about other ways of counting the years; see *VN* XXIX, 1.

55. *Con.* II, ii, 1. The time indicated is 3 years, 2 months (1,168 days). For a discussion of the very complex dating problems posed by this periphrasis, see *Dante's Lyric Poetry*, ed. K. Foster and P. Boyde, vol. 2, pp. 346–8.

56. Wisdom 3.7; Matthew 13.43; 1 Corinthians 15.43. See G. Ferguson, *Signs and Symbols in Christian Art* (New York, 1954), p. 148; J. Hall, *Hall's Dictionary of Subjects and Symbols in Art* (London, 1974) *s.v. Halo.*

57. References in order: *Par.* III, 48, 59, 69, 109.

58. *Par.* VIII, 52–4; IX, 70–1. The tempering is described in *Par.* XXX, 46–60. After a

series of further transformations, described in lines 61–9, Dante can see the angels and the blessed distinctly at any distance.

59. The point of the last line in the simile is that there is no *essential* change, because the stars were believed to receive their light from the sun: 'del suo lume [sc. del sole] tutte l'altre stelle s'informano' (*Con.* II, xiii, 15; cf. *Par.* XVIII, 105; XXIII, 28–30). One of the fullest statements of the arguments in favour of this view will be found in St Albert's *De caelo*, II, ch. 6, *Et est digressio declarans qualiter stellae omnes illuminantur a sole* (the digression is occasioned by Aristotle's *De caelo* II, 7, 289a 34). Having considered five well-founded objections to the thesis, he continues: 'Sed quod hoc nullo modo sit verum, probant egregii viri in philosophia . . . Et *potior ratio* . . . est haec, quod *omne quod est in multis secundum unam rationem, primo est in uno aliquo* quod *est causa omnium illorum*, sicut omnium calidorum causa est ignis. *Lumen* ergo, quod est multiplicatum in caelo et multis modis est in luminibus caeli, *oportet, quod primo sit in uno*, quod est causa multitudinis huius. Ab illo autem quod est causa luminis, in omnibus causatur lumen. *Ergo oportet esse unum, a quo recipiatur lumen in omnibus quae lucent.* Hoc autem nihil ita convenienter ponitur sicut sol. *Ergo a sole lumen est in omnibus stellis* . . . Adhuc, hoc ipsum indicat nomen solis, quia dicitur "sol" quasi "solus lucens".'

Having noted that different stars receive the light in differing ways according to the degree of their 'nobility', St Albert insists: 'concedendum autem est absque dubio, quod haec receptio non est per reflexionem, sed potius . . . incorporatum est lumen stellis'.

60. *Par.* XIV, 97–9; XV, 13–21.

61. References in order: *Par.* XIV, 67–75; X, 42, 76, 78; XIII, 1–24.

62. 'E quale uomo terreno più degno fu di significare Iddio, che Catone? Certo nullo . . .' (*Con.* IV, xxviii, 15). 'E vita liber decedere maluit quam sine libertate manere in illa' (*Mon.* II, v, 15). When Dante is in this frame of mind he can speak of Cato's suicide as an *inenarrabile sacrifitium*. For Cato's 'rigida onestade', see *Con.* IV, vi, 9–10. For the 'vita pura' of Adam before the Fall, see *Purg.* XXVIII, 142; *Par.* XXVI, 139–40.

63. *Purg.* XXIX, 121–32; XXXI, 104–11.

64. *Purg.* I, 23; VIII, 85–7. In their discussion of the problems, Buti and Bertagno (*Commento*, pp. 124–7) assume that the constellations would have been lying east and west of the poles rather than 'above' and 'below'. On this view, the reason why Dante can no longer see the first constellation in the evening is that he has been moving round up the northern slopes of the mountain as he climbs, and so the mountain itself lies between him and the stars to the west of the pole. But, as the authors concede, this does not meet the objection as to why did Dante not see *both* constellations in the morning when his view was unimpeded.

7 The angels

1. *Purg.* VIII, 38, 53, 118; IX, 1–48, especially 7–9, 44.

2. *Purg.* IX, 62, 64–9, 73–84; cf. *Inf.* V, 4–6, 16–24; *Purg.* II, 30–48.

3. The same stress will be found in the protagonist's earlier sightings of angels: see *Inf.* IX, 64–90; *Purg.* II, 10–51; VIII, 22–42, 94–108.

4. The classic statement of this poetic is in *Par.* IV, 37–48.

5. Just as Dante displayed his acquaintance with the eye, the science of optics, and the behaviour of incident and reflected light in canto XV, 16–24, so here he shows his technical knowledge of the 'imagination', and of the ways in which images can be induced there by the power of an angel, as well as through the external organs of sensation; see XVII, 13–18, 22–5, 31–4, 43.

6. The meeting with the angel on the circle of Sloth is recounted, without any of the recurrent features being suppressed, in just three terzinas (XIX, 43–51), with the rapidity that characterizes all the events in that circle. The next is presented as a *fait accompli* with a Virgilian *Già era* in the opening two terzinas of canto XXII.

7. *Purg.* II, 10–51; VIII, 22–42, 94–108.

8. 'Disegnava uno *angelo* sopra certe *tavolette*; . . . ritornaimi a la mia opera, cioè del *disegnare figure d'angeli*' (*VN* XXXIV, I, 3).

9. 'Onde è da sapere che di tutte quelle cose che *lo 'ntelletto nostro vincono*, sì che non può vedere quello che sono, *convenevolissimo* trattare è per li loro effetti: onde di Dio, e *delle sustanze separate*, e de la prima materia, così trattando, *potemo avere alcuna conoscenza*' (*Con.* III, viii, 15).

10. 'Et ecce terrae motus factus est magnus. *Angelus enim Domini* descendit de caelo, et accedens revolvit lapidem, et *sedebat super eum*. Erat autem *aspectus* eius sicut *fulgur*, et *vestimentum* sicut nix.'

11. For general definitions, cf. Psalm 103.20–1: 'Benedicite Domino, *omnes angeli* eius, potentes virtute, *facientes verbum* illius . . . Benedicite Domino, omnes *virtutes* eius, *ministri* eius qui *facitis voluntatem eius.*' Hebrews 1.14: 'Nonne omnes [sc. angeli] sunt *administratorii spiritus, in ministerium missi* propter eos qui hereditatem capient salutis?' For the meaning of the Greek word (*angelus 'nuntius' dicitur*), cf. *Inf.* IX, 85; *Purg.* XXII, 78; XXX, 18. Angels appear in a dream, e.g. Matthew 1.20, 2.13, 19; in a vision, e.g. Acts 10.3–7; in person, e.g. Judges 13.3; Daniel 8.16; 9.21. The title 'legate' is used of Gabriel by Dante in *Con.* II, v, 4; cf. Daniel 8.16; 9.21; Luke 1.19, 26–38.

12. For the general definition, cf. Psalm 91.11: 'Quoniam *angelis* suis mandavit de te, ut *custodiant* te in omnibus viis tuis'. Exodus 23.20: 'Ecce ego mittam angelum meum, qui praecedat te, et *custodiat in via.*' Other references in order: 1 Kings 19.5; Matthew 4.11; Luke 22.43; Acts 27.23; Exodus 14.19; Daniel 3.25; 6.22; Acts 5.19; 12.7–11. For Raphael, see the Book of Tobit, *passim*. He appears in 3.25. He takes the name of Azarias (5.18). He finally reveals himself with the words: 'Ego enim sum Raphael angelus, unus ex septem qui adstamus ante Dominum' (12.15).

13. For angelic massacres, see: Joshua 5.13; 2 Samuel 24.16; 2 Kings 19.35; 2 Chronicles 32.21. For Michael, see Jude 9: 'Cum Michael archangelus cum diabolo disputans altercaretur de Moysi corpore' (the story is one of the models for *Purg.* V, 103–29). Revelation 12.7 is a prophecy, but it is treated as a past event in *Inf.* VII, 11–12. See also Revelation 20.1; Daniel 10.13, 12.1; cf. Zechariah 3.1 and 10.

14. Luke 16.22. Cf. *Rime* XX, 59–62; *Purg.* II, 28–51; 1 Chronicles 21.16.

15. Matthew 13.39–41; 24.31; 1 Thessalonians 4.16; 2 Thessalonians 1.7. Revelation, *passim*.

16. Angels in pairs: John 20.12; Acts 1.10. Angels in a group of three: Genesis 18 (they become two only in Genesis 19). Jacob's ladder is described as follows: 'Viditque in somnis *scalam stantem super terram, et cacumen illius tangens caelum; angelos* quoque *Dei* ascendentes et descendentes per eam' (Genesis 28.12; cf. John 1.51). The Vulgate version of the angels of the Nativity runs: 'Et ecce *angelus Domini* stetit iuxta illos, et *claritas* Dei *circumfulsit* illos . . . Et dixit illis angelus . . . "ecce enim evangelizo vobis gaudium magnum . . ." Et subito facta est cum angelo *multitudo militiae caelestis, laudantium* Deum et dicentium: "Gloria in altissimis Deo, et in terra pax hominibus bonae voluntatis" ' (Luke 2.9–14). Cf. also 'Dominus . . . apparuit . . . et cum eo *sanctorum millia*' (Deuteronomy 33.2).

17. For visions of the angels in heaven, see Psalm 148.2; Matthew 18.10; Hebrews 12.22; Revelation 4.8–11. For the other titles cf. Job 38.7; Psalms 29.1; 89.5–6. Cherubs are recorded as playing an active part in at least two important texts: Genesis 3.24 ('Eiecitque Adam, et *collocavit ante paradisum voluptatis Cherubim*, et flammeum *gla-*

dium'); and Ezekiel 28.14–16. The words quoted are used almost verbatim in the ordinary of the Mass. They run: 'Sanctus, sanctus, sanctus Dominus, Deus exercituum; plena est omnis terra gloria eius' (Isaiah 6.3: the words are spoken by the Seraphs). The angels are, says Dante, 'in lunghissimo numero', 'quasi innumerabili' (*Con.* II, v, 5; cf. iv, 14–15). The numbers quoted are from Daniel 7.10: 'Millia millium ministrabant ei, et decies millies centena millia assistebant ei' (cf. *Par.* XXIX, 134). See also Genesis 32.2; Matthew 26.53; Hebrews 12.22; Revelation 4.11; 9.16.

18. The angels clearly assume human form in the Book of Tobit (e.g. 5.5.); Genesis 18.2; 19.5; Mark 16.5. The whiteness of their clothing is specified in: 2 Mach. 11.8; John 20.12; Acts 1.10; Revelation 7.13–14; 15.6; 19.14, etc. They carry a sword in: Genesis 3.24; Numbers 22.23; Joshua 5.13; 1 Chronicles 21.16. The oscillation between the narrative conventions is most striking in Genesis 18, where it supports the traditional explanation that the three 'angels' are really a manifestation of the Trinity. See also: Exodus 3.2–6; 13.21 and 14.19; Judges 6.12 and 14; Acts 8.26, 29, 39.

19. 'Vidi *Dominum sedentem super solium excelsum* et elevatum; et ea quae sub ipso erant replebant templum. *Seraphim* stabant super illud: *sex alae* uni, et sex alae alteri: *duabus* velabant *faciem* eius, et *duabus* velabant *pedes* eius, et *duabus volabant*' (Isaiah 6.1–2). 'Et in medio eius *similitudo quatuor animalium*; et hic aspectus eorum, similitudo hominis in eis. *Quatuor facies* uni, et *quatuor pennae* uni. *Pedes* eorum, pedes recti . . . Et *manus* hominis sub pennis eorum . . .', etc. (Ezekiel 1.5–8; see also 10.4–14). The necessary mediation between the *animalia* of Ezekiel and the evangelists was provided by the clearer descriptions found in Revelation 4.6–8. Dante alludes explicitly to both books in *Purg.* XXIX, 100–5. Medieval art gave six wings to both Seraphs and Cherubs, distinguishing them by colour (red and blue respectively); cf. *Par.* IX, 77–8.

20. References in order: *Inf.* IX, 85; *Purg.* I, 98–9; II, 30; XV, 29; XVII, 55; XXX, 18.

21. References in order: the golden ladder, *Par.* XXI, 25–42, XXII, 100–11; the procession and pageant, *Purg*, XXIX, 43–105, esp. 100 and 105; Lot, Genesis 19.17. We reach the Song of Songs (5.9; 6.1, 13, etc.) via *Con.* II, v, 5 and *Purg.* XXX, 11.

22. Ezekiel 28.13–14. Dante quotes the beginning of the passage in *Epist.* XIII, 76, where he shows that he accepts the traditional interpretation by which the words are addressed to Lucifer (or Satan), and where he clearly refers the *coelum delitiarum Domini* to the Empyrean (not to the Earthly Paradise). But the association of 'Eden', 'cherub' and 'holy mountain' is certainly suggestive.

23. References in order: *Par.* IV, 40–8; Michael, *Inf.* VII, 11–12, *Purg.* XIII, 51, *Inf.* IX, 64–105; Gabriel, *Par.* IX, 138, XIV, 36–7, *Purg.* X, 34–40.

24. There is by no means universal agreement that the *amore angelico* of *Par.* XXIII is to be identified with Gabriel, but the weight of the evidence favours the identification. The second appearance comes in *Par.* XXXII, 94–114.

25. In the Vulgate the crucial texts read as follows: 'Neque mors, neque vita, neque *angeli*, neque *principatus*, neque *virtutes*, . . . neque creatura alia poterit nos separare a caritate Dei' (Romans 8.38–9); 'Supra omnem *principatum*, et *potestatem*, et *virtutem*, et *dominationem* . . . et omnia subiecit sub pedibus eius' (Ephesians 1.21–2); 'quoniam in ipso [sc. Filio] condita sunt universa in caelis et in terra, visibilia et invisibilia; sive *throni*, sive *dominationes*, sive *principatus*, sive *potestates*: omnia per ipsum, et in ipso creata sunt' (Colossians 1.16).

26. Acts 17.34.

27. All the texts and facts considered in this section will be found in *S.T.* 1a. 108, esp. a.5. In a.1 Aquinas correctly states the meaning and etymology of 'hierarchy' as *sacer principatus*.

28. 'Sic igitur *Dionysius* exponit ordinum nomina *secundum convenientiam ad spirituales*

345

perfectiones eorum. *Gregorius* vero, in expositione horum nominum, *magis attendere videtur exteriora ministeria*' (*S.T.* 1a. 108, 5, resp.). 'Superiores angeli habent *universaliorem cognitionem veritatis* quam inferiores' (*ibid.*, a.1., resp.). '*Prima* hierarchia accipit rationes rerum *in ipso Deo*; *secunda* vero in *causis universalibus*; *tertia* vero secundum determinationem ad *speciales effectus* (*ibid.*, a.6, resp.; see also *C.G.* III, 80, esp. §2554). Aquinas quotes Dionysius (ch. 3 §2; PG 3, 165): 'ordo hierarchiae est alios quidem purgari, et illuminari et perfici, alios autem *purgare* et *illuminare* et *perficere*' (*ibid.*, a. 1, resp.).

29. Aquinas again quotes Dionysius (ch. 7 §1; PG 3, 205): 'Propria nomina singulorum ordinum proprietates eorum designant' (*ibid.*, a.5, resp.: cf. *VN* XIII, 4).

30. 'Nomen *Seraphim* . . . imponitur . . . a caritatis excessu, quem importat nomen *ardoris* vel *incendii* . . . Similiter etiam nomen *Cherubim* imponitur a quodam excessu scientiae; unde interpretatur *plenitudo scientiae*' (*ibid.*, a.5, ad 5). 'Cherubim vero supereminenter divina secreta cognoscunt' (*ibid.*, a.6, resp.; cf. *C.G.* III, 80, §§2550–1).

'In rebus humanis est aliquod *bonum commune*, quod quidem est *bonum civitatis vel gentis*, quod videtur ad *Principatuum* ordinem pertinere . . . Est etiam *aliquod humanum bonum*, quod non in communitate consistit, sed *ad unum aliquem* pertinet secundum seipsum, *non tamen uni soli utilia* sed multis; sicut quae sunt ab omnibus et singulis credenda et observanda . . . Et hoc ad *Archangelos* pertinet, de quibus Gregorius dicit, quod "*summa* nuntiant" . . . Quoddam vero humanum bonum est ad unumquemque singulariter pertinens. Et huiusmodi ad ordinem pertinent *Angelorum*, de quibus Gregorius dicit quod "*infima* nuntiant" . . . ' (*C.G.* III, 80, §§2559–61, making more explicit the ideas in *S.T.* 1a. 108, 6, resp.).

'Et quia *Deus* est finis creaturarum sicut *dux est finis exercitus* . . . potest aliquid simile huius ordinis considerari *in rebus humanis*; nam quidam sunt qui hoc habent dignitatis, ut per seipsos *familiariter accedere possunt ad regem* vel *ducem* . . . etc.' 'In executione autem cuiuslibet actus, sunt *quidam* quasi *incipientes actionem et alios ducentes*, sicut in cantu praecentores, et *in bello illi qui alios ducunt et dirigunt*' (*S.T.* 1a. 108, 6, resp.).

31. St Gregory proposed two orderings, both different from that of Dionysius. Dante, following Brunetto Latini's *Tresor* I, 12, chose the less common, viz.: Seraphs, Cherubs, *Powers*; Principalities, Virtues, Dominions; *Thrones*, Archangels, Angels; cf. *Par.* IX, 61. See the article *Gerarchia angelica* in the *Enciclopedia dantesca*.

32. *Par.* XXVIII, 102–11, confirming what was said in *Con.* II, v, 9: 'li Serafini, che veggiono più de la Prima Cagione che nulla angelica natura'.

33. See Kenelm Foster, 'Order in Paradise X' and 'The Son's Eagle: Paradise XIX', now in *The Two Dantes* (London, 1978), pp. 121–2 and 140.

34. References in order: *Par.* XXIX, 49–51, 55–7; *Inf.* VIII, 82–3; *Purg.* XII, 25–7; *Con.* II, v, 12; *Inf.* VII, 11–12; XXXIV, 28, 127; VII, 1.

35. References in order: *Con.* II, v, 12, *Inf.* XXXIV, 46–51; XXVII, 113. The military terminology is suggested by Matthew 26.53; *Inf.* XXI, 120; XXII, 1–12, 94.

36. The early appearance is of the 'more than a thousand who were "rained" from heaven', and who try to prevent Dante and Virgil from entering the city of Dis (*Inf.* VIII, 82–117). Charon is called a *demonio* (*Inf.* III, 109), but the guardians of the upper circles are drawn from classical mythology: Cerberus, Pluto, Phlegyas, the Minotaur, the Centaurs, the Harpies. Description of the penultimate circle does, however, begin in canto XVIII, that is, only just over half-way through the narrative.

37. References in order: outward appearance, *Inf.* XVIII, 35, XXI, 33–4, XXIII, 35–6; premature collection of souls, *Inf.* XXXIII, 139–47; the two Montefeltros, *Purg.* V, 85–129, *Inf.* XXVII, 61–129.

346

38. The devils as tormentors: *Inf.* XVIII, 35–81; XXI, 55–7, 71, 75, 86, etc. The devils of the fifth bolgia: *Inf.* XXI, 58–XXIII, 57.

39. For Lucifer before and after his fall, *Purg.* XII, 25–7; *Par.* XXIX, 56–7; *Inf.* XXXIV, 34, 108, 121. For the colours, one must set texts like *Purg.* XXIX, 121–9, XXX, 31–3, and *Par.* XXXI, 13–15 against *Inf.* XXXIV, 37–45. For the sinister connotations of the Italian 'vermiglio', see: *Inf.* III, 134; VIII, 72. For the 'wind', one must contrast *Purg.* XXIV, 145–50, XI, 6, and *Par.* IV, 35–6, XIV, 76, XVI, 28–9 with *Inf.* XXXIV, 4–9, 50–2.

40. For Dante's use of these other names, see: *Con.* II, ii, 7; iv, 2, 4, 15; *Mon.* I, iii, 7; *Par.* II, 129–31, 136; IX, 61; XIII, 59; XXVIII, 78; XXIX, 32, 76, 144.

41. Lucan, *Bellum civile* IX, 580, quoted in *Epist.* XIII, 63. Modern texts have 'quod*cunque*' for the second 'quocunque'; and J. D. Duff translates the line as: 'All that we see is God; every motion we make is God also.'

42. *Metaphysics* XII, 8, esp. 1074b 1–15, is particularly relevant to this chapter. For Dante's interpretation of the story of Orpheus, see *Con.* II, i, 3.

43. References in order: *Inf.* I, 72; *Con.* II, iv, 6–7; *Par.* IV, 62–3; VIII, 1–12.

44. See the objections considered by Aquinas in *S.T.* 1a. 50, 1–2.

45. See *S.T.* 1a. 52–3.

46. The angels' incorporeality and incorruptibility are established by Aquinas in the first *quaestio* devoted to the angels in the *Summa Theologiae* (1a. 50, 1 and 5). Dante's acceptance of both points makes it likely that he would have followed Aquinas in his contention that every angel constitutes a different species (*ibid.*, a.4). If an angel cannot die, there is no need of a multiplicity of individuals to ensure the survival of the species; and God does nothing in vain. And if the angels are *substantiae separatae*, they cannot be individuated and differentiated by their 'material cause' (as is the case with all species existing on earth); they must therefore be differentiated by their 'formal cause'; and every difference in the formal cause entails a difference of species. Dante does not make these points explicitly; but he does suggest that even individual human beings are so different one from another that they almost seem to belong to distinct species; and he does insist that the angels seen in the Empyrean are 'distinct in kind and in brightness' – 'ciascun distinto di fulgore e d'arte' (*Par.* XXXI, 132; cf. XXIX, 137–8).

For the angels' intellect and will, see: *Mon.* I, iii, 7; *Par.* I, 118–20; V, 19–24; XXIX, 72.

47. Cf. *Con.* III, iii, 11.

48. ' "Intellectus" et "ratio" differunt quantum ad modum cognoscendi, quia scilicet *intellectus* cognoscit *simplici intuitu*, *ratio* vero discurrendo de uno in aliud' (*S.T.* 1a. 59, 1, ad 1). 'Sic igitur patet quod ex eodem provenit quod *intellectus noster intelligit discurrendo, et componendo et dividendo*; ex hoc scilicet quod non statim in prima apprehensione alicuius primi apprehensi, potest inspicere quidquid in eo virtute continetur . . . Unde cum in angelo sit lumen intellectuale perfectum, cum sit "speculum purum et clarissimum", ut dicit Dionysius, . . . *relinquitur* quod *angelus, sicut non intelligit ratiocinando*, ita non intelligit componendo et dividendo' (*ibid.*, 58, 4, resp.). 'Sunt igitur aliquae *substantiae perfectae intellectuales* in natura intellectuali, *non indigentes acquirere scientiam a sensibilibus rebus*' (*ibid.*, 51, 1, resp.).

For Dante's description of the angels' mode of intellection, see *Con.* III, vi, 5–6. The following passages, strictly descriptive of the blessed in the Empyrean, may also be applied to the angels: *Par.* III, 32–3; VIII, 85–90; IX, 20–1, 73–81, XVII, 36–45; XXI, 83–90. *Sine interpolatione* occurs in *Mon.* I, iii, 7.

49. Psalm 8.6 translated by Dante in *Con.* IV, xix, 7.

50. More precisely: 'inclinantur ad bonum cum *cognitione* qua *cognoscunt ipsam boni rationem*, . . . *quasi inclinata[e] in ipsum universale bonum*' (*S.T.* 1a. 59, 1, resp.).

51. All 'intelligent creatures' (angels and men) have the divine gift of freedom in the

will (*Par.* V, 19–24). For 'inquisition', cf.: 'Ipse intellectus dicitur "ratio", inquantum *per inquisitionem* quamdam pervenit ad cognoscendum intelligibilem veritatem' (*In De anima* III, 9, 432b 28, *lect.* 14, §812).

52. This paragraph is a paraphrase of *Par.* XXVIII, 106–14; XXIX, 49–66; *Mon.* I, xii, 5: 'Et hinc etiam patere potest quod *substantiae intellectuales*, quaram sunt *inmutabiles voluntates*, necnon animae separatae bene hinc abeuntes, *libertatem arbitrii ob immutabilitatem voluntatis non amictunt*, sed perfectissime atque potissime hoc retinent.'

53. The same concern was already evident in the earlier chapters devoted to the heavens (*Con.* II, ii–iii); and it is particularly marked in iv, 2, 8, and v, 1.

54. In the passage from the first book (I, 3), Aristotle is studiously vague, referring in the neuter plural to 'quae ibi sunt apta nata esse' (279a 19–22). But Aquinas is probably correct in his commentary: 'convenientius est quod *hoc intelligatur de Deo et de substantiis separatis*, quae manifeste neque tempore neque loco continentur, cum sint separatae ab omni magnitudine et motu' (§213). In the second book, he says: 'Caelum autem est animatum, et habet principium motus' (*In De caelo* II, 2, 285a 30, *lect.* 3, §314). Dante will come very close to this formulation in *Par.* II, 130–44. The proposition was condemned by Bishop Tempier of Paris in 1277, but, as Aquinas goes on to observe: 'Nec multum refert, quantum ad hunc modum movendi, utrum moveatur a substantia spirituali *coniuncta* quae dicatur *anima* eius, vel tantum a substantia spirituali *separata* . . .' (§315).

55. 'Praeter *simplicem motum localem universi*, qui est motus diurnus, quo totum caelum revolvitur, et est uniformis, et est simplicissimus, *quem motum causat prima substantia immobilis*, videmus aliquos motus locales planetarum, qui etiam sunt sempiterni . . . Unde necesse est quod *quilibet horum motuum* moveatur a motore per se immobili et a *substantia sempiterna* . . . Unde manifestum est quod necesse est, *quot sunt lationes astrorum, tot esse substantias* . . . Manifestum est igitur, quod *sunt aliquae substantiae immateriales secundum numerum motuum astrorum*, et quod earum etiam ordo est secundum ordinem eorumdem motuum' (*In Meta.* XII, 8, 1073a 30, *lect.* 9, §§2556–7).

56. See *Republic* VI, 508–9 (Plato there considers the 'form' of the Good to be supreme. Plotinus would later identify the 'forms' of the Good and the One); *Timaeus*, 30, 40–1, especially 41 C.

57. A. H. Armstrong, ed., *The Cambridge History of Later Greek and Earlier Medieval Philosophy* (Cambridge, 1967), pp. 250–6. J. M. Rist, *Plotinus, The Road to Reality* (Cambridge, 1967), pp. 118–19.

58. Armstrong, *Cambridge History*, pp. 297–301.

59. See, in particular, the tenth of the thirty-two propositions contained in the work, quoted by Dante in *Epist.* XIII, 61. The pioneering study of Dante's knowledge and use of the *De causis* is that by Bruno Nardi: 'Le citazioni dantesche del *Liber de causis*', now in *Saggi di filosofia dantesca* (2nd edn, Florence, 1967), pp. 81–109; see also the *Enciclopedia dantesca, s.v.*

60. Avicenna combines early Aristotle and late Aristotle by assigning a 'soul' *and* an 'intelligence' to each heaven; while he takes from Platonism the idea that 'le Intelligenze de li cieli sono *generatrici* di quelli' (*Con.* II, iv, 5). The 'agent intellect' will reappear in the last chapter. For the moment we may note that Avicenna's account of the *intellectus agens* is significantly close to the description of 'Fortuna' that Dante puts into the mouth of Virgil in *Inferno* VII, esp. lines 77–8, 86–8, 95–6.

Aquinas quotes from and summarizes Avicenna's theory in several places, e.g. ' "*Deus* intelligendo se *produxit intelligentiam primam*, in qua, quia non est suum esse, ex necessitate incidit compositio potentiae et actus . . ." Sic igitur *prima intelligentia*, inquantum intelligit causam primam, *produxit secundam intelligentiam*; inquantum autem intelligit se secundum quod est in potentia, *produxit corpus caeli*, quod movet; inquantum vero intelligit se secundum illud quod habet de actu *produxit animam caeli*' (*S.T.* 1a. 47, 1, resp.). A similar passage in his Commentary to *Metaphysics* XII, 8 concludes: 'Secundum autem quod [intelligentia] intelligit suum principium, *causat intelligentiam sequentem*, quae movet *inferiorem orbem, et deinceps usque ad sphaeram lunae*' (§2559). And a little later, he explains: 'Lunae autem proprie competit immutatio materiae, et dispositio ipsius ad recipiendum omnes impressiones caelestes: et propter hoc videtur quasi esse deferens impressiones caelestes, et applicans inferiori materiae' (§2561).

61. *Con.* II, iv, 8–17; v, 4.

62. The description of the circles is given in *Par.* XXVIII, 22–39. Only later, at lines 90–3, is it made clear that they are made up of *scintille* whose number 'più che 'l doppiar de li scacchi s'inmilla'.

63. 'E ciascheduno / più tardo si movea, secondo ch'era / in numero distante più da l'uno' (33–6).

64. 'Da quel punto / *depende* il *cielo* e *tutta* la *natura*' (*Par.* XXVIII, 41–2). Moerbeke's translation has; 'Ex tali igitur principio *dependet caelum et natura*'; *Metaphysics* XII, 7, 1072b 14. Aquinas's paraphrase (§2534) adds '*tota natura*'.

65. The most important lines are quoted below. The gist of the argument will be found in this short paragraph: 'Sic igitur quanto corpus caeleste est *superius*, tanto habet *universaliorem, diuturniorem* et *potentiorem effectum*. Et cum corpora caelestia sint quasi instrumenta substantiarum separatarum moventium, sequitur quod *substantia quae movet superiorem orbem sit universalioris conceptionis et virtutis*; et per consequens oportet quod sit *nobilior*' (*In Meta.* XII, 8, 1073a 30, lect. 9, §2562). Cf. further *Par.* II, 113–14.

66. Dante makes some very characteristic additions to the opening of the Lord's Prayer: 'O Padre nostro che *ne' cieli stai*, / *non circunscritto, ma per più amore* / ch'ai primi effetti di là sù tu hai' (*Purg.* XI, 1–3).

67. 'Dintorno al punto che mi vinse, / parendo *inchiuso* da quel ch'elli 'nchiude' (*Par.* XXX, 11–12).

68. *Theologicae regulae*, no. 7.

8 Images of God as maker

1. '*Derisibile* est, si quis putet aliquid *planum* dixisse, dicens *mare esse sudorem terrae*, et ob hoc esse salsum, sicut Empedocles dixit. Forte enim sufficienter dixit, si intendit *metaphorice* dicere, *secundum modum poeticum: dicere enim aliquid per metaphoras pertinet ad poetas*, et probabile est quod Empedocles, qui *metrice scripsit*, ut dicitur, *multa metaphorice* protulerit. Sed tamen sic aliquid dicere non sufficit ad cognoscendam naturam rei: quia *res naturalis per similitudinem quae assumitur in metaphora, non est manifesta*' (*In Meteor.* II, 3, 357a 25, lect. 5, §167).

The principal target for Aristotle's reprimands on this score is Plato. As Aquinas notes: 'isti poetae et philosophi, *et praecipue Plato*, non sic intellexerunt secundum quod sonat secundum superficiem verborum; sed *suam sapientiam* volebant *quibusdam fabulis et aenigmaticis locutionibus occultare*' (*In De caelo* I, 10, 279b 15, lect. 22, §228; cf. further §298). 'Sciendum tamen est quod Aristoteles hic loquitur contra *Platonem, qui talibus metaphoricis locutionibus utebatur*, assimilans materiam matri et feminae, et formam masculo' (*In Physic.* I, 9, 192a 22, lect. 15, §138); cf. further *In Meta.* I, 3, 983b 28, lect. 4, §§83–4; VII, 11, 1036b 25, lect. 11, §1518.

2. 'Multa namque per intellectum videmus quibus *signa vocalia desunt*: quod satis Plato insinuat in suis libris *per assumptionem metaphorismorum*; multa enim per lumen intellectuale vidit quae *sermone proprio nequivit exprimere*' (*Epist.* XIII, 84).

3. Aquinas covers similar ground in this passage: 'Est autem naturale homini ut per

sensibilia ad intelligibilia veniat, quia *omnis nostra cognitio a sensu initium habet*. Unde convenienter in Sacra Scriptura traduntur nobis *spiritualia sub metaphoris corporalium* . . . Non enim cum Scriptura nominat Dei "brachium" est litteralis sensus quod in Deo sit membrum huiusmodi corporale, sed . . . virtus operativa' (*S.T.* 1a. 1, 9, resp.; 10 ad 3). This stress on man's dependence on images goes back to Aristotle: '*Sine sensu non potest* aliquis homo *addiscere* quasi de novo acquirens scientiam, *neque intelligere*, quasi utens scientia habita. Sed oportet, *cum aliquis speculatur* in actu, quod simul formet sibi aliquod *phantasma*. Phantasmata enim sunt similitudines sensibilium . . . Postquam aliquis acquisivit habitum scientiae, *necesse est ad hoc quod speculetur, quod utatur phantasmate*' (*In De anima* III, 8, 432a 3–10, *lect.* 13, §§791–2).

This proposition was most often quoted in the form: 'Nihil in intellectu quod non fuerit prius in sensu'. Aquinas's own stricter formulation runs: 'Intellectus autem noster possibilis secundum statum praesentis vitae est natus informari similitudinibus rerum materialium a phantasmatibus abstractis; et ideo cognoscit magis materialia quam substantias immateriales' (*S.T.* 1a. 88, 1, ad 2).

In this same important *quaestio*, Aquinas quotes Dionysius to the effect that 'non est possibile *humanae menti* ad *immaterialem illam* sursum excitari caelestium hierarchiarum *contemplationem, nisi secundum se materiali manuductione utatur*'. But he himself adds the qualification: 'Ex rebus materialibus ascendere possumus *in aliqualem cognitionem* immaterialium rerum, *non tamen in perfectam* . . . *Similitudines*, si quae a materialibus accipiuntur ad immaterialia intelligenda, *sunt multum dissimiles*, ut Dionysius dicit' (*S.T.* 1a. 88, 2, ob. 1 and ad 1).

4. 'Lumen autem actus est huiusmodi diaphani, secundum quod est diaphanum' (Aristotle, *De anima* II, 7, 418b 9). 'Prima substantiarum est lux' (*Liber de intelligentiis*, prop. 6). 'Formam primam corporalem quam quidam corporeitatem vocant, lucem esse arbitror' (Grosseteste, *De luce seu de inchoatione formarum*, opening words, quoted by B. Nardi, *Saggi di filosofia dantesca*, p. 203n. 'Lux est qualitas activa consequens formam substantialem solis, vel cuiuscumque alterius coporis a se lucentis, si aliquod aliud tale est' (*S.T.* 1a. 67, 3, resp.: the whole *quaestio* forms a convenient introduction to the subject).

5. See Schütz, *Thomaslexikon, s.vv. lumen, lux*. For the relevance of these metaphorical 'lights' to the *Comedy*, see C. S. Singleton, *Journey to Beatrice* (Harvard U.P., 1958) ch. 2, 'The Three Lights'.

6. In the *Comedy*, Dante rather ostentatiously airs his knowledge of some of the more elementary propositions – for example, that the angle of reflexion is equal to the angle of incidence (*Purg.* XV, 16–24; *Par.* I, 49–50; cf. II, 85–105). It has been plausibly suggested that one of the unwritten books of the *Convivio* would have been largely given over to a treatise on 'Perspective' (A. Parronchi, 'La perspettiva dantesca', *Studi danteschi*, 36 (1959), pp. 5–103; see p. 44). The treatise would have taken the form of a commentary to Dante's *canzone, Amor, che movi tua vertù da cielo* (*Rime*, XC).

7. *De luce seu de inchoatione formarum*, ed. L. Baur (Münster, 1912), p. 51.

8. 'Nullo sensibile in tutto lo mondo è più degno di farsi essemplo di Dio che 'l sole' (*Con.* III, xii, 7). Cf. Plato, *Republic*, 508–9. The usage is biblical (Isaiah 60.19; Wisdom 5.6). 'Sed Dionysius dicit, IV cap. *De div. nom.*, quod *radius solaris maxime habet similitudinem divinae bonitatis*. Ergo est ad imaginem Dei' (*S.T.* 1a. 93, 2, ob. 2; Aquinas will accept the comparison only 'quantum ad causalitatem', *ibid.*, ad 2; see further *S.T.Suppl.*, 69, 1, ad 2).

9. References in order: 'luce etterna', 'lume reflesso', *Par.* XXXIII, 124 and 128; 'punto', XXVIII, 16 and 41–2. For New Testament allusions to God as light, see John 1.4–5, 9; Revelation 21.23; 22.5.

10. *Liber de intelligentiis*, prop. 6, quoting Augustine, *Super Genesim ad litt.* IV, 28; cf. *S.T.* 1a. 67, 3, resp.

11. *Par.* XXIX, 136; XIX, 89–90.

12. *S.T.* 1a. 67, 2, resp.; 45, 3, ad 3.

13. 'Diligis enim omnia quae sunt . . . Quomodo autem posset *aliquid permanere* nisi tu voluisses? aut quod a te vocatum non esset *conservaretur*' (Wisdom 11.25–6). '*Nulla alia* est rerum omnium sensibilium et intelligibilium *subsistentia* praeter divinae bonitatis *illuminationem* et *diffusionem*' (John Scotus, *Expositiones super 'Ierarchiam caelestem'*, 1, P.L. 122, 127). 'Sic autem se habet omnis creatura ad Deum, sicut aer *ad solem illuminantem* . . . Conservatio rerum a Deo non est per aliquam novam actionem, sed *per continuationem actionis qua dat esse*' (*S.T.* 1a. 104, 1, resp. and ad 4). 'La *divina bontade* in tutte le cose discende, *e altrimenti essere non potrebbero*'; 'ratio manifestat divinum *lumen*, id est *divinam bonitatem*, sapientiam et virtutem, *resplendere* ubique' (*Con.* III, vii, 2, glossed by *Epist.* XIII, 61).

14. *Par.* I, 111, cf. 1–3. Apart from the references given in note 16, cf. '*Quanto magis* creaturae intellectuales *distant* a primo principio, *tanto magis dividitur illud lumen et diversificatur*, sicut accidit *in lineis a centro egredientibus*' (*S.T.*, 1a. 89, 1, resp.).

15. For St Bonaventure's appearance in the *Paradiso*, see XII, 28–145. The texts translated are: '*Propriissime . . . Deus lux* est, et quae ad ipsum magis accedunt, plus habent de natura lucis . . . Corpora mundi, secundum quod *plus et minus participant de luce*, sunt *magis* et *minus nobilia* . . . Lux est forma substantialis corporum, secundum cuius *maiorem et minorem participationem corpora habent verius* et *dignius* esse in genere entium. Unde *nobilissimum corporum*, sicut est *empyreum* illud, *est praecipue luminosum*, infimum vero, sicut terra, maxime est opacum, *intermedia vero secundum quod sunt magis et minus nobiliora, participant plus et minus* . . . Lux, cum sit forma nobilissima inter corporalia . . .' (quoted from B. Nardi, *Saggi di filosofia dantesca*, pp. 202–3).

16. *Con.* III, vii, 3–5. *In De sensu* 3, 439a 20, *lect.* 6, §84–6. *Par.* XXXI, 22–3.

17. See Chapter 6, note 59.

18. References in order: *Par.* XXX, 100–8; XXIX, 136–45, 64–6; II, 112–48; *Epist.* XIII, 60.

19. 'Et cum omnis vis *causandi* sit *radius* quidam *influens* a prima causa quae Deus est . . . Sic, mediate vel inmediate, omne quod habet esse habet esse ab eo; quia ex eo quod causa secunda recipit a prima, *influit* super causatum *ad modum recipientis et reddentis radium* . . . Patet quod omnis essentia et virtus procedat a prima, et intelligentiae inferiores recipiant quasi a *radiante*, et *reddant radios* superioris ad suum inferius *ad modum speculorum*. Quod satis aperte tangere videtur Dionysius de Caelesti Hierarchia loquens . . . Patet ergo quomodo ratio manifestat *divinum lumen*, id est divinam bonitatem, sapientiam et virtutem, *resplendere* ubique' (*Epist.* XIII, 70, 56, 60–1).

20. 'Licet causa prima non sit *causa impedibilis*, ipsa tamen producit *effectus inferiores per causas medias* et non *immediate*; quae causae mediae, licet accipiant ex ordine causae primae quod producant effectus et tunc et quod non impeditae, *non tamen quin in natura sint impedibiles*; et sic, quamvis causa prima non sit impedibilis, *producit tamen effectum per causam impedibilem*, propter quod ille effectus, etiam relatus in causam primam, *non necessario fuit* futurus antequam esset' (Sigier of Brabant (attrib.), *De necessitate et contingentia causarum*, quoted by B. Nardi, *Saggi di filosofia dantesca*, p. 48).

21. 'Quindi discende a l'ultime potenze / giù d'atto in atto, *tanto divenendo* [i.e. becoming so weakened] / che *più non fa* che *brevi contingenze*; / e queste contingenze essere intendo / le cose generate . . .' (*Par.* XIII, 61–5).

22. 'Quidam posuerunt *gradatim* res a Deo processisse: ita scilicet quod *ab eo immediate processit prima creatura, et illa produxit aliam*, et sic inde usque ad creaturam corpoream' (*S.T.* 1a. 65, 3, resp.). 'Quidam vero *attribuerunt distinctionem rerum secundis agentibus.*

351

Sicut Avicenna, qui dixit quod "Deus intelligendo se produxit intelligentiam primam, in qua, quia non est suum esse, ex necessitate incidit compositio potentiae et actus . . ." Sic igitur *prima intelligentia* . . . produxit *secundam intelligentiam* . . . [et] *corpus caeli* . . . [et] *animam caeli.* Sed hoc non potest stare . . . quia secundum hanc positionem, non *proveniret ex intentione primi agentis* universitas rerum, sed *ex concursu multarum causarum agentium.* Tale autem dicimus provenire *a casu.* Sic igitur *complementum universi, quod in diversitate rerum consistit,* esset *a casu;* quod est impossible' (47, 1, resp.). For the *secundorum agentium ordo,* see *C.G.* II, 42. For the image of a message amplified and distorted as it passes from mouth to mouth, see *Con.* I, iii, 7–10. For 'le secondarie cagioni' as causes of diversity, see *Con.* III, ii, 4.

23. Aquinas expounds and refutes these views in *S.T.* 1a. 46, 1–3.

24. 'Lux inter omnia apprehensioni est maxime delectabile' (*Liber de intelligentiis,* prop. 12). 'Et videt Deus lucem quod esset *bona*' (Genesis 1.4).

25. Dionysius, *De divinis nominibus,* ch. 4, quoted in *C.G.* I, 37, §307; III, 24, §2053.

26. Revelation 21.6; 22.1; *Par.* XXXIII, 12; XXXI, 93.

27. The Latin spelling is given to avoid quoting both the Latin and the Italian forms; but the verbs are quoted in the infinitive rather than the first person singular of the present indicative. For *descendere/discendere* as a verb of 'flowing', *Inf.* V, 98; *Par.* I, 138; XVII, 42, etc. Rivers 'flow', because water 'descends' to seek its 'natural place'.

28. *Purg.* XV, 132. 'Siquidem ex *fonte totum flumen* . . . manat, et per eius *alveum aqua,* quae primo surgit in *fonte,* in *quantamcunque longitudinem* protendatur, *semper* ac sine ulla intermissione *defunditur.* Sic divina bonitas, et essentia, et vita, . . . quae in *fonte* omnium sunt . . . *defluunt* . . . et . . . *decurrunt* . . .' (*De div. nat.* III, 4, P.L. 122, 632).

In his *Anticlaudianus,* VI, 234–49 Alan of Lille makes play with *fons, rivus* and *flumen* as images of the Trinity ('cum sint diversi, *fons, rivus, flumen,* in *unum* / conveniunt *eademque* trium *substancia* . . .' lines 245–6). He then passes immediately to light imagery used in the same way (*sol, radius* and *calor,* lines 250–72).

29. *Mon.* III, xvi, 15; *Par.* I, 113.

30. Revelation 21.6; 22.13; *Epist.* XIII, 90.

31. Cf. 'Però ne la giustizia sempiterna / la vista che riceve il vostro mondo, / com' occhio per *lo mare,* entro s'interna; / che, ben che da la *proda veggia il fondo,* / in *pelago* nol vede; e nondimeno / è li, ma cela lui *l'esser profondo*' (*Par.* XIX, 58–63); 'mai creatura / non pinse l'occhio infino a la *prima onda*' (*ibid.,* XX, 119–20).

32. Light imagery can also exemplify this process, since the 'secondo raggio' of reflected light can '*risalire* in suso / pur come *pelegrin* che *tornar* vuole' (*Par.* I, 49–51).

33. References in order: *Par.* III, 89–90; XXIV, 135; *Rime* C, 67–8; *Par.* VII, 67 and 70; *Par.* XXVII, 111; *Par.* XXV, 78.

34. References in order: *Mon.* II, ii, 2–3 ('*fluitans* materia'); *Inf.* II, 108; *Par.* XIV, 27; *Purg.* XXXI, 91–105; XXXIII, 127–9.

35. Cf. *Par.* II, 23–4; V, 91–2; *Inf.* XVII, 136.

36. Cf. *Con.* IV, xxii, 2–3; *Epist.* I, 6; *Par.* XIII, 105; XXVI, 24.

37. 'Deus *nihil* facit *frustra,* quia, cum sit agens per intellectum, agit *propter finem.* Similiter etiam natura nihil facit frustra, quia agit sicut mota a Deo velut a primo movente; sicut *sagitta non movetur frustra,* inquantum *emittitur a sagittante* ad aliquid certum' (*In De caelo* I, 4, 271a 32, *lect.* 8, §91). The comparison will be found in Aristotle's *Ethics* I, 1 1094a 24; and not infrequently in Aquinas's own works.

38. *In Meta.* X, 1. 1052b 25, *lect.* 2, §1939.

39. Aristotle gave repeated warnings about the danger of confusing the two main senses of 'one': 'unum quod est principium numeri', and 'unum quod convertitur cum ente'; but

his words fell on deaf ears. See *In Meta.* III, 4–5, *lect.* 12 and 13, §§489, 499, 501, 514; *Metaphysics* XIII–XIV, *passim*.

40. *De divina natura* III, 5, P.L. 122, 637, In the response of one article, Aquinas brings together relevant texts from St Paul, Aristotle and Plato, as well as developing his own line of argument. St Paul is quoted as saying: ' "ex ipso, et per ipsum, et in ipso sunt omnia" [Romans 11.36]. Respondeo . . . Necesse est igitur quod omnia quae diversificantur secundum diversam participationem essendi, ut sint perfectius vel minus perfecte, causari *ab uno primo ente*, quod perfectissime est. Unde et Plato dixit quod necesse est *ante omnem multitudinem ponere unitatem*. Et Aristoteles dicit, in II *Metaph.* [993b 25] quod "*id quod est maxime ens* et maxime verum, *est causa omnis entis* et omnis veri"; sicut "id quod maxime calidum est, est causa omnis caliditatis" ' (*S.T.* 1a. 44, 1, resp.).

41. 'In VIII *Metaphys.* Philosophus dicit quod *species rerum sunt sicut numeri*, qui specie diversificantur secundum additionem unius super alterum (*In De causis*, lect. 4, §115: cf. *S.T.* 1a. 76, 3, resp.; *C.G.* II, 44, §1211; *In De sensu* ch. 4, *lect.* 10, §137, where the subject is 'formae substantiales rerum').

Aristotle's remark occurs in *Metaphysics* VIII, 3, 1043b 33 as part of a critique of Pythagoras and Plato, in particular of their belief that numbers were the elements of things.

42. 'Quod autem est *propinquius Ei* quod est per se unum *est magis unitum*, quasi magis participans unitatem. Unde Intelligentia quae est *propinquissima* Causae primae *habet esse maxime unitum*' (*In De causis*, lect. 4, §103). 'Ita vero suis quisque numeri proprietatibus terminatur, ut *nullus eorum par esse cuicumque alteri possit*' (Isidore, *Et.* III, ix, 2). 'Mensura autem nihil aliud est quam *id quo quantitas rei cognoscitur. Quantitas* vero rei cognoscitur *per unum aut numerum*. . . Ulterius autem *omnis numerus cognoscitur per unum*, eo quod unitas aliquoties sumpta quemlibet numerum reddit. Unde relinquitur quod *omnis quantitas cognoscatur per unum* . . . Unde sequitur, quod ipsum unum, quod est *prima mensura*, sit principium numeri . . .' (*In Meta.* X, 1, 1052b 20, lect. 2, §§1938–9; cf. also §1944).

43. '*Numerus* nihil aliud est quam *pluralitas* et *multitudo* mensurabilis uno. Alio modo dicitur multum absolute . . . et sic *multum opponitur uni*, non autem pauco' (*In Meta.* X, 6, 1057a 1–5, *lect.* 8, §§2090 and 2082). 'Unum quod est principium numeri, est omnino indivisibile, *nullamque additionem aut subtractionem suscipiens manet unum*' (*ibid.*, lect. 2, §1945). 'Unde et ipsa *duo*, quae sunt numerus quidam, *sunt multa* secundum quod multa opponuntur uni' (*ibid.*, lect. 8, §2083).

44. Par. XXI, 91–6.

45. *In Meta.* IV, 2, *lect.* 2–3, §§562, 567; I, 2, 983a 15, *lect.* 3, §66).

46. *Dve* I, xvi, 5.

47. A 'perfect' number is the sum of its aliquot parts. 6 is divisible without remainder by the numbers 1, 2 and 3; and $1+2+3=6$. The same property is shared by 28 and 496. '*Perfectus* numerus est, qui suis partibus adinpletur, ut senarius . . .' 'Senarius namque numerus qui partibus suis perfectus est, *perfectionem mundi* quadam numeri sui significatione *declarat*' (Isidore, *Et.* III, v, 11; iv, 2).

48. Wisdom 11.21.

49. *Con.* II, xiv, 2–4. As Busnelli points out in his commentary *ad loc.*, the number 'million' was not in common use.

50. *Et.* III, iv, 4; *Con.* II, xiii, 18. The *locus classicus* for the serious study of the 'mathematics of created forms' will be found in Plato's *Timaeus*, 54–7.

51. Aquinas, *Quodlibet* VI, q.11.

52. *Mon.* I, vi, 2 (cf. v, 5). Aristotle develops the simile of God as general and king in the last chapter of the *Metaphysics* ('last' in medieval editions): '*Universum habet* et bonum

separatum, et *bonum ordinis*. Sicut videmus *in exercitu*: nam bonum exercitus est et *in ipso ordine exercitus*, et in duce, qui exercitui praesidet . . . *Ordo* autem *exercitus* est *propter bonum ducis adimplendum*, scilicet *ducis voluntatem in victoriae consecutionem* . . . *Totus enim ordo universi* est propter primum moventem, *ut* scilicet *explicatur in universo ordinato id quod est in intellectu et voluntate primi moventis*. *Dispositio enim entium naturalium* est qualis *optima* potest esse . . . *Totum universum* est *sicut unus principatus et unum regnum*. Et ita oportet quod ordinetur *ab uno gubernatore*' (*In Meta*. XII, 10, 1075a 15, 1076a 4, *lect*. 12, §§2629–31, 2662–3).

53. References in order: *Purg*. XIX, 63; *Par*. XII, 40 (cf. XXXII, 61); XXV, 39, 40–3; XXIV, 115; XXV, 17; XXVIII, 114. Cf. further *Par*. XXI, 8; XXX, 109–32; XXXI, 47–8, 67–9; XXXII, 7–18.

54. Cf. *Mon*. I, xiv, 4 ('minima iudicia cuiuscunque municipii . . .').

55. The first axiom runs: 'Causa nobilior est effectu'. Cf. *Con*. II, iv, 14: 'nullo effetto è maggiore de la cagione'. In *Mon* II, vi, 1, it is said to be impossible that 'effectus superaret causam in bonitate'. The second axiom is taken from *Metaphysics* II, 2, 994a 1 (translated by Moerbeke) 'At vero quod sit principium quoddam et non infinitae causae existentium . . . palam'. Cf. *Epist*. XIII, 55. The third axiom is quoted by Aquinas in the form 'Natura de uno extremo ad aliud transit per media' (*S.T*. 1a. 71, ad 4).

56. Dante's contemporary Pietro d'Abano could quote Aristotle and Averroes to the effect that 'Deus nihil potest in haec [inferiora] operari absque medio' (Nardi, *Saggi*, p. 47).

57. To avoid ambiguity, 'signet' will be used for the metal stamp, and 'seal' for the product. In Dante's Italian, the characteristic vocabulary includes: *suggello, sigillare*; *imprenta, imprentare*; *segno, segnare, stampa*; *impresso, impressione*. In scholastic Latin, *impressio* and *imprimere* were used so freely to denote causal activity – especially the activity of the heavens – that they became 'proper' terms.

58. *Con*. III, xiv, 2; cf. *C.G*. II, 43, §1201. In their note *ad loc*., the editors of the Marietti edition collect 30 other references from the same work.

59. 'Dixit [Plato] *species rerum* esse aeternas, quae sunt quasi quaedam *sigilla impressa* rebus generabilibus: et cum *sigillatur* materia, quod fit per illarum participationem, tunc res generantur; et cum eicitur *forma sigilli*, manet quidem perpetua, sed *destruitur individuum* per eiectionem talis formae' (*In De gen*. II, 9, 335b 10, *lect*. 9, §246); cf. also Nardi, *Saggi*, p. 105.

60. *Con*. IV, xxiii, 5. Both the Latin tags are used by St Thomas in framing objections to be turned aside. It is worth noting that the Platonists also used foot – and footprint-imagery (*pes* and *vestigium*); and that scholastic philosophers like St Bonaventure and Aquinas set up a 'scale' of such communicated likenesses, *viz*.: *umbra, vestigium, similitudo, imago*.

61. The *locus classicus* is *Timaeus* 50. See also *De anima* II, 1, 412b 8. The allusions to Dante are from *Par*. VII, 109; XIX, 43–5. The quotation in the text is wrenched from its context where the *imago* refers to the Eagle formed by the souls of the just in the Heaven of Jupiter.

62. The Pauline text is from Romans 1.20; Dante quotes it again in *Epist*. V, 23. See also *Con*. III, vi, 11. Lucifer, the highest of the angels before his Fall, was called *signaculum similitudinis* in Ezekiel 28.12–13 (a text to which Dante alludes in *Epist*. XIII, 76); and Gregory the Great commented: 'angelus dicitur *signaculum* similitudinis, quia in eo *similitudo divinae imaginis* magis insinuatur *expressa*' (quoted in *S.T*. 1a. 93, 3).

63. 'Est quasi quaedam *pictura*, quia scilicet sensibile *imprimit suam similitudinem* in sensu . . . Motus qui fit a sensibili in sensum, imprimit in phantasia quasi quamdam *figuram sensibilem, quae manet* sensibili abeunte, ad modum quo *illi qui sigillant cum annulis*

imprimunt figuram quamdam in cera, quae remanet etiam sigillo vel annulo remoto' (*In De mem.* ch. 1, 450b 2, *lect.* 3, §328. See also *De anima*, III, 12, 435a 10.

64. *Con.* III, vii, 2. Cf. further I, i, 12; iii, 7; II, ix, 6–7; xiii, 5; IV, xx, 7; xxii, 11–12; *Epist.* V, 3.

65. 'Secondo dice lo Filosofo nel secondo de l'Anima, " le cose convengono essere disposte a li loro agenti, e a ricevere li loro atti" [cf. II, 2, 414a 12]; . . . sì come se una pietra margarita è male disposta, o vero imperfetta, la vertù celestiale ricever non può, sì come disse quel nobile Guido Guinizzelli in una sua canzone che comincia: *Al cor gentil* . . .' (*Con.* IV, xx, 7).

66. Strictly speaking, the principle of individuation is 'materia *signata*' or 'materia *individualis*', which denotes '*haec carnes*' and '*haec ossa*', whereas 'materia *communis*' refers simply to 'caro et os' (*S.T.* 1a. 75, 4, resp.; 85, 1, ad 2).

67. Cf. *Mon.* II, ii, 3; *Con.* III, xii, 9. On *praeter*, *supra* and *contra*, cf. *In De caelo* I, 2, 269b 1–10, *lect.* 4, §47. The following phrases from Aquinas's commentary on the *Ethics* indicate the range of meaning: 'quod autem est *praeter intentionem* est per accidens', §327; '*praeter voluntatem* . . . non dicitur involontarium sed *non* voluntarium', §406; 'quae a fortuna *non* possunt esse *ex nostra praemeditatione*, quia sunt *improvisa*, et *praeter intentionem*', §463. His commentary on the *Liber de causis* yields these two clear similes, both relevant to our image-clusters. 'Invenimus enim causas ordinari dupliciter . . . "Per se" quidem quando intentio primae causae respicit usque ad ultimum effectum per omnes causas medias. Sicut cum *ars fabrilis movet manum, manus martellum qui ferrum percussum extendit*, ad quod fertur intentio artis. "Per accidens" autem quando intentio causae non procedit nisi ad proximum effectum. Quod autem ab illo effectu efficiatur iterum aliud est *praeter intentionem* primi efficientis, sicut *cum aliquis accendit candelam, praeter intentionem eius est quod iterum accensa candela accendat aliam et illa aliam*' (*lect.* 4, §41).

68. *Physics* I, 9, 192a 22. Aristotle quotes the image but objects to it: 'Dicere quod materia appetat formam *sicut femina masculum*, est *figurate* loquentium, scilicet *poetarum*, et non *philosophorum*' (*In Physic., lect.* 15, §137; see note 1 above).

69. '*Impressiones* enim causarum naturalium recipiuntur in effectibus secundum recipientium modum. Haec autem inferiora sunt *fluxibilia* et *non semper eodem modo se habentia, propter materiam*' (*C.G.*). See *Mon.* II, ii, 2 (*fluitans*); *In De gen.* II, 10, *lect.* 10, §260 (*inaequalitas*); *Con.* IV, xxiii, 7 (*impedire*); *Quaestio*, 44 (*inobedientia*).

70. *Con.* III, vi, 6; iv, 7.

71. 'Et ponit exemplum, sicut si aliquis tangat *ceram liquefactam*, usque ad illud *terminum* mota est, quousque *per actionem caloris* actio tangentis pertingit. Sed *lapis*, quia durus est, non est susceptivus talis impressionis. In *aqua* autem talis actio magis protenditur procul, quam in *igra* . . . Et esset simile de *cera* et *sigillo*, si *figura sigilli imprimeretur* in *ceram* usque *ad ultimum terminum eius*, sicut visibile *imprimit* speciem suam in aerem usque ad visum' (*In De anima* III, 12, 435a 10, *lect.* 17, §864). Moerbeke's literal translation runs: 'sicut utique si in *ceram sigillum* ingrederetur usque ad finem'. See *Timaeus*, 50 E.

One does not know whether to be more astonished at the density and mixing of the images (the omitted lines introduce 'seed' and 'craftsman' language), or at the attribution of such sentiments to St Thomas. In fairness, one must point out that Dante uses the wax-image 'in reverse' on one occasion, stating that 'the wax is always good, but not all impressions are': 'però che forse appar la sua *matera* / sempre esser *buona*, ma non ciascun *segno* / è buono, ancor che buona sia la *cera*' (*Purg.* XVIII, 37–9).

72. *Par.* I, 41–2; X, 28–9.

73. 'Che *drizzan* ciascun *seme* ad alcun *fine*' (*Purg.* XXX, 110); 'dispongono a lor *fini* e lor *semenze*' (*Par.* II, 120); cf. *Con.* IV, xxiii, 3; xxv, 13.

74. Cf. *Con.* II, iv, 3; viii, 10; III, xv, 3–4, 9–10; *Mon.* I, iii, 3; II, v, 20; vi, 5.

75. Announced in the third book of the *Convivio* (vii, 13), the image recurs again and again in the fourth book; see i, 11; ii, 6–8, 10; vii, 3–4; xix, 6–7; xx, 3, 5, 9; xxi throughout, esp. 12–14; xxii, 4–5, 11, 12; xxiii, 3; xxiv, 8–9; xxv, 1, 13; xxvii, 3–4, 7; xxviii, 4, 17; xxix, 3, 6.

76. For 'weeding' and 'tidying', see *Par.* XII, 71, 72, 86–7, 95–6, 100, 103–5; and cf. *Con.* IV, vii, 3–4; xxii, 12. For 'grafting', see *Con.* IV, xxii, 12 (Dante may well have seen his own activity as 'grafting' in this sense). For 'gathering in', see *Par.* XXIII, 20–1, 130–2. For the angels' *germogliare*, see *Par.* XXVIII, 115–16.

77. *Con.* IV, xxvii, 4; *Par.* XXII, 52–7, 62–3; (cf. xxv, 36).

78. See E. Gilson, *Introduction à l'étude de S. Augustin* (3rd edn, Paris, 1949), pp. 269–72. Cf. *S.T.* 1a. 45, 8, resp.; 115, 2, resp.

79. *Artefice*, in Italian, as in *Con.* III, iv, 7. In Latin, *artifex*, as in *Mon.* II, ii, 2–3; III, iv, 1 ('velut *artifex inferior* dependet ab *architecto . . .*').

80. *S.T.* 1a. 45, 6, resp.; *Inf.* XI, 100.

81. 'Sì come ciascuno *maestro ama* più la sua opera ottima che l'altre, così *Dio ama* più la persona umana ottima che tutte l'altre' (*Con.* III, vi, 10). Cf. *Con.* I, xii, 4–9; *Rime* LXXIX, 60.

82. '*Artifex* enim producit determinatam formam in materia, propter *exemplar* ad quod inspicit, sive illud sit exemplar ad quod *extra* intuetur, sive sit exemplar *interius* mente conceptum' (*S.T.* 1a. 44, 3, resp.).

83. '*Domus* quae fit ex lateribus et lapidibus *generatur a domo quae est in anima artificis.*' 'Onde nullo *dipintore* potrebbe porre alcuna figura, *se intenzionalmente non si facesse prima tale*, quale la figura essere dee' (*Con.* IV, x, 11). Cf. *VN* XXXIV; *Purg.* XXII, 74–5.

84. 'Exemplar est idem quod idea. Sed ideae secundum quod Augustinus . . . dicit, sunt "formae principales . . . quae divina intelligentia continentur" ' *S.T.* 1a. 44, 3, *sed contra*).

85. Cf. *Con.* I, xiii, 4; IV, iv, 12 (the knife is a very common example).

86. *Par.* XXIV, 101–2; cf. II, 27.

87. I have emended Mr Nicholl's translation of *praeter* from 'contrary to' to 'is no part of'; see note 67 above.

88. *Par.* IV, 40–8; see note 3 above.

9 Creation

1. 'Secundum Chrysostomum, primo Moyses *summarie* dixit quid Deus fecit, praemittens: "In principio creavit Deus caelum et terram"; *postea per partes explicavit.* Sicut si quis dicat: Hic artifex fecit domum istam, et postea subdat: Primo fecit fundamenta, et postea erexit parietes, tertio superposuit tectum' (*S.T.* 1a. 68, 1, ad 1).

2. The Authorized Version of the text from Ecclesiasticus (18.1) has not 'at once' but 'in general'. St Augustine's views are set out in his *Super Genesim ad litteram* which is a vast storehouse of the many acceptable and unacceptable interpretations of every detail in the text. It was freely excerpted in Peter Lombard's *Sentences* and in works like Aquinas's *Summa Theologiae*. Aquinas reports the last point made in this paragraph as follows: 'Secundum Augustinum . . . ea quae leguntur facta in operibus sex dierum, *simul facta fuerunt*' (*S.T.* 1a. 62, 1, ob. 3). The six days designate not the *temporis successio* but the *ordo naturae* (68, 1, resp.) St Thomas plays down the differences between Augustine and the majority of commentators (74, 2).

3. 'Augustinus enim videtur dicere quod non fuerit conveniens Moysen *praetermisisse spiritualis creaturae productionem*. Et ideo dicit quod cum dicitur: "In principio creavit

Deus caelum et terram", per "caelum" intelligitur *spiritualis natura adhuc informis*, per "terram" autem intelligitur *materia informis corporalis creaturae*' (*S.T.* 1a. 67, 4, resp.). 'Augustinus enim ponit duo primo creata, scilicet *naturam angelicam* et *materiam corpora-lem*' (66, 4, resp.). Augustine also held that the creation of Light on the First Day referred to the *formation* of spiritual natures ('unde oportet dicere quod per *lucis productionem* intelligatur *formatio spiritualis creaturae*' (67, 4, ad 4). In short, Augustine said that '*angeli non sunt praetermissi* in illa prima rerum creatione, sed significantur nomine "caeli" aut etiam "lucis" ' (61, 1, ad 1).

4. 'Considerandum est quod *Moyses rudi populo loquebatur, quorum imbecillitati condes-cendens, illa solum* eis proposuit, *quae manifeste sensui apparent*' (*S.T.* 1a. 68, 3, resp.). 'Non enim poterat Moyses *rudi populo* primam materiam exprimere, nisi sub similitudine rerum eis notarum' (66, 1, ad 1; cf. ad 2). 'Ideo autem [angeli] vel praetermissi sunt, vel *nominibus rerum corporalium significati*, quia *Moyses rudi populo loquebatur*, qui nondum capere poterat incorpoream naturam; et si eis fuisset expressum aliquas res esse super omnem naturam corpoream, *fuisset eis occasio idololatriae, ad quam proni erant*, et a qua Moyses eos praecipue revocare intendebat' (61, 1, ad 1; cf. 67, 4, resp.).

5. 'Dicendum quod, sicut Augustinus docet, in huiusmodi quaestionibus duo sunt observanda. Primo quidem *ut veritas Scripturae inconcusse teneatur*. Secundo, *cum Scrip-tura divina multipliciter exponi possit*, quod nulli expositioni aliquis ita praecise inhaereat quod, si certa ratione constiterit hoc esse falsum, quod aliquis sensum Scripturae esse asserere praesumat; *ne Scriptura ex hoc verbo ab infidelibus derideatur*, et ne eis via credendi praecludatur' (*S.T.* 1a. 68, 1, resp.). 'Unde mundum incoepisse *est credibile, non autem demonstrabile vel scibile*. Et hoc utile est ut consideretur, *ne forte aliquis, quod fidei est demonstrare praesumens, rationes non necessarias inducat*, quae praebeant materiam irri-dendi infidelibus . . .' (46, 2, resp.).

6. 'Dicendum quod illud verbum . . . "In *principio* creavit Deus caelum et terram", *tripliciter* exponitur ad excludendum tres errores. Quidam enim posuerunt *mundum semper fuisse, et tempus non habere principium*. Et ad hoc excludendum exponitur: "In principio, scilicet temporis". Quidam vero posuerunt *duo* esse *creationis principia, unum bonorum, aliud malorum*. Et ad hoc excludendum exponitur: "In principio, idest in Filio" . . . *Principium exemplare appropriatur Filio* propter sapientiam; ut sicut dicitur [Ps. 103. 24] "omnia *in sapientia* fecisti", ita intelligatur *Deum omnia fecisse in principio, idest in Filio*; secundum illud Apostoli *Ad Coloss.* [1, 16]: "*In ipso*", scilicet Filio, "condita sunt universa". Alii vero dixerunt *corporalia esse creata a Deo mediantibus creaturis spiritualibus*. Et ad hoc excludendum exponitur: "In principio . . . idest ante omnia." Quatuor enim ponuntur simul creata, scilicet caelum empyreum, materia corpora-lis, . . . tempus, et natura angelica' (*S.T.* 1a. 46, 3, resp.). St Thomas adds the adjective *empyreum* to his source (see note 7); Dante would understand *caelum* as referring to the physical heavens in their totality.

7. The quotations from Dante are in *Par.* XXIV, 130–5. To gain some idea of the range of errors circulating in the middle of the thirteenth century it is enough to scan the chapter headings in Aquinas's *Summa contra gentiles* II, 15–45, or to read the complete list of errors condemned by Bishop Tempier in 1277 (in the *Chartularium Univ. Parisiensis*, vol. I, 543–55: they are reproduced as an appendix to the Marietti edition of the *Contra gentiles*, under the title 'De Aristotelismo heterodoxo', vol. 3, pp. 493–502. The last text quoted in this paragraph ends: 'de quatuor coaequaevis, scilicet materia prima, tempore, caelo et angelo'. It comes from the *Summa de Creaturis* by St Albert, and is quoted by the Dominican Fathers of Ottawa in their notes to the *Summa Theologiae* (1a. 66, 4, resp.). Aquinas again understands *caelum* as meaning the Empyrean (see note 6).

8. Porena's article was first published in 'Noterelle dantesche', *Studi Romanzi*,

20(1930), pp. 5–10. The substance can be read in the long note, 'Ancora un monito a certa critica', appended to his commentary on this canto. His most telling point is that the phrase 'dilibrarsi da quel cinto' should be equivalent to 'non essere più tagliati dall'orizzonte'; and that the average time required for this to happen is 'alquanto più di un minuto'.

9. References in order: *Par*. XXX, 39; XXVII, 118–20; *Purg*. XI, 1–3; see also the last pages of Chapter 7 above.

10. References in order: Genesis 1.14–18; *Par*. X, 31; *Inf*. I, 38–40.

11. Cf. *Par*. III, 2–3: 'di *bella verità* m'avea scoverto, | *provando e riprovando*, il *dolce aspetto*'.

12. 'Dixit Deus ad Moysen: EGO SUM QUI SUM. Ait: Sic dices filiis Israel: QUI EST, misit me ad vos' (Exodus 3.14).

13. Dante's language is closer to Hesiod (as reported by Aquinas) than to Genesis: 'Et [Hesiodus] posuit rerum principium *amorem*, qui condocet omnia immortalia. Et hoc ideo, quia *communicatio bonitatis ex amore provenire* videtur. Nam *beneficium est signum et effectus amoris* . . . Iste autem Hesiodus ante philosophorum tempora fuit *in numero poetarum*' (*In Meta*. I, 4, 984b 29, *lect*. 5, §102).

14. The allusion is to Genesis 1.2 'And the spirit of God moved upon the face of the waters' (*Et Spiritus Dei ferebatur super aquas*). One cannot understand the force of the allusion, however, until one is familiar with the exegetical tradition of the word 'waters'. Origen had referred it directly to the angels, and Augustine to the *materia informis* (cf. *S.T*. 1a. 68, 2, resp.; 74, 3, ad 3). But the most influential view in Dante's century identified these waters with the 'waters above the firmament' (cf. v. 7), which was interpreted to mean a transparent heaven above the stars, a *caelum crystallinum*. This in turn was later identified with the *primum mobile* postulated by the astronomers (68, 2 and 3). Hence with the expression '*these* waters' Beatrice is referring to the heavenly sphere in which she and the pilgrim find themselves; and the whole sentence implies that time 'began' with the movement of the ninth heaven (cf. *Par*. XXVII, 109–20). See B. Nardi, *Nel mondo di Dante* (Rome, 1944), pp. 307–13.

'Ieronimo vi scrisse *lungo tratto* | *di secoli* de li angeli creati | [=from the creation of the angels] *anzi che l'altro mondo fosse fatto*' (*Par*. XXIX, 37–9). St Thomas reports that St Jerome's view was upheld by all the Greek fathers (61, 3, ad 1); and he indicates that it is not 'erroneous', but simply 'less probable' than the interpretation followed by Dante (*ibid*., resp.). The Greek interpretation does not entail the belief that the angels took an active part in the creation of the world. It is nevertheless a precondition of that seductive belief; and we may surmise that Dante was anxious to concede no ground at all to the Neoplatonist cosmogonies, all of which favoured 'creation by relay' (see note 22 to Chapter 8).

15. Where other Christian writers distinguish three aspects in creation, they will normally relate them to the distinct contributions made by Father, Son and Holy Spirit. This is clearly *not* the case in Dante.

16. 'Illuminatio autem fit *in instanti*. Nec potest dici quod fiat in tempore imperceptibili. Quia in parvo spatio posset tempus latere, *in magno autem spatio, puta ab oriente in occidentem, tempus latere non posset*; *statim* enim cum sol est in puncto horizontis, *illuminatur totum hemisphaerium* usque ad punctum oppositum' (*S.T*. 1a. 67, 2, resp.).

17. The characterization is possible only in this context. Universally speaking, only God may be described as 'pure act' (see *S.T*. 1a. 3, 1; 50, 2, ad 3; 115, 1, ad 1). For the argument, cf. *C.G*. II, 30, §1064.

18. Any residual doubt is banished a few lines later when Beatrice refers to the angels as Movers (*motori*) and develops the further argument that they could not have existed for a 'long tract of centuries' before they were provided with the *means* (the heavens) to exercise their function as Movers; for this is their specific activity (*operatio*) which constitutes the full 'perfection' of their being (*Par.* XXIX, 43–5).

19. *Par.* XXIX, 49–54. In a controversial area, Dante is arguing for the view that the angels were not created in a state of grace (cf. *S.T.* 62, 1–9), and that there was a brief but distinct interval between their creation and the fall of some of their number (cf. 63, 6). St Thomas supplies the detail that the faithful angels outnumbered the fallen (63, 9 resp.). The brief allusion to '*quest'* arte, / che tu discerni' (*Par.* XXIX, 52–3) reminds us that Dante-poet never forgets the narrative context of even the longest doctrinal speech.

20. Cf. *Inf.* XXXIV, 121–6; *Purg.* XII, 25–7. That this phrase can refer to Earth is shown by e.g. *Quaestio*, 37 (*ipsam* [*terram*] *substare omnibus corporibus*); *In De caelo* I, 3 269b, *lect.* 5, §55 (*sicut terra, quae substat omnibus*).

21. Cf. also *Con.* II, xiv, 11 ('le cose *incorruttibili*, le quali ebbero da Dio *cominciamento di creazione e non averanno fine* . . .').

22. The phrasing is suggested by Exodus 8.19, as mediated by Aquinas and Dante in their definition of a miracle: 'Sicut dicit Thomas in tertio suo *contra Gentiles*, "miraculum est quod praeter ordinem in rebus comuniter institutum *divinitus* fit". Unde ipse probat *soli Deo* competere miracula operari; quod autoritate Moysi roboratur ubi . . . magi Pharaonis . . . dixerunt: "*Digitus Dei est hic*". Si ergo miraculum est *immediata operatio Primi* absque cooperatione secundorum agentium – ut ipse Thomas . . . probat sufficienter . . .' (*Mon.* II, iv, 2–3).

23. 'Et sic, *mediate* vel *inmediate*, omne quod habet esse habet esse ab eo [sc. Deo] . . . Omne ergo quod est causatum, est causatum ab aliquo intellectu vel *mediate* vel *inmediate*' (*Epist.* XIII, 56, 58).

24. The Vulgate has: 'Didici quod omnia *opera* quae fecit Deus perseverent in *perpetuum*'; but the scholastics often use the form given in the text.

St Thomas does not dispute Dante's belief in the sempiternity of the angels, the heavens and primary matter, but he gives a different reason: 'Ostensum est . . . quod solus Deus potest creare. Multa autem sunt rerum quae non possunt procedere in esse nisi per creationem: sicut omnia quae *non* sunt composita ex forma et *materia contrarietati subiecta*; huiusmodi enim *ingenerabilia* oportet esse, cum omnis generatio sit ex contrario et ex materia. Talia autem sunt *omnes intellectuales substantiae*, et *omnia corpora caelestia*, et etiam *ipsa materia prima*. Oportet igitur ponere omnia huiusmodi *immediate a Deo* sumpsisse sui esse principium' (*C.G.* II, 42, §1189). There are, admittedly, a number of passages like the following in Aquinas's writings, where he seems to take up a position close to Dante's: 'Unde ea quae non possunt causari nisi *per creationem*, a *solo Deo* producuntur; et haec sunt *omnia quae non subiacent generationi et corruptioni*' (*S.T.* 1a. 47, 1, resp.). However, he makes all the necessary qualifications and distinctions in the last paragraph of his commentary to Book I of *De caelo* (*lect.* 29, §287).

25. 'Schiettamente neoplatonica è l'origine di questa dottrina' says Nardi (*Saggi*, p. 44); and T. Gregory writes: 'È una dottrina caratteristica del platonismo . . . Deriva da questo presupposto la distinzione, nell'opera della creazione di ciò che Dio chiama direttamente all'essere, e di ciò che invece lascia alle cause seconde: è dottrina ben nota a Chartres' (*Platonismo medievale* (Rome, 1958), p. 94). And he quotes this version from an anonymous *ninth*-century commentary on the *Consolatio*: 'nullum opus Dei subiacet corruptioni' (p. 92). Gregory also reminds us (p. 73) that the distinction goes back to the opening words of Plato's myth of creation in the *Timaeus*: 'We must in my opinion begin by distinguishing that which always is and never becomes (*quod semper est carens generatione*) from that which is always becoming but never is (*quod gignitur nec semper est*)' (27 D, trans. H. D. P. Lee, with phrases from the Latin translation by Chalcidius).

Plato goes on to say (41A) that the heavens are immutable, not because their matter is free from 'contraries', nor because this is a condition of created things, but *because it is God's will*. 'Quod autem quaedam corpora sint incorruptibilia, Plato adscribebat non conditioni materiae, sed *voluntati artificis*, scilicet Dei, quem introducit corporibus caelestibus dicentem: "Natura vestra estis dissolubilia, *voluntate autem mea indissolubilia*, quia voluntas mea maior est nexu vestro" ' (*S.T.* 1a. 66, 2, resp.).

In this connection it is worth noting that the phrase 'la divina bontà che da sé *sperne* | ogne *livore*' (*Par.* VII, 64–5) can also be traced back to the *Timaeus*: 'He was good, and what is good has no particle of envy in it' (. . . *omnis invidia relegata est*, 29 E). In this case, however, the immediate source is Boethius's hymn to the Creator in which we read 'verum insita *summi* | forma *boni livore carens*' (*Cons. phil.* III, m. 9, 5–6).

26. Nardi, *Saggi*, p. 44. Nardi notes that the thesis was condemned in the anonymous treatise *De erroribus philosophorum* in the form: 'quod a Deo *invariabili nihil variabile immediate* progredi poterat'.

27. Dante's position with regard to the *End* of the World may also have been heterodox; see 2 Peter 3, especially vv. 10 and 12: 'But the day of the Lord will come as a thief in the night; in the which the heavens shall pass away with a great noise (*in quo caeli magno impetu transient*), and the elements shall melt with fervent heat, the earth also and the works that are therein shall be burned up . . . the day of God, wherein the heavens being on fire shall be dissolved (*caeli ardentes solventur*).' Aquinas's solution to the difficulty is that the word 'heavens' here refers to the atmosphere (*caelos aërios terrae vicinos*), and that the heavenly spheres will not be destroyed but cease to move (cf. *Con.* II, xiv, 13). Time will therefore come to an end. Generation will cease. All species of minerals, plants and animals will disappear. But the four elements will survive in their spheres (*C.G.* IV, 97; *S.T. Suppl.* 74, 4).

10 Generation and universal nature

1. This first paragraph is what Aristotle called a 'circumscription'. 'Vocat "*circumscriptionem*" notificationem alicuius *per aliqua communia, quae ambiunt* quidem *ipsam rem*, non tamen adhuc per ea in speciali declaratur natura illius rei . . . Oportet quod aliquid *prius figuraliter* dicatur, id est secundum quamdam similitudinariam et extrinsecam quodammodo descriptionem . . . *Ad hominem pertinet paulatim in cognitione veritatis proficere*' (*In Ethic.* I, 7, 1098a 22, *lect.* 11, §131–2). Aristotle enunciates the same principle many times in the *Ethics*, where the adverbs used instead of *figuraliter* (in Aquinas's commentary) include: *superficialiter, similitudinarie, exemplariter, verisimiliter, summarie, in capitulo, in universali et in typo*: Dante used *typo* in just this kind of context in *Mon.* I, ii, 1.

The 'either–or' principle is formulated by Aquinas as follows: 'Omne enim quod in esse producitur, *vel generatur* per se aut per accidens, *vel creatur*' (*C.G.* II, 87, §1715). For the poet's activity as *generazione*, see *Con.* III, ix, 4. Another synonym for *generatio* (but little used in the Middle Ages) is *propagatio*: 'Augustinus . . . distinguit opus *propagationis*, quod est opus *naturae*, ab opere *creationis*' (*S.T.* 1a. 45, 8, *sed contra*).

For the meaning of 'creation', and its strict association with God, cf.: '*Creare* est aliquid *ex nihilo* facere' (*S.T.* 1a. 45, 2, *sed contra*). '*Creatio* autem est productio alicuius rei secundum totam suam substantiam, *nullo praesupposito* . . . Nihil potest aliquid creare nisi *solus Deus*, qui est *prima causa*' (65, 3, resp.).

2. 'Veramente per diversi filosofi de la differenza de le nostre anime fue diversamente ragionato: . . . ma però che ne la prima faccia paiono un poco lontane dal vero, non secondo quelle procedere si conviene, ma *secondo l'oppinione d'Aristotile e de li Peripatetici*' (*Con.* IV, xxi, 3).

3. '*Communium non est generatio, sed particularium* (non enim est generatio hominis simpliciter, sed *huius* hominis)' (*In De caelo* III, 2, 302a 5, *lect.* 8, §598: Aquinas is quoting Simplicius). 'Ad hoc ergo quod aliquid fiat simpliciter, *requiritur quod prius non fuerit simpliciter*, quod accidit in iis quae substantialiter fiunt. Quod enim fit homo non solum prius non fuit homo, sed simpliciter verum est dicere ipsum non fuisse' (*In Physic.* I, 7, 190a 33, *lect.* 12, §107).

4. *Substantia* will be used only in the primary sense distinguished by Aristotle ('quae proprie et principaliter et maxime dicitur' cf. *Metaphysics* V, 8, 1017b 10; VII, 3, 1028b 33). It refers to a complete individual thing existing independently ('individuum completum, per se subsistens, in se indistinctum, ab aliis distinctum'). It is opposed to *accidens*, a quality, such as a colour, that can only exist in a concrete, primary substance ('accidens sine substantia esse non potest'). In this sense it is virtually synonymous with *synolon*, *compositum* or *subiectum* as they will be used in this chapter ('accidentia individuantur per *subiectum* quod est substantia': these quotations are taken from L. Schütz, *Thomaslexikon* s.v.).

Aristotle's word *synolon* is defined by Aquinas as ' "simul totum", id est singulare compositum ex materia et forma' (*In Meta.* III, 4, 999b 15, *lect.* 9, §453). For the use of *compositum* as noun or as adjective in these contexts, cf.: 'Non enim est possibile quod sit aliqua domus praeter *hanc domum sensibilem compositam ex materia et forma* . . . quia formarum non est generatio, sed *compositorum*' (*ibid.*, §§454–5).

5. '*Formae non* proprie *habent esse*, sed magis sunt *quibus* aliqua habent esse . . . *Formae* enim proprie *non fiunt*, sed educuntur de potentia materiae. *Forma* enim proprie non fit, sed *compositum* . . . Quod *generatur* est *compositum*' (*ibid.*, VII, 8, *lect.* 7, §§1419, 1423, 1428).

Aristotle examines the subject in great detail in *Metaphysics* VII, 7–8, 1032a 12–1034a 10. Aquinas condenses one of the main lines of his argument in this passage (where the verb *fieri* may be replaced by *generari*): 'Omne quod fit, ad hoc fit quod sit: est enim fieri via in esse. Sic igitur unicuique causato convenit fieri sicut sibi convenit esse. *Esse autem non convenit formae tantum nec materiae tantum, sed composito . . . Unde restat quod compositum proprie sit. Eius igitur solius est fieri*' (*C.G.* II, 43, §1196; cf. II, 50, §1262; *S.T.* 1a. 65, 4, resp.; 91, 2, resp.).

6. *Metaphysics* 1033b 30. Dante quotes the dictum in the following forms: 'Nichil igitur agit nisi *tale existens quale patiens fieri debet*; propter quod Phylosophus in hiis quae *De simpliciter ente*: "Omne" inquit "quod reducitur de potentia in actum, reducitur *per tale existens actu*" ' (*Mon.* I, xiii, 3). 'Nichil est quod dare possit quod non habet; unde *omne agens aliquid actu esse tale oportet quale agere intendit* . . .' (*ibid.*, III, xiii, 6). See also note 27 below.

7. 'Ex *materia* autem sub quantitate existente, et *forma substantiali* adveniente, corpus physicum constituitur . . . Praeterea quaelibet forma substantialis *propriam dispositionem requirit* in materia, sine qua esse non potest' (*In De gen.* I, 10, 327b, *lect.* 24, §172; cf. *Con.* II, i, 10). 'Corruptio unius generatio est alterius' (*Epist.* III, 4; cf. *De gen.* I, 3, 318a 25).

8. 'Nam ipsum nomen "naturae", ut Philosophus dicit in V *Metaph.* [1014b 16], primo impositum fuit ad significandum *generationem* viventium, quae "nativitas" dicitur; et quia viventia *generantur ex principio coniuncto, sicut fructus ex arbore, et foetus ex matre*, cui colligatur, consequenter tractum est nomen naturae ad omne principium motus quod est in eo quod movetur' (*S, T,* 1a. 115, 2, resp.). 'Hoc quod est *agere* facit *tactu*; nam *corpora tangendo agunt*' (*In Physic.* III, 2, 202a 5, *lect.* 4, §301). 'Cum nullum corpus agat *nisi tangendo vel movendo*' (*S.T.* 1a. 45, 5, resp.).

'Manifestum est autem quod principium activum et passivum generationis rerum viventium sunt *semina ex quibus viventia generantur*' (*S.T.* 1a. 115, 2, resp.; cf. *In De anima*

II, 4, 415a 30, *lect.* 7, §312). '*Virtus enim formativa*, quae est in spermate maris, naturaliter est ordinata ut *producat omnino simile ei, a quo sperma est decisum*' (*In Meta.* VII, 8, 1034a 4, *lect.* 7, §1433).

It was known that some plants reproduced by suckers, cuttings, etc., but reproduction of this kind does not infringe the rules. The most important exception was constituted by the so-called *animalia imperfecta*, e.g. the worms and maggots that appear, apparently spontaneously, in slime or in putrefying corpses. These were held to be generated by the power of the heavens alone. 'Animalia enim perfecta videntur non posse generari nisi ex semine; *animalia* vero *imperfecta*, quae sunt vicina plantis, *videntur posse generari* et ex semine *et sine semine*; . . . *sufficit* ad agendum *sola virtus caelestis*' (*In Meta.* VII, 7, 1032a 30, *lect.* 6, §§1400–1; cf. *ibid.*, §§1455–7).

9. 'Istarum qualitatum duae sunt activae, scilicet calidum et frigidum . . . *Calidum* est quod est congregativum similium, *frigidum* vero est *congregativum similium et dissimilium* . . . Est ergo simplex et naturalis generatio *permutatio facta ab istis virtutibus activis* . . .'

'Frigidum . . . est activum dupliciter. *Primo* quia corrumpere est quoddam agere: *frigidum autem est corruptivum* . . . *Secundo* . . . quia circumstat calidum, et ex hoc calidum per . . . contrasistentiam frigidi fortificatur, et sic *frigidum fortificando calidum per accidens agit ad generationem*' (*In Meteor.* IV, 1, 378b 26, *lect.* 2, §313–14; IV, 5, 382b 8, *lect.* 8, §327).

10. 'Hic [Philosophus] determinare intendit breviter de his, *quae generantur in profundo ipsius terrae* . . . Sicut . . . supra terram est duplex exhalatio, . . . ita similiter *in partibus terrae est duplex exhalatio*, ex qua generantur duo genera corporum, quorum quaedam dicuntur *fossibilia* . . . et generantur ex *sicca* exhalatione: alia vero dicuntur *metallica*, quae magis generantur *per coagulationem*' (*In Meteor.* III, 7, 378a 15, *lect.* 9, §307).'

In this chapter, and in the fourth book of the *Meteorologica*, Aristotle tried to relate all the secondary tangible qualities such as malleability, fusibility, ductility, compressibility (cf. IV, 8, 385a 12), to the four primary qualities; and the context did not require him to specify that nothing can be *generatum* except from an existing *generans*. But the alchemists were true to his principles when they asserted that gold grows from gold, and when they likened the process of mineral 'growth' to the action of leaven in dough, or of rennet in cheese. The inference is that, given sufficient time, a vein of gold could be regenerated after mining provided that the vein were not exhausted. See E. J. Holmyard, *Alchemy* (London, 1957), pp. 22, 72, 111, 132, 134, 139, 143, 147; S. Toulmin and J. Goodfield, *The Architecture of Matter* (London, 1965), pp. 129, 130, 137–43.

11. '*Sol solus sufficiens est facere aestuantem calorem* in istis inferioribus: nam *calor* qui fit ex aliis corporibus caelestibus est *quasi (!) insensibilis* respectu caloris qui fit a sole' (*In Meteor.* I, 3, 341a 18, *lect.* 5, §34). 'Cum *superiora agant* in ista inferiora per *motum* et *lucem* . . . *illi maxime* attribuenda est virtus generandi, quod *maxime lucet*, et quod, lucem suam omnibus tribuens, ipsam a nullo participat. Huiusmodi autem est *sol*' (*In De gen.* II, 10, 336b 18, *lect.* 10, §260. Similar references to the sun are legion in all writers on the subject. Even Dionysius knows that 'sol *generationem* visibilium corporum confert, et *ad vitam* ipsa *movet*, et *nutrit* et *auget* et *perficit*' (*De div. nom.* IV, 7, quoted in *C.G.* III, 83, §2581).

12. *Physics* II, 2, 194b 13. Dante quotes it as follows: 'Humanum genus filius est caeli . . .: "generat enim homo hominem *et sol*", iuxta secundum *De naturali auditu*' (*Mon.* I, ix, i).

13. Aristotle insists that the *daily* passage of the sun is the cause of *continuity* rather than change. 'Motus corporis caelestis est causa *continuae* generationis. Cum autem generatio et corruptio sint contraria, non contingit fieri ambo . . . si sit tantum . . . unus motus localis; quia *idem manens idem et semper* similiter se habens, *semper natum est facere*

idem . . . Cum autem *motus primi orbis*, qui dicitur motus *diurnus*, semper *uniformiter* se habeat super circulos aeque distantes a circulo aequinoctiali, non potest esse causa generationis et corruptionis . . . Causa ergo *continuitatis est motus totius orbis*' (*In De gen.* II, 10, 336a 15, *lect.* 10, §258).

'Sed motus *circuli obliqui*, qui dicitur *zodiacus*, est causa sufficiens utriusque [sc. generationis et corruptionis] propter motum *accessionis* et *recessionis solis* in eo . . . Causa *praesentiae* et *absentiae* est *inclinatio* et *elevatio* ipsius *zodiaci*: . . . et ideo contingit quod ipsum *generans quandoque* est *prope* locum generationis, et *quandoque longe*; . . . et ideo sicut in *adveniendo* et in prope esse generat rem, ita in *recedendo* et in longe esse corrumpit idipsum . . . quia cum recedit, respicit *obliquiori radio*, et tunc dominatur frigus mortificans . . . Videmus enim ad oculum quod sole adveniente ad punctum Arietis, quando *directe locum nostrum tangit, incipit esse generatio* terrae nascentibus, *recedente* autem *sole* a principio Librae, incipit *rerum deminutio et corruptio*' (*ibid.*, §§258, 260). Cf. *Con.* II, xiv, 16, quoted in Chapter 6.

14. For the moon's influence on tides, see *Par.* XVI, 82–3. 'Sphaera lunae est nata movere aquam' (*In De gen.* I, 10, 327b, *lect.* 24, §172: this whole *lectio* by the so-called 'pseudo-Aquinas' offers a fascinating example of the way in which Aristotle's simple teaching was filled out by later 'science').

15. For the communication of circular movement from the sphere of the moon through the sphere of Fire to the sphere of Air cf.: 'Sphaera ignis movetur circulariter, et etiam sphaera aëris, licet non tota, *per raptum firmamenti*' (*ibid.*). '*Ille aër* qui excedit omnem altitudinem montium, *in circuitu fluit* . . . quia *simul trahitur cum circulatione caeli*: ignis enim est continuus . . . cum corpore caelesti, aër autem cum igne' (*In Meteor.* I, 3, 340b 35, *lect.* 5, §30). 'Videmus *ignem* imitari *circulationem caeli* . . .' (*Quaestio*, 84). Seeds were carried from the Garden of Eden, says Dante's Matelda, by the steady prevailing wind in the upper air (*Purg.* XXVIII, 103–20).

'*Superior pars aëris fertur circulariter secundum motum caeli* . . . et . . . *iste aer* [sc. inferior] *aliquid participat de motu superioris*, licet ista circulatio non compleatur. Et ex hoc contingit quod exhalationes commoventes aerem, *non movent ipsum in sursum aut in deorsum* . . . sed commovent aerem *in obliquum* . . . Unde non oportet quod semper motus venti sit ad occidentem, sicut est motus caeli, sed fit in oppositum exhalationis compellentis . . .' (*In Meteor.* II, 4, 361a 22, *lect.* 8, §188).

16. The story has been told by many historians of ideas. A good general introduction and bibliography for English-speaking readers will be found in the relevant chapters of two books by S. Toulmin and J. Goodfield: *The Fabric of the Heavens* (London, 1961), and *The Architecture of Matter* (London, 1962). Both have been reissued as Pelican books.

The following passage from an anonymous commentary to the *Timaeus* illustrates the general assumptions (we may disregard the initial 'ifs', just as the author does): 'Si enim verum est quod *planetae calorem* et siccitatem, *frigus* et humiditatem conferunt in terris, si *vitam* herbis et arboribus, si *temperiem* vel *distemperiem* humanis corporibus, quid mirum si *in conceptione, in utero*, in nativitate, *in vita, corpora contrahunt temperiem* qualitatum ad diu vivendum et animam conservandam, vel *intemperiem* ad contrarium. Huic ergo constellationi non est heresis credere' (quoted by T. Gregory, *Anima mundi*, p. 163).

17. 'Item, cum *omnes formae substantiales* inferiorum corporum sint *ex virtute caelestium corporum* . . . Dicendum est ergo quod *omnia* corpora caelestia, secundum communem virtutis luminis habent calefacere; sed *secundum alias proprias virtutes singulis corporibus attributas*, habet *non solum calefacere et infrigidare, sed etiam omnes alios effectus corporales efficere in istis inferioribus*' (*In De caelo* II, 7, 289a, *lect.* 10, §393). This is a typically cautious account by Aquinas speaking more or less in his own person and not just paraphrasing Aristotle. More detail is given by the anonymous continuator of his commentary to

Politics VII, lect. 5, §1121, which sums up the limits of their influence on human beings, and also in *Contra gentiles* III, 84, §2596.

The mature Dante waxes eloquent on this theme: 'licet *caelum stellatum* habeat unitatem in substantia, habet tamen *multiplicitatem in virtute*; propter quod oportuit habere diversitatem illam in partibus quam videmus, ut *per organa diversa virtutes diversas influeret*; et qui haec non advertit, *extra limitem phylosophiae se esse cognoscat*' (*Quaestio*, 70).

18. 'Videmus in eo differentiam in *magnitudine* stellarum et in *luce*, in *figuris* et *ymaginibus* constellationum; *quae* quidem *differentiae frustra esse non possunt*, ut *manifestissimum esse debet omnibus in phylosophia nutritis*. Unde alia est virtus huius stellae et illius, et alia huius constellationis et illius . . . etc.' (*Quaestio*, 71: cf. further *Par.* II, 64–72, 115–20, 136–8). Nardi quotes a less cautious view from the anonymous *Summa philosophiae* in his *Saggi di filosofia dantesca*, p. 23.

19. It also seemed to explain the mechanics of the derivation of the Many from the One in Neoplatonist metaphysics: cf. 'Ciascuna forma sustanziale procede da la sua prima cagione, la quale è Iddio, sì come nel libro Di Cagioni è scritto, e non *ricevono diversitade per quella*, che è semplicissima, *ma per le secondarie cagioni* e per la materia in che discende' (*Con.* III, ii, 4).

20. For the 'heat' of Mars and the constellation of Leo, see *Con.* II, xiii, 21; *Par.* XXI, 14. For the coldness of Saturn and the Moon, see *Rime* C, 7.

21. 'Et primo assignat [Aristoteles] *causam fossibilium* . . . Principium activum *principale* est *virtus caelestis*, quae dicitur *virtus mineralis*: a qua habent fossibilia quaedam, puta *lapides pretiosi*, quandam *virtutem caelestem et occultam*, per quam occultas operationes vere exercent; principium autem *instrumentale* est *caliditas* . . .'(*In Meteor.* IV, 7, 378a 15, lect. 9, §308).

22. Cf. S. Toulmin and J. Goodfield, *The Architecture of Matter*, p. 129; E. J. Holmyard, *Alchemy*, pp. 18–19. Chaucer's Canon Yeoman lists the correspondences thus: 'Sol *gold* is, and Luna *silver* we threpe, / Mars *iren*, Mercurie *quyksilver* we clepe, / Saturnus *leed*, and Juppiter is *tyn*, / And Venus *coper* . . .' (*Canterbury Tales*, VIII (G), 826–9).

23. 'Sphaera autem *stellarum fixarum* . . . in qua sunt multae imagines et figurae, *movet terram*; unde et in ipsa figurantur imagines multae in generatis' (*In De gen.* I, 10, 327b, lect. 24, §172). See note 33 below.

24. The most elaborate synthesis will be found in the work of Avicenna (whose *dator formarum* is the intelligence governing the moon); but the less 'suspect' *Liber de causis*, to which Dante refers several times, can provide all the documentation required. On the origins and influence of this work, see the article *s.v.* in the *Enciclopedia dantesca*. The following sentence from St Albert is wholly characteristic: 'Sicut enim sol ex se producit luces, *ita quaelibet intelligentia ex se producit formas* suorum naturalium operum, quae *operatur explendo eas per motum sphaerae quam movet*' (quoted by Nardi, *Saggi*, p. 97). Cf. further *S.T.* 1a. 110, 1, ad 3; 2, resp.

Aristotle attacked Plato's position many times, notably in *Metaphysics* VII, 7, 1032a 12. This is how Aquinas introduces the section in his commentary: '*Philosophus* . . . hic intendit ostendere, quod quidditates et *formae existentes in istis sensibilibus non generantur ab aliquibus formis extra materiam existentibus, sed a formis quae sunt in materia*. Et hic erit unus modorum, *quo destruitur positio Platonis ponentis species separatas* . . .' (*lect.* 6, §1381).

The following passage by the continuator of Aquinas's commentary to the *De generatione* gives an excellent summary of the Platonist position as it was understood in Dante's time (it will be seen that seal-imagery plays a prominent part): 'quidam somniaverunt naturam specierum, idest ipsas species separatas quas Plato appellavit *"ideas"*, *esse sufficientem causam ad hoc quod res generentur* . . . Et supponit [sc. Plato] quod entium quaedam sunt substantiae separatae, quaedam vero *participantia specierum sicut materiae*, et quod unumquodque compositum dicitur "esse actu" secundum speciem, *"generari"* autem secundum illius speciei susceptionem, et dicitur *"corrumpi"* secundum illius speciei *abiectionem*. Dixit enim species rerum esse aeternas, quae sunt quasi quaedam *"sigilla"* impressa *rebus generabilibus*; et cum *sigillatur materia*, quod fit per illarum participationem, *tunc res generantur*, et cum eiicitur *forma sigilli*, manet quidem perpetua, sed *destruitur individuum* per eiectionem talis formae . . .' (II, 9, 335b 10, *lect.* 9, §246).

25. E.g.: *'Omnis* . . . *motus ad formam* fit mediante *motu caelesti* . . . Per motum autem caelestem *non possunt produci multae formae sensibiles nisi mediantibus determinatis principiis suppositis*: sicut animalia quaedam non fiunt nisi ex semine . . . Mutatio generationis est eadem totius et partis. Partes autem horum generabilium et corruptibilium *generantur acquirentes formas in actu a formis quae sunt in materia, non autem a formis extra materiam existentibus*, cum *oporteat generans esse simile generato* . . .' (*C.G.* II, 43, §1198–9).

The following excursus from Aquinas's commentary on the *Metaphysics* is of interest for the way he applies the argument to the theories of 'hidden forms' and 'seminal forms': 'Omnes, qui non consideraverunt hoc, quod Philosophus supra ostendit, *quod formae non fiunt*, passi sunt *difficultatem* circa *factionem formarum*. Propter hoc namque *quidam* coacti sunt dicere, *omnes formas esse ex creatione*. Nam ponebant *formas fieri* . . . E contrario autem quidam posuerunt . . . *formas praeexistere in materia actu*, quod est ponere *latitationem formarum* . . . Sententia autem Aristotelis, qui ponit *formas non fieri, sed compositum*, utrumque excludit. Neque enim oportet dicere, quod formae sint causatae ab aliquo extrinseco agente, neque quod fuerint semper actu in materia; sed *in potentia tantum. Et quod in generatione compositi sint eductae de potentia in actum*' (*In Meta.* VII, 8, 1033b 20, *lect.* 7, §§1430–1).

26. The word 'inducing' is chosen with reference to the title of a chapter in *Contra gentiles* (II, 43), to which we shall return when we consider the *opus distinctionis* below: 'Quod rerum distinctio non est per aliquem de secundis agentibus *inducentem in materiam diversas formas*.' Cf. further: *'Corpora caelestia causant formas* in istis inferioribus, *non influendo, sed movendo*' (*S.T.* 1a, 65, 4, ad 3: the whole 'response' in this article is a magnificent exposé of the subject).

27. Cf. note 6 above and: 'Ove è da sapere che, sì come vuole lo Filosofo, tutte le cose che fanno alcuna cosa, *conviene essere prima quelle perfettamente in quello essere*; onde dice nel settimo de la Metafisica: "*Quando una cosa si genera da un'altra, generasi di quella, essendo in quello essere*". Ancora è da sapere che ogni cosa che si corrompe, sì si corrompe precedente alcuna alterazione, *e ogni cosa che è alterata conviene essere congiunta con l'alterante cagione*, sì come vuole lo Filosofo nel settimo de la Fisica e nel primo De generatione' (*Con.* IV, x, 8–9).

28. Dice [Timeo] che l'alma a la sua stella riede, / credendo quella quindi esser decisa / quando *natura per forma la diede*' (*Par.* IV, 52–4). 'La virtù informante / in queste stelle . . .' (*Par.* VII, 137–8). See the context quoted in the text below.

29. References in order: sun and ecliptic, *Par.* XXII, 116, X, 14, 28–9, *Con.* III, xii, 7–8; stars' light from sun, *Con.* II, xiii, 15; the heavens as a system, *Par.* XIII, 65–6, VIII, 127 (cf. *Con.* II, xiii, 5; III, xv, 15; *Purg.* XXX, 109–10; *Par.* II, 112–13; XXVIII, 127–9; *Mon.* II, ii, 2); each mirrors the heavens, *Mon.* III, xv, 12; *Quaestio*, 71–2.

30. References in order: luminary as organ, *Quaestio*, 67 (cf. *Mon.* III, iv, 18); distinct effects of distinct stars, *Par.* II, 64–72, 130–41; *Quaestio*, 71–2; importance of constellations in the Zodiac, *Con.* II, iii, 15; influence in light-ray, *Con.* II, vi, 9; heaven as 'tool' of an intelligence, *Con.* III, vi, 5–6, *Par.* II, 127–9, VIII, 109–11 (cf. *Con.* IV, iv, 12).

31. *Con.* III, xiv, 3; *Par.* XIII, 67–9, 73–5.

32. 'Le corpora composte prima, sì come sono le *minere*, hanno *amore* a lo *luogo dove la loro generazione è ordinata*, e in quello *crescono* e *acquistano vigore e potenza*; onde vedemo la *calamita* sempre da la parte de la sua generazione *ricevere vertù*' (*Con.* III, iii, 3; and cf. *ibid.*, 6–8). 'Per *algente freddo* | l'*acqua* diventa *cristallina petra* | là *sotto tramontana* ov' è il gran freddo' (*Rime* CII, 25–7; cf. *ibid.* C, 59–60; *Con.* IV, xviii, 4).

33. In *Con.* IV, xx, 7, Dante alludes with approval to the second stanza of Guinizzelli's *canzone, Al cor gentil*: 'come *vertute* in *petra preziosa*, | che da la *stella valor* no i *discende* | anti che 'l *sol* la faccia gentil cosa; | poi che n'ha tratto fore | per sua forza lo *sol* ciò che li è *vile*, | *stella* li da *valore*' (lines 12–16, cf. *ibid.*, 31–40). Dante also refers to the purifying and 'disposing' role of the sun in his canzone *Amor, che movi tua vertù da cielo*, *Rime* XC, 3–7. Dante's few references to the lapidary 'virtues' come, not unexpectedly, in the *canzoni* for the 'donna-petra': *Rime* CI, 19; CII, 11–24; CIII, 5.

34. '*La nostra vita . . .*, ed ancora *d'ogni vivente* qua giù, [è] *causata dal cielo*' (*Con.* IV, xiii, 6; cf. *ibid.*, II, xiv, 17). 'De la quale *induzione*, quanto a la prima *perfezione*, cioè de la *generazione sustanziale*, tutti li filosofi concordano che *li cieli siano cagione*' (*Con.* II, xiii, 5).

35. '*L'anima* d'ogne *bruto* e de le *piante* | di *complession potenzïata tira* | lo *raggio* e 'l *moto* de le *luci sante*' (*Par.* VII, 139–41). Dante is more 'guarded' there because he prefers *tirare* to the more controversial *indurre*: cf. *Con.* II, xiii, 5. For the 'passive' force of *potenziata* we may quote from the *Quaestio*: 'simul et *virtuatum* est *caelum* ad agendum, et *terra potentiata* ad patiendum' (76).

36. 'Le *fronde* | che *trasse* fuor la *vertù* d'Ariete' (*Rime* C, 40–1); 'per *ovra* de le *rote magne*, | che *drizzan* ciascun seme ad alcun fine | secondo che le *stelle son compagne*' (*Purg.* XXX, 109–11).

37. The paragraph in question is really describing the first months of the embryonic life of a *human being*; and this does present certain difficulties that are not entirely resolved by leaving out Dante's account of the final, miraculous stage in the making of a man. There are also other, unconnected ambiguities in Dante's language (which is less cautious, more Platonist, than in the corresponding passage in *Purgatorio* XXV which will be analysed in the last chapter). It is by no means certain that the three 'virtues' have been distinguished correctly (these being: 'la vertù del cielo', carried in the seed; 'la vertù celestiale che produce . . . l'anima in vita'; and 'la vertù del motore del cielo'). It is possible – to put the matter briefly for the moment – that the second and third 'virtues' both refer to God's direct action in the making of the human soul. But in any case this interpretation does not invalidate the account given in the text (where the third 'virtue' has been omitted and the second referred to the heavens).

38. 'E però dico che quando l'umano [cf. previous note] *seme cade* nel suo *recettaculo*, cioè ne la matrice, esseo porta seco la vertù de l'anima generativa e la vertù del cielo e la vertù de li elementi legati, cioè la complessione; e *matura e dispone la materia* a la *vertù formativa*, la quale diede l'anima del generante; e la vertù formativa *prepara li organi* a la *vertù celestiale*, che *produce* de la potenza del seme l'*anima* in vita' (*Con.* IV, xxi, 4).

As regards the first stage: 'in *ciascuna cosa*, naturale ed artificiale, è *impossibile procedere a la forma, sanza prima essere disposto lo subietto* sopra che la forma dee stare: sì come impossibile la forma de l'oro è venire, se la *materia*, cioè lo suo subietto, *non è digesta e apparecchiata*' (*Con.* II, i, 10; cf. *Purg.* XXV, 49–51).

39. 'Però che . . . la *disposizione del cielo* a questo effetto puote essere buona, migliore e ottima (*la quale si varia per le constellazioni, che continuamente si transmutano*), incontra che de l'umano seme e di queste vertudi *più pura* e *men pura* anima si produce' (*Con.* IV, xxi, 7; cf. *ibid.*, ii, 6; xxi, 10; *Par.* XIII, 67–75). Generically speaking, the heavens are best

disposed at the time of the vernal equinox. Specifically, they were perfectly disposed for the birth of the Saviour: see *Con.* IV, v, 4; *Par.* XIII, 84; *Mon.* I, xvi, 1–2; and cf. ix, 1–2.

40. In *Con.* II, xiii, 5, Dante quotes Aristotle as saying that the heavens are the cause of 'substantial generation' through a *'vertude celestiale* che è nel calore naturale del seme'. I take this and 'la vertù del cielo' of the present passage to be synonymous.

41. *Con.* IV, xxi, 7; III, iii, 9 (diet); IV, xxiii, 12–14 (variations due to age, season, and time of day). Even the cautious Aquinas will say: 'Dispositio autem *corporis humani subiacet caelestibus motibus* . . . Damascenus dicit . . . quod *"alii et alii planetae* diversas *complexiones* et *habitus* et *dispositiones* in nobis constituunt" ' (*C.G.* III, 84, §2596). It must be remembered that, conversely, the celestial influences are received in differing ways according to the existing disposition of the recipient: 'effectus astrorum variantur *etiam* in *rebus corporeis,* secundum diversam materiae dispositionem' (*S.T.* 1a. 115, 3, ad 4).

42. This paragraph combines points and hints from the following texts: *Par.* XIII, 67–71; XXVII, 125–6, 144, 148; *Con.* III, xii, 10.

43. *Par.* I, 127–9; XIII, 76–8; *Con.* III, xii, 8.

44. Once again Dante is dealing explicitly with human beings and human society. But the arguments apply *a fortiori* to lower levels of existence. The five references to Providence come in lines 79, 99, 100, 104, 135; and the crucial text runs: 'Natura generata il suo *cammino* / *simil farebbe sempre* a' generanti, / *se non vincesse il proveder divino*' (*Par.* VIII, 133–5).

The same ideas are set out more fully in the following texts (both about *man*, but both relevant to animals): 'Lo tempo, secondo che dice Aristotile, . . . è "numero di *movimento celestiale*", lo quale *dispone* le cose di qua giù *diversamente* a ricevere alcuna *informazione*. Ché *altrimenti* è *disposta* la terra nel principio de la primavera a ricevere in sé la *informazione* de *l'erbe* e de *li fiori*, e *altrimenti* lo verno; e *altrimenti* è disposta una stagione a ricevere lo *seme* che un'altra; e così la nostra mente in quanto ella è *fondata* sopra la *complessione del corpo*, che a *seguitare la circulazione del cielo altrimenti* è *disposto* un tempo e *altrimenti* un altro' (*Con.* IV, ii, 6–7).

'Phylosophus *naturam semper* agere *propter finem* in secundo *De naturali auditu* probat. Et quia ad hunc finem natura pertingere non potest per unum hominem, cum *multae* sint *operationes* necessariae ad ipsum, quae *multitudinem* requirunt in operantibus, necesse est naturam producere hominum *multitudinem ad diversas operationes* ordinatorum: ad quod multum conferunt, praeter *superiorem influentiam*, locorum inferiorum virtutes et proprietates' (*Mon.* II, vi, 6: the whole chapter should be compared with the commentary by the pseudo-Aquinas to Aristotle's *Politics* VII, 7, 1327b 20, *lect.* 5, §§1118–22).

45. All the points made in this introductory 'circumscription' (cf. note 1) are explained and substantiated below. The fundamental texts to which allusion is here made are: *Purg.* XVI, 67–9, 73; XVIII, 14–15, 26–7, 43–5, 49–60; *Par.* VII, 71–2.

46. 'Nomen "motus" etiam *ad spiritualia* derivatur dupliciter. Uno modo, secundum quod *omnis operatio* "motus" dicitur . . . Alio modo, *desiderium in aliud tendens* quidam "motus" dicitur' (*S.T.* 1a. 73, 2, resp.). 'Res autem quas considerat *Naturalis*, sunt *motus* et *mobile* . . . *Quaecumque mota movent*, sunt *physicae speculationis*' (*In De gen.* I, 1, *lect.* 1, §1). 'De his vero quae *dependent a materia* . . . est *Naturalis*, quae *Physica* dicitur. Et quia *omne quod habet materiam mobile est*, consequens est quod *ens mobile* sit *subiectum naturalis philosophiae* . . . Non dico autem *"corpus" mobile*, quia *omne mobile esse corpus* probatur in isto libro' (*In Physic.* I, 1, *lect.* 1, §§3–4). See also *Con.* II, xiii, 17.

'Illa autem dicimus *a natura moveri*, quorum *principium motus in ipsis* est . . . Manifestum est enim quod ea quae *per violentiam* moventur, *ab alio* moventur, ex ipsa violenti definitione. Est enim *violentum* . . . cuius *principium* est *extra*, nil conferente vim passo' (*In*

Physic. VIII, 4, 254b 12, *lect.* 7, §§1023–4). The definition of 'violent' motion is from *Ethics* III, 1, 1110b 5, and is quoted by Dante in *Par.* IV, 73–4.

47. The much quoted dictum is from Dionysius, *De divinis nominibus* ch. 4, §12. It is the remote source of Dante's definition of human love: 'Amore . . . non è altro che *unimento* spirituale de l'anima e de la cosa amata; nel quale unimento *di propia sua natura l'anima corre* tosto e tardi, secondo che è libera o impedita' (*Con.* III, ii, 3; cf. *ibid.*, 8–9). For the example of a predator and its prey, see note 54 below.

48. *S.T.* 1a. 48, 1, resp. Cf. Dante: '. . . *ciascuna cosa* massimamente desidera la sua *perfezione*, e in quella si queta ogni suo desiderio, e *per quella ogni cosa è desiderata* . . .' (*Con.* III, vi, 7; and cf. *ibid.*, xv, 3).

49. *Con.* III, i, 5.

50. '*Naturaliter quaelibet res seipsam amat*; et ad hoc pertinet quod quaelibet res naturaliter conservat se in esse *et corrumpentibus resistit quantum potest*' (*S.T.* 2–2ae. 64, 5, resp.). 'Ogni animale, sì come elli è nato, razionale come bruto, *se medesimo ama*, e teme e *fugge quelle cose che a lui sono contrarie, e quelle odia*' (*Con.* IV, xxii, 5; cf. *Purg.* XVII, 106–8).

'*Quies* enim demonstrat *motum consummatum.*' '*Requies* . . . accipitur . . . pro impletione desiderii' (*S.T.* 1a. 73, 1 ad 2; 2 resp.). The wording is suggested by the juxtaposition of texts such as that quoted in the following note, or these: '*Pax* importat . . . ut *desideria* nostra *conquiescant* in uno' (*S.T.* 1–2ae. 70, 3 resp.). 'Et ipsum etiam *bellum* est propter *pacem*, non autem e converso' (*In Polit.* II, 9, 1271b 5, *lect.* 14, §319).

51. *Con.* III, iii, 2. 'Philosophus proponit quod in *eundem locum* feruntur naturaliter pars et totum, sicut *tota terra* et *unus bolus* eius. Et hoc patet ex quiete: quia *unumquodque movetur naturaliter ad locum in quo quiescit naturaliter* . . .' (*In De caelo* I, 3, 270a 5, *lect.* 5, §56; cf. *Mon.* I, xv, 6).

52. *Con.* III, iii, 3; cf. *S.T.* 1a. 76, 4, ad 4.

53. 'Le *piante*, che sono prima animate, hanno *amore* a *certo luogo* più manifestamente, secondo che *la complessione* richiede: e però vedemo certe piante lungo l'acque quasi cansarsi, e certe sopra li gioghi de le montagne, e certe ne le piagge e dappiè monti: le quali se si transmutano, o muiono del tutto o vivono quasi *triste*, sì come cose disgiunte dal loro *amico*' (*Con.* III, iii, 4; cf. *Par.* VIII, 140–1).

54. Dante insists that the powers and loves of the lower level are subsumed in the higher: 'queste potenze sono intra sé per modo che l'una è *fondamento* de l'altra' (*Con.* III, ii, 12). He exemplifies the elemental, mineral, vegetative and animal loves in man with many picturesque details in *Con.* III, iii, 5–10.

'*Omne animal,* inquantum est animal, necesse est quod *habeat sensum aliquem* . . . Sensus communes et necessarii omni animali sunt illi, qui sunt *cognoscitivi* eorum *quae sunt necesse animali* . . . *Odoratus, auditus* et *visus* insunt *illis de numero animalium, quae* . . . *motu progressivo moventur* . . . propter unam causam communem, scilicet *causam salutis,* ut *a remotis* scilicet *necessaria cognoscant;* . . . ut . . . *prosequantur* conveniens *alimentum,* et *fugiant mala et corruptiva* quaecumque, sicut *ovis fugit lupum* ut corruptivum, *lupus autem sequitur ovem* visam vel auditam aut odoratam, ut conveniens alimentum' (*In De sensu* ch. 1, 436b 8, *lect.* 2, §§20, 21, 24).

55. *Differentiation* of tangible qualities is the primary function of touch, which is the foundation of the other senses and is possessed by all animals. 'Habent enim animalia *imperfecta* de sensibus *solum tactum.*' '*Necessarium* est animali debita *commensuratio* calidi et frigidi, humidi et sicci, et aliorum huiusmodi, quae sunt *differentiae corporum mixtorum* . . . Ad hoc igitur quod *cognoscat* ea, quae sibi sunt *necessaria vel contraria* secundum rationem corporis mixti, ordinatur *sensus tactus,* qui est *cognoscitivus praedictarum differentiarum*' (*ibid.*, §§11, 21).

For the operation of pleasure and pain, cf.: 'Epicuro . . . veggendo che *ciascuno animale*, tosto che nato è, quasi da *natura dirizzato* nel debito *fine*, che *fugge dolore* e *domanda allegrezza . . .'* (*Con.* IV, vi, 11). '*Gustus* autem est ei necessarius propter *alimentum*; quia per gustum animal *discernit delectabile et tristabile*, sive *sapidum* et *insipidum* circa cibum, ut unum eorum *prosequatur* tamquam *conveniens*, alterum *fugiat* tamquam *nocivum*' (*In De sensu* ch. 1, 436b 10, *lect.* 2, §22).

On the faculty called *aestimativa*, cf.: 'Ipsa *vis cogitativa . . .* est *propria homini, loco cuius alia animalia* habent quandâm *aestimativam naturalem*. Huius autem cogitativae virtutis est *distinguere intentiones individuales et comparare eas* ad invicem' (*C.G.* II, 60, §1370). 'Etiam quaedam animalia participant aliquid *prudentiae* et aliquid sapientiae, scilicet quod *recte iudicant de agendis* per *aestimationem naturalem*' (*In De anima* III, 3, 427b 8, *lect.* 4, §629). 'Per *experientiam* fit . . . *existimatio* quod aliquid sit . . . possibile . . .' (S.T. 1–2ae. 40, 5, resp.). Aquinas, however, comments: '*deceptio* videtur esse *magis propria animalibus quam cognitio* secundum conditionem suae naturae' (*In De anima* III, 3, 427b 1, *lect.* 4, §624).

56. These paragraphs are essentially a paraphrase of *Purg.* XVIII, 19–33, 43–5, 49–60. For Dante's use of *piegare*, see also *Par.* IV, 79. He uses *istinto* and *amore naturale* as synonyms (cf. *Par.* I, 114; *Purg.* XVII, 92–3; *Con.* III, iii, 2–10).

57. Cf. *Par.* VII, 71–2; and: '*Animalia irrationalia*, quae *solo appetitu sensitivo aguntur* in suis motibus, ut plurimum *insequuntur impressiones corporum caelestium*' (*In De anima* III, 3, 427a 22, *lect.* 4, §617). 'If man were like other animals', says Aquinas in his own person, '*non esset dominus suarum actionum*, quia ageretur voluntate cuiusdam substantiae separatae [i.e. one of the intelligences controlling a heaven]; et in ipso essent tantum potentiae appetitivae cum passione operantes, scilicet irascibilis et concupiscibilis, quae sunt in parte sensitiva, sicut et *in ceteris animalibus, quae magis aguntur quam agunt*' (*C.G.* II, 60, §1374).

58. Psalm 104.9; quoted by Dante in *Con.* IV, xxiii, 8. *Par.* XVI, 79–81.

59. '*Privatio* nihil aliud est quam *absentia formae* quae est nata inesse' (*In De caelo*, I, 3 270a, *lect.* 6, §63). '*Materia nunquam* est *sine privatione*: quia quando habet unam formam, est cum privatione alterius formae . . . Secundum intentionem Aristotelis . . . *privatio . . .* non est aliqua aptitudo ad formam, vel inchoatio formae, vel aliquod principium imperfectum activum, . . . sed *ipsa carentia formae* vel *contrarium formae* quod subiecto accidit' (*In Physic.* I, 7, 190b 27, *lect.* 13, §113; cf. *Quaestio*, 45). 'Sic igitur in omni mutatione naturali requiritur *subiectum* [sc. materia] et *forma* et *privatio* (*ibid.*, §116). 'Li *principii* de le cose naturali . . . sono *tre*, cioè *materia, privazione* e *forma* . . .' (*Con.* II, xiii, 17).

60. 'Secundum conditionem causae proximae, effectus habet *contingentiam* vel *necessitatem*' (*S.T.* 1a. 25, 3, ad 4; cf. 14, 13 ad 1). 'In entibus ita est, quod *quaedam sunt contingentia* esse et non esse, et *quaedam* non contingunt non esse, sed *sunt ex necessitate*' (*In De gen.* II, 11, 337b 10, *lect.* 11, §268). '*Quaedam* sunt *de necessitate* in esse: sicut sunt aeterna, ut *corpora caelestia*, quae in sua substantia et in suis motibus sunt necessaria, et similiter *substantiae separatae . . .* Quaedam vero sunt *possibilia esse et non esse*: et ista sunt generabilia et corruptibilia, quae *quandoque sunt et quandoque non sunt*' (*ibid.*, II, 9, 335b, *lect.* 9, §245).

'Che più non fa che *brevi contingenze*; / e queste contingenze essere intendo / le *cose generate*' (*Par.* XIII, 63–5). The two terms derive from Aristotle's logical writings, as Dante clearly knew: cf. *ibid.*, 98–9: 'se *necesse* / con *contingente* mai *necesse* fenno'.

61. 'La contingenza, che *fuor* del quaderno / de la vostra *matera non si stende*' (*Par.* XVII, 37–8; cf. line 16). 'In quibus vero *forma non complet totam potentiam materiae*, remanet adhuc in materia *potentia ad aliam formam*. Et ideo *non* est in eis *necessitas essendi*' (*C.G.* II, 30, §1073; cf. *Quaestio*, 45).

62. 'Componitur enim corpus animalis *ex quatuor elementis,* quorum *nullum tenet proprium locum' (In De caelo* II, 6, 288b 15, *lect.* 9, §375).

63. '*Omnia* quae . . . *ex contrariis* sunt, *corruptibilia* sunt' *(C.G.* II, 30, §1073. See *Con.* IV, xxiii, *esp.* 7–8, 12 and Busnelli's commentary *ad loc.; Rime* XXV, 18–19 = *VN* XXXI, 10; Nardi, *Saggi,* pp. 115–23. Underneath, there persists the picture-language used by Empedocles, well described in *Metaphysics* III, 4, 1000a 25, and in Aquinas's commentary, *lect.* 11, §§473–82.

64. '*Proxima principia corruptibilium* sunt ipsa *corpora caelestia,* ut dicit Philosophus' *(In De gen.* II, 9, 335a 30, *lect.* 9, §245). 'Motus *circuli obliqui,* qui dicitur *zodiacus* est *causa* sufficiens utriusque [sc. *generationis et corruptionis*], propter motum accessionis et recessionis solis in eo' *(ibid.,* 336a 32, *lect.* 10, §258). Cf. note 13.

65. 'Onde, con ciò sia cosa che ciascuno effetto ritegna de la natura de la sua cagione – sì come dice Alpetragio quando afferma che *quello che è causato da corpo circulare ne ha in alcuno modo circulare essere' (Con.* III, ii, 5; cf. Nardi, *Saggi,* pp. 112, 165, as corrected by D. Bigongiari in his long and important review, in *Speculum,* VII (1932), p. 147).

'Onde, con ciò sia cosa che la . . . vita . . . d'ogni vivente qua giù sia causata dal cielo, e lo cielo a tutti questi cotali effetti, *non per cerchio compiuto,* ma *per parte di quello* a loro si scuopra; e così conviene che *'l suo movimento* sia sopra essi *come uno arco quasi; e tutte le terrene vite,* . . . *montando e volgendo,* convengono essere quasi *ad imagine d'arco assimiglianti* . . . Aristotile . . . parve volere che la nostra vita non fosse altro che uno salire e uno scendere' *(Con.* IV, xxiii, 6, 8).

66. The moment of 'culmination' is usually hidden, as Dante points out, because the middle section of the arc is close to the horizontal and 'poco di flessione si discerne' *(Con.* IV, xxiv, 3). '*Aequale est tempus generationis et corruptionis* . . . Et ideo *in astrologia* septimum signum vocatur *domus mortis,* et ascendens vocatur *domus vitae' (In De gen.* II, 10, 336b 10, *lect.* 10, §260). Cf. *Con.* IV, xxiv, 3 ('. . . *tanto* quanto questa etade ha di *salita, tanto* dee avere di *scesa'*).

67. Cf. note 7. 'Sicut igitur *finis naturae* in *generatione* . . . est . . . *perpetuitas rerum,* per quam ad *divinam similitudinem* accedunt; ita *finis motus caelestis* . . . est . . . *assimilari Deo in causando' (C.G.* IV, 97, §4287). 'Alio modo complevit Deus *materiae desiderium, perpetuando* scilicet eius *esse* per *continuam generationem' (In De gen.* II, 10, 336b 25, *lect.* 10, §261). 'Quia igitur *non* possunt communicare inferiora viventia *ipsi esse sempiterno et divino* per modum continuationis, idest ut maneant eadem numero, . . . sequitur, quod *unumquodque communicet perpetuitate secundum quod potest* . . . et . . . *permanet semper per generationem* . . . in *simili secundum speciem,* . . . quia unumquodque generat sibi simile secundum speciem' *(In De anima* II, 4, 415b 1–8, *lect.* 7, §317).

68. For *praeter* and *contra intentionem,* see note 67 to Chapter 8. 'Omnis autem impotentia et defectus est *praeter naturam* . . . Quod est intelligendum quantum ad naturam *particularem,* quae est *conservativa uniuscuiusque individui quantum potest:* unde *praeter intentionem* eius est quod *deficiat in conservando. Non autem est praeter naturam universalem, ex qua causatur non solum generatio, sed etiam corruptio* . . .: dicitur autem "*natura universalis*" *virtus activa* in causa universali, puta *in corpore caelesti' (In De caelo* II, 6, 288b 15, *lect.* 9, §375). '*Natura universalis* non frustratur suo fine; unde, licet *natura particularis* aliquando propter inobedientiam materiae ab intento fine frustretur, *Natura* tamen *universalis nullo modo potest a sua intentione deficere,* cum *Naturae universali* aequaliter actus et potentia rerum, quae possunt esse et non esse, subiaceant. Sed *intentio Naturae universalis est ut omnes formae, quae sunt in potentia materiae primae, reducantur in actum,* et secundum rationem speciei sint in actu; ut *materia prima secundum suam totalitatem sit sub omni forma materiali* . . .' *(Quaestio,* 44–5). See also *In Meta.* VII, 7, 1032a 15–30, *lect.* 6, §1403; *In De caelo* I, 3, 270a 12, *lect.* 6, §63.

69. 'Dicendum est quod illa circulatio ignis vel aeris [cf. note 14] *non est eis naturalis*, quia non causatur ex principio intrinseco; *neque* iterum est *per violentiam*, sive *contra naturam*; sed est quodammodo *supra* naturam . . . *Quod* autem *inest inferioribus corporibus ex impressione superiorum, non est eis violentum nec contra naturam*, quia *naturaliter apta sunt moveri a superiore corpore'* (*In De caelo* I, 2, 269a 15, *lect.* 4, §39).

'Unde cum *intentioni Naturae universalis omnis natura obediat, necesse fuit* etiam praeter simplicem naturam terrae, quae est esse deorsum, *inesse aliam naturam per quam obediret intentioni universalis Naturae*; ut scilicet pateretur elevari in parte a virtute caeli, *tanquam obediens a praecipiente* . . .' (*Quaestio*, 48).

70. When we refer to the divine 'labours', says Aquinas, we must understand *opus* in three ways: 'scilicet *opus creationis*, per quod caelum et terra producta leguntur, sed informia. Et *opus distinctionis*, per quod *caelum* et *terra* sunt perfecta; . . . *et* . . . *opus ornatus*, [ad quod] pertinet *productio illarum rerum* quae *habent motum* in caelo et in terra' (*S.T.* 1a. 70, 1, resp.). Thus for Aquinas, Genesis 1, 1–2 refer to *creation*; 1. 3–13 (the first, second and third days) refer to *distinction*; while 1. 14–31 refer to *adornment*). This division does not accord well with Dante's account (e.g. his heavens are produced 'in lor essere intero', not *informia*). *Opus distinctionis* is therefore used here for all the labours after the first day that culminate in the making of Adam.

71. Cf. *Par.* VII, 85–6, 148. 'Individua quae nunc generantur, praecesserunt in primis individuis suarum specierum' (*S.T.* 1a. 73, 1 ad 3).

72. Obviously it was not exactly like generation because there could not have been any *generans actu tale*, nor any seed, nor any growth from infancy to maturity.

73. 'Cum *omnes formae materiales generabilium* et *corruptibilium*, praeter formas elementorum, requirant materiam et *subiectum mixtum* et *complexionatum* ad quod tanquam ad finem ordinata sunt elementa in quantum elementa, et *mixtio* esse non possit ubi *miscibilia* simul esse non possunt, ut de se patet; *necesse est esse partem* in universo *ubi omnia miscibilia*, scilicet elementa, *convenire possint*; haec autem esse non posset, *nisi terra in aliqua parte emergeretur*, ut patet intuenti . . .' '[Terra] patitur elevari in parte . . . *ut mixtio sit possibilis.*' '[Et] *de causa finali* . . . huius elevationis terrae . . . sufficiant quae dicta sunt . . .' (*Quaestio*, 47, 49, 59).

74. *Quaestio*, 34, 63, 67–8.

75. 'Cum igitur non sint plura corpora mobilia, praeter *caelum stellatum*, quod est octava sphaera, *necesse est hunc effectum in ipsum reduci* . . . *Caelum stellatum* . . . habet . . . *multiplicitatem* in virtute [see notes 17 and 18] . . . Consequens est quod . . . similitudo virtualis agentis consistat *in illa regione caeli quae operit hanc terram detectam*. Et cum ista terra detecta extendatur a linea aequinoctiali usque ad lineam quam describit polus zodiaci circa polum mundi [i.e. the Arctic circle] . . . manifestum est quod *virtus elevans est illis stellis quae sunt in regione caeli istis duobus circulis contenta* . . .' (*Quaestio*, 69–73).

76. 'Sed nunc quaeritur: cum illa regio caeli circulariter feratur, *quare illa elevatio non fuit circularis?*' (*ibid.*, 74). '[*Via*] inquisitionis in naturalibus oportet esse *ab effectibus ad causas*. Quae quidem via, licet habeat *certitudinem* sufficientem, *non tamen habet tantam*, quantam habet via inquisitionis in *mathematicis* . . .; et ideo *quaerenda est illa certitudo quae sic demonstrando haberi potest'* (*ibid.*, 61–2: cf. *Con.* IV, xxi, 1, 10, 11).

77. *Quaestio*, 75–6.

78. '*Natura* certo, quando *lasciò l'arte* / di sì fatti animali, assai fé bene' (*Inf.* XXXI, 49–50. For 'l'arte di natura', cf. *ibid.*, XI, 99–100; *Purg.* XXV, 71).

79. This reconstruction of Dante's position makes him a 'modern heretic' in the context of the following paragraph by Aquinas: 'Sunt autem quidam *moderni haeretici* qui dicunt Deum omnium visibilium creasse materiam, sed *per aliquem angelum diversis formis fuisse distinctam*. Cuius opinionis *falsitas* manifeste apparet . . . *Prima* igitur *institutio* *harum formarum*, ad quarum productionem non sufficit motus caelestis sine praeexistentia similium formarum in specie, *oportet quod sit a solo creante . . . Neque* igitur *totalis acquisitio formarum* in materia potest *fieri per motum ab aliqua substantia separata*, cuiusmodi est angelus' (*C.G.* II, 43, §§1193, 1198–9).

'*Formae corporales*, quas in *prima* productione corpora . . . habuerunt, *sunt immediate a Deo productae*, cui soli ad nutum obedit materia tanquam propriae causae' (*S.T.* 1a. 65, 4, resp.; cf. 45, 5 and 65, 3 which discuss the same range of problems). 'Quidam posuerunt . . . *corpora caelestia* esse *causas* istorum inferiorum non solum quantum ad motum, sed etiam quantum ad *primam* eorum *institutionem . . . ut sic . . . sint media* inter Deum et ista corpora inferiora *etiam in via creationis* quodammodo. Sed *hoc alienum est a fide*, quae ponit naturam *omnium immediate* a Deo esse conditam secundum *primam institutionem*' (*De veritate*, qu. 5, a. 9).

80. For the orthodox Thomist view of the role of the first Two Persons in Creation, see *S.T.* 1a. 45, 6 and 7, where we read: 'Secundum . . . quod [quaelibet creatura] est quaedam substantia creata . . . demonstrat Personam Patris . . . Secundum autem quod habet *quandam formam et speciem, repraesentat Verbum*; secundum quod forma artificiati est ex conceptione artificis . . .' (a. 7, resp.).

81. See the texts quoted in *Quaestio*, 77; *Con.* III, viii, 2; IV, xx, 6 etc.

82. *Con.* III, vi, 5. The whole paragraph gives a very explicit account of the derivation of all things from God, via the minds of the 'Intelligenze motrici' and the heavens.

83. In all these passages 'virtue' means the active, causal influence exercised by the heavens.

11   The makings of a man

1. The opening of the Casella episode (*Purg.* II, 76–87) is modelled primarily on the meeting between Aeneas and Anchises in the Elysian Fields (*Aeneid* VI, esp. 700–2); but Virgil had used the same motif and the same three lines in the earlier meeting between Aeneas and the shade of his first wife, Creusa (II, 792–4). Both episodes derive from Odysseus's leave-taking from his dead mother (*Odyssey* XI, 206). For the reference to the tangible qualities of heat and cold, see *Purg.* III, 31–3.

2. Aquinas tackles the problems in *C.G.* II, 79–81; *S.T.* 1a. 75, 6; 77, 8.

3. The quotation is from *Epist.* XIII, 24. The 'reminders' come in repetitions of the vain embrace in *Purg.* VI, 75 and XXI, 130–6. The 'anticipations' will be found in Virgil's speeches in *Purg.* III, 28–45 and XVIII, 49–60. The answers that he, as a pagan, cannot give, are supplied by Statius in the discourse to be expounded in the first half of this chapter.

4. *Purg.* XXV, 20–1.

5. 'Quod enim nutritur, *assimilat* sibi nutrimentum: unde oportet in nutrito esse virtutem nutritionis activam, cum *agens sibi simile agat*' (*C.G.* II, 89, §1736).

6. 'Et talis est operatio animae vegetabilis; *digestio* enim, et ea quae consequuntur, fit instrumentaliter per actionem caloris' (*S.T.* 1a. 78, 1, resp.). 'Sed hoc [sc. menstrual discharge] est purgamentum quoddam illius *puri sanguinis*, qui *digestione quadam est praeparatus ad conceptum*, quasi purior et perfectior alio sanguine' (*S.T.* 3a. 31, 5, ad 3).

7. This section leans heavily on the article by Bruno Nardi, entitled 'L'origine dell'anima umana secondo Dante', now in his *Studi di filosofia medievale* (Rome, 1960), pp. 9–68. There is a long and very clear exposition of Aristotle's teaching in the introduction to A. L. Peck's edition of *The Generation of Animals* (Loeb Library). The chapters entitled 'Hellenistic Biology and Medicine' and 'Galen' in G. E. R. Lloyd's *Greek Science after Aristotle* (London, 1973), pp. 75–90 and 136–53, offer a very helpful guide to later developments in antiquity. Subsequent notes will provide references to the works of Aquinas.

As regards Galen's theory of the blood it must be remembered that he believed there to be two *distinct* systems – the veins and the arteries. The former had its seat in the liver, the latter in the heart. The only interchange between the two systems consisted in the 'seepage' of blood through the invisible (and, in fact, non-existent) pores in the inner wall of the heart. The *movement* of the blood (and Dante will speak of blood 'fleeing' and 'running', *Rime* CIII, 45–7) was thought to be limited to an ebb and flow: in neither system was there a *circulation*.

The wording of the description of the third and fourth 'coctions' is based on modern paraphrases of Galen's theory. Nardi follows Avicenna and St Albert who give a slightly different version: 'la terza [si compie] nelle vene, ove il sangue grezzo e imperfetto, uscito dal fegato, vien depurato dalle superfluità acquose e si converte in sangue perfetto che si raccoglie nel lago del cuore; finalmente la quarta digestione avviene nelle singole membra, delle quali l'alimento sanguigno ristora le perdite e produce lo sviluppo' (*Studi*, p. 47). Statius's account is so dense that we cannot be sure which authorities Dante would have had in mind.

8. *Generation of Animals*, 765b 8–766b 25. For the contributions made by the mother and father, cf.: 'Habet autem hoc naturalis conditio, quod in generatione animalis *femina materiam* ministret, *ex parte* autem *maris* sit *principium activum* in generatione, sicut probat Philosophus [726b 25]' (*S.T.* 3a. 31, 5, resp.). On the *menstruum*, and its 'digestion' from the 'perfect blood' of the mother, cf.: 'Haec autem materia, secundum Philosophum in libro *De Gen. Anim.* [727b 33] est *sanguis mulieris*, non quicumque, sed *perductus ad quandam ampliorem digestionem* per virtutem generativam matris, ut sit materia *apta ad conceptum*' (*ibid.*). Later Aquinas describes it as 'quiddam imperfectum in genere seminis' (*ibid.*, ad 3). For the difficulties inherent in the concept of a 'formative power', see A. L. Peck, Introduction, §§29 and 34. The phrases concerning the 'perfect place' and 'making provision' are from *Purg.* XXV, 48, 59–60.

9. *Generation of Animals* 724b 26; 726a 26; 736b 28; 766b 8.

10. On the mother's 'passivity', see note 8, and *Generation of Animals* 716a 1–25; 730b 1; 733b 20; 740b 25; *S.T.* 1a. 118, 1–2. For the 'curdling' metaphor, see *Generation of Animals* 737a 15; 739a 5; 739b 20. Job 10.10; Wisdom 7.2. The verb *constare* is the Latin translation of Aristotle's *synistanai*. The double translation reflects the excellent note by A. L. Peck, Introduction, §54.

11. *Generation of Animals* II, 3, 736a 35; *C.G.* II, 89, §1736.

12. 'Intermedia non habent speciem completam, sed sunt ut *in via* ad speciem; et ideo non generantur ut permaneant, sed ut per ea ad ultimum generatum perveniatur' (*C.G.* II, 89, §1744). For the 'a riva' metaphor, see *Purg.* XXV, 54, quoted in text below. For the association between 'perfection' and the ability to reproduce, cf.: 'Unde et *signum perfectionis* est alicuius quod *simile possit producere*, ut patet per Philosophum in IV *Meteor.* [380a 13–15]' (*C.G.* I, 37, §307).

13. 'In uno animali non est nisi *unum principium formale*, quod est *una anima*.' 'Nihil enim est simpliciter unum nisi *per formam unam*, per quam habet res esse; ab eodem enim habet res quod sit ens, et quod sit una' (*S.T.* 1a. 118, 1, ob. 4; 76, 3, resp.).

'Dicendum est quod cum generatio unius semper sit corruptio alterius, necesse est dicere quod *tam in homine* quam in animalibus aliis, *quando perfectior forma advenit, fit corruptio prioris*; ita tamen quod sequens forma habet quidquid habebat prima, et adhuc amplius. Et sic *per multas generationes et corruptiones pervenitur ad ultimam formam substantialem, tam in homine* quam in aliis animalibus' (*S.T.* 1a. 118, 2, ad 2; see also *C.G.* II, 89, §§1743–5).

14. St Albert's (and, apparently, Dante's) views are expounded and rejected by Aquinas in the following terms: 'Neque tamen potest dici quod *in semine ab ipso principio* sit *anima secundum suam essentiam completam,* cuius tamen operationes non appareant propter organorum defectum . . . *Sequeretur* etiam, si a principio anima esset in semine, quod *generatio animalis esset solum per decisionem:* sicut est in animalibus anulosis, quod ex uno fiunt duo.

. . . *Neque* etiam dici potest, quod quidam dicunt: etsi a principio decisionis in semine non sit anima actu, sed virtute, propter deficientiam organorum, tamen *ipsammet virtutem seminis* (quod est corpus organizabile, etsi non organizatum) *esse proportionaliter semini animam in potentia,* sed non actu; et quia vita plantae pauciora requirit organa quam vita animalis, primo semine sufficienter ad vitam plantae organizato, *ipsam praedictam virtutem fieri animam vegetabilem; deinde,* organis magis perfectis et multiplicatis, *eandem perduci ut sit anima sensitiva;* ulterius autem, forma organorum perfecta, *eandem animam fieri rationalem,* non quidem per actionem virtutis seminis, sed ex influxu exterioris agentis . . . Secundum enim hanc positionem, *sequeretur* quod *aliqua virtus* eadem numero *nunc esset anima vegetabilis tantum, et postmodum anima sensitiva:* et sic ipsa forma substantialis *continue* magis ac magis perficeretur. Et ulterius *sequeretur* quod . . . *generatio esset motus continuus, sicut et alteratio. Quae omnia sunt impossibilia* in natura' (*C.G.* II, 89, §§1737–8, 1740; cf. *S.T.* 1a. 118, 2, ad 2).

15. The word *virtute (virtù)* is twice repeated here, once with the adjective *attiva* (line 52), and once with an adjectival clause (59). It is identical with the *virtute formativa* of line 41, as is confirmed by the repeated statements that this is the power which forms 'all members' (40, 60) and that it derives from the father's 'heart' (40, 59). In other words, the same *virtute* is operative throughout embryonic life. Statius does in fact use the word *operare* for its first action (49) and again for the activity that leads to the first stirrings of sensation and movement (55). Most important of all, he says that it is the *virtute* which *becomes* the plant-like soul: this is precisely the formulation condemned by St Thomas (see previous note). And finally he complicates the issue by describing this nutritive soul as the 'seed' (*semente,* 57) of the powers which it unfolds in the third stage of development.

Aquinas's position is summarized in this sentence: 'Relinquitur igitur quod *formatio corporis,* praecipue quantum ad primas et principales partes, *non est ab anima geniti, nec a virtute formativa agente ex vi eius, sed agente ex vi animae generativae patris,* cuius opus est facere simile generanti secundum speciem' (*C.G.* II, 89, §1742).

16. The following formulation of this commonplace is precise and representative: 'Homo habet propriam operationem *supra* alia animalia, scilicet *intelligere* et *ratiocinari,* quae est operatio hominis inquantum est homo, ut Aristoteles dicit in I *Ethicorum* [I, 6, 1098a 1–5]' (*C.G.* II, 60, §1371). Aquinas's paraphrase of the quoted passage ends: 'Homo *speciem* sortitur ab hoc, quod est *rationale',* §126.

17. The example of the stone comes from *De anima* III, 8, 431b 30: 'Non enim *lapis* in anima est, sed species.' The following passages from Aquinas use the same example and illustrate the terminology, especially the distinction between sense and intellect, particular and universal, *phantasma* and *species intelligibilis.* 'Anima autem intellectiva cognoscit rem aliquam *in sua natura absolute,* puta *lapidem* inquantum est *lapis absolute* . . . Si enim anima intellectiva esset composita ex materia et forma, formae rerum reciperentur in ea ut individuales; et sic *non cognosceret nisi singulare, sicut accidit in potentiis sensitivis, quae recipiunt formas rerum in organo corporali'* (*S.T.* 1a. 75, 5, resp.).

'Intellectus autem noster . . . intelligit abstrahendo speciem intelligibilem ab huiusmodi materia. Quod autem a materia individuali abstrahitur, est *universale.* Unde *intellectus noster* directe *non est cognoscitivus nisi universalium'* (86, 1, resp.). 'Primum quod intelligitur a nobis secundum statum praesentis vitae, est *quidditas rei materialis, quae est nostri intellectus obiectum*' (88, 3, resp.). '*Intelligitur enim natura communis, seclusis principiis individuantibus . . .*' (76, 2, ad 4).

'Posset autem diversificari actio intellectualis mea et tua per diversitatem phantasmatum, quia scilicet aliud est *phantasma lapidis* in me et aliud in te, si ipsum phantasma . . . esset forma intellectus possibilis . . . Sed *ipsum phantasma non est forma intellectus possibilis, sed species intelligibilis quae a phantasmatibus abstrahitur*. In uno autem intellectu a phantasmatibus diversis eiusdem speciei *non abstrahitur nisi una species intelligibilis*. Sicut in uno homine apparet, in quo *possunt esse diversa phantasmata lapidis*, et tamen ab omnibus eis *abstrahitur una species intelligibilis lapidis*, per quam intellectus unius hominis operatione una *intelligit naturam lapidis non obstante diversitate phantasmatum*' (76, 2, resp.).

18. In other contexts it would be necessary to distinguish and contrast these activities of the intellect, in the light of texts such as the following: '*Duplex est operatio intellectus: una* quidem, quae dicitur indivisibilium intelligentia, per quam scilicet intellectus *apprehendit essentiam* uniuscuiusque rei in seipsa; *alia* est operatio intellectus, scilicet *componentis* et *dividentis*. Additur autem et *tertia* operatio, scilicet *ratiocinandi*, secundum quod ratio procedit a notis ad inquisitionem ignotorum' (*In Periherm.* I, I, *lect.* I, §I: these are the opening words of Aquinas's own *prooemium*).

19. Dante will make Statius refer both to our own self-awareness (=the intellect's knowledge of itself, line 75; cf. *De anima* III, 4, 429b 9), and to our recognition of mind in others through their command of language (line 61). For Dante's grasp of the distinctively human faculty of speech ('*Soli homini* datum est loqui'), see *Dve* I, ii–iii.

20. '*Visio est substantialis forma oculi* . . . Vigilantia est actus animae sensitivae, sicut incisio est actus cultelli, et *visio est actus oculi*' (*In De anima* II, I, 413a 1–4, *lect.* 2, §§239, 241).

'Rationabile est quod [intellectus] *non misceatur corpori*, idest quod *non habeat aliquod organum corporale* . . . Eiusdem rationis est ponere quod intellectus non habeat organum corporale, et quod non habeat aliquam naturam corpoream determinatam . . . *Nullum est organum intellectivae partis* sicut est sensitivae' (*In De anima* III, 4, 429a 25, §§684–5). It must of course be remembered that 'la nostra anima conviene grande parte de le sue operazioni operare con organo corporale . . .' (*Con.* IV, xxv, 11; cf. *ibid.*, III, iv, 9; viii, 1, etc.).

The intellect is said to be 'divine' and 'from outside' in *Generation of Animals* II, 3, 736b 28. It is called 'immortal' and 'perpetual' in *De anima* III, 5, 430a 23; cf. also I, 4, 408b 18–30.

21. 'In omni natura quae est quandoque in potentia et quandoque in actu, oportet ponere *aliquid*, quod est sicut materia in unoquoque genere . . . et *aliud*, quod est sicut *causa agens*, et factivum; quod ita se habet in faciendo omnia, sicut *ars* ad *materiam* . . . Necesse est igitur in anima intellectiva esse has differentias: ut scilicet unus sit intellectus, in quo possint omnia intelligibilia fieri, et hic est *intellectus possibilis* . . .; et alius intellectus sit ad hoc quod possit omnia intelligibilia facere in actu; qui vocatur *intellectus agens*' (*In De anima* III, 5, 430a 10–15, *lect.* 10, §728).

The following passage from the *Summa Theologiae* brings out another important strand in Aristotle's reasoning about the agent intellect. 'Intellectum vero posuit Aristoteles [429a 24] habere *operationem absque communicatione corporis. Nihil autem corporeum imprimere potest in rem incorpoream.* Et ideo ad causandam intellectualem operationem, secundum Aristotelem, *non sufficit sola impressio sensibilium corporum, sed requiritur aliquid nobilius*, quia "agens est honorabilius patiente" [430a 18], ut ipse dicit. *Non* tamen ita quod intellectualis operatio causetur ex sola impressione aliquarum rerum *superiorum, ut Plato posuit*; sed *illud superius et nobilius agens quod vocat intellectum agentem . . .* quod facit phantasmata a sensibus accepta intelligibilia in actu per modum *abstractionis* cuius-dam ... *Phantasmata non sufficiunt immutare intellectum possibilem, sed oportet quod fiant intelligibilia actu per intellectum agentem'* (1a. 84, 6, resp.).

Earlier commentators of Aristotle, chief among them the Arabs, had tended to place *either* or *both* these intellects *outside* the individual human soul, and to treat them as Intelligences or *substantiae separatae*. Aquinas insists that both are located *within*: 'Est etiam praedicta positio contra Aristotelis intentionem: qui expresse dixit, has differentias duas, scilicet *intellectum agentem* et *intellectum possibilem, esse in anima*: ex quo expresse dat intelligere, quod sint *partes animae, vel potentiae, et non aliquae substantiae separatae'* (*In De anima* III, 5, 430a 18–20, *lect.* 10, §§736; cf. §734).

Dante never refers to the *'agent* intellect' as such. There are, however, passages in the *Convivio* where his use of the imagery of intellectual light does suggest that he thought of the mind as being illuminated from *without* (see II, iv, 16–17; viii, 13–15; III, i, 1; iv, 2, 10; vii, 5, 8; xv, 5–6).

22. *'Anima* dicitur esse *primum principium vitae* in his quae apud nos vivunt' (*S.T.* 1a. 75, 1, resp.). 'Anima enim est primum quo nutrimur, et sentimus, et movemur secundum locum; et *similiter quo primo intelligimus'* (76, 1, resp.).

'Natura enim uniuscuiusque rei *ex eius operatione ostenditur* [cf. *Purg.* XVIII, 49–54]. *Propria autem operatio hominis*, inquantum est homo, est *intelligere*; per hanc enim omnia alia transcendit ... Oportet ergo quod homo secundum illud speciem sortiatur, quod est huius operationis principium. Sortitur autem unumquodque speciem per propriam formam. Relinquitur ergo quod *intellectivum principium sit propria hominis forma'* (*S.T.* 1a. 76, 1, resp.).

23. 'Hoc ergo principium quo primo intelligimus, sive dicatur intellectus, sive *anima intellectiva*, est *forma corporis*. Et haec est demonstratio Aristotelis in II *De anima* [414a 12]' (*S.T.* 1a. 76, 1, resp.). 'Dicendum est quod *nulla alia forma substantialis est in homine nisi sola anima intellectiva*; et quod ipsa, sicut virtute continet animam sensitivam et nutritivam, ita *virtute continet omnes inferiores formas*, et facit ipsa sola quidquid imperfectiores formae in aliis faciunt' (76, 4, resp.). *'Anima intellectiva continet in sua virtute quidquid habet anima sensitiva brutorum, et nutritiva plantarum'* (76, 3, resp.).

24. Cf. *Con.* III, ii, 10–15; iii, 11. *'Anima intellectiva quandoque nominatur nomine intellectus, quasi a principaliori sua virtute*; sicut dicitur in I *De anima* [408b 18], quod "intellectus est substantia quaedam"' (*S.T.* 1a. 79, 1, ad 1).

25. Aristotle uses the famous image of the mind as a wax tablet: 'Oportet autem hoc sic esse, *sicut contingit in tabula*, in qua nihil est actu scriptum, sed plura possunt in ea scribi. Et *hoc* etiam *accidit intellectui possibili* ... Et per hoc *excluditur* ... opinio Platonis, qui posuit naturaliter animam humanam habere omnem scientiam, sed esse eam quodam-modo oblitam, propter unionem ad corpus' (*In De anima* III, 4, 430a 1, *lect.* 9, §§722–3).

'Unde oportet quod, sicut hoc individuum est *animal* propter *sensum* ... ita sit *homo* propter *id quo intelligit*. Id autem quo intelligit anima, vel homo per animam, est *intellectus possibilis*, ut dicitur in III *De anima* [429a 10–11]. *Est igitur hoc individuum homo per intellectum possibilem'* (*C.G.* II, 73, §1493). See also the terminology used by Dante in *Con.* IV, xxi, 5–7.

26. *'Impossibile* est quod *virtus quae est in semine, sit productiva intellectivi principii* ... Virtus intellectivi principii, prout intellectivum est, *non potest ad semen pervenire*. Et ideo Philosophus, in libro *De Gen. Anim.* [736b 27], dicit: "Relinquitur intellectus solus de foris advenire" ... *Haereticum* est dicere quod *anima intellectiva traducatur cum semine'* (*S.T.* 1a. 118, 2, resp.; see also *C.G.* II, 86–9).

On the role of the 'spirit', cf.: 'Non oportet quod ista vis activa [quae est in semine ex anima generantis derivata] habeat aliquod organum in actu; sed fundatur in *ipso spiritu incluso in semine*, quod est *spumosum*, ut attestatur eius albedo. *In quo etiam spiritu est quidam calor ex virtute caelestium corporum . . .*' (*S.T.* 1a. 118, 1, ad 3).

27. See *Inf.* IV, 144; *Mon.* I, iii, 9; *Con.* IV, xiii, 8, etc.

28. 'Fuerunt autem et *alii* alia adinventione utentes in *sustinendo* quod *substantia intellectualis non possit uniri corpori ut forma*. Dicunt enim quod *intellectus*, etiam quem Aristoteles "possibilem" vocat, est quaedam *substantia separata non coniuncta nobis ut forma*' (*C.G.* II, 59, §1353. The whole chapter sets out and refutes Averroes's reasoning; see also ch. 73, §1488, and *In De anima* III, 4, 429a, *lect.* 7, §§689–99).

Averroes identified the specifically human soul with a third kind or aspect of intellect, the 'passive' intellect, which he located firmly in the middle of the brain: 'Dicit enim praedictus Averroes quod homo *differt specie* a brutis per intellectum quem Aristoteles vocat "*passivum*", qui est *ipsa vis cogitativa, quae est propria homini,* loco cuius *alia animalia* habent quandam *aestimativam* naturalem. Huius autem cogitative virtutis est distinguere *intentiones individuales*, et comparare eas ad invicem: sicut intellectus qui est "separatus et immixtus" comparat et distinguit inter intentiones *universales* . . . Praedicta virtus vocatur nomine "intellectus" et "rationis", de qua *medici dicunt quod habet sedem in media cellula capitis*. Et secundum dispositionem huius virtutis *differt homo unus ab alio* in ingenio et in aliis quae pertinent ad intelligendum . . . Et *hic intellectus "passivus" a principio adest puero, per quem sortitur speciem humanam,* antequam actu intelligat' (*C.G.* II, 60, §1370). The verbs used for the 'participation' or 'union' of this 'passive' intellect with the separate and unique 'possible' intellect are *copulari, coniungi,* and *continuari*.

29. Averroes's argument is set out in *C.G.* II, 70, §1614. For Aquinas's counter-attacks, see *C.G.* II, 59–62, 68–79, esp. 60 and 73; *S.T.* 1a. 76, esp. a. 2, where the reply begins: 'Dicendum quod *intellectum esse unum omnium hominum*, omnino est *impossibile*.' Elsewhere he calls Averroes's theses 'ridiculous' and 'frivolous'.

30. In the Vulgate text of Genesis 2.7, the crucial words are '*inspiravit . . . spiraculum* vitae'. Dante's choice of the more suggestive word *spirito* is influenced by texts such as Ecclesiasticus 12.7: 'Revertatur pulvis in terram suam, unde erat, *et spiritus redeat ad Deum qui dedit illum*' (cf. *S.T.* 1a. 75, 6, ad 1). See also *Aeneid* VI, 726.

31. 'Sicut semen viri, in generatione communi hominum, *in suam subsistentiam trahit* materiam a matre ministratam, ita eandem materiam, in generatione Christi, Verbum Dei ad suam unionem assumpsit.' 'Non autem Verbum Dei subsistentiam habet ex natura humana, sed magis *naturam humanam ad suam subsistentiam* vel personalitatem *trahit*; non enim per illam, sed in illa subsistit' (*C.G.* IV, 45, §3818; 49, §3839; see also §§3826, 3841, 3848). The first passage is quoted by Busnelli in the tenth appendix to his commentary on *Convivio* IV (vol. 2, p. 399).

32. It is not in fact likely that Dante is inviting us to see the three powers of the human soul as the image of the Trinity in man. That likeness was traditionally located wholly in the divine part, the intellect; and it was identified by St Augustine with memory, intelligence and will – to which Statius will soon allude (*Purg.* XXV, 81, 83; cf. *S.T.* 1a. 45, 7; 93, 1, 2 and 6). On the contrary, Dante makes Statius insist on the *unity* of the soul to 'exclude' another error found in Plato and other *moderni*, who held that there were three distinct souls in man. The original error had already been exposed and dismissed by Aristotle (*De anima* I, 5, 411b). In the *Contra gentiles*, St Thomas demolishes the Platonic position in the chapter immediately preceding his attack on Averroes's exposition of the *intellectus possibilis* (II, 58, 59; cf. also *S.T.* 1a. 76, 3–4). Dante follows Aquinas closely in his earlier reference to the error in *Purg.* IV, 1–12 (for which, see Aquinas, *In Ethic.* X, 5, 1175b 1–15, *lect.* 7, §§2045–7).

33. See also *Purg.* XVI, 89; *Par.* XXXII, 64.

34. All the allusions to and quotations from the second part of Statius's speech will be

found in *Purg.* XXV, 79–108. For Aquinas's account of the separated soul, see *S.T.* 1a. 89, 1–8 ('De cognitione animae separatae'); *Suppl.* 70, 1–3 ('De qualitate animae existentis a corpore separatae et poena ei inflicta ab igne corporeo'). The four adverbs (*dubitando*, etc.) come from 1a. 89, 8, resp. and *Suppl.* 70, 2 and 3. St Thomas insists that only the intellectual faculties persist; that memory will not entail memory of *particularia* in the past; that the soul will have no sensitive powers and no vision. His explanations of the sufferings caused by fire could not be used as a basis for poetic representation.

35. Now, finally, we understand why Statius kept insisting on the *virtute informativa* – alias *virtute attiva*, alias *ciò che trova attivo* – at every stage in his account of the formation of the embryo.

36. References in order: foundations. *Par.* VIII, 143; lovers and Venus, IX, 33, 95–6; crusaders, XIV–XVII, *passim*, IV, 58–60; Gemini, XXII, 112–23.

37. See the texts quoted in notes 16–29; *Mon.* I, iii, *passim*; *Par.* IV, 124–9; etc.

38. '*Vis appetitiva . . . in parte rationabili . . . est voluntas . . .* Appetitus qui sequitur apprehensionem intellectus, est unus tantum . . . *Intellectus non est principium motivum . . .*; *neque ratiocinativa . . .* videtur esse *movens . . . Speculativus intellectus* non *speculatur aliquid agibile*, neque dicit aliquid de fugibili et persequibili; et sic non potest movere . . . Aliquando autem intellectus considerat aliquid agibile, non tamen practice, sed speculative, quia considerat ipsum in universali . . . *Sed intellectus non iubet timere vel desiderare . . .*' (*In De anima* III, 9 432b 25, *lect.* 14, §§802, 804, 812, 814). For Aquinas's own account of the will in intellectual beings, see *S.T.* 1a. 19; 59; 82–3; 1a–2ae. 6–17.

39. *Purg.* XVIII, 62–3.

40. *Epist.* XIII, 25. See also *C.G.* II, 60, §1374.

41. 'Haec *libertas* sive *principium hoc totius nostrae libertatis*, est *maximum donum humanae naturae a Deo collatum . . .*' (*Mon.* I, xii, 6).

42. *Con.* IV, xii, 14. The same chapter develops the image of a journey from one *albergo* to the next and from a smaller good to a greater good; it is the first place where Dante speaks of the '*cammino* di questa vita' (15). The idea is expressed with greater exactitude in *C.G.* II, 87, §1719.

The conclusion can also be reached in other ways which bring out the importance of the likeness between God and man: e.g. Every effect must resemble its cause (*agens agit sibi simile*). Likeness is the cause of love (*similitudo est causa amoris*, cf. *Rime* CVI, 63, 136; CXVI, 36; *Con.* III, i, 5; *Par.* VII, 73; *Mon.* I, xi, 15). Therefore, every effect must love its cause.

43. 'Questa *prima voglia* / *merto* di lode o di biasmo *non cape*' (*Purg.* XVIII, 59–60; cf. XVII, 97–9, 111).

44. Cf. *Purg.* XXX, 130–2; XXXI, 28–36, 56; and, earlier, XVII, 133–5; XIX, 16–33.

45. *Purg.* XVII, 127–9; XXVIII, 139–41. This was the spirit he recognized in Aristotle and Virgil (cf. *Purg.* III, 43), and which drew him so powerfully to their works; this too is the source of the tragic pathos in his characterization of Virgil as an actor in the *Comedy*.

46. On charity (love for God) as the ground of the moral life, see *Purg.* XVII, 91–139; XVIII, 46–75. For man's 'natural place', see *Purg.* XXVIII, 77–8, 92–3; *Par.* I, 55–7. For his unimpeded ascent, see *Par.* I, 121–6, 139–41; II, 19–21 (cf. *Purg.* I, 71; XXVII, 131, 140).

47. St Paul had of course been 'caught up into paradise' but 'whether in the body, or out of the body' he could not tell (2 Corinthians 12.3; cf. *Par.* I, 73–5). A happy ending is essential to Dante's definition of 'comedy': '*Comoedia* vero inchoat asperitatem alicuius rei, *sed eius materia prospere terminatur . . .*' (*Epist.* XIII, 29).

48. *Con.* II, viii, 8. For *carità*, and Dante's love for Florence, see *Inf.* XIV, 1; *Rime* CXVI, 76–9; *Par.* III, 43; *Dve* I, vi, 3; II, vi, 4. For the 'true city', see *Purg.* XIII, 94–5.

49. References in order: Psalm 8.5–7 (quoted by Dante in *Con.* IV, xix, 7); man's desire for immortality, *Con.* II, viii, 10–12, III, xv, 7–9, IV, xiii, 6–9 (cf. *C.G.* II, 79, §1602); Dante's affirmation, *Con.* II, viii, 10, 16.

50. Cf. *Inf.* III, 8; IV, 42; *Purg.* III, 34–45; VII, 25–6; XXI, 16–18.

51. In the original, the verb *videri* occurs in a subordinate construction which takes the subjunctive mood (*videatur* not *videtur*): 'Cum igitur homo non naturae instinctu, sed ratione moveatur, et ipsa *ratio* vel circa discretionem vel circa iudicium vel circa electionem *diversificetur in singulis*, adeo ut *fere quilibet sua propria specie videatur gaudere . . .*' (*Dve* I, iii, 1); cf. *Con.* III, xi, 7. The following passage from Aquinas's commentary to the *Ethics* is illuminating: 'Cum delectatio consequatur operationem, videtur *quod unicuique rei sit propria delectatio*, sicut et propria operatio . . . *Operationes sequuntur formas* rerum secundum quas *res specie differunt* . . . Manifestum est enim, quod *alia est delectatio equi* et alia *canis* et alia *hominis* . . . Sic igitur patet quod eorum quae differunt specie, sunt delectationes specie differentes. Sed eorum quae *non* differunt specie, rationabile est quod sit *indifferens delectatio consequens naturam speciei* . . . et ita sit in aliis animalibus; *tamen in hominibus*, qui omnes sunt eiusdem speciei, *multum differunt delectationes*, sicut et operationes. Cuius ratio est, quia operationes et delectationes aliorum animalium consequuntur naturalem inclinationem, quae est eadem in omnibus animalibus eiusdem speciei. *Sed operationes et delectationes hominum proveniunt a ratione, quae non determinatur ad unum*' (*In Ethic.* X, 5, 1176a, *lect.* 8, §§2057–60).

There are some fascinating paragraphs on the general problems of individual, species and genus in Aquinas's Commentary to *De caelo* II, 11, 291b, *lect.* 16, §449, where he makes short work of Averroes's contention that 'omnes stellae sunt individua eiusdem speciei'.

52. 'Definitio personae quam Boethius assignat in libro *De duabus naturis* [ch. 3, *P.L.* 64, 1343], quae talis est: "*Persona* est *rationalis naturae individua substantia*" ' (*S.T.* 1a. 29, 1, introd.). 'Boethius dicit: "Nomen *personae* videtur traductum ex his personis quae *in comoediis tragoediisque* homines repraesentabant" . . . Quia enim in comoediis et tragoediis repraesentabantur *aliqui homines famosi*, impositum est hoc nomen "persona" ad significandum *aliquos dignitatem habentes*' (29, 3, ob. 2 and ad 2).

Aquinas will allude to the etymology in a phrase like: 'manus Socratis, quamvis sit quoddam individuum, non tamen est *persona*, quia non *per se* existit, sed in quodam perfectiori, scilicet in suo toto' (*S.T.* 3a. 2, 2, ad 3; *quaestiones* 2, 3 and 4 are all relevant). The final quotation ('id quod est perfectissimum' is from *S.T.* 1a. 29, 3, resp.

53. *Purg.* II, 91; *Par.* III, 49; VI, 10; XXVI, 83–4.

54. Significantly, Dante reports the common view that mankind was in fact created to make good (*restaurare*) the loss caused by the Fall of the rebel angels (*Con.* II, v, 12).

55. *Con.* III, iii, 5–11; IV, ii, 7; xxi, 4–9.

56. The image is pursued in the following terzina. Men are like imperfect insects ('*antomata* in difetto'), or like a caterpillar in which the process of formation is defective ('come *vermo* in cui formazion falla'). The image of soaring upwards is resumed briefly in XII, 95. See Hugh Shankland, 'Dante *aliger*', in *Modern Language Review*, 70 (1975), pp. 764–85, for a thorough survey of all the images relating to flying and soaring in the *Comedy*.

57. Like so many other moralists, including Aristotle (cf. *Ethics* X, 7, 1177b 18–1178a 5), Dante often seems to forget this simple truth. When he is wearing his Aristotelian hat, he often limits his attention to the highest reaches of human activity, that is, to the kind of mental life possible only for the privileged few. When he speaks as a Christian, he will hold up the single mirror of Christ as the perfect man, and urge us to imitate him (cf. *Mon.* III, xiv, 3–5): but few medieval works are less like the *Comedy* than Thomas à Kempis's *Imitation of Christ*.

58. For Dante's acceptance (and qualification) of Aristotle's dictum that man is a 'political animal', see *Con.* IV, iv, 1; *Par.* VIII, 115–48.

59. 'E a vedere li termini de le nostre operazioni, è da sapere che solo quelle sono *nostre* operazioni, che subiacciono a la *ragione* e a la *volontade*; che se in noi è l'operazione digestiva, questa *non è umana*, ma *naturale*' (*Con.* IV, ix, 4).

60. Aristotle, *Ethics* I, 7, 1098a 8.

61. 'Natura nihil facit frustra, neque deficit in necessariis' (*In De anima* III, 9, 432b 22, *lect.* 14, §811). Dante develops two long and important lines of argument from this axiom: *Con.* II, viii, 10–13; III, xv, 8–10.

62. Strictly speaking, Aristotle would say that animals can experience 'joy' or 'delight' (*gaudium, delectatio*), but not 'happiness' (*felicitas*). 'Animalia irrationalia . . . carent felicitate . . . *Nullum aliorum animalium est felix*, quia in nullo communicant speculatione. Et sic patet, quod *quantum se extendit speculatio, tantum se extendit felicitas*' (*In Ethic.* x, 8, 1178b 23–30, *lect.* 12, §§2124–5).

63. *Con.* IV, vi, 7–8; xxiii, 8; *Inf.* IV, 131.

64. *Mon.* III, xv, 3–8, translated by D. Nicholl. His one error of translation has been corrected, and the punctuation modified in a few places to accommodate the phrases from the original.

Suggestions for further reading

The following list is limited to the dozen works which I believe will be of most use to the readers for whom the present book is intended. It includes all the authors (but by no means all their relevant works) to whom I feel most indebted. Readers who require a more detailed and up-to-date bibliography on topics covered in this book are referred to the corresponding entries in the *Enciclopedia dantesca* (6 vols, Rome, 1970–9), and to the new edition of Dante's Latin works published by Ricciardi (*Opere minori*, vol. 2, Milan–Naples, 1979).

Foster, K. *The Two Dantes and Other Studies* (London, 1977).
Gilson, E. *Dante et la philosophie* (2nd edn, Paris, 1953), translated into English by
    D. Moore as *Dante the Philosopher* (London, 1948).
    L'Esprit de la philosophie médiévale (2nd edn, Paris, 1948), translated into English by
    A. H. C. Downes as *The Spirit of Mediaeval Philosophy* (London, 1936).
    Le Thomisme. Introduction à l'étude de Saint Thomas d'Aquin (5th edn, Paris, 1948),
    translated into English by L. K. Shook as *The Christian Philosophy of Saint Thomas
    Aquinas* (London, 1961).
Lewis, C. S. *The Discarded Image. An Introduction to Medieval and Renaissance Literature*
    (Cambridge, 1964).
Limentani, U. (ed.) *The Mind of Dante* (Cambridge, 1965).
Lloyd, G. E. R. *Aristotle: The Growth and Structure of his Thought* (Cambridge, 1968).
Moore, E. *Studies in Dante* (4 vols, Oxford, 1896–1917) reprinted with new introductory
    matter edited by C. Hardie (Oxford, 1969); especially vol. 3, 'Miscellaneous Essays'.
Nardi, B. *Saggi di filosofia dantesca* (Naples, 1930; 2nd edn, Florence, 1965).
    Nel mondo di Dante (Rome, 1944).
    Dante e la cultura medievale (Bari, 1942; 2nd edn, 1949).
    Dal 'Convivio' alla 'Commedia'. Sei saggi danteschi (Rome, 1960).

Index of longer quotations from Dante's works

Index

Abano, Pietro d', on God acting through intermediaries, 354

Abati, Bocca degli (*Inf.*), 309

actuality, pure:
  First Cause defined as, 63, 358
  angels described as, 244

Adam (*Par.*), 55, 91, 166
  creation of, 279, 377

admiratio (*ammirazione*)
  Dante's use of term, 50, 311
  opposed to *stupor* by Aquinas, 311

adolescenzia (*youth*)
  Dante's age of, 21–2
  length of, 22, 261, 308
  qualities characteristic of, 48

Aeneas, 101, 327

Aether, the fifth element, 133–4, a sphere with circular motion outside the sphere of Fire, 134–6, subdivided into spheres for sun, moon, planets, and fixed stars, 136–8
  etymology and meaning of (Aristotle), 337
  heavenly bodies formed of, 136, 244
  rotation of spheres of, used in geocentric astronomy to explain the apparent movements of heavenly bodies, 150

agens, agit sibi simile, 225, 255, 271, 341, 360, 361, 365, 370, 372, 378

Air, one of the four elements, composed of the contrary qualities Heat and Wetness, 58
  close to modern idea of 'gaseous', 59
  possesses Lightness, tends to rise, 64
  sphere of, 64–5, 77, 86; emergence of Earth into, *see terra discoperta*
  transmutation of, to Water, 60, 76; 'pregnant' with Water, 75

upper layer moved by sphere of Fire, 363

Alan of Lille, 201, 352

Albert of Cologne, St
  in the assimilation of Aristotle's work to Christian theology, 300, 307
  on the Creation, 238, on the heavenly bodies, 338, 343, on Intelligences, 364, and on the Scale of Being, 335
  other references, 339, 357, 374

alchemy, 60
  punishment for use of, to falsify metals (*Inf.*), 114

Alfraganus, Arab astronomer, as source for Dante, 220, 326, 338, 340, 342

alteration, 60–1, 275

Angelitti, Filippo, challenges accepted fictional date for the *Comedy*, 163–4

angels
  in art of Dante's time, 179, 345
  in the Bible, 179–81, 344–5; Biblical, in the *Comedy*, 181–4; not mentioned in the Biblical account of the Creation, 236
  in the *Comedy*: *Inferno*, sent to crush opposition to entry of Dante and Virgil, 83–4, 324; *Paradiso*, visions of, 83–4, 198–9, 231; *Purgatorio*, in Antepurgatory, 178, at gate, 173, on seven terraces, 173, 174, 175–8, and piloting boat bringing newly dead souls, 44, 81, 94–5
  creation of, in Dante's account, 241, 242, 262, 359, 379
  fallen, *see* demons
  hierarchy of, 184–7; *see also* Dionysius
  nature of: as Intelligences and Movers, 194–8, 200, 358–9; as substances separate from matter (pure form),

385

angels *cont*.
191–3, 347; their loving-kindness,
179
anima (soul, vital principle)
composed of atoms (Lucretius), 8, 11
possessed by all *corpora animata*, 127,
333, 376
see also soul
animals
in the *Comedy*, 118–20
as *corpora animalia*, 128
heat in development of, 249
organs of sense and locomotion
possessed by, 258–9, 368
scale of nobility among, 120, 128
Annunciation, by the Archangel Gabriel,
180, 182
Antepurgatory, 49, 114, 161, 178
Dante and Virgil in (the 'day of
marvel'), 44–7, 79–80, 323
Apennines, to Dante a linguistic as well
as geographical watershed, 100, 327
appetites (or 'loves'), characterizing each
level of existence, 129
Aquinas, St Thomas
in the assimilation of Aristotle's work
to Christian theology, 307; a faithful
interpreter of Aristotle, 252, 300
a cautious Aristotelian, 208, 209
as a character in the *Comedy*, 234
commentaries on Aristotle's works by,
300, 307
on God as a craftsman, 232, 236
on philosopher and philomythes
(paraphrasing Aristotle), ix, 50
Summa contra Gentiles by, 307, 315;
condemns Averroes's interpretation
of Aristotle, 278; on the end of the
world, 360; prologue to, 40
Summa Theologiae by, 307, 333; on
creation and generation, 265; on
interpretation of *Genesis*, 236–7; on
persona, 289
*for other references to his works, see the
subjects concerned*
Arab philosophers, 196
their experimental knowledge of light,
207
see also Averroes, Avicenna
archangels: Gabriel (messenger),
Michael (warrior), and Raphael
(guardian), 180, 182, 345
in the celestial hierarchy, 184, 185

Aristotelians, Christian, 6
held matter to be good, 228
their problems about angels, 191
their problems about primary matter,
and the creation of the world from
nothing, 62–3
Aristotle
Dante on, 36, 133
Dante's devotion to, 31, 294, 378
Dante's study of works of, 31, and
commentaries on, 306–7
Dante and his theories of generation,
252
his thought enriched by Dante with
Christian elements, 279
placed by Dante in Limbo in the
Comedy, 313
speaks of God in the singular, 190
Aristotle's works, 299–300
De anima, 128, 294
De caelo et mundo, 133; on the fifth
element (Aether), 133–6, 160; on
the heavenly spheres, 136–8, 156,
160, 195
De generatione et corruptione, 60–1,
248–50, 252
Ethics, 26, 48, 68, 282, 294
Generation of Animals, 271–3; rival
interpretations of, with respect to
the transformations of the embryo,
273–5
Metaphysics, 50, 195, 221, 252; all men
desire to know, 25, 51, 283; on
philosopher and philomythes, ix,
50; rejects atomic theory, 58; on
species, 131, 218
Meteorologica, 73, 74, 314; comment
on Empedocles in, 205
Physics, 57, 252; on causes, 51–2; on
the elements, 57–8
Poetics, 48
Politics, 73
Rhetoric, 48
On Sensation, 210
*for other references to his works, see the
subjects concerned*
art, medieval: angels in, 179, 345
astrology, 196, 307
impact of, on theory of generation,
250–2, 363
astronomy
Dante's simile from, to illustrate a
'point of time', similar to a point of

qualities of Heat and Cold as efficient causes of, 63

translations
'always a betrayal', 299
of Aristotle, Dante notes differences between, 79, 323
of Dante: by Cary, 312; by D. L. Sayers, 89–90

Trinity, the, Dante's Lucifer as a terrible parody of (*Inf.*), 70
as object of contemplation of the angelic orders, 186–7

tropics of Cancer and Capricorn, 147, 148

truth
Aristotle loved more than Plato, 27, 307–8
happiness found in contemplation of, 25
offered by philosophy, 26
philosophic and Christian, made one truth for Dante, 39
'shall make you free', 7–8, 18
vision of the whole of, 8, 26, 283; the *Comedy* as a journey to, 40, 51
see also certainty, intellect, knowledge, wisdom

typus (*in typo*, 'in a general way', 'by analogy'), 62, 315, 360

Ugolino (*Inf.*), 309

Ulysses
Dante's encounter with (*Inf.*), 106
he tells of his voyage over Ocean, to end in destruction before reaching the island of Purgatory, 107–9, 111, 328

unity, 332, 352–3, *see also* One

universe, uniqueness of (Aristotle), 337

vapor (moist exhalation), drawn from water or damp earth by the sun, condenses to cloud on rising and cooling, 74–5, 77, 317, 319

vapore, used of Holy Spirit, 317

variability in Nature
explicable by changes in the heavenly bodies, 251, 254, 259

Venus (goddess), Lucretius's hymn of praise and prayer to, 14, 302

Venus (planet)
Dante uses movements of, to give a date, 166

as morning star, seen from Purgatory, 44, 164, 169
sphere (heaven) of, 137, 142; Dante's encounters in (*Par.*), 89, 104; moved by third order of angels, 198

vergogna (shamefastness), a desirable quality in *adolescenzia*, 48, 49, 310

Verona, Dante at court of Can Grande della Scala at, 34, 38

vero primo (*notizia prima*), self-evident truth, 339

Vestibule (*Antinferno*), between gate of hell and Acheron river: inhabited by angels neither rebels against God, nor loyal to him (*Inf.*), 188

Vigna, Pier della (*Inf.*), 73, 309

Virgil, 3, 16, 310, 312
Dante's quotations from, 101, 327

Virgil, as guide through Hell and Purgatory in the Comedy, 36, 378
in Antepurgatory, during the 'day of marvel', 44–7, 79–80
in Hell, 82; on the Harrowing of Hell by Christ, 91, 92–3; *maraviglia* expressed by, 309; in Wood of Suicides, 71; making a way out of Hell, 70–1, 91–2
in Purgatory, 172, 173, 176, 177, 311

Virgilio, Giovanni del, 302

Virgin Mary: vision of Gabriel and, in Starry Heaven (*Par.*), 182, 183

virtues
cardinal (temporal), Cato as embodiment of, 170
theological, 295, colours associated with, 329
theological plus cardinal, 341; symbols of, 170–1

virtute formativa, in development of embryo, 272–3, 275, 280, 374

virtutes, secondary active qualities in composite bodies, 126, 332
in plants, 128

Visconti, Nino, friend of Dante (*Purg.*), 47, 161, 172

Vita Nuova, by Dante, 23
autobiographical matter in, 179, 306, 308
number nine in, 166, 220
reference in, to *primum mobile*, 158
see also Index of Quotations

water
in Aristotle's meteorology, 75–6